S0-AFT-717

THE NEW ILLUSTRATED ENCYCLOPEDIA OF AUTOMOBILES

105 HYY

THE NEW ILLUSTRATED ENCYCLOPEDIA OF AUTOMOBILES

EDITED BY DAVID BURGESS WISE
Revised and updated by Lance Cole

CHARTWELL BOOKS, INC.

Published by Chartwell Books
A Division of Book Sales Inc.
114 Northfield Avenue
Edison, New Jersey 08837
USA

ISBN 0-7858-1106-0

QUMEOAT

This book is produced by

Quantum Publishing
A division of Quarto Publishing PLC
The Old Brewery
6 Blundell Street
London N7 9BH

Project Manager : Joyce Bentley
Designer : Peter Laws
Editor : Phillip Jarrett
Author : Lance Cole

Printed in Indonesia by APP Printing Pte Ltd
Manufactured in Singapore by United Graphics Pte Ltd

Contents

Introduction

Originally written and researched by David Burgess-Wise and a team of contributors, the Complete Encyclopedia of Automobiles now appears with updated and expanded information, and a wider perspective that complements the century of the motor car and the new millennium.

It seems incredible that, in the passing of a century, the motor car could have come so far and changed so much. The word "revolution" seems somehow inadequate. Since the 1880s, the car as a commercial entity has existed and, since the early years of the 20th century, the car has been raced and rallied. Car manufacturers, engineers, designers, stylists, car buyers, and collectors have come and gone. A core of great marques and great engineers and designers has created the motor industry and the motor car. Good ideas and bad ideas, like good cars and bad cars, have passed along the highway of automotive history and left their mark upon its legends. A nucleus of motoring publications and a supporting cast of motorsport teams have serviced the enthusiasm of mankind for the motor car. Automotive technology has raced ahead; perhaps only matched by the pace of events in the aviation industry.

There are some still alive who can recall when a man with a red flag had to walk in front of the new-fangled motor car as it drove through the roads of Victorian and Edwardian England. There are those who can remember early Fords, and other makes, trundling along the roads of America at the scandalous speed of 24mph, the best top speed in 1920-something. Yet now we can storm down autobahn, motorway, autostrada and freeway at anything from 80mph to 200mph. Sleek, double-glazed, supersafe, aerodynamically sculptured automobiles whisk us along while we listen to CDs and relax in comfort. We also sit in traffic, and have created a pollution problem of worrying proportions.

A hundred years – the 20th Century of the car – has passed. What will the next hundred years, the new millennium, bring for the car and its driver? Time will tell. Meanwhile, this book, with its original theme and its evolved viewpoint, records what has passed and what is upon us. Above all, it charts the magic of man's motoring.

Lance Cole

Morgan, the Classic Sportster, essence of a classic car.

4
MORGAN
4

Pre-History

Man's search for some form of motive power to replace the horse goes back over 300 years. Clockwork, wind power and elaborate clockwork gearing were all tried before the power of steam became tractable enough to be used to drive a vehicle. Not that it was initially successful. The oldest surviving self-propelled vehicle, Cugnot's 1770 fardier, owes its preservation to the fact that, on its trial run, it ran amok and knocked down a wall! Put into store, it survived the French Revolution, was acquired by the Conservatoire des Arts et Métiers in Paris in 1799, and has been a major exhibit there ever since.

It was followed by a number of even less practical designs from optimistic French, English and American engineers, and it was not until 1801 that the first successful road carriage appeared. The work of Cornish mining engineer Richard Trevithick, it led to his London Carriage of 1803, which made a number of successful runs in the capital before it was dismantled to power a hoop-rolling mill. Trevithick lacked the staying power to perfect either this or his other great invention, the railway carriage. He was succeeded by a lunatic gaggle of inventors who proposed machines driven by articulated legs, tiny railway engines running inside a drum like squirrels, compressed air, gunpowder. and "vanes, or fliers, like the sails of a windmill."

Then, between 1820 and 1840, came a golden age of steam, with skilled engineers devising and operating steam carriages of advanced and ingenious design. Men such as Gurney, Hancock and Macerone produced designs which were practicable, capable of achieving quite lengthy journeys and of operating with a relatively high degree of reliability. Walter Hancock, a better mechanic than businessman, operated his steam coaches on regular scheduled services in London in the 1830s, but was rooked by his associates. He eventually called it a day after 12 years of experiment had brought him little more than unpaid debts and the hostility of those with vested interests who, fearing that the steam carriage would prove a threat to the thousands whose livelihood depended on the horse, promoted swingeing tolls on the turnpike roads. An 1831 Parliamentary Commission, though largely favorable to the steam carriage, failed to prevent such injustices, and the final blow to the builders of steam carriages came with the advent of the railroad age. Railroad engines, running on smooth, level rails, had none of the problems experienced by steam carriages running on uneven, badly maintained roads, and this newer form of locomotion soon eclipsed the steam carriage, even though legislation restricting the speed and operation of steam carriages was not enacted until 1863, when it was decreed that all "road locomotives" should have a man with a red flag walking ahead.

It was the advent of the bicycle in the 1860s which revived touring by road.

The James's steam carriage of the 1830s (right), Johann Hautsch of Nüremburg devised this curious clockwork carriage in the seventeenth century (below)

Dr Church's Birmingham Road Carriage, which was never completed (above.) The Hancock steam drag of c. 1830 represents the high point of early British steam carriages (below)

The first gasoline car conceived as an entity was the 1885-86 Benz three-wheeler

1880 TO 1900

The lordly Bollée Mancelle steam carriage of 1873

The internal combustion engine appeared early in the history of the motor vehicle, but took over three-fourths of a century to be perfected to the level where it could be used in a vehicle capable of running on the roads. An 1805 powered cart of the Swiss Isaac de Rivaz was no more than an elaborate toy, only capable of crawling from one side of a room to another, and the 1863 car built in Paris by J J Etienne Lenoir took three hours to cover six miles. It was not until the mid-1880s that the first successful gasoline cars appeared, developed independently by two German engineers, Gottlieb Daimler and Karl Benz.

Of the two vehicles, that of Benz was incontestably superior, for it was designed as an entity, using the new technology of the cycle industry, while Daimler's carriage was no more than an adapted horse vehicle. Benz went into limited production with his three-wheeled carriages (described in his catalogue as "an agreeable vehicle, as well as a mountain-climbing apparatus") in 1888. Daimler was more interested in selling his engines as a universal power source.

Neither man found immediate success, but neither did the great geniuses of the steam vehicle who were their contemporaries. The Bollée family of Le Mans, France, built some truly advanced steam carriages between 1873 and the mid-1880s, vehicles which pioneered independent front suspension, while blacksmith's

Serpollet's 1888 three-wheeler used his high speed flash boiler

son Léon Serpollet conceived the "flash boiler" for instantaneous generation of steam, and held the first driving license issued in Paris. And while the Comte De Dion and his engineers Bouton and Trépardoux built some excellent steam vehicles during the 1880s and early 1890s, they were to achieve their greatest fame as manufacturers of light gasoline vehicles, from 1895 onward.

The crucial event in the story of the motor car was the 1889 Paris World Exhibition. It was there that the French engineers Panhard and Levassor saw the Daimler "Steelwheeler" car, powered by the Daimler vee-twin engine. Levassor's lady friend, an astute widow named Louise Sarazin, held the French rights to the Daimler engine in succession to her late husband, and Panhard and Levassor began manufacturing these power units in 1890. Because they could see no future for the motor car, they granted the right to use Daimler engines in self-propelled vehicles to the ironmongery and cycle firm of Peugeot, which had just decided not to go ahead with its planned production of Serpollet steamers.

It was in France, too, that Benz enjoyed his first limited success, for his Paris agent, Emile Roger, managed to sell one or two Benz cars in Paris (and, coincidentally, garaged his first Benz in Panhard and Levassor's workshop.) But it was not until he produced his first four-wheeler, the 1893 Viktoria, that Benz began serious production.

Peugeot was already established as a motor manufacturer by that date, for in 1891 it had sold five cars, boosting production to a dizzy 29 the following year.

The success of the Peugeot cars caused Panhard and Levassor to reconsider their opinion of the horseless carriage, and, after building a couple of crude dogcarts with the engine at the rear, Levassor devised the famous Systéme Panhard, with the engine at the front, driving the rear wheels via a sliding pinion gearbox inspired by the mechanism of a lathe; a layout which, however "brusque et brutale" its inventor thought it, has been used on the majority of motor cars built since.

In the USA, the motor car was evolving along different lines and, in January-February 1891, the New World's first gasoline vehicle – a friction-driven three-wheeler built by John W Lambert of Ohio City – made its first tentative runs. In 1895, America's first motor manufacturing company was founded by the Duryea brothers, Charles and Frank, whose prototype dated from 1893. The following year they exported a couple of vehicles to Britain. Anti-motoring prejudice in

1898 Hurtu is a typical horseless carriage (above.) 1899 Fiat $3^{1}/_{2}$hp (left)

that country was, though, running high so there was little encouragement for motor vehicles, either home grown or imported. Even so, the company promotions of the so-called "father of the British motor industry," H J Lawson, succeeded in extracting a large amount of cash from a good many credulous investors.

Lawson had influential friends and, in 1896, succeeded in getting the ridiculous requirement for motor cars to be preceded by a man on foot – a legacy of the old Locomotives on Highways Acts of 1865 and 1878 – to be repealed. He held a commemorative run to Brighton on 14 November 1896 to celebrate the raising of the speed limit to 12 mph, but some of the participating machines covered the distance by railroad and were cosmetically muddied after they had been unloaded. Worse, the first machine home, a Duryea, was not one of the marques under Lawson's aegis (he had expensively purchased a great number of motor car patents in a forlorn effort to monopolize the nascent British car industry.)

The demand for motor cars grew steadily during the latter part of the 1890s, and the Benz became the world's most popular car, the 2,000th production vehicle being delivered in 1899. Motoring was still the sport of a few rich eccentrics, however, and many people had never seen a car.

In 1900, to remedy this problem, the Automobile Club of Great Britain and Ireland held its famous 1,000 Miles Trial, which took in most of the major cities of England and Scotland. A total of 65 cars, many English Daimler and MMC models built by Lawson's empire, set out from Hyde Park Corner, London, in April. The majority finished the run without major mishap, proving that the motor car had at last become a (relatively) reliable touring vehicle after a century's gestation.

1895 tricar utilized the power unit from the Leyland steam lawnmower (left.) De Dion, Bouton, and Trépardoux built this neat little steam car in 1885 (below)

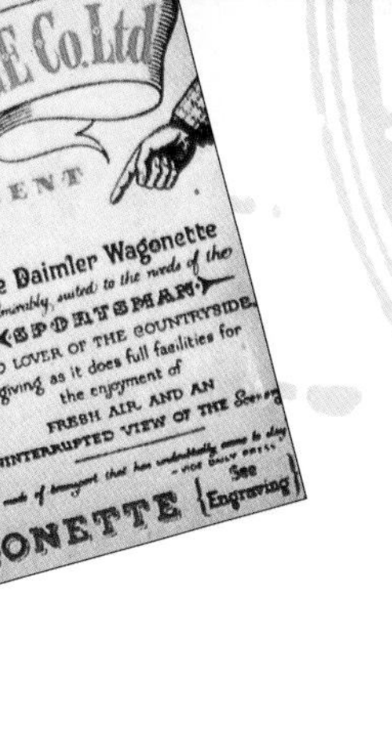

Couched in glowing Victorian prose, this advertisement is a pastiche conceived for Daimler's 40th anniversary

Badges & Mascots

Radiator badges were the heraldry of the early motor car. Starting simply as makers' plates fixed to the radiator, badges quickly developed into a minor art form. Some badges, indeed, were masterpieces of the enameler's craft; the Invicta was endowed with a polychromatic butterfly badge delicate enough for jewellry. As for mascots, they began as good luck charms, such as teddy bears tied to the radiator, but soon the techniques of statuary were being employed to produce mascots of real beauty. The Hispano stork and the Rolls-Royce "Spirit of Ecstasy" became marque symbols, though owners also commissioned individual mascots, like the Wagnerian soprano whose Métallurgique was endowed with a sterling silver Seigfried clad in chain mail.

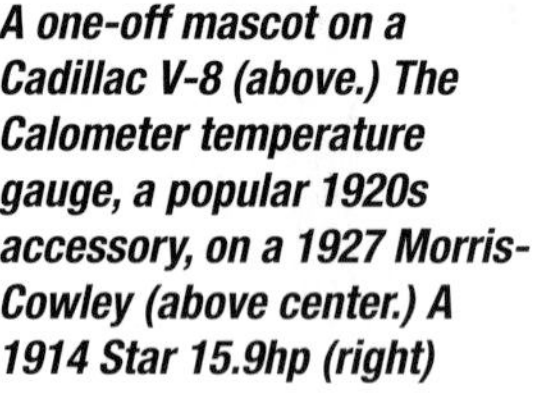

A one-off mascot on a Cadillac V-8 (above.) The Calometer temperature gauge, a popular 1920s accessory, on a 1927 Morris-Cowley (above center.) A 1914 Star 15.9hp (right)

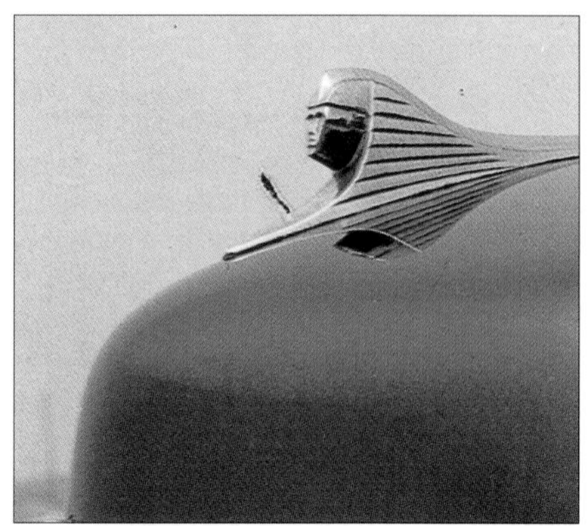

The Hotchkiss badge recalls the firm's origin (top.) Packard's emblem – "a pelican in her piety" (center.) The Armstrong Siddeley sphinx (above)

Chrome and colors, the very heart of badges

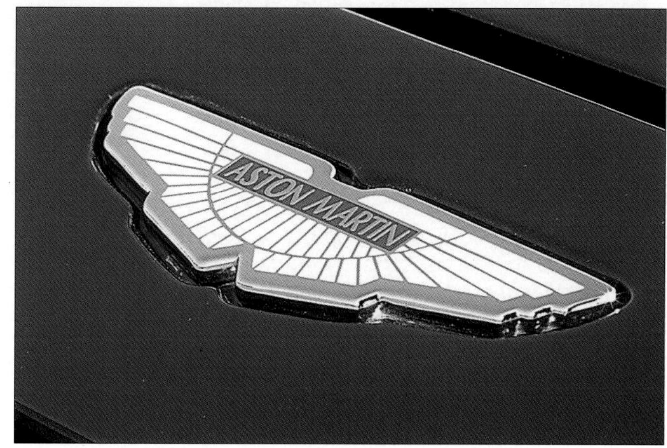

BMW's badge derives from a pre-war logo depicting an aircraft propeler as it rotated – indeed BMW engines are still used to power aircraft (above left,) the three pointed star of Stuttgart's super brand – Mercedes-Benz (left,) the Aston Martin Legend (right)

1901 To 1914

The popular impression that motor cars were "engines of death" is illustrated by this 1904 cartoon (above.) A 1901 Curved-Dash Oldsmobile (right)

The new century was spectacularly ushered in by "the car of the day after tomorrow" – the Mercedes, designed by Daimler's engineer, Wilhelm Maybach. The contract to produce the first batch of 30 cars had been signed within a month of Gottlieb Daimler's death in March 1900. They had been ordered by the wealthy Austro-Hungarian Consul at Nice, Emil Jellinek, who insisted that they be christened for his daughter, Mercedes, a name which found such favor with the wealthy car-buying public that all German Daimler cars were soon known as "Mercedes," too.

The advanced design of the Mercedes, which combined, in one harmonious whole, elements such as the honeycomb radiator, pressed steel chassis and a gear-lever moving in a gate rather than a quadrant, "set the fashion to the world." Soon many high-priced cars were copying its layout, even comparatively small cars like the Peugeot were built on Mercedes lines.

These cars did not, however, represent the "popular motoring" of the early 1900s. This was the province of single-cylinder runabouts such as the De Dion and Renault. Again, these well-built cars were widely imitated, in America first by light and temperamental steam cars like the Locomobile, and then by gas buggies, of which the most famous was the Curved-Dash Oldsmobile.

But the development of the motor industry in America was being hampered by the shadow of monopoly, as it had been in Britain a few years earlier. A patent lawyer named George Baldwin Selden drew up a "master patent" for the motor vehicle in 1879, published it in 1895 and claimed that all gasoline-driven vehicles infringed his patent. His claims were eventually given commercial teeth by the Association of Licensed Automobile Manufacturers (ALAM), established to administer the Selden Patent in 1902, and which most major American car firms were persuaded to join.

One of the great names of motoring in the Edwardian era was Napier: this 1907 60hp six-cylinder has been constructed as a replica of the car on which S. F. Edge averaged over 60mph for 24 hours to inaugurate the Brooklands race track (top.) Another, if humbler, "immortal" of the period was the twin-cylinder Renault AX for this chassis was used on the taxis which ferried troops to the Battle of the Marne and saved Paris in 1914 (left.) 1914 Prence Henry Vauxhall (far right)

However, Henry Ford, who founded his Ford Motor Company in June 1903, decided to stand against the ALAM, which began proceedings against him in 1904. After lengthy litigation, which resulted in the ALAM building a car to Selden's 1879 design, and Ford building a car with an engine based on that of the 1863 Lenoir, Ford won the day in 1911 (not long before the Selden Patent would have expired anyway,) and the victory established him as a folk hero.

Ford's great achievement, after five years' work, was to introduce in October 1908 the immortal Model T, which became so popular that he was forced to introduce the car industry's first moving production line to build sufficient cars to satisfy demand. His "Universal Car" changed the face of motoring. More than 16.5 million were built before production ended in 1927 – truly "putting the world on wheels" and transforming society.

Although the Edwardian era saw motoring become more popular, it also saw the finest and most elegant cars of all time, built to a standard of craftsmanship which could never be repeated. After the First World War many of the great marques faded away in a genteel decline. Delaunay-Belleville, "the Car Magnificent," the favorite marque of the Tsar of Russia and one of the very best of the French cars of the pre-1914 era, became just a petit bourgeois in the 1920s.

Napier, the British company which popularized the six-cylinder engine, enjoyed perhaps even greater acclaim than its rival, Rolls-Royce, while its sales were controled by that bombastic character Selwyn Francis Edge. When Napier gave him a £160,000 ($256,000) "golden handshake" after a dispute over policy in 1912, however, the company's fortunes seemed to leave with him. Having agreed to leave the motor industry for seven years, Edge became a successful Sussex pig farmer. Napier built very few cars after the war, concentrating instead on aero engines.

Such ostentatious machinery relied for its existence on a pool of highly skilled, low-paid craftsmen with a surpassing pride in their work. The big luxury cars stood little chance against the onslaught of cheap machines produced in America by unskilled labour using production techniques which eliminated most of the human factor. They represented only a tiny fraction of the potential market for the motor vehicle and, even if their production had not been decimated by the drying-up of the car market as a result of the war, they would inevitably have died out as a result of the social changes in the post-war world.

Europe, indeed, experienced an outburst of popular motoring in the 1910-14 period which

V 2948

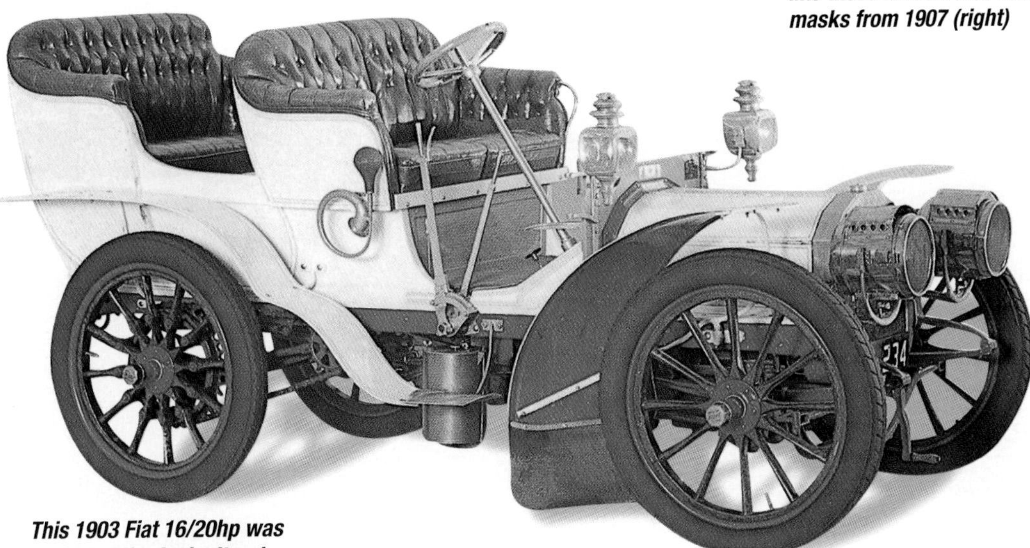

Some of the ignorant fear of motoring may have been caused by the strange garb affected by early motorists, like these sinister anti-dust masks from 1907 (right)

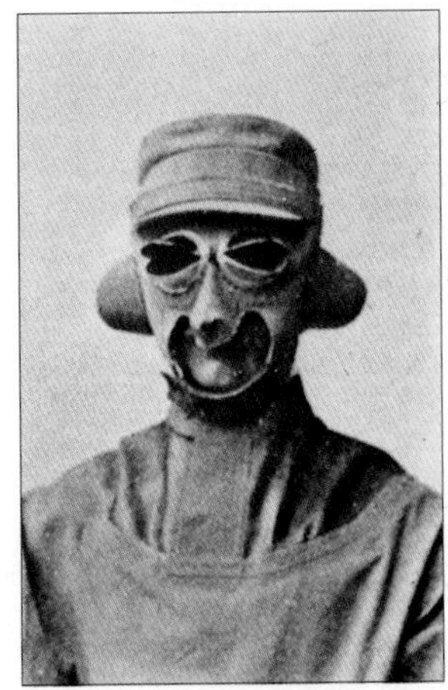

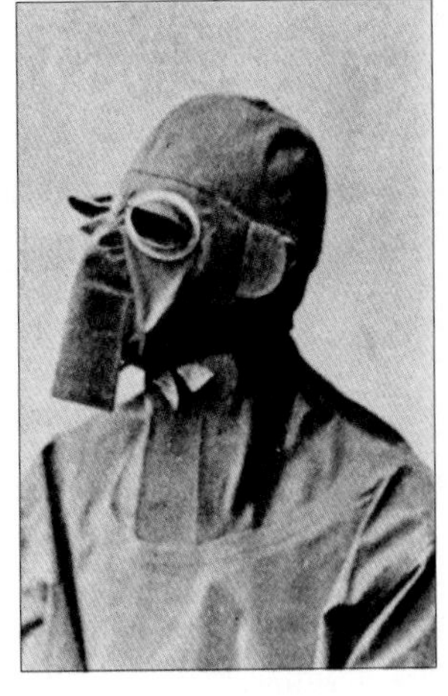

This 1903 Fiat 16/20hp was shown at the Agricultural Hall Exhibition in London: its Grosvenor tonneau body is English-built (above.) A more idealized concept of motoring is shown in the 1908 Argyll advertisement (below)

owed nothing to American concepts of mass production. Instead, it grew out of the motorcycle industry, whose engines – single-cylinder or vee-twin – offered lightness and power. Optimistic enthusiasts installed these engines in chassis of often suicidal crudeness, with cart-type center-pivot steering in many cases, as well as other unmechanical devices such as wire cables coiled round the steering column instead of a conventional steering box, drag link, belt and pulley transmission and tandem-seat layouts with the driver in the second row of the stalls. These crude devices, known as cyclecars, flourished, especially in England and France, but attempts to transplant them to America failed because they were simply unsuited to the very different motoring environment there.

However, the worst of the cyclecars were shortlived. The designs of the late Edwardian period which promised perhaps the most for the future were the new light cars like the Morris-Oxford, the Standard and the Hillman – all "big cars in miniature" of around 1100cc, with four cylinders and built on proper engineering lines. These admirable machines were the patterns for the popular family cars of the 1920s.

Radiators

Even if they had radiators to cool their engines, the earliest cars had them slung at the rear of the chassis or in some other anatomically improbable position, and therefore lacked a certain amount of character. However, when Mercedes developed the honeycomb radiator into a recognizable marque symbol, cars began to acquire personality. And, although radiators are now hidden behind grilles, it is still front-end treatment that gives a car its character.

When Ettore Bugatti originally adopted a shape for the radiators of his cars, he apparently followed the outline of a chairback designed by his furniture-designer father, Carlo (top centre.) The 1949 Bristol 400 took its functional radiator openings from the BMW with which it was closely connected (above.) The 1936 Railton cloaked its American origins behind a very English radiator (left)

Typical of its era, the 1913 Unic radiator reflects honest craftsmanship (top.) The crude front end of the 1921 Carden cyclecar is purely a dummy, aping larger cars (above)

Radiator grill of the 1936 Triumph Dolomite (left.) The "dollar grin" of the 1947 Buick Eight (below.) Americana captured in chrome (below left,) Mercedes-Benz has always had a distinctive face (below right)

Chrome plated grille detail (top;) the instantly recognizable BMW "Kidney" Grille (above,) Volvo's traditional badge and grille – always to the fore (left)

1915 TO 1930

The technology of the motor age revolutionized the way in which the First World War was fought. The internal combustion engine gave new mobility to the infantry which, before hostilities in Europe came to a standstill in the trenches, could be rushed to reinforce weak points in the front line; most notably when the French General Gallieni sent 6,000 reinforcements to repel Von Kluck's attack on Paris in 1914. It also provided motorcycles for despatch riders, permitted H G Wells's forecast of "land ironclads" to be fulfilled in the angular shapes of the first armored cars and tanks and, perhaps most significantly, gave warfare a new dimension by taking it into the air.

One way and another, most of those who fought in the war were given an insight into the utility of the motor vehicle and, when peace came, many returning soldiers were only too anxious to spend their demobilization pay on cars of their own. The result was a boom such as the motor industry had never known. In Britain and France, especially, the established manufacturers found themselves contending for the favors of the car-buying public with a whole new sub-industry of optimists who, working from inadequate back-street premises,

The Hispano H6B was one of the great designs of the 1920s (above.) The Blackhawk of 1929 was a short-lived attempt by Stutz to build a lower-priced car (right)

Typical of American quality car design in the late 1920s is this 1929 Packard 640 six-cylinder phaeton (left.) The Morris-Cowley "Bullnose" (below)

assembled light cars and cyclecars from proprietary components in the hope that they might make their fortunes. Most found only commercial failure, like the British firm which, with the bailiffs mounting a 24-hour watch outside the doors of its London factory, broke an exit through the unguarded rear wall, loaded as much of its machinery as possible on to the finished chassis and drove off to seek new (but unforthcoming) fortune in the Midlands.

If the American industry had already developed to the extent where success in popular car sales would inevitably go to the established big battalions (even Chrysler, founded in 1924, sprang from the established Maxwell-Briscoe grouping,) there was still room in Europe for new mass-producers. Most spectacular of these was André Citroën, a former gear manufacturer, who, with the aim of bringing Ford-style mass-production to France, enjoyed an immediate success with his 10hp, launched in 1919. However, the rise of Citroën spelt doom for the dozens of optimistic assemblers who clustered most thickly in the north-western suburbs of Paris.

The boom collapsed in 1920-21, speeded on its way by strikes, hold-ups, shortages, loss of stock market confidence in the car industry, restrictions on lease-purchase sales, costlier raw materials and the introduction of a swingeing horsepower tax in Britain.

Only the fittest survived. Ford, whose example was followed by a number of American and European makers, gained a brief respite by cutting prices in order to boost falling sales. He compensated for the loss on the cars by compelling the dealers to take $40-worth of spare parts on which there had been no reduction but still had to close down for some months to clear unsold stocks. It was not until 1922 that the motor industry was back on course and a second generation of post-war popular cars began to emerge, most notably the Austin Seven.

Many of the cars of the 1920s profited from the technology of the aero engines developed during the war, particularly the overhead-camshaft Hispano-Suiza V-8. Wolseley built this engine under license and used an overhead camshaft on its post-war cars, but it was not until after the 1927 takeover by Morris that this Wolseley design realized its full potential, especially in MG sports cars.

Hispano-Suiza used its aero-engine expertise to full advantage in the 1919 32cv of 6.6 litres, a splendid machine with servo-assisted four-wheel brakes and delightful handling characteristics whose overall conception was several years ahead of any of its rivals.

Bentley, which had built rotary aero engines during the war, brought out an in-line four with an overhead camshaft in 1919, but it did not go into production until 1921. This 3-liter was to become one of the immortal sporting cars.

Many leading manufacturers adopted the overhead-camshaft layout during this period, but Rolls-Royce, which had used this layout for its aero engines, stuck resolutely to side valves on its cars until the advent of the 20 in 1922. This had pushrod ohv, a configuration followed on the 1925 Phantom which was to supplant the Silver Ghost, which had side valves until the end.

Oddly enough, apart from honorable exceptions like the Hispano, it was the cheaper cars which pioneered the use of brakes on all four wheels, one of the most positive advances in car equipment in the early 1920s. Possibly it was felt that luxury cars would be handled by professional drivers who would be less likely to

The Model T Ford (right.) A 1925 aluminum-bodied sports version of the 10.8hp Riley, normally known as the "Redwinger" (below)

indulge in the kind of reckless driving that would require powerful brakes! Moreover, some American popular-car makers, appalled at the cost of retooling their cars to accept brakes on the front wheels, actually campaigned against their introduction on the grounds that they were dangerous.

As the decade wore on, more features designed to make motoring more comfortable and safer became commonplace. Windscreen wipers, electric starters, safety glass (first standardised on the 1928 Model A Ford,) all-steel coachwork, saloon bodies, low-pressure tires, cellulose paint and chromium plating all became available on popular cars. Styling and the annual model change became an accepted part of the selling of motor cars, bringing huge tooling costs which could only be borne by the biggest companies. Many old-established firms just could not keep up, and were swept away by the onslaught of the Depression in 1929.

WHEELS

The wheel is one of man's most fundamental inventions, as it has no parallel in nature. The earliest cars rolled into the world on wire wheels derived from cycle practice, or on wooden wheels developed from those used on carriages. These basic types have been followed by many different patterns of wheel; only the roundness has remained constant.

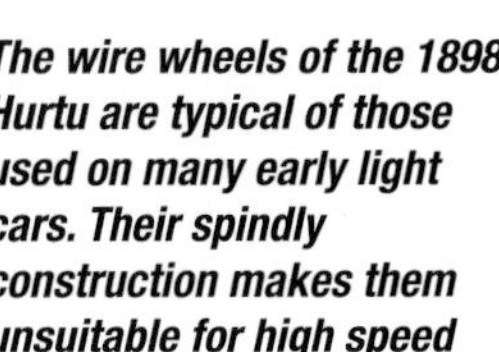

The wire wheels of the 1898 Hurtu are typical of those used on many early light cars. Their spindly construction makes them unsuitable for high speed

One of the odder inventions of Edwardian times was this hub-mounted tire pump, here fitted to a wooden-wheeled Gladiator (above.) Bugatti's famous spoked aluminum wheels were developed for racing use. Cheap to make and light in weight, they could be changed complete with brake drum (right)

Wooden artillery wheels were common on most pre-World War One European cars, and were still being used in America throughout the 1920s (above)

The spokes on the wheels of this Model A Ford are electrically welded to the rim, not located by adjustable nipples as on conventional wire wheels

This wheel trim was considered vulgar for its time (above.) That (above right,) was more elegant and was used to protect a wire spoked wheel and make it easier to clean. The wheels on this 1923 Calcott are pressed steel simulating wooden artillery wheels, a popular fashion on British light cars of the 1920s (right)

Hub caps and spokes with chrome plated themes

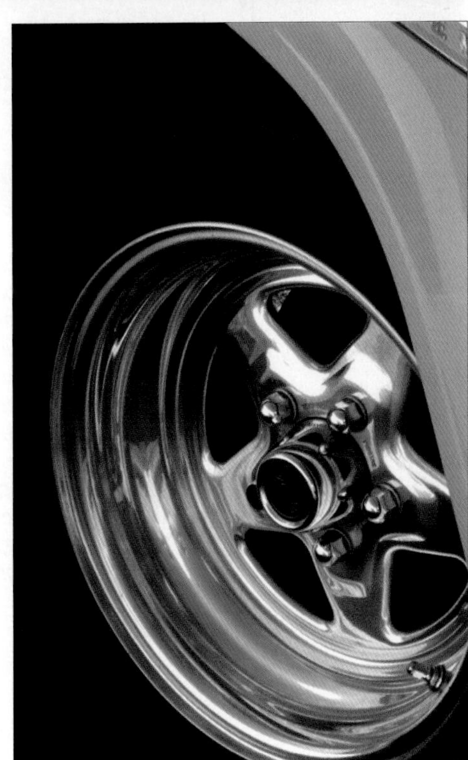

The wheel as an art form. Forged alloys – Porsche style (left,) Audi "designer" wheel (below,) MGF – 6 spoker essential 1990s kit (bottom left,) a BMW multi spoke design (bottom right)

1931 TO 1945

Perhaps the most significant pointer to the changing status of the motor car is the fact that, at the beginning of the 1920s, most cars were open tourers. By 1931 sedan bodies were fitted to 90 per cent of the cars produced. A contemporary editorial sums up the more functional, utilitarian role of the typical 1930s motor car: "Today there is no room for the cheap and shoddy, or for immature design. The day has passed when unmechanical contraptions can claim the serious attention of the public ... manufacturers no longer expect the public to carry out the testing of new productions for them".

However, the public was also calling for smaller engines, more suited to the economic climate of the times. To cope with the weight of sedan bodywork and all the popular accessories, these little engines had to be geared low. Consequently they revved high and hard, and their bores wore alarmingly. The days when durability was a feature taken for granted on all but the shoddiest of cars, seemed long past.

The design of cars now began to change radically as well. The demand for more capacious bodywork on small chassis led to the engine being pushed forward over the front axle. The radiator became a functional unit concealed behind a decorative grille which became more elaborate and exaggerated as the decade wore on, until on some cars it resembled a chromium-plated waterfall or fencing mask.

During 1930-35, there was a vogue for streamlining which found its full flower in devices like the Chrysler Airflow, the Singer Airstream and the Fitzmaurice-bodied Ford V8. Even on

Austin Seven (above.) Henry Ford's "last mechanical triumph" was his 1932 V8, seen here with phaeton bodywork (right)

Rolls-Royce made some concessions to fashion while retaining its innate dignity (left)

more staid cars, the angularity of line that had characterized the models of the late 1920s gave way to more flowing contours. Though most cars still retained running boards, the separate side valances were eliminated by bringing the lower door edges down to give a lower, more bulbous look, accentuated by the adoption of wings with side panels, often blended into the radiator and hood.

The swept tails of the new-style coachwork now usually concealed some kind of luggage accommodation as well, a feature sadly lacking on most 1920s models, which usually boasted a luggage grid and nothing more.

"Well-rounded and commodious," the cars of the 1930s offered greater comfort and convenience than their forebears. The stylist, however, had taken over from the engineer and the craftsman bodybuilder and, as a result, the new cars were often deficient in handling because the main masses were now concentrated at either end, like a dumb-bell. New suspension systems, especially independent front springing, also brought their handling problems, and some cars had to be fitted with bumpers incorporating a harmonic damping device to prevent them from shimmying right off the road on their supersoft springing.

It was not all gloom and despondency in the 1930s. Some manufacturers produced excellent cars during the decade. Morris and Austin continued to build soundly engineered small cars (though Herbert Austin was distinctly upset when his designers insisted on moving the radiator behind a dummy grille, as he felt that it was a kind of heresy,) while the last two new models in which Henry Ford was personally involved, the 8hp Model 19Y and the V-8, both of which appeared in 1932, were instantly and deservedly successful.

And, of course, there was the famous front-wheel-drive Citroën, which made its debut in 1934. Although its development costs all but bankrupted André Citroën, who was forced to sell out to Michelin, this was one of the truly great cars.

A lesser, though no less significant, happening was the metamorphosis of the SS marque from a merely meretricious styling exercise into a modestly priced, excellently finished, well-equipped sedan; the first Jaguar.

The same year that the SS Jaguar was launched, 1936, Dr Porsche built the prototype Volkswagens, the "Strength through Joy" cars sponsored by the Nazi Party and intended to be sold to the German public at $80-$88 to keep them from buying imported models; the first of over 20 million of this most popular car of all time. Few Volkswagens, however, were built before the war (though the design was readily adapted for military purposes.)

In many ways the 1930s were a watershed. They saw the last of the big luxury cars from makers such as Hispano-Suiza, Duesenberg and Minerva, as well as the end of many small, independent manufacturers and coachbuilders (victims of the swing to mass-produced cars with pressed-steel bodies.) The motor industry

The traditionally-shaped 1930s Zagato-bodied 2.3-litre Alfa Romeo. The Jaguar "SS" 1930s supercar (below)

had reached the point where it had become vital to the economic well-being of the major industrialized countries. Now it was to prove just as vital in providing weapons of war.

In Britain, five of the largest motor manufacturers set up "shadow factories" in the late 1930s which could be used to produce aero-engine parts in the event of war. They produced many thousands of aero engines and complete aircraft during the hostilities. Ford joined the five soon after the outbreak of war and was soon building Rolls-Royce Merlin engines on a moving production line in Manchester, while in the USA Ford mass-production expertise was given its greatest test in manufacturing Consolidated Liberator bombers on a gigantic production line at Willow Run, Michigan.

From the ubiquitous Jeep, through staff cars, trucks, tanks, and powerboats to the biggest bomber aircraft, the motor industry played a crucial role in the Second World War. Readapting to peacetime production was, however, to prove a big a test of the industry's abilities.

The avant-garde Cord designed by Ray Dietrich was deemed worthy to be shown in New York's Museum of Modern Art (top.) The Type 57 Bugatti has saloon coachwork (centre.) The 1930s Packard (left)

Fiat's little "Model 500" was first produced in the 1930s but was removed after the war (aboveleft.) An advertisement for the 1939 two-door saloon Studebaker (above.) The opening of the Volkswagen plant in Germany, 1939 (left.) Known as the "people's car," it was originated during the Nazi regime

Body Styles

Since the dawn of motoring a bewildering lexicon of words has been used to describe automobile bodywork, many descending from horse-carriage practice, others coined by car manufacturers. Some became standard practice, like the use of the word "torpedo" to describe an open four-seater touring car; others, like the similar "gunboat roadster", vanished into limbo. Fashion, too, has played its part in determining names. In America, "touring" was superseded by "phaeton" in an attempt to standardize coachwork nomenclature. And, of course, there are the national differences in usage. A "saloon" is a closed car in England but a public bar in America, where the car becomes a "sedan". Henry Ford devized the names "Tudor" (two-door) and "Fordor" (four-door) to describe the Model T sedan; more than 50 years later these names are still in use internally in the Ford Motor Company. Today there is little variation in body styles. Most cars are sedans, though "hatchback" and "notchback" are specialized subdivisions of the type. Legislation has all but killed off the convertible, save for specialist sports cars, and the word coupé, once used for two-seaters with a folding hood that was kept erected, now means any sporting sedan that is lower than average.

The pane of glass ahead of the folding rear roof section of this Fiat Tipo 4 of c.1914 vintage identifies it as a three-quarter landaulette: a landaulette has the rear roof folding from immediately behind the door pillar (above.) Two-seaters like this 1938 Citroën 7cv, are often known as roadsters (below)

A sedan of the traditional pattern is mounted on this 1931 Chevrolet (right.) Designed to eliminate body rattles, the Weymann sedan, here mounted on a Peugeot (below)

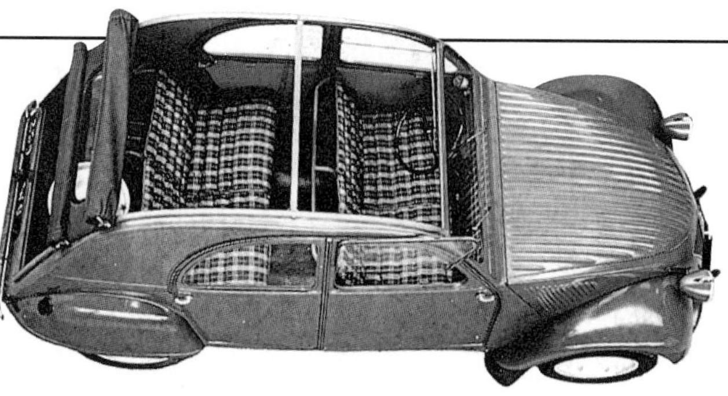

Wicker-bodied Bugatti (far left.) Boulanger's little "Deux Chevaux," designed for the Citroën (left)

John Tjaarda styled the 1937 Lincoln-Zephyr V12, one of the pioneering aerodynamic cars (above.) This 1949 two-seater emphasizes the "sporty-formal" ethos of that model (left)

Jeep (top,) typical American heavy metal (center,) Volvo's definitive estate car, a benchmark in design (right)

The essential spirit of Lotus re-born, the Elise (left.) Toyota's mid-engined MR2 (below.) Ford's elegant Taurus estate sells well in the USA (below left.) Chrysler's beach buggy concept (below right)

1946 TO 1960

Although they were beset by post-war materials shortages and government interference, motor manufacturers soon returned to production, inevitably with slightly modernized pre-war models in most cases, though some actually managed to produce all-new cars, notably Armstrong Siddeley in Britain.

Despite shortages of fuel and tires there was a vast demand in Britain for cars, but the government forced manufacturers to export half their output, even though these cars had been designed mostly for the very insular requirements of pre-war Britain. To curb speculators who were buying new cars and selling them at an inflated profit, purchasers had to sign a "covenant" guaranteeing that they would not resell for initially one year, later two.

There was much talk of technical developments arising from wartime projects, but devices such as automatic transmission were only generally adopted in the USA, and reports that hydraulic suspension, or springing by rubber or torsion bars, were about to be adopted on British cars, proved to be more than a little premature. Indeed, some makers seemed unready to come to terms with the future, as one report noted: "Since wind resistance is an important factor in brake performance, streamlining may lead to braking difficulties, as was shown in experiments carried out in France."

European manufacturers faced the problem of rebuilding war-shattered plant. In France the industry had lost machine tools, equipment and labor to Germany, and had suffered much bomb damage. Shortages of sheet steel and tires also

Built by the most traditionally minded motor company of all, the Morgan 4/4 of the 1950s (above,) was little changed in appearance from its ancestor of the mid-1930s. A classic post-war sports car, the Jaguar XK 120 (right)

played their part in keeping production to about a sixth of the 1938 level in 1946-48, though some recovery was apparent by 1949, when the first post-war Salon de l'Automobile was held in Paris and production had risen to about four times the 1938 monthly level.

Other manufacturing countries had similar difficulties, those of Germany being compounded by the division of the country and the replacement of the Reichsmark (\$1 = RM15) by the Deutschmark (\$1 = DM7.5,) an effective devaluation of around 100 per cent. Nevertheless, the country's most prolific manufacturer, Volkswagen, continued to make progress despite the opinions of British experts (and of Henry Ford II) that the VW was too noisy and uncomfortable to be competitive. And though the BMW factory had ended up in the Russian Zone, the first (and only) "war reparation" design to come out of Germany became the BMW-based Bristol 400.

That was only one of the classic sports cars to appear after the war. More famous still was the Jaguar XK 120, with a twin-cam engine reportedly developed during wartime fire-watching duty. It made its debut in 1948, along with a pair of more utilitarian designs, the Morris Minor and the Citroën 2 cv.

The 1950s saw the motor industry entering a period of traumatic change. Those brave attempts by independent companies such as Kaiser and Crosley to carve a foothold in the American market against the Big Three corporate giants, Ford, GM, and Chrysler, came to nothing, and the most respected of the old-established independents such as Packard, Nash and Studebaker were in decline and would soon vanish, either by attrition or by merger. The American car industry had become stereotyped. Its typical product, generally superlatively hideous, had either a six-cylinder engine (often of fairly antique provenance) or a V-8, and boasted excruciatingly named accessories and components like Hi-Fyre or Firedome engines, HydraMatic or UltraMatic transmissions, and even FlightSweep styling. This was the era of the exaggerated tailfin, the grinning chrome grille and the "performance car" that could only go fast in a straight line. The announcement of small "compact" cars in 1959 brought, as well as the Ford Falcon and Chrysler Valiant of conventional design, the unorthodox rear-engined Chevrolet Corvair, whose unAmerican handling activities ensured that the US industry went straight from nadir to Nader.

There were mergers in Europe, too, like the shotgun wedding between Austin and Morris, a union born out of strife which would lay the seeds of trouble for that British Motor Corporation's ultimate descendant, British Leyland. But at that time their products, small family cars, were just what the public wanted. Fuel economy became even more significant after the 1956 Suez War, when gasoline was rationed, and the event created a new race of cyclecars, only now they were called "bubblecars". Many

The 1946 Lincoln shows how even quality post-war American cars adopted extreme styling for their radiator grilles (top.) Classic styling and design of the 1950s (above)

See for yourself how much more Chevrolet offers-

came from German firms grounded in the aircraft industry, such as Heinkel and Messerschmitt.

In the main these bubblecars were beastly machines whose only merit lay in their economy. Their death knell was tolled by the advent of an epochal design by Alec Issigonis, the 1959 Mini Minor, which gave a new word to the popular vocabulary and heralded a new race of decently engineered small cars with sports-car-like handling. Its layout of front-wheel drive and transverse engine was to set the pattern for the coming 20 years and more.

But the 1950s had their glamor cars, too. Britain produced the big Healeys, the Triumph TRs and the first MG to abandon the perpendicular lines of the 1930s, the slippery profiled MGA, even available with a temperamental twin-cam engine. Italy built big powerful sports cars like the Ferrari America and Super America, while France, which had taxed the grand'routiers like Delahaye out of existence, introduced the avant-garde Citroën DS. Germany, once again persona grata after its post-war isolation, brought out the unique and distinctive Mercedes 300SL coupé, with its stylish, if not entirely practical, gull-wing doors.

Designs like these captured the spirit of America in the late 1950's

Cadillac set the fashion for fins in the 1950s: by the 1954 models this vulgar trend had reached its peak (below)

The essential Ford Thunderbird, circa 1957 (above.) An Oldsmobile advertisement of the 1950s (left)

One of the most sought-after sports cars of the 1950s, both then and now, was the world class Gull Wing SL model 300SL Mercedes (left.) The timeless baby Fiat – the ultimate city car (below)

Citroën's amazing time-warped DS model (left.) A rare Jaguar – the Mk1 "S" type – later restyled with slimmer detailing to create the classic "Jag" (below)

ENGINES

The 1908 Hutton with its electrolytically-deposited copper water-jackets and dual ignition (right.) The 1934 Graham straight-eight, with its centrifugal supercharger, was a short-lived way of obtaining increased performance (below)

Sophisticated and powerful though the engine of a modern car may be, it operates on principles first successfully applied more than a century ago. The first car engines were simple affairs, usually with one or two cylinders, though since the turn of the century multicylinder power units have predominated, normally with four, six or eight cylinders, though non-conformist configurations with three, five, twelve or sixteen cylinders have been tried. Rotary engines have also made sporadic appearances, too. But the main changes in the power unit have been technical improvements: the replacement of the atmospherically operated automatic inlet valve by mechanical inlet valves in the early 1900s, the adoption of monobloc cylinder castings instead of cylinders cast singly or in pairs, the general use of detachable cylinder heads, and the change from side to overhead valves. Today the overhead camshaft, once the premise of high-powered sports and racing cars, is a common feature of family cars, thanks to the invention of the cogged driving belt, which replaces the complex gear trains of earlier designs and is cheap to install and silent in operation.

The 1908 Grand Prix Benz unit, which promised plenty of ram with pushrod ohv and drainpipe exhaust (right.) The Jaguar XK120 engine, with its twin ohc, was a classic 1940s design capable of great development (far right)

A more modestly priced dohc power unit was the Lotus Twin Cam, here seen in a 1971 Lotus Super Seven (above.) The 1936 Morris Eight (right)

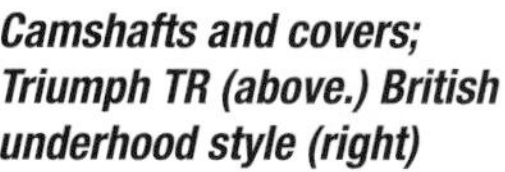

Camshafts and covers; Triumph TR (above.) British underhood style (right)

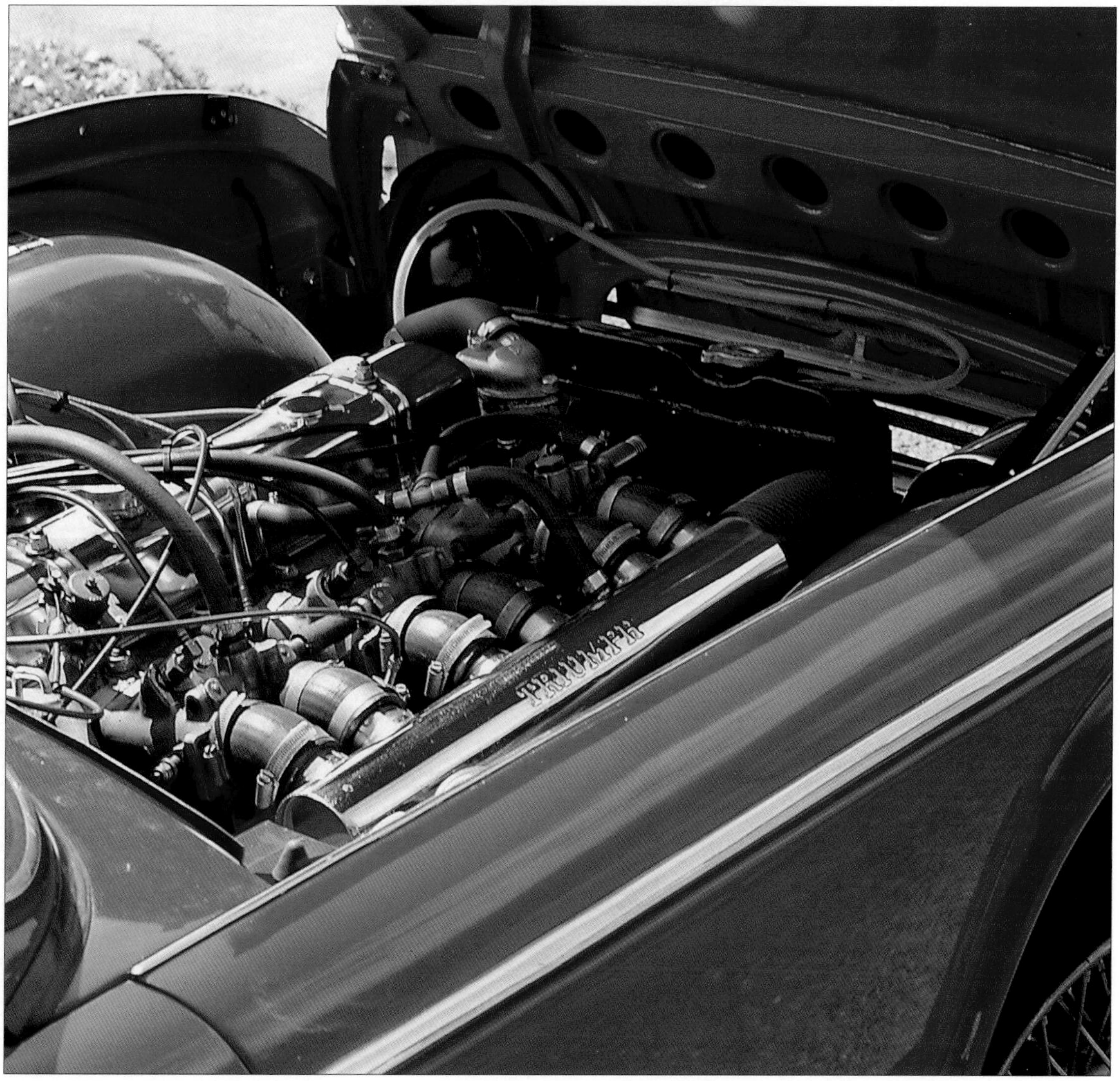

The classic iron-block engine exists among a world of alloy engines. Despite fuel injection the "Iron lumps and classic carbs" are still popular today

Porsche air cooled flat four – the magic sound (right.) Ford and Volvo multivalve designs of the 1990s (below)

BMW "M power," GM eco tec, or just plain "turbo" engines took on a greater identity in the 1990s

1961 TO 1979

The very success of the American compact cars brought new problems to their makers in the early 1960s. For, instead of capturing a whole new market, they encroached into established sales areas, and American dealers began the decade with upwards of a million unsold "full-size" cars on their hands. Not only that, but the compacts also hit exports of European cars to the USA, and many dealers just stopped selling foreign cars. The only two makes which really managed to hang on to their American sales were Volkswagen and Renault. Interestingly enough, in the late 1970s these two firms were to remain most heavily committed to the USA market, VW opening a plant in Pennsylvania in 1978 which gave it third place in sales in a remarkably short space of time, and Renault tying up a sales deal with AMC, which VW had pushed into fourth place.

America was making its presence felt in Europe, too. Ford of America took control of its English affiliate for a record sum of money, and Chrysler began a step-by-step takeover of the Rootes Group with governmental blessing, the

An early advertisement for the Volkswagen Beetle (above.) VW's basic Beetle sold in an age when the ultimate Ferrari was this "Dino"246 (right)

CTO508K

task of sorting out the company's financial problems having been judged beyond the powers of mere government officials.

Mergers were the order of the day. Standard-Triumph joined up with the Leyland Group in 1960, and that same year Jaguar and Daimler combined. Jaguar-Daimler was itself absorbed by the BMC in 1966, while Leyland took over Rover, which had acquired Alvis. Finally, Leyland and the BMC merged early in 1967 after much hard bargaining (though a prime reason for the merger had been political rather than commercial, the huge and complex group faced extraordinary difficulties right from the start.) The result was British Leyland, which later became BL. The problems it inherited included model lines which competed with one another, thus reducing group efficiency, and the fact that its most outstanding popular model, the Mini, was being produced at a loss. Indeed, it was to reach its twentieth birthday before it showed a profit.

German manufacturers were uniting, too. Mercedes had already linked with Auto-Union-DKW, and Volkswagen and NSU also became part of the same grouping during the decade, while the old two-stroke DKW was succeeded by a revived Audi marque. In France, Citroên took over Panhard, one of the industry's oldest marques, in 1965, but ended car production there two years later.

A straighter edged 1960s American-style Chrysler (left.) 1980s styling of a Talbot (Chrysler) Sunbeam (below left)

In Britain, these Vauxhall Vivas captured the feel of their times (above.) An icon, the 1970s Ford Capri – impossible to replace although many tried (left)

The Lyons look – the superb XJ from Jaguar (right)

A Corvette with a difference (right.) Classic 1960s Mercedes Dignity (below)

Shelby, Cobra; a legend (right)

There were many reasons why Europe's manufacturers were joining together. As well as direct mergers, the decade also saw the start of programs of co-operation jointly to develop components such as engines for the benefit of several makers, who perhaps could not stand the ever-increasing cost of developing new powerplants on their own.

And there was a new source of competition as well, for the Japanese were beginning to send their cars to Europe in small numbers. It was the start of an onslaught which was to become such a torrent that, in little over a decade, manufacturers from some European countries, especially Britain, had to strike a "gentleman's agreement" with the Japanese manufacturers that the latter would hold down exports to a "prudent" level, since it was felt that their products were placing too much stress on the indigenous manufacturers. Just how good the Japanese products had become was to be emphasized in 1979, when BL announced that it was to build a Honda model as a stopgap.

A crucial turning point in the history of the automobile came with the Arab embargo on oil exports following the Arab-Israeli War of late 1973. Though supplies were gradually restored to something approaching normality, the system had suffered a shock from which it will perhaps never fully recover, for the era of cheap oil was over.

For America, the experience was particularly traumatic, for the public had become accustomed to unlimited use of big, 'gas-guzzling' cars. Shortages in gasoline supply gave Americans a chilling reminder of what life without cars could mean. The eventual result, once panic measures like the virtually overnight switching of production from large models to compacts had subsided, was an almost nationwide blanket speed limit of 55 mph and government insistence on the production of more fuel-efficient cars for the 1980s. There was even, following post-revolutionary cuts in gasoline supplies from Iran, the introduction in 1979 of rationing in California, where three-car families were common. This represented a dramatic turnabout in future model policies, and involved vast expenditure. For Ford in 1978, the outlay needed to develop new, more economical cars for the early 1980s, fuel consumption limits was greater than the total sum of investment over the company's previous 75 years. For General Motors it represented an annual bill of $3.2 billion from 1975 onward to revise its model range, an increase of 135 per cent on previous years. And for Chrysler, finance had to be found by selling off most of its foreign holdings, notably Chrysler Europe, acquired by Peugeot-Citroên.

Europe had become the focus of the world car industry, and by the end of the 1970s was producing some 20 per cent more automobiles than the Americans. But the world industry was poised for an even more dramatic change. The Japanese, having conquered the motorcycle industry with amazing speed, were now poised to take the lead in car manufacturing too. Motor industry executives began, belatedly, to warn of a "Trojan Horse" and to attempt to match Japanese productivity levels.

MUSTANG CLUBS
RACING TEAM
Ford
16
BOSS
302

Known instantly the world over the Jaguar E type (right.)The pure bred, Chapman's GRP Lotus Elan (below)

Bertone styled the Fiat X19 for the late 1970s (above)

Aston Martin's elegance (left.) E type – a hallmark of design and graphics (above)

Mk1 Range Rover, a timeless design icon

Classic Japanese auto design. The Celica from Toyota (above,) and the Datsun Z car that stormed America and Europe (right)

Porche perfection (right.) A larger Lotus – the Elite (below)

Mid-size mediocrity US style (above). Mazda's unique rotary engined RX7, 1980s model (left)

DASHBOARDS

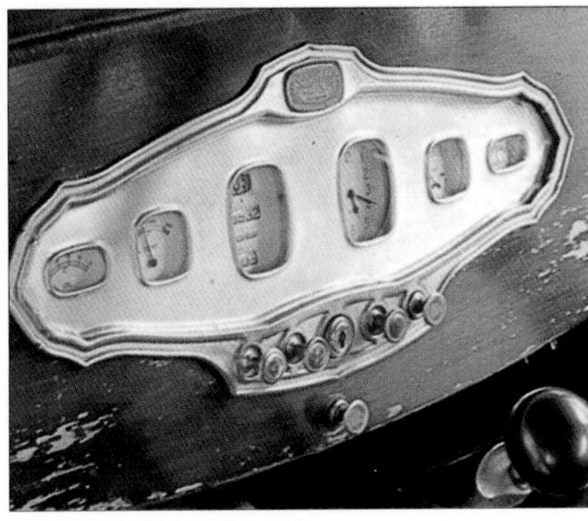

The instrument panel on the 1959 R-Type Continental Bentley (left.) 1929 Stutz Blackhawk in which style was set against the easy interpretation of the instruments (above)

Though the very first cars were devoid of instruments, by 1899 enterprising accessory manufacturers had begun to offer speedometers. "Motor timepieces" soon followed, along with voltmeters, gradient meters, odometers and gasoline gauges. The first "idiot lights" appeared in 1908, in the shape of a patent oil indicating device which glowed white when there was sufficient oil and red when the level was too low. The invention of the dipstick soon rendered this "Lubrimeter" superfluous. By 1910 there was even an instrument to measure gasoline consumption. Some of these ingenious devices, too far ahead of their time to be commercially viable, have been reinvented and, in modern form, appear on some of the latest cars.

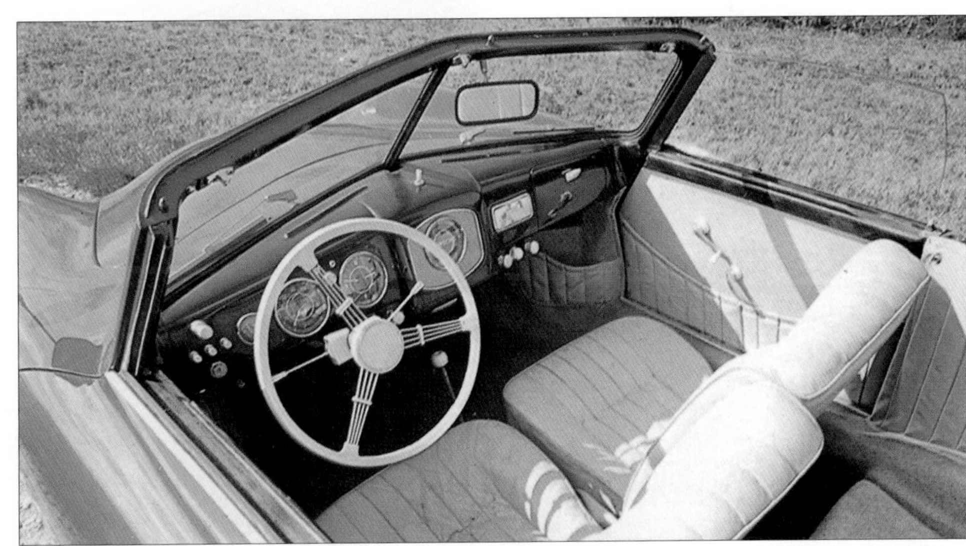

The 1959 Porche 356 Speedster's instrument panel reflects the character both of the car and era in which it was built (above)

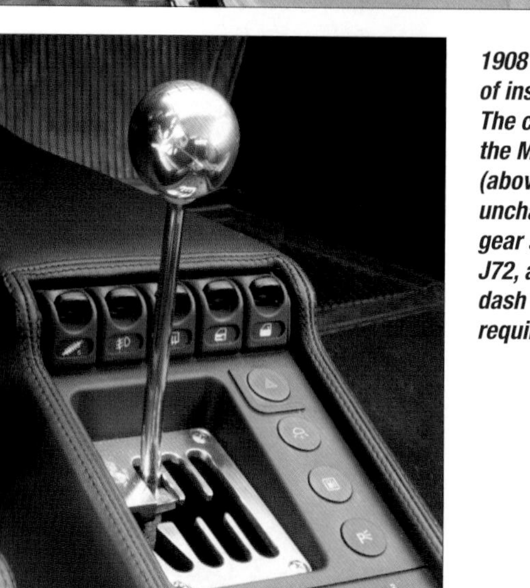

1908 Benz with the minimum of instruments (above left.) The complex instruments of the Mercedes 38/250SS (above right.) The classic, unchanged Ferrari open gate gear shift (left,) 1979 Panther J72, a blend of traditional dash layout with modern requirements (right)

Chrome and vinyl made a definitive style statement in the 1960s

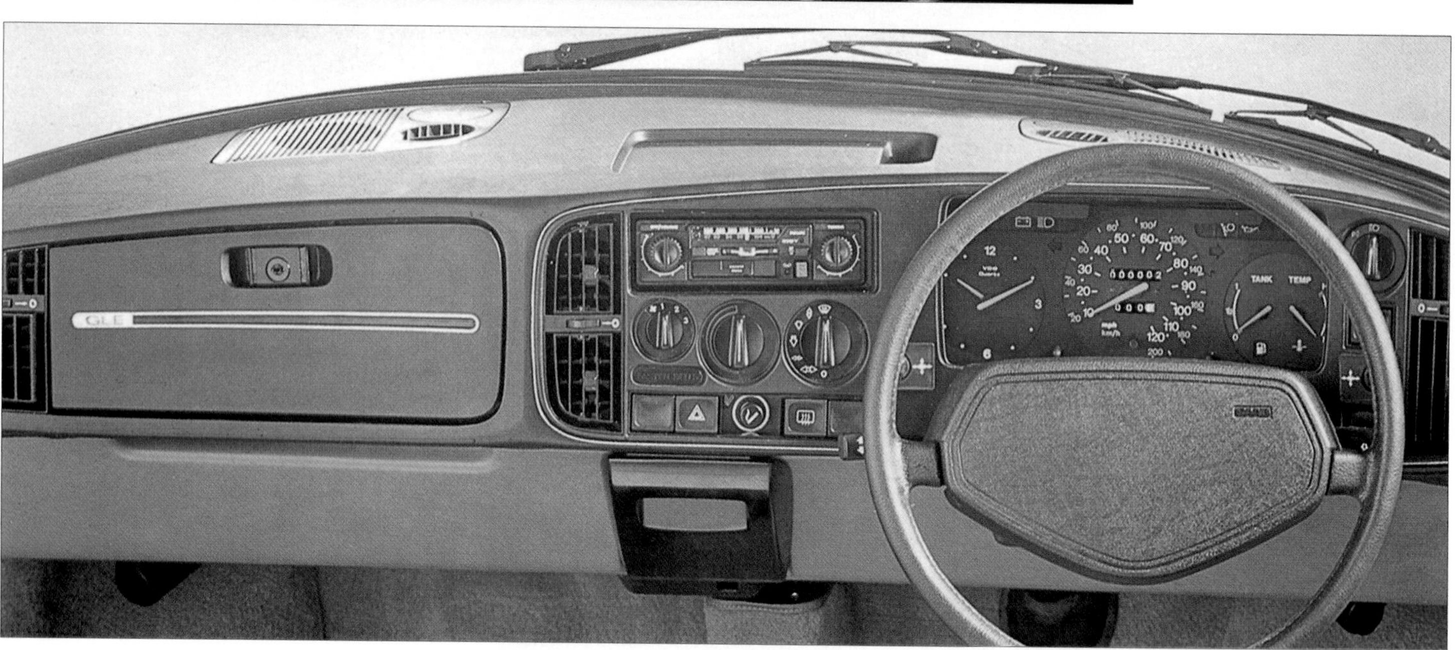

Style – but not much safety in this interior (top,) 1979 Saab 900 saloon with the padded steering wheel for safety (above.) Citroën's curves extended to the interior of the CX range. This version has dials (right)

The new Jaguar S type tried to capture the "woody" feel (top.) Push-button style (above.) MGF – moulded plastic – all the rage in the 1990s (right)

BMW's state-of-the-art 1990 Fascia (left.) Volvo's traditional square edges gave way to curves (above)

Tradition captured by Jaguar in the XK concept (below)

Mass Production

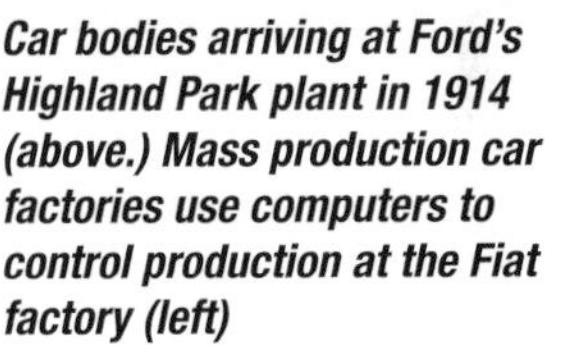

Car bodies arriving at Ford's Highland Park plant in 1914 (above.) Mass production car factories use computers to control production at the Fiat factory (left)

"Traditional'" hand production methods for limited-production cars at the Panther factory

The 1980s saw another fundamental shift in the focus of car manufacturing, as the Japanese swept past the American industry in terms of production and made huge inroads into the popular car market on both sides of the Atlantic. Held back in the past by protectionist sales quotas, the Japanese established bridgehead production plants in Europe, particularly in Britain, and the USA. By the start of the 1990s they had 14 factories in the USA producing one-fifth of all the new cars bought by Americans, and were even producing the country's best-selling model. Moreover, they were moving into the luxury-car market and challenging the world's best. Although it took them some time, the traditional American luxury brands responded and a fine clutch of new models emerged. In Europe, the opening of new factories was an obvious preparation for the lifting of trade barriers between the member countries of the Common Market at the end of 1992. This affected some of the bastions of nationalist motoring preference, notably in the French and Italian markets. In both of these countries the market has traditionally been dominated by the national producers, who have enjoyed a high level of government protection. Indeed, if Fiat and its subsidiaries are taken away from the Italian market, there is virtually nothing left! Recently, the car has been under pressure from legislators for its contribution to atmospheric pollution (about 20 per cent in "motorized" countries, and 5 per cent worldwide.) However, the other sources of harmful emissions, jet aircraft, diesel trains, power stations and factories, have so far largely escaped the expensive solutions imposed on the car makers, who have to spend half of their engineering budgets on pollution control. Mazda has even started planting a set number of new trees for each car sold in the UK! In fact, the motor car has been shown to be the most efficient way of moving people, in terms of fuel used, by a significant degree. The exhaust catalysts beloved of legislators notably use more fuel and actually do not work when the engine is cold, when 75 per cent of pollutants are produced. If there was a singular design theme to the 1980s, it was the growing importance of aerodynamics, which suddenly became an important tool in the quest for fuel efficiency. It had become a primary consideration after the dramatic raising of oil prices by OPEC in 1978/79 coincided with the Iranian revolution, in which the pro-Western Shah was toppled by Moslem fundamentalists headed by the Ayatollah Khomeini, effectively cutting off a major source of the West's oil. On both sides of the Atlantic, Ford, kept afloat only by its successful European operations, gambled with high stakes by switching to an aerodynamic look for its most popular lines. Top management told the designers to create the sort of cars they would like to be seen driving and, though there was some reaction from the more conservative customers, who dismissed the new cars as "jelly moulds," the new streamlined Fords spearheaded an industry-wide shift to the production of cars that had been shaped in windtunnels. The results were dramatic. The new streamlined Fords spearheaded a dramatic recovery in the firm's fortunes that led to its profits actually overtaking those of GM for the first time in decades. Needless to say, GM responded, and it was recalled that other makers had used aerodynamics long before Ford's giant PR machine claimed the science of aerodynamics as its own with the Sierra model. It was in Europe, however, that Ford made the running in the new global game of takeovers and alliances. By the 1990s others would compete for the big league, too. In 1984 Ford held discussions with Fiat which, had they come to a successful conclusion, would have

created Europe's biggest automotive grouping. Ford then offered to take over the Austin Rover group, which was all that remained of the former British Motor Corporation, which had undergone a bewildering series of identity changes. In the 1970s,

As British Leyland, the group had got itself into deep financial problems through a combination of ramshackle management structures and a popular car range of perverse styling and imperfect reliability. An ill-advised government bailed out BL in a vote-catching attempt to preserve jobs in an overmanned group, without rectifying the fundamental causes of the problem.

The company remained a steady drain on the national exchequer and an embarrassment to the Conservative government of the1980s. Ford developed a detailed rationale for the future of Austin Rover, but the plan was scuttled by political pressure (as was a GM plan to buy Land Rover,) and Austin Rover (by now simply called Rover) was taken over by British Aerospace instead. Having acquired shares in Mazda, Ford also attempted to buy the Italian manufacturer Alfa Romeo in 1986. This time Fiat forestalled the American company, buying loss-making Alfa itself. In the luxury car segment, Ford was more successful, taking over Aston Martin and Jaguar at the end of the decade. Denied Jaguar, GM bought Saab on the rebound. Honda relinquished its share of Rover, and German BMW stepped to secure itself a traditionally English brand and the increasingly popular four-wheel-drive market of Land-Rover. The "olde worlde" styling of the new Rover 75 underlined such niched pretensions. Volkswagen swallowed up SEAT of Spain and Skoda, which it turned into a quality brand with quality cars that shared VW floorpans, engines and components. A similar outcome resulted from the cross-fertilization that was the Audi A3/VW Golf model liaison. Ford swallowed Volvo Car AB of Sweden for a stunning billions-of-dollars figure that Ford hoped would take it up-market in the USA, where Volvo's old and new image was enviable. This affected the previous tie-up between Volvo and Mitsubishi, who had even got as far as sharing metal and factories. Peugeot and Citroen retained their link, yet are seeking to create more individual identities, as is Renault. The link-up between Daimler-Benz and Chrysler created the biggest of car makers, and opened up new futures for both companies.

Meanwhile, in South America and Australia, the existing badge engineered brands, peculiar to their respective markets, continued. Such

Mass production at the Panther factory (top.) Checking for surface defects at the Ford plant in Dagenham (above)

moves seemed to support the contention of Fiat head Gianni Agnelli that only four or five independent car manufacturing groups would be left by the turn of the century. Certainly at a lower level, just about every major car maker either owned shares in, or was involved in joint ventures with, companies that were ostensibly its rivals. As the motor industry enters the 21st century it is certain that its future shape will be even more complex, but paradoxically this will be based on a far smaller number of independent manufacturers, giving the appearance of a slimmer, simplified motor industry. Few car buyers will really know just what parts of other cars their cherished, favoured badge of marque preference will contain beneath the skin. The concept of the "world" car has arrived, albeit hidden behind alliances and reskinned metal and shared components.

Workers check and trim and the rear fender clips on the Corvette (above.) The old Corvette customer delivery garage at Flint became a sports car factory (right)

The various stages of mass production at the Ford plant in Dagenham. These include robot studding of the underbody, stages in body assembly, the final highligting and engine timing belt assembly

1980 Onwards

The 1980s saw Japanese econoboxes like this Toyota Starlet (above.) Despite safety legislation, soft tops made a comeback in the US in the 1980s (right)

Until the end of the 1970s, car making and car design had followed an established pattern of furthering perceived wisdom. Design, manufacture, and marketing, could be said, with a handful of glorious exceptions, to have taken an evolutionary course – not a revolutionary course. In the 1980s and 1990s, all that changed.

The car as a global institution offered many paradoxes at the end of the 1970s. On the one hand, companies like Ford produced solid, conservative cars for a middle of the road mass market expectations. Renault, British Leyland , Volkswagen, Rover, Toyota, Chrysler, and many others did likewise. Yet amongst these standard bearers of the motor industry, there were companies like Alfa Romeo Saab, NSU, and Citroên who dared to be different – happy to occupy small market shares appealing to a select band of devotees with a range of cars of decidedly design and engineering type.

As the motor industry went in to the 1980s, such boundaries remained intact, in fact the 1980s saw major car makers all turn to churning out what the motoring press called, in Europe at least, the "Eurobox". These cars all came to have similar styling themes and similar engine and trim specifications – often set by company car considerations rather than for the private buyer. The cars from major manufacturers all took on a similar look – with a black

MUSTANG GLX
1983

Reliability personified – Toyota Corrolla (right,) the privately built Saab EX concept propsal (center.) Audi's A3, based on a shared VW chassis (bottom)

slatted rectangular grille, square headlamps and a range of 1.6 to 2 liter engine options tied to basic and luxury trim offerings. From Ford Cortina to Morris Italy from Tagora to Vauxhall Cavalier, the similarities were obvious.

In America, fuel crisis inspired downsizing saw the car makers cut the length out of their cars and try to create smaller, more efficient ranges – the Chrysler K car series of square rigged, yet smaller dimensions being the first step on the road to the end of "dinosaur" – chrome-laden 25 foot long sedans that had been the norm. AMC created the daringly styled (for its context) Pacer – a curvaceous three door hatch back that struggled to enter the higher mpg economy car arena. Ford pinto tackled a similar niche whilst the Japanese – through the likes of Toyota Celica, Datsun Cherry and Mazda offerings, scooped up their opportunity in the market place as the traditional American makers floundered and treaded water.

In Europe, British Leyland turned itself into Austin Rover and tried to survive through sharing car designs with Honda and taking badge engineering to the end of the road. Several European car makers posted huge losses, and the industry searched for what to do next – simply perpetuating and re-hashing old engines and old body designs had served therm well for decades, now they had to deliver more – the motoring public and the motoring press wanted more; styling, crash safety, handling, and performance all came under scrutiny.

Typical people carrier layout (top,) RAV 4, Toyota's stylish 4WD accessory (below)

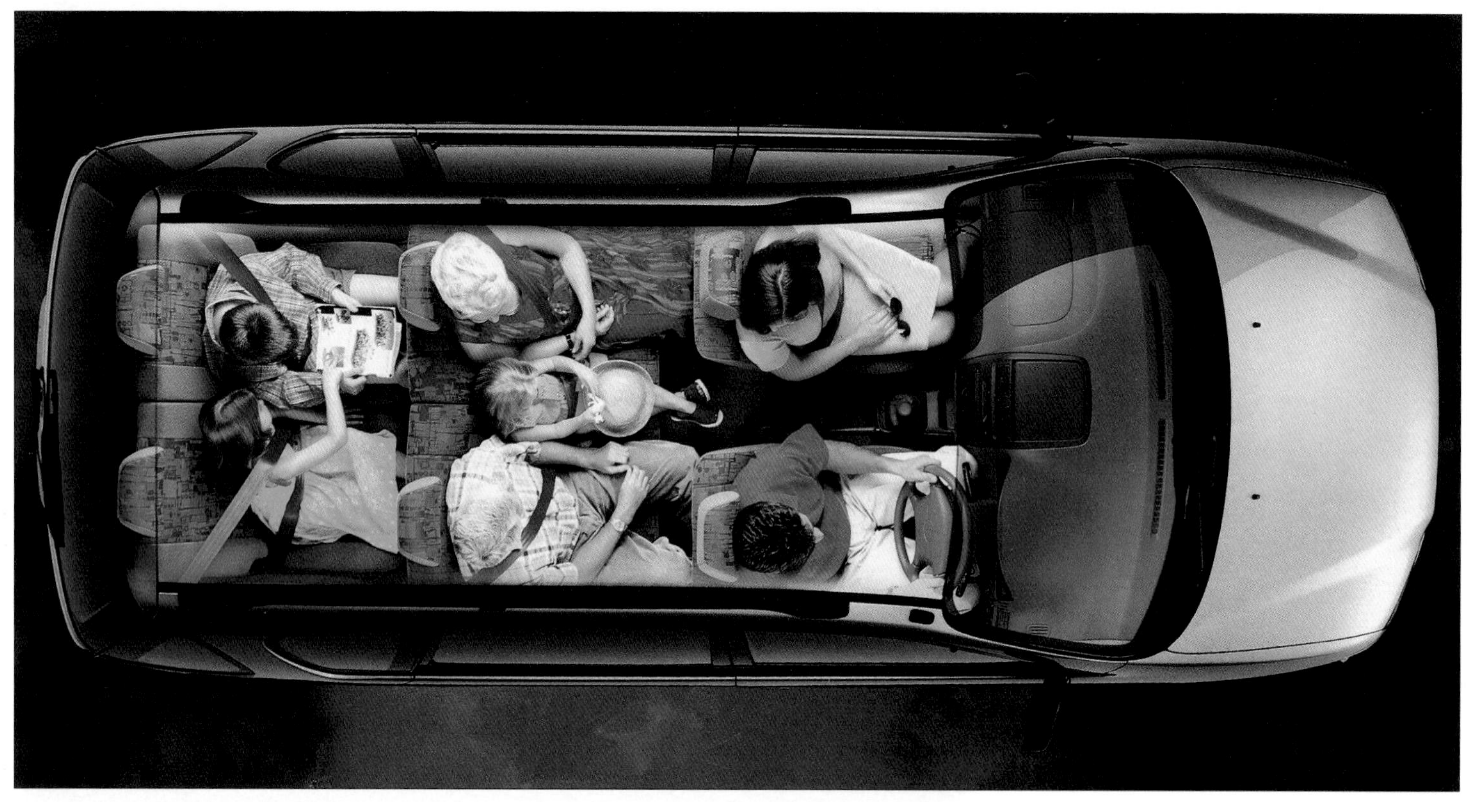

Ford's excellent Taurus – US late 1990s market star (top.) 1999 saw the Toyota Yaris – a remarkable entry into the mini-car sector (above)

Corvette style (above.) Galaxy, Ford's own people carrier built on a shared VW platform (left)

Chrysler's new face for the new millennium (right). Mustang – back on track for the late 1990s (below)

Hummer – the ultimate off-roader (left.) Convertible Charisma – the American way (below)

A Global Industry

Although the motor industry had its roots in Europe and was subsequently dominated by the United States, by 1970 Western Europe had once again outstripped the USA. Since then, however, the focus has increasingly shifted to the Pacific Rim countries, most notably Japan, where Toyota overtook General Motors in 1990 to become the world's highest-output manufacturer. Yet the cyclic switching of production numbers continues to this day, not least as a result of the alliances formed between the big manufacturers. Thus the fact that Ford now owns Aston Martin, Jaguar, and Volvo changes the figures. Similarly, the growth of Volkswagen/Audi, and the alliance between Daimler-Benz and Chrysler to form DaimlerChrysler, changes much in the world of the corporate heavweights. In the 1970s the big European and American manufacturers moved into new countries and competed with one another for market supremacy. During the 1980s the tide turned, and the Japanese manufacturers began establishing bridgeheads in Europe and America, where their impact had hitherto been restricted by import quotas. They also started to build their cars in Europe and America.

By the same token, BMW and Mercedes opened up production lines in the USA. Export became essential when the Japanese began producing cars by the million, because their home market could not absorb all of the output. Another new factor was brought into play by the break-up of the USSR and the collapse of the Communist Party at the beginning of the 1990s, for a potential market of millions, denied cars for decades through enterprise-sapping socialist dogma and a moribund economy throttled by centralist planning, was opened up virtually overnight.

American and European manufacturers were quick to establish footholds in the former Eastern Bloc countries, for once market forces were unleashed nobody wanted the crudely-made cars that had previously been all that was available. Makes that had been established for decades vanished within weeks. The rise of Korean car makers such as Hyundai and Daewoo also created a new sector, as did the grand alliances and takeovers of the late 1990s. Smaller players, like Malaysia's Proton, ably stepped into the market niche once occupied by cheaper Soviet and Eastern Bloc marques. With Rolls-Royce and Bentley broken up in a confused deal with BMW and Volkswagen, BMW buying Rover, and Saab coming under GM's control, the historical face of the motor industry changed. New brands and new models proliferated, and the Asian economic crisis also played its part in the first real slowdown in the Japanese market.

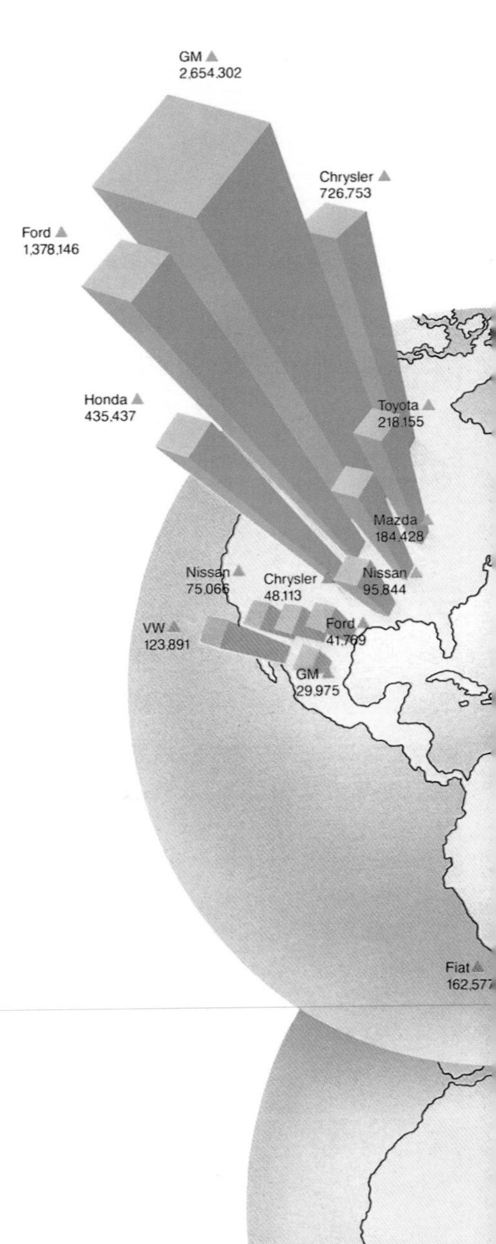

The world's leading car manufacturers (1990 figures)

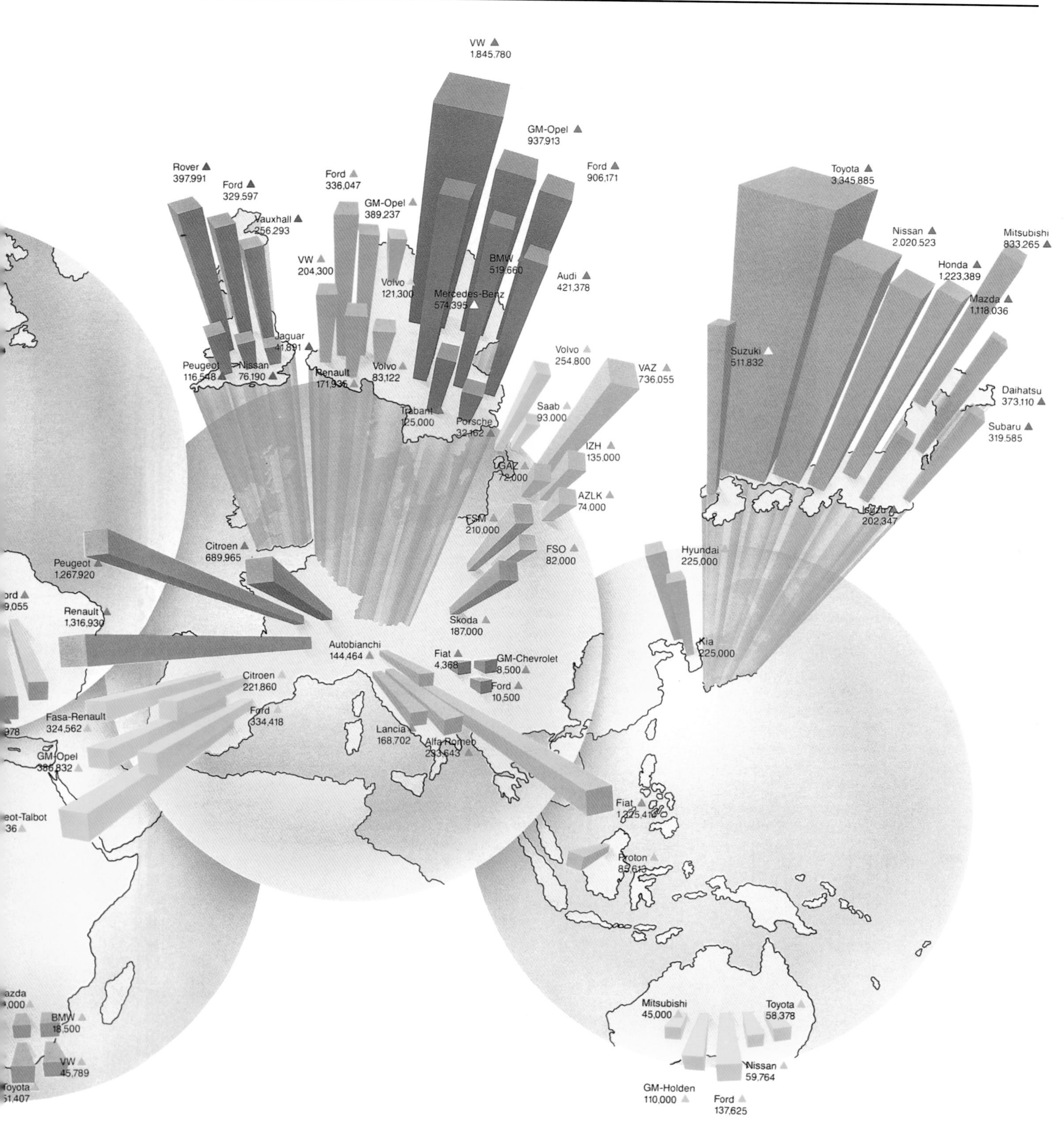
VW 1,845,780
GM-Opel 937,913
Ford 906,171
Rover 397,991
Ford 329,597
Ford 336,047
GM-Opel 389,237
Vauxhall 256,293
VW 204,300
BMW 519,660
Volvo 121,300
Mercedes-Benz 574,395
Audi 421,378
Jaguar 41,891
Peugeot 116,548
Nissan 76,190
Renault 171,936
Volvo 83,122
Volvo 254,800
VAZ 736,055
Trabant 125,000
Porsche 32,162
Saab 93,000
IZH 135,000
GAZ 72,000
AZLK 74,000
FSM 210,000
FSO 82,000
Citroen 689,965
Peugeot 1,267,920
Renault 1,316,930
Skoda 187,000
Autobianchi 144,464
Fiat 4,368
GM-Chevrolet 8,500
Ford 10,500
Citroen 221,860
Fasa-Renault 324,562
Ford 334,418
GM-Opel 386,832
Lancia 168,702
Alfa Romeo 233,643
Fiat 1,325,410
Proton 85,613
Toyota 3,345,885
Nissan 2,020,523
Mitsubishi 833,265
Honda 1,223,389
Mazda 1,118,036
Suzuki 511,832
Daihatsu 373,110
Subaru 319,585
Isuzu 202,347
Hyundai 225,000
Kia 225,000
BMW 18,500
VW 45,789
Mitsubishi 45,000
Toyota 58,378
Nissan 59,764
GM-Holden 110,000
Ford 137,625

Car Design

The Ford Thunderbird returns to its roots in styling terms for the year 2000 model (right.) The Mercedes Vision SLR (far right)

Cars have always been designed, but the term design has had many interpretations. Design can mean engineering in the form of suspension, engine, handling, drive train, and structure, but it can also mean styling, shaping, and the needs of a car's form as well as its function. Thus, when we talk of car design, we have to be specific about what aspect of design we mean. Above all, and throughout the history of the automobile, cars have had their own individual appearances, their own marque identities, and their own visual evolution. In the early days of motoring, the car's body was almost an addendum to the engine and drive line that formed the very core of this new type of transport. Early cars had the driver and passenger perched on top of a chassis with little in the way of bodywork. Such bodywork as there was resembled that of the horsedrawn carts and buggies that had gone before, and which had had early engines mounted upon them to form the first cars. Yet by the early 1900s car bodies had begun to take on their own individual shapes, most often focusing upon the grille and engine cover as the styled or artistically tailored area of the vehicle.

Certainly, a glance at the various Renault, Vauxhall, Cadillac, Pierce-Arrow and other types of the 1905-1920 era reveals cars with standard-type open tourer cabins, but with more individual frontal styling tailored to each marque's chosen image or signature. In such a manner was born the look, or "face" of each marque. Yet from that period on, right up until the 1940s, the car body was seen as a completely separate entity from the chassis and engine which it cloaked. Indeed, it was even constructed as such; as a separate bolt-on addition to the chassis. Although car makers could and did provide standard, or stock, body designs to go with their chassis, it was the normal and accepted fashion to commission, from a specialist coachbuilder, a body of distinct individualism and often unique design, to be mounted upon the chosen chassis. Through this technique was born the tradition of coachbuliding or carroserie/carrozzeria, which led to the creation of the great pre-First World War coachbuilding and styling firms of America and Europe, which concentrated on creating special car body designs and highly individual shapes.In such companies lay the foundation of specialist design and styling houses which dominate the trends in car design to this day. Yet, after the huge growth in industry and technology afforded by the Second World War years, 1939-1945, the trend for every car to be ordered with an expensively commissioned, perhaps even one-off body design, changed. The advent of mass production on a global scale and the spread of motoring down through society saw car makers take the styling and design of their car bodies in-house, and initiated a series of trends and styles conceived and perpetuated by the big American car companies. Special car body design remained an option for the rich and famous but, in general terms, car styling and design was reclaimed by the manufacturers, who devoted massive resources to the marketing implications of constant styling reviews.Perhaps the years 1955 to 1965 signify the greatest period for this scenario, when styling houses and styling chiefs of the likes of General Motors (GM), Ford, and others churned out year-on-year styling changes, all based on the then-current chrome and jet-age-inspired finned styling shapes of the era.

Harley Earl, at the GM styling centre, was perhaps the best-known advocate of the genre. Such was their impact that the Europeans followed the trend, and another era was born. Other distinct styling trends in the 1930s to 1960s saw the likes of Boulanger's Citroën 2CV shake off the conventions of the age, as did the Breer designed 1934 Chrysler Airflow, with its advanced streamlining. Some designers, such

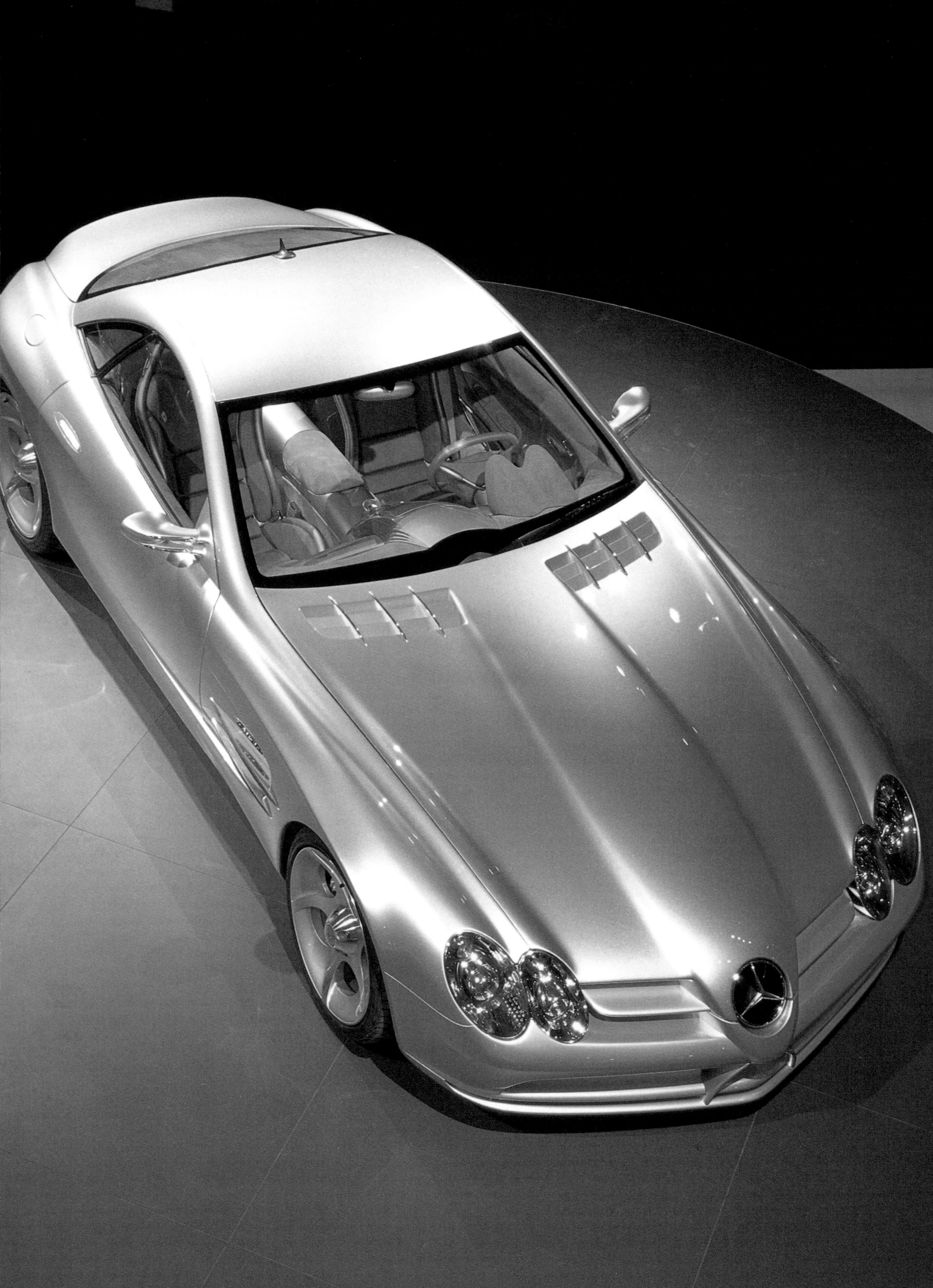

Pininfarina - The Perfection of Car Design

Italian car design company Pininfarina surely represents the apogee of taste, decorum and design excellence in the automotive field. Above all, perhaps, Pininfarina is the story of great car design. Founded in 1930 by one man, the firm sprang from the coachbuilding or carrozeria of Battista Farina. Farina incorporated his nickname, 'Pinin', into his own name and into the name of his coachbuilding and body design company based in the northern Italian city of Turin. That city, close to the home of other great car designers, became the Mecca for auto manufacturers the world over, and Farina, latterly assisted by his son Sergio and son-in-law Renzo Carli, created some of the greatest car shapes, styles and designs the world has seen. Farina started out in the late 1920s, designing and fabricating special one-off coachbuilt bodies for well known Italian society figures, and won many awards for his skills in shaping and sculpting car bodies. He also undertook other fabrication and construction work and, with the help of investors, established himself as a coachbuilder in 1930. He never looked back, and the talent with which he was born, and which he passed on to his son, has become the hallmark of timeless, elegant car design. As early as 1936 Pininfarina sculpted an aerodynamic body for the Lancia Aprillia without the aid of a windtunnel, and it was later found to be accurate in all ways. Over the succeeding decades, his own and the company's intuitive feel for airflow control would manifest itself in many subsequent aerodynamically designed cars. Pininfarina also built its own windtunnel and research unit in 1973. Through creating design studies and presentation bodies of ideas for major car makers, Pininfarina began to receive contracts for its design input from the world's leading car manufacturers. In 1952 the company designed a saloon and a roadster for American manufacturer Nash. At the same time it made a body for Ferrari which marked the beginning of a long line of Ferrari cars that would wear the Pininfarina badge to denote the origins of their elegant, sculpted, bodies. In the 1960s the British BMC company called in Pininfarina to create a complete range of cars, French maker Peugeot did likewise, and Cadillac of the USA began a long association with Pininfarina as early as 1959. Alfa Romeo, Bentley, Rolls-Royce, BMC, Jaguar, Lancia, Fiat, Abarth, Cistalia, Peugeot, Cadillac, and Nash, all of these and more produced models carrying the Pininfarina signature. That signature was a look of elegance and purity of line, a shape that captured the essence of a manufacturer, and what it wanted its car design to say. Such was the talent and success of the Pininfarina look. Today, some of the world's most desirable classic cars have the Pininfarina shaping. The rare 1947 Cistalia coupe, the Alfa Spyder, the Lancia Aurelia, the Ferrari 250, 275 GTB, Dino, Daytona, 512BB, and 308, all are Pininfarina, as are the latest Ferraris and Alfas. The Pininfarina company also undertakes research and prototype construction work, and windtunnel testing. Throughout the 1960s Pininfarina presented safety-car ideas, racing-car suggestions and advanced structural and engineering proposals. The firm's latest designs of the 1990s exude the elegance that has become its trademark. The all-aluminum Argento furthers the use of that alloy by Honda and Audi, while some details of Peugeot's Nautilus grand sedan concept will surely be passed to the company's latest big executive sedan. At the millennium Pininfarina remains one of the greatest names, if not the greatest name, in car design in the history of the automobile.

as Citroën's Bertoni, Tatra's Hans Ledwinka, and Saab's Sixten Sason, extended the art of aerodynamics in car design, while others, like Jaguar's Sir William Lyons and Malcolm Sayer, drew historical shapes that evoked a solid marque identity or graphical image. Men such as Raymond Lowey tapped into the themes of the moment for American design, notably through the glassfiber-bodied, elegantly shaped Studebaker Avanti, and the Robert Bourke styled Hawk. Despite the differences between the American and European markets, and the differences between the cars, there was a cross-fertilization of ideas and themes between the markets and the trends. At the same time there was a golden age of design diversification and marque individualism; an era of badge identity. This dichotomy of design direction was perhaps summed up by the differences in engineering and styling approaches seen between designs such as those by Alec Issigonis for the British, Austin/Morris/BMC, car maker and the transatlantic styling of the Ford and Vauxhall models of the time. Again, in Europe, the maverick aerodynamic shapes of Citroën and Saab were out of stylistic synchronization with equivilent period products from the likes of Volkswagen, Opel, or Fiat. In this diverse and regularly facelifted styling world of the late 1960s and early 1970s, car design perhaps achieved its greatest span of coverage. Advanced designs such as the Citroën DS, NSU R080, Alfa Sud, and others were created in a market that contained the freedom and resources to support them while still offering conventional cars such as the Ford Cortina, Ford (USA) Ltd Sedan, and Renault 12 to the mass-market buyer. In the same period, distinct schools of design emerged which saw periods where a straight edged, folded paper type of styling was fashionable, only to be superseeded by a more curved, moulded look that took its lead from the increasing dominance of aerodynamics.The rise of the Japanese auto industry also saw the American influence on styling manifest itself through the Japanese manufacturers' early model ranges. By the late 1980s, however, these makes had also developed their own looks and their own marque identities, often with help from specialist designers.Beside this contemporary trend, there was still room for the individual styling houses, whose role was to produce one-off show car specials for big makers, or to suggest a look or style in an attempt to win a commission from a car maker to oversee a new model's styling direction. Greatly reduced in numbers, and with the once great names of British, German, French, and American spe-

The 1980s Citroën's CX (above.) Citroën XM – square edged eccentricity for the 1990s (left)

cialist coachbuilders depleted, their remained a core of exotic design houses to advance the art of the automobile through their freedom from manufacturer's marketing restraints. It was through just such work that the likes of Battista and Sergio Pininfarina, Nuccio Bertone, Giovanni Michelotti, Sergio Scaglietti, Zagato, Gandini, Fioravanti, and, latterly, Giorgetto Guigario's Ital Design, cornered the market in providing visual styling expertise in what became an Italian trademark of automotive couture.Throughout the 1960s and 1970s, and on beyond the 1980s and 1990s, such design houses have created concept cars, show cars, and themed production car styling proposals that have earned them a living with European, American, and Japanese car makers. Complete car body designs, detail input and model facelifts have all been created by the leading Italian firms. Of notable success in styling terms have been the Pininfarnia styled Cadillac Allante convertible and the Peugeot 504, amid an entire range that Pininfarina penned for Peugeot; the Bertone shaped Fiat X19, Lancia Stratos, and Citroën BX; the Michelotti penned Triumph 2000 sedan and TR sportscars; and the Guigario shapes and input that produced VW Golf, Fiat Uno, Lancia Delta, and several Japanese- and Korean-made cars with Ital Design genealogy, notably the successful Daewoo Matiz and Eleganza ranges. Undoubtedly, the stunning show-car proposals of Bertone and the swish, silver hued styling suggestions of Guigario's Ital

Futurevision – 1950s style (right.) Fins – defining an age (below)

Design have, with Pininfarina, influenced nearly every car manufacturer in the world. Their influence cannot be underestimated.As a response to the success of such firms, and as a response to a period of blandness and uniformity in car design and styling which manifested itself in the 1980s, when one car tended to look very much like another and even once-daring marques such as Citroën became more conservative in design, a renaissance in design and the art of styling began in the 1990s. This led to the big manufacturers each setting up styling centres in America and Europe to push the leading edge of design trends and filter the wilder ideas into production cars. Design schools flourished as never before, and the long track record of the car design course offered by the Auto Design Unit of Britain's Royal College of Art once again came to the fore, many of its past students reaching the top of the auto design world. For the first time in decades, the ideas of design and of visually tailored styling came back into consideration, rather than being looked down upon by certain engineers who also had had ideas on how to clothe their chassis designs, but would never have wanted to be called designers, let alone stylists! By the 1990s several trends were at work. Some car makers, in a search for a visual heritage to tap into for their new models, and encouraged by marketing needs, started to evoke shapes from their own past marques and work them into their new models. This became known as the "retro" trend, and saw several cars being tailored or styled in a deliberate manner which evoked a time past. Many agree that cars such as the new Ford Thunderbird, Chrysler PT, new Volkswagen Beetle, BMW Z07, Rover 75, Nissan Z-Car, and Jaguar S type may be classics of either the retro movement or of heritage design, depending upon the viewer's standpoint. Conversely, other manufacturers trod different ground.

Mercedes-Benz introduced the unique A Class mini-sized MPV and Ford created the Focus, a car of rare undiluted design purity which replaced the Escort with the sort of radical futurism once the preserve of Citroën. Volvo cleverly reinvented itself with the Peter Horbury designed C70 and S80 models, which looked forward as well as back. Chrysler's new Dodge Charger managed to do the same thing, while Mercedes, through its Vision SLR coupe, signaled its intent to retake the sporting grand tourer ground.From the days of highly individual coachbuilt bodies, through the various schools of design development, then on through the years of corporate blandness and back to cars of individual appearance with distinct identities and visual graphics, we have seen car design (or car styling, call it what you will) evolve, come full circle and bloom again into a specialist world of tailored, individual design. At the turn of the century the world of car design has confirmed itself as an art form, and as a symbol of all the ages of the history of the motor car.

Mustangs across the decades (above.) Lamborghini Countach – the ultimate 1980s supercar (left)

Bentley Hunadiniere arrives out of the Volkswagen take-over of Bentley and asserts a more sporting format (above.) Bentley Hunadiniere interior leather and chrome for a new era (right)

Ferrari's new baby sportster, the 360 Modena, contains all the classic ingredients of Ferrari and Pininfarina

The Beetle RSI's interior advances the art of interior design with its combination of techniques and finishes

The interior of the Pagani Zonda is as striking as its exterior

Mitsubishi's, Super Sports is a hint at the direction of the off-road MPV wagon

Cadillac EVOQ at the Detroit debut in 1999 (above.) Aston Martin DB7 V12. The definitive new V12 Aston at the 1999 Geneva show (right)

Mazda's sporty and smart MPV concept idea

Pagani Zonda C12 (above.) Renault's Avantime is an advanced MPV which will go into production in the year 2000 (left)

DEVELOPMENT

The manufacture of a modern popular car is a highly-automated process, making the fullest use of robots and computer technology. In place of the huge stockpiles of components that once dominated car factories, manufacturers now employ a "just-in-time" system which ensures that parts flow into the factory only as they are needed.Assembly and testing of power units is increasingly automated.

Among the many highly-automated operations is the ingenious use of pneumatic tubes to blow bolts and studs required for engine assembly to automatic assembly tools. While the individual components for the car's systems are manually loaded on to platens which supply a special subassembly loop, each set of parts is selected according to scheduling instructions issued by the computer which controls the production lines, and assembled by automatic machines. Huge presses stamp out body sides in one piece to ensure maximum precision in manufacture. The outer panels are placed in jigs and tack-welded before robots position and weld the inner panels and wheel arches.The underbody panels are brought together in multi-welder jigs which give a consistent and extremely accurate performance, and robots then add the finishing touches to the completed floorpan.

The pre-assembled engine compartment is then installed and the complete unit is automatically transferred to a new work station where robots finish the welding and add the studs to which components will be attached. Computers then select the correct bodystyle for the particular floorplan, and robots weld them together in a "framing buck" before the assembly moves to a second buck for the addition of the roof and scuttle panels. A final welding process completes the body assembly.

For maximum protection against corrosion, vulnerable areas of the body shell are now made from zinc-coated steel. The entire shell is then dipped in a bath of protective phosphate paint which is electrolytically deposited into every crevice. Primer and enamel coats are applied by robot spray guns which color each car in accordance with instructions from the master computer. The days when all of the cars on an

Thousands of hours of wind-tunnel work helps reduce drag and increase efficency in a new model. This is a Mercedes soft top

A draughtsman makes a full-size drawing of a proposed new model so that critical dimensions can be evaluated (right.) Because of the cost of building full-size prototypes, fifth-scale models of a new car are made so that wind-tunnel tests can be carried out to "fine-tune" the aerodynamics before a project is committed to sheet metal (below)

assembly line had to be painted black, so that production was not slowed down, are long gone!

After painting, the doors are removed from the car. Because modern doors contain so many electrical components (motors for the windows, solenoids for the locks, loudspeakers for the in-car entertainment system), this ensures that work can be carried out more accurately, and with less risk of operator fatigue or damage to the paintwork. Then, instead of manual labour being used to bolt the door hinges to the body frame, the doors are precisely positioned by sensor-guided robots before automatic welders secure the hinges, eliminating a source of leaks, rattles, and wind noise. Instrument clusters and wiring harnesses, too, are now assembled and tested off-line by robots. Assembly of the soft trim is becoming increasingly mechanized.

Headlinings are now made as preformed pads and bonded in place, and many manufacturers are molding seat pads and fabric covering in a single automated sequence that eliminates all stitching, clips, and wires. At the end of the production line the completed vehicle is given its first shot of fuel, started up and tested using a plug-in diagnostic computer. Hydropulse machines, which reproduce the worst road surfaces a vehicle is likely to encounter, are used to carry out quality audits, enabling possible sources of squeaks and rattles to be identified and eliminated. It takes three to four years to develop the average European-built car, which currently has a production life-span of some six years, depending on market and model conditions.

Tradionally, the Japanese makers have had much shorter model lives for their cars, and even shorter design and development profiles. Whatever the case, the car designer has to be able to forecast with some accuracy what will be fashionable and acceptable several years in the future, and to ensure that it remains that way for several years more. A new car generally starts as a designer's concept based on a number of assumptions known collectively as a "package". These include the possible power unit, the number of passengers and the required load-carrying capacity.Traditionally, the concept has progressed from sketches to full-size clay models, but in recent years computers have completely transformed the design process. Now a designer can create a shape round the package "hardpoints" on a computer screen, using an electronic stylus. Once the basic parameters are in place, the computer can develop the design in the round, rotate it for inspection and modification, color it, make the brightwork sparkle and even show it in animated "motion" against a simulated scenic background.The design can be changed, stretched, shortened, and revised without anything solid being created. It can even be presented for approval by the company's board, who will be able to see inside and out on the computer screen, and view an infinity of alternative concepts. In short, modern computer technology makes it possible to do everything but touch and drive the car, and, given the progress in virtual-reality computer graphics,

Using modeling clay, highly skilled modelers create not only full-size mockups of a new design, but also interior features like the facia panel (right)

Wind-tunnel tests on the completed prototype produce much valuable information (below)

extra step will soon be taken. It is already possible to crash-test a future car, which exists only as a series of electrical pulses in a computer program, so accurately that "real-world" testing produces identical results. Once a concept has been accepted, the computer can control a scanning machine which cuts a full-size model of the proposed car from clay or styrofoam, not only for windtunnel testing, but also so that glassfibre molds can be taken and "bucks" made for final assessment of interior trim and exterior shape. Once the design is finalized, the computer can transmit the crucial dimensions directly to the manufacturing area in digitized form, so that machine tools can be programed and stamping dies cut to form the body panels. Nowadays, design and manufacturing staff work closely together from the earliest stages, a process known as "simultaneous engineering," so that a design is not only attractive to look at but also feasible to manufacture. By reducing the time spent on the design stage, "simultaneous engineering" can speed up of new models and eliminate needless waste. Computer technology and satellite communication also enables design studios round the world to work simultaneously on the same project. Despite all these advances, however, there is one test that cannot be simulated, and that is whether customers will buy the car once it is in the showrooms. Now, more than ever, engineering, design, safety, and handling are of paramount importance, even to the average buyer. The standards now achieved in the average car are far higher than they were even ten years ago. With one or two exceptions, all manufacturers are now offering uniformly high standards of excellence in many areas.

The average sedan or small hatchback is now a definitive markof the power of the car makers and the strength of car buyers' knowledge and demands. To advance further, other avenues of technology might have to be explored. Now that the car has been honed almost to engineering perfection, perhaps the 21st century will bring another step in automotive evolution.

SAFETY

As far back as the postwar era, some car manufacturers concentrated on the issue of a car's safety as part of its overall design. To some, safety meant designing a car that would handle and drive so well that it would have a better chance of avoiding an accident in the first place. To others it meant making their cars stronger to better survive a crash. To many car makers, however, safety was not a major selling point. All cars were safe in that they were not designed to be deliberately unsafe, but, as history has proved, some cars were stronger, or safer, or handled better, than their direct rivals.

The work of the controversial, yet hugely important, Ralph Nader proved this point for the consumer. However, even in the 1950s there were no industry wide safety standards that could be applied to every new car. There was, however, an active safety lobby in the USA, and a safety inspired group of concerned engineers within certain of the American and European manufacturers' design departments.

Thus it was that the late 1950s saw the first of the crash tests that today are the obvious and public face of car safety designs. In that era the so-called "crash test dummies" were conceived, life-size human shaped models that could be strapped into a car and filmed to see how they, and the car's structure, were affected by an impact. In later years they would carry measuring sensors and replicate details and behavior of the human body by incorporating expensive data gathering equipment.

The giant American car manufacturers carried out their own early crash test research programs, and began to learn how to minimize dangers from a car and within a car as it crashes. But despite this voluntary work there was no consumer knowledge of the subject and, thus, no consumer demand with regard to it. As Nader's work and safety engineering gained a wider currency, a demand developed for safety features to be incorporated into cars or enhanced further.

From the 1950s to the late 1980s, safety standards in cars improved, yet the fact remained that some cars incorporated more-safety features in their design than others. But in the short decade of the 1990s the issue of

A Volvo sedan undergoes a frontal impact test

Saab 9-5s undergo "offset" frontal impact in real-life, car-to-car crash testing

car safety not only rose to prominence, it also became an important marketing tool for all car manufacturers, and brought greatly increased crash safety improvements to all types of new cars.The original work into creating safer cars stemmed from the observations of manufacturers such as Volvo, Mercedes-Benz, and Saab, with American experts also playing a major, if more personally orientated, role.

These people and firms pioneered the art of improved car safety from as early as the 1950s. A Mercedes engineer noticed a box of eggs lying unbroken within the trunk of a car that had crashed, injuring its occupants. The idea of cocooning passengers in a box, in the same manner as the eggs in their box, with the surrounding structure absorbing the impact, had not previously occurred. Indeed, at that time, many cars had very strong engine compartments to support the engine and drive train, but a weaker, softer passenger compartment to carry the lighter passenger loads. By reversing this, and creating a safety cage or safety cell of strength, with the engine and outer body made more shock-absorbent, Mercedes created the concept of a safety-cell type of car design. Similar research led Volvo to design into its cars a stronger central passenger cell with impact absorbing crush zones. Saab, too, incorporated reinforcing beams in the windscreens and roof pillars of its cars. All three manufacturers were early pioneers of padded interiors and collapsible steering columns. Volvo, notably, made seatbelts standard equipment from 1959 onward.

Few other manufacturers did this, and even a decade later some were charging extra for the option of fitting seatbelts. Similarly, as early as 1972, the Swedish manufacturers incorporated anti-intrusion beams in the door panels of their cars. Other manufacturers carried out safety work at this time, notably Audi, Volkswagen, Rover, and NSU. In the USA, experts concerned about safety lobbied hard, and several special safety cars were constructed for demonstration purposes. Nonetheless, legislation and crashworthiness standards still varied widely between carmakers, and the safety issue was deflected and debated for some time. For more than 30 years most cars had to pass only one main type of legally required crash test before they were put on the market.

This was the full head-on impact test, in which a new car was crashed at around 30 mph, squarely head-on into a concrete barrier. Although it measured and limited the amount of steering wheel intrusion that resulted within the car's cabin, the test checked a car's crash test performance in only one, 100 per cent head-on, impact scenario. However, as safety studies developed, it became clear that most frontal accidents involved cars hitting each other at angles, or at an offset percentage overlap, not squarely and head-on as the legislation tested for. It was revealed from real life, rather than laboratory crash testing, that a car might

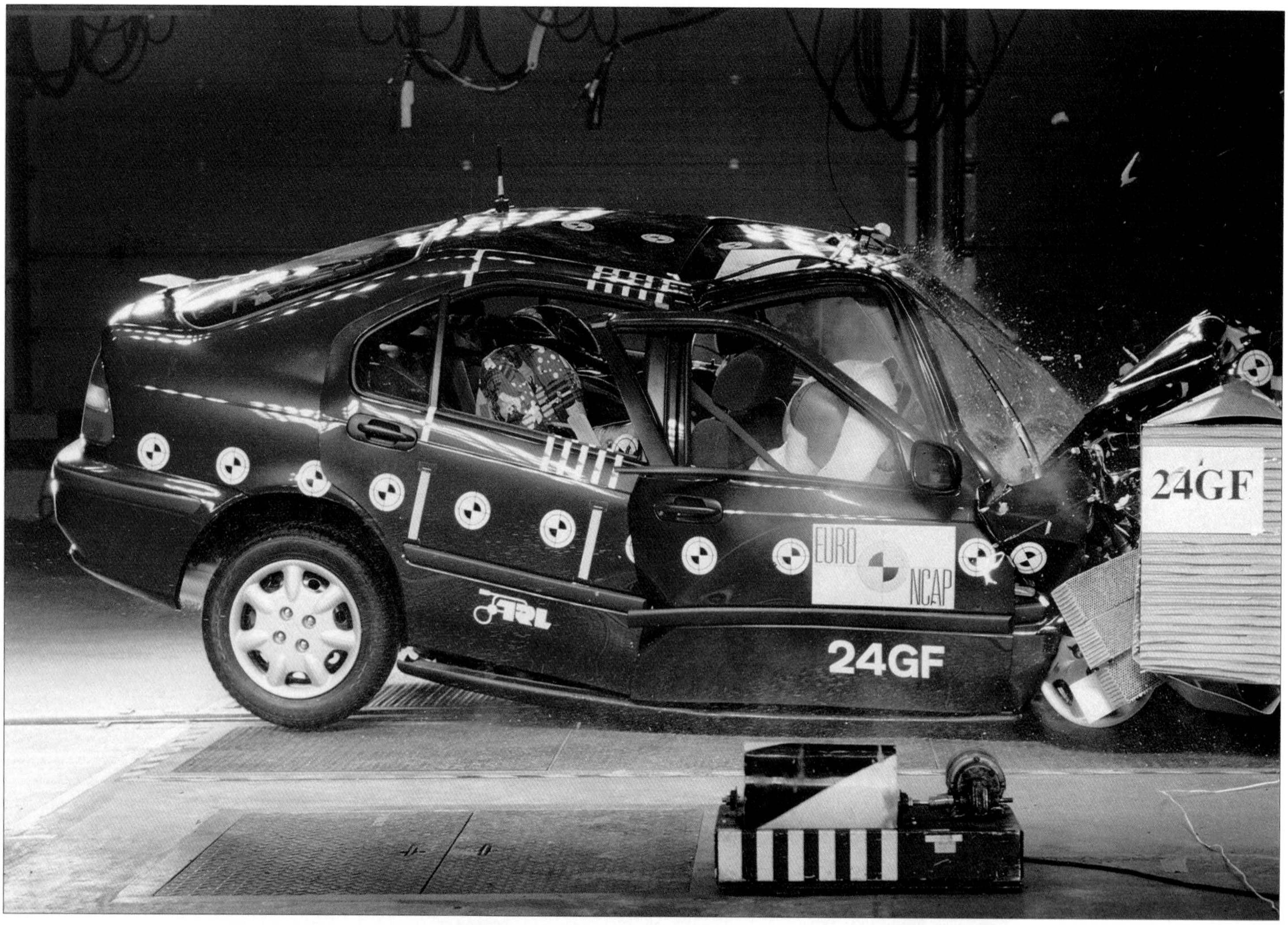

Honda Civic and Citroën Xsara (lower picture) during NCAP crash testing

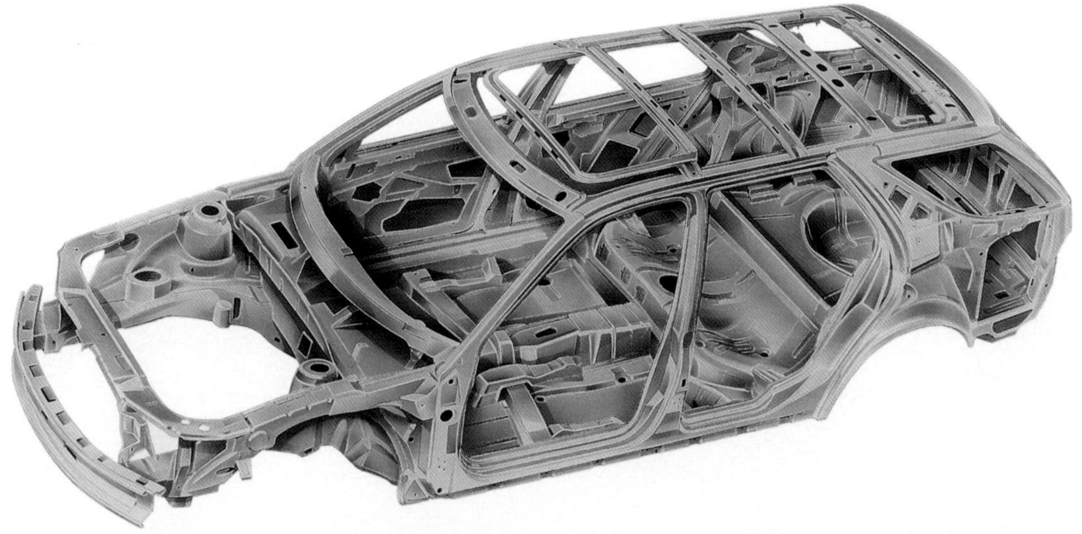

Saab safety structure (above.)
Side impact testing (right)

more easily pass the required legislative test than perform well in a real life, offset or overlapped, angled crash impact, despite the advent of crush zones and collapsable steering wheels. Similarly, the introduction of airbags took place at a differing pace throughout the world car markets, and some anomalies within the airbag's protective intent became obvious. Seatbelt legislation had differed around the world, and the airbag had initially been promoted in the United States as a way of reducing injuries to those drivers who remained unbelted or who were only using a lap belt, rather than a full three-point lap and chest belt.

These differences account for the varying sizes of frontal airbag seen on the market, some car makers installing 70-litre-capacity airbags and others opting for 130-litre airbags with differing rates of inflation. Yet despite certain problems with the airbag, most notably in relation to their effects upon children in child seats and shorter passengers sitting nearer the steering wheel, where the airbag is housed, there is no doubt that a massive reduction in chest injuries has resulted from its introduction. This in turn focused attention on lower-limb injuries caused by footwell intrusion in crashes, and underlined discoveries made as long ago as the 1960s regarding the collapse of cabin space and firewall/footwell intrusion characteristics in all cars, even the larger models on sale in Europe and America. Air bags later manifested themselves as side airbags that, on smaller scale, offered protection against intrusion in a side impact. Perhaps the most intriguing development of the airbag idea is the inflatable-curtain-type airbag that many makers have adopted for their latest models. This device offeres an all-round protective shield within the car, and greatly improves protection for all the occupants.These new areas of focus and research, and the work of investigators on both sides of the Atlantic, led to the changes in crash test legislation that came into effect in the late 1980s in America and in the 1990s in Europe. This new legislation forced car makers to design cars that could perform well in such offset impacts, and also addressed the issue of side impacts.

Similarly, work was done on the safer location of fuel tanks and on greater roof strength for all types of car. As a result of well intended safety legislation in America, open topped convertible cars had to meet new roll-over accident rules, and this led to the development of "pop-up" roll bars and roll hoops.In a side impact the thin sidewall of the car has to absorb the impact of the heavy force of the opposing vehicle, placing occupants at great risk from chest and head injuries caused by the intrusion of the side panels and doors into the car. The widespread fitting of so-called door bars in the 1990s created an impression of strength being added, but because there was surrounding structure to complement the door's anti-intrusion bar, the increase in side-impact protection was not always optimized. Once again Volvo came to the fore with its Side Impact Protection System (SIPS), in which the door worked with the surrounding roof and floor members to dissipate the impact forces and reduce the threat of tho-

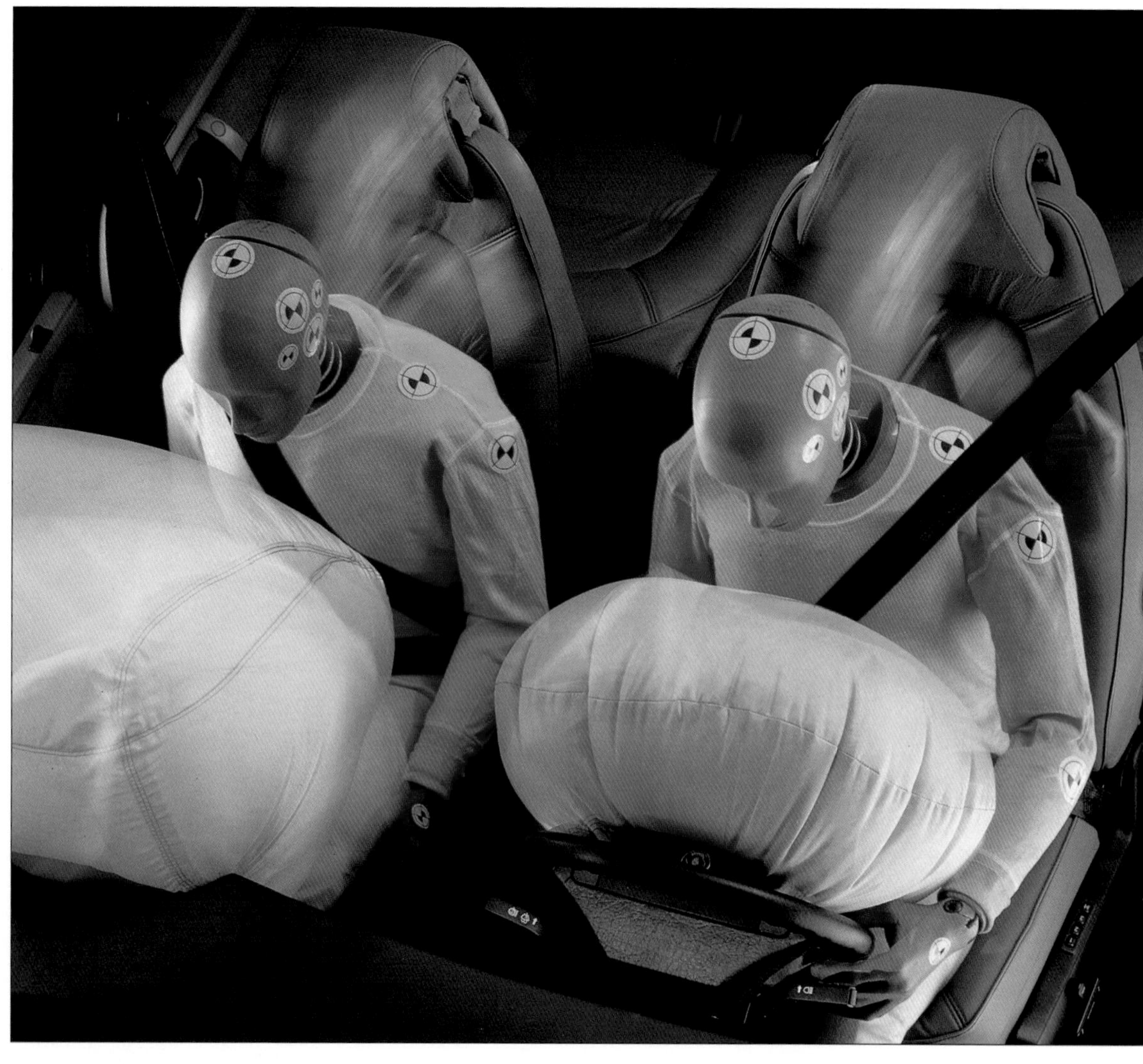

Crash, test dummies, and airbag deployment

racic and abdominal injury to the car's occupants. In independent tests the Volvo system, and others like it, have been proved to have significant benefits.The rise of consumer pressure groups and general awareness of safety as a purchasing factor came to prominence after a long period when the adage "safety does not sell," was a truism. At that time many car makers put more emphasis on other aspects of their vehicles, producing cars that met the safety legislation but did not exceed or extend it. Through the work of the Highway Loss Data Institute in the USA and the German auto society (ADAC) crash test scheme in Europe, car buyers were shown how cars performed in crashes in publicly featured tests funded by magazines and consumer groups. In Europe this culminated in the Euro-NCAP (New Car Assesment Programme,) in which brand new models were bought and then submitted to higher-speed (40mph) offset frontal impacts, as well as side impacts and pedestrian safety tests. The publicity surrounding the NCAP scheme, and the fact that it was run and supported by leading transport agencies and magazines, and received European Community funding, caused a deep seated change in the car-buying public's perception of safety.

Although some car manufacturers baulked at the singular nature of the tests, and at the test speed and type of impact barrier used, it soon became clear that car makers were modifying existing models to perform better in the NCAP rating and designing new models to pass its standards, as well as the new European and worldwide crash test legislation. For the first time, cars from all manufacturers, and of all sizes, began to reach an improved standard of average crashworthiness, and their manufacturers used such safety performances to boost their sales. In America similar tests made their mark, as did the pioneering Australian crash test program initiated in that country in the mid-1980s. With attention being paid to airbags, footwell intrusion, side impact resistance, and ease of escape, the safety story took on a new chapter that saw such research and improved crash survivability applied to a far wider section of cars; notably the small to medium sized car sector, where good safety levels had traditionally been harder to achieve than in larger cars. Larger cars, MPVs, or "People Movers," and off-road four-wheel-drive cars also came under the spotlight, and the weaker crash perfomers in these sectors were also exposed. Much work has also been done since the 1950s on making cars that can better avoid an accident situation in the first place, as well as enabling cars to survive an accident when it occurs.

Thus the five decades that took car safety design from the postwar era through to the millennium have seen great increases in such active and passive safety features, though not without hiccups, heated debate and some unfortunate events within the car industry. The safety story has come a very long way. Whereas a 40mph offset crash was once unsurvivable, or a side impact fatally devastating, such accidents can now be survived in many cars, even the smallest. Safety now sells.

Motor Sport

From the dawn of the car age, humans wanted to go faster for the sake of nothing else but going faster. This led to the competitive edge, the competitive spirit and ulitmately to the competition that is motorsport. For decades the sporting aspect of racing and rallying was the reason for its existence. Yet the influence of marketing, sponsorship, and sales has brought an era when motorsport may well exist for sport, but also exists to sell cars and car related products. There has always been an element of marketing and money associated with motorsport, but in the last quarter of the 20th century the spirit of the sport has been refocused upon the material-and marketing-led aspects of a century of motorsport and its achievements.The first gatherings to race cars began before 1900, and in 1907 the world's first racing circuit opened at Brooklands, near Weybridge, Surrey, in southern England. With car manufacturers making cars on the site and testing their high-speed capabilities around the circuit, England soon began to lead the high speed field. With the establishment of a series of French, German, and Italian circuits, where car makers could do the same thing in the 1920s and 1930s, the racing of cars truly became a new and exciting international sport, with dedicated teams, heroic drivers and interest from car manufacturers. The golden days of the late 1930s saw a world championship established, with international venues and fierce competition between makers. Large teams like those of Mercedes, Alfa Romeo, and Ferrari vied for honors while smaller teams from Lotus, Cooper, BRM, and others formed the new nucleus of dedicated racing and grand prix manufacturers. In fact they created a new era for the moved it on from the days of Bentley at Le Mans, Bugatti, Maserati, and Mercedes fighting on European circuits, and of front and rear engined racing cars slugging it out in a mixed field. By the 1950s some of the heavyweight team names and their heavyweight cars had gone, replaced by the new formula of lightweight racing cars with their engines bolted directly on to a monocoque tub in which the

NASCAR "stock"car – US-style super coupé racing

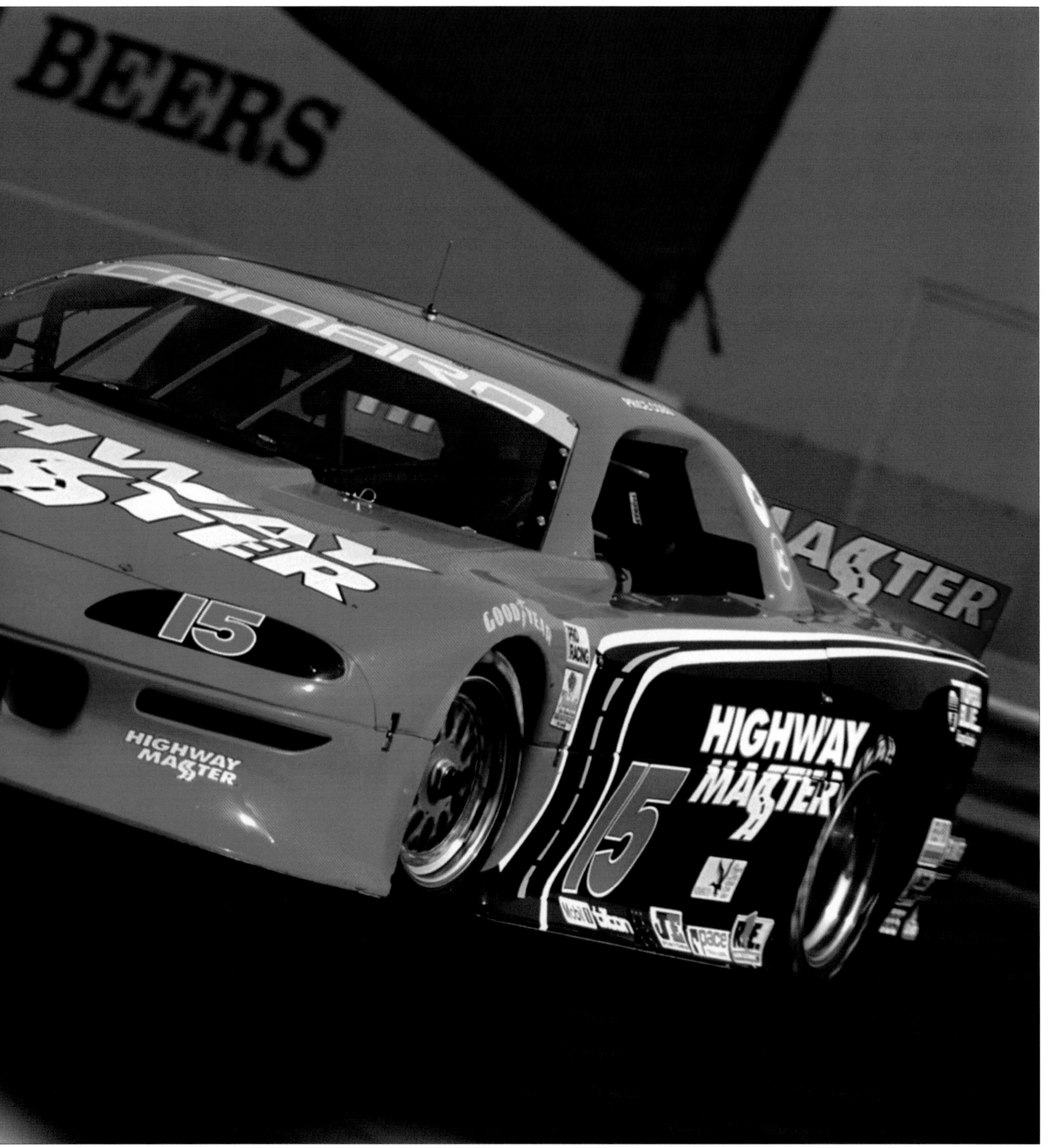
BEERS
15
GOODYEAR
HIGHWAY
MASTER
HIGHWAY
MASTER
15

The 1960s at the Silverstone race track, England, shows how all aspects of race construction have changed, from the lack of aerodynamic

driver sat, and from which the suspension and wheels were hung. From the 1930s to the late 1960s a roll of honor of grand prix heroes emerged. Drivers such as Ascari, Caracciola, Nuvolari, Farina, Fangio, Bira, Moss, Ireland, Hill (Graham, Great Britain), Hill (Phil, USA), Collins, Hawthorn, Surtees, Brabha, and Clark became the greats of Grand Prix. Mille Miglia, Targo Florio, Nurburgring, Silverstone, Reims, etc, were the great circuits that saw true sport and, sadly, true tragedy. Despite great technical developments, and the growing importance of aerodynamics, which culminated in the "ground-effect" era, grand prix racing, whether at top level Formula One or at the Formula Two or entry levels, still drew massive crowds of ordinary motorists as spectators, and saw marketing spin-offs into the everyday world of the motor car. However rarefied the cars, the drivers, the circuits and the fashion, grand prix racing retained its historical allure amid the inevitable deaths. In the late 1960s and on into the 1970s the Grand Prix Drivers Association made strenuous efforts to improve the safety aspect of motor racing, reaching a summit of achievement in the 1980s.

Headed by the work of Scottish World Champion Jackie Stewart, various improvements to grand prix cars and the circuits upon which they raced were enacted. The death toll was reduced, but still many famous drivers of this era died at the wheel. Rindt, Courage, and Petersen are just three of the great names on the fatal roll-call of that era; there were many others. Despite the introduction of immensely strong carbonfibre cockpits, safety suits, and run-off areas on the circuits, the dangers

The javelin form of the "Golden Arrow" in which Henry Segrave broke the land speed record in 1929

1970s style aerofoils in action (above.) The controversial Brabham "Fan" car, which had two electrically-powered fans mounted at the back of the car to suck air from beneath it and create more vacuum. It was so effective that it won its first race, but was subscequently banned (left)

When Formula One cars first began experimenting with wings, the attention was at the rear, to improve braking and cornering in turns by increasing the downforce on the rear wheels. This Lotus used a huge rear wing, but no aids at the front

DAYTONA
500
76
UNOCAL
UNOCAL
UNOCAL
Bud
94
10
Tide

remained. Nonetheless, there was a period of great safety, when years passed without a fatality.

Sadly, at the height of the Williams team's dominance of Formula One, their star driver, Ayrton Senna, was killed. However, some drivers have walked away from very serious crashes with minor injuries, testament indeed to the work of the teams, drivers, designers, and officials who are part of the new Grand Prix world. The 1970s, 1980s, and 1990s saw battles between the BRM, Maclaren, Williams, Ferrari, Lotus, Benneton, and Jordan teams, with massive sponsorship and big money coming to play an increasingly large part in the sport and in the running of it. In America the presence of Formula One waned, the days of the Watkins Glen GP and other races faded. The stars of the European F1 circus were less well known, despite the success of Mario Andretti with Lotus in the late 1970s and early 1980s, and despite other American drivers achieving much success in grand prix racing. In place of the Formula One circus the American Indy Car racing sector came to prominence, with equally big names and big sponsorship coming to dominate this entirely US home-grown sport. In these races high-speed, grand-prix-style single-seat racing cars hurtle round a standard oval racetrack, often in close proximity to an outer retaining wall that edges the banked circuits, speeds of up to 200mph often being reached.

Some drivers transferred betwen the American Indy Car scene and the Formula One world, but not all met with success. Whatever the differences between these two types of racing, they retain a common bond, as do their drivers. The quest for speed, as always, is the heart of such racing. Speed manifests itself in a different manner in the less-exotic yet very popular world of sedan car racing. This formula, which came to prominence in Europe in the 1990s, pits tuned and modifed production cars against each other in a more accessible manner, which the public can enjoy and relate to.

Pitstop perfection, F1 style (top.) Direct downloading of technical data helps tune F1 cars (above)

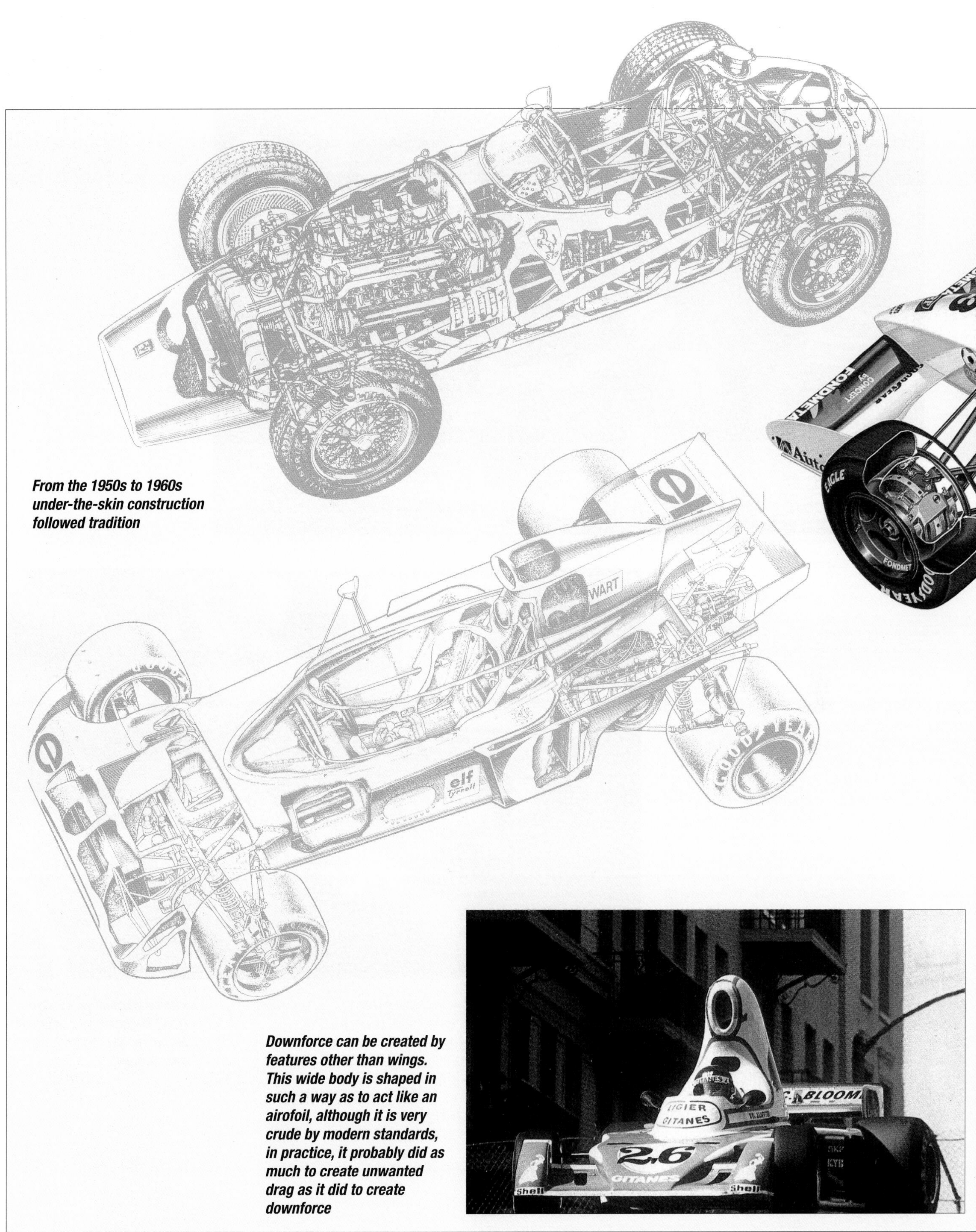

From the 1950s to 1960s under-the-skin construction followed tradition

Downforce can be created by features other than wings. This wide body is shaped in such a way as to act like an airofoil, although it is very crude by modern standards, in practice, it probably did as much to create unwanted drag as it did to create downforce

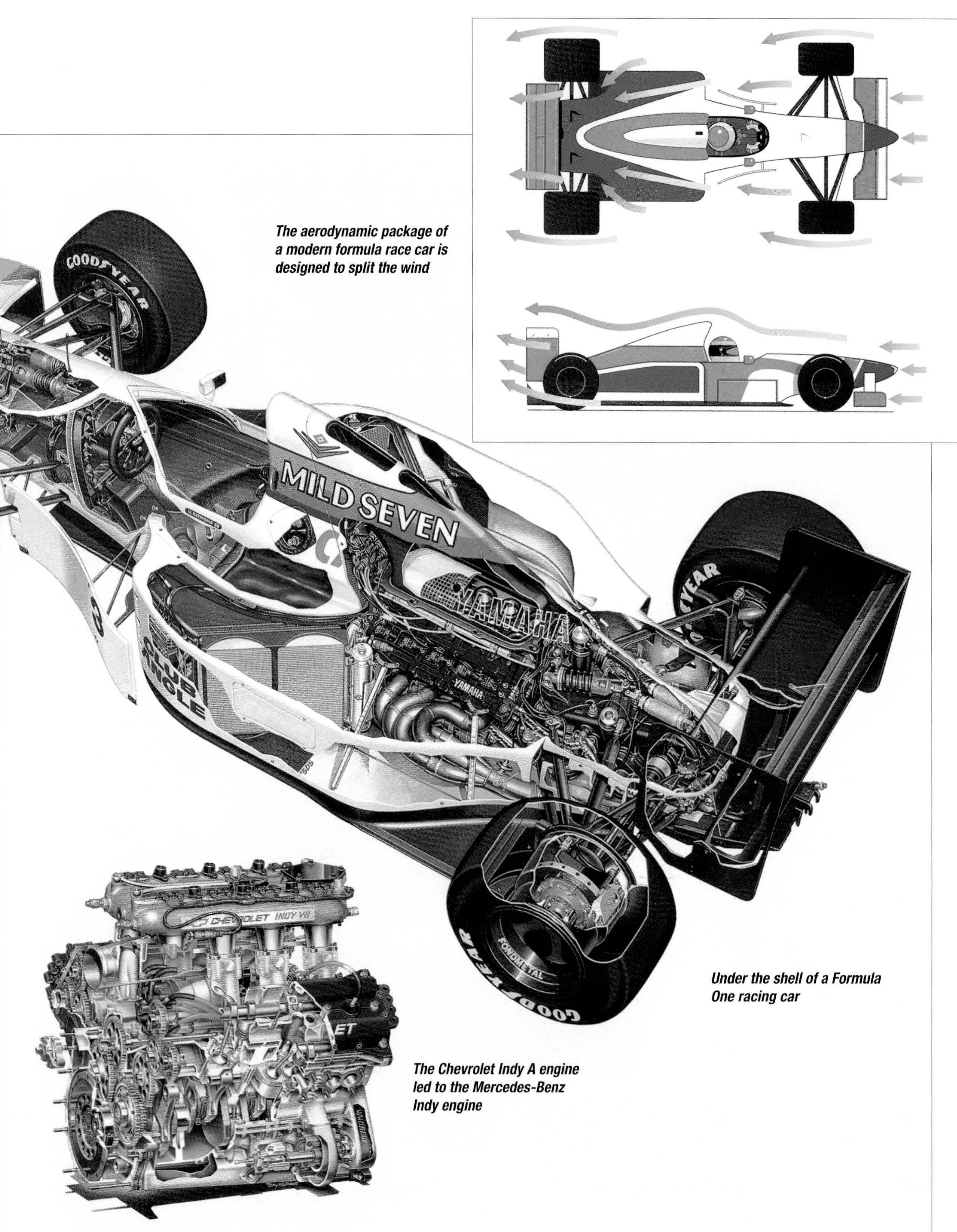

The aerodynamic package of a modern formula race car is designed to split the wind

Under the shell of a Formula One racing car

The Chevrolet Indy A engine led to the Mercedes-Benz Indy engine

Long straightaways and turns, where very little braking is required, force Formula One teams to set the wings so that they do not generate so much downforce that they significantly decrease top speed (left.) After exhaustive tests Raynard established the definitive 941 shape (right)

With his hands free from having to work an H-pattern shifter to select the proper gear, Damon Hill can concentrate on working the best line through a turn in his Williams car

Despite the modernity of the sedan car series, it has its roots in the 1950s, when even big names in grand prix racing were willing to drive production based sedan and sports car racers in a series of races that were extremely popular. In the USA this kind of racing also evolved at state and national level, and is known as "stock car" racing (not to be confused with the British habit of racing specially built, one-off oddities also called "stock cars"). In Europe, the big car makers fund the series, and the likes of Ford, Renault, and Volvo slug it out for racing and marketing honors. Even the Williams grand prix team have entered a sedan car in the series, thus underlining its growing importance. In Australia the Hardy 1000 (kilometre) race confirms that nation's support for stock car racing. Speed has dominated throughout the history of the car, but straight-line speed or circuit speed is not the whole story. From the early days, rallying has formed an important part of the motorsport scene. Rallying has taken on several incarnations, from running near-production-standard sedans in the 1930s to competing with "tweaked" sedans and sportscars in the 1960s and 1970s, and on to the high-tech four-wheel-drive behemoths of the 1980s.The original concept was of long-distance, time-trialled events over public roads, in which production cars could be mildly modified and raced against the clock; not really against each other. Naturally, the car makers realized that public relations and marketing spin-offs would come from such demonstrations of reliability and strength. At that time the Saab 93-96, Mini, and Austin Healey 3000 became the most obvious symbols of rallying.

But by the 1970s the rallying format had changed to racing on specially selected routes, mostly through forests, on mountains, on ice and snow, and on African dust and mud. Thus the world rally championship developed, cars

TARGET
GOODYEAR
GOODYEAR
TARGET
EAGLE
8
Scotch
Videocassettes
DIET PEPSI
7UP
RUST TOUGH
RAYOVAC
Ford
COSWORTH
BOSCH
RAYOVAC
reynard

such as the Ford Escort, Lancia Stratos, and Triumph TR7 excelling in its early years.

Drivers like Roger Clark, Stig Blomvqist, Timo Makinen, and Ari Vatenen dominated. After a brief flirtation with specially-built non-production rally cars known as Group B cars, which were sold in limited batches of 200 to the car-buying public to satisfy the rules, the rally-car world returned to modified production cars rather than highly powered, unique and hugely expensive specials like the special-build Ford RS200 and Audi Quattro Sport that had dominated rallying in the mid 1980s. Thus came a revival in rallying's fortunes that saw the sport regain its high profile as an activity accessible to the ordinary man at club level, as well as being enjoyed at super-star level. Known as the World Rally Car (WRC) series, it saw variously modified and homolgated cars like the Toyota Celica, Ford Escort Cosworth, Lancia Integrale, Subaru Imprezza, Ford Focus, and Mitsubushi EVO driven by men such as McRae, Makinen, Sainz, and Kankunnen. These vehicles are the ultimate incarnations of 50 years of rally car development, and the acme of an enormously popular sport.

US Indy car (above.) Pitlane refuellers (left)

The jewel race in the NASCAR circuit is the Daytona 500, which starts the season in February and always features close running among more than 40 cars

24-year-old Jeff Gordan became the phenomenom of NASCAR in 1995 when he took the championship, although Gordon won the title, 16 drivers visited the winner's circle that year

Winston
Drag Racing
TOOLS
Bud
403
NHRA
SIMPSON

Hot rods race the 1/4 mile in a test of straight-line speed

Art & the Automobile

Since automobile art first arose in Paris at the turn of the century, mainly taking the form of caricatures and allegorical posters, it has embraced many forms and schools of art, being particularly evident in the Pop Art and Photo Realism movements in the USA. Popular items for collectors of "automobiliana" include posters, sculptures, mascots, ornaments, glassware, and even "polychrome sculptural masses" formed from car components fed into an hydraulic press.

An 1898 poster by Belgian racing cyclist Georges Gaudy. This was one of the first posters to advertize a motor race

A squared-up drawing and water-color by the famous French illustrator, Geo Ham

The Michelin Tyre Company's building in Fulham Road, London, was the work of architect Français Espinasse. Dating from 1910, it is decorated with colored tiles depicting contemporary racing successes. This is the 1907 French Grand prix

An Art Deco poster, by Faltucci, depicting the 1930 Monaco Grand Prix (above)

The Hispano-Suiza catalog was illustrated by René Vincent, a leading motoring artist from before World War I up to the 1930s

Motoring ornanments are widely collected items of "automobiliana." This is a porcelain Art Deco model (below)

"In the Car" by artist Roy Lichtenstein, 1963

A 3.5-litre BMW decorated by American sculptor Alexander Calder, inventor of the "mobile" (left)

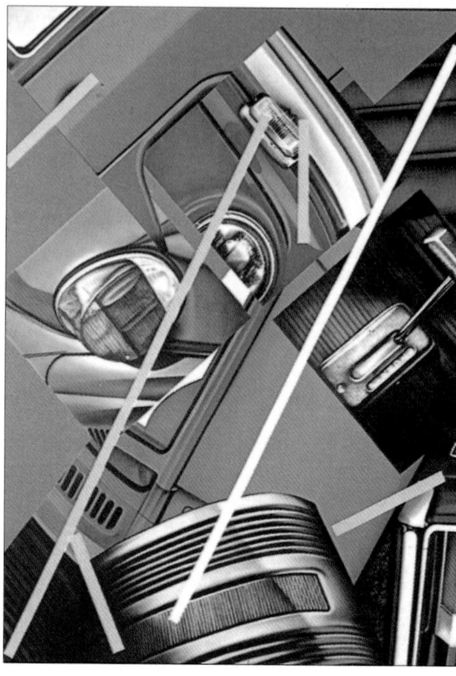

An example of the Photo Realism school is "Wrecking Yard III" by the American Don Eddy (above.) "Automobilia" is a pop art composition by Peter Philips 1972–3 (left)

Alternative Power

Though the four-stroke internal combustion engine has been around for over a century, it has had remarkably few challengers to its supremacy. In the early days of motoring, steam and electricity both had their advocates, but their shortcomings led to their general demise. Steam (external combustion) needed a boiler and water tank, and was complex to operate and maintain, while the electric car needed heavy accumulators to give even the most modest of ranges; it enjoyed something of a vogue in America as a town car, however, up to the 1920s.

Once the electric starter was a commonplace item of equipment, the supremacy of the gasoline engine was assured, until, that is, fuel shortages inspired manufacturers to search for viable alternatives. During the First World War cars had been run on coal gas carried in bags like embryo Zeppelins, either on the roof or in trailers; during the Second World War private cars were fitted with gas producers generating combustible gas from carbon, usually in the form of charcoal.

Serious development of alternative power sources did not begin, however, until the 1950s. Rover, in Britain, led the way with production of gas turbine prototypes, and both General Motors and Ford began experiments along these lines. The major American manufacturers also began looking anew at steam and electric vehicles.

Turbines failed to meet the requirements of the car industry, though they had some attraction to truck builders. Their main fault was a "time-lag" when accelerating; also, their application to mass-produced cars depends on the development of low-cost, high-temperature components designed for satisfactory engine efficiency and performance.

Another candidate which was tried and found wanting was the Stirling "hot-air" engine, appropriately designed by a preacher in the early 1800s. Powered by a closed-circuit system using heat expansion of an inert gas, the external-combustion Stirling was at one time seriously considered by Ford as a possibility for the production cars of the late 1980s, but the programme got no further than the building of mobile test beds.

Rotary piston engines, long a fruitful field for hopeful inventors, came to the fore with the Wankel trochoidal engine pioneered by NSU in 1963, but failed to stay the course. Although rotaries are more compact than conventional reciprocating engines, they are costlier to produce and maintain, and are not so fuel-efficient.

Even the "pollution-free" and noiseless electric car has not overcome the problems which bedevilled it at the turn of the century. It still relies on heavy storage batteries with limited range, and needs to be recharged at frequent intervals. And, if its batteries are recharged from a conventional oil-fired generating station, the source of the atmospheric pollution is only transferred from the car to the power station.

One of the more promising alternative power sources is the stratified-charge engine, basically a more efficient variant of the conventional gasoline engine. There are two main types, the divided-chamber engine and the fuel-injected stratified-charge engine. The first is typified by Honda's CVCC engine, which features a dual carburetor and a precombustion chamber, while the second type is represented by Ford's PROCO (programmed combustion) engine. This has a special cylinder and piston head design, and uses fuel injectors to deliver a finely atomized spray of fuel directly into the combustion chamber.

But perhaps the most successful "alternative engine" is also one of the oldest; the diesel, first devized in the 1890s. Long proven in trucks, by the late 1970s diesels were appearing in a small VW family car, the Golf. Able to run on cheaper, less volatile oil fuel than the gasoline engine,

1979 Ford Mustang (top.) The Blitz Bertone is a 1992 sports car prototype (above)

In the mid-1960s Ford of Britain developed a small urban electric car prototype, the Comuta (above.) The Vauxhall Electric Astra being power charged (left)

Cars of the Future

Tomorrow, as far as the motor industry is concerned, comes every motor show. But, like good card players, motor manufacturers never reveal every card in their hands when they unveil those glamorous concept cars, designed to reveal the future shape of motoring. Rather, these eyecatching models are pointers to features that might appear on future models, a method of promoting new powerplants or a simple way of testing public reaction to new bodystyles or accessories.

"Dream cars" have been a potent force in guiding and monitoring public taste ever since General Motors' larger-than-life styling chief Harley Earl unveiled his famous Buick Y-Job in 1938 to educate the public to the forthcoming fullwidth body styles.

Today's dream cars look ahead to the new century, with safety and environmental protection as key issues. Good aerodynamics, the big theme of the 1980s, are now taken as normal. The ability to recycle components when the car's useful life is over is becoming increasingly important, particularly as more lightweight materials, especially plastics, are used to reduce fuel consumption.

As roads become increasingly congested, new ways of avoiding accidents are being investigated. Among them are a cruise-control incorporating sensors that maintain a safe distance between vehicles relative to their speed, a system which warns drivers when their vehicles cross a lane marker without signalling (the idea is to prevent accidents caused by drowsiness or inattention) and a computerized guidance system which controls steering, throttle, brakes and transmission to back the car automatically into its garage.

Satellite navigation systems are increasingly seen on concept cars, and "drive-by-wire" computer control of throttle and gearshift uses technology already in service on the most modern jet aircraft.

Over the years many new powerplants, from engines running on hot air to small nuclear reactors, have been proposed on concept cars, but the good old reciprocating internal combustion engine remains virtually universal. Ford has been

GM's electric dream car, inspired by Californian legislation

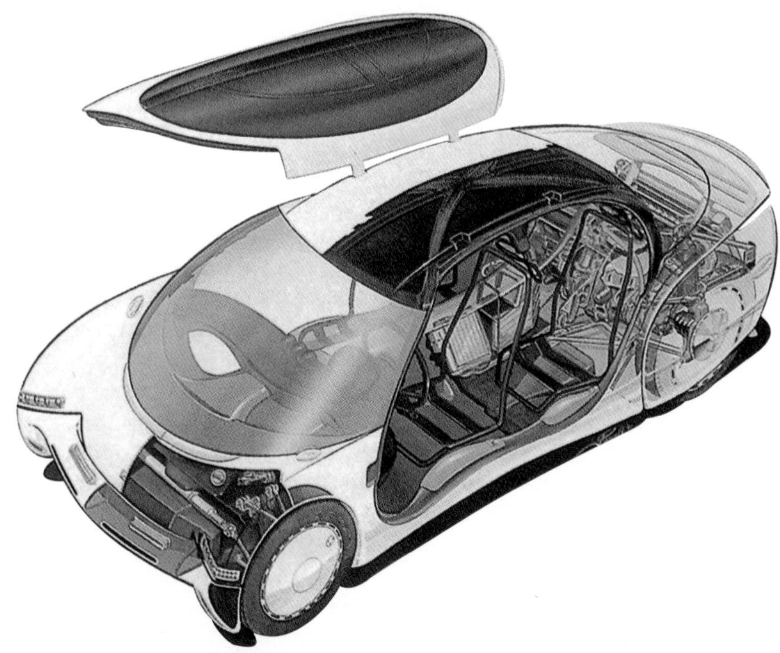

An example of a "Dream car," the GM Ultralite cross-section and prototype (right and below)

involved in the development of an engine largely made from plastics, which is said to be quieter and have 20 per cent lower emissions than a conventional engine. Another field of experiment involves the "Orbital" engine, a lightweight valveless three-cylinder two-stroke with low emission levels and improved power and fuel economy.

Only one maker, Mazda, has persisted with rotary-piston engines. Early electric cars suffered from restricted range and performance, but technological developments in electric power have been slow to come to fruition. Hybrid vehicles are one possibility. A small internal combustion engine and alternator can extend the operating range of an electric vehicle to at least 250 miles.

The GM Ultralite dashboard

The Ford Probe (right.)
A prototype from Audi with all-aluminum body (below)

What will tomorrow's car look like? The evidence is that it will have a shorter hood, thanks to more compact power units, more glass area, far more space for people and luggage, and less front and rear overhang. The influence of aerodynamics will surely remain paramount, and perhaps ensure that the windcheating curved look, rather than the sharp edged school of styling, will remain dominant.

Changing lifestyles (more wealth and leisure, a slowing birthrate, and increased life expectancy) are creating new "niche" markets. These include so-called "multipurpose" vehicles which combine the space of a minibus or light van with car-type performance, meeting all the needs of a family in a single vehicle, and

"speciality" cars which offer the style and performance that affluent "empty nesters" are seeking to recapture after years of more family orientated family transportation.

Whatever the future, cars will surely always have an individual character and a degree of nationalistic trait. It seems unlikely that we will all be driving identical, faceless "blobs" of vehicles that are all tuned to a common, legislated formula, even if the constraints of new rules and new problems make advancement harder to secure. New materials, aluminum, carbonfibre and plastics will surely rise to prominence in the mass car market, as opposed to the current supercar and executive car classes to which they are currently limited. Some argue that the car has passed its zenith as a part of our society, and that environmental and population issues will see the car become a far more controlled and restricted vehicle. Others feel that they are wrong, and that man's fascination with all things wheeled will see a new millennium filled with cars just as exciting and varied as those that have passed into recent and distant history.

Jaguar chopped the roof of its XK to create this concept model (top.) Honda (above)

Nissan return to Z car legend – a tangible "dream" car designed for the year 2000 (left.) Interior view (below)

FOUNDERS OF THE MOTOR INDUSTRY

Karl Benz

APPERSON, Edgar (1870-1959)

Collaborated with Elwood Haynes to build one of America's first cars in 1894, later forming Haynes-Apperson. After they broke with Haynes they founded the Apperson Brothers Motor Car Company.

AUSTIN, Herbert (1866-1941)

Briton who worked for the Wolseley Sheep Shearing Company in Australia, then returned to England to build the first Wolseley car (1895). Left Wolseley to found Austin (1906), where landmark designs included the Seven and the 12/4. He was knighted in 1917and became Lord Austin in 1936.

Herbert Austin

BENTLEY, Walter Owen (1888-1971)

Trained as a railway engineer, fitted some of the first aluminium pistons to DFP cars in 1914. After building aero engines during the First World War he launched the Bentley car in 1919. He later worked for Lagonda.

BENZ, Karl (1844-1929)

Began development of a petrol engine in 1878, founding Benz & Co in 1883. Built his first motor car in 1885/86, the first petrol car conceived as a unity and owing nothing to horse-drawn carriages.

BIRKIGT, Marc (1878-1953)

Swiss engineer who moved to Spain and became designer of Hispano-Suiza cars and aero engines.

BOLLEE, Amédéé Père (1844-1916)

French bell-founder and designer of steam carriages who pioneered independent front suspension and other technical features well ahead of their time.

BOLLEE, Amédéé Jils (1867-1926)

Began with steam carriages, but turned to gasoline cars in 1896, building a streamlined racer in 1899 with underslung chassis, rear-mounted twin carburetor and four-cylinder engine with hemispherical combustion chambers.

BOLLEE, Léon (1870-1913)

First achieved fame with the invention of a calculating machine, then, in 1895, devised a sporting tandem-seat voiturette. In contrast, from 1903 he built refined and silent quality cars of advanced design.

BRISCOE, Benjamin (1869-1945)

Founded, with Jonathan Maxwell, the Maxwell-Briscoe Motor Company in 1903, and in 1910 organized the United States Motor Company, a combine of some 30 firms, which folded in 1912. In 1913 Briscoe began building cars under his own name. A visit to the 1912 London Motorcycle Show introduced him to cyclecars, which he built in France and America in conjunction with his brother Frank (1875-1954).

BROWN, Sir David (born 1904)

Industrialist who bought Aston Martin and Lagonda in 1947. His backing ensured the survival of both of these famous marques until 1972 and brought Aston Martin victory at Le Mans.

BUGATTI, Ettore (1881-1947)

Born in Milan, he was designing for De Dietrich before he was 21. Moved to Mathis, and in 1910 built the first Bugatti car at Molsheim (Alsace.) "Le Patron," rarely seen without his bowler hat, also affected digitated shoes.

David Buick

BUICK, David Dunbar (1855-1929)

Applied the money he made from the invention of the enamelled bathtub to the development of a car engine with ohv. Then in 1903 he organized the Buick Motor Car Company with backing from the Briscoe brothers, but was bought out by Billy Durant late in 1904.

CHADWICK, Lee Sherman (1875-1958)

Built his first car in 1899, joining Searchmont in 1900. His Chadwick company lasted from 1903 to 1911, and his racing cars pioneered the use of superchargers. His latter years were spent as the head of a stove company.

CHAPIN, Roy (1880-1936)

Started with Olds, then, in 1906, helped found Thomas-Detroit (later Chalmers). In 1909 he organized, along with Howard Coffin, the Hudson Motor Car Company. He was an active crusader for better roads for America.

CHAPMAN, Colin (1928-1982)

English designer/constructor of Lotus sports and racing cars.

CHARRON, Fernand (1866-1928)

French cycle and car racer who collaborated (with Girardot and Voigt) in the CGV car, having made a "killing" from holding the sole agency for Panhard-Levassor at a time of great demand. Sold his share of Charron Ltd (as CGV became) to work for his father-in-law, Adolphe Clement but they split up and Charron eventually built the "Alda" car. Though he was very bald, the fashionable M. Charron rarely wore a hat, a matter which drew some comment at the time.

CHEVROLET, Louis (1878-1941)

Swiss racing driver who arrived in the USA in 1900 to sell a wine pump he had invented. He became a team driver for Buick and, with Etienne Planche, designed the first Chevrolet Six in 1911.

Louis Chevrolet

He left Chevrolet to found the Frontenac Motor Company, building racing cars and "go-faster" equipment for Model T Fords.

CHRISTIE, John Walter (1886-1944)

Pioneered front-wheel drive in the USA, even competing in the French Grand Prix with huge, if not particularly reliable, fwd racers. He also produced fwd tractor units for fire appliances and built an advanced tank in the 1930s.

CHRYSLER, Walter Percy (1875-1940)

A locomotive engineer who joined Buick in 1911, rising to become President, as well as first Vice-President of General Motors. Moved to Willys in 1920, saving this company, and Maxwell-Chalmers, from bankruptcy. He converted Maxwell into the Chrysler Corporation, acquiring Dodge in 1928.

CITROËN, André (1878-1935)

Frenchman who worked with Mors before the First World War, and devised a double chevron gear which was used as the emblem of the car-producing company he founded in 1919. Development of a magnificent new factory and of the classic fwd Citroën car caused his death.

Georges Bouton (left) and Albert de DIon

CLEMENT, Adolphe (1855-1928)

French cycle manufacturer who made a fortune from the French rights for the Dunlop pneumatic tire and his exceedingly complex business dealings when he entered the motor car industry. As a result of selling the manufacturing rights to the "Clement" car, he changed his name to "Clément-Bayard." His company also pioneered airplanes and airships.

COATALEN, Louis (1879-1962)

Breton engineer who came to England in 1900, working for Crowden, Humber, and Hillman. His greatest designs were for Sunbeam, where he became managing director and built the first V-12 racing car in 1913.

CORD, Erret Lobban (1894-1974)

Dynamic entrepreneur who created the Auburn-Duesenberg-Cord empire and also owned Lycoming engines, American Airlines, Stinson Aircraft, and New York Shipbuilding before he was 35.

Gottlieb Daimler

DAIMLER, Gottlieb (1834-1900)

Born in Württemberg and trained as an engineer. Becoming interested in gas engines in the 1860s, he helped develop the Otto gas engine. During the 1880s he set up on his own to develop a "universal power source" in the shape of a light gasoline engine, in collaboration with Wilhelm Maybach. This engine was fitted into a carriage in 1886, creating the first Daimler car.

DARRACQ, Alexandre (1855-1931)

Born in Bordeaux, Darracq entered the cycle industry in 1891, building "Gladiator" cycles. Selling out in 1896, he moved first into components and then into motor vehicles. Darracq voiturettes were particularly famous. He retired in 1912 to take a financial interest in the Deauville casino. Though Darracq built many thousands of cars, he never drove, and disliked riding in them.

DE DION, Albert (1856-1946)

Famous as a duellist and gambler, Comte De Dion sponsored two brothers-in-law, Bouton and Tré) pardoux, in the construction of steam carriages. The first practicable De Dion Bouton gasoline engines appeared in 1894 and were fitted to tricycles, voiturettes (for which the marque became renowned) appearing in 1899. De Dion also founded the motoring daily L'Auto. He became a Marquis in 1901.

DELAGE, Louis (1877-1947)

French builder who supplied components to marques such as Helbe, then made complete Delage light cars from 1906. After 1919 Delage also built luxury cars.

DOBLE, Abner (1890-1961)

Built his first steam car in 1906, and drove a prototype to Detroit in 1914 to seek backing. Began production in San Francisco in 1920. Output was always limited, but he gained great acclaim. He later acted as a steam power consultant for overseas firms, including Sentinel steam waggons in England.

DODGE, John (1864-1920) and Horace (1868-1920)

Machinists and cycle makers, the Dodges built transmissions for Olds (1901/02,) then made chassis and engines for Henry Ford in return for a tenth of his company. They sold their Ford shares for $25,000,000 and founded the Dodge Brothers company, coining the word "dependable" to describe their products.

Henry Ford

S.F. Edge on a 1903 Napier

DUESENBERG, Frederick (1877-1932)

Designed his first car in 1904, and by 1913 had organized the Duesenberg Motor Company to build engines. During the 1930s Fred and his brother August built the Duesenberg luxury cars, though E. L. Cord took control of the company in 1927. Fred Duesenberg died in a car crash.

DURANT, William Crapo (1860-1947)

Having become a major force in the carriage industry, Billy Durant took over Buick in 1904 and then, in 1908, founded the General Motors group. Ousted in 1910, by 1915 he was ready to take over again via his Chevrolet company. However, a share crash in 1920 put him out of GM again, so he established a "Second Empire" which survived until the Depression.

DURYEA, Charles (1861-1939) and Frank (1870-1967)

In 1893 built the first practicable American car to lead to a production company, the Duryea Motor Power Wagon Company (1896).

EARL, Harley (1893-1969)

In the early 1920s was a director of Don Lee Corporation, which built custom coachwork for the wealthy. Became director of "art and color" at GM in 1927, and is recognized as the first mass-production stylist. Among his styling innovations were tailfins.

EDGE, Selwyn Francis (1868-1940)

Born in Sydney, New South Wales, Australia, came to England and became known as a racing cyclist. Promoted the Napier car and achieved some notable racing victories, including the only British victory in the Gordon Bennett Cup series (1902.) In the 1920s backed AC and Cubitt cars.

FLANDERS, Walter (1871-1923)

One of the US car industry's first mass production experts. He was hired by Ford as production manager in 1908, but left in 1909 to found EMF. Later he founded the United States Motor Company group.

FORD, Henry (1863-1947)

Son of an immigrant Irish farmer, Henry Ford wanted to take the drudgery from farm life, and became an engineer in Detroit. In 1896 he built his first car. After two unsuccessful attempts to found manufacturing companies he established the Ford Motor Company on June 16, 1903. He successfully defied the Association of Licensed Automobile Manufacturers monopoly group.

Hans Ledwinka

FRANKLIN, Herbert (1867-1956)

Newspaper proprietor who became a pioneer of die casting, then in 1902 put the first air-cooled Franklin car on the market.

FRAZER, Joseph W. (1894-1973)

Having worked for Packard, GM and Pierce-Arrow, Frazer became President of Willys-Overland in 1939 and, with Henry Kaiser, founded Kaiser-Frazer in 1946 in an attempt to break the monopoly of the "Big Three" in the popular car market.

HAYNES, Elwood G. (1857-1925)

Built his first car in 1894 with the help of the Apperson Brothers, and started the Haynes Automobile Company in 1898. He was also a pioneering metallurgist.

ISSIGONIS, Sir Alexander Arnold Constantine (1904-1988)

Designer of Morris Minor (1948,) Mini-Minor (1959,) and other fwd British Motor Corporation family cars.

JANO, Vittorio (1891-1965)

Italian designer for Fiat, Alfa Romeo, and Lancia, for whom he created some of the finest sports and racing cars of all time.

JEFFERY, Thomas B. (1845-1910)

An Englishman who emigrated to the USA in 1863 and in 1879 began manufacturing "Rambler" bicycles. He invented a "clincher'" tire in 1891 and built his first successful car in 1900. Production of Rambler cars started in 1902.

JOHNSON, Claude (1864-1926)

First Secretary of the ACGBI (later the Royal Automobile Club). Introduced Rolls to Royce, and was first managing director of Rolls-Royce.

JORDAN, Edward (1882-1958)

A journalist who became advertizing manager of the Thomas B. Jeffery Company, leaving to found the Jordan Motor Car Company in 1916. He became better known for his evocative advertizing copy than for his cars.

KELSEY, Cadwallader (1880-1970)

Having built an experimental car in 1897, began production of Auto-Tri three-wheelers. Worked for Maxwell as sales manager 1905/09, then produced the Motorette car (1910/1912) and the Kelsey car (1921/1924.)

KETTERING, Charles F. (1876-1958)

"Boss Ket" organized Delco laboratories to develop an electrical ignition system, and subsequently perfected the electric self-starter for the 1911 Cadillac. In 1920 he became head of the GM research laboratories.

KING, Charles Brady(1868-1957)

Built Detroit's first motor vehicle in 1896, and later designed the "Silent Northern" and "King 8" cars, turning to aero engines in 1916.

LANCHESTER, Frederick William (1868-1946)

British pioneer who built an advanced car in 1895. Apart from his contributions to automobile engineering, he was a pioneer of aerodynamics.

LAWSON, Harry J. (1852-1925)

Company promotor, nicknamed "Father of the British Motor Industry". Attempted, from 1896, to form a patent monopoly to control the industry, and floated a number of over-capitalized companies, notably Daimler of Coventry (which survived the collapse of his empire in the early 1900s.)

LEDWINKA, Hans (1878-1967)

Austrian designer who worked for Nesselsdorf, Steyr, and Tatra, where he devised backbone chassis, all-independent suspension and air-cooled engines, latterly rear-mounted.

LORD, Sir Leonard (1896-1967)

Chairman of BMC (1952/61,) Lord was a brilliant production engineer, who resigned in anger over Morris to join Austin in 1936. His bitterness created damaging internal rivalries within BMC.

LYONS, Sir William (1901-1985)

Founder in 1922 of Swallow Sidecars, which evolved into Jaguar. A brilliantly innovative stylist, he had an unrivalled instinct for designing hardsome, keenly-priced cars for sporty drivers.

LELAND, Henry M. (1843-1932)

"The Master of Precision" learned his art in the arms industry. He also invented the mechanical hair-clipper and began building engines. He reorganized the Henry Ford Company as Cadillac after Ford resigned in 1902, and later founded Lincoln.

LENOIR, J-J. Etienne (1822-1900)

A Belgian, he invented a successful method of enamelling clock faces in 1847, and in the late 1850s devised a gas engine. He built his first horseless carriage in Paris in 1862, later selling it to the Czar of Russia.

LEVASSOR, Emile (1844-1897)

Co-founder of Panhard-Levassor and inventor of the Systéme Panhard, in which the engine was at the front, under a hood, driving the rear wheels via a sliding-pinion gearbox. Died from the delayed effects of a racing accident.

Ferdinand Porsche

MARKUS, Seigfried (1831-1898)

Austrian inventor who built a number of experimental internal combustion-engined test-benches from 1868. His first true car, long claimed to have been built in 1875, is now known to date from the late 1880s.

MAXWELL, Jonathan Dixon (1864-1968)

Starting in the cycle industry with Elmer Apperson, he worked on the 1894 Haynes-Apperson. In 1903 he joined Ben Briscoe to found the Maxwell-Briscoe company.'

METZ, Charles (1864-1937)

Famed for his Orient cycles, Metz began production of the crude Orient Buckboard. In 1909 he introduced the low-priced friction-drive Metz 22, sold initially for home assembly.

MORRIS, William (1877-1963)

Starting as an Oxford cycle agent, Morris (who became Lord Nuffield) built his first Morris-Oxford light car in 1912, and came to dominate the British motor industry in the 1920s. He was renowned for his philanthropy.

NASH, Charles W. (1864-1948)

An itinerant farm worker, Charles Nash joined the Durant-Dort carriage company, then moved to Buick with Billy Durant, becoming president of the company in 1910 and of the whole GM group in 1912. He left to take over Jeffery and transform it into the Nash Motor Company.

OLDS, Ransom Eli (1864-1950)

Claimed to have built his first steam car in 1896, and his first gasoline car in 1894. Success came with the 1901 Curved-Dash Oldsmobile. He later founded Reo, and also invented an early motor mower.

PENNINGTON, Edmund Joel (1858-1911)

American "mechanical charlatan," who "invented" an airship in 1885 and produced a number of eccentric motor vehicles which seemingly defied normal mechanical laws.

PEUGEOT, Armand (1849-1915)

Son of one of France's leading ironmongers, Peugeot translated his firm's expertise in making steel rods to replace whalebone in crinoline skirts into the manufacture of cycles. In 1889 the Peugeot company built a steam car designed by Serpollet, but then constructed tubular-framed Daimler-engined cars, France's first production cars.

POPE, Albert Augustus (1843-1909)

Colonel Pope founded a successful cycle manufacturing group in 1879, and moved into the motor industry via electric vehicles as early as 1896. Pope's motor group was dragged down by the decline of the cycle business.

PORSCHE, Ferdinand (1875-1952)

Austrian designer for Steyr, Austro-Daimler, Mercedes, Auto-Union, Cisitalia, and Porsche, he created the original Volkswagen in the 1930s.

PORTER, Finley Robertson (1872-1964)

Designed the classic Mercer Raceabout, as well as FRP and Porter cars, becoming chief engineer of Curtiss Aircraft in 1919.

Henry Royce

The Hon C.S. Rolls

RENAULT, Louis (1877-1944)

Son of a rich Parisian button maker, Louis Renault rebuilt his De Dion tricycle into a shaft-driven voiturette in 1898, and received so many orders that he began production of similar vehicles. By 1900 Renault was building 350 cars a year and was established as one of France's leading makes. Louis Renault died in prison during the Second World War, having been accused of collaborating with the Germans during the Occupation of France.

RIKER, Andrew L. (1868-1930)

Built his first electric tricycle in 1884, but did not begin production until 1899. In 1902 joined Locomobile to design their first gasoline cars.

ROESCH, Georges (1891-1969)

Brilliant Swiss engineer who became chief engineer of Clement Talbot of London at 25, designing highspeed tourers of great refinement.

ROLLS, The Hon. Charles Stuart (1877-1910)

Interested in machinery from an early age, Lord Llangottock's youngest son was a pioneer motorist and racing driver who entered the motor trade. Anxious to sell a car bearing his own name, he joined with the engineer Royce. Rolls died in a flying accident at Bournemouth, having been the first man to fly the English Channel in both directions.

ROYCE, Henry (1863-1933)

Electrical engineer who built a twin-cylinder car in 1903 and went on to construct the "best car in the world", as well as some outstanding aero engines.

SELDEN, George Baldwin (1846-1932)

A patent attorney who experimented with engines from 1873 to 1875, and designed a self-propelled vehicle on which he filed a patent in 1879, the patent being granted in 1895. He sold the patent to Columbia Electric on a royalty basis in 1899, when it was used to try and create a monopoly group (Association of Licenced Automobile Manufacturers.)

SERPOLLET, Léon (1858-1907)

Frenchman who devised the flash boiler for rapid production of steam and built a steam tricycle in 1887. He built a number of steam three-wheelers in the 1890s, but did not seriously begin car production until the turn of the century. His sprint racers broke many speed records. His aim was to build a steamer that was as simple to control as a gasoline vehicle, but his death from consumption ended the Serpollet company.

SIMMS, Frederick R. (1863-1944)

Brought the first Daimler engines into Britain in 1891, and fitted them into motor launches tested on the Thames. Formed the Daimler Motor Syndicate in 1893, which was taken over by Lawson interests in 1896. He invented the term "motor-car" and helped to found the Automobile Club of Great Britain and Ireland (later the Royal Automobile Club) and the Society of Motor Manufacturers and Traders. He also built Simms cars.

SLOAN, Alfred P. (1875-1966)

At Durant's behest, formed the United Motors Corporation of accessory manufacturers, later absorbed by GM. An administrative genius, Sloan reorganized the corporate structure of GM, becoming its president from 1923-1936.

STANLEY, Francis E. (149-1918) and Freelan O. (1849-1940)

The Stanley twins used the proceeds from the sale of their photographic dry-plate business to develop a steam car, the rights to which were bought for $250,000 to create Locomobile. The Stanleys came up with an improved design, Stanley steamers being built into the 1920s.

STUTZ, Harry (1871-1930)

Designed an improved rear axle, then became sales manager for Schebler carburetors, engineer for Marion and designer of the American Underslung. Manufacture of Stutz cars began in 1911; Harry Stutz resigned in 1919, later founding HCS. He was also a talented saxophonist.

THOMAS, Edwin Ross (1850-1936)

Though he founded the E. R. Thomas Motor Company in Buffalo, NY, in 1900 (it built the Thomas Flyer, which won the round-the-world New York-Paris Race of 1908,) Edwin Thomas never learned to drive.

VOISIN, Gabriel (1880-1973)

French aviation pioneer who went into car production between the wars with advanced and unorthodox sleeve-valve cars.

WHITE, Windsor (1866-958), Rollin (1872-1968), Walter (1876-1929)

Rollin and Windsor built the first White Steamer in 1900, and Walter was sent to London the next year to develop the European market. Rollin left the White Company (Windsor was its president) in 1914 to build Cleveland tractors, and launched the Rollin car in 1923.

WILLS, Childe Harold (1878-1940)

Childe Harold Wills

A brilliant metallurgist who helped Henry Ford develop his first cars (and also designed the famous "Ford" script logo) and became chief engineer of the Ford Motor Company. He developed vanadium and molybdenum steel alloys for the motor industry. With his severance pay from Ford he founded Wills Ste Claire. In 1933 he became Chrysler's chief metallurgist.

WILLYS, John North (1873-1933)

In 1906 undertook to sell the entire output of Overland, then mounted an effort to save the company when it got into difficulties in 1907, moving production to Toledo. He built Overland production up to 95,000 units, second only to Ford, in 1915.

WINTON, Alexander (1860-1932)

Scots marine engineer who jumped ship in America in 1880, starting bicycle production in 1896. Built his first car in 1896, founding the Winton Motor Carriage Company next year. In 1903 he launched an eight-cylinder "Bullet" racer. His designs featured pneumatic controls. When car production was suspended in 1924 he began manufacture of diesel engines.

Frederick Simms

A-Z OF THE WORLD'S AUTOMOBILES

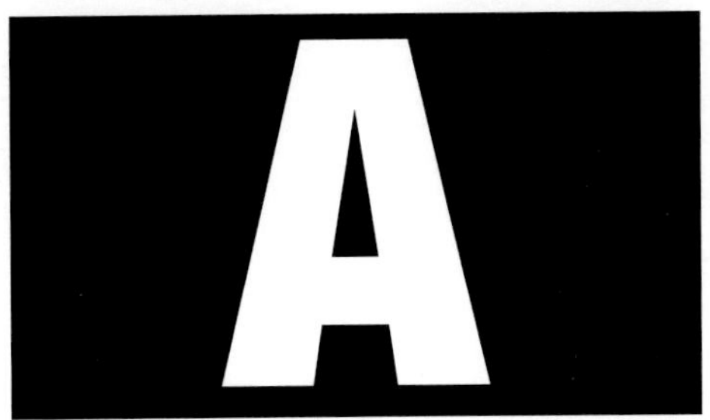

AAA • France 1919-1920

The Ateliers d'Automobiles et d'Aviation of Paris offered electric 'voitures de luxe' on petrol car lines.

AACHENER • Germany 1902

The Aix-la-Chapelle Steel Works made engines of 1.3 /4hp to 11 hp, and components as well as complete cars - later marketed as 'Fafnir'.

AAG • Germany 1900-1901

Produced 5 hp voiturettes to the design of Professor Klingenberg. A leading politician and head of the AEG group, Emil Rathenau, bought the AAG factory and founded the 'Neue Automobil Gesellschaft', which built NAG cars until 1934.

AAG • Germany 1906-1907

A four-cylinder, four-speed, shaft-drive car designed by an engineer named Burchardt.

ABADAL • Spain 1912-1923

Francisco Abadal was a forceful Hispano-Suiza salesman who began building fast luxury cars in Barcelona in 1912. These had 3104cc four-cylinder and 4521cc six-cylinder engines closely patterned on the Hispano. Abadals were soon being built under licence by Impèria of Belgium as Impèria-Abadals. Abadal acquired the Buick agency in 1916, and Barcelona Abadals after that date had Buick power units and custom coachwork. In Belgium M A Van Roggen, formerly of Springuel, took over Impèria, and built about 170 more Impèria-Abadals, including a 2992cc 16-valve four-cylinder ohc sports model and three prototype 5630cc straight-eights.

AAA electric 'voiture de luxe', 1919

ABARTH • Italy 1950-1971

Founded by former racing motorcyclist Carlo Abarth in Turin, this factory concentrated on sports and racing cars. It also produced a wide range of tuning equipment for various Fiat models from 500cc upwards. There were also Abarth sports-racing cars with own make dohc engines of 1098cc, 1496cc and 1966cc, as well as very fast Fiat-Abarths of 598 to 2323cc. In 1964 there was a 695cc, 66 bhp model and a 982cc 'Bialbero' dohc model with 114 bhp. There were numerous prototypes, which included a dohc V-12 5980cc racer, and a 2986cc V-8 with dohc and 310 bhp. Abarth also co-operated with Simca and created some fast Simca-Abarth cars. In 1971 Abarth, whose pre-war home was at Vienna, decided to 'slow down' and Fiat took over his works.

ABBEY • England 1922

The short-lived friction-drive Abbey was an assembled car with a 10.8 hp Coventry-Climax engine.

Autobianchi A 112 Abarth

ABBOTT-DETROIT • USA 1909-1919

The Abbott-Detroit was a powerful, well-designed luxury car with a Continental engine. By 1913 electric lighting and starting had been standardised, and the cars were guaranteed for life. The 1913 range cost from $1,700 for the 34/40 hp four-door Roadster, to $3,050 for the seven-passenger Limousine, and included a 44/50 hp Battleship Roadster at $2,150. In 1914 three models were offered; the 34 hp Model F, the 32 hp Model L, and the 27 hp Model K.

1923 ABC four-seater chummy

ABC • USA 1906-1910

'The cheapest high-grade car in America', the St Louis-built ABC was available with 18 hp twin and 30 hp four-cylinder engines, solid or pneumatic tyres, and friction drive.

ABC • England 1920-1929

The ABC was a light car powered by a 1203cc flat-twin air-cooled engine designed by Granville Bradshaw, who was also responsible for the ABC motorcycle. The company was based in Hersham, Surrey and, during the earliest years of its existence, was part of the Harper Bean combine. The car was not cheap, selling for £414 in 1920. Although it was initially unreliable, later examples were

c. 1908 Adams 40/50 hp V-8 phaeton

more refined, having enclosed pushrods, stronger valve gear and a better lubrication system. Surprisingly, the 'radiator' cap was the petrol tank filler! A Super Sports version with twin carburettors appeared in 1925, and was the only model available in the last four years of the car's production.

ABC • USA 1922

Although planned and advertised by the Arthur-Boynton Co of Albany, New York, this light car (which would have sold for $300) never materialised.

ABERDONIA • England 1911-1915

The 20 hp Aberdonia, built in Park Royal, London, cost £500 with seven-seated touring coachwork, or £700 with 'special landau body'. This was a weird mid-engined, forward-control device.

ABINGDON • England 1902-1903

The Abingdon range for 1903 consisted of a 61.2 hp De Dion-engined two-seater, tonneau-bodied 12 hp and 16 hp twins and a 24 hp four-cylinder.

ABINGDON • England 1922-1923

An assembled car, powered by an 11.9 hp Dorman engine, the Abingdon was built only in small numbers. Motorcycles were produced until 1925. In 1905-1906 the company had built the 5 hp AKD tricar.

ABLE • USA 1917-1919

Featuring its own engines, but otherwise proprietary components, the Able was a small production car built at Mount Vernon, New York. It became the Vernon in 1920.

ABLE • France 1920-1927

A small cyclecar made at Avignon by Paul Toulouse, with proprietary engines like SCAP, Chapuis-Dornier and CIME, from 1100cc to 1500cc. Some of them were sold under the 'Toulouse' name.

AC • England 1908 to date

See panel overleaf

ACADEMY • England 1906-1908

A dual-control 14 hp model built by West of Coventry, mainly for Motor Schools, London (who offered a course of 12 lessons for £3.3s), but also shown at the 1906 Olympia Show.

ACADIAN • Canada 1962 to date

Chevrolets built in the Oshawa, Ontario, plant of General Motors, differing in styling details from their USA counterparts.

ACCLES-TURRELL • England 1899-1902

Accles-Turrell began in 1899 with a two-seater 3 hp light carriage, equipped with an engine of the company's own make (fitted with the 'A-T Sponge Carburettor'). In 1901 the rights to the 'New Turrell' car ('vibrationless, very simple, quiet and efficient'), which had a 10/15 hp engine designed by F H De Veuille under the front seat, were acquired by Pollock Ltd of Ashton-under-Lyne, who soon joined forces with Accles to form the famous tube-making company Accles & Pollock.

ACE • England 1913

An 8 hp £125 four-cylinder chain-driven light car from the same manufacturer as the Salmon and Baguley.

ACE • USA 1920-1922

This assembled car emphasised 'square' coachwork lines which set it apart from its contemporaries. Both Continental and Herschell-Spillman six-cylinder engines were used, as well as a Gray four. The Ace was taken over by the American Motor Truck Co.

ACE CLASSIC • USA • New Zealand 1991 to date

Built in New Zealand and assembled near Los Angeles, this is a replica AC Cobra.

ACHILLES • England 1904-1908

Built in Frome, Somerset, the Achilles was a shaft-drive voiturette of 8 or 9 hp.

AC • England 1908 to date

The original AC was the 5/6hp Sociable, evolved from the company's commercial three-wheeler, the Autocarrier, with a passenger chair replacing the box body. The single rear wheel was driven by a one-cylinder air-cooled engine with two-speed epicyclic gearbox in the hub of the back wheel. These durable little three-wheelers were made up until 1914. However, in the previous year AC announced their four-wheeler, having an 1100cc Fivet engine with gearbox fashionably placed in the rear axle. This reappeared after the First World War, though by this time powered by a 11/2-liter Anzani engine, which remained in production until 1927. At the 1919 Motor Show AC displayed John Weller's remarkable 1991cc overhead-camshaft wet liner six-cylinder engine, though it did not go into production until 1922. Nevertheless the engine was produced up until 1963, by which time output had been boosted threefold, from 35 to 103 bhp. In 1921 S F Edge became chairman and governing director and his influence was no doubt responsible for the company's active participation in long-distance record work. Unfortunately all was not well with the company's finances and it went into voluntary liquidation, no cars being built between 1929 and 1931. In 1930 William and Charles Hurlock bought the company and production restarted, with the faithful Weller 2-liter six continuing to give sterling service. The designs were intelligently updated, the rear-mounted gearbox being replaced by a Moss box in unit with the engine, while underslung chassis frames were introduced. These good-looking sports cars attained some popularity in the 1930s, the handsome coachwork originating from the company's Thames Ditton factory. After the Second World War an AC saloon appeared, though rather surprisingly it retained a leaf-sprung front supension until it ceased production in 1957. Much more significant was the Ace of 1954, having an all-independent tubular framed Tojeiro designed chassis. Initially the famous 2-liter six was pressed into service, though this was replaced by 2- and 2.2-liter Bristol and 2.6-liter British Ford power units. In 1963 the car received an even more significant transplant, an American Ford 4.2- (and later 4.7-) liter V-8. The Cobra had arrived! The models sporting pedigree was amply reflected by Cobras being placed 4th at Le Mans in 1964 and 1966. Yet another variation on the theme came with the Cobra 427, fitted with a 7-liter Ford engine and having handsome bodywork by Frua. In 1967 a slightly larger V-8 — also by Ford — of 7016cc was fitted, and this model, designated the 428, was available until 1973. The next AC offering was a sports car powered by a 3-liter Ford V-6 engine mounted transversely behind the driver. Though first shown in 1972, the AC ME3000, based on the Bohanna Diablo and with a mid-mounted 3-liter Ford V6, did not go into production until 1979, as AC moved into other fields and sold its factory. The ME3000 design (and the rights to a Ghia-bodied version) were acquired by the Glasgow company AC (Scotland) in 1984, but only prototypes were built. Meanwhile, the AC Cobra had been put back into production as the MkIV by Autokraft at Brooklands, Surrey, which held rights to the marque on 'Cobra-shaped cars' and later took over the entire company with plans to build a new Ace. Ford took a 50 per cent share in 1987, and then, under Brian Angliss, a new AC ACE two-seat convertible was designed. Through various incarnations it, and its exquisitely styled body, finally made it into production and instantly assumed, 'classic' status. Using Ford mechanicals and handcrafted coachwork, the car re-established the marque.

AC 3000 ME coupé, 1972 (above)

1914 AC 10hp four-cylinder

1934 AC March Special

1910 AC three-wheeler

1965 AC Cobra S/C (below)
AC Cobra in racing trim (right)

ALFA ROMEO • Italy 1910 to date

Founded in 1906 as a branch factory of the French Darracq company, the works were sold in 1910 to the Italian Anonima Lombarda Fabbrica Automobili (ALFA), which started with a 4084cc 24 hp four, followed in 1911 by a 2413cc 12 hp of similar design. In 1912 came the big 6082cc 40-60 hp, and the company built its first dohc engine on a one-off Grand Prix car. Nicola Romeo added his name to ALFA in 1920, when the first post-war model, the Merosi-designed 2916cc RL six, made its debut. The vee-radiatored RL Sport (1922-25) and Super Sport (1925-27) had 2944cc engines. The RM four (1923-26) had a 1944cc engine. In 1924 the new chief designer, Vittorio Jano, began work on a high-performance 1.5-liter six-cylinder car, which emerged in 1927 as the brilliant overhead camshaft 6C1500 in twin overhead cam sport and Super Sport versions (the latter available with a supercharger). From 1929-33 Alfa Romeo built the 6C1750 in single- and twin-cam versions (dohc engines were available supercharged or unsupercharged). A dohc 6C1900 was built in 1933, followed by the 6C23000. Most glamorous of the road-going 'Jano' Alfas were the supercharged 8C2300 of 1931-34, which were victorious in the Le Mans 24 Hours and Mille Miglia Targa Florio sports-car races in racing 'Monza' guise, and the 8C2900 of 1935-39.

Financial problems forced a government takeover of Alfa Romeo in 1933. The dohc 6C2500 of 1939 was developed from the 6C2500 by Bruno Trevisan, Jano's successor, and survived until 1952. True mass production arrived in 1950 with the monocoque-bodied dohc 1900, designed by Orazio Satta Puliga. In 1954 came his Guilietta (Juliet) with a 1300cc engine - the smallest Alfa then built. A sports coupé version, the Guiletta Sprint, and a Spider two-seat convertible were also available in addition to the TI (Touring International) saloon. At this period Alfa also built some exciting small series of sports-racing cars, such as the 'Disco Volante' and the 6C3000 CM. There were also potent sporting versions of the Guilietta, the Bertone-bodied 'Sprint', 'Sprint Speciale' and the Zagato-bodied 'SZ'. In 1962 came the new Guilia and, a year later, Alfa Romeo opened a new factory at Arese near Milan, which began production in 1963 with the Guilia Sprint GT. The Zagato-bodied Giulia TZ (Tubolare Zagato) also went on the market that year. In 1966 Alfa Romeo launched Battista Pininfarina's last design, the 1600 Spider; which was still in production 25 years later. A curious venture of 1965 was the 'retro' look 4R with Zagato bodywork based on the 6C1750. Just 92 were built. A new 1750 saloon was launched in 1968. In 1972 Alfa opened a factory near Naples to build the Rudolf Hrushka-designed Alfasud, the first front-wheel-driven Alfa Romeo. It lasted until 1984, when it was replaced by the joint-venture Alfa-Nissan Arna, which failed to catch on. At this time Alfa also brought out the Montreal model – it had supercar aspirations, but sold only in limited numbers. Another 1972 introduction was the Alfetta, with a De Dion-type transaxle, joined in 1972 by the Alfetta, a new Guilietta in 1976, the Alfa 6 and GTV6 in 1979, the angular 33 in 1983 and the 164 in 1986. That year Ford attempted to buy the loss-making Alfa Romeo business, but was headed off by Fiat, which united Alfa and Lancia. This ended the Arna venture. In conjunction with Zagato, Alfa Romeo then brought out a brutally-styled 100-off super-

1981 Alpha Romeo GTV6

1978 Alpha Romeo Giulia Spider

car, the SZ, in 1989. In 1991 the company became an operative division of Fiat. The 164 model was derived from the joint venture 'Type 4' car, a shared floorpan between Fiat, Lancia, Alfa, and Saab. With its classic Pininfarina styling and 3.0-liter V-6 and 2.0-liter Twin Spark models, the model was a huge success. It was replaced in 1999 by the 166. Before that the 156 range had really re-established the marque in the upper middle ranges of executive cars. Although not a true replacement for the Sud, the 145 and 146 hatchback ranges with adventurous styling and new engines (signalling the end of the classic Alfa flat-four 'boxer' engine) also reaffirmed Alfa Romeo's postion in that sector of the market. The reborn GTV range, notably in 3.0-liter form and again sporting 'Diseno di Pininfarina' badges, made a stunning impact in 1996 and became the enthusiasts' benchmark for purity of concept in its market arena.

Clockwise from top, 1929 Alpha Romeo Spider AR 1750 SS, 1938-39 Alpha Romeo 6C 2300 Berlinetta, 1992 Alpha Romeo Alfa 155 GTA, Alpha Bertone Bella (bottom left), Alpha Romeo SZ 1989 Classic (left)

few production cars were built from 1937, basically two-seater Ford V-8s, but from 1945 came the first true Allards – the K1, the L and the J1; still Ford-based but with long-nosed bodies designed by Godfrey Imhof. The J-type could also be specified with a 3917cc Mercury V-8. A drophead coupé version of the L, the M-type, appeared in 1947. In 1949 came the immortal J2 Allard, with coil spring ifs, de Dion rear axle and a 4375cc Mercury. With Ardun ohv conversion, the stark J2 could top 110 mph (177 kmh). Production of Allard cars ceased in the 1960s with the Ford Zephyr-engined Palm Beach model.

ALL-BRITISH • Scotland 1906-1908

George Johnston, formerly of Arrol-Johnston, set up this company at Bridgeton, Glasgow, to build a 54 hp eight-cylinder car of curious design, with the cylinders arranged as two parallel fours - the pistons being actuated by rocking beams driven by connecting rods from a conventional four-throw crank. This unit was needlessly complex, and only a dozen All-British cars saw the light of day.

ALLDAYS & ONIONS • England 1898-1918

Founded in the mid-1800s, the Alldays & Onions Pneumatic Engineering Company of Birmingham entered the car field with the Traveler quadricycle. In 1900 Alldays showed a rear-engined flat-twin 7 hp four-seater of 'novel construction' at the National Show, which combined shaft, belt and gear transmission with great inefficiency. A shaft-drive single appeared in 1903, followed in 1905 by a twin-cylinder 10/12 hp which lasted until 1913. A 20/25 hp four followed, joined in 1908 by a 14/18 hp. A 30/35 six of 4891cc was introduced for 1911, and a vee-twin light car, the Midget, appeared in 1913. There was a neat bull-nosed 9 hp four in 1914. In 1918 Alldays merged with Enfield (which it had owned since 1907).

ALLEN • USA 1913-1914

Friction-drive two- and four-cylinders from a Philadelphia manufacturer.

ALLEN • USA 1913-1921

Built at Fostoria, Ohio, the Allen used Sommers four-cylinder engines, the company acquiring this power-unit manufacturer in 1915. The 1920 Allen 43, with bevel-sided touring coachwork and a high-shouldered radiator, was a handsome car which nevertheless failed to avert the company's bankruptcy. Willys acquired the remnants.

ALLEN KINGSTON • USA 1907-1909

Designed on European lines to avoid the 45 per cent duty on imported cars, these 45 hp 7400cc four-cylinder cars were built by the New York Car & Truck Company for motor agent Walter C Allen of New York. The Allen Kingston combined 'the best features of the Fiat, the Renault and the Mercedes in a harmonious new construction of the highest quality'.

1902 Alldays Traveler Voiturette

Allen Classic phaeton from Ohio

ALLIANCE • Germany 1903-1905

A supplier of components for car production, Alliance of Berlin also built complete cars with two- and four-cylinder engines. Early versions had De Dion motors.

ALLIANCE • France 1905-1908

With a similar radiator to the Mass, this Parisian marque was also known as 'Aiglon'. In 1908 an 18 hp four with Tony Huber engine was listed, which sold in England for £450.

ALLRIGHT • Germany 1908-1913

Known in Germany as 'Allreit', this Cologne-Lindenthal factory also built Allright, Tiger, Roland and Vindec-Special motorcycles and bicycles. The Allright-Mobil had 5 hp or 7 hp vee-twin engines; the last ones had sv 960cc engines with air-cooling.

ALLSTATE • USA 1952-1953

'The lowest-priced full-sized sedan on the US market' claimed Sears Roebuck's Allstate auto accessory chain (though it was similar to the even cheaper Henry J). Offered with either a four-cylinder 68 hp or an L-head six 80 hp engine, only 2,363 were sold in 12 months and the line was discontinued after the second model year.

ALL-VELO • Sweden 1904-1906

Starting with importing bicycles, the Allmanna Velociped-Aktiebolaget of Landskrona decided to buy unassembled Waltham Orient Buckboards from the USA. They were sold as All-Velos, and possibly around 50 were assembled. Most parts except engine, axles and steering were wood, and the car had a single-cylinder aircooled engine at the rear, with friction drive. Brakes were fitted only on the right rear wheel and there was tiller steering.

ALMA 6 • France 1926-1929

Very few cars were made by this Courbevoie factory, which made its own engines instead of using proprietary units. The Alma engine, developed by aircraft engineer Vaslin, was a 1643cc with three valves per cylinder.

ALP • Belgium 1920

Designed by the former chief engineer of Mètallurgique, this 2121cc light car was built by Automobiles Leroux-Pisart of Brussels.

ALPENA • USA 1910-1914

Designed for speed, the Alpena Flyer featured unit engine/gearbox construction with three-point suspension (and the Alpena Company was fined $400,000 in a court case brought against it by the patentee of this design, Emile Huber).

ALPINE • France 1952 to date

Jean Rèdelè founded this well-known marque of rear-engined sports cars in Dieppe in 1952. Having built some prototypes for racing, he started production in 1956 with the 4cv Renault-based Alpine A106, followed by the 'Milles Miles'. Two new models were presented in 1958, the A108 roadster and the 'Tour de France' with a top speed of 180 km/h (112 mph). From 1959 the Alpine was built under licence in Brazil by Interlagos. At the beginning of the 1960s Rèdelè presented a new car, the long-lived Alpine A110, which began with Dauphine or Dauphine-Gordini engines, and was then R8 and R8-Gordini engined. With the latter engine the car could reach 209 km/h (130mph). The car was later equipped with Renault engines such as the 1108cc and 1296cc Renault-Gordini, R16 TS and R12-Gordini. Alpine had many victories in rallies, as well as in road-racing, and was a regular entrant at Le Mans for many years. The R16 TS-engined Alpine A310 presented in 1971 eventually supplanted the A110. A 2664cc A310 V-6 subsequently became available. Renault took over Alpine in 1974, the new GTA V-6 of 1985 being presented as a Renault Alpine.

1992 Alpine A610 Turbo

ALSACE • USA 1920-1921

Built by Piedmont for export, the Alsace had right-hand drive and differed from other Piedmont products in its Rolls-Royce-shaped radiator. The wheelbase was 116 inches and a four-cylinder Herschell-Spillman engine was used.

ALTA • England 1931-1954

Geoffrey Taylor's Altas were initially powered by an 1100cc engine of his own design, having an aluminum block, wet liners and shaft-driven twin overhead camshafts. This was mounted in a low-slung chassis frame and, in 1935, 1496cc and 1961cc engines became available. From these sports cars, racing machines naturally evolved, 1937 seeing an all-independent suspension 11.2-liter supercharged car offered for sale. After the war Taylor built a car for the current Formula One, and later supplied engines for HWM and Connaught racing cars.

ALTENA • Holland 1900-1906

Altena of Haarlem-Heemstede built between 40 and 50 cars, initially using De Dion engines.

ALTER • USA 1914-1917

A four-cylinder from Plymouth, Michigan.

ALTHAM • USA 1896-1899

George J Altham of Fall River, Massachusetts, was one of the pioneer manufacturers of 'hydrocarbon carriages'. The company collapsed at the end of 1899 when the treasurer absconded with most of the stock and real-estate deeds.

ALUMINUM • USA 1920-1922

The Aluminum was built by Aluminum Manufacturers Inc of Cleveland, Ohio, in a research attempt to emphasise and prove the advantages of this metal in automobile construction. In all, six were built; five-passenger touring cars weighing 1080 kg (2,400 lb), with a 126-inch wheelbase and four-cylinder Alcoa engines. In 1922 Pierce-Arrow interests entered the picture and the cars built after that point were under Pierce-Arrow direction and known as Pomeroy cars.

ALVAREZ • Spain 1921-c1923

Also known as 'MA', this was a sporting cyclecar with brakes on all four wheels, built by Jesus Battlo of Barcelona.

ALVA SPORT • France 1913-1921

The Alva Sport made in Courbevoie used two different four-cylinder engines, an ohc 1496cc and an ohv 2651cc unit. Even when fitted with Perrot front-wheel brakes, Alvas suffered from archaic features such as a cone clutch.

ALVIS • England 1920-1967

See panel Overleaf

AMAZOON • England 1921-1922

A light car with a rear-mounted 6.9 hp Coventry-Victor power unit.

AMBASSADOR • USA 1921-1926

The Ambassador had been known as the Shaw before Yellow Cab bought the business. A few large cars were sold under the name before the Model D-I was introduced as a 'drive-yourself' car in 1924. The car became the Hertz in 1926.

AMC • England 1900

The Automobile Manufacturing Company of London offered this 10 hp steam car with flash boiler, 'absolutely safe in the hands of a novice'. Top speed was said to be 64 km/h (40 mph).

AMC BORGWARD ISABELLA • Mexico 1979

A sedan with Mexican Borgward engine and AMC coachwork.

AMCO • USA 1919-1920

The Amco was an export automobile with optional left- or right-hand steering. Amco cars were marketed in a single colour, beige, and carried a radiator especially designed for tropical climates. A GB & S four-cylinder engine was used and the cars had a wheelbase of 114 inches.

1961/62 Alvis TD21 drophead coupé

ALVIS • England 1920-1967

The Alvis took its name from an aluminum piston designed by G P H de Freville, who was responsible, along with T G John, for the design of the first model, the 10/30. In 1922 Captain T G Smith-Clarke joined the company as chief engineer and, along with chief designer W M Dunn, created the famous 12/50 of 1923. The uncertainty of the company's financial state was reflected by the appointment of a receiver in 1924, but, once production of the 12/50 got under way, prospects brightened considerably. This pushrod-engined car was available with long-stroke (1598cc) touring or short-stroke (1486cc) sports form being replaced by the similar 12/60. In its turn the four-cylinder theme was continued by the 11.2-liter Firefly.

Alvis played a progressive role in the development of fwd in Europe. In 1925 it produced a low-slung sprint car, powered by a 12/50 engine mounted back to front and, in the following year, a 11.2-liter supercharged dohc straight-eight grand prix car. In 1928 came the Front Wheel Drive production car using an ohc four-cylinder 1482cc engine, with the option of an Alvis designed and built supercharger and all-independent suspension. Although it remained in production for only two years, a few straight-eight examples were also built. A six-cylinder Alvis of 1870cc appeared in 1928, but the capacity was upped to 2148cc the following year , the model then being named the Silver Eagle. From this power unit sprang the successful six-cylinder Alvises of the 1930s; the Speed 20 (2.5- and 2.7-litres), Speed 25 (3.5-litres) and the 4.3-liter, plus the touring Crested Eagle and Silver Crest. These well-engineered cars were among the handsomest thoroughbreds of their day and also some of the fastest. At one time the 4.3 model was one of the quickest saloons on the British market, being capable of over 160 km/h (100 mph).

In 1933 the company's progressive technical outlook was reflected by the last-named model, which had independent front suspension and an all-synchromesh gearbox. Not that four-cylinder models were neglected. George Lanchester was responsible for the design of the 12/70 which replaced the Firebird of 1935 in 1938. After the Second World War Alvis adopted a one-model policy, the TA 14 appearing in 1946, having evolved from the pre-war 12/70. Its four-cylinder pushrod engine was of 1892cc. This cart-sprung model survived until 1950, when it was replaced by the six-cylinder TA 21, with a 3-liter engine which produced 90 bhp. This in its turn was succeeded by the TC 21/100 with a guaranteed 100 mph, though this was dropped in 1956. That year the gracious Graber-designed saloon appeared on what was basically a TC 21/100 chassis and, in 1959, it was named the TD 21 – evolving into the TE 21 in 1964. The following year the company was acquired by Rover, and private car production ceased in the summer of 1967, though military vehicles are still being manufactured.

Alvis 12/50 `ducksback', c. 1925, at Brooklands

1928 Alvis fwd team at Le Mans

1900 American Electric Golf Trap

AMERICA • Spain 1917-1922

The four-cylinder 'valveless' Tipo A America of 1917 had a primitive form of synchromesh gearbox and worm final drive, but this Barcelona firm's main product was the Tipo B of 1097cc, and the Tipo C – an ohv racing model.

AMERICAN • USA 1899

The American Automobile Company of New York offered 'hydrocarbon carriages' which could be started from the seat by chain-and-sprocket gearing.

AMERICAN • USA 1902-1903

A wheel-steered gas buggy from Cleveland, Ohio.

AMERICAN • USA 1916-1924

The American was one of many assembled cars built during its time, and Amco, Rutenber and Herschell-Spillman engines were employed over the years. For a time, racing driver Louis Chevrolet served as head of American's engineering department. Never a large producer, its peak year was 1920, when some 1,500 units left the factory at Plainfield, NJ. In 1923 the American car became connected with the Bessemer Truck Corporation and, that October, the new combine became Amalgamated Motors, which also included the Northway and Winther companies.

AMERICAN AUSTIN, AMERICAN BANTAM • USA 1930-1941

This was America's version of the Austin Seven, introduced with the hope of creating a large market of small-car enthusiasts and users in the USA. The cars with their four-cylinder engines rather resembled miniature Chevrolets with horizontal hood louvres à la Stutz or Marmon. The coupé, at $445, was billed as a sedan and at that price should have appealed to more buyers than it did. But the Depression and the appeal of known secondhand cars at a lower price did not help Austin sales. Slightly more than 8,000 were sold during the car's first year of sales, and they subsequently fell to the point when production was suspended in 1934, until 1937. That year, the car was redesigned by Alexis de Sakhnoffski and the name changed to Bantam. The facelift and new name helped a little, as did a new line of body styles, including light trucks and a station wagon. The Bantam pioneered the design for the first Jeep, and the first of these were built by Bantam for the US Army; by which time passenger car production had ended.

AMERICAN CHOCOLATE • USA 1903-1906

Well known as makers of coin-in-the-slot confectionery dispensers, American Chocolate of New York began assembling 30, 40 and 50 hp cars from imported components, under the supervision of the Swiss engineer William Walter, who had built his first car in 1898. From 1906, when the company relocated in Trenton New Jersey, cars were built under the name Walter.

AMERICAN ELECTRIC • USA 1899-1902

Based in New York, this company built a wide range of electric carriages capable, it was claimed, of running 35 to 50 miles; 'very few private carriages would ever be subjected to such a test,' claimed this optimistic manufacturer.

AMERICAN ELECTRIC • USA 1913-1915

An amalgamation of three electric car companies: Argo, Borland and Broc.

AMERICAN MOTORS CORPORATION • USA 1954 to 1988

See panel overleaf

AMERICAN SIMPLEX, AMPLEX • USA 1906-1915

A four-cylinder 50hp two-stroke engine powered the American Simplex, 'a motor car symphony', from Mishawaka, Indiana. From 1910 the name was shortened to 'Amplex'. The 1911 30/50 hp toy tonneau sold for $4,300.

AMERICAN STEAM CAR • USA 1924-1931

This car, produced by Thomas Derr, catered largely for former Stanley owners, and most of the company's operations were limited to conversions. Most used Hudson chassis and bodies.

AMERICAN STEAMER • USA 1922-1924

Not to be confused with Thomas Derr's American Steam Car, the American Steamer was a product of the American Steam Truck Company of Elgin, Illinois, and was typical of the renaissance of steam cars which tried to get on the American automobile market in the early 1920s. Featuring a twin-cylinder compound double-acting motor, the American Steamer line offered a touring car, roadster,

1958 Ambassador

AMERICAN MOTORS CORPORATION • USA
1954 to 1988

Financial difficulties forced Nash and Hudson to merge under the presidency of George Romney, who concentrated on the 1950-introduced Rambler, largely to the exclusion of the two older marques – which vanished in 1957. That year, the Rambler range was expanded to 20 models, including the new 5359cc Rebel V-8. Rambler was still marketing the Metropolitan sub-compact built by Austin, a legacy of Nash days. In 1959 AMC revived the six-cylinder Rambler as the American, and brought back the Nash Ambassador with the 5359cc V-8 as a top-of-the-range model. There was now a complete line of Rebels. Unable to match the competition from the 'Big Three' compacts, the Metropolitan ceased production in 1960, but unsold stocks were still being cleared in 1962. Sleek new styling earned Rambler and Ambassador Motor Trend's Car of the Year award in 1963, while the little American was remodelled in 1964, offering superior specification to its rivals. AMC's entry in the 'musclecar' stakes was the four-seater Javelin Sports coupé of 1968, with 4752cc, 5621cc or 6391cc V-8s, or a 3802cc six. Front disc brakes were optional on the V-8s. The Javelin was followed in mid-season by the AMX two-seater with the 6391cc V-8, featuring disc brakes and sports suspension. The Rambler name was dropped in 1970 when a famous name, the Hornet, was revived for a 3261cc six. (Three V-8 engines were optional). In mid-March that year AMC announced the Gremlin sub-compact, little bigger than a VW, with lift-up rear window and 3621cc or 3802cc six-cylinder engine. An intermediate model, the Matador, was built in 1971 – available as sedan, wagon or sport coupé. Ambassador production ended in 1974, and a new model 'designed around the passenger compartment', the Pacer, appeared. Just 171 inches long, it was 6 inches wider than the Cadillac Seville, and windows covered a third of its exterior. The 3802cc six was standard until 1978, when a 4982cc V-8 was offered. Hornet production ceased in 1978, 400,000 units having been sold, and it was replaced by the Concord luxury compact. In 1979 the Gremlin (dropped a year earlier) was replaced by the Spirit – available as hatchback or sedan – while a 'Limited' edition of the Concord boasted a high level of specification including leather trim. There were also a 'Limited' Pacer and a new sporty AMX with four-speed manual gearbox. AMC's fortunes were aided by a 1970 merger with Kaiser Jeep and, in 1979, an agreement with Renault provided for the production and sale of the Renault R18 by an AMC factory in the USA. The Pacer was replaced in 1980 by the more-conventional Spirit and, in 1981, America's first 4x4 passenger cars, the Eagle range, was launched. Renault's increasing share of AMC resulted in the 1982 Alliance, an American Renault 9, which was joined two years later by the Encore - a modified Renault 11. A further model based on the Renault 21 was conceived but, by 1987, Renault's losses were so great (over $700 million) that it was glad to sell out to Chrysler for $600 million. In grabbing the brand, Chrysler had secured itself the Jeep label, which it went on to exploit with great success. AMC as a name died. The Renault alliance cars drifted on for a short while with new badges until the parent group outlined the new Eagle Talon range.

AMC Pacer De Luxe Hatchback, 1978

1968 AMC Javelin

AMC Rambler Classic Wagon, 1965

1924 American Steamer

coupé and a sedan. At least 16 cars are known to have been built, and possibly as many as 20 may have left the factory.

AMERICAN UNDERSLUNG • USA 1905-1914

One of the classic marques of its day, the American Underslung from Indianapolis was the brainchild of Harry Stutz. An underslung chassis and big 41 x 41.2 inch wheels gave the American Underslung its distinctive appearance. Prices ranged from $1,250 to $4,500, and Teetor-Harley engines of 40 hp and 50 hp were used. From 1905 to 1908 the car was also available with a conventional chassis as the 'American Tourist'.

AMES • USA 1910-1915

A beetle-backed 'gentleman's roadster' and a five-passenger tourer were the initial products of this Owensboro, Kentucky company.

AMG • Sweden 1903-1905

From 1897 the AB Motorfabriken i Gèteborg built stationary engines. In the first years of the century it imported French Richard-Brasier cars. Swedish production of cars based on this marque was proposed, but the plans failed. In 1903 a new model was shown, using twin-cylinder air-cooled engines bought from the German Fafnir company. These tended to overheat and were soon changed to watercooling. Only engines were imported, the rest of the car being manufactured in Sweden. About 10 were built.

AMHERST • Canada 1912

The 'Two-in-One' Amherst 40 could be converted into a truck by removing the rear seats. Only nine were completed.

AMILCAR • France 1921-1939

This well-known French marque started in 1921 as a small cyclecar, designed by Jules Salomon and Edmond Moyet,

Amilcar Pegase sports, 1937 Le Mans

and bore a close resemblance to the pre-war Le Zëbre. The first model was the 903cc CC, available in a sport version, the CS, and the family C4. The sv engine had splash lubrication, and there was a three-speed gearbox. But the most famous of all was the CGS 'Grand Sport' of 1924 with a sv engine of 1074cc and four-wheel brakes, which evolved into the more sporty CGSS 'Grand Sport Surbaissë'. These were made under licence as Pluto in Germany and Grofri in Austria. In the mid-1920s the marque entered proper motor racing, building a batch of supercharged dohc 1100cc six-cylinder cars that used a roller bearing crankshaft in the full racing version but were also available with plain bearings. Amilcar also built a light touring car, the M-type, with a sv 1200cc engine, launched in 1928, followed by M2, M3 and M4 versions. It also made a straight-eight in 1928, with an ohc 2-liter engine. This C8 proved unreliable and expensive and disappeared very quickly. In the late 1930s Amilcar introduced two new models, the 14cv with a four-cylinder Delahaye engine and the Compound. The latter was made when Amilcar was taken over by Hotchkiss. Very advanced in design, the fwd Compound featured a monocoque frame made out of light alloy and independent suspension all round. The engine was an ohv four-cylinder of 1185cc. Production was not resumed after the Second World War.

AMIOT (AMIOT-PENEAU) • France 1897-1902

A fwd power-pack for converting horse-carriages into motor cars, the Amiot, from Asniéres, originally had a 6 hp Cyclope engine. An electric version was also available.

AMITRON • USA 1967

Powered by two lithium-nickel fluoride batteries, the Amitron was a three-passenger vehicle produced by American Motors and Gulton Industries. Capable of travelling 240 km (150 miles) at 80km/h (50 mph) on a single charge, the Energy Regeneration Brake system automatically switched the motors to generators, which recharged the batteries and increased the range.

AMOR • Germany 1924-1925

Another small car built in limited numbers. It had a 16 hp four-cylinder proprietary engine.

AMPERE • France 1906-1909

The Ampére, built at Billancourt (Seine), had a 10/16 hp four-cylinder engine driving through an electric clutch ('variation of speed by electric transmission, with neither dynamo nor accumulators').

AMPHICAR • Germany 1961-1965

Designed by Hans Trippel, who had produced amphibian cars at the Bugatti factory at Molsheim during the war, the Amphicar, built by the Quandt Group at Lübeck but mainly at Berlin-Borsigwalde, had an English 1147cc Triumph four-cylinder engine with 38 hp at 4750 rpm. Most cars were sold in the USA. Total production was about 2,800 units.

AMX • Italy 1969-1972

Made at the former Bizzarini factory at Turin, the Italian-built AMX was another Bizzarini design and contained many parts made by the American Motor Corporation, which had taken over the small Bizzarini works. Ital Design supplied the bodywork for the mid-engined car, which had a 6383cc AMV V-8 engine developing 345 PS (SAE) at 5,100 rpm.

ANADOL • Turkey 1966 to date

Turkey's first production car, the Reliant-Ogle styled Anadol is built in Istanbul and powered by Ford, currently 1300cc and 1600cc.

ANAHUAC • USA 1922

Patterned on a contemporary Polish car, the Anahuac was to have been marketed in Mexico by a Mexican concern. Wheelbase was 115 inches, and only four units were ever

The amphibious Amphicar of the early 1960s (see page 159)

completed by the builder, Frontenac Motor Corp. of Indianapolis, Indiana.

ANASAGASTI • Argentina 1912-1914

Horacio Anasagasti of Buenos Aires is credited with building the first Argentinian car, a 15 hp Ballot-engined vehicle. In 1912-1913 he came to Europe to prove his designs in competition, entering a team for the 1912 Tour de France and a Picker-engined racer for the 1913 Coupé de l'Auto. He returned to Argentina and is said to have built about 50 touring Anasagastis.

ANCHOR BUGGY • USA 1910-1911

A high-wheeler from Cincinnati, Ohio.

ANDERHEGGEN • Holland 1901-1902

A light 4 hp four-seater vis-à-vis built in Amsterdam. Total production was under ten.

ANDERSON • USA 1916-1925

Anderson, the most successful of all American cars built in the southern states, was the outgrowth of a South Carolina carriage works. Andersons were sold throughout the country by an active dealership. Using Continental six-cylinder engines, the make was noted for its attractive body styles and colour combinations, production reaching nearly 2,000 units in 1923.

1913 Coupé de l'Auto Anasagasti

ANDERSON ELECTRIC • France 1912

A costly electric car with five speeds and Edison batteries which was shown at the 1912 Paris Salon. The 3/9 hp cost Fr 13,500 and the 4/12 hp Fr 18,500.

ANDRE • England 1933-1934

This lightweight two-seater sports car used a vee-twin ohv JAP engine of 728cc. Only half-a-dozen were made.

ANGLADA • Spain 1902-1908

Angladas were built in Puerto de Santa Maria (Andalucia), as one- or four-cylinder cars of 6 to 36cv. A 24 hp four was the first Spanish car bought by Alfonso XIII, in 1904.

ANGLIAN • England 1905-1907

Tricars built in Beccles, Suffolk, with either 31.2 hp single-cylinder De Dion or 5 hp 'twin coupled' power units.

ANGLO-AMERICAN • England 1899-1900

This York company claimed that these 'exceptionally powerful motors were manufactured throughout in our own works', but they were probably Continental imports. Motor tricycles with 2 hp engines were also offered.

ANGLO-DANE • Denmark 1902-1917

H C Fredriksen of Copenhagen was building bicycles in the 1890s using British parts; hence the name. The first cars were light trucks with single-cylinder Kelecom engines. Later cars had single-cylinder 4.5 hp engines and friction drive, and a few passenger cars were also built with twin-cylinder engines.

ANGLO-FRENCH • England 1896-1897

Leon l'Hollier's Anglo-French Motor Carriage Company of Birmingham modified Roger-Benz cars for the British market.

ANGUS-SANDERSON • England 1919-1927

The Angus-Sanderson was, in concept, rather like the Bean and Cubitt. The intention was to mass-produce one model, following the successful Ford practice. An assembly of proprietary parts, the Angus-Sanderson had a 2.3-liter engine by Tylor, a Wrigley gearbox and rear axle, springs by Woodhead and wheels by courtesy of Goodyear. Unfortunately all the brave words of the day failed to produce many cars. Production moved from County Durham to Hendon, Middlesex, in 1921 and a smaller 8 hp car was toyed with in 1925, but production finally ceased two years later.

ANHUT • USA 1909-1910

Open two- and four-seat 3785cc ohv sixes built in Detroit; taken over in 1910 by Barnes.

ANKER • Germany 1919-1920

This small company, based in Berlin, built cars up from war-surplus car components, mainly of the 1145cc four-cylinder Wanderer.

ANSALDO • Italy 1921-1931

Ansaldo, a leading armaments concern, entered car manufacture with an ohc 1847cc four-cylinder model which developed 36 bhp at 3,600 rpm. A sports version had a 1981cc engine, and there was also a six-cylinder version

of 1991cc. Later six-cylinder models had engines of 2179cc. Among the last cars made by Ansaldo was an ohv straight-eight of 3532cc. The Ansaldos were cars of good quality and modern design, and they competed in many races. When Wikov in Czechoslovakia began manufacture in 1928, they built the 1453cc Ansaldo Tipo 10.

ANSBACH • Germany 1910-1913

Forerunner of Faun, Ansbach was famous for lorries and buses. Its 1559cc four-cylinder 14 hp touring car was known as the Kautz.

ANSTED • USA 1922

The Ansted or Ansted-Lexington was actually a custom-designed Lexington roadster marketed under the Ansted emblem, the engine being an Ansted six. Luxuriously appointed, this sporty car cost $4,500.

ANSTED • USA 1926-1927

Following the sale of Lexington's plant in Connersville, Indiana to Auburn, the Lexington-Ansted interests marketed their last cars as Ansteds. These differed from the Lexington only in the radiators, emblems and hubcaps.

ANTOINE • Belgium 1900-1905

V Antoine of Liège was an engine manufacturer who also offered a 4 hp voiturette and, in 1905, a 15/25 hp car.

ANTOINETTE • France 1906-1908

Better known as a builder of aeroplanes and aero engines, Antoinette of Puteaux showed a car with a 32 hp V-8 engine and hydraulic clutches instead of a gearbox and differential at the 1906 Paris Salon. The following year a 16 hp four and 30 hp V-8 were available.

ANZANI • Italy 1923-1924

Famous as a producer of proprietary engines for motorcycles, cars, aeroplanes and boats, Anzani also built a number of 1098cc cyclecars.

APAL • Belgium 1981 to date

Plastic-bodied replica of the Porsche 356 Speedster, built on a VW Beetle floorplan.

APOLLO • Germany 1910-1927

Ruppe & Son of Apolda (Thuringia) produced first Piccolo then, from 1910, Apollo cars. The first Apollo, the 'Mebbel', had an air-cooled 624cc single-cylinder ioe engine. There were also air-cooled 1608cc in-line fours and a 1575cc V-4. Four separate cylinders in line powered the 1770cc model 'E'. Designed by racing driver Karl Slevogt, the model 'B' had an ohv 960cc four-cylinder engine; another of his superb creations had an ohv 2040cc engine. Other Apollos had sv four-cylinder engines of up to 3440cc. Some models after 1920 had wishbone suspension, and the last Apollo cars had ohv 1200cc four-cylinder engines or sv 1551cc Steudel four-cylinder power units. Hugo Ruppe, son of the factory founder, was a famous two-stroke engine designer. He built the air-cooled MAF cars which, in 1920, became part of Apollo. Slevogt raced Apollo cars with streamlined Jaray bodies during the mid-1920s.

1921 Angus-Sanderson

Anderson Sport roadster, 1921

APOLLO • USA 1962-1964

The Apollo was a well-engineered, fast sports/personal car with Italian handmade two-seater aluminum convertible or fastback bodywork and a V-6 or V-8 Buick engine. Ninety were produced before it was renamed the Vetta Ventura.

APOLLO • England 1971-1972

The Can-Am racer-inspired Apollo was the brainchild of Allen Pearce. Originally intended purely for his own use, this dramatic-looking VW-based glassfibre sports car very nearly entered serious production in 1972.

APPERSON • USA 1902-1926

After the Apperson brothers broke away from Haynes-Apperson (q.v.) they continued for a while with a front-mounted flat-twin engine, then used a horizontal four. Vertical fours were the order of the day by 1904, when 24 hp and 40 hp models were offered. In 1906 a 95 hp four was catalogued at $10,500 and, a year later, came the first of the famous Jackrabbit speedsters – a 60 hp selling at $5,000. For a time the entire range was known as the 'Jack Rabbit'; a 32.4 hp four and a 33.7 hp six were listed in 1913; a 33.8 hp 90 degree V-8 of 5502cc appeared during 1914. In 1916 the 'Roadaplane' six and eights were announced. A sporty tourer designed by Conover T Silver, the 'Silver-Apperson', was launched in 1917. After 1919 it was known as the 'Anniversary'. In 1923 a proprietary six of 3243cc appeared, and a Lycoming eight was also available from 1924. By now both Apperson and Haynes were losing sales, but a rumoured remarriage came to nothing, and the introduction of four-wheel brakes on the 1926 Appersons failed to halt the company's end.

APPLE • USA 1917-1918

The $1,150 Apple 8 from Dayton, Ohio, was, agents were assured, 'a car which you can sell!!!' Unfortunately the public did not buy.

1917/18 Apple 8

AQUILA-ITALIANA • Italy 1906-1914

Designed by Guilio Cesare Cappa, these were big four- and six-cylinder cars with ioe engines of advanced design. After 1908 there was an interruption in manufacture, but new models appeared late in 1911. These had 4192cc six-cylinder engines and proved successful in many races. Among their drivers were Meo Costantini, who afterwards joined Bugatti at Molsheim, where he became a racing driver and eventually Chef d'Equipe, and Carlo Masetti, elder brother of Count Giulio Masetti.

ARAB • England 1926-1928

That enigmatic genius Reid Railton was responsible for the design of the Arab, a sporting 2-liter which appeared in 1926. The engine was an ohc four-cylinder, with leaf-valve springs as on Parry Thomas's Leyland Eight, a reminder that Railton had worked for Thomas. But after the Welshman's death attempting to break the world land speed record in 1927, Railton lost heart in the Arab project. A pity, for the two-seater was good for 129 km/h (80 mph) and the more potent Super Sports was able to touch 145km/h (90 mph).

ARBEE • England 1904

A 6 hp two-speeded car with 'slow running engine'. Hardly a compelling sales gimmick!

ARDEN • England 1912-1916

Starting life as a crudely finished vee-twin JAP-engined cyclecar with wooden chassis, the Arden grew up into a well-built four-cylinder 1096cc Alpha-engined light car, eventually with full four-seater coachwork.

L'ARDENNAIS • France 1901-c.1903

This voiturette, from Rethel (Ardennes) came with interchangeable water- and air-cooled cylinders, for summer and winter use.

ARDSLEY • USA 1905-1906

W S Howard, who had built cars under his own name, designed this 30/35 hp four.

ARGO • USA 1915-1916

A short-lived attempt to rival Ford in producing 'a motor car for the millions', the 1916 Argo from Jackson, Michigan, sold for $405 in two-seater form. The firm originally made a cyclecar; the four-cylinder 'Motorvique', based on the Briscoes' French-built Ajax.

1913 Arden four-seater tourer

1916 Argo

ARGONAUT • USA 1959-1963

The first name applied to this proposed behemoth was the 'Argonaut State Limousine', but the name was soon changed to the 'Argonaut Motor Machine' as the car was planned to be the finest and most luxurious in the world. The prototype of the Argonaut was mounted on a Chrysler chassis. Prices quoted ranged from $26,800 to $36,000, and a variety of stainless and special steels were planned for the car's manufacture. A 12-cylinder ohc aluminum air-cooled engine developing some 1010 bhp was designed and all Argonauts were to have carried a four-year guarantee. In its catalogue Argonaut claimed that two of its models, the 'Smoke' and the 'Raceway', had a maximum speed of 240 mph (386 km/h). One Argonaut is known to have reached private hands.

ARGONNE • USA 1919-1920

The Argonne, 24 of which constituted the firm's entire output, was a sports roadster with a 118-128-inch wheelbase and a four-cylinder Buda engine, although a Rochester-Duesenberg powerplant could be had as an option. The radiator of the Argonne was sharply pointed, similar to that of the Austro-Daimler.

ARGUS • Germany 1901-1909

Founded by Paul Jeannin, Argus originally built copies of the Panhard & Levassor cars. They also had P & L engines and most other components came from France. Engines of Argus's own design and manufacture appeared in 1903; Argus cars had now 2380cc two-cylinder and 4960cc and 9240cc four-cylinder engines. They were luxurious and expensive cars.

ARGYL • Scotland 1976 to date

Ex-Mini racer and supercharger expert Bob Henderson is also builder of Scotland's only sports car. Based on a sturdy tubular chassis, the striking mid-engined Caledonian is powered by a variety of engines including a supercharged version of the Rover V-8.

1976 Argyl coupé

ARGYLL • Scotland 1899-1932

See panel opposite

ARIEL • England 1900-1915, 1922-1925

Ariel of Birmingham began with motor tricycles and quadricycles but, by 1902, a 10 hp twin-cylinder car was being built. In 1903 came the company's first four-cylinder, the 16 hp. A design peculiarity of these cars was a leather cone clutch entirely separate from the flywheel. A six-cylinder model, whose tubular chassis seemed totally inadequate, appeared early in 1904. That year, a 16 hp Ariel was the first car up Snowdon. A completely new range was announced at the end of 1905 under the name 'Ariel-Simplex', which were Mercedes-inspired fours of 15 hp and 25/30 hp and a 35/40 hp six. In 1907-1908 the monstrous 50/60 hp six was launched, which offered 15.9 litres for a chassis price of £950. In 1907 Ariel sold its Bournbrook, Birmingham, factory to British Lorraine-Dietrich, and Ariel cars were thereafter assembled at the Coventry Ordnance Works. The outbreak of the First World War put paid to a 1.3-liter light car. After 1918 the Ariel Nine with a flat-twin air-cooled engine (and made by A Harper Sons and Bean) was an abortive attempt to cash in on the small car market.

ARIES • France 1903-1938

Ariés began building two- and four-cylinder cars in a large factory at Asnières (Seine), building 20 chassis at a time. These shaft-drive cars used a curious double rear axle,

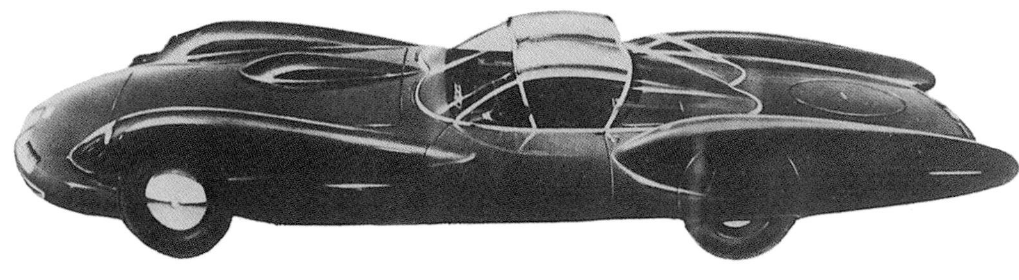

Argonaut State Limousine

ARGYLL • Scotland 1899-1932

Alex Govan's first voiturette was copied from the contemporary Renault and had a 2/3/4 hp De Dion engine and shaft-drive. 1901 models had a 5 hp engine, 1902 cars an 8 hp unit. A 10 hp twin with radiator tubes forming the bonnet sides soon appeared and, in 1904, there was a range of front-radiatored Aster-engined cars; a 10 hp of 1985cc, and fours of 3054cc, 3686cc and 4849cc. All had Govan's awkward gearbox with T-shaped gate and separate change-speed and reverse levers. Argyll was now Scotland's biggest make, and moved from Bridgeton, Glasgow, into a grandiose terracotta factory at Alexandria, on the outskirts of the city. It was never used to capacity and, with Govan's death in 1907, Argyll began a gentle decline. The famous 'Flying Fifteen' joined the range in 1910, as did a six-cylinder. Rubury four-wheel brakes were available in 1911 and, in 1912, the single sleeve-valve engine designed by J P McCollum and Argyll director Baillie P Burt made its debut. By 1914 all the range had Burt-McCollum engines. Argyll changed hands in 1914, and 1920s production – starting in 1920 with the revived pre-war 15.9 hp, and joined in 1922 by a 11.2-liter - was on a small scale.

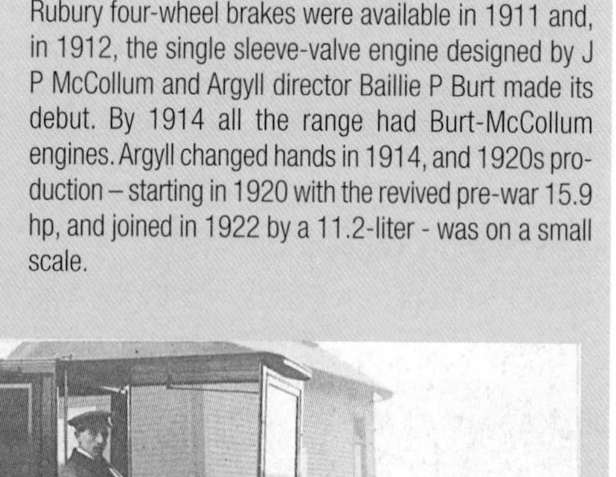

c. 1906 Argyll 15 hp landaulette

1908 Argyll 14 hp tourer

1923 Ariel 10 hp tourer

1924 1.5-liter Arés at Le Mans

and the engines were made by Aster. In 1907 the company made a V-4 engine with desmodromic valves, as well as six-cylinder cars. In 1910 it entered the field of commercial vehicles, mainly supplying the French Army and, during the war, the works built many military lorries, and Hispano-Suiza aero engines. After the war Ariés presented a 7 cv ohc 1085cc four-cylinder and a 15cv 3-liter in two versions. The first had a sv Aster unit, and the second a sporty ohc engine. Some with the ohc 3-liter engine were successful in racing events. During the financial crisis of the 1930s Ariés stopped production of the 1100cc and the 3-liter cars, which had become outdated. They were replaced by new 1500cc and 2-liter models with a curious arrangement of a three-speed gearbox augmented by two-speed gears in the back axle, giving six speeds forward. Very few were made. At the outbreak of war production of both touring cars and lorries was suspended. After the war Ariés briefly made moped engines under the ABG name.

ARIMOFA • Germany 1921-1922

Starting with a small cyclecar with a 12 hp Steudel twin-cylinder engine built in limited numbers, Arimofa continued in 1923-1925 with the Ari two-stroke motorcycle.

1913 Armstrong-Whitworth 17/25 hp tourer

1971 Arkley sports two-seater

ARISTA • France 1912-1915

Taking its name from its founder, P Arista-Ruffier, the Arista marque was built in Paris. There were eight models in its natal year; a 720cc single and fours of 1460cc, 1726cc and 1847cc. All had friction drive and were sold complete with bodywork and tyres, and fours of 1460cc, 1593cc, 1847cc and 2001cc with conventional gearboxes, all sold as untyred chassis.

ARISTA • France 1956-1963

A garage in Paris made these glassfibre-bodied cars with Panhard engine and components.

ARKLEY • England 1971 to date

A bug-eyed, glassfibre panelled sports car, the Arkley SS kit was designed by Morgan man, John Britten, to allow rusted Sprites and Midgets to live another day. Several hundred have been sold since the car was introduced in 1971.

ARKON • England 1971-1972

Strictly a one-off, the 33-inch-high Arkon was the product of a year's devotion by students Richard Moon and Neil Morgan. The exotic-looking GT is powered by a rear-mounted 1mp engine set on a Triumph Spitfire chassis.

ARMADALE • England 1906-1907

This 'perfect little three-wheeler' was built by Toboggan Motors of London, and featured infinitely variable friction drive and a pressed steel chassis – an unusual feature on a tricar.

ARMSTRONG • England 1902-1904

Claimed to be 'the best hill-climber extant', the Armstrong had an 8 hp International engine.

ARMSTRONG SIDDELEY • England 1919-1960

See panel

ARMSTRONG WHITWORTH • England 1904-1919

The famous Tyneside engineering and shipbuilding company began by taking over construction of the flat-four Wilson-Pilcher, with its preselective transmission, which had first appeared in 1901. From 1906 it was increasingly preoccupied with the Armstrong Whitworth, a handsome machine on Mercedes lines, with engines from 12/14 hp to 40 hp, mostly fours, though a 30/50 hp six appeared in 1912.

ARNO • England 1908

Introduced at the 1908 Stanley Show, the Coventry-built Arno had a 25b hp White & Poppe engine and shaft drive.

ARNOLD • England 1896

Arnold, an agricultural engineering company of East Peckham, Kent, built a dozen cars based on the Benz. One survives.

ARNOLT • USA 1953-1964

S H Arnolt Inc of Chicago combined an MG chassis and engine with Italian Bertone coachwork of steel and aluminum to produce four-passenger coupés and convertibles. British Bristol 404 chassis with six-cylinder 130 hp engines were later used to produce Arnolt Bristols.

ARROL-JOHNSTON (ARROL-ASTER) • Scotland 1895-1929

When his experimental steam tram went up in flames in 1894, locomotive engineer George Johnston turned to internal combustion, building a heavy dog-cart with an opposed-twin engine with four pistons. A syndicate formed to produce this 'Mo-Car' was headed by Sir William Arrol, engineer of the Forth Bridge. High, slow and fired by pulling on a rope through the floorboards, the dog-cart was built until 1906. In 1905 it was joined by a 3023cc 12/15 hp model of more modern appearance but still with an opposed-piston engine. There was also a three-cylinder version of the dog-cart, an uncouth 16 hp with the center cylinder of greater bore than the outer pair. In 1906 came a 24/30 hp vertical four of 4654cc, followed in 1907 by a 38/45 hp of 8832cc. The 12/15 hp twin survived until 1909, in which year T C Pullinger, ex-Darracq and Humber, joined Arrol-Johnston, sweeping away the old range in favor of a new 15.9 hp of 2835cc, with a dashboard radiator and four-wheel brakes (dropped in 1911). An 11.9 hp was introduced for 1912 and, in 1913, production

1907 Arrol-Johnston used on Shackleton's South Pole expedition

ARMSTRONG SIDDELEY • England 1919-1960

Armstrong Siddeley was created by an amalgamation of Armstrong Whitworth and Siddeley Deasy of Coventry. The outcome of this union was a fairly massive first car – a 5-liter 30 hp – although a smaller 18 appeared in 1922, and a 2-liter 14 hp came in 1923. The year 1928 saw the introduction of a 15 hp six, while the following year a 12 hp car joined the range. It was also a pioneering year for the marque, with the Wilson preselector gearbox being offered, originally as an optional extra, though it became standard equipment on Armstrongs from 1933. In 1930 four models were being marketed, of 12, 15, 20 and 30 hp; the last costing £1,450. Armstrong Siddeley's rather staid image was endorsed during the 1930s by a range of six-cylinder cars with ohv engines, although a four-cylinder 12 hp was produced up until 1936. A reminder that Armstrong Siddeley was one of the country's largest manufacturers of aero engines came in 1933, when the 5-liter six-cylinder Siddeley Special was announced with Hiduminium aluminum alloy engine. The model cost £950.

The very week the war in Europe ended, Armstrong Siddeley announced its first post-war models; the Lancaster four-door saloon and the Hurricane drophead coupé, echoing the names of aircraft built by the Hawker Siddeley Group (as it had become in 1935) during the war. These cars were powered by 2-liter six-cylinder engines, although the capacity was increased to 2.3 litres in 1949. In 1953 the company announced the Sapphire, with a six-cylinder engine of 3435cc and, in 1956, the number of models was increased. These were the 234, a 2.3-liter four, and the 236, with the older 2.3-liter six-cylinder engine. Armstrong Siddeley's last model was the Star Sapphire of 1958, with a 4-liter engine and automatic transmission. In 1959, however, Bristol Aero Engines merged with Hawker Siddeley to form Bristol Siddeley. A casualty of this union was Armstrong Siddeley cars. The last one left the Coventry works in 1960.

1921 Armstrong Siddeley six-cylinder tourer (above) 1956 Armstrong Siddeley 346 saloon (left)

shifted from Paisley to Dumfries, where 50 electric cars were built for Edison. Arrol-Johnston's 1919 'Victory' model, designed by G W A Brown, had an ohc 2651cc engine but proved 'unsellable and unreliable' and was replaced by a modernized 15.9 hp. A short-lived 14 hp appeared in 1924, replaced in 1925 by a 12.3 hp. There was also a 3290cc 'Empire' model for the Colonies. In 1927 Arrol-Johnston merged with Aster. Alongside sleeve-valve Arrol-Asters there were pushrod Arrol-Johnstons of 15.40 and 17.50 hp. Final folly was the straight-eight sleeve-valve Arrol-Aster 23.70 hp of 3292cc.

ARSENAL • England 1898-1899

A Bollèe-like 'reputed 31.2 hp' tricycle built at St Albans, Hertfordshire, by a company boasting 'practically the control of one of the largest and best-equipped plants of American Automatic Machinery'. Costing £59, the tiller-steered Arsenal could carry 'two or three persons, or four children'.

ARZAC • France 1926-1927

A small cyclecar made in Paris with fwd, independent suspension on all four wheels and a two-stroke engine available in 483cc and 500cc forms.

AS • France 1924-1928

The AS made by Automobiles Serrano was a small car from la Garenne-Colombes with such proprietary engines as Chapuis-Dornier, Ruby and CIME.

ASA • Italy 1962-1969

A small, high-efficiency 'dream car', created by Bizzarini and, as far as the ohc 1032cc four-cylinder engine was concerned, by Enzo Ferrari. It was built in a small factory at Milan, owned by the De Nora Electrochemical Group of companies. A racing version of the 1000 GT Coupé had 1092cc and 95 bhp; later even 105 bhp. Only a few ASA cars were made, but they gained successes in Italian sporting events. A few larger four- and six-cylinder cars, mainly prototypes, were also individually built to order. All had glassfibre bodywork.

ASARDO • USA 1959-1960

The American Special Automotive Research and Design Organisation of Bergen, NJ, built this sport coupé with an Alfa Romeo four-cylinder engine and four-speed gearbox. A glassfibre body was mounted on a lightweight tubular space frame.

AS Type A2S 7/30cv sports

Ashton-Evans two-seater, c. 1922

ASCORT • Australia 1958-1960

Though unrecognizable as such, this four-seater grand touring coupé was basically a Volkswagen Beetle. The locally-made, roomy, double-skinned glassfibre body was remarkably well conceived and appointed. The 1.2-liter Beetle engine was modified with an Okrasa kit to produce 54 bhp. Total vehicle weight was 33 per cent less than a standard sedan, giving brisk acceleration. More than a dozen were built before the project collapsed.

ASCOT • England 1904

The 31.2 hp engine of the Ascot Forecar was equipped with a 'patented method for mechanically-controlling valves, doing away with useless pinions and cams'.

ASCOT • England 1928-1930

Cyril Pullin was responsible for the Ascot, and he produced the Ascot-Pullin motorcycle at the same time. The Ascot was largely based on the Hungarian Fejes, being assembled from welded steel pressings, but it never went into production. A larger 21.4-liter six did become a reality, however.

ASHLEY • England 1954-1962

The Ashley name was first attached to sports bodies for Austin Sevens, and over 500 were built during the 1950s. Ford-powered Ashleys followed, first with proprietary chassis and then with the company's own. The Sportiva was its final car; special bonnets and hardtops for Sprites its last commercial projects.

ASHTON-EVANS • England 1919-1928

The first of this Birmingham marque had a rear track of only 8 inches, but from 1920 a normal rear-axle was used. All had 11.2-liter Coventry-Climax engines and constant-mesh gearboxes.

ASPA • Czechoslovakia 1924-1925

Made by a small machine factory at Pribram, the Aspa, successor to the Stelka, had a Ford Model T engine and many other Ford parts. Only a few were built.

ASQUITH • England 1901-1902

Built by a Halifax machine-tool works, the Asquith had a front-mounted De Dion engine and, originally, a belt-drive, but this was replaced by a two-speed gearbox because the belts slipped disastrously. Probably only one car was built, as the firm decided to concentrate on building boring machinery.

The Ascort coupé

ASQUITH • England 1981 to date

Founded to build 'Retro-style' delivery vans based on the Ford Transit chassis, Essex-based Asquith announced a 1930s-style taxi cab on a purpose-built chassis in 1991.

ASS • France 1919-1920

'L'automobile pour tous', the ASS was powered by a 12 hp two-stroke Thomas engine. Ambitious plans for mass production were unrealised.

ASTATIC • France 1920-1922

Made at Saint-Ouen, the Astatic was another attempt to market a car with independent suspension all round, by means of leaf-springs. The engine was an 1100cc SCAP.

ASTER • France 1900-1910

Best known as suppliers of power units to manufacturers such as Gladiator, Ariés, West, Argyll, Whitlock and Dennis, this firm from St Denis (Seine) also built chassis. It seems unlikely that a complete car was marketed by the Aster company, although a four-cylinder chassis was exhibited at the 1907 Paris Salon.

ASTER • England 1922-1930

Aster made only six-cylinder cars; the first, the 18. 50, had a 2618cc engine, being enlarged to 3 litres in 1926. Later examples of this marque had Burt-McCollum single-sleeve-valve engines.

ASTON MARTIN • England 1922 to date

See panel overleaf

ASTRA • USA 1920

Built by a subsidiary concern of the Dorris, the 108-inch wheelbase Astra was shown in its native St Louis in 1920. It used a Leroi four-cylinder engine and featured a slightly pointed radiator. An estimated five to ten units were made before the company failed in June 1920.

ASTRA • France 1922

A small cyclecar with a twin-cylinder two-stroke engine of 496cc which featured independent suspension on all four wheels plus friction drive.

ASTRA • England 1956-1959

Claimed to be the smallest and cheapest four-wheeler on the British market, the utility Astra had a rear-mounted 322cc engine and all-round independent suspension. It was built by British Anzani of Hampton Hill, Middlesex.

1920 ASS four-seater

This is the heavyweight 1998 Aston supercar - the Vantage - based on the Virage model's genes

1959 Aston Martin DB4

ASTON MARTIN • England 1922 to date

The original Aston Martin was built in 1914 by Lionel Martin and Robert Bamford; the Aston prefix being derived from the Aston Clinton hillclimb in which the car had successfully competed. This first car used an Isotta-Fraschini voiturette chassis, powered by a 1.4-liter Coventry-Simplex engine. Car production proper started in 1921, the cars having sv 11/2-liter engines. More exciting developments came in 1922 when a four-cylinder 16-valve car was designed for Count Zborowski, who held the company's purse strings. Unfortunately it failed to live up to expectations on the race tracks, but became available to private customers the following year. Single-cam variants were also available. After Zborowski's death at Monza in 1924 the company struggled on until the 1925 Motor Show, but was wound up a few weeks later. At the end of 1925 Bamford and Martin Ltd was purchased by W S Renwick for £6,000. He had met a fellow engineer, A C Bertelli, at Armstrong Siddeley and they had formed an engineering concern which produced just one car, the R and B. It had an ohc 11.2-liter four-cylinder engine and formed the basis of the Bertelli-designed Aston Martins until 1936. This 11.2-liter model established a good competition record at Brooklands, Le Mans and the Mille Miglia, thus perpetuating the marque's sporting pedigree. Finance was also a problem, and after a brief flirtation with Frazer Nash in 1931 and later with L. Prideaux Brune, the company came under the control of R G Sutherland in 1933. A new 2-liter model succeeded the 11.2-liter series for 1937 and, although superficially resembling the smaller-capacity car, it lacked the commercial and competition success. The first Aston Martin of the post-war years had a Claude Hill-designed pushrod 2-liter engine and independent front suspension, but only a few were made before the company was taken over by the David Brown group in 1947. Experiments continued in 1948-1949, the resultant cars being dubbed DBls. Meanwhile, David Brown had also acquired Lagonda and the outcome of this liaison was that the dohc 2.6-liter six-cylinder engine which W O Bentley had designed for the post-war Lagonda was fitted in a square-tube space frame and entered in the 1949 Le Mans; emerging the following year as the DB2. The DB3 of 1954 was a sports-racer actively campaigned by the factory, while the Eberan von Eberhorst-designed DB3S maintained the company's sporting activities. The DBR that followed gave Aston Martin a car with which to win Le Mans (in 1959) along with the Sports Car Constructors' Championship. However, the DB4 which appeared for the 1960 season was a completely new car, having a Tadec Marek-designed all-aluminum dohc 3.7-liter engine and a platform-frame chassis, trailing link and coil rear suspension and handsome coachwork constructed on the Superleggera principle (a tubular metal cage clad in hand-fashioned aluminum). The DB5, announced in 1963, offered a 4-liter engine with many of the troubles that had plagued the earlier DB4s ironed out, while the 1966 DB6 offered true four-seater motoring coupled with sensational performance. The follow-

The DB7 - rebirth of a classic Aston line, 1997

The 1966 DB6 - culmination of the classic Aston line

ing year saw the DBS 6 and DBS Vantage, a more expensive and powerful variant that remained in production until 1973. A new 5.4-liter all-aluminum V-8 appeared as the DBS V-8 of 1970, being renamed the V-8 in 1972. It was also used to power the William Towns styled Lagonda model which reached full production status in 1978. David Brown sold out to Company Developments Ltd in 1972 and, in 1975, the company was again reconstructed. Under the chairmanship of Victor Gauntlett from 1981, after a takeover by Pace Petroleum and CHI (Gaunt and the Livanos family bought them out in 1983), Aston Martin brought out a spectacular 50-off Zagato coupé in 1985 and a 25-off convertible two years later. In 1987 Ford acquired 75 per cent of Aston Martin. The Vantage V-8 continued to be the mainstay of the company until 1990, when the new Virage, perhaps the last of the company's famous handcrafted supercars, went into production. A convertible version followed in 1992. Development of a more affordable Aston Martin car (codenamed DP1999) was being undertaken. Victor Gauntlett resigned in 1991.

The new Aston model emerged as the Callum styled DB7, and its styling and power took the model to the headlines. The Ford influence, however, was evident in its interior fittings. Despite this the model has sold in large numbers. As with the Virage (re-launched as the V-8), the DB7 featured superchargers and a wonderful engine note. In 1999 it evolved into a mildly restyled 420 bhp V-12 Vantage model that sprinted from 0-96 km/h (0-60mph) in 5.0 sec with a claimed top speed of 299 km/h (187mph). Building on the relaunch of the DB model line brought about by the DB7, Aston Martin has strengthened its foundations and has pointed to its future through the wild, lighter shape of the Project Vantage show car concept. Despite one or two telltale signs from the Ford parts bin, the fact is that, even under Ford, Aston Martin has kept its heritage and its unique essence.

1973 Aston Martin V-8

Elegant Motors' 1979 Auburn replica

ASTRESSE • France 1898

Using engines built under Grivel licence, this Levallois-Perret manufacturer claimed to build two to three cars monthly.

ASTRO-GNOME • USA 1956

Built by the Richard Arbib Co, NY, the Astro-Gnome looked like something from a Flash Gordon film, with its fluted aluminum side panels anodised in different blending hues. A bubble canopy, giving unobstructed vision all round, covered the passengers, but could be raised to allow walk-in entry and exit. Only one prototype was made.

ATALANTA • England 1915-1916

Built in Staines, this was a £195 light car with an own-make four-cylinder 1097cc engine.

ATALANTA • England 1937-1939

The Atalanta sports car, which featured all-independent suspension, used Albert Gough's slightly erratic 11.2- and 2-liter engines, previously fitted to some Frazer Nashes. More popular was the 4.3-liter V-12 Lincoln-Zephyr option. After the war Richard Gaylard Shattock revived the name with the RGS Atalanta, offering complete cars with glassfibre bodywork or kits of parts until 1958.

ATHMAC • England 1913

A friction-drive 1110cc cyclecar from Leyton, Essex.

1920 Astra phaeton

ATLA • France 1957-1959

Another small car using small Renault 4 cv engines and glassfibre body. Made by Jacques Durand (who later made CG and Jidé sports cars), the Atla boasted gull-wing' doors.

ATLAS • USA 1907-1913

The 'two-cycle' Atlas, built in Springfield, Mass., was available with 22 hp twin-cylinder and 34 hp three-cylinder engines. Knight sleeve-valve engines were used from 1911.

ATS • Italy 1963-1964

Connected with Count Volpi's 'Scuderia Serenissima' Formula One racing team, only a very few of these V-8 sports coupés, with engines up to 245 bhp, were built. Like the 'Serenissima' which followed them, they were never fully developed.

ATTILA • England 1903-1906

The Hunslet Engine Company of Leeds could not resist calling these three-cylinder 20 hp vehicles after the most famous Hun of all.

ATVIDABERG • Sweden 1910-1911

A Holsman high-wheeler was imported from the USA in 1910 by Atvidabergs Vagnfabrik AB, and used as a pattern. The engine was a flat-twin and top speed was about 45 km/h (28 mph). Some of the later engines had four cylinders. There was a two-speed gearbox and, to engage reverse, the whole engine was slid backwards under the frame. Thirty-five cars were planned, 12 were built and the rest converted for railway inspection use.

ATW • Germany 1983 to date

Electric minicar whose monocoque plastic body is supplied by a French boat builder.

AUBURN • USA 1900-1936

The Frank and Morris Eckhart's Auburn (Indiana) Carriage Company, dating from 1874, built its first car in 1900 and went into production with a 'one-lunger' two-seater in 1903. It was followed in 1905 by a twin-cylinder and, in 1909, by a 25 .30 hp Rutenber-engined four. A Rutenber-engined six appeared in 1912. A range of proprietary-engined sixes took Auburn through to a change of ownership in 1919, followed by the launch of the Continental-engined 26 hp 'Beauty-Six'. Its lack of sales success brought in the dynamic Errett Lobban Cord as first general manager, then as president. Early in 1925 came the 'Eight-in-Line', developed into the 4523cc '8-88' with a range of striking body styles. In 1928 the first of the boat-tailed Auburn Speedsters appeared, capable of over 174 km/h (108 mph) with its 115 hp engine. In 1929 over 22,000 Auburns were sold, falling to under 14,000 the next year, but boosted to a record 28,000 in 1931 by restyled coachwork on the new 8-98 model. The 6407cc Lycoming-engined V-12 of 1932-1933 proved a near-flop; however, Gordon Buehrig's blown outside-exhaust 851/852 Speedsters of 1935-36 were an all-time classic, but they sold at a loss.

1930s Auburn

AUBURN • USA 1966 to date

Three companies currently offer glassfibre replicas of the 1935-1937 Auburn Speedster, with power ranging from Ford Galaxie to Jaguar XJ6 engines. Glenn Pray's Auburn Replicar appeared in 1966, with a 7-liter Ford V-8, while Elegant Motors of Indianapolis launched its version in 1974. The 1979 range consisted of the 856 Speedster, 898 2+2 Phaeton and 898 Phaeton Elegante – all using Chevrolet Corvette frame and running gear. In 1976 the Custom Coach Company of Pasadena launched its 876 Speedster in kit form, followed by a phaeton in 1978. Kits are now being phased out in favor of complete cars.

AUDI • Germany 1909 to date

See panel opposite

AUDI • Germany 1909 to date

Audi's current high profile as a world leading center of excellence in styling and engineering belies the fact that just, two decades ago, the company's name was associated with solid but staid cars derived from the shared components of a larger named car maker. In the cycle of a handful of model ranges it has taken itself to a premier place in its home sector within Germany, and to a premier place throughout Europe and also in America. Founded by the creator of Horch cars, August Horch, at Zwickau in East Germany, Audi became part of the Auto-Union in 1932, was nationalized in 1945, and became defunct until 1965, when the name 'Audi' was resumed at the 'new' Auto-Union works at Ingolstadt in Western Germany. The Audi of today is one of Germany's leading cars, now part of the great VW Group, following Audi's merger with NSU's car operations.

Horch's first Audi was a 2612cc car; other superb-quality four-cylinder models of 3564cc, 4680cc and 5720cc followed. Driven in major sporting events, they proved to be very successful. Pre-war models had ioe engines. After the war, new sv engines of 2071cc were introduced, and there was also an ohv 3500cc 50 hp. The first six-cylinder motor, an ohc 4655cc unit, appeared in 1924, and the first straight-eight sv 4872cc appeared in 1928 after J S Rasmussen, then head of DKW, bought the remains of the American Rickenbacker car works and began building the Rickenbacker eight-cylinder engines in Germany. At about the same time he also bought Audi (Horch had left the works in 1920). In 1929 came the introduction of the Audi Zwickau 4371cc and 5130cc eights, followed in 1931 by a 3838cc six-cylinder and a small 1.1-liter four with a Peugeot motor. Most Audis were luxurious cars with special coachwork. Audi joined Wanderer DKW and Horch in the newly formed Auto-Union in 1932, and the 1933-built front-engined 1963cc Audi had a Wanderer six-cylinder ohv engine. It was followed by a similar 2255cc model and a 3281cc car with an ohc Horch six-cylinder motor. Mercedes controlled the destiny of Audi in the mid-1960s, and also designed the first post-war Audi 1.7-liter four-cylinder engine. Before the first new Audi was on the market they had sold Auto-Union to VW. The new range consisted of cars from 1496cc to 1871cc and, with the Audi 50 of 1974, also 1093cc and 1272cc cars of first-class design and workmanship. There was also a 1984cc 100GL. All of these new Audis were front-wheel-drive cars.

Audi revised its strategy in the 1980s and concentrated on advanced technology (*vorsprung durch technik*, or forward through technology, was its slogan), with the aim of competing directly with BMW. It entered new ground with four-wheel 'quattro' transmissions, five-cylinder engines and smoothly-styled bodies with flush glazing. The 100 model of the 1980s boasted a drag co-efficient (cd) of 0.31 – low for the time. It started a trend with its smooth detailing, and moved the marque on from its then highlight of the famous, sharp-edged 4wd Quattro coupé, which became the large performance car icon of that era. This car and its shorter-wheelbased Quattro Sport rallying variant took the sport by storm. The 1994 model year saw the 100 and 200 range revised and then subsequently labelled A6. After that, Audi turned out the superbly tailored A4 range that took on the mid-range business class sector icon that was the BMW 3 series, and won. An all-new A6 model with state-of-the-art technology appeared with advanced styling that was drawn and developed from the Audi A8 flagship, the industry-first, all-aluminum-bodied car that by then had become the apogee of Audi's achievement.

In 1999 the company took a design lead with the TT sports car and a performance lead with the A3 sport model. Although it has to share components with its Volkswagen partners, Audi remains an individualistic, advanced design house and car creator.

1930 Audi Zwickau eight-cylinder limousine

The more straight-edged Audi's of the 1980s saw models such as the Coupé

The A3 Audi of 1999, typical of Audi's smooth design skills

Austin Grand Prix in road-going guise (boxer Jack Johnson at the wheel)

AUDIBERT & LAVIROTTE • France 1894-1901

The oldest makers of motor cars in Lyon, Audibert & Lavirotte built Benz-like cars of up to 6 hp, with rear-mounted engines and belt drive. In 1900 the company built three 36hp racers. It built an interior-drive 'Berline de Voyage' (the first saloon car?) as early as 1898.

AULTMAN • USA 1901

A light steam carriage built in Canton, Ohio. Its makers also built a four-wheel-drive steam truck.

AUREA • Italy 1921-1930

A small producer, whose ohv four-cylinder cars had initially 1460cc, later 1497cc, engines. They were well-made but heavy. Production ceased around 1926, but a few more cars were assembled from existing parts.

AURORA • England 1904

The Aurora Tri-Motor was a 31.2 hp tricar on motorcycle lines.

AURORA • USA 1957-1958

Father Alfred A Juliano, a Catholic Priest, built this safety-inspired car of extraordinary appearance on a Buick chassis with a choice of Chrysler, Cadillac or Lincoln engine.

AUSTIN • USA 1901-1921

Big, powerful touring cars from Grand Rapids, Michigan: the 1907 60 hp Austin was an eight-seater tourer, while the 1908 90 hp six was, according to Walter S Austin, the 'sportiest kind of car it is possible to get'. A V-12 appeared in 1917.

AUSTIN/England 1906 -1989

See Panel

AUSTIN/England 1906 -1989

Herbert Austin started his motoring career as Wolseley's general manager, leaving in 1905 to set up his own company in an old printing works at Longbridge – seven miles (11 km) south of Birmingham. He began production the following year. His cars were conventional but well-made, having T-head engines with separate cylinders. His first was a 25/30 hp model but, three years after its formation, the company was able to offer a range of three four-cylinder models (15, 18/24 and 40 hp) and a 60 hp six-cylinder. This last-named model formed the basis of a racing variant that Austin entered for the 1908 French Grand Prix, finishing in 18th and 19th places. The year 1910 saw the appearance of a 1.6-liter four-cylinder car. Initially for export, it became available on the home market 12 months later, together with a single-cylinder 1100cc car (in effect a re-radiatored Swift) which appeared in 1909. At the outbreak of the First World War Austin was offering three four-cylinder models, the largest being close on 6-litres capacity. Austin's marketing philosophy experienced a marked change after the First World War, for he offered just one model; the 3.6-liter 20 of 1919. Unfortunately, this large car failed to sell in sufficient numbers, and it was not long before the company was placed under receivership. A new model, virtually a scaled-down 20, the famous 1.6-liter Twelve, was rushed into production in 1921, and this solid and reliable car remained in production until 1936, though the car was slightly scaled-up and the engine capacity increased to 1861cc in 1927. The famous Austin Seven was announced in 1922. When it appeared, the Seven was the smallest British four-cylinder car, being initially of 696cc, although this was soon increased to 747cc. Inspired by the Peugeot Quadrilette, its tiny splash-lubricated engine was designed by an 18-year-old draughtsman, Stanley Edge. The four-wheel brake car, with transverse suspension at the front and quarter elliptics at the rear, remained in production until 1939, by which time 290,000 had been made. It was also manufactured under licence in France, Germany, Japan and America. Its sporting successes included a third place in the 1929 TT and a win in the 1930 500 Miles Race at Brooklands. A fashionable 3.4-liter six-cylinder 20 went on sale in 1927, but the older four-cylinder model remained in production until the following year. The six was scaled down to produce the 2.3-liter Sixteen of 1928, but a less happy variation was the 12.6 of 1931. The successful Ten (1125cc) was introduced the following year, a Ten remaining a feature of the Austin range until 1947. The Light 12/4 (1535cc) appeared in 1932, sharing a similar production run. The famous Seven was replaced in 1939 by the 900cc Eight, this again being phased out in 1947. Austin's first overhead valve engine, the 2199cc Sixteen, was fitted in the 1940 12 body and chassis in 1945, though independent front suspension had to wait for the 1948 Princess and Sheerline and the 1.2-liter A40.

Austin and Morris merged in 1952 to form the British Motor Corporation, and that year saw the appearance of the A30 with 803cc ohv engine, which was also Longbridge's first unitary construction car. The quaintly styled

The Austin A40 Devon of the 1950s (top). 1979 Austin Maxi 1750 HLS (above). 1920's Austin

Metropolitan, made initially for Nash, appeared in 1954, powered by an A40 engine. New models in 1955 included the Cambridge, with A40 or A50 power units, together with the Westminster, which was fitted with a 2.6-liter six. Farina styling was a feature of the 1959 range, which saw further rationalisation with MG, Morris, Wolseley and Riley offering badge-engineered versions of the Austin Cambridge theme.

Britain's most revolutionary car appeared in 1959. Alec Issigonis's fwd Mini was initially sold as the Austin Seven and powered by an A series 848cc transversely-mounted engine with four-speed gearbox mounted beneath. Rubber suspension by Alex Moulton, 10-inch wheels and a distinctive box-like shape were unconventional features of the design that subsequently altered small-car technology throughout the world. It was followed in 1964 by the Pininfarina designed 1100 with Hydrolastic suspension (also appearing under the Morris trademark), and the larger 1800 two years later. Rear-wheel drive lingered on until the shortlived 3-liter was phased out in 1971. The Harris Mann designed 'Princess' (and as an Ambassador facelift) range later took over this sector of the large saloon market for Austin. Earlier years had seen the engulfment of BMC by Leyland to form British Leyland, and, in the following year, came the Maxi – powered by an ohc 1485cc engine, and using a fashionable tailgate. A more powerful 1748cc engine became available for the 1971 season. The fwd Allegro of 1973 was offered with a range of 1100, 1300, 1500 and 1750cc power units. Production quality problems blighted the car's image and perhaps signalled the death knell for the brand. In 1980 Austin launched the Metro 'super-mini'. The Maestro hatchback of 1983 and its notchback/estate derivative, the 1984 Montego, was still built under the Rover banner after the Austin marque had died and its remaining last model, the Metro, had been rechristened the Rover 100. After it died in 1998, only the Mini remained in production. In a supreme irony, it had outlived all the cars that came after it in Austin or Austin-Morris, BLMC and BL form.

1955 Austin-Healey 'Frog-Eye' Sprite with Donald Healey

AUSTIN-HEALEY • England 1953-1971

The Healey 100 was the undisputed star of the London Motor Show in 1952. Graceful but sturdy and very competitively priced, it caused an immediate sensation, as did the ensuing announcement that production was going to be on a very large scale and undertaken not by the Donald Healey Motor Co, but by Austin at Longbridge; enter the Austin-Healey. When production of the 'Big Healey' finally ceased in December 1967, nearly 74,000 cars had been completed. Of course the Austin-Healey name was also carried on 'Frog-Eye' Sprites, 48,999 of which were made, as well as thousands of the subsequent Sprites, Mks II-IV, which were mechanically identical and bodily similar to the equivalent MG Midgets.

Austin Healey 3000s Fixed Head (top), 1960s soft top Healet Sprite with glassfibre roof (center), 1960s Healey Sprite (left)

AUSTRAL • France 1907

'Touring tricars' and motorized delivery tricycles were offered by this Parisian company.

AUSTRALIAN SIX • Australia 1919-1930

This grandiose attempt to compete against imported US cars consisted of a mixture of local and imported parts,

Australian Six tourer, 1922

AUSTRO-DAIMLER • Austria 1899-1934

Originally a branch of the German Daimler factory, the works at Wiener-Neustadt became independent in 1906 and built some excellent cars. The firm's first designer was Paul Daimler, son of the great Gottlieb Daimler, followed by Ferdinand Porsche (responsible for the Mercédès-Electrique-Mixte of 1902-1907), Karl Rabe, Oskar Hacker and others. The factory also competed successfully in sporting events. Among A-D cars, the 'Prince Heinrich' model of 1911 with an ohc 5714cc four-cylinder engine became famous. It developed 95 bhp at 2100 rpm, while a less potent version had side-valves and a 6900cc engine developing 60 hp at only 1200 rpm. Both were Porsche designs. The smallest model was a 2212cc four-cylinder. In the early 1920s Porsche also created the 1.3-liter 'Sascha' racing cars, financed by Count 'Sascha' Kolowrat and built at the A-D works. The outstanding production car of that era was the ADM with ohc six-cylinder engines of 2540cc, 2650cc and 2994cc. The last model, ADM III, developed 110 hp at 4000 rpm and was one of the great cars of the late 1920s. The 100 hp ADR was a luxurious, less sporting version. The year 1931 saw the introduction of a 4624cc eight-cylinder A-D, a superb, very expensive luxury motor car. The last great car built at Wiener-Neustadt was the six-cylinder 'Bergmeister' with an ohc 3614cc engine developing 120 hp at 3600 rpm and a top speed of 145 km/h (90 mph) . In 1928 Austro-Daimler amalgamated with Puch and in 1930 with Steyr. Porsche, who had left in 1923 for Daimler-Benz at Stuttgart, later designed a big car for Steyr: Steyr afterwards joined Austro-Daimler.

Austrian (Austro-) Daimler touring car, 1913

1907 Austro-Daimler Mercedes-Electrique driven by Porsche

with a conventional chassis layout and a choice of five locally-made bodies. Most Australian Sixes were fitted with Rutenber six-cylinder engines and Muncie or Grand Lees gearboxes, but some had an imported ohv Anstead engine. High local production costs forced the company to close after 900 cars had been built. Several survive.

AUSTRALIS • Australia 1897-1907

The company started with a quadricycle, and then produced a 7 hp twin-cylinder light buggy, selling for $270.

AUSTRO-DAIMLER • Austria 1899-1934

See panel

AUSTRO-FIAT • Austria 1912-1936

Originally a branch factory of Fiat (Turin), Fiat at Vienna became independent after the First World War and built touring cars with 2072cc and, later, 1300cc sv four-cylinder engines. The factory eventually became part of the Austro-Daimler, Steyr, Puch combine and, after 1936, built commercial vehicles only.

AUSTRO-GRADE • Austria 1923-1925

The Grade was an 808cc two-stroke twin-cylinder car, designed by German aeroplane and two-stroke-engine pioneer Hans Grade. In the design Grade incorporated many aircraft principles, especially in the 'streamlined' body. The Austrian branch was at Klosterneuburg, near Vienna.

AUSTRO-RUMPLER • Austria 1920-1922

Edmund Rumpler was a famous aeroplane and car designer. In 1921 he created rear-engined streamlined cars and, in 1922, designed the Benz 'Teardrop' racing

1959/60 Auto Union

car with the engine in the back. In Austria he tried to build 10 hp cyclecars with a newly formed company, but few were made before the factory ran out of funds.

AUSTRO-TATRA • Austria 1932-1948

There was always a close connection between the Czechoslovakian Tatra works and its Austrian branch at Vienna. For many years it assembled cars in Vienna, especially the models 11 and 12, and afterwards built the Tatra 57, a 1260cc four-cylinder with the transverse-mounted flat air-cooled engine in front, under licence.

AUTOBIANCHI • Italy 1955 to date

These excellent small cars are built in the old Bianchi works. Autobianchi, controlled by Fiat since 1967, concentrated for many years on the Fiat-based two-cylinder 499cc Bianchina, which was available in various forms, mostly with 17.5 bhp and 21 bhp engines. Subsequently, 792cc and 1221cc four-cylinder models were added. From 1969 onwards Autobianchi also built 903cc and 1403cc Fiat-based four-cylinder cars. In 1975 Autobianchi merged with Lancia, another Fiat-controlled car factory. The company still produces the 499cc two-cylinder Giardiniera, the A 112 four-cylinder transverse-engined model, and the A 112 Abarth with a 1049cc 70 bhp engine and a 160 km/h (100 mph) top speed. Since 1985 Autobianchi has been alter ego for the Lancia Y-10 minicar.

Autobianchi A 112 Elegant saloon

AUTO-BOB • USA 1914

'My Boy's Delight', this $150 3-5 hp cyclecar was intended for 10- to 15-year-olds.

AUTO-BUGGY • USA 1906-1911

A high-wheeler with a 1647cc two-cylinder engine, built by International Harvester.

AUTOCAR • USA 1899-1911

The first Autocar was built at Swissvale, Pa., in 1899. It was a single-seater 4 hp buggy with tiller steering. In January 1900 a flat-twin Stanhope was announced. 1901 saw a 'high-powered touring carriage' with a front engine of 18 hp and left-hand-drive. Big two- and four-cylinder cars appeared in 1907, but only trucks were built after 1911.

AUTOCAR • England 1903

A 20 hp model from Manchester.

AUTOCRAT • England 1911-1926

A Birmingham-built light car, originally available with 1088cc or 1300cc four-cylinder engines. By 1921 the 11.9 hp Autocrat had a Lucas dyno-start as standard.

AUTOETTE • USA 1952-1957

The Autoette Electric Car Co of Long Beach, California, built this three-wheeled electric car for town use.

AUTO LEGER • France c. 1906-1910

This light car from Lyon had 'a bonnet in the form of a flying dragon, whose head and wings were shaped into radiator and mudguards'.

AUTOLETTE • Holland 1905-1906

A three-wheeler built in Rotterdam.

AUTOMATIC ELECTRIC • USA 1921-1922

Very few of these cars were manufactured, production being confined to a two-passenger roadster at $1,200.

L'AUTO-MIXTE • Belgium 1905-1912

Petrol-electric cars built in Liége. A Knight-engined model appeared in 1912.

AUTOMOBILE COMPANY OF AMERICA • USA 1899

Originally known as the 'American Motor', the power units built by this company were built in single- and twin-cylinder form. A complete car, the Stanhope, 'one of the newest and most approved styles on the market', was made.

AUTOMOBILE CONSTRUCTION • USA 1914

An assemble-it-yourself chassis for the trade from Philadelphia, with a 1557cc Continental.

AUTOMOBILETTE • France 1911-1924

Starting before the First World War with a small cyclecar with vee-twin engines and belt drive, Automobilette resumed after the war with a more conventional four-cylinder car. Some were sold under the name of CAB ('Construction Automobile de Bellevue'), from the name of the town where the works were situated. Some time after the closure the constructor, M Coignet, started again with the Coignet-Delaage.

AUTOMOTETTE • France 1898

A light tiller-steered three-wheeled carriage with a 3 hp horizontal single-cylinder engine and dual-ratio belt-drive.

AUTOMOTO • France 1901-1907

Also sold in England as the Automotor, this make was originally known as the Chavanet (1898-1900). Automotos were available either as complete cars, from a 4 hp single-cylinder voiturette to a 24/30 hp four, or as a kit of parts for home assembly.

AUTOMOTOR • USA 1900-1904

Designed by Hinsdale Smith, this car originally appeared as the Meteor. It was a light runabout powered by a De Dion engine. 31.2 hp and 5 hp models were offered.

AUTOMOTRICE • France 1901-1907

Henri Popp began production of these cars in Bergerac, though it later shifted to Paris. It is thought that l'Automotrice was the successor to the Cyrano. By 1903 the company had become known as the Socièté Française d'Automobiles, and offered a 6. 9 hp single, 9.12 hp twin and fours of 12, 16 and 24 hp. What is thought to be an early six-cylinder appeared in the touring car class at the November 1903 Dourdan hillclimb, driven by Gastè.

AUTO PARTS • USA 1909

Like the Metz, this 23 hp shaft-drive car from Chicago was sold in 'instalments' for home assembly. $450 got 'ten outfits of our $600 car'.

AUTO-PRATIQUE • France 1912-1913

A single-cylinder 601cc shaft-drive voiturette from Paris.

AUTO-TRI • USA 1898-1900

The Auto-Tri was a three-wheeled car built by C W. Kelsey,who later built the Motorette and Kelsey automobiles. The one-cylinder Auto-Tri existed as a prototype only, although the Auto-Tri Company was formally set up at Chestnut Hill, Pennsylvania and maintained its existence, despite its lack of output, until 1900.

AUTOTRIX • England 1913

A three-wheeled cyclecar with a choice of 6hp or 8hp twin-cylinder power units.

AUTO UNION • Germany 1932 to date

The Auto Union was the result of a merger in 1932 of DKW, Horch, Wanderer and Audi for financial reasons. Only DKW, thanks to big motorcycle sales, was really financially sound. There was at that time no real car bearing the Auto Union sign only, with the exception of the Porsche designed rear-engined racing cars. A DKW became an Auto Union-DKW, and that was also the case with the three other factories. Everything finished after the Second World War, when these factories, then in East Germany, were nationalized. It was not until the 1950s, when Auto Union was established in the western part of Germany at Ingolstadt and Düsseldorf, that the Auto Union insignia appeared once more on DKW cars. Years later the name was changed to Audi NSU Auto Union AG, with the old NSU works as the HQ. The great VW group is now the 'parent' of all cars built under the Auto Union banner.

c. 1914 Averies chassis

Another Avro venture, the 1924 two-wheel Monocar

AUTOVIA • England 1937-1938

A Riley subsidiary, the V-8 Autovia was of 2.8 litres capacity and, no doubt, inspired by the Ford V-8. A preselector gearbox was fitted and also, surprisingly, a worm-driven rear-axle. The project died with the Riley collapse in 1938.

AV • England 1919-1926

This cyclecar was initially a single-seater, but two passengers were later catered for. Engines were vee-twin, either by JAP or Blackburne, and mounted at the rear.

AVALLONE • Brazil c. 1976 to date

Builds a GM-powered replica MG-TF, as well as stretched VW and Opel bodies and a VW Beetle cabriolet.

AVANTI II • USA 1965 to date

Two businessmen acquired part of the defunct Studebaker factory and, employing ex-Studebaker personnel, formed Avanti. Produced in limited numbers, the Avanti II is indistinguishable externally from the original. Under new ownership from 1986, Avanti launched four-door and convertible models in 1989.

AVERIES • England 1913-1915

Marketed by John Averies, who imported La Ponette cars, this 1094cc light car was based on the Dupressoir 'Rolling'.

AVIETTE • England 1914-1916

A gawky belt-driven cyclecar sold by Hurlin, with 4 hp and 8 hp JAP or Blumfield power.

AVIS • Austria 1925-1928

Made in limited numbers by an aircraft firm at Wiener-Neustadt, the Avis had sv 798cc two- and 1096cc four-cylinder engines.

AVON • England 1902

Built in Bristol, the Avon was a wheel-steered three-wheeler with car-type bodywork with a 3.3/4 hp engine and twin radiators, one each side of the seat. Its three-speed gearbox was controlled by Bowden cable.

AVRO • England 1919-1920

Built by the aircraft manufacturer A. V Roe, the Avro was a short-lived affair powered by a 1300cc four-cylinder engine, although a two-stroke and five-cylinder radial were options.

AWS-SHOPPER • Germany 1973-1974

A small, simple shopping car built mainly from Goggomobil parts, with a 248cc two-stroke engine. It was expensive and of limited appeal.

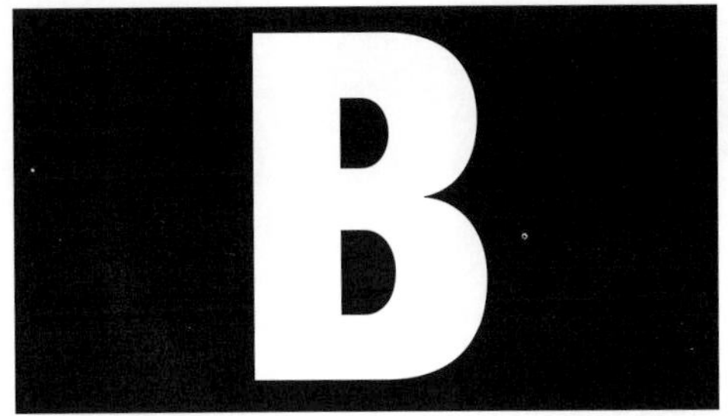

BABCOCK • USA 1906-1912

"A contented woman is she who operates a Babcock Electric – she knows there is nothing to fear," boasted the Buffalo, NY, makers of this marque.

BABY BLAKE • England 1922

The unusual thing about the Baby Blake was that it was fitted with two engines, both two-strokes. An ingenious friction drive was employed.

BABY-RHONE • France 1941

A single-seater electric voiturette.

BAC • England 1921-1923

The BAC, with its handsome radiator, used a 9.5 hp Peters engine and gearbox, and had some sporting pretensions.

BACHTOLD • Switzerland 1898-1899

A motor tricycle from Steckborn was based on the Egg, and was shown at the 1899 National Show in London.. Only six were made.

BACON • USA 1920-1921

The Bacon was built in prototype form only as a two-passenger roadster featuring wire wheels and a four-cylinder Herschell-Spillman engine.

BACS • England 1906

This 18/24 hp model was sold by the British Automobile Commercial Syndicate of London.

BADENIA • Germany 1925

Ex-Benz employees built this 2860cc car which had a modified six-cylinder sv Benz engine.

BADGER • USA 1908-c. 1910

An early fwd car with a 55/60 hp four-cylinder engine.

BADGER • USA 1910-1912

A 30 hp four built in Columbus, Wisconsin.

BADMINTON • France • England 1907-1908

An early "joint venture," the round-radiatored Badminton had a French chassis and English coachwork. It was built by Teste & Lassen and was available with 20 hp and 25 hp fours.

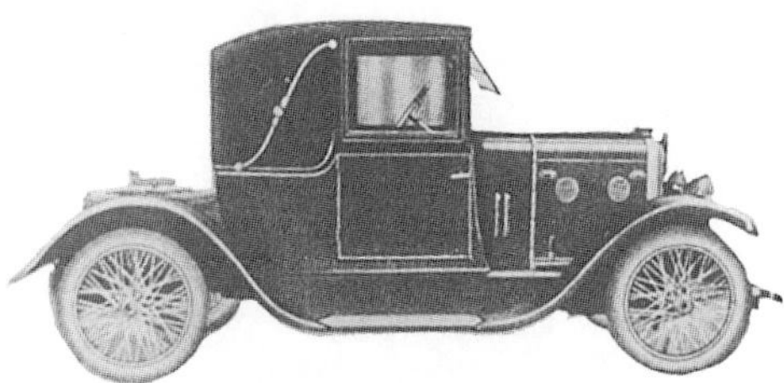

1923 Baer 4/18 PS Cabriolet

1923 Baker steam car

BAER • Germany 1921-1924

Paul Baer was a two-stroke enthusiast, like many others in the Berlin of the 1920s. He built a 770cc two-cylinder car with a double-diameter piston, and also produced proprietary two-stroke double-piston engines. His power units were also used in BF racing cars.

BAGULEY • England 1911-1914

The 15/20 hp Baguley was a well-designed, conventional car, available with either plate or cone clutch and worm or bevel final drive. The standard model had semi-elliptic rear springs; the de luxe three-fourth elliptics.

BAILEY • USA 1907-1915

Electric runabouts and victorias from Amesbury, Mass.

BAILLEAU • France 1901-1914

M Bailleau's 1902 light motorcar was "specially built to meet demand for a popular-priced two-seater vehicle." A 16 hp four was listed in 1906.

BAJA • Austria 1921-1924

The Baja cyclecar was driven by 490cc single-cylinder or 678cc vee-twin JAP engines.

BAJA GT • England 1969 to date

A survivor of the "Buggy" era, the Baja has rakish glass-fibre bodywork adorning the inevitable VW chassis. Engine choices have varied from "Beetle" 1200 to Chevrolet Corvair.

BAKER • USA 1899-1914

Most Baker Electrics were little more than wheeled battery boxes but, in 1902, Walter Baker unveiled his super-streamlined electric "Torpedo" land speed record contender – the first car to have seat-belts fitted – and capable of over 75 mph. He also built an electric brougham for the King of Siam in 1909. In 1914 Baker merged with Rauch & Lang.

BAKER STEAM CAR • USA 1920-1924

Probably no more than half-a-dozen Baker Steamers were built, although the 1921 calendar year saw a touring car, roadster and a 21.2-ton truck completed; all disc-wheeled and of conventional appearance. Boilers designed by the company's head, Dr H O Baker were, however, used as replacements for Stanley boilers.

BALBOA • USA 1924-1925

The Balboa was a California-built car with a factory in Fullerton which never went into actual production, although three prototype models were made. The 1924 pilot model featured a Kessler eight-cylinder engine, this being supplanted by another powerplant, probably of Balboa design, a year later. The cars were disc-wheeled and had 127-131-inch wheelbases. Balboas had distinctive lines and were ahead of their time in general appearance.

BALDWIN • USA 1896-1899

Based in Providence, Rhode Island, Baldwin built chain-drive steamers with either surrey or dos-á-dos coachwork. Unlike other light American steamers, the Baldwin had a condenser so that the exhaust steam could be recycled.

BALDWIN • USA 1900-1901

Baldwin, of Connellsville, Pa., claimed to have materials on hand for the manufacture of 180 steam cars, but went bankrupt amid accusations of fraud.

BALLOT • France 1919-1932

Ballot really originated as early as 1905, when the brothers Edouard and Maurice Ballot started manufacturing marine engines and proprietary power units. After the First World War they entered motor racing when ex-Peugeot engineer Henry designed a straight-eight 4.9-liter car for the 1921 French Grand Prix. They later evolved a 2-liter racing car from which was developed a touring version, the 2 LS. This was a dohc 1944cc four which stayed in production until 1924. In 1923 Ballot presented the ohc 2 LT with three-bearing crankshaft, and a sport version,

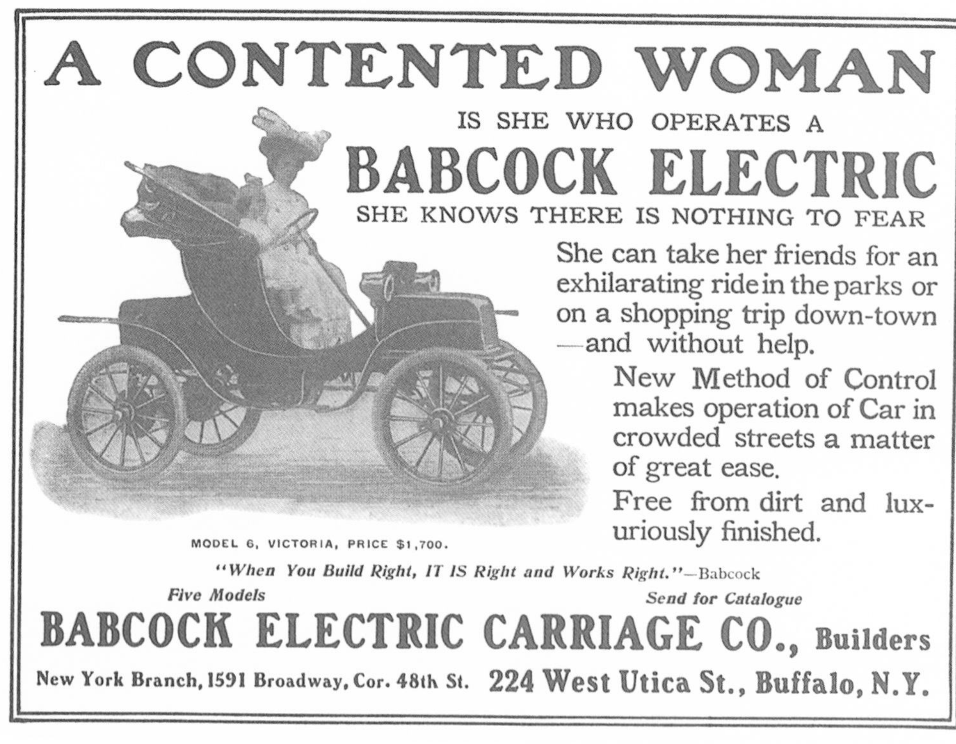

1908 Babcock Electric Victoria, Model 6

the 2 LTS, was soon evolved with larger valves. In 1926 a six-cylinder was presented at the Paris Show but never went into production, and it was replaced the following year by the ohc 2.8-liter type RH straight-eight. The engine was then enlarged to 3 liters, but the car was too heavy to enjoy success. In 1931 the Ballot factory was taken over by Hispano-Suiza. The Ballot HS 26, which had been launched at the Paris Show in 1930, was renamed Hispano "Junior." The six-cylinder engine of 4580cc was designed by Birkigt and made at the Hispano Works. Ballot provided only the chassis but, nevertheless, the Ballot factory closed its doors in 1932.

1930 Ballot RH-3 3-litre tourer

BALZER • USA 1894-1901

Steven Balzer of New York was a pioneer builder of motor carriages. In 1899 he received an order for ten cars from "Paris, France." His 1901 8 hp had a three-cylinder 2500cc rotary.

BAMBER & LEWIS • England 1898

A two-seater "oil motor car" from Meopham, Kent, said to be of the company's own manufacture. May also have been known as the "Vesta."

BANDINI • Italy 1948-1956

Four-cylinder 746cc sports cars with Fiat-based engines, built in limited numbers. The highly tuned engines had ohv and also ohc cylinder-heads and proved fast in many races, but failed as far as consistent reliability was concerned.

1925 Balboa five-passenger phaeton

BARAUF • USA 1920

Probably only one Barauf car was built, and this was exhibited in February 1920. It was a five-passenger touring model featuring a 108-inch wheelbase and a four-cylinder Leroi engine. It could be converted into a utility.

BARBARINO • America 1924-1925

Salvatore Barbarino was an automobile engineer and designer who took over the assets of the defunct Richelieu automobile and announced a new Barbarino car late in 1924. Only ten were completed. The cars featured a Leroi four-cylinder engine, disc wheels and a high rounded radiator reminiscent of Fiat or Kissel. All bodies for this 110-inch wheelbase car were supplied by Chupurdy & Co of New York City.

BARCLAY • England 1933

The Birmingham-built Barclay was an assembled family sedan with a 10 hp Coventry-Climax engine, Moss gearbox and ENV rear axle.

BARD • England 1899-1900

Forerunner of Calthorpe, George Hands"s Bard Cycle Company showed Grappler-tyred motor tricycles and quadri-

1903 Bardon 12 hp

BARDON • France 1898-1906

Like the Gobron-Brillié, the Bardon used an opposed-piston engine, but in this case there were two pistons and four flywheels. Engines of 5 hp to 12 hp were offered.

1913 Barimar 8 hp cyclecar

BARIMAR • France 1913

Welding engineers Barimar of London could carry out spectacular repairs on broken or cracked castings. The 8 hp Barimar car seemed out of character for this company, as it was a spindly single-cylinder model imported from France.

BARLEY • USA 1922-1925

The Barley was named for Albert Barley and built by the Barley Motor Car Co of Kalamazoo, Michigan, as a companion car to the Roamer which had been made by Barley since 1916. Strictly an assembled car, Barleys featured both Continental and Herschell-Spillman engines, a wheelbase of 118 inches, and prices starting at $1,395. In 1925 the name was dropped and the Barley became the Roamer 6-50, with the exception of the taxicab line, which was continued under its old name of Pennant.

BARLOW STEAM CAR • USA 1923

This 130-inch wheelbase $3,000 touring car appeared in a single pilot model only. The company's plan to manufacture buses also failed to materialize.

1913 Barré 3-liter sports in the Tour de France

BARNARD • England 1921-1922

An American Henderson four-cylinder motorcycle engine powered this chain-driven device, which was built in East London.

BARNES • England 1905-1906

Tricars from Deptford, Kent, with own-make 6/8 hp and 12 hp twin-cylinder engines.

BARNES • USA 1907-1912

Builders of an air-cooled four-cylinder, who acquired Anhut in 1910.

BARRE • France 1902-1930

Barré, of Niort (Deux-Sévres), began production with light cars powered by De Dion, Aster or Buchet engines flexibly mounted on springs. In 1908 Barré added a Ballot-engined car. In 1920 came a car with a SCAP 1600cc engine. The company changed its name to Barré & Lamberthon in 1923, but never reattained its pre-war success, as sales were confined to local customers.

BARRELLIER • France 1919

This three-wheeler was a "voiturette for war-wounded," powered by an air-cooled horizontal twin.

BARRIERE • France 1898-1900

Barriére of Paris built a "Sociable Tricycle" seating two side-by-side, as well as a 2 hp tricycle of more conventional layout.

BARRINGTON • England 1932-1936

Barrington Budd hoped to market a car powered by a two-stroke three-cylinder engine of his own design, but the project never reached production status. A 782cc version mounted in a two-seater body was built, but further ideas came to nothing.

BARRON-VIALLE • France 1909-1929

The founders of this firm, Barron and Vialle, joined forces at Lyon in 1912 when the coachbuilder Vialle (established in 1909) decided to build trucks. After the war Barron and Vialle acquired the manufacturing rights of the Automobiles Six of Strasbourg. They presented their car in 1924; an ohc six-cylinder of 2078cc ("Super Six".) The same year the firm also presented a straight-eight ("Super Huit") of 2771cc. It also made another version with the eight-cylinder engine in the six-cylinder chassis. Until 1924 the name of Barron-Vialle was never featured on the radiator. The firm enjoyed steady local sales but nevertheless closed its doors in 1929. Vialle continued truck production in another works at Arandon.

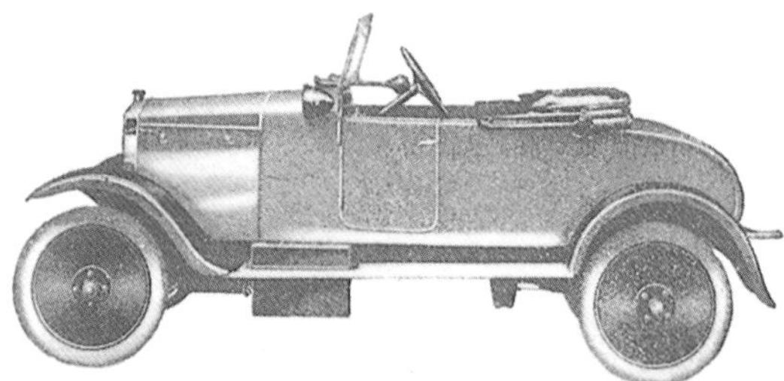

9/19 hp Bayliss-Thomas Popular, 1923

The 1936 Batten-Special range

BARROWS • USA 1896-1899

A fwd electric tricycle built in New York. The maker planned to offer these machines for lease rather than for sale.

BARTLETT • Canada 1913-1917

With air suspension and solid tires, the Bartlett appeared in prototype form with independent front suspension and four-wheel brakes augmented by retractable spikes which dug into the road through the tires – and caused a 26-car pile-up when they were tested. The ifs and spike braking were omitted from the 600 Bartlett cars and trucks produced in the firm's Toronto works. Production was halted when Bartlett"s USA suppliers went over to war work.

BASSETT • England 1899-1901

A two-speed light car with 4 hp Schwanemeyer twin-cylinder engine.

BASSON"S STAR • USA 1956

Basson's Industries, of New York, offered a glassfiber single-cylinder two-stroke three-wheeler for $999. It was no more successful than the company's previous attempt, the Martin Stationette of 1954.

BASTAERT • France 1907-1908

A Parisian voiturette manufacturer which exhibited at the 1907 Paris Salon.

BASTIN • Belgium 1908-1909

A round-radiatored light four-cylinder from Liège.

BAT • England 1904-1909

The 6 hp twin-cylinder Bat-Kar was a three-seater, three-wheeled voiturette from a well-known Penge motorcycle maker. In 1909 a curious four-wheeler, the Carcycle was launched, with a 7/9 hp JAP twin incorporating a detachable belt-driven cycle.

BATES • USA 1903-1905

"Buy a Bates and keep your dates" was the slogan of this unsuccessful venture by gas engine manufacturers Madison F Bates and J P Edmonds of Lansing, Michigan.

BATTEN • England 1935-1938

Batten-Specials were based on the Ford V-8 chassis, with stark open two- and four-seat er bodies.

BAUGHAN • England 1922-1929

The 1922 Baughan, from Stroud, Gloucestershire, was a 998cc twin-cylinder cyclecar with chain drive.

BAYLEY • England 1905-1907

This 18/20 hp four-cylinder worm-drive model was produced by the English Motor-Car Company of London, which also made the Lipscomb car.

BAYLISS-THOMAS • England 1922-1929

From the Birmingham-based manufacturer of Excelsior motorcycles, this was an assembled car, which started with a 11.2-liter Coventry Climax engine, an 1100cc ohv Meadows four being added in 1923. Sports two-seaters were available, but production was on a limited scale after 1925.

BAY STATE • USA 1906-1907

Rossell Drisko's Bay State Forty, from Boston, was powered by a 5.8-liter four-cylinder engine.

BAY STATE • USA 1922-1924

A successful small-production car, the Bay State was manufactured by R H Long in Framingham, Mass. and, in its three years of production, some 2,500 were sold. The car featured a Continental six-cylinder engine and proven standard components on a 121-inch wheelbase. It was designed by a former Winton designer, which probably explains the similarity of the radiator shape. A complete line of body styles was offered in both open and closed models, including a sports phaeton. Prices ranged from $1,800 to $2,850.

BEACON • England 1912-1914

A vee-twin cyclecar available with woven cane bodywork.

BEAN • England 1919-1929

A Harper, Sons & Bean was a well-established Dudley engineering firm which wished to emulate Henry Ford by mass-producing its first car, the 11.9 of 1920. As time was of the essence it updated the pre-war 1174cc Perry, producing it in a specially acquired factory with moving assembly line in nearby Tipton. Despite a good start in 1920, the company was soon placed under receivership owing to the collapse of its holding company, which included ABC, Swift and Vulcan, plus a host of component manufacturers. By the time production restarted in 1922 it had lost out to William Morris's Cowley. In 1923 the overweight 14hp was announced, with unit-construction engine and gearbox, and detachable cylinder head – something that the Edwardian-inspired 11.9 had not offered. A scaled-down 14, the 12 with the same engine capacity as the old 11.9, appeared in 1924.

Hadfields, a Sheffield steel company which had been associated with Bean since 1919, took over the company in 1926, ironically their centenary year, and production later moved exclusively to Tipton. A six-cylinder model, the 18/50, with Meadows engine and gearbox, appeared in 1927, though the Imperial Six with a 3.8-liter Bean engine aimed at the colonial market reached only the prototype stage. In 1928 the 14/40 Hadfield Bean appeared with

1923 Bean 11.9hp tourer

1924 Bean 14 hp and 3 m (10 ft) Eccles caravan

separate gearbox and worm-driven rear axle. The car was hopelessly unreliable and production ceased in 1929, but not before a sporting version, the 14/70, put in a fleeting appearance. Commercial vehicle production, which had begun in 1924, continued until 1931.

BEARDMORE • Scotland 1920-1928

The first three Beardmore models were built in three separate plants at Glasgow, Coatbridge, and Paisley. These were a 10 hp (1486cc), a 15hp (2413cc), and a 20 hp (4071cc). The 10 hp was developed into the ohc Eleven 1860cc of 1922 which, in turn, produced the 2-liter Sports, with aluminum pistons and a 70 mph top speed, which took the Shelsley Walsh record in 1925. A side-valve 16 hp followed but, after 1928, Beardmore concentrated on taxicab construction.

1903 Beaufort 6 hp single-cylinder

BEATRIX • France 1907-1908

Monobloc six-cylinders of 46 hp (5184cc) and 58 hp (6574cc) built by Tisserand of Paris.

BEAUFORT • England • Germany 1902-1910

The Beaufort was built in Germany with English capital, solely for the British market. The 1902 range consisted of 6 hp and 8 hp singles and 12 hp and 16 hp twins. A 20 hp four was introduced for 1903. In 1902, a Beaufort was the first car to climb the Round Tower, a notable Copenhagen landmark.

BEAUJANGLE CAN-AM • England 1972-1974

Supposedly inspired by the great Can-Am racers, the Beaujangle was a sports two-seater based on VW chassis and running gear. Changes to the suspension gave the Beaujangle superior handling to the much more conventional "Buggies."

BEAUMONT • USA 1966-1969

The Beaumont was GM's Canadian Chevelle, having only minor alterations from the American version. Phased out in 1969, it was replaced by Canadian-built Pontiac Tempests and Le Mans.

BEAVER • USA 1916-1923

One of the very few cars to have been built in the state of Oregon, the Gresham-made Beaver was an assembled six-cylinder car with worm drive. Only a few were built in the company's eight years of business.

BECHEREAU • France 1924-1925

Coming from the aeronautics industry (he had made record-breaking airplanes), Louis Bechereau started in Paris making cars based on the Salmson cyclecar, but with independent suspension on all four wheels by means of

coil springs and swinging arms. With an aerodynamic body, the Bechereau was too advanced for the public.

BECK • France 1920-1922

This Lyon marque presented its first car at the 1920 Brussels Show. The car had coil spring independent suspension all round. A second car was presented at the Paris Show the following year. The ohc four-cylinder engine had a swept volume of 1500cc.

BECKMANN • Germany 1900-1926

Early Beckmann cars had much in common with Panhard designs. Later, the company built good cars with engines ranging from 1768cc to 7320cc. After the First World War models with 2072cc and 2583cc four-cylinder engines were produced in limited numbers, the last version being fitted with a 2015cc four-cylinder Selve sv engine. Opel bought Beckmann"s Breslau factory in 1927.

BEDELIA • France 1909-1925

Certainly one of the very first cyclecars in the world, the Bèdèlia was built in Paris by Bourbeau & Devaux. It was noteworthy for having the pilot seated at the rear and the passenger at the front. The car was made of wood and plywood, and used firstly single-cylinder Aster engines, then the company's own 1056cc vee-twin. The car was belt driven. Bèdèlias sold very well until the war, and in 1920 the firm sold the manufacturing rights to M Mahieux, who made modifications, including seating the passengers side-by-side. The marque collapsed in 1925.

BEESTON • England 1899

This well-known Coventry cycle and motorcycle maker built a number of 31.2 hp single-cylinder tricycles, quadricycles, and voiturettes.

BEECHCRAFT • USA 1948

Built by the Beech Aircraft Company, the Beechcraft could have revolutionized the industry had production not been prevented by development costs! Advanced features included independent air-bag suspension, air shock absorbers, and a unitized aluminum body. Power was to be by a four-cylinder Franklin air-cooled engine driving an electric generator which, in turn, powered electric motors, one for each wheel.

BEGBIE • England 1903-1904

A wood-framed 61.2 hp Aster-engined voiturette built at Willesden Junction, London. The company also offered "chassis for coachbuilders."

1922 Beck 12hp

BEGGS • USA 1918-1923

The Beggs was a typical assembled car, the Continental engine being used exclusively throughout its existence. Successor to a flourishing line of buggies and farm wagons, it had a 120-inch wheelbase and could be bought as both open and closed models priced at $1,495 to $2,150. Several hundred were made,and prices were lower in its last years of production.

Family outing in a 1913 Bedelia

BEGOT ET MAZURIE • France 1900-1902

Known to a disgruntled British owner as the "Bag o" Misery," this 750cc voiturette from Reims was notable chiefly for the tasteful arabesques cast into its gearbox casing.

BEIJING • China 1958 to date

Founded as a repair works in 1938, Beijing started actual manufacture with the engagingly-named Jing Gang Shan, Beijing, and Dong Fang Hong marques. Now partly owned by Chrysler Jeep, it builds the Jeep Cherokee BJ 2021 and the utilitarian BJ 2020.

BELCAR • Switzerland 1955

A three-wheeled 197cc minicar produced in limited numbers.

BELGA • Belgium 1920-1921

The Belga, from Marchienne-Zone, was a 10/12 hp Ballot-engined light car with a Domecq-Cazaux eight-speed friction transmission incorporated in the cone clutch assembly.

The Bedelia range – "tourisme," "sport," and "livraison" – in 1913

Post First World War advertising for the Bellanger

1914 Bellanger 15 hp chassis

BELGICA • Belgium 1902-1909

Built by a cycle company established in Brussels in 1885, Belgica cars initially consisted of an 8 hp single, a 12 hp twin, and a 20 hp four. In 1905 came a 24/30 hp four, joined in 1907 by a 60 hp six. The company's latter cars were known as Saventhem-Belgicas. At the 1908 Agricultural Hall Show in London the cars it exhibited included a 24 hp and 30 hp fours and a 58 hp six with pair-cast cylinders; "a very fine piece of work." Excelsior subsequently acquired the company.

BELGRAVE • England 1904-1905

This 16.24 hp double-phaeton was sold by the Donne & Willans company, which imported the Rochet-Schneider into England.

BELL • England 1905-1914

Bell Brothers of Ravensthorpe, Yorkshire, began with an 8/10 hp twin, followed by fours of 16, 20, 24 and 30 hp. After the First World War the Co-operative Wholesale Society took over the company and built CWS lorries to Bell design in Manchester, although the cars were theoretically available until 1926.

BELL • USA 1915-1922

"The sensation of the year 1915," the four-cylinder Bell Model 16 from York, Pa., sold for only $775. Between 1916-1918 Bells were also license-built in Barrie, Ontario.

BELL • France 1923-1925

Built in Paris by M Bellois, this was a cyclecar with independent suspension and brakes on all four wheels. The engine was a 1308cc flat-four.

BELLAMY • France 1904

Bellamy, who enlivened the early days at Brooklands with a hilariously unsuccessful flying machine (and who eventually vanished in a balloon race), built this monstrous 38,507cc eight-cylinder for a young American lady.

BELLANGER • France 1912-1925

Most Bellanger cars were used as Paris taxis. The first models made at Neuilly from 1912-1914 were fitted with Daimler-Knight engines of 9.13 hp (2001cc), 15 hp (2548cc), 20 hp (3308cc,) and 38 hp (6280cc). After the war Bellanger used American Briscoe sv engines from 1920 to 1923 for the 15 hp "Tourisme" and "Sport" (3231cc,) and the 24 hp Sport (4253cc.) In 1921 it launched a luxury car, the 50hp V-8 of 6361cc. Bellanger halted car production in 1923, continuing only with aero engines. It started to sell De Dion Bouton cars under the name of "Bellanger" in 1928, but closed down soon after.

BELLE • England 1901-1903

Ex-Hewetson engineer E J Coles, of Holloway, London, claimed to have built this car himself, although it was probably based on an imported chassis. It was built with an inclined 7 hp engine and belt drive, and was normally fitted with solid tires.

BELMONT • USA 1909-1910

"Possessed of snap, style and finish," the four-cylinder $1,650 Belmont 30 from New Haven, Conn., had overhead exhaust valves.

BELSIZE • England 1896-1925

Marshall & Company of Manchester, forerunners of Belsize, began work in 1896 on a Benz-like car based on the French Hurtu, initially with tiller steering. The name "Belsize" was first used in 1901. Cars of up to 40 hp were produced, but in 1911 a 10/12 hp of advanced design, with unit engine/gearbox, made its bow. This was built up to the outbreak of the war, along with a 15.9 hp; Belsize was then building 50 cars and trucks a week. HE shells and aero engines were built during the war, and production resumed with a four-cylinder "15 hp" of 2799cc. In 1921 came the Belsize-Bradshaw, with a twin-cylinder "oil-boiler" engine. Last products were a 1696cc six (1924) and a 2.5-liter straight-eight (1925).

1923 Belsize Bradshaw two-seater

BENHAM • USA 1914-1917

Designed by Skelton and Goodwin, the Benham successor to S & M was a left-hand-drive luxury six-cylinder which sold for $2,585.

BEN HUR • USA 1916-1918

An assembled car produced in limited numbers at Willoughby, Ohio, the Ben Hur was powered by a six-cylinder Buda engine.

BENJAMIN • France 1921-1931

Benjamin made light cars and cyclecars at Asniéres. Production started with a cyclecar in 1921 with a 751cc four-cylinder engine which proved to be a great commercial success. In 1924 Benjamin presented a very interesting new model with a 547cc twin-cylinder two-stroke engine with pumping piston. It also made a three-cylinder car based on the same design. It quickly returned to more conventional cars with a voiturette with sv or ohv Chapuis-Dornier engines but, in 1924, presented another original car with a rear-mounted twin-cylinder four-stroke of 636cc, later of 616cc. The car was a complete failure. Following financial difficulties in 1927, the marque turned back to Chapuis-Dornier-engined cars, but went into liquidation until production was resumed under the name of "Benova." The revived company built cars with various proprietary engines, including a straight-eight SCAP of 1502cc. The last cars were Ruby engined. The final closure occurred in 1931.

BENNER SIX • USA 1908-c. 1909

An ohv pair-cast six of 3784cc, in unit with a two-speed gearbox, powered this $1,750 roadster from New York.

BENNET • England 1904

A 12hp four-cylinder model shown at the 1904 Cordingly Exhibition in London.

BENTALL • England 1906-1913

Agricultural engineers since 1792, Bentall of Maldon, Essex, offered a number of round-radiatored cars of 8 and

Benjamin

Benjamin "Bagatelle" sports, 1924

BENTALL • England 1906-1913

Agricultural engineers since 1792, Bentall of Maldon, Essex, offered a number of round-radiatored cars of 8 and 11 hp (two-cylinder), 16hp (four-cylinder) and an over-square 16/20 hp four. A former employee claimed production ceased because Bentalls paid its engineers only "farm wages,; being in a mainly agricultural area.

BENTLEY • England 1920 to date

See panel

BENZ SOHNE • Germany 1905-1926

After Karl Benz left Mannheim he headed – with his sons Eugen and, later, Richard – this new Ladenburg-based car factory. Karl Benz retired in 1912. It built some excellent cars with engines from 2608cc to 3565cc and also sleeve-valve models under Henriod-License. Production after the war was on a small scale. The range included sv 1638cc and 3560cc fours.

BERG • USA 1902-1905

Panhard-like four-cylinder chain-drive cars of 15/20 and 24 hp from New York. In 1905 Berg merged with the Worthington Automobile Company, which modified Leon Bollées for the US market and also sold an 18 hp five-seater called the Meteor.

BERGANTIN • Argentina 1960-1962

A forerunner of IKA-Renault, with a Willys-Jeep engine in an Alfa Romeo 1900 bodyshell.

BERGDOLL • USA 1908-1913

Louis J Bergdoll, from a well-known Philadelphia society family, boasted that the Bergdoll 30 was "backed by millions." It was assembled from proprietary components, including a Westinghouse engine and Driggs-Seabury chassis, and sold at prices ranging from $1,500 to $2,500.

BERGE • France 1922-1923

R Caillat of Le Pré-St-Gervais offered 7 and 10 hp

1922 Berge 10/14 hp cabriolet

BENTLEY • England 1920 to date

One of the truly great British sports cars, the first Bentley appeared at the 1919 Motor Show but did not reach the public until 1921. This was a long-stroke ohc 3-liter model, with a fixed head and four valves per cylinder. Although this remained in production until 1929, the next model was a more sophisticated six-cylinder 61.2-liter car which appeared in 1926. W O Bentley reverted to his four-cylinder theme with the 41.2-liter of 1927 (and supercharged by Sir Henry Birkin for 1930,) although the mighty 8-liter of 1930 was a further development of the 61.2-liter layout. Although today the Bentley represents to most of us the personification of the vintage sports car, many were fitted with stately and elegant sedan bodywork. However, the open four-seater cars are for ever associated with the Le Mans 24 Hour Race. The Cricklewood company chalked up no fewer than five wins – in 1924, 1927, 1928, 1929, and 1930 – the last three victories going to a car driven by Woolf Barnato, who had taken the company under his financial wing in 1927. The results of the Depression of 1929 were the last straw as far as the company's finances were concerned and, in 1931, it was bought by Rolls-Royce, pipping Napier to the post. In 1933 the first Rolls-Royce-built Bentley appeared, based on the Derby company"s 3.7-liter 20.25 model. 1936 saw this capacity increased to 41.2 liters. Independent front suspension put in a brief appearance in 1940 on the Mark V car. The first post-war model, the Mark VI, was the same capacity (4257cc) as its pre-war counterpart, but the engine featured an overhead inlet/side exhaust layout. It was offered with a standard steel body by Pressed Steel, the very first Rolls-Royce product to be so equipped. Although 1952 saw the announcement of the 4566cc Mulliner-bodied Continental, the marque's identity became more closely allied to Rolls-Royce, and 1960 saw the disappearance of the faithful six; this being replaced by a 6.2-liter V-8. These models used a 6750cc V-8 engine; the Corniche was available in sedan and convertible form, and the T series car shared the same monocoque body as the Rolls-Royce Silver Shadow.

During the 1980s Rolls-Royce Motors began to re-establish the separate identity of Bentley, first with the launch of the Mulsanne Turbo in 1982 and then with the 1985 Turbo R which, by 1990, accounted for 65 per cent of Bentley sales. In 1991 Bentley launched the Continental R two-door, four-seat coupé, the first all-new Bentley since 1952. With a top speed of 145 mph it is the fastest production Bentley ever. A further revised model, the Continental T, expanded on this theme. At this time the Bentley sedan lineage was enhanced by the new Arnage model. As usual it was a spin-off from the Rolls stable via its similarly bodied Seraph. Both cars were fitted with a BMW sourced engine, yet the Arnage was more individual than the previous T series version of the Rolls-Royce Shadow, and it received rave reviews in the motoring press. In a shock move soon after the launch of the Arnage, the Bentley name was sold off to Volkswagen in a bitter fight with BMW which, by this time, had engulfed Rolls-Royce. In less than a year the new VW influence manifested itself through the stunning Bentley Hunaudieres super car concept design that stormed the 1999 Geneva motor show; pointing as it did to a more sporting, futuristic image. Despite now being under German influence, Bentley seems set to retain its unique character.

1927 "works" 3-liter Bentley with Le Mans trim at Brooklands

1929 Speed Six Bentley (left)

1933/34 3½-liter Derby Bentley (far left)

1985 Bentley Turbo R

1887-1888 Benz three-wheeler

A modified Benz Viktoria, c. 1898

1902 front-engined 10 hp Benz

1921 Benz Sportwagen

BENZ • Germany 1885-1926

Karl Benz of Mannheim built his first motor car in 1885-1886. Three-wheelers of similar design followed, but proved more popular in France than in Germany. The 1893 "Viktoria" had a 2000cc water-cooled single-cylinder engine, but there were also 1730cc and even 2900cc versions. Another model, built until 1902, was the 3 hp "Comfortable" with a 1045cc single-cylinder engine. 1902 saw the introduction of the "Parsifal" with 10, 12, and 14 hp two-cylinder and 20 and 30 hp four-cylinder engines. This design created much trouble in the factory because both Benz and Marius Barbarou claimed responsibility. Benz resigned in a huff. Barbarou became chief designer, followed by Fritz Erle and Hans Nibel. Many superb cars – from 1950cc to a big 10,080cc developing 105 bhp (at 1400 rpm!) – left the Mannheim factory which, after the war, built a sporty ohc 1570cc car; the popular 6.18. Less sporty was the sv 2080cc 8 .20 hp. In 1923 a sv 2860cc six-cylinder appeared and also a sporty 4130cc six-cylinder which was built until 1926, when Benz merged with Daimler (Mercedes.) Benz racing cars, included, in 1909, the 200 hp "Blitzen"-Benz and, in 1922-1924, the rear-engined Edmund Rumpler-designed 1980cc Benz "Teardrop" racing car.

BERG ELECTRIC • USA 1921-1922

Few Berg Electric cars were ever completed, those units known to have been made being sold as town cars and limousines for private use as well as for lease. Artillery-wheeled, the 126-inch wheelbase Bergs had a General Motors 60 volt, 28 amp motor. The limousine cost $2,650.

BERGEON • France 1897-c. 1898

Using 5 hp Landry & Beyroux engines, this Bordelais manufacturer constructed four-seated victorias with the advanced feature of a vee windscreen.

BERGMANN • Germany 1909-1922

This electricity company built a 50 hp car and soon afterwards took over the license for Belgian Métallurgique cars. On the payroll was Ernst Lehmann, one of Germany's leading car designers, also connected with Métallurgique. Among his designs were 1560cc and 1728cc twin-cylinder and 2800cc to 6320cc four-cylinder Bergmann-Métallurgique cars. Other four-cylinder models included 9880cc, 7320cc, 3365cc, and 1560cc sv-engined versions. The last Bergmann designs had 55 hp four-cylinder and 45 hp six-cylinder side-valve engines.

BENZ • Germany 1885-1926

See panel

BERKELEY • England 1913

A low-priced 14/18 hp four-cylinder car.

BERKELEY • England 1956-1962

Small, glassfiber-bodied, motorcycle-engined sports cars. Performance of the later versions was very good, thanks to more powerful engines and a weight of around 355 kg (7 cwt). Designed by Laurence Bond at the request of Charles Panter of Berkeley Caravans, the cars sold in steady numbers until the company's demise.

BERKSHIRE • USA 1905-1913

The first production Berkshires used Herschell-Spillman engines. From 1907 they used own-make 6211cc fours.

BERLIET • France 1895-1936

Marius Berliet started building single-cylinder cars in a small shed in 1895. In 1900 he also offered twin-cylinder cars. After taking over Audibert & Lavirotte in 1901 he built two- and four-cylinder cars and, a year later, introduced a completely new design with a honeycomb radiator and steel chassis frame instead of wood. In 1906 Berliet sold the US license for his design to the American Locomotive Co. From 1907 to the outbreak of war Berliet

1923 Berliet 12cv tourer

production was mainly centered on three models: fours of 2412cc and 4398cc and a six of 9500cc. A 1539cc model was current from 1910-1912. Berliet made cars until 1917, but developed its truck department during the war for the needs of the French Army. After the war it resumed production of cars with a 12 hp (2613cc), 15 hp (3308cc), and 22 hp (4398cc), plus other minor models. The sv engines were all of pre-war design. In 1924 Berliet presented new ohv engines; a 7 hp (1159cc) would-be popular car, a 12 hp (2484cc) and an 18 hp (3969cc) – these models co-existing with the old side-valves. With the growth of truck sales, Berliet had less and less interest in making cars. Nevertheless it launched two new six-cylinders of 1800cc and 4000cc in 1927. In 1933 only two car models were listed; a 1600cc and a 2000cc, available in side-valve as well as ohv form. The last model, presented in 1936, was the Dauphine, a car similar to the Chrysler Airflow, with independent front suspension. When Marius Berliet died after the war, a change of policy had already suppressed cars in favour of trucks. Berliet, which was taken over by Citroên in 1967, still makes trucks.

BERNA • Switzerland 1902-1907

One of the great Swiss truck firms, Berna of Berne began with a rear-engined car on De Dion lines and curious three-seater coachwork in which the front-seat passenger sat sideways. A front-engined 8 cv appeared in 1903, joined by a 5 cv the following year. The last Berna touring cars were six monobloc fours built in 1907.

BERNARDET • France 1946-1950

A well-known builder, Bernardet started to build economy cars with 750cc and 800cc two-stroke engines just after the Second World War. The company had no great success, so it returned to sidecars and also made scooters.

BERSEY • England 1894-1899

Walter C Bersey's first experimental electric vehicle, an omnibus, appeared in 1888, but it was not until he and Desmond FitzGerald had developed a suitable dry cell for propulsion purposes that he began to promote his designs commercially, starting with a parcels van which ran for

A 40 hp Berliet in the 1905 Coupe des Pyrenees

1,000 miles in London during 1894. Bersey concentrated on vans, formal landaus and cabs (he built London's first taxi fleet in 1897, and also supplied electric cabs to Paris) because he felt that no form of pleasure car could ever replace the horse.

BERTRAND • France 1901-1902

Two-speed voiturettes from Paris with Clément, De Dion, Buchet or Aster engines.

BESSEYRE & RAYNE • France 1908

Remarkable for what it omitted from the expected specification, this was a two-stroke four "without gearchange or water circulation."

1896 Bersey Cab undergoing Scotland Yard testing

1901 Bertrand

1913 Bianchi 25/30 hp Prince Henry Torpedo

BEVERLEY-BARNES • England 1924-1931

The straight-eight ohc Beverley-Barnes was made in small numbers by Lenaerts and Dolphens and varied in engine capacity from 21.2 to 5 liters. At least one was Bean-engined! These luxury cars were made only in small numbers and did not survive the Depression.

BF • Germany 1922-1926

A small factory, concentrating on fast two-stroke cars. Bolle-Fiedler of Berlin also built 1096cc and 1496cc racing cars, with three- and four-cylinder engines, which were driven by the designer Max Fiedler. Production versions had 1026cc motors.

BIANCHI • Italy 1898-1938

Founded in 1885 by Edoardo Bianchi this Milan factory, still well known for bicycles, commenced manufacture of motorcycles and cars in 1898. It built many touring car models over the years. Some had ohv 8-liter in-line engines, but most were of 1460cc, 2690cc, or 2890cc; there was also a popular ohv 1287cc four-cylinder. Bianchi cars were of sound, sturdy design. Attempts to revive production with new designs after the Second World War failed, partly as a result of the great demand for bicycles and motorcycles, and partly because of the high costs of developing the new cars.

1904 Bijou 5 hp voiturette

BIDDLE • USA 1915-1923

A highly regarded small luxury automobile, distinguished by a pointed radiator similar to that of the Mercedes or American Singer. With prices ranging from $2,950 to over $5,000 for custom-bodied models, Biddle cars were known for their exquisite individually designed coachwork. Although a Buda engine was standard equipment, the Rochester-Duesenberg engine was used on 1918 models and available as an option after.

BIFORT • England 1914-1920

A 10 hp light car built in Fareham, Hants.

BIGNAN • France 1918-1931

In 1920 Bignan (which had made proprietary engines before the First World War) started to build the Bignan Sport in the Grégoire factory at Poissy. There were two models, of 2951cc and 3457cc, with fixed-head sv engines. Bignan also made a real sports-racing car whose Causan-designed ohc 2959cc engine had four valves per cylinder. In 1922 Bignan made another, very raceworthy sports car. This, the famous 2-liter with desmodromic valves,was replaced in 1924 by another 2-liter, with four valves per cylinder. On the touring side, Jacques Bignan presented in 1922 an ohc 1693cc 10 hp, followed with an 11 hp in 1923. After a first failure in 1926, Bignan quickly resumed production with a new management and launched a car with two valves per cylinder. Of minor interest, for they were not true Bignan cars, the marque also made 8 hp 1200cc and 10 hp 1500cc SCAP-engined cars and a 10 hp with 1600cc Ballot engine. It also turned to badge-engineering with Salmson cyclecars bearing Bignan radiators. Forced to meet more and more financial demands, Bignan started to run his business under the new name of "La Cigogne" and built a new six-cylinder 2.5-liter and an eight-cylinder SCAP-engined car in 1929. Between 1930 and 1931 Bignan only repaired cars, and then closed.

BIJOU • England 1901-01904

The Protector Lamp and Lighting Company of Eccles, near Manchester, built a tiny motor fire engine in 1901. Its Bijou light cars had 5 hp water-cooled engines and were capable of 20 mph.

BIJ"T VUUR • Holland 1902-1906

Aster-engined cars from Arnhem. Only a few were built.

BILLINGS-BURNS • England 1900

Designed by E D Billings of Coventry, this voiturette was powered by a 21.4 hp De Dion engine.

A Bignan Sport in the 1925 Le Mans Race

1920 Bignan Sport 3-liter

BINGHAMTON ELECTRIC • USA 1920

The Binghamton Electric Truck Co of Binghamton, NY made only two or its threetwo-passenger electric coupés.

BINNEY & BURNHAM • USA 1901-1902

An ineptly named twin-cylinder steamer from Boston.

BIOTA • England 1969-1976

The Biota was a striking, open-topped two-seater with a Mini engine mounted in the nose of a light tubular chassis clothed in a neat glassfiber body. About 31 Biotas were built for road and track, one winning the 1972 Castrol BARC Hillclimb Championship, driven by Chris Seaman. Weighing a mere 8 cwt, all Biotas enjoyed lively performance.

BIRCH • USA 1916-1923

Like the Bush, the Chicago-based Birch was strictly a mail-order car. A complete line of four- and six-cylinder models featured Leroi, Lycoming, Beaver, and Herschell-Spillman engines. Production was limited to open models until 1921, when a sedan augmented the line. Wheelbases ranged from 108 to 117 inches and the car's main appeal was probably its low price. From the aesthetic point of view, little could be said for the Birch.

1922 Blériot 739 cc "conduite interieure"

BIRD • USA 1897-1898

A rear-engined friction-drive dos-á-dos built by Henry Bird of Buffalo, NY.

BIRMINGHAM • USA 1921-1922

The Birmingham of Jamestown, NY, featured independent suspension by transverse semi-elliptic springs and a fabric-covered body; a novelty in America. Some 20 units were produced, powered by a Continental six-cylinder engine and other proven components. The design, without the independent suspension or fabric body, was used later on the Canadian Parker car.

BISCUTER • Spain 1953-1958

Gabriel Voisin's last production vehicle was unlike anything he had produced before, save in the originality of its conception. It was a tiny two-seater with a duralumin monocoque body and a 197cc Spanish-built Villiers engine driving the front wheels. Built in Barcelona, it proved a popular solution to the problem of providing basic transport for the car-hungry Spaniards during the 1950s.

BITTER • Germany 1973 to date

Produes luxurious 5354cc V-8 230 hp coupés with ohc Opel Diplomat engines and bodywork by Baur of Stuttgart. In 1992 Bitter launched the Opel-powered Type 3 sports car, with coupé or convertible coachwork, built in conjunction with Bertone and trimmed with leather and rosewood.

BIZZARRINI • Italy 1965-1969, 1991

Giotto Bizzarrini, who mainly built prototypes at Livorno, first created the Iso-Grifo, then a couple of cars bearing his own name. They were of advanced design, although his very sporty cars had front engines when other designers were already switching to rear engines. Best known were his GT Strada 5300, a high-efficiency coupé with Type 327 Chevrolet Corvette engine and the GT Europa 1900 with an 1897cc ohv four-cylinder Opel motor. In 1989 Bizzarrini announced he would be starting production of a new 160 mph two-seater, the Picchiom, in 1991.

BJERING • Norway 1919-1920

A great problem in Norway was the narrow roads, especially in winter, when ordinary cars were too wide for the narrow track left by the snow plow. The Bjering car from Gjovik was designed for this, with tandem seating, the driver sitting in the rear seat to obtain better traction. The engine was an air-cooled V-4 of Norwegian design placed in the middle of the car. Four cars were built before it was redesigned, with a four-cylinder engine at the rear. Only two of these were built.

1922 Black Prince 2¾ hp cyclecar

BLACK • USA 1899

Phaetons, dos-á-dos and "business wagons" of 21.2 hp to 8 hp were offered by this Indianapolis manufacturer.

BLACK • USA 1903-1909

"Speed! I guess yes!" was the optimistic slogan used to advertise this 10 hp, twin-cylinder high-wheeler from Chicago, with a maximum velocity of 40 km/h (25 mph).

BLACKBURN • England 1919-1925

Built by the well-known aircraft company, the Blackburn was a conventional enough car with a 3160cc Coventry-Simplex engine.

BLACKHAWK • USA 1929-1931

The Blackhawk initially appeared as the Stutz Model B-B in 1928 but, a year later, it was given marque status. Both an own-make six and a Continental eight were featured. Despite certain efforts to give the Blackhawk an image of its own, it was almost always regarded as just another model of Stutz.

BLACK PRINCE • England 1920

The shortlived Black Prince was a belt-driven cyclecar, largely made of wood and driven by a 2.3/ 4 hp Union air-cooled engine.

BLAKE • England 1899-1904

Blake"s first car, built in 1899, was a Benz-like vehicle with a 3 hp horizontal Blake engine, which he planned to fit with a Dawson dynamo/starter unit. The 1902 4 hp voiturette had a twin-cylinder horizontal engine of Blake"s own construction. The company subsequently concentrated on building engines for motor launches.

BLERIOT • France 1921-1922

Made by Blèriot Aeronautique at Suresnes, the Blèriot cyclecar had a small twin-cylinder two-stroke engine of 739cc, and a wooden chassis. Only a few were made by the firm, which was also making motorcycles at this time.

BLERIOT-WHIPPET • England 1920-1927

Infinitely variable transmission by pulley and belt was an unconventional feature of this cyclecar. The engine was a centrally mounted Blackburne vee-twin. Later variants were shaft- and chain-driven.

BLM • USA 1906-1908

A sporting four-cylinder built in New York by Breese, Lawrence and Moulton. Engines of up to 11,120cc were used.

BLODGETT • USA 1922

Only one prototype was built, a five-passenger touring car featuring disc wheels and a six-cylinder Continental engine. The manufacturer was Blodgett Engineering & Tool Co of Detroit.

BLOMSTROM • USA 1906

Blomstrom of Detroit built the Gyroscope, a friction-drive flat-twin model with vertical crankshaft and fore-and-aft cylinders for "gyroscopic stability in running – no skidding!" The company later merged with De Luxe.

LE BLON • France 1898

Benz-like voiturettes with 4 hp twin cylinder engines, sold in England as the "Lynx."

BLUMBERG • USA 1920

A handful of four- and eight-cylinder automobiles were built by this manufacturer of tractors. A V-8 was offered, with a wheelbase of 124 inches and a price of $3,000.

BMF • Germany 1904-1907

This Berlin-based factory was the predecessor of Oryx, which in 1909 merged with Dürkopp. BMF built 22 hp Fafnir-engined cars and supplied many Berlin taxicabs. Some models had friction drive.

BMW • Germany 1928 to date

See panel

BMW • Bayerische Motoren Werke Germany 1928 to date

When BMW bought the Dixi car works at Eisenach they also acquired the license for the Austin Seven. They were soon building the "Wartburg." This sports car with a two-seater body and an 18 hp engine gained the first racing successes on four wheels for this Munich-based company. The first true BMW design was an ohv 788cc four-cylinder in 1931. Other versions followed. with 845cc and, in 1933, the first six-cylinder BMW – an 1173cc Fritz Feidler design. The 1490cc six-cylinder developing 34 bhp was built also as a two-seater 40 bhp sports car and, from 1936 onwards, a 1911cc six-cylinder was made. The most famous version was the 328, developing 80 bhp at 4500 rpm, which won many races with drivers including Prince Bira and Dick Seaman. The last pre-war model was a 3485cc six-cylinder touring car with 90 bhp at 3500 rpm. In England BMW cars were sold by Frazer Nash and raced under the Frazer Nash name.

As a result of the war BMW lost the Eisenach works, but bought the Glas car works at Dingolfing in 1966, where it also built a new factory. The first post-war car was the 501 with a 1971cc six-cylinder engine, built from 1952 onwards. Improved versions, and also a 2077cc model, followed. A V-8 appeared in 1954; firstly with 2580cc, later with 3168cc and up to 160bhp at 5600 rpm. Using modified 246cc single-cylinder ohv motorcycle engines, from 1955 BMW built the Italian Isetta bubble cars under license. There was also a 298cc model and a 582cc BMW-Isetta, which used an ohv flat twin of BMW's own manufacture. New small cars with 697cc flat-twin engines appeared on the market in 1959. They saved BMW during a recession, when even motorcycle sales slumped. New, larger car models came into production in 1962 with four-cylinder ohc engines of 1499cc, 1573cc, 1773cc and 1990cc capacity; subsequently ohc six-cylinder engines of 2494cc to 3295cc. All of these engines came in a variety of models. Among later models were the 316, 318, 320, and 320i with 1573cc, 1766cc, 1990cc, and 2315cc ohc engines and the 518, 520, 520i, 525, 528,.530i range, which also included six-cylinder ohc in-line engines of 1990cc, 2494cc, and 2788cc. The 630 and 633 CSi cars use 2986cc and 3210cc engines developing up to 200 bhp, while the 728, 730, and 733i were powered by 2799cc, 2986cc, and 3210cc six-cylinder ohc engines

In 1978 BMW launched the high-performance M1, the first model developed by BMW Motorsport. All BMWs from 1979 had fuel injection. The 1979 732i was the world"s first production car with digital motor electronics, and the 1980 745i had a 3:2-liter turbocharged engine plus antilock brakes. A new 5 series appeared in 1981, and five-speed manual or four-speed automatic transmissions were standardized from 1983. The new 3 series of 1986 reintroduced a Cabriolet model. The top-of-the-range 7 Series was renewed in 1986, and the 750i.750iL offered the first German V12 power unit since the 1930s. A third-generation 5 Series arrived

1929 BMW Wartburg sports (top)

BMW 327 Cabriolet, 1938

Mark II incarnation of the 3 series BMW (left,) BMW 3 Series coupé in M3 variant (below)

The "ultimate" BMW 5 Series (far right.) 1990s 5 series BMW (right.) BMW Z coupé (below.) A Classic BMW interior (near right)

in 1988. The Z1 roadster developed by BMW's independent R & D company and built 1989-91 had unorthodox doors that retracted into the sills. A new 3 Series appeared in 1991, though the old-style Convertible and Touring estate continued alongside the new sedan for some time.

Alongside them BMW had the 8 series coupé, which became an icon of its time and of the type of person who aspired to BMW ownership. With a new model 7 series, a new 3 series Compact Coupé and the new Z3 roadster and its later M Coupé variant, the company's model range covered all bases. However, a certain degree of derivation and conservative evolution was observed in some of BMW's cars by the motoring press, and the company responded with hints of more adventurous things to come. The new 5 series quickly became its class leader, and remained so despite strong competition. It is available with a range of six-cylinder engines and also with BMW's class-leading turbo-diesel unit. The top-of-the-range 540 comes with a V8 engine and can also be ordered as an estate variant. The glimpse of a revived large two-seat convertible aping the old 507 helped refocus BMW's sporting claims. Labelled Z7, it debuts in 2000. Through buying the Rover (and Land Rover) brands as well as gleaning a part of the Rolls-Royce empire, BMW tried to expand its market coverage further. This was not easy, and led to boardroom troubles as well as factory-floor concerns for BMW and Rover. BMW's plants in South Africa and America also saw changes, yet the strong brand image of BMW's blue and white badge, derived from an aircraft propeller, will surely see it through.

1926 BNC 1100cc sports

BNC • France 1923-1950

Bollack, Netter et Cie built many excellent sports cars, initially evolved from the Jack Muller cyclecar. The first models used SCAP and Ruby engines from 900cc to 1100cc in sv or ohv form. They started with true sports cars in 1927 with the "Montlhéry," "Monza," and "Miramas" models with Ruby and SCAP engines. Some of these, mainly the SCAP engined models, were supercharged. They sold very well. Under the management of M de Ricoux the company entered the field of larger cars with the ill-fated AER in 1930. BNC took over Lombard in 1929. Some BNC racing cars used 1500cc Meadows engines. The firm closed its doors in the late 1930s. The BNC marque was taken over by its agent, M. Sirejols, who continued to assemble cars from parts until 1950, some of them using BMW 328 and Ford Ten engines.

BOB • Germany 1920-1925

A small producer who fitted 990cc and 1268cc Siemens & Halske four-cylinder engines into own-make frames. Bob cars had a "sporting touch" and competed in many German races. The last 1268cc versions had own-make engines.

BOBBI-KAR • USA 1945-1948

Produced by the Bobbi Motor Car Corp., first in California and then in Birmingham, Alabama, the Bobbi-Kar had Torsilastic independent suspension consisting of rubber welded to steel, combined with torsional rigidity. Rear-mounted water- or air-cooled engines ranged from one to four cylinders. Some bodies were of plastic, but a coupé

Bock & Hollender sporting two-seater, 1907

Léon Bollée

1900 Amédée Bollée 6 hp phaeton

BOLLEE • France 1873-1924

The Bollées, a gifted family of bellfounders from Le Mans, sired three marques; the steam carriages of Amédée Bollée père, built between 1873-1881 (his Mancelle of 1878, with independent front suspension, set the style for cars to come, and was built in a small series.) the advanced gasoline cars of Amédée Bollée père fils (1896-1913;) and the fiery three-wheeled Lèon Bollée (1896) – the first vehicle to bear the name "voiturette." The 1896 Amédée Bollée was the first shaft-driven car with spiral bevel gearing. Amédée fils subsequently built the streamlined racing torpilleurs, the 1899 model featuring a 20 hp monobloc four, with twin carburetors, a chassis independently sprung at the front and underslung at the rear. But their disappointing performance inspired Amédée to concentrate on refined limited production cars. His 1907 Type E, the first ergonomically designed car, featuring hydraulic tappets. The last Amédée Bollées left the works in 1913, but some were assembled from spares until 1919. Lèon Bollée's factory built large, conventional cars from 1903 to 1924, when it was taken over by Morris.

Amédée Bollée limousine, 1902

with removable steel top and a wood-panelled sedan almost went into production.

BOBBY-ALBA • France 1920-1924

Made by Lucien Bollack (later of BNC), these light cars had sv Ballot engines of 1131cc.

BOCAR • USA 1958-1960

Bob Carnes designed and built a high-performance two-seater sports car with a plastic body and tubular frame. Powered by a supercharged or fuel-injected Corvette engine with Volkswagen suspension, Buick brakes and Jaguar wire wheels, this limited production car was priced at $4,146.

BOCK & HOLLENDER • Austria 1899-1910

Bock & Hollender built cars, known also as the "Regent," and motorcycles. The cars mainly had four-cylinder engines of 16 hp, 24 hp and, eventually, 40 hp. Early models had chain drive. Works driver Karl Trummer won many hill-climbs in these cars.

BOES • Germany 1903-1906

Like other early German producers, Boes built cars with vee-twins and also with in-line four-cylinder proprietary engines.

BOISSAYE • France 1901

A "real racing carriage so dear to quick speeds amateurs," the Boissaye was a 24 hp four.

BOITEL • France 1946-1949

The small Boitel used 400cc and 589cc two-stroke engines, but few were sold.

BOLLEE • France 1873-1924

See panel opposite

BOLIDE • France 1899-1908

Léon Lefévbre started production with a range of high-built belt-drive racing cars with horizontal engines with one, two and four cylinders; the largest being 11,699cc. Chain-drive came in 1901 and, by 1902, Bolides were of conventional design, with vertical engines of various proprietary makes. Lefévbre left around 1906 to make the Prima car, and the last new Bolide design was a six-cylinder shown at the December 1906 Paris Salon.

Bond Equipe GT, 1962

BOLIDE • USA 1969 to date

The Bolide prototype Can-Am I, designed by Andrew J Griffith, was immediately followed by Can-Am II with a 5752cc Ford V-8 engine. A fwd ORV Bolide using the 3687cc Jeep 160 hp V-6 engine is also produced.

BOLSOVER • England 1907-1909

A three-cylinder steamer from Durham.

BOLWELL • Australia 1963-1974

The Bolwell brothers started in business building glass-fiber kit cars and, by 1970, had graduated to the factory-built Nagari sports coupé. This beautiful and exciting machine was powered by a Ford V-8 302 engine. The Lotus-type backbone chassis incorporated four-wheel independent suspension of Bolwell design. The firm had planned to export to the US market, but tough safety and emission regulations made this impracticable. Nearly 100 Nagaris (and hundreds of the earlier Mark 7 models) were sold in Australia. Many survive.

BOND • England 1922-1928

Powered by a six-cylinder American Continental engine, the Bond also appeared as a sports car in 1925 with a 1496cc four-cylinder Meadows engine.

BOND • England 1949-1976

Now part of Reliant, the Bond started life as a basic three-wheeler with a 122cc (later 197cc) Villiers two-stroke driving the front wheel by chain (and only with a kick-starter until 1952). The Minicar lasted into the mid-1960s, by which time Bond also offered the Triumph-Herald-based Equipe, with glassfiber bodywork. The Bond Bug was a sporty three-wheeler of idiosyncratic design.

BONDIS • France 1910-1911

Showed a range of cars with 8, 12, 16 and 20 hp engines at the 1910 Paris Salon.

BONNEVILLE • France 1898

A "train-cycle" consisting of a quadricycle with trailer attachment.

BONSTETTIN • France 1897

The weird transmission of this voiturette consisted of a pyramidal flywheel with surface teeth engaged by a movable crown wheel linked to a complex belt and edge-bevel final-drive

BORBEIN • USA 1903-1909

A component manufacturer of St Louis which sold cars complete, except for engine and tires. The 1909 four-passenger roadster cost $598.

Bolwell Nagari sports

Borgward Isabella coupé

BORDEREL-CAIL • France 1905-c. 1908

Ironmaster Borderel was, it seems, the keeper of Meg Steinheil, the grande cocotte who caused the embarrassing death of French President Félix Faure in 1899; La Société Cail was one of France's oldest locomotive builders. F Gros was the designer of this curious four-cylinder six-wheeler, on which the center axle drove and the front and back axles steered.

BORGWARD • Germany 1939-1961

Carl F Borgward was 73 when he died in 1963, and his large car works had closed down two years earlier. Forerunners of his Borgward cars were the Hansa, Hansa-Lloyd, and some other makes, which he either founded or bought when the former manufacturer of car radiators was on the way up. The first model bearing the Borgward name had an ohv four-cylinder 1498cc engine; the next cars were of 1758cc and there was also a diesel-engined model. The popular Borgward "Isabella" was built from 1954 in various models with ohv 1493cc four-cylinder engines. Borgward also competed in sports car events with 1493cc ohc cars. The small-car ranges were built under the Lloyd and Goliath trade marks and, when the Bremen works finally disappeared, these makes also became victims of the collapse.

BORLAND • USA 1913-1914

A six-speed, shaft-drive electric built by Borland-Grannis of Chicago.

BORO GT • England 1971

A very professional one-off on the lines of the Unipower. Designed and built by Eric Lacey, the alloy-bodied, two-seater Boro featured its own tubular chassis and was powered by a rear-mounted Mini engine.

BOSS • USA 1903-1907

Boss Knitting Machines, of Reading, Pa., built this 8 hp twin-cylinder steam car designed by one James L Eck.

BOTYS • France 1907

A single-cylinder voiturette of 942cc. One competed in the 1907 Coupe des Voiturettes.

BOUDREUX • France 1907-1908

This Parisian voiturette maker offered the "simplified" Boudreux-Verdet engines in "monoduplex, biduplex, tetraduplex and quadruplex" forms.

BOULET • France 1903

A "suspended quadri-voiturette" with 4 hp, 6 hp, and 9 hp rear-mounted Aster engines; one was entered for the Paris-Madrid race.

BOULT • France 1898

A three-wheeler voiturette on similar lines to the Bollée.

BOUND • England 1920

The friction-drive Bound monocar, built in Southampton, used a 31.2 hp Precision engine.

BOUQUET, GARCIN & SCHIVRE • France 1899-1906

The 1899 BGS electric was "an elegant and stately design for a private pleasure carriage," which could cover 60 miles on one charge of its 70lb battery pack, at speeds up to 15 mph.

BOURASSA • Canada 1899-1932

Henri-Emile Bourassa of Montreal built one-off cars to special order. He tried for six years to raise finance for his 1926 Bourassa Six design, then broke up the prototype in despair.

BOUR DAVIS • USA 1915-1922

The Bour Davis was a conventionally assembled car featuring a Continental six-cylinder engine and other well-known components, initially produced at Detroit. The company failed in 1917 but, within two years, operations were re-established in Shreveport, Louisiana, where cars were built with prices starting at $1,650. In 1922 the name was changed to Ponder and one final car, essentially a Bour Davis, was produced with a Ponder emblem on its radiator.

BOURGUIGNONNE • France 1899-early 1900s

Chesnay de Falletane & Cie, of Dijon, invented a curious "sprinkling" cooling system for the 3 hp single-cylinder power unit of its voiturette. Nominally air-cooled, the cylinder barrel was sprayed with water from a tank pressurized by the heat of the exhaust, which was also used to vaporize the fuel.

BOUVIER-DREUX • France 1897

A lightweight voiturette powered by an opposed-twin air-cooled engine, the Bouvier-Dreux sold for Fr 3000 in two-seater form.

BOVY • Belgium c. 1908-c. 1914

A Brussels truck builder offering a limited number of cars, mostly twin-cylinder landaulettes.

BOWEN • England 1906-c. 1908

A 1305cc two-cylinder car built in London by Bowen & Co of the Phoenix Brass Foundry, Mount Pleasant.

BOWMAN • USA 1921-1922

Bowman of Covington, Kentucky, produced a handful of roadsters and touring cars in its short lifespan. Powered by a four-cylinder engine of its own manufacture, the 108-inch wheelbase Bowman sold in a price range of around $1000.

BOW-V-CAR • England 1922-1923

The integral chassis/body Bow-V-Car was a brief essay on the cyclecar theme using a 10 hp vee-twin Precision engine.

1907 Brasier 30/40hp limousine

BOYER • France 1901-1907

A light car that made its name by being driven without a breakdown from Paris to Barcelona; no mean feat in that era. The Boyer had a tubular chassis and final drive by side chains, and was available with De Dion, Aster, Buchet, or Meteor power units of 71, 2, 12 hp. It was built at Neuilly-sur-Seine. In 1905 a 16cv Boyer won a gold medal for easy starting, springing into life (on the handle) in 0.8 second. The firm"s last offering was a six-cylinder, shown at the 1906 Paris Salon.

BOZIER • France 1901-1920

Bozier began as makers of motor tricycles and a gear-change system which were used, among others, by Dennis. From 1905 the firm built tricars under Austral license, as well as a 41.2 hp De Dion-engined voiturette. Single, twins, and fours of up to 24 hp were listed up to 1914, when production almost certainly ceased.

BPD • England 1913

An 8 hp cyclecar from Shoreham, Sussex.

BRADBURY • England 1905

Better known as motorcycle manufacturers, Bradbury of Manchester also built a range of "Peerless" forecars with 41.2 hp watercooled engines.

BRADLEY • USA 1920-1921

An undistinguished assembled car, the Bradley featured both four- and six-cylinder Lycoming-engined touring cars.

BRAMWELL-ROBINSON • USA 1899-1901

A "very natty little three-wheeled sociable" built by a firm of paper box machinery manufacturers from Hyde Park, Mass. Bramwell built cars under his own name to 1904.

BRASIER • France 1905-1930

After Georges Richard left to found Unic, Richard-Brasier became simply "Brasier," offering reliable cars such as the 10 hp twin of 1526cc and the 1847cc four. The 1551cc 11 hp, introduced in 1909, lasted until 1915. A new range was launched in 1911, with a pair-cast six-cylinder of 4766cc and a four-cylinder derivative of 3177cc, plus other models including a 24 hp four of 3562cc. In 1914 the flat radiator gave way to a round one, and four new cars were introduced; of 9 hp, 12 hp, 16 hp, and 22 hp. After the First World War the Brasier factory resumed production in 1919 with a 3404cc 18 hp model which had an electric starter. This remained in production only until the end of 1920. The next year a new car appeared, the 2120cc 12 hp, current until 1926. A 9 hp of 1452cc was introduced in 1924. In 1926 the marque name was changed to Chaigneau-Brasier, presenting a fwd straight-eight of 3078cc. This, in the late 1920s, proved to be too far ahead of its time.

1914 Brasier 30 hp chassis

BRAUN • Austria 1899-1908

Designed by August Braun, the Austrian Braun cars had no connection with the German car of the same name. August Braun built cars with one, two, and four cylinders, of 5 hp, 9 hp, 15 hp, and 20 hp. They were of good quality. By 1902, magneto ignition was standard.

BRAUN • Germany 1910-1913

A fire-fighting equipment factory, Justus Christian Braun of Nuremberg was connected with Premier of Coventry and built not only Premier motorcycles but also four-cylinder Kaiser cars in limited quantities, with, among others, Fafnir engines from 18 hp to 70 hp.

BRAVO • Germany 1921-1922

Built a small 10 hp two-cylinder car, but was soon taken over for the production of the Mannheim-built Rabag-Bugatti (license-built Bugatti Type 22 and 23).

BRECHT • USA 1901-1903

Built three styles of steam car, and three of electric.

BREESE-PARIS • USA • France 1921-1925

Built to special order only, the Breese-Paris was a sports roadster designed by the American Robert Breese, whose brother had built the BLM. An ohc 1390cc four was used on some cars; others had side-valve Ballot fours.

BREEZE • USA 1909-1910

A range of 14 hp high-wheelers priced from $425 to $850, built in Cincinnati.

BREGUET • France 1942-1944

During the German Occupation the Ateliers d"Aviation Louis Bréguet built some electric cars in its Toulouse works.

BREMS • Denmark 1900-1907

The first of the Brems cars from Viborg was clearly inspired by the German Wartburg car (two members of the family had been working at the Wartburg works in Eisenach!). Six single-cylinder cars were built and sold and, finally, another twin-cylinder 9 hp car with a three-speed gearbox was built.

Brennabor Juwel 3147cc eight-cylinder, 1930

BRENNABOR • Germany 1908-1934

Brennabor built prams, bicycles, motorcycles, three-wheelers, and cars, and was for some time the biggest car manufacturer in Germany. The firm initially used Fafnir two- and four-cylinder engines, afterwards units of its own make. It produced in pre-First World War days cars from 904cc to 3800cc which, in England and other export markets, were known as "Brenna." Most models were designed by Carl Reichstein, one of the founders of Brennabor at Brandenburg-Havel. They were of good quality and advanced design. In the early 1920s daily production was around 120 cars, many of them the 1569cc with ohv and ioe engines of 20 hp and 25 hp. In 1927 a new sv 2090cc four-cylinder and a sv 3080cc six-cylinder appeared. Another six-cylinder, the Juwel, had a 2460cc engine. Added to this model in 1930 was the 3417cc eight-cylinder Juwel and also a fwd version of the Juwel 6. The last Brennabor range consisted of the rear-wheel-driven 995cc Model D and two (1950cc and 2500cc) six-cylinder models. The factory also built low and fast racing cars in the 1920s which were driven by Reichstein, Mitzlaff, Bakasch, Neidlich, and other works drivers. Brennabor also competed successfully in major trials, such as the Alpine trial and the Europa-Fahrt 10,000 km. The racing cars had dohc 1499cc four-cylinder engines.

1931 Brennabor 1-liter sedan

BREW-HATCHER • USA 1904-1905

A five-passenger 16 hp tourer from Cleveland.

BREWSTER • USA 1915-1925, 1934-1936

The original Brewster automobile was manufactured by the carriage firm of Brewster & Co at Long Island City, NY. The Brewsters were powered by a four-cylinder Knight engine and distinguished by an oval radiator, an option of either left- or right-hand steering, and a complete line of exquisite open and closed coachwork. Brewster cars were quite popular in New York City and its environs, selling at prices in the $10,000 range. Very little change marked the outward appearance of these Brewsters from the first car built to the last models before the company suspended production. Roughly 300 cars were built between 1915 and 1925.

In 1934 the late John S Inskip, who had been president of Rolls-Royce of America Inc, set up the Springfield Manufacturing Company in the former Rolls-Royce works and began production of a second Brewster automobile, American Rolls-Royce having bought out Brewster & Company in 1926. The new line of cars was essentially examples of Brewster bodies mounted on lengthened Ford V-8 chassis although, in a few cases, Buick, Oldsmobile, and even one Rolls-Royce chassis were used. The chassis featured heart-shaped grilles, flared fenders, and split bumpers, and most of them were town-cars listed at $3,500. A few convertible-sedans and convertible-coupés were also produced. Approximately 300 of these Brewsters were completed and sold before production was phased out and Springfield Manufacturing closed its doors. Inskip became US distributor for Rolls-Royce.

1936 Brewster station wagon

1936 Brewster Town Car

BRICKLIN • USA 1974-1976

Malcolm Bricklin hoped to break into the Corvette market with his SV-1 sports car, but never remotely approached his planned output of 12,000 units a year. The Bricklin bristled with unusual features including a color-impregnated acrylic outer skin bonded to a glassfiber body, gull-wing doors and 19 km/h (12 mph) crash-resistant bumpers. The steel perimeter frame encircled the passenger compartment at bumper height, and AMC suspension, brakes and 5899cc V-8 were used (though a change was made to a 5161cc Ford unit in 1975).

BRIERRE • France 1900-1905

Brierre of Paris started with a 31.2 cv voiturette, then built Cottereau cars under license.

BRILLIE • France 1904-1908

Eugéne Brillié left Gobron-Brillié in 1903 to produce a range of four-cylinder cars with conventional ioe engines and shaft drive, built by the Schneider armaments company. His Brillié-Schneider buses and trucks enjoyed greater success.

1977 Bristol 412

BRISCOE • USA 1914-1921

The car with the "half-million-dollar motor" was originally designed in France by Benjamin Briscoe, who built the Ajax cyclecar at Neuilly (Seine) in 1913-1919. Early examples of this 2514cc four-cylinder car had a "cyclops" headlamp incorporated in the radiator header tank; later models had conventional lighting. A few V-8s were built in 1916. from 1921 to 1923 the four-cylinder Briscoe was produced under the name "Earl." Total Briscoe and Earl production was in the region of 75,000.

BRISTOL • England 1902-1907

Motor agent Arthur Johnson built his first car, a 10 hp twin, in 1902. At first, cars were built solely for lease but, from 1902, cars were sold on a limited basis; about six 10 hp and 18 of the four-cylinder 16/20 model of 1905-1907.

BRISTOL • England 1945 to date

The car division of the Bristol Aeroplane Company was formed in 1945, with the intention of building high-performance cars of quality, a maxim as applicable today as it was then. The aeronautical ancestry of the early 400 Series was very evident in the unusual styling, but the marque soon found success. Bristol"s 2-liter engine powered many racing as well as road cars with success in the 1950s, not least the Formula 2 Cooper-Bristols. Nowadays, though production still continues at Filton, Bristol Cars Ltd, as the company is now known, has no direct links with the aircraft industry and is owned and run by former racing driver and business wizard Anthony Crook. Fast and very luxurious, today's Bristols use American V-8s. Despite this, Bristols, with their hand-built, artisan-built bodies, separate chassis, exquisite interiors and old-world charm, have become perhaps the last quintessentially British icon of a great history of car making. The Blenheim 2 model achieved celebrity status in the 1990s and found a higher profile for this quiet, yet tenacious little company, which will surely always find buyers for its hand-built offerings.

1914 Briscoe 2514cc tourer with cyclops headlamp

BRIT • England 1914

The two Brit cyclecars (8 hp and 9.5 hp) built by the Britannia Engineering Company of Nottingham.

BRITANNIA • England 1896-1899

Electrics designed by Vaughan-Sherrin, whose first car dated from 1897.

BRITANNIA • England 1899, 1906-1908

Britannia Lathes of Colchester first catalogued the "Facile" heavy oil cars in 1899. In 1906 it announced fours of 12/18 hp and 24/40 hp and a 30/45 hp six, all with round copper radiators.

BRITISH • England 1905-1907

The 61.2 hp twin-cylinder and 10/12 hp four-cylinder cars from this maker had "tilting steering wheel, dashboard starting, patent change speed gear."

BRITISH DUPLEX • England 1906-c. 1909

Built in Clerkenwell, the British Duplex had a curious two-stroke "air scavenging" engine ("no crankcase as pump, no outside moving parts.")

BUGATTI • Germany • France 1909-1956 Italy 1991 to 1994

After nearly ten years of working for firms such as De Dietrich, Mathis, and Deutz, Ettore Bugatti established himself in his own premises at Molsheim, near Strasbourg. He started with the ohc four-cylinder Type 13 of 1327cc. One of his early successes was the "Bébé," made by Peugeot to Bugatti's design. Pre-war he also built fours of 1368cc and 5027cc, first with 8, later with 16, valves. In 1913 there was a 2906cc straight-eight. In 1922 came the first production eight-cylinder 1990cc Type 30. It was in 1924 that Ettore presented the archetypal Bugatti, the eight-cylinder Type 35 of 1990cc, subsequently developed into versions such as the 35A (1990cc) and the 35B (2261cc) or the 39A (1492cc). All were supercharged. To meet popular demand Bugatti also evolved sports models with a 1496cc four-cylinder engine. The four-cylinder Type 40 and eight-cylinder Type 43 were also good sports cars. On the touring car front, Bugatti made the excellent Type 44 (3 liters) and the Type 46 (5.3 liters). He also made the fabulous Royales, whose engines (eight-cylinder 12,762cc) were later used in railcars. In 1931 Bugatti's first dohc engine appeared on the Type 51 racing car, with eight cylinders displacing 2261cc. The last of the great line of racing cars from Molsheim was the Type 59, made in 2.8-liter, 2.9-liter and 3.3-liter forms. The Type 55 was a fantastic 2.3-liter dohc sports car.

From 1934 up to the war Bugatti made the Type 57 of 3257cc, also available in supercharged form as the 57S and 57SC. It was the last of the production cars made by "le Patron," who died in 1947, although some Type 101 models were built post-war. Bugatti Automobili SpA under the control of Romano Artioli acquired the rights to the marque in 1986 and produced the first examples of its high-tech 4x4 V12 3.5-liter supercar in its showcase factory near Modena in 1992. With a top speed of 215 mph, the reborn Bugatti was christened the EB110 as it was launched on the 110th anniversary of Ettore Bugatti's birth. The EB110 boasted remarkable styling, a superb interior and amazing performance. The company also bought a share of Lotus at this time. Sadly, despite the new car's brilliance, financial implications came to the fore yet again and the company was absorbed by Volkswagen (Lotus remained separate), which kept its new brand name acquistion on the shelf until it presented a show car proposal for a new Bugatti sedan in 1999.

1927 Bugatti Type 41, "La Royale"

c. 1925 Bugatti Type 35A "Tecla" in touring trim

1991 Bugatti EB 110

1928 Bugatti Type 43 straight-eight

Type 46 Bugatti, bodied by Neuss of Berlin for Prince Gustav Adolf

made for company officials. A handsome sports sedan was announced for 1921 but failed to materialize.

BSA • England 1907-1926, 1933-1936

The early BSAs were, in effect, scaled-down Daimlers; this applying in particular to the sleeve-valve cars from 1911 onwards – a reminder of the company's takeover of Daimler in that year. However, an earlier 1908 model had been a copy of the Italian 40 hp Itala, so originality was never the watchword! A change came after the First World War with the vee-twin-powered Ten, although this lasted only until 1924, while sleeve-valve-engined cars continued until 1926. BSA re-emerged in 1933 with a car similar to the Lanchester Ten, the group having taken over the old-established concern in 1931.

BSA • England 1929-1940

BSA Cycles Ltd (the motorcycle division of BSA) produced a fwd three-wheeler powered by a 1000cc vee-twin air-cooled engine in 1929. A fourth wheel was added in 1932 and, the following year, an 1100cc four-cylinder was fitted. This remained in production until 1940 (with a break in production in 1934), being renamed the Scout for the 1935 season.

BUC, BUCCIALI • France 1922-1933

The Bucciali brothers started making a small cyclecar under the name of Buc at Courbevoie. It was powered by a twin-cylinder two-stroke engine of 1340cc and was followed in 1925 by a 1600cc SCAP-engined car available in two versions; "Tourisme" and "Quatre Speciale" supercharged. The company also built a 1500cc six-cylinder car. In 1928 Buccialis made cars caused a great sensation; the TAN six-cylinder and an eight-cylinder fwd with Sensaud de Lavaud automatic gearbox. This attempt was followed in the 1930s by the Double Huit, also fwd, powered by two straight-eight Continental engines mounted side-by-side. The last of these prototypes was made with a Voisin 12-cylinder engine. Very few of these fwd Bucciali cars ever reached the road.

BUCHET • France 1910-1930

The Buchet marque established its fame before the war, making proprietary engines for automobile, aircraft and motorcycle manufacturers. Their first car, the 12-20 hp, was presented in 1910 with a four-cylinder 1996cc engine. After the war it made 1131cc and 1551cc cars which remained in production, largely unchanged, until Buchet closed down. At the very end a six-cylinder of 1737cc was introduced.

1955 Buckle coupé

1914 La Buire 15 hp in the Melbourne-Sydney trial

BUCKBOARD • USA 1956

The McDonough Power Equipment Co of Georgia offered a lightweight, 3 hp air-cooled machine with a top speed of 15 mph.

BUCKBOARD • USA 1960

A 43 hp Ariel motorcycle engine powered an oak-framed, mahogany-panel-bodied, two-passenger car built by the Automotive Assoc Co of White Plains, NY. Four-wheel independent suspension and steering gear came from Renault, and the headlights turned with the front wheels.

BUCKINGHAM • England 1914-1923

A bullnosed, belt-drive cyclecar built in Coventry and designed by Captain Buckingham, inventor of the tracer bullet. Inevitably, the coupé version was called the "Palace."

BUCKLE • Australia 1955-1959

Locally designed with a glassfiber four-seater coupé body, the Buckle GT tourer employed a Ford Zephyr six-cylinder engine. The advanced design included fold-down rear seats, an adjustable steering column plus an electrically-operated door locks. The car was raced with distinction. Twenty were built. Several still survive.

BUCKLER • England 1947-1962

One of the more prominent firms concerned with the manufacture of light, strong-bodied sports cars to which Ford mechanicals could be fitted. Its most successful car, the Buckler 90, had an all-enveloping body, weighed less than 9 cw) and was fitted with a De Dion rear axle for ultimate road-holding.

BUCKMOBILE • USA 1903-1905

A 15 hp twin-cylinder roadster from Utica, New York.

BUFFALO • USA 1901-1902

Light, tiller-steered runabouts which were powered by gasoline or electricity.

BUFFALO • USA 1912-1915

Formed by a merger of leading electric carriages (Babcock, Van Waggoner, and others), the Buffalo Electric Vehicle Company offered elegant vehicles styled on petrol car lines under the slogan "The Best of America."

BUFFUM • USA 1901-1906

Built in Abington, Maryland, the Buffum is chiefly remembered for a spectacular flat-eight which appeared in 1904. Herbert Buffum also designed a lighting dynamo in 1905, but his ingenuity was not matched by his business acumen, and the company folded in 1906.

BUGETTA • USA 1969 to date

Powered by a 4949cc Ford V-8, this mid-engined car from Costa Mesa, California, has a one-piece moulded glassfiber body with the choice of hard or soft top and two or four doors.

BUGATTI • Germany • France 1909-1956
Italy 1991 to date

See panel

BUICK • USA 1904 to date

See panel overleaf

LA BUIRE • France 1902-1930

La Société de l"Horme et de La Buire was founded at Lyon in 1847, specializing in railroad and tramway rolling stock, and was an early builder of steam carriages and traction engines. Its early success as a car builder was achieved

with the Type Fraignac – a Mercedes-like 20 hp with pair-cast cylinders, introduced at the 1904 Paris Salon at the behest of their most energetic agent, the engineer Fraignac. There was a 30 hp version with direct drive in third and fourth gears. The new 20-30 hp was one of the sensations of the 1905 Paris Salon. By 1907 there was also a 15 hp six in the range, with a 9500cc engine, and selling in Britain as a chassis. Smaller sixes of 16 hp (3619cc), 24 hp (4786cc,) and 30 hp (6374cc) joined it in a complex range for 1909, which also included five four-cylinder models from 12 hp to 28-35 hp. The large La Buires were actively campaigned in British sprint and hill-climb events by wealthy Stockport businessman J A Higginson, but the marque was not otherwise involved in racing. The immediately pre-First World War range went from an 8-10 hp four of 1726cc to a 24 hp six of 4767cc, all with notably long-stroke engines (the 4071cc 20 hp four had bore and stroke of 90 mm x 160 mm) but, when the marque reappeared post-war, its vital force was spent. Undistinguished fours of up to 2650cc constituted the remainder of La Buire's story, the only advanced feature being the addition of four-wheel brakes from 1922.

BUKH & GRY • Denmark 1904

Both Bukh & Gry had been working in car factories in the USA. Their one and only car, built at Horve, was exhibited at Tivoli in Copenhagen in 1905. It had a water-cooled 10-12 hp two-cylinder engine and friction drive. No more cars were built.

BULLOCK • England 1972

A rather ugly, open-top fun car designed by Andrew Ainsworth, the Bullock featured a glassfiber body mounted on a pre-drilled box-section chassis. Power came from a Ford Anglia unit.

BURLAT • France 1904-1909

Burlat Fréres of Lyon built cars with rotary X-formation four-cylinder engines, though its swansong was a rotary eight, incorporating two of these unorthodox power units in which, instead of ignition leads, there were curved contact strips against which the tops of the sparking plugs rubbed as they came round. Despite this, one Burlat was said to have covered 24,800 miles.

BURNEY • England 1930-1933

Sir C Dennistoun Burney, designer of the R100 airship, created this all-independently sprung, rear-engined streamline car, of which only a dozen (plus a prototype based on a back-to-front fwd Alvis chassis) were built, using Beverley-Barnes, Lycoming, or Armstrong Siddeley engines. The Prince of Wales bought one, and the design was taken up by Crossley. Unfortunately it overheated, and was not a commercial success.

BUICK • USA 1904 to date

Scots plumber and David Dunbar Buick built his first prototype in 1903 using his own ohv flat twin engine, and started production (backed by the Briscoe Brothers) in 1904. He soon ran out of finance, and Billy Durant took over. Buick was elbowed out in 1908, by which time the twin had been joined by three fours, of 2.7, 4.2, and 5.5 liters, all with ohv (Buick has never built a side-valve-engined car.) The firm, by now one of the "Big Four," was the cornerstone of Durant"s 1908 formation of General Motors, and was managed by Charles Nash from 1910-12 and Walter Chrysler from 1912-20. Walter Marr designed the first Buick Six in 1914, and from 1919-26 Buick sales were the largest, in dollar terms, in the US car industry. Four-wheel brakes came in 1924, along with a Packard-like radiator. From 1925-30 a wide range of sixes from 3.1 to 5.4 liters was offered. A sales slide was incurred by the 1929 "pregnant Buick," and not halted by the introduction in 1931 of 3.6-, 4.5, and 5.7-liter straight-eights. The 1934 range had ifs and new styling, but revival of Buick's fortunes had to wait until 1936, when the new general manager, Harlow H. Curtice, and stylist Harley Earl, collaborated to produce a new line, Special, Century, Roadmaster, and Limited, with more powerful engines, aluminum pistons, and hydraulic brakes. Another line, the Super, was added in 1940.

A Bedford-Buick in the 1913 Coupé de l"Auto

The 1942 Buick"s had radical styling with full-width front fenders flowing into the rear fenders; this line was continued after the war, along with the toothy grille. In 1948 Buick became the first American manufacturer to offer a torque-converter drive, the famous "Dynaflow," on the Roadmaster. In 1949 came the first hardtop coupe, the Riviera. Buick remained faithful to straight-eights until 1953, when a short-stroke was announced. This powered the limited edition Skylark which celebrated Buick's golden jubilee, in which year the company built its 7-millionth car. The Century appeared in 1954, capable of 110mph with the V-8 unit; that season over 200 single and dual-tone colour schemes were

BURNS • USA 1908-1910

The $800 Burns Hi-Wheel Buggy came from Havre de Grace in Maryland. In 1908 Burns offered a "transformable coupé on the company"s 18-20 hp high-wheeler chassis.

BURROW, STRUTT • England • Germany 1900

A three-wheeled, three-seater motor carriage whose maker claimed factories in London and Berlin. It had "seat adjustable either to back or front at pleasure."

BURROWES • USA 1905-1908

This Portland, Maine, manufacturer built a few cars, latterly a 30 hp four.

BURY • USA 1927

Billed as the first "Bug" car, the Bury was an early attempt to market a miniature car of the Austin type in America. Designed by Charles W Bury of New York City, the car sported a 73-inch wheelbase and in its two-passenger form was the smallest car in the USA at the time. Power was by a 1368cc four-cylinder Model "H-2" engine.

1947 Buick Special sedan (below,)1930 Buick Standard Eight Empire Sedan (right,) 1964 Buick Wildcat (left)

available. Buick took third place in sales from the Plymouth in 1955-57, but drastic restyling in 1958, with lashings of chrome (including a 160-piece grille) failed to stop sales from falling below the 250,000 mark. The 1959 models featured compound curve windscreens and canted fins fore and aft, with names including LeSabre, Invicta, Electra, and Electra 225, all except the LeSabre having a new 6571cc engine. Styling was subdued for 1960, but Buick nevertheless fell to ninth place in sales. The Special compact with an all-alloy 3359cc V-8 appeared in 1961 followed in 1962 by a cast-iron V-6 of 3245cc (which supplanted the V-8, sold to British Leyland, in 1964.) The Riviera Sport Coupe of 1964, with V-8 power (6571cc or 6965cc), was joined in 1966 by the 6965cc Skylark Gran Sport (succeeded in 1967 by the 6555cc GS400.) The Riviera was restyled for the third time in 1971, with raked-forward front and boat-tail rear. Convertibles were a dying breed (two were built in 1972, one in 1973 and 1974,) and were replaced by electric sunroofs. New bodies and an old name, Century (replacing Skylark), appeared on the 1973 intermediates, with 5735cc or 7456cc V-8s. The Riviera was restyled in 1974, and the Apollo compact, with a 4097cc straight-six, launched. The V-6, dropped in 1967, was reannounced in 1975 in the subcompact Skyhawk, together with a new Skylark, Century and Apollo. A new Century, the Regal, became a series in its own right in

1977, with a turbocharged V-6, while the 1979 Riviera, with V-6 or V-8 power, shared the fwd all-independent suspension layout of the Olds Tornado and Cadillac Eldorado. May 1979 saw the launch of Buick's version of the GM X-car range.The 1980s saw Buick, like its American contemporary marques, enter a period of sharing components from its parent group. Buick's of this period were smaller, and moved away from their traditional glitzy or luxury image. A downturn in the marque's profile ensued, and gladly, for the 1990s, Buick returned to its upmarket branding, at the same time switching to fwd for many of it s cars, and also eschewing the traditional V-8 powerplants. A stylish range of coupes badged "Riviera" with V-6 engines, re-established Buick's credentials alongside a range of classy sedans named Regal, le Sabre, and the flagship Park Avenue model.

BUSH • USA 1916-1924

Like the Birch (also built in Chicago,) the Bush was a car sold by mail order only. Built by various manufacturers, including Piedmont, a complete line of open and closed models wore the Bush emblem. Standard components were used throughout, four-cylinder cars using Lycoming engines and the sixes, Continentals.

BUSHBURY ELECTRIC • England 1897

Electric three- and four-wheeled cars built in the Star Cycle Factory at Wolverhampton. Some were controlled by reins.

BUSSON • France 1907-1908

The smallest six-cylinder car at the 1907 Paris Salon, the Busson-Bazelaire (built by de Bazelaire) had a 15-20 hp engine of 3318cc. The firm also sold six-cylinder Nagants as "Busson-Dedeyns," and built a few voiturettes under its own name.

BUTTEROSI • France 1919-1924

The Butterosi, made in Boulogne-sur-Seine, had a sv four-cylinder engine of 1327cc.

BZ • Germany 1922-1925

One of the many small cars built after the First World War, the BZ had a 493cc flat-twin BMW motorcycle engine. It was a light 60 cwt car with a two-seater body of duralumin.

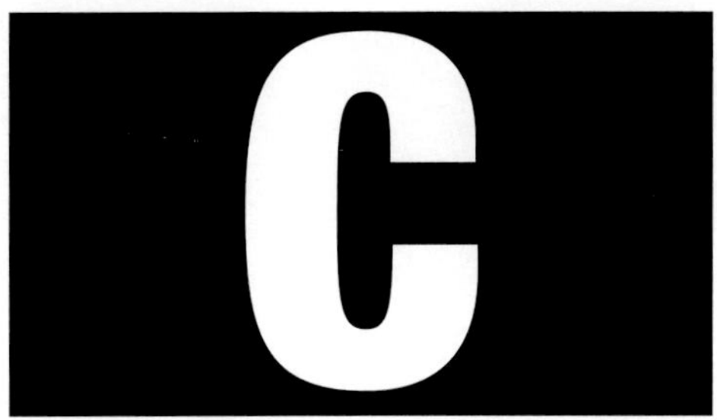

LE CABRI • France 1924-1925

A small cyclecar from Asniéres with a sv 980cc Ruby engine. Few were made.

CADILLAC • USA 1902 to date

See panel

CADIX • France 1920-1923

Made at Cadix-Martinville, this car was Ballot-engined. Two engines were available, a 10 hp of 1593cc and a 12 hp of 2297cc. M Jannel, the builder, was previously involved in manufacturing the Métropolitaine car in Paris.

1907 16/20 hp Cadogan Landaulet

CADOGAN • England 1902-1907

The first Cadogan cars had a 12 hp vertical-twin water-cooled engine and "perfect construction of steering." In 1907 Cadogan offered a twin-cylinder 14-16 hp and fours of 16-20 hp and 28-32 hp under the name "Leander."

CAFFORT • France 1920-1922

The Caffort brothers of Marseilles started as marine-engine builders. They moved to Paris in 1921 to build a cyclecar using their own 1206cc four-stroke vee-twin engine. These were sold mainly as delivery vans.

CALCOTT • England 1914-1926

The Calcott, with a shouldered radiator like the contemporary Standard, was the product of a famous Coventry cycle company. Pre-war cars had engines of 1460cc; post-war models had 1645cc power units. In 1926 Singer took over.

CALDWELL VALE • Australia 1907-1913

Very few technical details have survived, except that this touring car had fwd plus a 30 hp six-cylinder engine. One

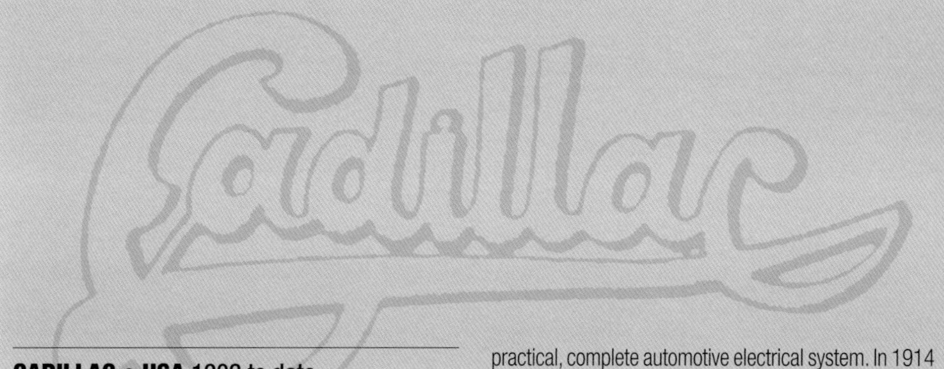

CADILLAC • USA 1902 to date

Originally the Henry Ford Company, this firm adopted the name of Antoine de la Mothe Cadillac, founder of Detroit in 1701, after Ford was replaced as chief engineer by Henry Leland, "master of precision." Leland practised rigorous interchangeability of parts, and his single-cylinder Cadillac (16,126 were sold between 1903 and 1908) won the 1908 Dewar Trophy in a spectacular demonstration of this, when three new Cadillacs were disassembled, their parts scrambled, and three cars built up from the pile of parts without any hand fitting. Durant took Cadillac into the new General Motors concern in 1909, by which time the firm was only building four-cylinder cars. In 1912 the "self-lighting, self-starting, self-igniting" Cadillac with Delco electrics appeared, and won a second Dewar Trophy for this first practical, complete automotive electrical system. In 1914 Cadillac standardized on the 5150cc V-8 engine. During the First World War Henry Leland and his son Wilfred left to found the Lincoln Motor Company, initially to build Liberty aero engines and later to make fine cars. Cadillacs of the 1920s were, like so many of their contemporaries, well engineered but dull in appearance. A dynamically-balanced crank came in 1924, a year after four-wheel brakes. In 1928 a new 5.6-liter engine (based on the 1927 LaSalle unit) appeared, along with chromium plating and synchromesh gear change. Chief engineer Ernest Seaholm's masterpiece, the world's first production V-16, was unveiled in January 1930. Fleetwood coachwork was standard, and 3,863 of this ohv 7.4-liter were built, until it was replaced by a sv V-16 in 1938 (just 511 of these were built up to 1940.) A V-12, using the V-8 chassis, was also listed until 1937; these

1947 Cadillac Sedan

1954 Cadillac Fleetwood

rear view of 1959 Cadillac El Dorado (above.) 1992 Cadillac Eldorado TC (left)

were Cadillac's only deviation from the V-8 path. Stylist Harley Earl introduced a bold "egg-crate" grille in 1941 and, in 1948, came his legendary tailfins, inspired by the Lockheed P-38 Lightning fighter plane's twin-boom empennage. A new short-stroke V-8 of 5.4 litres appeared in 1949 and, in 1950, Hydramatic four-speed automatic transmission, hitherto optional, was standardized on the 1950 Series 60 Special and 62, and on all cars except the 75 from 1952. In 1953 air conditioning was offered, and a limited-edition convertible, the Eldorado, made its debut. Its successor, the 1957 Eldorado Brougham, was a $13,074 handbuilt model with quad headlamps and self-levelling air suspension. Just 904 were made (1957-1960.) Tailfins reached their apotheosis on the supremely vulgar 1959 Cadillacs then gradually atrophied until, by 1965, they had almost disappeared. Comfort Control single-unit heating/air-conditioning appeared on 1964 models, all powered by the 1963-introduced 7030cc V-8. In 1967 came the razor-edged, front-wheel-drive Eldorado (President Nixon gave Soviet leader Brezhnev a 1972 version as a gift), which by 1970 had the world's then-biggest production car engine of 8.2 liters. This unit was standard on all but one of the 1975 series.

Following the energy crisis, Cadillac introduced the Chevy Nova-based Seville, with 5.7-liter Olds power, to combat European luxury cars. Full-size Cadillacs had their engine displacement trimmed to 7 liters in 1978 (when Sevilles were specified with an on-board computer showing distance elapsed, fuel-to-empty and other information.) The Eldorado emerged as a totally new car in 1979; shorter and with improved handling, using a common power unit with the Seville Since the 1970s, Cadillacs have been downsized and rationalization has meant that smaller and cheaper Cadillacs have been little more than upmarket Buicks.

In 1988 Cadillac brought out a Pininfarina-bodied "ultra-luxury roadster," called the Allante. In the 1990s the marque began to reassert its separate identity, and the 1992 Seville and Eldorado had completely new bodywork and 4.9-liter V-8 engines. By 1992 the only Cadillac type to retain the rear-wheel drive was the 5.5 m-(18ft 4in-)long 5.0-liter V-8 Brougham. These truly large Cadillacs finally finished production as the last examples of the magnificent art of the American dinosaur car, yet their market segment remained and the Eldorado-de Ville models of the 1990s still served that niche of true Americana.

The introduction of the 300 bhp "Northstar" engine changed Cadillac's fortunes and, by adding it and state-of-the-art technology including adaptive damping suspension, the new Cadillacs stood firm against the rise of competitors such as the Lexus brand, which had made huge inroads into the American market. Through smaller models such as the Cimarron, and then through its replacement, the GM brand, Omega model based Catera, Cadillac has expanded its appeal and can offer the American market a homegrown competitor to the likes of the BMW 3 series and various Saabs, Volvos, and small Mercedes that vie for the same buyers. Right-hand-drive cars are also now made, and the Seville STS has become the most powerful front-drive car in the world and is available in the UK.

1907 Certain Tri-Voiturette

Tourist was a tiller-steered gas buggy on the lines of the Oldsmobile.

CENTURY • England 1899-1906

Although the first Century, like its cousin, the Eagle, was a tricar powered by a 21-4 hp single-cylinder engine, later models were conventional four-wheelers. From 1903, 8 and 12 hp two-cylinder and 22 hp four-cylinder Aster engines were fitted. Century fitted the gear quadrant of its 1902, 9 hp Aster-engined model with an indicator lamp so that the driver could easily change gear after dark.

CERTAIN • France 1907

A belt-driven two-seater "tri-voiturette" with a single-cylinder Lurquin-Coudert engine.

CERTUS • Germany 1928-1929

The Certus was made in very small numbers at Offenburg, mainly from French components. SCAP supplied the sv 1170cc and 1476cc engines.

CEYC • Spain 1923-1931

The 4-10 cv CEYC was built by the Electronic and Communications Center of the Spanish Army, using a 396cc two-cylinder duplex two-stroke engine devised by Captain of Engineers J Hernandez Nunez. Two- and three-seat tourers and coupés were built, all for Army use.

CFB • England 1920-1921

Final drive by rubber belts was a novel feature of the CFB, which was powered by an 8 hp vee-twin engine.

CG • France 1967-1973

The CGs were made at Brie Comte Robert by Chappe, Gesslin and Durand, using mostly Simca parts. The bodies were made of glassfiber. They were only sold as sports-racing cars. The marque was succeeded by the Jidé.

1904 CGV 15 hp of French Premier Rouvier

CGV, CHARRON • France 1901-1930

In 1901 three ex-racing cyclists – Charron, Girardot, and Voigt – began production of a four-cylinder 3300cc chain-driven car in Puteaux, followed by various models including one of the very first straight-eights in the world, built in 1903. At that time they sold their USA rights to Smith and Mabley. Most CGVs were chain driven, and it was only in 1906 that the first shaft-drive model appeared. Girardot then left the factory and the name was turned into Charron Ltd after a British concern had taken over. For many years the Charron remained an old-fashioned car, with the radiator behind the engine. Notable among the various models manufactured between 1907 and the war were the 12 hp (2412cc) and 29 hp (5710cc) four-cylinders, the only six-cylinder (3619cc) and the tiny 7-10 hp (1592cc) introduced in 1912. At the outbreak of war Charron presented a new car, a 6 hp of 1056cc named "la Charronette." After the war Charron resumed production with civilian models, having been one of the few French manufacturers continuing to make cars for the Army during hostilities. From a total of seven models in 1919, of which "la Charonnette" was the most significant, production fell steadily over the years to three models. Then, in 1925, a new 12-14 hp six (2770cc) appeared. The Charronette remained in production until the end, latterly bodied as a small van which could be quickly converted into a family tourer.

CHABOCHE • France 1900-1906

M Chaboche's twin-cylinder flash-boilered steam cars came in two guises, a light two - four-seater with paraffin or gasoline-fired boiler and shaft-drive, or a heavy chain-driven six-eight-seater with coke or coal-fired boiler.

CHADWICK • USA 1905-1916

One of the great sporting marques, the Chadwick originated from Chester, Pennsylvania, although production shifted to Philadelphia in 1906 and Pittsburgh in 1907. Lee Sherman Chadwick's first production model was a pair-cast but, in 1907, came the first Great Six, with a copper-jacketed engine of "general simplicity of construction" and 11.581cc swept volume. The 1909 60 hp "Semi-racer Runabout" had exhaust cutouts in the hood-sides for "speeding." In 1911 the engine design was altered from T-head to F-head, with the overhead inlet valve in the center of the combustion chamber. Some 1908 racing Chadwicks had forced induction by centrifugal supercharger, but this did not appear in production.

CHADWICK • USA 1960

Weighing 680 lb and powered by a BMW 13 hp single-cylinder air-cooled motor, the 87-inch long Chadwick was designed as a shopping car. Chassis was tubular, with independent front suspension, and quarter-elliptic leaf springs at the rear.

CHAIGNEAU-BRASIER • France 1926-1930

This luxury car was an attempt by the manager of the Brasier works to make a car under his own name. The engine was a straight-eight of 3079cc, and fwd was featured.

CHAINLESS • France 1900-1903

Shaft-driven voiturettes with Abeille motors of 10, 16, and 20cv, built, apparently, by a M Chain.

CHALMERS-DETROIT, CHALMERS • USA 1908-1924

Hugh Chalmers, former vice-president of National Cash Register, took over Thomas-Detroit in June 1908, changing the name and introducing a new F-head 30 hp designed on European lines. A 20 hp appeared in 1909, but was taken over by the newly formed Hudson Motor Car Company. In 1911 the cars and the company became known as plain "Chalmers," and a 36 hp four was added to the existing models the following year. Chalmers's first six, a pair-cast 56 hp with compressed-air starting, made its debut in 1911 and became known as the Master Six. It was joined by the 30 hp Light Six in 1914. A new chief designer, C C Hinkley, brought out a new ohc 6-40 hp Model 32 six in 1915, which replaced the 4-36. A similar 6-30 model appeared in 1916, Chalmers' best year, with 21,000 cars produced. Output fell to 12,000 in 1917, and Maxwell, now headed by Walter Chrysler, took over, completely absorbing Chalmers by 1921. Hydraulic band brakes on all four wheels were added for 1924 but, in January that year, the Chalmers was supplanted by the new Chrysler four.

CHAMBERS • Ireland 1904-1925

One of the few cars to be built in Ulster, the Chambers was made in limited numbers in the Cuba Street Works, Belfast, starting with a 10 hp twin, also marketed as "Downshire." In 1913 the firm was offering 11-15 hp and 12-16 hp four-cylinder models with three-speed gearing. Only a 3181cc six was being built when production ended.

CHAMEROY • France 1907-1909

A manufacturer of cars, light cars and voiturettes with infinitely variable belt-drive, from Le Vèsinet (Seine-et-Oise.)

CHAMPION • England 1899

A four-seater dog-cart powered by a 1.3-4 hp De Dion engine was fired by a pedal.

CHAMPION • USA 1908-1909

A 10-12 hp tiller-steered high-wheeler "roadster" from East Chicago, Indiana.

CHAMPION • USA 1917-1923

The first Champions were built in Pottstown, Pennsylvania, and drove through gearing mounted in the rear wheel rims. Subsequently, operations moved to Philadelphia where four-cylinder cars, using both Herschell-Spillman and Lycoming four-cylinder engines, were built.

CHAMPION • USA 1920

Not to be confused with the Philadelphia-built car of the very same name, the Champion of Cleveland, Ohio, was exhibited at an industrial meeting in its home city in April 1920, but failed to survive the prototype stage.

1915 Chalmers Six tourer

CHAMPION • Germany 1948-1956

This Holbein-designed two-seater was built by various producers in Germany and even Norway. It had 246cc double-piston TWN two-stroke or 398cc Ilo and Heinkel twin-cylinder two-stroke engines mounted in the rear. Maico, still famous for motorcycles, took over production in 1956 and fitted 452cc Heinkel two-stroke engines.

CHANDLER • USA 1913-1929

"The Marvelous Motor" was built in Cleveland. For most of its production span a 29 hp, 4736cc bi-block six of Chandler's own make was used although, in 1927, the monobloc Standard Six of 2954cc was offered, joined by two straight-eights the following year. From 1923 a constant-mesh "Traffic Transmission" was used on the 29 hp six. Between 1919 and 1926 Chandler also built the ohv 3529cc Cleveland Six.

CHANNON • England 1905

Edward Channon & Sons of Dorchester, Dorset, built approximately six 10 hp cars using modified Brit stationary engines from nearby Bridport. The price was 225 guineas.

CHAPMAN • USA 1899-1902

A light "sulky electromobile" with two 1-2 hp motors, built by the BelKnap Motor Company of Portland, Maine.

CHARLES TOWN-ABOUT • USA 1958-1959

Based on the Karmann-Ghia coupé body, the Charles Town-About was powered by two electric motors driving the rear wheels. Using a 48 volt electrical system, each motor developed 3.2 hp, giving the car a 77-mile range. Top speed was a claimed 58 mph. Manufactured by the Stinson Aircraft Tool Corp of San Diego, Ca, the car was conceived by the company vice-president, Dr Charles H Graves, whose name it bore. Torsion-bar suspension was used.

1951 Champion two-seater

CHARLON • France 1905-1906

A belt-driven voiturette, "built under Mahout license."

CHARRON-LAYCOCK • England 1920-1926

The 1460cc four-cylinder Charron-Laycock was so called because Charron Ltd acquired a controlling interest in the railway equipment manufacturer W S Laycock of Sheffield. This 10-25 model was pricey; in 1925 the four-seater tourer cost £525, the sedan another £100.

CHARTER • USA 1903

James A. Charter's "Mixed-Vapor" car operated on a mixture of gasoline and water, the theory being that the ignition of the gasoline in the cylinder would flash the water vapor into superheated steam.

CHASE • England 1904-1905

A 7 hp twin-cylinder "four-wheel tandem car," the "exquisitely designed" Chase from Anerley, SE London, predated the cycle car craze by several years.

Chandler"s 1923 Cleveland Six 19.8 hp

CHATEL-JEANNIN • Germany 1902-1903

Despite the French name, these cars were made in Germany, as Mulhouse (Alsace) was then part of the German Empire. It was a very unorthodox design with 6.5 hp single-cylinder and 12 hp twin-cylinder engines.

CHATER-LEA • England 1907-1908, 1913-1922

A maker of cycles and components, Chater-Lea showed a four-wheeled "Carette" at the 1908 Stanley Show. It had a 6 hp vee-twin engine mounted on the right of its coach-built body, with clutch and two-speed gear on a transverse shaft which drove the left rear wheel by chain. An 8 hp light four was built from 1913.

CHATHAM • Canada 1906-1909

Starting with flat-twin Reeves-engined tourers, by 1907 Chatham was concentrating on a 25 hp four. In 1908 the company was acquired by a dentist named Cornell. Production ended soon after.

CHECKER • USA 1923 to date

Up to 1948 when a "pleasure car" was cataloged, Checker had catered solely for the taxi trade. Post-war models were much the same as pre-war designs, powered by a sv 3704cc Continental six, which was to remain Checker's main engine until 1965. The 1956 A8 was totally new, and its slab-sided modern appearance was uncompromisingly practical; ifs replaced the old beam axle. In 1958 an ohv six was offered on the new 12-passenger A9 "Airport Limousine" on a 189-inch wheelbase (there was also a smaller 9-seat version.) In 1960 Checker surprisingly produced its first model for general public sale, the Superba, available as sedan or station wagon but sharing body and mechanicals with the A8. The 1963 Town Custom Limousine was Checker's most prestigious model to date, with optional air-conditioning and center division. From 1965 the base powerplant was Chevrolet's 3769cc six, although various V-8s have been offered as options. A 1970 Ghia-designed prototype had not reached production in 1979, and the Checkers of that period still used the 1956 body, but the standard engine was now the 4097cc Chevrolet six, with a 5736cc V-8 available in the Marathon line.

CHELMSFORD (CLARKSON) England 1899-1903

Successor to the elaborate Clarkson steamers of 1899-1901, the Chelmsford steam cars were built by the Clarkson & Capel Steam Car Syndicate of Moulsham Works, Chelmsford, Essex, which also supplied double-deck steam buses to the National omnibus fleet in London. Chelmsford steam cars were large, heavily-built machines, usually featuring distinctive curved glass windscreens. They were described as "safe, strong, speedy, simple," and the passenger compartment could be heated by steam in cold weather. They also had the great advantage that "a nice cup of tea can be quickly made by steam at any time."

CHELSEA • USA 1914

A four-cylinder 1557cc light car from Newark, New Jersey.

CHELSEA • England 1922

This electric car had the outward appearance of a gasoline-engined vehicle but the under-hood area consisted mostly of batteries! A BTH electric motor was used.

CHENARD & WALCKER • France 1901-1946

The Chenard & Walcker factory, based in Asniéres, started with tricycles and two- and four-cylinder light cars until it was forced to close its doors in 1907. Promptly resurrected under the name of Société Anonyme des Anciens Etablissements Chenard et Walcker in new premises in Gennevilliers, the firm presented two new models in 1908;

CHEVROLET • USA 1911 to date

Billy Durant, recently ousted from General Motors, backed racing driver Louis Chevrolet (assisted by engineer Etienne Planche) to produce four- and six-cylinder prototypes in a Detroit garage. The six went into production for 1912, and 2,999 units were sold that year. In 1913 manufacture was shifted to Flint, where a sister marque, the Little Four, was built. Louis Chevrolet resigned that year. The Little was phased out in 1915, but a similar design was followed in the new Model H Chevrolet with an ohv 2.4-liter four built by Mason. Chevrolet was by now so successful that Durant was able to exchange its shares for those of GM, thus regaining control of the group. Late in 1915 Chevrolet moved into direct confrontation with Ford by introducing the 490. By 1920 sales had soared to 150,226, but a financial crisis forced Durant out of GM for a second and final time. The 1923 Superior, succeeding the 490, offered better equipment than Ford at a slightly higher price, and sold 480,737 units in its first year. However, the 1923 "copper-cooled" Chevrolet was a disaster, and most of the 100 units released were recalled and destroyed. In 1927 Chevrolet became America's best-selling marque, producing over a million cars for the first time, and consolidated its lead with the new International Six, a 3.2-liter ohv unit launched in 1928. Ford regained the lead in 1929-30, but Chevrolet was back on top in 1931 and has maintained the lead virtually uninterrupted ever since. Master and Standard ranges appeared in 1933, with "knee-action" ifs from 1934. The range was extensively redesigned in 1937, and endowed with the 3.55-liter "Blue Flame" six.

Chevrolet 490 c. 1918

1954 Chevrolet Bel Air sedan

1971 Chevrolet Camaro SS coupé

Pre-war designs lasted until 1949, when the Special and the De Luxe appeared, still with the old "stove bolt six" and, in 1950, Chevrolet was the first low-priced marque with a fully-automatic transmission; the two-speed Powerglide. The Corvette sports car of 1953 was totally new, with two-seat fiberglass body and a new "Blue Flame" six of 3.8 liters, plus Powerglide. Also brand new from the ground up, the 1955 Chevies had the marque's first V-8 since 1919. With fuel injection, this engine (in 4637cc form) became the first American production engine to develop 1 hp cu in, in 1957. Chevrolet suffered a minor sales setback that year in face of the restyled Plymouth and Ford ranges, but recaptured the number one slot with all-new cars in 1958. Five different series were available on an x-member frame. The 4637cc engine was standard, but a 5702cc version with three two-barrel carburetors was a popular option. In line with other GM divisions. Chevrolet offered all-new bodies and frames for 1959, and now featured a "gull-wing" rear deck with huge peardrop tail lights. At the end of that year the dramatic styling was toned down, and the compact Corvair, Chevrolet's first unit-construction model, was launched. Power was by a rear-mounted 2294cc flat-six and suspension was independent all-round. Over 250,000 were sold in the first year.

A totally new line, the Chevy II, appeared in 1962, with an ohv four of 2507cc or an ohv 3179cc six. A new 6702cc V-8 was available, and there was a performance version of the Corvair, the Monza Spyder, with a turbocharged engine. In 1963 the Corvette was completely redesigned, emerging as the Corvette Stingray, and in 1963 came the intermediate Chevelle with a 3179cc six or 4638cc V-8. Chevrolet's five separate lines were augmented by the division's belated answer to the Mustang; the Camaro, with 3769cc six or 5359cc V-8 – a 5735cc V-8 being optional.

The Corvair, condemned as "unsafe at any speed" by consumers' champion Ralph Nader, was dropped in 1969. New for 1970 was the conservatively styled Monte

Chevrolet Corvette (right,) from the 1956 catalogue

1956 Chevrolet Bel Air (above,) 1980 Chevrolet Citation (below right)

a 14-16 hp (3020cc) and a 30-40 hp (5881cc). In 1912 they offered five different cars, from 7-9 hp (1592cc) to 20 hp (5881cc). More cars were presented the following year based on these engines, and a new six-cylinder 20 hp (4523cc) appeared. After the war the factory resumed production with the 14 hp (3015cc), which remained in production for several years. It was followed in 1920 by a 12 hp (2650cc) and, in 1921, by a 10 hp. In 1922 came the famous "3-liter" with a 2978cc engine. The ohc 2-liter, also of 1922, was the winner of the very first Le Mans 24 Hour Race in 1923, and 1924 saw the 22 hp straight-eight of 3945cc. In 1925 Chenard and Walcker launched a small 1095cc four-cylinder sports car with the much-admired streamlined "tank" body, capable of 14 mph unsupercharged and 106 mph supercharged. Chenard & Walcker followed this with some medium cars of 1286cc and 1495cc. At the end of the 1930s Chenard & Walcker were struggling desperately to survive with the fwd "Aigle" with Citroên four-cylinder or Ford V-8 engines. It also made some rear-wheel-driven cars with Citroên engines. Although taken over in 1946 by Peugeot, Chenard remained independent for the next few years, producing light vans.

CHESWOLD • England 1911-1915

Former Adams designer E C. Inman-Hunter was the progenitor of this Doncaster-built 15.9hp four with dashboard radiator and worm drive.

CHEVROLET • USA 1911 to date

See panel

Carlo, with the 5735cc V-8. The 1971 Vega, with all-aluminum ohc four, pioneered Chevrolet's sub-compact revolution and led to the 1975 Monza 2 + 2 hatchback with optional 4293cc V-8. The 1971 Chevette rapidly became a best seller. Overseas, GM subsidiaries built their own versions of this ohc 1393cc small car (although body panels and mechanical features were, oddly, not interchangeable.) The Vega, which had even featured a Cosworth dohc four, was killed off in 1977. Economics forced greater interchangeability between GM lines, and the GM B-body was used on the 1977 Capric/Impala range. However, the Corvette and Camaro continued with 1968 styling into 1979, except for a new Camaro Berlinetta, with a six or two V-8s available. In April 1979 the "1980" Caprice X-car was revealed as a replacement for the Nova, with a transverse four-cylinder engine driving the front wheels.

Chevrolet's version of the GMJ-car was the 1981 Cavalier. That year also saw the launch of the Celebrity, using I-4 or V6 engines in GM"s "A-body," and the Camero with 2.8-liter V-6, and 5.0-5.7-liter V-8 engines. A new Corvette appeared in 1983 and was updated in 1988, and again in 1991. The 1984 Monte Carlo coupé used the old Malibu chassis with V-6 4.3-liter engine. In 1985 Chevrolet began building the Toyota Corolla under the name "Nova." The mechanically-identical Corsica sedan and Beretta coupé appeared in 1987. In 1991 the Caprice limousine received new bodywork.

Revised versions of these cars further strengthened the marque's name, and subsequent model expansion saw both strengths and weaknesses emerge in Chevrolet's model line-up. The company's various shares in other manufacturers enabled it to call up GM sourced Isuzu sourced models with suitably badge engineered looks. Huge losses and an ageing model line-up meant that action was necessary and, in the early 1990s, a design-led recovery took place through such models as the Monte Carlo coupé, the Geo Prizm, Geo Metro compact and sub compact cars. An MPV range and the Lumina sedan helped revive the marque's image. Most importantly, the company took in hand the dated Corvette concept and revived its fortunes through the superb styling and handling of the 1998 Corvette. This, allied to a range of muscular pick-up trucks, put the Chevrolet name back on track as real piece of American auto legend.

The Corvette heritage, 1954-1999

$100,000

Chrysler

CHIC • Australia 1923-1929

Although advertised as a "Car for Australian Conditions," the Chic was a locally assembled tourer using British mechanical parts and an Australian body. An unusual idea was the choice of two Meadows overhead valve engines. The four-cylinder 2.1-liter unit developed 40 bhp, and the six-cylinder 2.7-liter 48 bhp. At least 50 Chics were sold, and two are known to have survived. The chassis layout was conventional.

CHICAGOAN • USA 1952-1954

Using a two-passenger glassfiber sports body and a six-cylinder Willys engine, the Chicagoan was produced by Triplex Industries of Chicago. Only fifteen were built over a two-year period although, as the Triplex, it apparently continued into 1955.

CHILTERN • England 1919-1920

The short-lived Chiltern, powered by a Dorman engine, was built in Dunstable, Bedfordshire, and had Vulcan connections.

CHINNOCK • England 1899-1900

The Chinnock-Davis Manufacturing Co of Penge, a cycle maker, built 31-2 hp aircooled single-cylinder voiturettes with two-seater dog-cart bodywork, and 2.3-4 hp tricycles.

CHIRIBIRI • Italy 1913-1929

Most Chiribiri cars, named after Antonio Chiribiri, the designer/manufacturer, were around 1.5-liters: 1593cc with a sv four-cylinder engine, 1453cc with an ohv motor and there was also a "hot" 1485cc ohc racing car, designed by Englishman Jack Scales. Built in 1925, it developed 72 bhp at 5100 rpm. Sufficient funds to develop this excellent engine were not forthcoming. Gigi Platé drove one in 1926 at the Berlin Avus, but crashed in practice.

CHOTA • England 1912-1913

This 6 hp cyclecar preceded the Buckingham.

CHRISTCHURCH-CAMPBELL • England 1922

This assembled car had a 10.8 hp Coventry-Simplex engine and gearbox. Only one was made.

CHRISTIE • USA 1904-1910

J Walter Christie is predominantly known as being the first serious proponent of fwd automobiles, and built half-a-dozen racing cars between 1904 and 1908. The initial Christie racer of January 1904 boasted a transverse four-

1947 Chrysler Town & Country

1956 Chrysler 300B

CHRYSLER • USA 1924 to date

Walter Chrysler"s gifted triumvirate of engineers – Breer, Skelton, and Zeder – created a remarkable car to succeed the old Maxwell marque. Its six-cylinder engine had a high-compression Ricardo-type head, and four-wheel hydraulic band brakes were an innovation on a popular-priced car; $50 million-worth were sold in the first year. A four appeared in 1925, and a luxury Imperial Six was added to the range. Chrysler expanded rapidly. The De Soto and Plymouth marques were created in 1928, in which year Dodge was taken over. The company's reputation for innovation was sustained by the widely copied "ribbon" radiators of the 1929 range. In 1929 a Cord L29-like radiator was adopted and two straight-eights of 3.9 liters and the 6.3-liter Imperial were announced. The 1932 models had automatic clutches and freewheels. Synchromesh came in 1933, followed in 1934 by automatic overdrive. That was the year of the Airflow, a technical tour de force and commercial failure which lasted only until 1937, although some of its advanced features were used on the more conventional Chryslers that had moved the company into second place in the sales league.

The 1942 models had a radical facelift, with full-width wraparound grilles, and the limited-production Town and Country was distinguished by external wood framing. Different grilles and trim were the only noticeable differences in the three postwar 1946 series, the C38 sv six, and the straight-eight C39, and C40 Imperial. The Town and Country was reintroduced, and standard transmission was the 1938-introduced clutchless "Fluid-Drive." New models celebrated Chrysler"s 1949 Silver Jubilee and, in 1951, came the marque's first V-8; the famous ohv "Hemi" of 5424cc which was the base engine in the New Yorker, Saratoga and Imperial series, and was also raced by Briggs Cunningham. The firm"s first fully automatic transmission – PowerFlite, and AirTemp – the first recirculating air-conditioning system, appeared in 1953 models, restyled with a curved one-piece windscreen. "Flight Sweep" styling by Virgil Exner on 1955 models revived flagging sales, with a long hood sloping down between well-defined wings and a windscreen wrapped around at top and bottom. Two series, Windsor and New Yorker, both powered by the Hemi, were offered; Imperial becoming a separate division. There was also the limited edition 300 series based on the New Yorker, America"s fastest and most powerful stock production car. In 1956 a 300B set up a world passenger car speed record of 139.9 mph.

Tailfins reached their zenith on 1957 models, which had TorqueFlite pushbutton automatic transmission. New wedge-head engines of 6276cc and 6768cc replaced the Hemi in 1959, and 1960 saw new unitary bodies; a 300C set a new speed record of 176.6mph. The 1963 cars were little changed mechanically, but had all-new styling devoid of chrome. In 1964 a limited series of 50 gas-turbine cars was built for evaluation purposes by Ghia, but all but ten were destroyed when the experiment ended in 1966. The 1965 models had sculptured side panels, slab-sided wings and minimal chrome; a style retained until 1969, when "fuselage styling" with a bulbous shape and narrow curved windows appeared. The last Chrysler convertible was built in 1970, and the Imperial line returned to the fold the next year, but poor sales caused the demise of this luxury car in 1975.

The smallest post-war Chrysler, the Cordoba of 1975, was aimed at the "personal luxury" market. In 1978 it gained a new "lean burn" engine of 5211cc and a power sunroof. That year, too, the LeBaron model name – dating back before the war – was revived for a luxury compact with either a 3687cc six or V-8s of 5211cc or 5899cc. For 1979 the New Yorker/Newport series lost 7 cwt in weight by extensive use of aluminum and engineering improvements including electronic spark control instead of "lean burn," as well as an electronic feedback carburetor with catalytic convertor to reduce emissions.

Rescued from financial disaster by former Ford president Lee Iacocca, Chrysler transformed its image during the 1980s and based its range on the front-wheel-drive K-car platform, which had first appeared in 1981. An Italian-built Chrysler-Maserati appeared in 1986. Using

1949 two-seater Chrysler Cabriolet (above.) 1961 Chrysler 300G (left)

a traditional Chrysler model name, the LeBaron convertible and coupé were launched for 1987; the convertible being claimed to be the world's best-selling open car. A LeBaron sedan made its debut in 1990. All 1992 LeBarons had a choice of 2.5 or 3.0-liter V8 power units. Above the LeBaron came the 3.3-liter V6 New Yorker Salon and 3.3/3.8-liter V-6 New Yorker Fifth Avenue luxury models. An all-new New Yorker due for launch in the mid-1990s was previewed at the 1992 Detroit Show. Flagship of the 1992 range was the luxury Imperial, launched in 1990 with the 3.8-liter V-6 engine, and a wide range of luxury equipment including a ten-speaker radio. At this time Chrysler absorbed the American Motors Corporation and inherited the Renault derived "alliance" cars. These were briefly given a new title as the Eagle brand. A Mitsubishi Starion sourced coupé known as the "Conquest" also appeared. The Eagle brand was also expanded with the Talon, a small but smart coupé.

By this time the Chrysler model line-up, although improved, was overpopulated. Like so many other American brands under the onslaught of Japanese and European imports, the firm had to sharpen up. This it did, culminating in the superb "cab forward" designed, type LH – labelled "Cirrus," "Stratus," "Sebring," and "Concorde" ranges in the 1996-1999 model years. The Jeep Grand Cherokee had also established a worldwide following and was produced in right-hand-drive form in Europe. The successful Neon range also expanded Chrysler"s appeal in the small sedan market, and the Viper models have achieved near-super-car status. A stake in Lamborghini and a massive tie-up with Germany's Daimler-Benz in 1998 saw the creation of the $25 billion entity that is Chrysler-Daimler, with 43 per cent owned by Chrysler and 57 per cent owned by Daimler-Benz. With each developing separate brand areas, this car company will have massive breadth and the ability to share much design and production material, with massive inherent cost savings.

The Jeep Wrangler Rubicon (top,) The Jeep Grand Cherokee (bottom)

The 1999 Chrysler Pronto Cruiser (above.) The 1999 Chrysler Pronto Spyder (center.) The 1999 Chrysler Grand Voyager 2.5 Turbo Diesel SE (below)

1914 CID Baby

cylinder engine, the crankshaft taking the place of the front axle. Subsequent cars were all different from one another. Christie built two (possibly three) touring cars in 1905 and, in 1909, built a taxicab. In 1911 he began producing fwd tractor conversions for fire apparatus, and later made tanks.

CHRITON • England 1905

Built at Saltburn-by-the-Sea, Yorkshire, this was a horizontal-engined 1715cc 10 hp four.

CHRYSLER • USA 1924 to date

See panel on previous page

CHRYSLER • England • Scotland 1976-1979

The old Rootes Group marque names were suppressed after the Chrysler takeover in 1970, though the Sunbeam name has been revived on a hatchback, based on the Avenger floorpan. A 2.2-liter Lotus-engined performance version was launched in 1979. The old 180 sedan died at this time and the Talbot name briefly came into being to carry Chrysler's hopes in a deal that saw Peugeot-Citroên take over the brand. It was not to last long. Despite sharing pan-European-American models such as the Horizon, and creating the excellent but instantly forgotten Tagora model, the Talbot – out of Peugeot via Chrysler out of Rootes names – died in 1986 and left the UK automotive scene.

CHRYSLER VALIANT • Australia 1962 – 1990

After initially importing US-made Valiants, Chrysler Australia embarked on local manufacture. Over the years the design grew steadily away from those of the US counterpart. The early Valiants were highly successful, having more power (140 bhp) than rival Falcon and Holden models, but the Valiant's popularity diminished during the 1970s. The 1979 model came in three basic styles – sedan, wagon, and van – with a choice of 4.3-liter six-cylinder engine or an imported 5.2-liter V-8. The design was conventional throughout, apart from the use of torsion bar front suspension. Up-market versions with the same mechanical specifications are called Regal and Le Baron.

CID • France 1912-1914

Constructions Industriels Dijonais (successor to Cottereau) was best known for the 8 hp Baby with single-cylinder Buchet engine and transverse front suspension, although big sleeve-valve fours were also offered.

CIEM • Switzerland 1904-1906

Convinced that the gasoline engine was not reliable enough on its own, the Compagnie de l"Industrie Electrique et Mècanique of Geneva equipped its cars with electric motors as well as vee-formation engines with two or four cylinders. Vertical-twins and fours appeared at the end of 1905 and, the following year, the cars became known as "Stella."

CINCINNATI • USA 1903

A steam runabout with side-tiller steering and "reachless running gear."

CIPHER • England 1980

Eight running prototypes of this neat Reliant-based sportscar were built before the project ran out of steam. In 1990 a plan to build 70,000 Ciphers a year in Lithuania was announced.

Citroên light 15 model, the highlight of European car design

CITROEN • France 1919 to date

Engineer Andreé Citroën had spent many years in the automotive industry, making gears then, during the First World War, he manufactured munitions. His first car, the Type A launched in 1919, had a sv 1327cc engine. In 1922 came the Type B of 1453cc. The same year saw the first of the famous Citroën expeditions with the Citroën-Kégresse halftrack across the Sahara. It was also the year of the popular "Cloverleaf" Type C of 855cc. This remarkable car was very popular owing to its low price and high reliability. Between May 1922 and May 1926 80,232 Cloverleaves were built, but Citroën's record during the vintage period was for the C4, with 134,000 cars built in a little more than four years. Citroën introduced mass production on the American pattern into France. With the B10 of 1925 he also introduced France's first all-steel body. The C-Series followed, of which the most interesting was the C6 six-cylinder, available in two versions (2442cc and 2650cc). In 1934 Citroën presented the revolutionary 7 cv "Traction Avant", but its development costs bankrupted him and the firm was taken over by Michelin.

Between 1934 and 1940 the factory made the Traction Avant in no fewer than 21 different versions, the three basic models being the 7 cv and 11 cv fours and the 15 cv six. It also presented a prototype of a sensational V-8-engined front-wheel-drive which never saw production. After the Second World War Citroën resumed production with the 11 cv and the 15 cv, sold only in black. At the Paris Motor Show of 1949 Citroën launched the amazing Pierre Boulanger designed 2 cv; a strange

CISITALIA • Italy 1946-1965

Founded by ex-racing driver Piero Dusio, a 1930s Italian industrialist, Cisitalia started building cars after the Second World War, using Fiat engines which developed around 60 bhp. Dusio was the creator-manufacturer of these light cars with tubular frames, mainly sold to private customers, and he also built a range of sports cars with hotted-up 1089cc and 1346cc Fiat power units. In 1947 came the acme of Cisitalia cars, the 202 coupé with Pininfarina bodywork. Very few were produced. In 1949 Ferdinand Porsche designed a 1492cc Grand Prix car for Dusio, with a 12-cylinder engine with two superchargers, mounted in

Citroën XM (right.) Citroën CX (below right.) 1948 Citroën 2cv (below)

1948 Citroën 2cv

and spartan car, front-wheel driven with a 375cc air-cooled flat-twin engine. For many years the Traction Avant and the Deux Chevaux were the only models. In 1954 the 15 cv was equipped with hydropneumatic suspension.

The year after, Citroën presented the car of the new era, the immortal, daring Bertoni design that was the DS 19. The old "Traction" nevertheless remained in production until 1957. A simpler version of the DS, the ID 19, was presented in 1956, and 1961 was the year of the Ami 6 – a sort of "super 2 cv". The DS 21 followed the DS 19 in 1967 and, a year after that, the Dyane appeared; still with the air-cooled flat-twin. In 1968 a strange vehicle left the works; the plastics-bodied Mehari which resembled a Jeep. The most significant car of that year was the GS (later the long lived and popular GSA), with a flat-four engine, and 1969 saw the luxurious SM with the dohc Maserati V-6 of 2675cc. In 1975 the DS gave way to the futuristic looking CX 2000, later enlarged to 2200cc, 2400cc and 2500cc. Having come under the control of Puegeot, Citroën presented the LN, a marriage of a Peugeot body with a Citroën engine.

Launched in 1978, the Visa hatchback had a choice of 652cc (Citroën) or 1124cc (Peugeot) power units. From 1982 the BX hatchback, with power units ranging from 1.4 to 1.9 liters and Bertone-influenced styling, slotted into the range between the CX and GSA. The 1129cc Axel of 1984 was built in Romania. In 1986 came the all-new AX "supermini" with engines of 954cc, 1124cc and 1360cc. The 16 valve BX 19 GTI was introduced in 1987. French production of the 2CV (built in the 1890s Clèment factory at Levallois) ended in 1988 and was transferred to Portugal, where the last 2CV was built in July 1990. The 1989 XM luxury sedan pioneered electronically-controlled hydractive suspension. A more conservative, less eccentric Citroën appeared in the form of the ZX five-door sedan, with engines ranging from 1.4 to 1.9 liters. It was replaced by the Xsara in 1997. The Saxo, a small hatchback based on the Peugeot 106 floorpan, gave Citroën an entry-level model at a crucial time, and the Xantia range took over from the BX. The XM, perhaps the last great eccentric Citroën, is due to be superseded by a return to daring design in the form of a large four-door coupé-type sedan. Although part of the Peugeot alliance, Citroën seems set to make a return to its individualism and daring design legend. Press and public alike hope for a replacement for the 2CV in the early years of the new century.

the rear of the tubular frame. At that time Dusio ran out of money and transferred operations to Argentina, but never regained the position which he had held in Turin. Among his designers was an Austrian who soon became famous in his own right; Carlo Abarth. Another owner tried to resume Cisitalia production in Italy but was not successful. His last cars had 847cc Fiat-based engines, while earlier attempts to revive the Cisitalia included the production of 1095cc, 1248cc and even 2760cc coupés. By 1965 nothing was left. Piero Dusio was equally unsuccessful in Argentina, where he built Jeep-like cars. Cisitalia went out of business in 1965.

CITO • Germany 1905-1909

A bicycle and motorcycle factory which produced small Fafnir-engined two- and four-cylinder cars of 704cc, 1648cc, 1808cc, 2012cc and 2608cc. Some of the later cars had French Aster motors. Cito used many components of French manufacture.

CITROEN • France 1919 to date

See panel

CITUS • Denmark 1900-1903

Citus tri- and quadricycles were probably little more than modified De Dion Bouton products, even if the maker, Fyens Cycle Vaerk, Odense, tried to deny it. The name "Citus Motor" was, however, cast on the crankcase of the single-cylinder air-cooled 2.5 hp engines.

CITY AND SUBURBAN • England 1901-1904

The City and Suburban Electric Carriage Company supplied its vehicles, or Columbia electrics bearing its nameplate, to high society. Among its long list of illustrious clients

1903 City & Suburban Grand Victoria

were Queen Alexandra, the Dowager Empress of Russia, Dame Nellie Melba, and the Countess of Wilton. Hire vehicles were based at Niagara, a former skating rink in Westminster. A wide range of formal coachwork was offered.

CIZETA • Italy 1988 to date

Taking its name from the initials of its builder, Claudio Zampoli, plus the name of the company's backer, composer Giorgio Moroder, the Cizeta Moroder V-16 T was created by ex-Lamborghini engineers. Its 560 bhp engine, the only modern production V-16, produces a top speed of 328 km/h (204 mph). By 1992 four had been built.

CLARENDON • England 1902-1904

This Coventry company built a 7 hp two-seater car as well as motorcycles.

CLARK • USA 1899-1909

A 6 hp twin-cylinder steam dos-à-dos, with its controls laid out so that the car could be driven from either the left or the right, depending on the driver's whim, was the product of a marine engine and boiler-maker in Boston, Mass. In 1899 Clark also built the first 4wd, four-wheelsteer motor car; a light steamer designed by an inventor named Shaw, of Hyde Park, Mass.

CLARK • USA 1910-1912

Tourers of 30 hp and 40 hp were listed by this Shelbyville, Indiana, firm at $1,400 to $1,750.

CLARKMOBILE • USA 1903-1906

A 7 hp wheel-steered "gasoline buggy," the Clarkmobile from Lansing, Michigan, was claimed to be the "easiest rider built,"and was said to have been tested for two years before being marketed.

1899 Clément-Panhard

CLASSIC • USA 1916-1917, 1920-1921

A 3.2-liter Lycoming four powered this Chicago marque. Featuring a slanting windscreen, the Classic was available only in open form. Failing in 1917, the Classic reappeared three years later after reincorporation with a factory at Lake Geneva, Wisconsin. Lycoming engines were again used, but these cars were more expensive than their Chicago forebears.

CLASSIC • France 1925-1929

Made by the Compagnie Générale des Voitures in Paris, the Classic was available with engine options; the 2120cc sv Sergant and a sleeve-valve unit of 1593cc. Classics were mainly used as taxis.

CLAUDE DELAGE • France 1923-1927

Having no relationship with the other Delage, these cars were made at Clichy with four-cylinder engines of 8 hp (1131 cc), 10 hp (1847cc) and 12 hp (2297cc).

CLAUDIUS • France 1903

A voiturette "remarkable for its low, yet elegant form," with a 41.2 hp Aster engine on the rear axle, "doing away with chains, belt, or cardans."

CLAVEAU • France 1923-1950

Made in Paris, all Claveau cars were highly unorthodox in design. The first was rear-engined, with a streamline body and independent suspension all round. The engines were a 9 hp flat-four and a 7hp flat-twin of 739cc. The following model had fwd. A postwar V-8 prototype was never produced.

CLC • France 1911-1913

A single-cylinder "valveless" voiturette with a circular radiator, built by MM. Cockborne, Lehucher and da Costa in Paris.

CLEM • France 1911-1914

The CLEM was assembled in Lyon using Belgian Fondu engines of 1131cc and 1327cc and Rolling (Dupressoir) chassis. It took its name from Mme. Clémence Servoz, wife of the first customer, a journalist.

CLEMENT, CLEMENT-BAYARD France 1898-1922

Gustave-Adolphe Clément, having made his fortune in the cycle industry, floated the Clément-Gladiator-Humber ("Clediaber") company for Fr 22 million in 1896. The Humber connection was soon broken, but in 1898 the firm began building Clément and Gladiator cars. A new factory was built at Levallois-Perret (Seine), where the infamous Clément-Panhard, a beastly machine with center-pivot steering and rear-mounted tube-ignition engine, was built alongside a tiny 21.2 hp voiturette; also rear-engined. In 1901, 7 hp single- and 12 hp twin-cylinder cars designed by Marius Barbarou (who soon left to join Benz) were introduced. By 1903 a range of 9, 12, and 16 hp cars was available. The 12 and 16 hp were four-cylinders with automatic inlet valves, almost identical to the contemporary Gladiators, but with shaft instead of chain drive. In October 1903 Clément left the company, which was taken over by Harvey DuCros (of Dunlop tyres), and also lost the right to make cars under his own name. He therefore changed his name to Clément-Bayard after le chevalier sans peur et sans reproche, whose statue stood in front of his factory at Meziéres. Initially, Clément-Bayard cars were similar to the Clément-Gladiator but, in 1907, a 1.6-liter 10-12 hp model with unit gearbox and dashboard radiator was introduced. This type of high-quality light car characterized the subsequent history of Clément-Bayard. Post-war, only 8 hp and 17.6 hp models were available; in 1922 the sole remaining Clément factory was taken over by Citroên for the manufacture of spare parts.

1992 Cizeta Moroder V-16 T

1925 Clyno 10.8hp Sports

10.8 hp Clyno Royal Tourer, 1927

CLEMENT • England 1908-1914

After the foundation of Clement-Talbot, Clément-Gladiators were sold under the Clement name in Britain. All-British Clements were built in Coventry from 1908, based on contemporary Swift designs of 10-12 hp (twin), 14-18 hp and 18-28 hp (fours). A 12-12 hp four replaced the twin in 1913.

CLEMENT ET ROCHELLE France 1927-1930

Another interesting attempt to make a car with independent suspension on all four wheels (this time by leaf-springs,) the Clement et Rochelle was made in Clamart with an 1100cc Ruby.

CLENET • USA 1976 to date

Designed by French-born Alain Clenet after the style of Jaguar and Mercedes sports cars of the 1930s, each Clenet takes 1600 man hours to build and costs $50,000. A modified Continental Mk V chassis carries an all-steel body, Ford suspension, brakes and engine, with MG doors and windscreen. Hand-rubbed walnut from 1,200-year-old trees is used for the dashboard.

CLESSE • France 1907-1908

Friction-drive voiturettes and light cars were built by this firm from Levallois-Perret (Seine.)

CLETRAC • USA 1923

Cletrac is an acronym for Cleveland Tractor, whose Cletrac tractors are famous throughout the world. Cletrac was affiliated with White, and the first Rollin cars (named for Rollin White) were built by Cletrac and consequently carried that name, although subsequent cars were marketed under the Rollin emblem.

CLEVELAND • USA 1900-1901

"Pretty, agreeable and practical" electric cars from the Cleveland Machine Screw Company.

CLEVELAND • USA 1902-1909

"The car without one weak spot" was a shaft-drive 6435cc four-cylinder 30-35 hp which completed the 1906 Glidden Tour with only two penalty points. Chassis were initially built by Garford. From 1908 they were of own make.

CLIFT • England 1899-1902

An electric victoria with an "extra-special" top speed of 29 km/h (18 mph) "for quick manoeuvring in traffic". Sinclair gasoline cars of 5 hp (rear-engined) and 10 hp (front-engined twin) were also marketed by the same firm.

CLIMAX • England 1904-1907

"Pioneers of high-class cars at moderate prices," Climax of Coventry began production with a four-car range, 10-12 hp two-cylinder, 15 hp three-cylinder and fours of 16 hp and 20 hp but, in 1906, only 14 hp and 22 hp fours were listed. A 20 hp six appeared for 1907.

CLIMBER • USA 1919-1923

Featuring both four- and six-cylinder models of open and closed cars, as well as a few trucks, the Climber was the major effort made by the automobile industry in Arkansas. Using Herschell-Spillman engines exclusively, the cars were distributed by some ten agencies across Arkansas, Mississippi, and Tennessee.

CLINTON • Canada 1911-1912

When its thresher factory burned down, Clinton rebuilt it as a car factory, but assembled fewer than ten four-cylinder cars with US engines.

CLIPPER • USA 1956

In 1956 the Clipper became a separate marque for a season (instead of a lower priced Packard) before it again became a Packard Clipper. Available in three series, Custom, Super, and Deluxe, the Custom had Packard"s superior Torsion-Level ride combining torsion-bar suspension with the electronic load-levelling system. This was offered as an option on the Super and Deluxe, which had coils at the front and leaf springs at the rear. The Custom Clipper used a 245 hp V-8 Packard engine, while the Super and Deluxe had a smaller 225 hp version. Electric windows and Twin Ultramatic transmission were optional.

CLOVER • USA 1899-1900

Lieutenant H K Clover, USN, designed the twin-cylinder two-stroke engine of this Omaha, Nebraska, car. Its silencer incorporated a "deodorizing preparation" of magnesia, lime and charcoal, to be renewed every 30 days.

CLUA • Spain 1959-1960

A 398cc twin-cylinder two-stroke powered this sporty utility model from Barcelona.

CLUB • USA 1910-1911

Several New York bankers, determined to eliminate the middleman, decided to combine and build a limited number of cars for themselves and others entering their club. Members could buy up to five $100 shares, allowing them to buy one "Club Car" annually per share. The 40-50 hp Club was built by Merchant & Evans of Philadelphia, and had an American & British engine. A dual-ratio back axle gave direct drive on the top two ratios.

CLUB • Germany 1921-1925

Club, of Berlin-Charlottenburg, fitted 1305cc 18 hp Atos engines into sporting two-seater cars. Top speed of the 15 cwt car was around 43 mph.

CLULEY • England 1922-1928

Proprietary sv four-cylinder engines were used in the Coventry-built Cluley, the company initially having made bicycles. These 10 and 11.9 hp models were joined by the six-cylinder 16-40 in 1924. The final model was on ohv 14-50 which never went into production.

CLYNO • England 1922-1929

Already famous as a motorcycle manufacturer (the name came from the variable-ratio "Clyno" belt-pulley, designed by the company's founders, Frank and Allwyn Smith), Clyno of Wolverhampton built three prototype 10 hp ohv sports cars in 1920 before the post-war slump killed the project. Re-formed in 1922, it launched a low-priced 10.8 hp

Coventry-Climax-engined light car intended to compete with Morris. It proved an instant success. Early in 1924 a wide-track Colonial model (reflecting Clyno's interest in export markets) and an ephemeral Sports, with four-wheel brakes and external exhaust, were added to the range. At Olympia that year a refined Clyno range included "Royal" tourer, two-seater, and sedan. Right-hand gear change and balloon tyres were standard and four-wheel brakes were available. For 1926 an 11.9 hp four was added, initially with Coventry-Climax and then, from December 1925, with Clyno's own-make engine. Production peaked at over 12,000 in 1926, when Clyno was third-largest British manufacturer, and a vast new factory was built in the Wolverhampton suburb of Bushbury. In September 1927 a new 8.3 hp Clyno "Nine" appeared, designed by A G "General" Booth, who subsequently designed the AJS Nine and the Hillman Minx. Like the other cars in the 1928 range it had a new, square-cut radiator. By February 1928 Bushbury was turning out 70 Nines a week and, in May 1928, came a luxury 12.35 hp, the wirewheeled "Olympic." In an attempt to forestall the expected Morris Eight, Clyno launched the £112 "Century" Nine during 1928 (it had been planned as a £100 car.) This basic machine's unpopularity with agents and public, coupled with the cost of Bushbury, helped to bring Clyno down in 1929, when a prototype monobloc straight-eight (derived from two Nine engines) had just completed its trials. R H Collier of Birmingham, who bought up the spares and goodwill, built another six 12.35s. A plan for engine manufacturer Meadows to revive Clyno cars in the mid-1930s was scotched by its involvement in rearmament.

CLYDE • England 1899-1930

G H Wait of Leicester built cars, motorcycles and "tricarettes" for over 30 years, mainly for local customers. His 12-13 hp three-cylinder and 7-8 hp twin-cylinder cars of 1905 had transverse power units.

CM • France 1924-1930

Made by Charles Mochet, this was a tiny cyclecar with a single-cylinder 346cc engine mounted at the rear. The marque resumed after the war with the pedal-powered Vélocar Mochet.

CMN • Italy 1919-1925

Enzo Ferrari and Ugo Sivocci were with CMN at Milano-Pontedera before they joined the much larger Alfa-Romeo factory. CMN built a range of cars with 2180cc and 2960cc four-cylinder sv engines, but never gained any international fame.

COADOU ET FLEURY • France 1921

A small cyclecar made in Paris with a steel monocoque body and a 903cc sv Ruby engine.

1922 Colonial two-seater

Colombe cyclecar, 1924

COATES-GOSHEN • USA 1908-1910

Built four-cylinder cars of 25 hp and 32 hp.

COATS STEAM CAR • USA 1922-1923

Few of these $1,085 three-cylinder steam tourers designed by George A Coats were built. Never passing the prototype stage, the Coats boasted a two-speed and reverse gear with floor shift.

COCHOTTE • France 1899

A voiturette of untidy appearance, with an exposed water-cooled engine at the front.

COEY • USA 1913-1917

Coey of Chicago built the Coey Bear cyclecar and the six-cylinder Coey Flyer sporting car.

COGNET DE SEYNES • France 1912-1926

An 1124cc four built in Lyon.

COHENDET • France 1897-1914

This company was founded by an American in Paris, C R Goodwin, for whom its "Americaine" 792cc voiturette of 1910 was named. A 31.2 hp single-cylinder air-cooled engine powered Cohendet"s "nice-looking carriage" of 1897, which was driven by a leather belt strengthened by steel links to prevent stretching. By 1905 one-, two- and four-cylinder models were available. Cohendet, which built a wide range of components, also offered to build cars to his clients' own designs.

COIGNET • France 1912-1913

M M Coignet and Ducruzel, of Billancourt, built a varied range of belt-driven cyclecars with single- and twin-cylinder power units.

COLBURN • USA 1906-1909

The Colburn, from Denver, Colorado, was similar in appearance to the Renault, with the radiator behind a coal-scuttle bonnet. A 116 km/h (72 mph) roadster was offered in 1909.

COLBY • USA 1911-1914

An underslung 40 hp four from Mason City, Iowa.

COLDA • France 1921-1922

Cars made in Paris with 1847cc four-cylinder Sergant engines.

COLE • USA 1909-1925

J J Cole's Indianapolis carriage-building firm started with a 14 hp flat-twin high-wheeler, but soon turned to large, conventional four- and six-cylinder models. From 1913 these had electric starting and lighting. In 1915 Cole announced its first V-8, with a Northway power unit. The 1916 range was just Roadster, Sportster, and Touring (one

Coltman c. 1910, 20hp, four-cylinder

color option was "dustproof gray") but, by the early 1920s, "Sportsedan," "Sportcoupé," "Sportosine," "Tourosine," and "Toursedan" were also listed. Cole's penchant for appalling model names burst into full flower in its ultimate range with the "Aero-Volante" and a sedan called, for some reason, the "Brouette," French for "wheelbarrow".

COLIBRI • Germany 1907-1910

Built by the Norddeutsche Automobilwerke (NAW) at Hameln-Weser, the small Colibri was a popular car, and was also exported in large numbers. The first model had an ioe 860cc twin-cylinder engine, the larger version a sv 1320cc four-cylinder. Later models were known as the "Sperber."

COLLINET • USA 1921-1922

This was the successor to the earlier Collins built in Huntington, NY, but had a four-cylinder Wisconsin engine. The price in 1921 for the 132-inch-wheelbase, wire-wheeled Collinet chassis was $5,500. For 1922 this was reduced to $5,000 although a six was quoted at $6,500. A 1921 Collinet was exhibited late in 1920 in New York City. It might have been the only car actually built!

COLLINS • USA 1920

Built in Huntington, New York, by Albert H Collins, the car featured a four-cylinder Herschell-Spillman engine and 120-inch wheelbase. Wire wheels were standard, and the five-passenger touring car was listed at $2,500. The car may have existed only as a prototype and became the Collinet for 1921.

COLLINS • USA 1921-1922

The Collins was built by the Collins Motor Car Co of Detroit, Michigan (and later Cleveland, Ohio), by Richard H Collins, former president of Cadillac. The car was absorbed into the Peerless line when Mr Collins affiliated with that company. Cars carrying a Collins nameplate were prototypes only.

COLOMBE • France c. 1920-1925

Although this firm from Colombes started with an assembled car using a Model T Ford engine and transmission, by 1923 it had introduced an odd fwd cyclecar with a 345cc single-cylinder engine which, in single-seat form, set up world records in its class at Arpajon.

COLONIAL • USA 1920

Only one of these Colonials was built, but it is important in automotive history as the first car built in the USA with four-wheel hydraulic brakes. With an own-make straight-eight engine, the Colonial featured disc wheels and two side-mounted spare wheels, as well as a hard-top body (known in the USA as a "California top"), and could pass either as a touring car or a sedan at the driver's whim, given a few seconds to arrange the windows.

1919 Columbia Six tourer

COLONIAL • USA 1920-1921

The Chicago-based Colonial was nothing more than the Shaw automobile with another emblem. For some reason best known to Shaw, the Colonial name was substituted, briefly, before the car returned to its original "Shaw" designation. Soon after it was bought by Yellow Cab and renamed "Ambassador."

COLONIAL • USA 1921-1922

Built in Boston, Mass, probably fewer than a dozen Colonials ever got on the road, despite the company's prediction that it would produce "in excess of 100 units" in its first year. These were handsome cars with a 130-inch wheelbase and a six-cylinder engine by Beaver. Although a complete line of open and closed body styles was advertised, probably only a few open models were actually built. A 12-cylinder model using the Weidely engine was also proposed to augment the 1921 line, but it is doubtful whether it materialized.

COLT • USA 1907-1908

The sporty six-cylinder Colt 40hp was built at Yonkers, NY, and cost only $1,500. Top speed was a claimed 60 mph (97 kmh), which enabled it "to run away on the hills from any runabout of the season, bar none."

COLT • USA 1958

The Colt Manufacturing Co of Milwaukee, Wisconsin, offered this two-passenger glassfiber-bodied car powered by a one-cylinder four-stroke air-cooled engine with a top speed of 50 mph. Automatic transmission was standard equipment.

COLTMAN • England 1909-1920

Though this 20 hp four-cylinder from the Midland Ironworks, Loughborough, is supposed to have remained in production until 1920, it appears only to have been built between 1909-13.

CULEBRA • England 1989

A mid-engined Ferrari lookalike.

COLUMBIA • USA 1898-1913

One of America's leading manufacturers of electric vehicles, the Columbia and Electric Vehicle Company of Hartford, Connecticut, was part of Colonel Albert Pope's motor- and cycle-building empire. The 1899 models ranged from an electric phaeton (the original type of Columbia electric) through a dos-à-dos, a run-about, a victoria, a "Daumon Victoria," and a brougham to a 15-seat omnibus. Queen Alexandra of England used a Columbia Victoria around the grounds of Sandringham. The company began to manufacture "gasoline carriages" in 1899. By 1904 a 12-14 hp twin and 30-35 hp fours designed by H P Maxim were available; the smaller models acquiring left-hand drive for 1905, while the larger cars retained right-hand control. In 1906 a big four of 40-45 hp was listed. The 1909 29 hp four had the very curious designation, "Mark 48, Lot 3,"

Hugo Ogren driving the 1923 Commander

perhaps prophetically, for Columbia became part of the United States Motor Company combine the following year. Its last models were the Knight and Cavalier of 1911-1913. Along with Courier, Stoddard-Dayton, Brush, and Maxwell, Columbia went down with the collapse of the US Motor Company in 1913, and only Maxwell resurfaced.

COLUMBIA • USA 1917-1924

"Gem of the Highway," the Columbia Six was an assembled car of some quality which used a 24 hp Continental engine. It was noteworthy for its thermostat-controlled radiator shutters, "a constant source of delight to the Columbia owner". In 1923 Columbia took over Liberty.

COLUMBUS • USA 1903-1904

The Columbus Automobile & Manufacturing Co of Columbus, Ohio, was a motor agency which also advertised "machines reconstructed and special designs carried out." Flat-twin cars were produced, sometimes they were known as "Imperial."

COMET • Canada 1907-1908

This Montreal-assembled 24 hp four used a Clément-Bayard engine and chassis; there were (briefly) a six and a 40 hp four. Its promoter eventually went on to open an orange-juice cannery.

COMET • USA 1914-1915

A tandem-seated cyclecar from Indianapolis.

COMET • USA 1917-1923

Comet produced several hundred cars during its brief existence. The first cars used Lewis engines, but the company switched to Continentals thereafter. All Comet cars were six-cylinder automobiles, excepting a smaller four of which only a few were completed. Comet also built a Lycoming-powered truck. The company failed in 1922, and cars marketed as 1923 models were actually left-over 1922 units.

COMET • England 1921

"Designed by an engineer with considerable racing experience in France," this was a 1593cc sports car.

COMET • USA 1947-1948

The General Developing Co of Ridgewood, NY, built "the world's handiest run-around-in car." The three-wheeled Comet had a 41.2 hp air-cooled rear-mounted engine and a glassfiber body on a tubular frame.

COMIOT • France 1899-1904

Reversing the usual trend, Comiot of Paris imported frames and transmissions for his tricycles and quadricycles from Eadie of Redditch.

COMMANDER • USA 1922

The Commander was actually a re-emblemed Ogren automobile, the proposed Commander company being a scheme to build the basic Ogren under a different name and management. One $5,000 touring car was exhibited before the enterprise failed.

COMMERCE • USA 1922

This was a truck company which built a ten-passenger touring car during one year. Billed as a "charabanc," the Commerce open car used a Continental six-cylinder engine, sold for $2,350 and, if it looked very much like an open bus, it was certainly not considered as such by its manufacturer.

COMMODORE • USA 1921

Built only in prototype form, the Commodore was a six-cylinder assembled car with a Herschell-Spillman engine and a 124-inch wheelbase. The price for the touring car, complete with wire wheels, was quoted at $2,485.

COMMONWEALTH • USA 1917-1922

Formerly the Partin-Palmer, this was an assembled car built in Chicago, offering a complete line of open models and, for 1921, a sedan and a taxicab. With the exception of a "Victory Six" model in 1919, Commonwealth cars used four-cylinder Lycoming or Herschell-Spillman engines. The make failed in 1922. An attempt to continue the passenger-car line as a luxury make under the "Goodspeed" emblem unfortunately came to nothing. The taxicab became the Checker cab.

COMPACT • England • France 1907

Sold by the Newmobile Car Company, the Compact car had British-built engines in French-made chassis.

COMPACT • Italy 1991

This Turin company bought the rights to Giugiaro's twin-cockpit Aztec show car and was to build 50 for the Japanese market.

COMPAGNIE FRANÇAISE • FRANCE 1901-c. 1905

M Onfray's Cie Française des Cycles et Automobiles, of Paris, built a range of cars including 6 cv and 8 cv single-cylinders, and twins of 9 cv and 10 cv, at prices from Fr 4000-Fr 9500.

COMPONENTS • England 1899

Built at "Componentsville", Birmingham, these motor tricycles and quadricycles were known as "Ariels" after 1900.

COMPOUND • USA 1903-1907

The power unit of the Compound was unusual for a gasoline engine in having two high-pressure cylinders which exhausted into a central low-pressure cylinder, as on a steam engine. Made by the Eisenhuth Horseless Vehicle Company of Middletown, Connecticut, it survived only four years.

CONCORDIA • France 1903

This Parisian company offered a range of Buchet-engined cars from 10 cv to 20 cv, capable of running on gasoline or alcohol.

CONCORDIA • Canada 1977

A wedge-shaped "dream car" conceived by Ken Hill of Trebron Design as a "teaching platform" in conjunction with Concordia University. It went into production in a limited run, priced at $(Canada) 35,000-40,000.

CONDOR • Switzerland 1922

Only five Mag-engined cars (similar to the 5 cv Citroên) were built by this Courfaivre (Jura) cycle manufacturer.

LA CONFORTABLE • France c. 1920

A tiny cyclecar with a single-cylinder two-stroke Train engine of 344cc.

CONNAUGHT • England 1949-1957

Best known for its racing cars, this Send, Surrey, firm began production with a Lea-Francis-based 1767cc sports car with full-width bodywork.

1907 Continental voiturette

CONRAD • USA 1900-1904

Starting as maker of steam cars, Conrad (of Buffalo, NY) introduced a gasoline-engined range in 1903. Alfred Sloan, later head of General Motors, owned one. "It had a two-cycle engine with four cylinders ... it was a lemon."

1933 Continental Ace De Luxe Sedan

CONSTANTINESCO • England • France 1926-1928

Romanian-born engineer Georges Constantinesco made a car with a 494cc two-stroke engine of his own design (as was the torque converter which replaced the gearbox and clutch.) It never worked properly.

CONSULIER • USA c.1991 to date

A road-going version of a successful mid-engined sports racer, featured a Shellby-developed 2.2-liter turbo 1-4 power unit.

CONTINENTAL • USA 1909-1914

A four-cylinder 5539cc engine powered this tourer from Franklin, Indiana.

CONTINENTAL • USA 1933-1934

The Continental was an unsuccessful attempt by the Continental Motors Corp. to sell the De-Vaux automobile under a new name and revamped design. Built in three basic models, one four and two sixes, the "Beacon," "Flyer," and "Ace" constituted the line, with prices starting at $335. Despite the low price, attractive to the new car purchaser in the Depression, the cars did not sell and only 3,310 had been sold by 1 January 1934, when both the Flyer and Ace were dropped from the line and the four-cylinder Beacon was given a slight facelift to designate it a 1934 model. Only 983 units were sold, and the company ceased manufacture. Continentals were also sold in Canada under the Frontenac emblem.

1933 Continental Beacon Roadster

CONTINENTAL • USA 1958

An obscure do-it-yourself glassfiber sports car kit. Two models were available, the Sabre and the slightly larger Speedster, designed to fit small American or European chassis with the minimum of modification.

CONTINENTAL • USA 1956 to date

In 1956 a separate division of Ford built the Continental Mk II. The restrained chrome-free design (partly constructed by hand) was different from all others in the Ford range except for the Lincoln's 300 hp V-8 engine. Designed as a "status symbol", it cost almost $10,000. The Mk III of 1958 was a Lincoln Premiere with a different grille. For 1961 the Continental name was applied to a new range of the Lincolns and remained as such until 1968, when a separate line of Continentals reappeared. The new Mk III was mass-produced and evolved into the Mk IV in mid-1971, followed by the Mk V in 1977. The styling and RR-type grille remained almost unaltered from 1968, but the 7538cc V-8 engine was replaced by a 6555cc unit in 1979. Elaborate trim by Pucci, Cartier, or Givenchy is offered on limited versions.

COOPER • England 1909-1910

The Cooper Steam Digger Company of King's Lynn, Norfolk, built this curious four-cylinder two-stroke, the engine of which had rigid piston rods, cross-heads, and connecting rods like a steam engine, and a three-speed gearbox driving through a dual-ratio back axle. Only six were built, of which one survives.

COOPER • England 1922-1923

A 1919 three-cylinder prototype preceded limited production of 1368cc Coventry-Climax-engined light cars in Coventry.

COPE-BOHEMIAN • England 1905-1906

"The finest thing ever produced in tricars," the Cope-Bohemian was built in Manchester with 31.2 hp (air-cooled) or 41.2 hp (watercooled) single-cylinder engines or a 6 hp watercooled twin.

CORBIN • USA 1904-1912

Built in New Britain, Connecticut, the first Corbins featured an air-cooled engine. The 1906 Model G "High Powered Runabout" had a four-cylinder 24 hp engine and sold for $1,800. Corbin cars were available with watercooling as a sales option for 1908, apparently because of the sales

CORD • USA 1929-1932, 1936-1937

The first fwd car to get into serious production in America, the Cord was introduced in November 1929 by the Auburn Automobile Co of Auburn, Indiana; the third of the triumvirate of cars built by Erret Lobban Cord and designed to occupy a sales position between the Auburn and Duesenberg cars. The rakish, altogether beautiful and ahead-of-its-time Model L-29 Cord featured a 4894cc Lycoming straight-eight engine developing 125 bhp. The car's lines, strongly suggestive of the larger Duesenberg, adapted well to the car's height of only 61 inches and its 137-inch wheelbase. Four standard models comprised the Cord L-29 line, including sedan, brougham, cabriolet, and phaeton; at prices ranging from $3,095 to $3,295. In addition, two town cars were built to special order, as well as some boat-tailed speedsters. Sleek, aesthetically pleasing and powerful as the Cord L-29 was, it could not have been introduced at a more inauspicious time as the introduction coincided with the Stock Market crash. Sales, although consistent, were small. In early 1931 prices were reduced to $2,395 from $2,595, but to little avail, and the L-29 was phased out of production early in 1932 after some 4,429 cars had been built.

1937 Cord Convertible

Late in 1935 the name was revived with the modernistic Model 810, designed by Gordon Buehrig. Originally intended to be a smaller Duesenberg, a last-minute decision gave it the Cord nameplate and, like its other predecessor, it was front-wheel driven. Of a unique modernistic design, its flat hood was adorned with wraparound chromed louvres. Headlights were retractable and located in the wings. Powered by a 3547cc Lycoming V-8 engine, it developed 125 bhp at 3500 rpm and had a 125-inch wheelbase and an overall height of 58 to 60 inches. The ultra-modern car could be ordered in two sedan styles, as well as the two-seater "Sportsman" and four-seater convertible sedan-phaeton. In 1937 the 810 gave way to the 812, which featured a supercharger, upping the horsepower to 195! Added to the 812 line was a custom berline with glass division and lengthened wheelbase. Prices of the 1936-1937 Cord ranged from $1,995 for the 1936 sedan to $3,575 for the supercharged 812 berline. Only 2,320 810 and 812 Cord automobiles were made. The design, cited for its beauty by the Museum of Modern Art in New York City, was subsequently sold first to Hupp and finally to Graham; and the last models of these two cars closely resembled the Cord in appearance. Since then at least three different concerns have built Cord replicas.

1931 Cord L29 Sedan

resistance to air-cooling. The 1908 30 hp six cost $2,650 if air-cooled, $2,500 watercooled.

CORBITT • USA 1912-1913

A four-cylinder tourer built in Henderson, North Carolina.

CORD • USA 1964-1973

Glenn Pray of Tulsa, Oklahoma, made a plastic-bodied replica of the 1936 Cord which incorporated a Corvair flat-six air-cooled engine to drive the front wheels. In 1968 the third owners of the marque (it had gone to Philadelphia for a year) changed to rear-wheel drive, a Ford engine, a glassfiber body and fixed headlights. Production was spasmodic.

CORD • USA 1929-1932, 1936-1937

See panel

CORINTHIAN • USA 1922-1923

The Corinthian car was built in two sizes, a 130-inch-wheelbase Wisconsin-engined series with a touring car priced at $5,000 and a similar body style with a 110-inch wheelbase at $985, powered by Herschell-Spillman. Very few of either model were produced.

CORNELIAN • USA 1914-1915

This cyclecar, built by components manufacturer Blood Brothers of Alleghan, Michigan, had all-round independent suspension by double transverse springs.

CORNILLEAU • France 1910-1914

Cornilleau first showed at the 1910 Paris Salon. The company's offerings were two four-cylinder models, one of 4942cc, the other of 2001cc.

CORNILLEAU-STE BEUVE • France 1905-1909

Cornilleau's 16-24 cv four had engine and gearbox mounted as a unit in an aluminum casing which had side shields to keep the engine compartment clean. Well engineered and designed for ease of maintenance, the CSB was also built in England by Straker-Squire.

CORNU • France 1905-1908

Paul Cornu, designer of one of the first helicopters, built this curious voiturette with a complex tubular chassis and a separate single-cylinder engine, driving each rear wheel direct by belt, without any form of gear-change. The brake was actuated by the exhaust gas.

1905 16 hp Coronet tonneau

CORONA • Germany 1905-1909

Corona cars, built by a well-known bicycle and motorcycle factory at Brandenburg, were made under Maurer license and had friction drive. Maurer were also responsible for supplying the 1470cc single-cylinder 8 hp and 1526cc twin-cylinder 11 hp engines.

CORONA • France 1920

This was the first straight-12, with a pushrod ohv engine of 7238cc. A five-year guarantee was offered, but it is probable that no Coronas were sold.

CORONA • England 1920-1923

The two-seater Corona used a 9 hp flat-twin engine by Bovier, though in 1923 a 9.8 hp four-cylinder Coventry-Climax power unit was offered.

CORONET • England 1904-1906

Designed by MMC engineer George Iden's son Walter, these cars (8 hp single, 12 hp twin, 16 hp four) were built from British and French components in Coventry.

CORRE • France 1908-1914

In 1908 J Corré left the Corré-La Licorne company and built voiturettes of 8 hp, 10 hp and 12 hp under the "Corré" or "JC" marque at Rueil (Seine-et-Oise.)

CORREJA • USA 1908-1915

A shaft-driven 40 hp four (5808cc) built by Vandewater & Co of Iselin, NJ.

CORRE-LA LICORNE • France 1899-1950

The Société Française des Automobiles Corré was founded in 1901 in Levallois, and started production with motor tricycles and quadricycles. Various cars with proprietary engines were made until 1906. Until then the cars were sold under the name of Corré. When M Corré left the factory the name was changed to Corré-La Licorne. The range was then a twin-cylinder (1727cc) and a 15-20 hp four (2544cc). The old single-cylinder De Dion-engined 8 hp model of 942cc was in production until 1912 but, after that date, all Corré vehicles had four-cylinder engines. No fewer than nine models were available in 1914, from the 7 hp to 25 hp.

After the war Corré-La Licorne moved to Neuilly, and the first new model, presented in 1919, had a sv Ballot engine of 1244cc. During the 1920s the main models were the Ballot-engined 9-12 cv (1692cc) and the 12-15 cv (2997cc) and the SCAP-engined 8-10 cv (1393cc). A 1492cc six was offered in 1927, and raced with success. La Licorne, bolstered in decline by the 5 cv (905cc) and the 8 cv (1450cc), moved to Courbevoie and made some conventional front-engined, rear-wheel-drive cars using the fwd Citroên body. At the outbreak of the war two new cars, a 6 cv and an 8 cv, were made, but it was too late. After a prototype had been shown at the Paris Show in 1949 the works closed for ever.

A sporting 1924 Corré-La Licorne

M. Cottereau"s family with his 1901 range

COSMOS • England 1906-1907

A "do-it-yourself" chassis to which the purchaser could choose to fit an 8 hp or 10 hp engine.

COSMOS (CAR) • England 1919-1920

Roy Fedden, later of the Bristol Aeroplane Company, was responsible for the design of the three-cylinder radial rear-engined Cosmos. (A theme he returned to later with the experimental Fedden of the Second World War years.) The square (3x3 inch) engine was also available in the CAR, though with 1/4 inch greater bore and stroke.

COSTIN • England 1968-1972

The name of engineer/designer Frank Costin has been linked with many projects. The Costin Amigo featured a plywood monocoque body/chassis unit, as first seen on the Marcos, with mainly glassfiber panels. Seven were made, with all but one being Vauxhall-powered.

COTAY • USA 1920-1921

The Cotay (the name was an acronym of its builder, the Coffyn-Taylor Motor Co of New York City) was a sporting car built as a two-seater roadster only. It featured a four-cylinder air-cooled engine by Cameron, disc wheels and a wheelbase of 105 inches. Few were built.

COTE • France 1908-1913

Cote built a 3 hp voiturette in 1900. Its 1908-13 range consisted of two-stroke two- and four-cylinder-engined cars of up to 16-28 hp.

COTTEREAU • France 1898-1910

The original Cottereaus were known as "voiturines," and their hill climbing powers were "a revelation."Then in 1902 Cottereau of Dijon listed a 5 cv single-cylinder voiturette and tubular-chassis 7 cv and 10 cv vee-twins. The "irréprochable" tonneau riche" cost Fr 8000. There was also a 16 cv straight-four of 3191cc. The company was reorganized in 1906; its 15 hp four was described as "la plus chic voiture". There were also two singles, a twin, two threes, and another four. By 1910 the firm was experimenting with rotary-valve fours and sixes. From 1911 the marque was known as "CID."

COTTIN-DESGOUTTES • France 1905-1933

Cottin et Desgouttes of Lyon made many interesting cars from 1905. The best were the 9500cc six-cylinder of 1904, the four-cylinder series made from 1906 to 1914 using four different engines, and the 1908 six of 3619cc. After the war Cottin-Desgouttes recommenced production with one model, the 14-16 cv (3216cc), promptly followed by a 18-20 cv (4071cc,) and a 23-25 cv (5026cc). In 1924 a new range of cars appeared, with ohv engines of 2613cc, as well as the famous 2986cc three-valves-per-cylinder model; the latter sometimes presented in a racing "Grand Prix" version. In 1926 came the 2613cc "Sans Secousses" model with independent suspension all round. The last Cottin-Desgouttes was a 3813cc sv six. Having always made luxury cars, Cottin-Desgouttes were victims of the Depression.

COUDERE • France 1907

A single-cylinder voiturette which won its class in the 1907 Evreux Trials.

COURIER • France 1906-1908

The 18-24 hp Courier had a Gnome engine. A major selling point of this model was its makers" claim that a Courier car "had been driven 8,000 miles by a lady without any

M. Cottin in a 1907 Cottin-Desgouttes

mechanical trouble." There was also a 10-12 hp twin-cylinder Courier.

COURIER • USA 1909-1913

Related to the Stoddard-Dayton, this was a cheaper model with a 3245cc four-cylinder engine. From 1912 a 3638cc four was used, and the cars were then known as Courier-Clermont.

COURIER • USA 1922-1924

Lineal descendant of the Maibohm, the Courier was built in Sandusky, Ohio, and featured full-pressure lubrication. Using a Falls six-cylinder engine, the 116-inch wheelbase Courier was noted for its trim, sporty lines,with closed models carrying cowl lights resembling small carriage lamps. Probably 1,000 were produced before the firm failed in 1924.

COUTERET • France 1907

A fwd voiturette from Paris.

COUVERCHEL • France 1905-1907

Known as CVR following a move to Boulogne-sur-Seine from Neuilly in 1906, this firm offered cars from 12/16 hp to a 40-50 hp six.

COVENTRY MOTETTE • England 1896-1897

An Anglicized version of the Bollée voiturette, built in Coventry.

COVENTRY-PREMIER • England 1919-1923

The original Coventry-Premier was a three-wheeled vehicle, powered by a watercooled twin-cylinder engine. However, following a takeover by Singer in 1920 it acquired a fourth wheel and, the following year, a Singer Ten engine.

1921 Coventry-Premier three-wheeler

1920 16-valve Craig Hunt

COVENTRY-VICTOR • England 1926-1938

The three-wheeler chain-driven Coventry-Victor naturally used its own proprietary engine, a side-valve flat-twin of 688cc. The make lingered on until 1938, by which time 850cc, 90cc, and 1100cc engines were available.

COVERT • USA 1901-1907

Byron V Covert of Lockport, NY, started in 1901 building steam cars, then went on to light De Dion-engined runabouts which were subsequently then exported to England and renamed Covert-Jacksons.

1903 8 hp Covert

COWEY • England 1913-1915

With a 10 hp Chapius-Dornier engine and friction drive, the Cowey from Kew, Surrey, was distinguished by pneumatic suspension with automatic levelling.

COX • England 1967 to date

The Cox GTM (Grand Touring Mini) went on sale in kit form in 1967 for £330, requiring only Mini mechanical parts to complete it. A stumpy car with glassfiber body and strong backbone chassis, the GTM had rearmounted Mini power. Built initially under the Cox and latterly just the GTM banner.

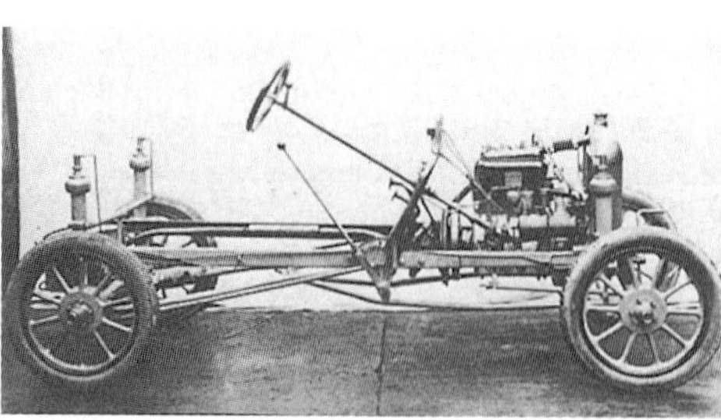

The chassis of the 1913 air-sprung Cowey

COYOTE • USA 1909-1910

A sporty 50 hp eight-cylinder model from Redondo Beach, California.

CRAIG-DORWALD (AILSA CRAIG) • England c. 1902-c. 1906

Some 12 cars of differing designs were built by this Putney engineering firm, starting with a single-speed 8 hp. Most used a two-cylinder Craig-Dôrwald marine engine of 3539cc or four-cylinder derivative (an uprated "50 hp" four was used in a 1904 barouche for the Earl of Norbury). Marine engines were the company's forte. In 1904 it built a 12,127cc ohc six and a 150 bhp V-12 of 21,234cc.

CRAIG-HUNT • USA 1920

Although the "Sixteen Valves" Craig-Hunt was widely advertised in the automotive press, probably only one pilot model was made. This "Character Car" resembled the Model T Ford in outward appearance, but had a conventional transmission.

CRAIG-TOLEDO • USA 1906-c. 1907

A $4,000 three-passenger runabout.

CRANE • USA 1912-1915

Forerunner of the Crane-Simplex, this was a 9226cc four priced at $8,000 in chassis form.

CRANE & BREED • USA 1912-1917

A 48 hp six was the 1912 offering from this Cincinnati

1917 Crane-Simplex six-cylinder

A surviving 1922 Crawford

company, which after this date built mostly ambulances and hearses.

CRANE-SIMPLEX • USA 1915-1917, 1922-1924

One of the most prestigious and expensive cars built in America, Crane-Simplex (correctly, Simplex-Crane Model 5) produced about 500 chassis between its organization in 1915 and the First World War, when its factory was converted to war production. An enormous car, this successor to the earlier Simplex sported a six-cylinder engine with a displacement of 9238cc and a wheelbase of 1431.2 inches. The $10,000 chassis carried coachwork from such custom body builders as Brewster, Holbrook, Quimby, and Kimball, and the car boasted 100 bhp at 1800 rpm. Following the First World War, Crane-Simplex, along with Locomobile and Mercer, was absorbed by Hare's Motors. Plans were announced in 1922 that a new Crane-Simplex would be made at the Locomobile plant in Bridgeport, Connecticut. Although the company technically existed, no cars were forthcoming.

CRAWFORD • USA 1905-1923

The Crawford was a highly regarded small-production car built in Hagerstown, Maryland. It was chain-driven until 1907, with transaxles featured on the 1911-1914 models. Later cars had brass trim, disc-covered wooden artillery wheels, and Continental six-cylinder engines. The Crawford interests were eventually purchased by the M P Moller Pipe Organ Co of Hagerstown, which brought out a sporting version of the Crawford in 1922, called the Dagmar. The last Crawfords were sold in 1923, but Dagmar continued until 1927.

CRAWSHAY-WILLIAMS • England 1904-1906

Four-cylinder Simms engines of 14-16 hp and 20-24 hp powered these handsome chain-driven cars.

CREANCHE • France 1899-c. 1905

In 1898 a Créanche tricycle won the Coupe des Motocycles; the following year a voiturette won the Louga-St Petersburg race. A Créanche electric car took first place in the 1899 Criterium des Voitures Électriques. The 1902 Créanche gasoline cars (6 cv, 9 cv, 12 cv) were De Dion-engined. The two larger cars were based on the Chenard-Walcker, while the smaller was a carbon copy of the De Dion Populaire.

CREMORNE • England 1903-1904

A steam car with a 25 hp horizontal four-cylinder engine, "designed and constructed for solid rubber tyres."

CRESCENT • USA 1900

This tiller-steered "tri-moto" from the Western Wheel Works of Chicago had a single-cylinder engine driving the single front wheel.

CRESCENT • England 1913-1915

Birmingham-built cyclecars of 8.96 hp and 9 hp.

CRESCENT • USA 1914-1915

A conventional four-cylinder tourer from Cincinnati. The 1915 Crescents had either a 40 hp Northway four or a 60 hp six. Bodies were patterned on the Lancia.

CRESPELLE • France 1906-1924

M Crespelle made his first cars with De Dion and Aster single-cylinder engines of 1694cc and 2199cc. These were followed by cars with 2982cc Janvier four-cylinder engines. After the First World War Crespelle used various four-cylinder Sergant engines; 1593cc, 2121cc, and 2413cc. Before it closed in 1924 it also listed a 1327cc four. After production ceased Crespelle remained in business making special ohv "conversion kits" for production side-valve engines.

CREST • CRESTMOBILE • USA 1899-1905

Crest, of Cambridge, Mass, was an engine manufacturer building single-cylinder 21.4 hp and flat-twin 4 hp air-cooled engines on De Dion lines.

CREWFORD • England 1920-1921

Largely made of Model T parts, the Crewford used an underslung T chassis and Ford engine. Two- and four-seaters were offered.

CRICKET • USA 1914-1915

The engine of this Detroit-built cyclecar was on the running board, driving the right rear wheel.

CRIPPS • England 1913

A cyclecar with a watercooled JAP vee twin.

CRITCHLEY-NORRIS • England 1906-1908

A limited production of 40 hp Crossley-engined chain-drive cars was undertaken by this Lancashire bus builder.

CROMPTON • England 1914-1915

An aggressively pointed JAP-engined cyclecar, available as a monocar or two-seater.

CROSLEY • USA 1939-1952

Radio pioneer Powel Crosley's first small cars had a 580cc twin-cylinder engine but, in 1946, he returned to production in Marion, Indiana, using the Cobra (*CO*pper *BRA*zed) sheet-steel engine, a 721cc four, originally developed for US Navy generators. In 1949 it was succeeded by the

1950 Crosley Hotshot

1904 22/28 hp Crossley

CROSSLEY • England 1904-1937

Crossley of Manchester made four-stroke gas engines in the latter quarter of the 19th century, so it was only natural that it should turn to motor car manufacture. Its first model was a 22 hp four-cylinder car, while an even larger 40 hp model appeared in 1906. A later variation was a 20 hp model which developed into the long-lived 20-25. After 1910 new 12 and 15 hp cars appeared. The latter model and the 25 hp car saw sterling service in the First World War, the Manchester firm being one of the few manufacturers to continue production throughout the hostilities. The faithful and uprated 25-30 continued in production until 1926, although the first new model of the decade was the 3.8-liter 19.9 hp, which was available until 1925. That year saw the arrival of the company's first six, the 18-50, which replaced the 25-30. Two years later its capacity was increased from 2.2 to 3.2 liters. Further six-cylinder models followed, the 2-liter in 1928 and the 20.9 hp Super Six of 1931. A sign of the times, however, was the Ten of 1932, with a Coventry-Climax overhead inlet/side exhaust engine of 11000cc. Three years later came the Regis range of smaller cars, a Ten and 11.2-liter six-cylinder with engines also by Coventry-Climax. They failed to save the company, and private car production stopped in 1937, although commercial vehicles were produced until 1956.

1912 15 hp Crossley chassis on test

15 hp Crossley, c. 1913

Crossley 18/50 hp six, c. 1928

more reliable CIBA cast-iron unit. The 1949 Crosleys were America's first disc-braked production cars, although the discs – prone to road salt damage – were replaced by drums in 1950. Four models were available; a two-door-sedan, a station wagon, a convertible and the nippy Hotshot roadster, which won the Performance Index at Sebring in 1950, and nearly won its class in the 1951 Le Mans 24 Hour Race. A Super Sports Roadster appeared in 1951, but sales had fallen to 4,839 from the 1948 peak of 24,871, and Powel Crosley, having sunk $3 million into the venture, ended it in 1952 after only 1,522 Crosleys had been sold that year.

CROSSLEY • England 1904-1937

See panel

CROSSLAND STEAM CAR • USA 1923

This twin-cylinder steamer presumably existed only in prototype form. Specifications cite a 125-inch wheelbase and disc wheels, with the touring car priced at $1,985.

CROUAN • France 1897-1904

A 6 bhp horizontal twin, the 1903 Crouan car was endowed with five speeds forward and reverse, and the column-mounted gear lever also controlled the throttle!

1903 Crouan

8 hp Crouch vee-twin, c. 1922

CROUCH • USA 1899-1900

W Lee Crouch, of New Brighton, Pa, built a handlebar-steered steam carriage, as well as the gasoline engine for the car built by Doctor Booth of Youngstown, Ohio. Production was centerd on Baltimore. From the spring of 1900 these cars were known as "Columbia."

CROUCH • England 1912-1928

The chain-driven three-wheeler 8 hp Crouch Carette was the first offering from this Coventry firm although, in 1913, a fourth wheel was added. The year 1922 saw the appearance of a front-mounted vee-twin (the first engine had been centrally mounted) with shaft final drive. The following year a four-cylinder Anzani engine was offered.

CROWDEN • England 1898-1901

Formerly the manager of the Great Horseless Carriage Co., Charles T Crowden invented the chain-geared front-driving cycle and had early experience with steam tramcars and fire engines. The dog-cart, which he built in his works at Leamington Spa, had a 5 hp single-cylinder engine and three-speed belt transmission. In 1899 Crowden also built a steam shooting brake.

CROWDUS • USA 1901-1903

An obscure make of electric runabout built in Chicago, with speed control and braking operated by the steering tiller.

1910 Croxton-Keeton 40hp tourer

CROWDY • England 1910-1911

Crowdy took over Weigel in 1910, and continued the 20-30 hp and 30-40 hp Weigels under their own name. To these it added a 19-24 hp four and 29-34 hp six, aimed at "the seeker after rational practical progress," with Cooper-Hewitt piston-valve engines and dashboard radiators. A curious body, the "Canadian Canoe," with a driver's seat adjustable for height and rake, was a feature of these cars (and of another Hewitt-engined car, the Davy.)

CROW-ELKHART • USA 1909-1924

The first Crow-Elkharts were 30 hp fours, the company's first six appearing in 1915 for $2,250. Pricing policy changed totally in 1916, when the 19.6 hp Crow-Elkhart cost only $750 in its cheapest form. Six-cylinder engines reappeared in 1919, this 4078cc model surviving until 1921, when production reverted to four-cylinder cars only. Some Crow-Elkharts were sold by Black under the name "Black Crow." About 100 were built in Ontario in 1916-18, known as the "Canadian Crow."

CROWN • England 1903

A 5 hp light three-wheeled car sold by a Holborn, London, firm.

CROXTED • England 1904-1905

Built in Herne Hill, South London, the Croxted car was available with either a 10 hp engine or a 14 hp four-cylinder power unit.

CROXTON-KEETON • USA 1909-1910

A brief-lived partnership between H A Croxton of Jewel and F M Keeton produced the 40 hp Jewel-based "German-type" and the dashboard-radiatored "French-type" Croxton-Keetons. The latter continued as "Croxton" until 1914, with four- and six-cylinder engines.

CRYPTO-DUPRESSOIR • England 1906-1906

In 1905 there were two models of this assembled car, a De Dion-engined 8 hp single and a 10-12 hp with a two-cylinder Tony Huber engine. The 1906 twin-cylinder 8-10 hp Crypto-Dupressoir used a Bentall engine.

CSONKA • Hungary 1909-1912

This Budapest commercial vehicle works also built a few single-cylinder private cars with two-seater bodies and circular radiators.

LA CUADRA • Spain 1898-1903

Artillery captain Emilio de la Cuadra began by building electric cars in his Barcelona factory. Then, on a visit to Paris, he met Swiss engineer Marc Birkigt, who designed first a gasoline omnibus for La Cuadra, and then a twin-cylinder car of 1101cc with shaft final drive. Few were built before lack of finance closed the factory.

CUBITT • England 1920-1925

The Cubitt was intended for mass-production along American lines. The engine was an orthodox 2.8-liter four with four-speed gearbox and worm drive. The cheaply made body did little to enhance the vehicle's rather hefty appearance, and the company later concentrated on making AC engines under license.

1921 Cubitt 15.9 hp tourer

CUDELL • Germany 1899-1908

The first Cudells had De Dion engines but, from 1904 onwards own-make engines were used. Cudell was one of the pioneers in Germany and used single-cylinder engines of 402cc, 860cc, and 942cc before the introduction of the Karl Slevogt-designed "Phoenix" models; large 6100cc four-cylinders developing 45 hp at 1400 rpm. Few of these were actually built, but a 2554cc four-cylinder of advanced design and excellent finish sold in large numbers. Experiments with new designs brought Max Cudell into financial difficulties. After 1905 the remains of the company were transferred from Aachen to Berlin, where Cudell's son Paul continued on a very small scale.

CUMBRIA • England 1913-1914

The Cockermouth-built Cumbria light car was available in two models, a 964cc 8 hp twin-cylinder and a 1107cc 10 hp four.

CUNNINGHAM • USA 1907-1937

One of the most prestigious automobiles ever made in the USA, the Cunningham car initially appeared on the motoring scene as an electric in 1907. The manufacturer was the renowned carriage-building firm of James Cunningham Son & Co. Inc of Rochester, New York, which had been in business since 1842. The first electrics were quickly succeeded by gasoline motor cars – assembled cars in the truest sense, with four – and six-cylinder types using engines by Continental as well as Cunningham's own four. After 1910 Cunningham began building cars from its own components and, for five years, these were assembled alongside horse-drawn carriages; the latter being discontinued in 1915. By 1916 the Cunningham had become considerably larger and more powerful, with a new V-8 engine, and much more expensive. Pleasure cars were built, along with some funeral vehicles and ambulances, which had a reputation second to none. In its halcyon years, 1917 to 1927, the Cunningham car occupied an enviable (if small) position in the American luxury car market, competing with such names as the American Rolls-Royce, largest McFarlan, Stevens-Duryea, Pierce-Arrow, Locomobile 48, and Packard Twin-Six. Prices on closed Cunninghams frequently exceeding $10,000. The company used its own coachwork almost exclusively, and quality was maintained up to the end of manufacture although, by 1931, the Cunningham was regarded by many as an anachronism. The last Cunninghams were built in 1931, although several of these were sold in 1932 and designated 1932 models. Cunningham then concentrated on its hearse and ambulance business, but continued to build an ever-increasing number of bodies for other chassis. The company also produced a number of town-car bodies for use on Ford V-8 chassis, the last of these being made in 1937. It survives to this day as a manufacturer of crossbar switches.

12 hp twin-cylinder Cudell, 1903

CUNNINGHAM • USA 1951-1955

Wealthy sportsman Briggs Cunningham's prototype C-1 sports car, produced in 1951, had a tubular chassis and was powered by Chrysler's new hemi-head V-8. This was closely followed by the C-2R in open and closed body styles, with the engine output boosted from 180 to 300 bhp. Three C-2Rs competed at Le Mans in 1951, but engine trouble put paid to their chances. The vastly improved C-4R, driven by Cunningham himself, came fourth in the 1952 Le Mans, and the torsion-bar-suspended C-5R came third overall the next year, with C-4Rs seventh and tenth. A 16-valve Offenhauser four powered the unsuccessful 1955 Le Mans contender, the C-6R. Cunningham, spending $50,000 annually on his Le Mans attempts, called it a day. There was a production Cunningham car, too, the Michelotti-designed C-3 coupé, with automatic transmission and a 220 bhp hemi. There was also a 200 bhp road-going C-4.

CURRAN STEAM CAR • USA 1923

Curran was a builder of commercial vehicles, and only two steam touring cars were made, using a three-cylinder motor and carrying a wheelbase of 128 inches.

CURTIS • USA 1921

A little-known Arkansas car, the Curtis used a Herschell-Spillman four-cylinder engine. Few were made.

CURTISS • USA 1920-1921

The Curtiss was a sporting car made in very limited numbers (perhaps as few as two) using a converted Curtiss OX-5 V-8 aero engine and a Phianna chassis. The car was made at Hammondsport, New York.

1899 Cyrano car from Bergerac

The curious 1921 Cyclauto

CUSSET • France 1896

Built at Levallois-Perret, this car had a single-cylinder horizontal engine with forced induction provided by a "compressing cylinder." The first supercharger, perhaps.

CUTTING • USA 1909-1912

Successor to the CVI, the Cutting 40 was a shaft-drive four selling for $1,650. A stripped chassis covered 200 miles at 65.75 mph in a race at Indianapolis in May 1910.

CVI • USA 1907-1908

Designed by Charles D Cutting, the first 6178cc CVI "Cutting Six" was completed in February 1907. The factory at Jackson, Michigan, built only some 50 roadsters and tourers annually.

CWS • Poland 1922-1929

A 3-liter four built in Warsaw, equipped with four-wheel brakes.

CYCAR • England 1920

A E Parnacott of Penge in Kent, motor agent and prolific correspondent to the light-car press, offered this 11.9 hp two/three-seater, claiming it to be "proof against road shocks and guaranteed to run 50 miles per gallon.."

CYCLAUTO • France 1919-1923

A small three-wheeled cyclecar made at Suresnes by the Compagnie Française du Cyclauto. The engine was at the front of the tubular cycle-style frame, and the car was driven by the back axle. The first engine was a two-stroke twin-cylinder SICAM of 497cc, and they then used four-cylinder sv Ruby engines of 903cc and 950cc.

CYCLOMOBILE • USA 1920

A small car with a vee-twin Spacke air-cooled engine and a 90-inch wheelbase, the Cyclo-mobile was marketed as a two-passenger wire-wheeled roadster at $425. The dummy radiator was the car's gasoline tank. The 1921 Manexall was a development of this vehicle.

CYKLON • Germany 1902-1929

Cyklon of Berlin was a pioneer motorcycle producer and, with its Cyklonette (1902-1922), also a leading manufacturer of three-wheelers. Its final product was an 1825cc car, nearly identical to a similar Dixi model which also had components in common with some other factories, including NSU, that were then controlled by the Schapiro concern. For this concern Cyklon also built, from 1923 to 1927, a very popular 1300cc four-cylinder 20 hp car with a sv engine. The bodywork was made by Schebera, another factory belonging to Schapiro, which was also closely connected with Benz. The French Zedel works supplied some engines to Cyklon.

CYRANO • France 1899

A voiturette built under Elie Lacoste patents at Bergerac by Richard Popp, similar in appearance to that built by Lorenz Popp in Basle, Switzerland. It had a twin-cylinder engine with belt drive, and two- or four-seater vis-à-vis coachwork.

1919/20 Cunningham phaeton Model V-3

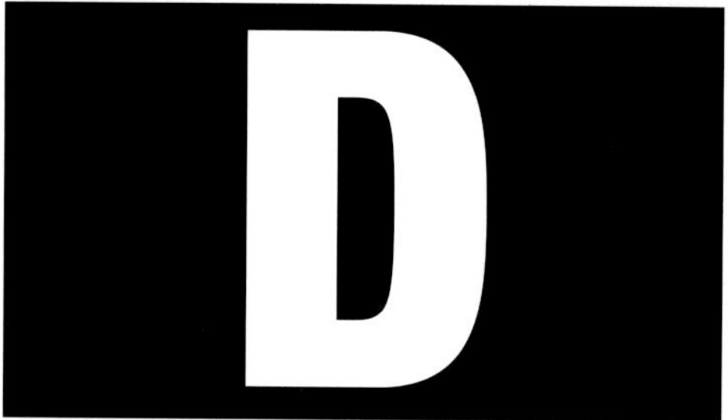

DAC • USA 1922-1923

Prototypes only were made of the V-6 Detroit air-cooled car. Featuring an own-make 2553cc engine, the car was mounted on a 115-inch wheelbase chassis. The list price of the touring car was $1,250.

DAEWOO • Korea 1980 to date

A new name from Korea, the Daewoo company is a massive industrial concern building components for everything from ships to cookers, computers and airliners. A home produced Daewoo for the Korean market was based on GM mechanicals, and it was no surprise that, when it wished to expand overseas, the company bought the rights to produce recently replaced models from the Vauxhall-Opel arm of the GM parts bin.

Entering the Australian and then British markets, Daewoo's first export cars were mildly facelifted versions of the old Astra-Kadett ranges, with revised trim but carried-over tooling, drive trains, and engines. Although these cars, named Nexia, were neither ancient nor brand new in design terms, they were solid and faithful; certainly not decades behind the times like some of the Soviet bloc imports in the bargain basement market sectors. What was different, however, was the way Daewoo sold its cars, cutting out the dealer and creating its own network of outlets. Fixed prices and set deals, allied to a long warranty with a free replacement car, proved very attractive to a certain type of particularly British buyer, but caused angst among the more traditional car sellers.

The marque introduced its own body designed, top-of-the-range, Espero model, based on the previous model GM Cavalier floorpan. Having established such a foothold, the company went on to create its own brand new models, with styling input from Ital Design. In 1998/9 the elegant and well equipped Leganza model sold well in Europe. In five short years Daewoo has become a success and now produces state-of-the-art cars. In 1999 it took over the ailing Ssanyong brand and rebadges their Musso and Korrando models as Daewoos, complete with the Daewoo corporate grille added.

Daewoo Nubira CDX four-door, 1999

1991 Daihatsu Fourtrak Estate 2.8 TDZ

DACIA • Romania 1968 to date

The Renault-derived Dacia is fastest – 99 mph - in its 1.4 diesel estate guise, which says quite a lot about the marque. More recent is the 500cc Dacia 500 mini car.

DAF • Holland 1958-1975

Truck and trailer maker at Eindhoven, DAF introduced a twin-cylinder 600cc car, the 'Daffodil,' with 'Variomatic' belt drive at the 1958 Amsterdam Show. A 750cc development, the '33,' appeared in 1962, followed in 1967 by the Michelotti-styled 850cc '44.' A four-cylinder 1100cc Renault engine was used on the '55' of 1968. A sports version appeared in 1969. Volvo of Sweden took a share in, and eventually control of, DAF after a 1974 reorganization. DAF's largest model, the 1300cc Marathon, formed the basis of a new model built as a Volvo.

DAGMAR • USA 1922-1927

Some of the sportiest-looking automobiles of their time, the first Dagmar cars, a spin-off of the Crawford of Hagerstown, Maryland, featured disc-covered artillery wheels, brass trim and straight 'military' wings. Generally painted in pastel colors, the cars were produced in two sizes, featuring Continental or Lycoming six-cylinder engines. Several hundred Dagmars were manufactured. The make also acted as a base model for both the Standish automobile and the Luxor taxicab.

DAGSA • Spain 1957-1959

Defensa Antigas SA of Segovia built this 500cc saloon car, also available as a pickup.

DAIHATSU • Japan 1954 to date

Starting with the 540cc Bee three-wheeler, Daihatsu introduced its first four-wheeler in 1963, the 797cc Compagno, and added a fuel-injected 958cc model in 1967. A 360cc minicar was also offered. In 1969 came the Consorte range, still in production ten years later, with 958cc and 1166cc engines. The 'Fellow Max,' a 550cc flat-four, appeared in 1970 and, in 1974, came the Charmont, with 1166cc and 1407cc power units. Expanding overseas, notably in third-world markets, Daihatsu made a name for

1893 Cannstatt-Daimler (Chicago World Fair Exhibit)

itself with small, cheap, lightweight cars of low capacity. In the 1980s it created its own sub-compact type niche in several markets with the Charade and Curore models, and expanded into the fwd market with the FourTrak model. 1999 saw the launch of the cute Terios model, a miniaturised MPV type fwd with youth appeal.

DAIMLER • Germany 1889-1902

In 1885 Gottlieb Daimler, one of the great motoring pioneers, built his first (and last!) motorcycle, fitted an engine to a carriage in 1886 and, in 1889, completed the 'Steel-wheeler,' with a 566cc vee-twin engine, designed by his assistant Wilhelm Maybach. He exhibited this car at the 1889 Paris World Exhibition and sold a production license to Levassor. 1890 saw the foundation of the Daimler Motoren Gesellschaft at Cannstatt (now part of Stuttgart). Daimler then introduced his 1060cc two-cylinder belt-driven car, succeeded in 1897 by the 5507cc four-cylinder Phoenix sports and racing car. This attracted the Consul-General of the Austro-Hungarian Empire at Nice, the wealthy Emil Jellinek, who influenced Maybach to design a lower-built, lighter car, which Jellinek named after his elder daughter, Mercédés. This appeared in 1901, shortly after Daimler's death. Mercedes cars soon showed their supremacy, even over a new car designed by Daimler's son, Paul, which was built at the Austrian Daimler factory at Wiener Neustadt.

DAIMLER • England 1897 to date

See panel

DAIMLER-MERCEDES (BRITISH-MERCEDES) • England 1907-1908

The British & Colonial Daimler-Mercedes Syndicate of London commissioned these license-built copies of the contemporary Mercedes from the Yorkshire Engine Company, locomotive engineers in Sheffield. Two models were available, a 35 hp four of 5322cc and a 50/60 hp six (7893cc). They differed from their prototype in mechanical detail, such as the use of a disc clutch instead of the famous Mercedes scroll clutch, and were considerably cheaper. The chassis price of the 35 hp was £680, against £1,010 for the comparable Mercedes. About 50 Daimler-Mercedes were built before the sales company's refusal to pay further royalties brought a lawsuit which ended the project.

DAIMLER • England 1897 to date

Floated in 1896 by H J Lawson, Daimler of Coventry began production a year later with a 4 hp two-cylinder car based on the Panhard. One of these was the first car to travel from John O'Groats to Land's End. Over the next five years a complex range of two- and four-cylinder cars was turned out under the aegis of J S Critchley, and these were succeeded in 1902 by a three-car line-up designed by Edmund Lewis. One of the first buyers of the new 22 hp model was King Edward VII, whose purchase of a 6 hp in 1900 had marked the start of a long Royal patronage for Daimler. Up to 1908 fours and sixes of 3.3 to 10.4 litres were produced. Daimler then exchanged performance for refinement with the adoption of the Knight sleeve-valve engine. A merger with BSA in 1910 saw some rationalization of the two ranges.

Post-war Daimlers, launched in November 1919, were two 30 hp models and a 'special' 45 hp. Four-wheel brakes were standardized in 1924, as were thinner sleeve-valves for greater power outputs. Four "57 hp" Daimlers were built for King George V that year. In 1926 Daimler"s chief engineer, Laurence Pomeroy, designed the complex "Double-Six," a sleeve-valve V-12. He also introduced, in 1930, the Fluid Flywheel which, combined with the Wilson preselector gearbox, gave a simplicity of control unrivalled until the advent of automatics. Sleeve-valves were phased out in the mid-1930s. Pomeroy introduced a 4.6-liter poppet-valve straight-eight in 1936, soon joined by three straight-sixes; although a few prestige poppet-valve V-12s were also built. Coil-spring independent front suspension appeared in the late 1930s on Daimler and the company's sister marque, Lanchester, acquired in 1931.

The post-war range, DB18 2.5-liter and DE27 4.1-liter sixes and 5.5-liter eight, was based on pre-war designs. A 3-liter six appeared in 1950, and a four-cylinder variant, used in a new Lanchester 14, formed the basis of the 1953 Daimler Conquest. A performance version, the 100 bhp Conquest Century, was current from 1954 to 1958. Also launched in 1953 was the 3-liter Regency, developed through a 3.5-liter version into the 3.8-liter Majestic of 1958, and Majestic Major 4.5-liter of 1960. In 1960 Jaguar bought Daimler and, thereafter, the marque (apart from specialist models like the glassfibre-bodied SP 250 sports designed by Edward Turner) was largely based on contemporary Jaguar bodies and running gear, although the pre-merger engines were used for a number of years. A V-12 Jaguar engine powered Daimler's 1973 Double-Six, while the limousine had a 4.2-liter XK power unit.

The Series 3 Sovereign, Vanden Plas and 4.2 were identical to the Jaguar XJ6 bar grille and trim. Since 1986 six-cylinder Daimlers have shared the "XJ40" style body with Jaguar and use the 3.6-liter twin-cam AJ6 engine. The Double Six models still use the classic Series 3 bodyshell, while a V-12 engine installation is developed for the new shape. In 1991 Daimler ceased building the Limousine after 23 years.

The Hon. John Scott-Montagu's 1899 12hp Daimler: the passenger is Edward VII, then Prince of Wales

Classic post war Daimler Dart (top,) 1950 Daimler DB 18 Special Sports Drophead Coupé (center left,) 1977 Daimler Sovereign 3.4 (center right.) 1946 Daimler DB-18 2½ litre (left)

DALE • USA 1974

A twin-cylinder three-wheeler claiming to incorporate "space-age technology," the Dale was a confidence trick perpetrated by a female impersonator, who persuaded investors to part with $3 million in deposits. The Dale was confected from Toyota and VW parts with a glassfiber body and a generator engine.

DALIFOL • France 1896

A horizontal-engined gasoline car from a firm better known for its steam motorcycles.

DALIFOL & THOMAS • France 1898-1899

Two separate De Dion engines powered this voiturette, built in the Dulac factory at Montreuil-sous-Bois. In 1899 came a motor tricycle with a "dust-proof" two-speed constant-mesh gearbox.

DALILA • France 1922-1923

A light car with all-round independent suspension on similar lines to the Citroën 2CV. Ruby engines of 903cc and 967cc were used.

DALLISON • England 1913

Weekly production of 50 of these five-speed, worm-drive cyclecars was envisaged.

DAMAIZIN & PUJOS • France 1910

Built chassis with a patented constant-mesh gear change. May also have been known as "Dux."

DANA • Denmark 1908-1914

The Copenhagen-built Dana cars had friction transmissions with belt final drive. Engines were first air-cooled single-cylinder Peugeots, then twin-cylinders from the same source. From 1913 a proper gearbox was used. The cars weighed only about (5 cwt, and were popular as long as heavy cars were banned on Danish minor roads.

DANIELS • USA 1915-1924

One of the highest regarded USA-built motor cars of all time, the Daniels of Reading, Pennsylvania, was built by G C Daniels, erstwhile president of Oakland. The car was powered by an own-make V-8 engine after 1919, and the stylish body styles for both open and closed models were in demand by the affluent. This was a large car with a high rounded radiator, identified only by the letter "D" on the hubcaps. In 1923 the car was sold to a Philadelphia motor combine which attempted to assemble and sell some Daniels sedans at $10,000, a considerably higher price than the earlier models. These later cars were not made with the care that had become associated with the Daniels name, and the 1924 cars were the last of the line. Many of the closed models sported bodies by Fleetwood.

1920/22 Daniels 8 phaeton with victoria top

Darmont-Morgan racer c. 1923

A Darl'Mat Peugeot in the 1937 Le Mans race

DANSK (DANSK FABRIKAT, CHRISTIANSEN) • Denmark 1901-1908

Cudell-engined three-wheelers and a prototype four-wheeler were built in 1899 by H C Christiansen, an enthusiastic cyclist and the owner of a Copenhagen cycle repair shop. In 1901 he founded the company, and nine cars were shown at the 1902 automobile exhibition in Copenhagen, ranging from 2 to 6 hp. Five cars were sold, having single-cylinder engines with two forward speeds. In 1902 Copenhagen's first taxi was delivered, but it was found to be too noisy and the rest of the fleet was fitted with Oldsmobile engines. The first four-cylinder engine came in 1906 in a more civilized car with three-speed gearbox and shaft drive. Probably around 75 chassis were built, many of these commercials.

DANVIGNES • France 1937-1939

A small sports car made by a motorcycle agent in Paris. Two-seater and roadster bodies were available. The power units were a 750cc twin or a 1100cc Ruby.

D"AOUST • Belgium 1912-1927

Light sporting cars were the forte of this Brussels-based firm. Its 1912 10/14 cv formed the basis of post-war production, along with a bored-out 2-litre sports model, which had fwb from 1924. There were also two light cars; a 6 cv and an 8 cv.

DARBY • USA 1909-1910

Billed as "the simplest automobile on earth" the $800 Darby, from St Louis, was claimed to "spin over the road like a monster touring car and dodge around city corners like a bicycle."

DARL"MAT • France 1936-1950

Parisian Peugeot agent Emile Darl'mat made sports cars based on the Peugeot 302 chassis with the 402 engine and these were successful at Le Mans. Made in very limited numbers, they were offered in three versions: roadster, coupé and drop-head coupé. After the war Darl'mat made several more cars based on the Peugeot 203.

DARMOUNT • France 1920-1939

Ex-Morgan racing driver and French agent for the Malvern three-wheelers, M. Darmont built replicas of the British trikes under his own name. These were powered by air- or watercooled 1084cc vee-twins by Blackburne or JAP. Darmont also built some vee-twin-engined four-wheeled cars in the late 1930s under the name of "Etoile de France."

DARRACQ • France 1896-1920

See panel

DARRIN • USA 1946

Howard "Dutch" Darrin of Los Angeles designed and built this $1,950 five-passenger car powered by a 90 hp Continental six-cylinder engine. The convertible body was constructed from four glassfiber panels. Torsion-bar suspension at the front and semi-elliptic springs at the rear were used.

DARRIN • USA 1955-1958

Using the Kaiser-Darrin sports car frame (originally designed for the now defunct Kaiser company) car stylist Howard Darrin fitted a Cadillac engine to increase performance. Despite mechanical and styling alterations, only five of these $4,350 cars were built.

DART • USA 1914

A vee-twin cyclecar built in Jamestown, NY, by the world's largest maker of voting machines.

DASSE • Belgium 1894-1924

Pair-cast 14/16 hp (2799cc) and 24/30 hp (4942cc) fours were offered in 1912 by this Verviers firm, which had started with a belt-drive single-cylinder three-wheeler. Few cars were built post-war, the firm turning to commercial and military vehicles, though two ohv fours, a 12/14 hp and a 30 hp, were shown at the Brussels Salon.

DARRACQ • France 1896-1920

Born in Bordeaux of Basque parents, Alexander Darracq sprang to notice when, in partnership with one Aucoc, he founded the Gladiator cycle company, selling out to a British combine five years later. His first motor cars were electric cabs, but the design was dismissed as "worthless" and he turned to the manufacture of tricycles and quadricycles, then spent £10,000 on the acquisition of Léon Bollée's patents, and turned out a horrid belt-drive machine called the Darracq-Bollée. A neat voiturette appeared in 1900, a 61.2 hp single; quickly followed by two- and four-cylinder models which in 1904 acquired Darracq's distinctive chassis, pressed, together with its undershield, from a single sheet of steel. British capital reformed the company in 1905, and thereafter a complex range was available, from a 1039cc 8 hp single to an 8143cc 50/60 hp six. Disastrous fours with Henriod rotary valves appeared in 1912, a 2613cc 15 hp (uprated to 2951cc the next year) and a 3969cc 20 hp. These proved so unreliable that profits dwindled to almost nothing. M Darracq quickly decided to retire (he had never really liked cars anyway, could not drive and did not like to be driven), and took a share in the Casino at Deauville. Darracq was taken over by Owen Clegg, who introduced a 1913 range based on his excellent Rover Twelve, with monobloc L-head engines of 2121cc and 2971cc. A 4084cc model was added in 1914. This was used by the French Army during the war, and was joined in 1919 by an advanced sv V-8 of 4595cc. A merger with Sunbeam-Talbot came in 1920, and Darracqs became "Talbots" in France (but were still sold as "Darracqs" or "Talbot-Darracqs" in England until 1939.)

1900 Darracq tonneau (above.) 1905 Darracq 8 hp, star of the film "Genevieve," (right.) 1907 Darracq 40 hp six-cylinder (below)

DAT • Japan 1914-1926

Predecessor of Datsun, DAT (from its founders Den, Aoyama and Takeuchi) built cars on a small scale. The 2.0-liter four-cylinder DAT 31 of 1915 was followed by the 2.3-liter DAT 41 of 1916-1926. In 1926 DAT merged with the maker of the Lila car. Between 1927 and 1931 only trucks were built under the DAT name.

DATSUN (NISSAN) • Japan 1931 to date

See under NISSAN

LE DAUPHIN • France 1941-1942

This tandem-seated cyclecar was made during the first year of the German Occupation in Paris to provide a cheap and economic means of transport. It was available with 100cc and 175cc two-stroke Zurcher motorcycle engines, or electrically powered.

1979 Datsun Cherry Coupé

DAVID • Spain 1914-1922, 1951-1957

José Maria Armangué, frustrated from representing Barcelona in a bobsleigh contest for lack of snow, fitted the sleigh with cycle wheels, starting a craze for engineless "down cars" which became a dangerous pastime for young Barcelonese. A club was formed, and Armangué and his three brothers fitted a JAP engine and belt drive to a "down car," creating a cyclecar which they christened the "David." A company, Fabrica Nacional de Cyclecars David, was formed on 14 July 1914, and was soon in full production, now using vee-twin MAG engines. Later Davids also had four-cylinder Ballot power units. A noteworthy feature of the David was its independent front suspension. David cyclecars enjoyed many sporting successes. In 1917 José Maria Armangué was killed in a flying accident, and the company passed into the ownership of his collaborators, José Maria and Ramon Moré. Oddly, the last production David cyclecars were taxis for Barcelona. The David company thereafter operated taxis and hire cars (mostly Citroëns) although, in the Civil War some electric cars were built. Between 1951 and 1957 three-wheelers powered by a single-cylinder 345cc two-stroke engine were produced in small numbers.

1898 David & Bourgeois four-cylinder cab

DAVID & BOURGEOIS • France 1898

This tiller-steered saloon had a "square-four" engine developed by Paul Gautier.

DAVIS • USA 1908-1930

Starting with four-cylinder Continental-engined models, by 1914 this Richmond, Indiana, company was offering a 50 hp Continental-engined six and, after 1915, built six-cylinder cars only. A small six, of 3670cc, was launched in 1915 and became the company's principal offering. The 1924 range had eccentric model names; "Legionaire," "Man O"War,"and "Broudan". An eight appeared in 1927 and, like its sister marque, "New York Six," had the Parkmobile easy parking device. The Davis also formed the basis of the Canadian Winnipeg (1923) and its successor, the Derby (1924-1927).

DAVIS • USA 1947-1949

Built by Glenn Gordon Davis, this well-known three-wheeler could seat four people abreast. It had a four-cylinder 60 hp Hercules engine, disc brakes all round and aerodynamic styling with a detachable metal roof and push-button-operated doors. It was claimed that this untippable car could turn a smaller circle than standard cars at 55 mph and that its top speed was 116 mph, making it the fastest American car of its day. Seventeen prototypes were built, but it never reached production owing to Davis' conviction on a fraud charge.

DAVIS STEAM CAR • USA 1921

The Davis Steam Car only existed in prototype form, if that! The twin-cylinder Davis was announced as having a 120-inch wheelbase. The touring car was priced at $2,300.

DAVIS TOTEM • USA 1921-1922

As many as ten Davis Totem cars were manufactured. The car boasted friction drive like the contemporary Kelsey and

1916 David

Metz and used a four-cylinder Herschell-Spillman engine. The five-passenger touring car was listed at $1,695.

DAVRIAN • England • Wales 1966 to date

Now based in Wales, Davrian Developments first produced its dumpy, rear-engined sports car in West London. Its glassfiber monocoque was designed to accept Hillman Imp subframes and engine, as well as Ford, Mini, and VW units.

DAVY • England 1909-1911

An unorthodox Manchester-built car, the 12/18 hp Davy had a 2.2-liter Hewitt piston-valve engine, "two-speed clutch, two-speed back axle" and two-seater "Canadian Canoe" bodywork "specially suited for Colonial use". There was also a long-stroke 18/24 hp 3.2-liter.

DAWSON • England 1899-1901

Like the vintage Dunelt motorcycle, the Dawson had a double-diameter "top-hat" piston, though Mr Dawson missed the supercharging potential of this layout. Instead, he used the lower piston to pump air into a reservoir, this compressed air being used to start the engine. A valve system also allowed the pumping piston to scavenge the

cylinder at the bottom of each exhaust stroke and inject pure air at the start of each induction stroke.

DAWSON • USA 1900-1902

A twin-cylinder steam "Auto-Mobile" from Basic, Virginia, capable of 25-30 mph.

DAWSON • England 1919-1921

Ex-Hillman works manager A J Dawson conceived this handsome quality light car with an ohc 1795cc four and Bentley-like radiator. Some 65 were built. Triumph took over the factory.

DAY-LEEDS • England 1913-1925

The first car built by Job Day of Leeds (makers of tea-packing machinery) was a twin-cylinder cyclecar of 804cc, succeeded in 1914 by a 10 hp four-cylinder 1287cc light car, which formed the basis of post-war production.

DAYTON • USA 1914

This factory built three to four Spacke-engined cyclecars daily at its peak.

DAYTON ELECTRIC • USA 1911-1915

A complex range of electric cars from Dayton.

DB • France 1938-1961

Charles Deutsch and René Bonnet started with a Citroën-engined racing car before the war. After the war they made a few more racing cars with Citroën engines but quickly turned to Panhard-engined "Racer 500s," following those successful cars with a larger version, the "Monomille" 750cc, built in sufficient numbers to justify their own junior formula in France. The company also made some Panhard-engined sports-touring cars with glassfiber bodies and engines from 850cc to 1300cc. After the end of their association in 1961 the two men made cars under two different names, CD and René Bonnet.

DEAL • USA 1905-1911

A four-seater high-wheeler with wheel steering.

DEASY, SIDDELEY DEASY • England 1906-1919

Designed by E W Lewis, formerly with Rover, the original Deasy (made in Coventry) was a 41.2 liter with ample braking and adjustable steering column. By 1909, however, two huge fours, of 8621cc and 11,947cc, headed the range. J D Siddeley joined Captain Deasy"s company that year, and introduced the JDS 4084cc four with coffin-nosed hood and dashboard radiator, plus Lanchester worm-drive and cantilever rear springs. It was soon joined by a 2654cc 14/20 hp. On 7 November 1912 the company changed its name to Siddeley Deasy and brought out two Knight sleeve-valve-engined models, these were a 3308cc 18/24 hp four and a 24/30 six of 4694cc, plus poppet-valve models of 1944cc and 3308cc. A poppet-valve 4962cc six was announced for 1914. War halted production, and the company merged with Armstrong Whitworth in 1919 to form Armstrong Siddeley.

DE BAZELAIRE • France 1908-1928

Famed for their voiturettes, by 1909 De Bazelaire was offering a twin-cylinder 12/14 hp available in two chassis lengths with gearbox in unit with the differential. In 1910 a sports model with a 1645cc engine and a Fischer slide-valve-engined six of 2540cc appeared. Other models used Ballot or Janvier engines; the 1914 Sport had a long-stroke (80 x 180mm) engine of 3619cc. After the war De Bazelaire built a wide range of four-cylinder cars from 6 to 15 hp with SCAP, Ballot and Janvier power units.

DECAUVILLE • France 1898-1911

Narrow-gauge locomotive engineers of Petit-Bourg (Seine et Oise,) Decauville acquired the rights to the Guédon car and christened it La Voiturelle. Its two-cylinder De Dion-based engine drove the rear axle through naked and unlubricated two-speed gears. Sliding pillar ifs (and no rear suspension save the air in the tires) characterized the Voiturelle, which was license-built in Italy by Orio et Marchand and, in Germany, as the Wartburg. In 1900 a front-engined 5 hp model appeared, joined by a snub-nosed 8 hp twin with horseshoe-shaped dashboard radiator. A 3-liter four arrived in 1901. The neat 10 hp twin of 1902

1905 Decauville Landaulette

1902 Dechamps Tonneau

with unit engine/gearbox construction inspired Henry Royce to build his first car. By 1906 the five-car range consisted of fours (12, 16, 24, 30, and 45 hp,) but was cut to only the 12 and 16 hp in 1907.

DE CEZAC • France 1922-1926

A manufacturer from Périgueux who, after the First World War, built a handful of cars with 1203cc CIM and 1692cc Ballot engines.

DECHAMPS • Belgium 1889-1906

Déchamps of Brussels made Panhard-type cars of 7 hp (single), 9 hp (twin,) and 20 hp (four). The 1902 Déchamps range was said to be the first to have electric starters fitted as standard. From 1904 to 1906 the company built the single ohc 15 hp and 25 hp Baudouin.

DECKERT • France 1901-1904

This Parisian firm offered a 6 hp single, 12 hp, and 16 hp twins and a 20 hp four.

DE COSMO • Belgium 1903-1908

The designer of the first FNs, J de Cosmo was responsible for these pair-cast fours of 24/30 hp (sold in Britain as the Wilkinson) and 30/35 hp. A 45/55 hp six appeared in 1906.

DE CROSS • USA 1913-1914

A tandem-seater 1100cc vee-twin cyclecar.

DE DION BOUTON • France 1883-1932

See panel opposite

DEEMSTER • England 1914-1924

The Ogston Motor Company of Acton, London, largely staffed by former Napier employees, was responsible for the Deemster, a light car of 1100cc capacity, and for its engine. Adventurous plans to manufacture the Deemster in America in 1923 at a price of $1,100 came to nothing. In 1923 the Deemster succumbed to a proprietary engine, a 12 hp Anzani being available. Although the vehicle was never in the sports car league, no less a personage than Kaye Don raced a Deemster.

1914 Deemster 10 hp

DEEP SANDERSON • England 1961-1969

Morgan devotee Chris Lawrence has been associated with a number of projects over the years, not least the Deep Sandersons. Fourteen of these rear-engined, Mini-powered 301 coupés were built, while various prototypes were raced at Le Mans.

DEERE • USA 1906-1907

Built by famous plow manufacturer John Deere of Moline, Illinois, this "car of quality and style" sold for $2,000.

DEERING MAGNETIC • USA 1918-1919

The Deering Magnetic was designed by Karl H Martin, designer of both Roamer and Kenworthy and builder of Wasp motor cars. Featuring a Dorris six-cylinder engine and the Entz electric transmission made famous by the Owen Magnetic, it sold for a substantially lower price. The car was probably overpriced for its time, some models selling in excess of $7,000, and it failed before many units had reached their market.

DEETYPE • England 1974 to date

Conceived by automotive engineer Bryan Wingfield, with bodies built by Grand Prix Metalcraft Ltd, the Deetype is a beautifully fashioned and remarkably faithful replica of

De Dion Bouton

DE DION BOUTON • France 1883-1932

Comte Albert de Dion backed the mechanics Bouton and Trépardoux in the production of steam carriages during the 1880s and early 1890s. Trépardoux devised the "De Dion axle" for power transmission on their heavy steam brakes, but resigned in 1894 because De Dion and Bouton were dabbling with petrol engines, which he regarded as heresy. Bouton's single-cylinder petrol engine of 1895 ran at speeds of up to 3500rpm on test, and powered sporting tricycles, built until 1901. A quadricycle appeared in 1899, and was quickly supplanted by the rear-engined 31.2 hp model D voiturette of 402cc. De Dion also produced engines in vast numbers for other manufacturers, By 1904 over 40,000 power units had been completed at its Puteaux factory. By 1902 the rear-engined model had a 6 hp engine, which was then supplanted by the 8 hp Model K, with a front-mounted engine under a crocodile hood. This retained the neat two-speed expanding-clutch transmission of its predecessor. Up to the war all De Dions had decelerator pedals. The firm's first twin-cylinder car, the 12 hp S, came in 1903, and fours of 15 and 24 hp appeared two years later. By the end of 1906 all models had conventional gearboxes, and the last 8 hp single was made in 1908. In 1910 De Dion introduced the first production V-8 of any real merit, a 6.1-liter model, subsequently available with swept volumes of 7 liters, 7.8 liters and 14.7 liters; the latter aimed at the US market. The De Dion axle was dropped in 1911, and the last single-cylinder-engined model, the DE 1, was built in 1913. The V-8 was produced up to 1923, alongside dated fours then, in 1923, came the ohv 12/28, with aluminum pistons and fwb available as an extra. In decline, the factory struggled on until 1927, then was temporarily closed down. It reopened with a new 2.5-liter straight-eight, offered alongside a 2-liter four, but few of either were sold, despite an uprating of the eight to 3 liters in 1930. The last car, an 11 hp, was delivered in 1932, but the company built trucks until the late 1940s, then became a service garage. The name was last seen on motorcycles in the 1950s.

1899 De Dion Quadricycle (top right.) 1907 8 hp single-cylinder De Dion Bouton (above right.) 1923 De Dion Bouton 12/28 hp (right)

1923 De France cyclecar

either the 1956 or 1957 (the choice is yours) Jaguar D-Type Le Mans cars. With laudable devotion, Wingfield constructs each car in his home workshop.

DE FRANCE • France 1923

A Ballot-engined light car from Vierzon (Cher.) Two ran in the 1923 Bol d'Or.

DEGUINGAND • France 1928-1930

After the closure of the Vinot-Deguingand works at Puteaux, the marque resumed production for a few ye[ars] with a 735cc two-stroke four-cylinder 5 hp cycl[ecar] designed by M Violet, which was made alongside the [...] and Huascar.

DEHN • Germany 1924

Built soon after Germany's runaway inflation, this was a shortlived, simple cyclecar with an air-cooled 346cc motorcycle engine.

DELAGE • France 1905-1959

See panel

DELAHAYE • France 1894-1954

See panel opposite

DELAUGERE ET CLAYETTE • France 1900-1926

Delaugére et Clayette, of Orléans, started with a Romain-engined 2 hp tricycle. The 1902 Delaugéres had 12 cv and 20 cv four-cylinder engines, and could run on gasoline or alcohol. Chain drive was available until 1908. In

1907 Coupé des voiturettes Delage

1920 Type CO 4 1/2 litre six-cylinder Delage sports torpedo

1949 Delage D6 3-litre

DELAGE • France 1905-1959

Louis Del,ge started in Courbevoie with a single-cylinder De Dion-engined car. This was later followed by a 1460cc four-cylinder 9 cv, numerous 12 cv models and a six-cylinder of 2588cc, but it was not until the post-war period that Delage production became really significant. The first of the much-admired Delage cars was the CO of 1918, with a six-cylinder 20 cv engine of 4532cc. That car became the CO2 in 1921. The 1920s saw many racing successes for Delage. The most successful touring cars of the period were the DI of 2120cc and the GL with an ohc 30 cv engine of 5945cc. Then came a long line of six-cylinders like the ohv DM of 3174cc and the sv DR of 2516cc. In 1929 Delage presented its first straight-eight, the 4060cc D8, from which the D8S sports evolved. In 1932 came the D6 11 of 2100cc, and two years later the new eight-cylinder D8 15 of 2700cc. When Delage was forced to sell to Delahaye some cars were continued, such as the 4300cc D8 100, the D8 120 and the 2700cc D6 70. After the war a six-cylinder model was advertised as a Delage by Delahaye, but the name eventually disappeared.

DELAHAYE • France 1894-1954

Founded in Tours by Emile Delahaye, a pioneer of motoring, this company started by making belt-driven single- and twin-cylinder cars. The founder left the factory in 1901, one year after a second factory was opened in Paris. From 1908 Delahaye made more interesting cars with four cylinders like the 9hp of 1460cc and the 12hp of 2120cc, which were continued until the war together with a V-6 of 2565cc. Delahayes were exported, but also made under license in Germany and America. After the war Delahaye was mainly involved in making trucks, motor plows and fire engines. Now little interested in cars, it nevertheless made some reliable models, like the four-cylinder 1847cc and 2950cc and six-cylinder 4426cc. In 1934 Delahaye presented two new cars, the four-cylinder 12 cv (2150cc) and the six-cylinder 18 cv (3200cc). In 1935 came the most famous Delahayes, the six-cylinder ohv 3.2 Coupe des Alpes and the 3557cc "135."

In the same year Delahaye bought Delage, perpetuating that marque on cars built with Delahaye components. Delahaye was successful in racing, and the touring cars sold very well. Famous coachbuilders such as Figoni, Chapron, and Letourneur et Marchand made lovely bodies for these cars. Delahaye was also involved in making trucks and armoured vehicles. After the war the 135 was resumed and the 175 of 4.5 litres was presented in 1948. In 1951 came the last new Delahayes; the Jeep-Delahaye, a very advanced vehicle, and the 235 of 3.5 liters. Hotchkiss took over Delahaye in 1954 and built only trucks. These were given the name of Hotchkiss-Delahaye for a few months, and were then known as Hotchkiss.

1896 Delahaye phaeton (above,) 1915 Delahaye 12/15 hp Type 64 (far left,) 1937-38 Delahaye Type 135 cabriolet by Henri Chapron (below)

1911 the company presented a six-cylinder model of 4252cc and, in 1913, a four-cylinder of 2723cc with a Fischer sleeve-valve engine. After the war it continued with four-cylinder models of 1692cc, 2155cc, and 3329cc, and a six of 4993cc. The works eventually collapsed, despite making small trucks.

DELAUNAY-BELLEVILLE • France 1904-1950

This famous engineering firm from Saint Denis started with Marius Barbarou as engineer, building 16, 24 and 40 hp four-cylinder cars. But the six-cylinder engine was to become a feature of Delaunay-Belleville design, and the four-cylinder an exception. The marque was considered in France as the ultimate in cars, and the round radiator, recalling the famous Belleville marine boilers, was well known. The smallest six-cylinder made before the First World War was the 12 hp of 2913cc, and the biggest was the 45 hp of 7998cc. After the Armistice Delaunay-Belleville resumed production with pre-war models, including the 1914 14/16 hp of 2129cc. In 1922 the 2613cc 12 hp four-cylinder acquired an ohc. By the late 1920s the Delaunay-Belleville had lost its "prestige," and some unimportant models were made with American engines like the Continental straight-eight. The last true Delaunay-Bellevilles were the 3180cc and 3619cc ohv sixes. At the very end, after the Second World War, the company built the tiny De Rovin cars in its works.

DE LA VERGNE • USA 1895-1896

A single-cylinder engine of 2234cc powered this Benz-derived car built by the New York Refrigerating Co. Its designer, La Vergne, built cyclecars in 1914.

DELCAR • USA 1947-1949

Built by American Motors of Troy, New York, the Delcar produced extremely compact delivery cars and station wagons. With a wheel-base of only five feet and a four-cylinder engine under the floor, the Delcar was able to use maximum carrying space in the smallest area.

1913 Delaunay-Belleville 40 hp limousine

De Tomaso Pantera

Carryall car-cum-station wagon was unique to De Soto. The L-head six was joined in 1952 by a 4525cc Firedome V-8, which sold 45,800 units in its first year and soon outsold the sixes two to one. Attractive new styling heralded the 1955 FireFlyte series, with a 200hp V-8 of 4769cc. From then on, V-8 engines powered all De Sotos except for the export-only Diploma (a thinly disguised Plymouth.) In 1956 came the limited-production Adventurer, with a gold-on-white paint scheme, gold trim and a 5595cc hemi-head V-8. New Flight Sweep styling (and the low-priced FireSweep series, powered by a new 5326cc V-8) boosted De Soto sales to a record 117,747 in 1957. However, poor quality control cut the next year"s sales to 35,556. The new wedge-head V-8s (5916cc or 6276cc) boosted 1959 sales slightly, but not enough. The 1961 models, with canted fins, "two-tier" grille and 5916cc engine, had only been out for four months before De Soto ceased production on 18 December 18 1960.

DE TAMBLE • USA 1908-1913

This 10/12 hp two-cylinder car was built by the Speed Changing Pulley Co of Indianapolis, maker of the Carrico air-cooled four-cylinder engine, which also sold complete shaft-drive chassis to other manufacturers. For 1910 the four-cylinder 4-34 model was announced.

DE TOMASO • Italy 1959 to date

Ex-racing driver Alessandro de Tomaso, born in Argentina, and his wife, American ex-racing driver Isabell Haskell, moved to Italy in the late 1950s. There De Tomaso built various prototypes, including racing cars. Today he owns Moto Guzzi and Benelli, two leading motorcycle factories, and his Modena-based De Tomaso car works, besides many other industrial interests. During an association with Ford came his first production car, the Mangusta, with a 4728cc V-8 Ford engine and a Ghia coupé body. Later, in 1970, the 5796cc V-8 Pantera appeared. It was a sports coupé with a top speed of 162 mph. That same year the Mangusta acquired a larger, 4949cc V-8 engine and there was now also the 5796cc Deauville, which had luxurious limousine bodywork. New in 1972 was the "Longchamp," a luxurious coupé. Built in small numbers, these expensive cars underwent steady development. By 1979 the range included the 300 bhp mid-engined Pantera L, the 330 bhp Pantera GTS and the 300 bhp Longchamp and Deauville. The Pantera GTS remained the sole survivor in a fast-dating model line-up, and the company went through various changes in the 1980s and saw several show car proposals come to nothing; the highlight of which had to be the 1993 Guara. These concepts remained in abatement until a completely new model was readied for 1999. Called the Mangusta (after the famous model of the 1960s), and with American financial backing, this stylish and technologically advanced super car seems set to return the marque to the front line of Italian performance cars.

DETROIT • USA 1899-1900

This was Henry Ford's first venture into the commercial manufacture of horseless carriages, although he had already built two experimental cars. The Detroit Automobile Company was shortlived; no more than a dozen cars and vans being built. One of thedistinctive features was a "single lever which, by a forward and backward movement through the space of about 12 inches, starts the engine and controls the forward speeds and backup; thus eliminating the confusion arising from a multiplication of levers."

1911 9900cc Deutz 38/65 hp Type 8a

DETROIT • USA 1904-1907

The Detroit 22/24 hp was a $1,500 flat-twin with shaft drive. Its main claim to fame was that its exclusive selling agent was John North Willys, subsequently of Willys-Overland.

DETROIT ELECTRIC • USA 1907-1938

Probably the best-known and best-selling electric car built in the USA. Detroit Electric sold upwards of 1,000 cars annually before the First World War; peak production being reached from 1912 to 1915. In 1920 a false hood was provided as an option for any buyer who disliked the boxy "museum showcase" appearance of the original design. Although to all intents and purposes electric cars were outmoded by 1920, a loyal but small clientele continued to purchase them. The final models featured Willys-Overland coachwork as a concession to modern design, but the older pattern featuring the fore and aft battery covers was still available; safety glass and balloon tires being the only noticeable changes. A few of the last Detroits used Dodge hoods and grilles.

DETROITER • USA 1912-1915

Also known as the Briggs-Detroiter, this 16/20 hp four-cylinder sold in Britain for £200. A 3.3-liter V-8 appeared in 1915.

DETROIT STEAM CAR • USA 1922-1923

Initially, this was advertised and marketed under the name "Trask-Detroit", the name being changed for the 1923 model year. Very few of these twin-cylinder automobiles were built; all touring cars. The makes carried a "Windsor" nameplate for cars to be sold in Canada.

DEUTZ • Germany 1907-1911

Ettore Bugatti designed this range of large cars with ohc engines of 4960cc, 6400cc, 9900cc, and even 10,500cc at Cologne for Gustav Langen, who then headed the Deutz factory. After producing yet more big cars, Bugatti also created a small 1327cc four-cylinder in which he competed in some events, but which was never built at Deutz. It was with this design that he founded his own works at Molsheim (Alsace,) although still continuing design and development work for Deutz. The last Deutz car had a 2600cc four-cylinder 30 hp engine; it was built in small numbers only, as these high-class Deutz cars were quite expensive.

DEVAUX • USA 1931-1932

The DeVaux was an economy car introduced at an economically inauspicious time, and the hoped-for sales of this six-cylinder line of automobiles did not materialize. With only a few thousand units built, the DeVaux failed in

The De Wande Ford, an 'elegant spider'

1932 after some 14 months of production. The assets of the company were taken over by the Continental Motors Co of Detroit and Muskegon, Michigan, which marketed the cars for the remainder of that year as the Model 80 or DeVaux-Continental. The cars were facelifted and sold as Continentals in 1933 and 1934. In Canada, as a part of Canadian Durant, they were marketed as "Frontenacs."

DE VECCHI • Italy 1904-1907

Fast and comparatively sporting cars which proved successful in many sporting events. Engines, mainly ioe four-cylinder, were made by De Vecchi: 1908 models were a 16/20 hp (shaft-drive) and a chain-drive 18/24 hp. Ugo Sivocci, killed at Monza in 1923 driving an Alfa Romeo, was a De Vecchi driver in his early years.

DEVIN • USA 1958-1960

Devin Enterprises of El Monte, California, normally manufactured glassfiber kits (starting price $295) suitable for small foreign car chassis. In 1959 it produced a complete car, the Devin SS, priced at $5,950. Powered by a 220hp V-8 Chevrolet engine, it attained 60 mph in 5.6 seconds.

1922 interior-drive DFP 12cv

DEW • USA 1928

The Dew was named for the initials of its builder, D E Willis, who gained a kind of prominence by designing the Willis nine-cylinder car the same year as the smaller three-cylinder Dew. Like the larger car, only one pilot model was built.

DEWALD • France 1902-1926

Dewald seems to have built only one-offs to order until 1912, when a complex line-up was offered, ranging from 10 hp to 60 hp. The following year only 14 hp and 24 hp fours were offered. A straight-eight of 4.8 liters was listed in 1924.

DE WANDRE • Belgium c. 1923

A wire-wheeled sports car based on the Model T Ford.

DEWCAR • England 1913-1914

The original 482cc single-cylinder Dewcar cyclecar was as basic as could be, as its main chassis/body structure consisted of two planks on edge, joined at the front. It sold for £60, a high price considering the crudity of its construction. There was also a 6 hp vee-twin. These models were replaced by 41/2 hp single and 8 hp twin Dewcars in 1914.

DEXTER • France 1906-1909

Sporting cars from Lyon with four- and six-cylinder engines of 50 to 100 hp.

DFP • France 1906-1926

The Doriot, Flandrin et Parant works in Courbevoie made lively single-cylinder 1100cc cars up to 1910 but, from 1909, it had also offered an 8/10 cv four of 1874cc. From 1911 it abandoned proprietary engines to build its own, the 12/16 cv of 3015cc and the 10/14 cv of 2001cc. The latter was still being made when DFP restarted production after the war. Forced to return to proprietary engines, DFP made cars with 2001cc ohc Altos, 1847cc Sergant, and even 1098cc CIME power units. In 1926 the DFP factory was bought by Théophile Lafitte.

DFR • France 1924

In 1924 the well-known motorcycle factory run by MM Desert and De Font-Reaulx built a number of 893cc SCAP-engined light cars.

1928 Dixi 3/15 hp (licence-built Austin Seven)

engined light cars.

DIABLE • France 1921-1924

A three-wheeled, two-speed cyclecar from Paris with a twin-cylinder 1096cc engine.

DIAL • England 1971-1974

Many improvements were made to the futuristic mid-engined Dial Buccaneer before its demise. Final examples featured alloy space-frame chassis and lightweight bodies, allowing exciting performance from almost any chosen power unit.

DIAMANT • France 1901-1906

"Combining all the improvements to date of any importance in motor engineering," the 1904 Diamant range consisted of a 12 hp twin and a 24 hp four-cylinder. (Also sold as "La Française.")

DIAMOND T • USA 1905-1911

Powerful touring cars (up to 70 hp) from a Chicago company later famed for its trucks.

DIANA • England 1900

A 5 hp three-seater voiturette built by Lewis & Lewis of Fulham, London, with "new patent-speed-changing arrangement." It sold at 165 guineas.

DIANA • USA 1925-1928

Introduced in mid-1925 as "Queen of the Eights," the Diana was a companion car to, and built by, Moon. Powered by an eight-cylinder Continental engine, the car had a radiator copied from that of the Minerva. The cars were popular; one sporting model, a roadster, featured bronze radiator, wire wheels, and bright bodywork. Prices ranged from $1,595 to $2,895, plus a hardly seen town-car, available to special order only, which retailed at $5,000!

DIATTO • Italy 1907-1929

Diatto originally built a range of Clément-based two- and four-cylinder models. During the 1920s it built superb cars, partly designed by the famous Alfieri Maserati, who established his own factory in 1926. Together with his brothers he also created a supercharged eight-cylinder ohc racing car, which eventually formed the basis for the first Maserati. Production Diatto cars had ohc 1990cc four-cylinder engines of advanced design and even had four-wheel brakes and four-speed gearboxes as early as 1922. There was also a 2980cc four-cylinder Diatto, which was built in limited numbers.

DIAZ Y GRILLO • Spain 1914-1922

The Diaz y Grillo (or D y G) was a sporting light car built in Barcelona. Initially a twin-cylinder Blumfield engine was used; latterly, four-cylinder Ballot and MAG engines were employed.

DIEDERICHS • France 1912-1914

Though the Diéderichs family had built prototype vehicles in 1878 and 1899-1901, production did not begin at Charpennes (Rhône) until 1912, using 10/12 cv Luc-Court four-cylinder engines.

DILE • USA 1914-1916

"Distinctively individual," the $485 Dile light car came from Reading, Pennsylvania.

DIM • Greece 1977 to date

The 594cc Dim, from Athens, is a two-door saloon with Fiat 126 mechanicals.

DININ • France 1904-1907

Long-range electric cars from Puteaux (Seine.)

DINO • Italy 1966 to date

A mid-engined car built by Ferrari at Modena. Named after Ferrari's only son, Dino, who died young, the original Dino was a superb car with Pininfarina bodywork and Ferrari-designed 2418cc V-6 mid-engine. Following this 246GT came the 246GTS in 1972, which now, like the 246GT, had an engine built by Fiat, of which Ferrari had become a part. A new Dino appeared in 1974, the 308GT4 with a 2926cc, 225 bhp V-8 engine and a 2 + 2-seater coupé body. Today's Dino range includes the improved 308 GT4, with Bertone-designed and Scaglietti-built coupé coachwork, and a dohc 225 bhp V-8 engine. A smaller model, the 1975-introduced 208 GT4, has a 1991cc 170 bhp engine. This too is a mid-mounted V-8.

DINOS • Germany 1921-1926

Successor to the LUC built by Loeb of Berlin (1909-1914,) the sporting Dinos was designed and also driven by Robert Dunlop, whose Dinos factory at Berlin was financed by the Stinnes Group, which also controlled AGA, Rabag-Bugatti and Stolle. After the death of Stinnes, Dinos became part of AGA. Dinos built a 2100cc four and a 4050cc six. Both had own-make ohc engines with detachable cylinder heads. Production was concentrated on the four.

DIRECT • Belgium 1904-1905

This 40/50 hp four-cylinder car from Brussels had no gearbox, but its clutch was said to give "speed reductions by variations in pressure."

DISK • Czechoslovakia 1925-1926

This 660cc twin-cylinder two-stroke car was the first attempt by the Brno-Zidenice Arms Factory ("Z") to produce a small, cheap car. Designer was B. Novotny. Only a few were built before the factory introduced the "Z" car.

1931 DKW 584cc Sportwagen

1962 DKW Junior 741cc

DIVA • England 1961-1966

During Diva's five-year reign a number of front-engined and six mid-engined competition cars were built and raced with success. Only three genuine road cars were made. Known as 10Fs, they were based on the front-engined GT but had heavier-gauge bodies.

DIXI • Germany 1904-1928

Dixi ("I have spoken") cars succeeded the Wartburg in 1904, in which year a 2815cc four-cylinder was introduced. That year also saw a new single-cylinder of 1240cc and a twin-cylinder of 2468cc. A 6800cc four-cylinder came into production in 1907. There were many more models built, including a 1320cc four-cylinder with side valves. Improved versions of 1568cc appeared after the war. Two six-cylinder models of 2330cc and 3557cc appeared in the mid-1920s. Before the Second World War the "Wartburg" trademark was changed to "Dixi" and, in 1927, this factory acquired the license for the manufacture of the Austin Seven. It built it at Eisenach but ran out of money, and BMW of Munich took over the design and the works.

DIXIE FLYER • USA 1916-1923

The Dixie Flyer was an assembled automobile using Lycoming and Herschell-Spillman four-cylinder engines throughout its relatively brief life. In 1922 Dixie Flyer and Jackson were both absorbed by National, and the Dixie Flyer became the National Model 6-31 for 1923, after existing "1923" Dixie Flyers had been sold.

DKW • Germany 1928-1966

Founded by Jôrge-Skafte Rasmussen, DKW built its first two-stroke motorcycles in 1919 and, after building SB and DEW electrics, used a similar wood-framed chassis-less construction on its first gasoline-powered DKW two-stroke cars at its Berlin-Spandau works in 1928. The first cars had 584cc twin-cylinder engines followed, in 1930, by watercooled V-4 models with two-stroke engines which had 780cc and, later, 992cc engines. The first fwd two-stroke 490cc and 584cc two-cylinder models left the works in 1931. Up to 1939 DKW produced two-stroke cars in 684cc and V-4 1047cc versions. They were good, but not always very economical. In 1928 Rasmussen bought engine production equipment from Rickenbacker in the USA and afterwards produced big six- and eight-cylinder engines for Audi and other firms. In 1932 DKW became part of the Auto Union Group, consisting of DKW, Audi, Horch, and Wanderer.

After 1945 all these works became nationalized, as they were located in an area which became the DDR. New Auto Union factories in West Germany at Ingolstadt and Düsseldorf came into being in 1949 and built fwd DKW cars with 684cc twin-cylinders and, soon after, three-cylinders of 896cc. They were again two-stroke cars with water-cooling and vertical cylinders in line. They developed 23 bhp and 34 bhp, while later three-cylinder versions developed 38 bhp and also 40 bhp. The Auto Union DKW "1000" of 1957 got a new three-cylinder 980cc engine which had 44 bhp, afterwards 50 bhp at 4500 rpm, while the "Special" was supplied with 55hp motors. They were two-stroke cars with fairly thirsty engines. The trend led to four-stroke engines and to the first "New" Audi. Mercedes (Daimler-Benz) bought the works in 1958 and sold it to VW in 1965, by which time Mercedes had developed the first engine for the Audi. The last two-stroke DKW was produced in February 1966.

DL • Scotland 1913-1915

A 10 hp monobloc 1307cc four-cylinder from Motherwell; an 8hp was also available.

DMC • England 1914

Taking its name from the local area of ducal seats, the Dukeries Motor Company of Worksop, Nottinghamshire, built two models of cyclecar; a 578cc 41/2 hp single-cylinder and a 964cc twin.

DOBELLI • Italy 1904

A "mechanical prodigy" from Rome, the Dobelli was a monstrous 180 hp two-seater with five forward speeds, which Friswells of London offered for sale. Its huge four-cylinder engine had a displacement of 31,625cc, valves 114mm in diameter, and was accommodated under a 5ft 6in-long hood.

DOBI • Spain 1919

A Madrid-built cyclecar with a British Douglas flat-twin engine.

DOBLE • USA 1914-1932

Abner Doble's first production steam cars appeared in 1915-1917, advertised as "Doble-Detroits." The war halted the project and production did not restart until 1924, in

The 180 hp Dobelli, a 'mechanical prodigy'

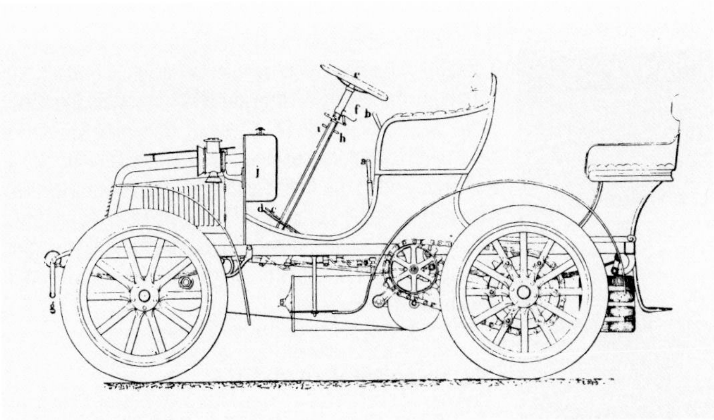

1901 Gaillardet (Doctoresse)

1922 Doble phaeton

Emeryville, California. But Doble's zeal for perfection prevented production from ever attaining anything like the anticipated momentum, and no more than 45 Doble steamers were built. However, in its final form the Doble could reach a full head of steam in under 90 seconds from cold, could run1,500 miles on 24 gallons of water – thanks to an efficient condenser – and had a 75 bhp four-cylinder engine giving exceptional acceleration and hill-climbing powers.

DOCTORESSE • France 1899-1902

Designed by Gaillardet, these 6 cv and 12 cv cars from Suresnes took their odd name from the fact that "like a doctor, they were always ready to render service."

DODGE • USA 1914 to date

See panel overleaf

DODGESON • USA 1926

John Duval Dodge, son of John F Dodge (one of the original Dodge brothers who built the Dodge Brothers car,) was engineer and designer of the Dodgeson, which featured a 3167cc straight-eight rotary-valve engine producing 72 bhp at 3000 rpm. Prototypes were built and experiments were made. Although the Dodgeson was pronounced a success, the car never went beyond the experimental stage.

1913 Dodson 12/16 hp tourer

DODSON • England 1910

Built in two models, a three-speed 12/16 hp and a four-speed 20/30 hp, the Dodson was "practically a replica of the Renault," built in Huddersfield by David Brown Ltd. Up to late 1912 the obsolescent quadrant gear change was standard.

DOHERTY • Canada 1895

Stove-maker Tom Doherty of Sarnia, Ontario, actually built and operated a three-wheeled prototype car worked by a giant clock spring.

DOLLY • England 1920

A four-cylinder watercooled engine was the motive power of the Dolly. A slanting engine/gearbox unit obviated the need for a universal joint in the propeller shaft.

1920 Douglas 8 hp cyclecar at Brooklands

DOLPHIN • England 1906-1909

The Dolphin used a two-stroke engine designed by Harry Ricardo which had separate pumping and working cylinders in vee formation. The prototype had a 12/15 hp "twin" power unit, but the majority of the dozen or so cars produced had 28/30 hp engines with four working cylinders. Most of the orders received seem to have come from indulgent members of the Ricardo family.

DOLSON • USA 1904-1907

The "mile-a-minute" Dolson, from Charlotte, Mich., had a 60 hp engine; 20 and 28hp models were also listed.

DOME-O • Japan 1978 to date

A limited-production "dream car" built by a group of enthusiasts.

DOMINION • Canada 1910-c. 1915

A 3942cc 35 hp four built in Walkerville, Ontario, to the design of E W Winans, formerly with Regal in Detroit. As New Dominion, the firm struggled on for three years after a 1911 liquidation.

DOMINION • Canada 1914

This American-backed company planned to assemble six-cylinder cars shipped from Britain at the port of St John, New Brunswick, which is ice-free all year round.

DONNET • France 1924-1933

The small Donnet was the successor to the Zedel. The company tried to survive by producing a small 7 cv of 1098cc and an 11 cv of 2120cc. In 1926 Donnet presented a six-cylinder model of 1866cc. Marcel Violet built a small car like his Huascar for Donnet, with a 750cc twin-cylinder two-stroke but, shortly afterwards, the works passed into the hands of Simca.

DONOSTI • Spain 1923

A 3-liter 16-valve sports car built by the Garage Internacional of San Sebastian.

DORA • Italy 1899-1907

This Genoa firm built a few electrics.

DORE & BOUISSOU (DORE) • France 1898-c. 1900

The steering pivot of this twin-cylinder carriage also acted as a shaft for the pinion driving the front axle. A gasoline car was later built under the "Doré" name, and the Doré motor was also used as the basis of a particularly ingenious fraud by Walter K Freeman, the "auto-acetylene swindler" (late of Sing Sing), who claimed it as a new type of motive power to attract credulous investors.

Doré fiacre, 1898

DOREY • France, 1912-1913

A French-Canadian resident in Paris, Dorey built both chassis and complete cars; in 1906-07 single (De Dion) cylinder and four-cylinder voiturettes and, in 1912, a twin cyclecar.

DORIGNY • France 1898

The "Inseparable" was a rear-engined tricycle seating two side-by-side on saddles, each with their own handlebars and brakes.

DORMANDY • USA 1903-1905

All told, only four Dormandy automobiles were built, combining the talents of a mechanic in a buggy works and an employee of a shirt factory! Four-cylinder air-cooled engines were used for all of them, the last being a Frayer-Miller. The cars were built at the request of J K P Pine, president of the United Shirt & Collar Co. of Troy, New York, and were used by Pine, his two sons and Gary Dormandy, an employee and the builder of the cars.

DORRIS • USA 1905-1926

George P Dorris, an early automobile manufacturer in St Louis, Missouri, produced several lines of cars from 1897 to 1905 named after the city of their origin (see St Louis). Thereafter all Dorris cars (and commercial vehicles) carried the name of their maker. After the First World War the Dorris became one of the country"s better-known luxury automobiles, limited production notwithstanding. Prices of the cars in the 1920s ran as high as $7,000 for closed models and, although "production" as such ceased in 1923, Dorris cars could be obtained on special order until 1926.

DORT • USA 1915-1924

In 1886 J Dallas Dort, a clerk in a hardware store, invested $1,000 for a half-share in the new Durant-Dort carriage company, which soon became America's largest, producing 150,000 vehicles in 15 plants, and went into the motor business in 1903, producing the Buick car. Dort began building cars under his own name in 1915. The first Dorts were 2720cc Lycoming-engined fours. The 1918 Model 11 had a 3146cc Lycoming and one pedal-operated clutch and parking brake; the other was the "emergency" brake. The 1921 range was totally restyled, with an angular radiator shell. This, however, was supplanted by a rounded, nickeled radiator a couple of years later. An ohv 3205 six joined the range in 1923 and became the sole Dort chassis in 1924.

DOUGLAS • England 1913-1922

A 10 hp flat-twin light car built by the famous Kingswood, Bristol, motorcycle company.

DOUGLAS • USA 1918-1920

The former Drummond car, the Douglas featured an eight-cylinder Herschell-Spillman engine. The few cars sold in 1920 were probably left-over 1919 models.

DPL • England 1907-1910

A 12/15 hp hood-less landaulet with flat-twin engine built by Dawfield Philips, of West Ealing, Middlesex.

DRAGON • USA 1907-1908

The son of tramcar builder, J G Brill of Philadelphia built this four-cylinder car, using proprietary components. In

1967 Dodge Dart GT convertible (right.) 1916 Dodge touring car (center,) 1929 Dodge Standard six (bottom)

DODGE • USA 1914 to date

Built at Hamtramck, Detroit, the Dodge car was a 3.5-litre four with a dynastarter which operated automatically if the engine stalled. By 1916 the marque was America's fourth largest, by 1920 the 'Dependable Dodge' was second only to Ford. All-steel coachwork was adopted as early as 1916, stop-lamps and anti-theft locks were offered from 1923. The new Senior Six, with hydraulic fwb, appeared in 1927. The four was replaced by a cheaper 'Victory' six in 1928, in which year Chrysler bought the company for $126 million. A Chrysler-based straight-eight appeared in 1930, as well as a 2.6-litre six. The eight was dropped in 1933, but Senior and Victory Sixes were now lavishly equipped. Dodges never adopted Chrysler's 'Airflow' styling, but were otherwise closely patterned on the sister marque. 1936 saw automatically engaged overdrive standardized on the Senior Six. Although post-war cars used the basic pre-war designs, styling was freshened, with fenders swept into the doors and a chequerboard grille; all models used the 3769cc six. All-new models, the Wayfarer, Meadowbrook and top-of-the-line Coronet, appeared for 1949, with the 3769cc six coupled to Fluid-Drive transmission (as before) or with the new option of GyroMatic semi-automatic transmission. In 1953 came Dodge's version of the Chrysler hemi-head V-8, the 3949cc Red Ram, initially only available in the Coronet. By 1955 this was standardised on Royal and Custom Lancers and optional across the rest of the range. The 1957 range had Virgil Exner's 'Forward Look' styling with high fins and compound-curved windscreens; and unitary construction arrived on the 1960 range. Standard models were renamed Matador and Polara, and the intermediate Dart range (Seneca, Pioneer and Phoenix) was launched. The faithful L-head six was replaced by an ohv slant six of 3687cc, standard in Seneca and Pioneer. Dodge styling had lost its fins by 1962, when the Lancer compact (based on the Plymouth Valiant) made its bow, powered by a 2785cc six.This lasted for only two seasons, the Dart taking over as Dodge's compact in 1963. The most

expensive 1963 model, the new Custom 880, shared a Chrysler bodyshell. In 1966 came the performance Charger model, with a 5211cc V-8 as standard, and units up to a 425 bhp V-8 of 6891cc as options; these engines also powered the handsome 1968 Charger, capable of 0-96 km/h (0-60 mph) in 4.75 sec. Only available for 1969, a limited-edition performance model, the Charger-based Daytona, had a long aerodynamic nose and two huge stabilizer fins.

The popular Dart series carried Dodge into the 1970s while, on the performance front, the Charger was joined by the Challenger, with the slant six as standard and the V-8s up to the 425 bhp version optional. Top of the range was the luxury Monaco. In 1972 Dodge introduced the Mitsubishi Colt of 1598cc to the US market, where it sold quite well. In 1975 the Charger was totally redesigned, with a bodyshell in common with Chrysler's Cordoba; its performance image was traded for a "personal luxury car" specification. New for 1976 was the Aspen compact with the 3687cc six (or optional V-8s of 5211cc or 5899cc), which supplanted the Dart, and offered a sporty "Super Coupé" with front and rear spoilers. A new Challenger appeared for 1978, based on the Colt, with 2540cc "Silent Shaft" engine, four-wheel disc brakes and five-speed manual transmission. Also new for 1978 were the Diplomat (based on Chrysler's LeBaron), the luxury Magnum XE, derived from the Charger SE, and the Omni fwd Compact, with a 1753cc VW engine. The Aries of 1983 had a transverse 2.2-liter engine. In 1984 Dodge announced the sporty Daytona hatchback, which was updated for 1992, with a new IROC R-T version powered by a turbocharged 2.2 liter I-4 engine added to the range. The Shadow of 1987 was built in three- and five-door versions, with a two-seat convertible (built in Toluca, Mexico) added in 1991. The mid-size Dynasty of 1988 had engines of 2.5 liters (I-4), 3.0 and 3.3 liters (V-6). The 1989 Spirit had European-influenced styling and 2.5-liter I-4 (with optional turbo) or multivalve 2.2-liter-turbo I-4 engine and a top speed of143 mph. The 1.5-liter Colt was aimed at young buyers looking for a Japanese-built vehicle. In 1990 Dodge launched the Canadian-built Monaco large car and, in the following year, came the best-selling Caravan minivan. Designed by Chrysler and engineered and built by Mitsubishi, the 159 mph Stealth sports car of 1991 boasted fwd and steering, and outstanding styling. The 1992 Viper sports car first appeared as a concept car in 1989, and public opinion compelled Dodge to put it into production. Performance from its unique 8.0-liter V-10 engine is "awe-inspiring," with a 165 mph top speed. In hard top GTS coupé form it found a wider buyer base.

The cars that really brought Dodge up to date were the Intrepid and Stratus sedans, which drew heavily from the parent Chrysler group's design work in the mid-1990s. A revised series of pick-ups and a Charger sedan concept were unveiled at the 1999 Detroit show, assuring the Dodge brand a characterful future.

1992 Dodge Viper RT/10 (left,) Chrysler Viper GTS coupé (below)

January 1908 the company changed hands. Only 35 hp two-seater roadsters were available to the public, as the main output became taxicabs.

DRAGON • USA 1921

Although the Dragon looked almost identical to the contemporary ReVere, there was no connection between the two. A 3620cc Midwest four-cylinder engine was used. Wire wheels were standard and open models only were available, although plans were made for a taxicab. Probably no more than a dozen units were completed.

DRAKE SIX • USA 1922

Built by the Drake Motor & Tyre Mfg Co of Knoxville, Tennessee, only a single prototype of the car (and one of a truck) was produced. The car featured a six-cylinder Herschell-Spillman engine, was equipped with disc wheels and was otherwise conventional throughout. Wheelbase was 127 inches and the touring car was listed at $2,195. A smaller model was planned but never built.

DREYHAUPT • Germany 1905

A simple car with a two-cylinder 10 hp De Dion engine built in very limited numbers. Most parts were supplied by other companies.

DRIGGS • USA 1921-1923

The idea of the Driggs car was to emphasize economic value in size with meticulous detail in construction or, as its slogan stated, "built with the precision of ordnance." Using a four-cylinder own-make engine of 1596cc, the 104-inch wheelbase Driggs was available in two open body styles as well as a coupé and a sedan. Relatively few were manufactured. In 1915-1916 the company built the Driggs-Seabury cyclecar, as well as Ritz, Sharon and Twombly light cars.

DRI-SLEEVE SPECIAL • England 1971-1972

Whether Ettore would have approved of it or not, the Dri-Sleeve replica of his type 37 Bugatti was built to exactingly high standards. A ladder chassis, housing a Cortina engine, supercharged or unsupercharged, was clothed in a mixture of aluminum and glassfiber. Despite anomalies like the large alloy wheels, the flavor was unmistakably Bugatti. Six were sold.

DRUMMOND • Scotland 1908-1909

The first Drummond was built as a personal car for D M Drummond of the North British Ironworks, Dumfries; 16/20hp cars of similar design were marketed in 1908 and 1909.

1928 Dixi 3/15 hp (licence-built Austin Seven)

DS • England 1978

Costing around £120, the DS Spyder kit does for the Triumph Spitfire what the Arkley does for the Sprite-Midget; gives a fresh, individual look to many ageing or rusting examples.

DSPL • France 1910-1914

Failed aeroplane builder Comte Pierre D"Hespel, of Premesques, near Pérenchies (Nord), built sporting four-cylinder cars with shaft drive. A 2815cc 12/13 hp DSPL was shown at the 1912 Paris Salon. D"Hespel not only built his own engines and coachwork, but also patented wheels with detachable rims.

DSR • France 1908-1909

This Parisian model had its epicyclic gearbox incorporated in the back axle.

DUAL-GHIA • USA 1955-1958

Gene Casaroll, head of Dual Motors, a haulage firm in Detroit, used Chrysler components, the 5162cc Dodge D-500 with engine and bodywork designed by Ghia, to make this Italian assembled car priced at $7,646. Available either as four-passenger hardtops or convertibles, the cars had Powerflite transmission, radio, heater and English leather upholstery. Rising costs put an end to production in 1958 after some 117 cars had been built.

DU BOIS • England 1903

This London-based company offered an 11 hp gasoline car and a 10 hp Steam Tonneau ("the most attractive steam car on the market.")

DUCOMMUN • Germany 1903-1905

Another small car factory in Alsace, Ducommun of Mulhouse built three models, all with square (4 1/4 x 4 1/4 inch) engines. There were a twin-cylinder of 2088cc and two distinct four-cylinder models of 4179cc. All had four speeds and shaft drive.

DUCROISET • France 1897-1900

Built on the "Berret" system, the 8 hp twin-cylinder Ducroiset of 1898 had a three-speed belt-drive transmission, and was sold in Britain as the "Hercules."

DUDLY BUG • USA 1914-1915

A bullnosed two-seater cyclecar manufactured in Menominee, Michigan.

DUER • USA 1907-1908

Rope final drive characterized this 12/15 hp high-wheeler from Chicago.

DUESENBERG • USA 1966 to date

One car was built by Ghia to the design of Virgil Exner in 1966, in an attempt to revive the Duesenberg car. In 1971 the Duesenberg Motor Corp of Gardena, California, launched a replica of the SSJ short-wheelbased Duesenberg of 1936. Although identical in appearance to the original, it was built on a modified Dodge truck chassis, powered by a 6210cc Chrysler V-8 engine and bodied in aluminum. It cost $50,000, and it is believed that 25 cars had been built by 1977.

DUESENBERG • USA 1920-1937

See panel

DUFAUX • Switzerland 1903-1909

Charles and Frederic Dufaux were well-known motorcycle makers from Geneva who had a 12.8-liter straight-eight racing car built in the Piccard-Pictet works with the aim of competing in the 1904 Gordon Bennett Cup. It was joined in 1905 by a 26.4-liter 150 hp four which set up a flying kilometre world speed record of 156.5 km/h (97.2 mph) at Salon. That year, too, the Dufaux built a partly successful gasoline-powered helicopter. The first touring Dufaux cars appeared in 1905, built in a new factory at Balexert, a suburb of Geneva. They had four-cylinder 35 cv engines. In 1906 a 16 cv of 4084cc also appeared. At least one straight-eight 70/90 cv limousine was built. An association with the Italian marque Marchand was agreed in 1907, but the Marchand-Dufaux lasted less than two years.

DU FURAN • France 1907

"Quadrivoiturettes" from this maker of cycles and car components appeared at the 1907 Paris Salon.

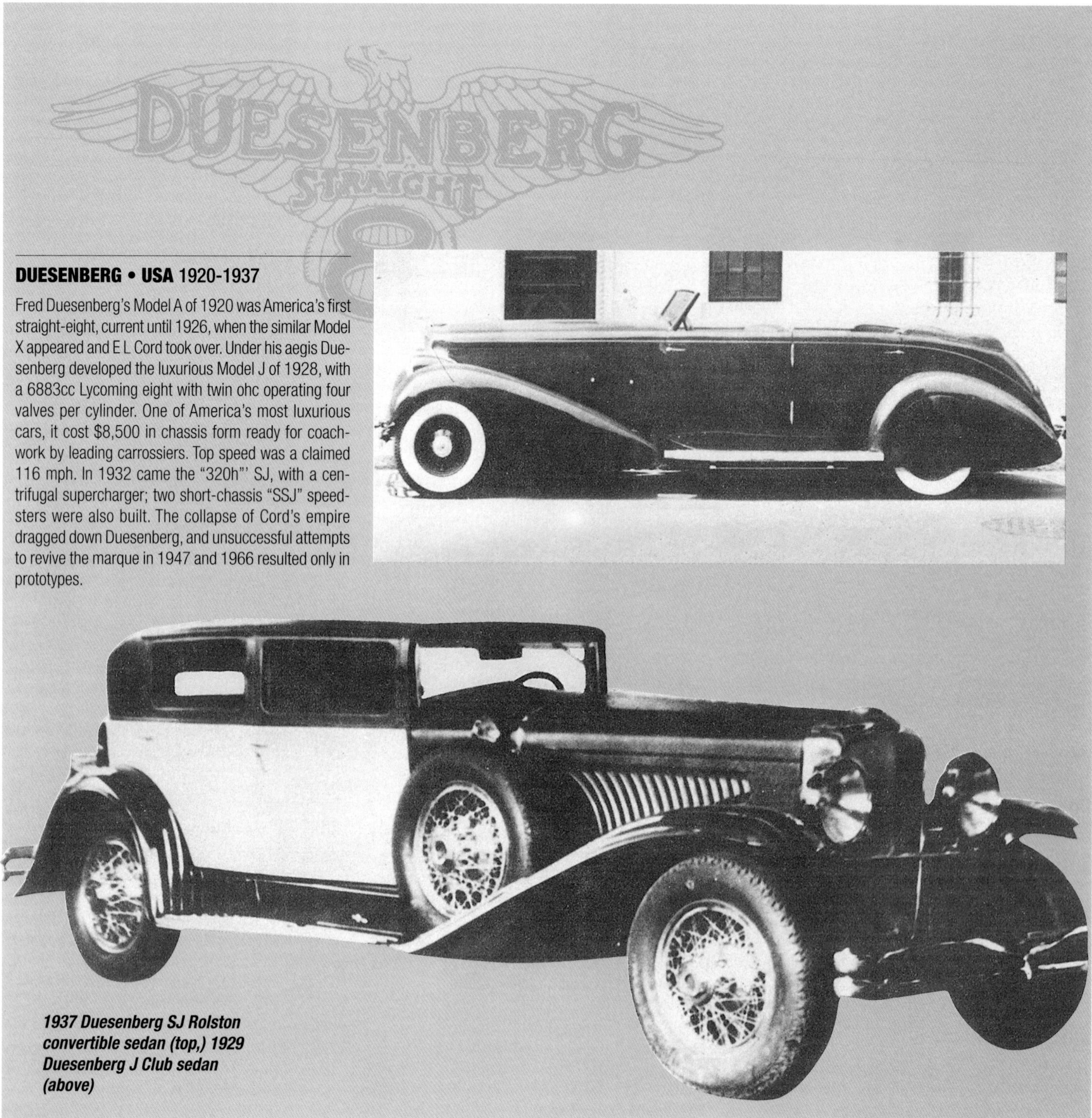

DUESENBERG • USA 1920-1937

Fred Duesenberg's Model A of 1920 was America's first straight-eight, current until 1926, when the similar Model X appeared and E L Cord took over. Under his aegis Duesenberg developed the luxurious Model J of 1928, with a 6883cc Lycoming eight with twin ohc operating four valves per cylinder. One of America's most luxurious cars, it cost $8,500 in chassis form ready for coachwork by leading carrossiers. Top speed was a claimed 116 mph. In 1932 came the "320h"' SJ, with a centrifugal supercharger; two short-chassis "SSJ" speedsters were also built. The collapse of Cord's empire dragged down Duesenberg, and unsuccessful attempts to revive the marque in 1947 and 1966 resulted only in prototypes.

1937 Duesenberg SJ Rolston convertible sedan (top,) 1929 Duesenberg J Club sedan (above)

DUHANOT • France 1907-1908

Best known as a builder of taxicabs, Duhanot of Paris began production with a six-model line-up, hastily reduced to three soon after the launch. The Duhanot"s most endearing feature was a tubular radiator which revolved like the blades of a fan. The 1908 range consisted of 12/4 hp and 17/20 hp fours, with conventional coolers.

D-ULTRA • England 1914-1916

A 995cc Lister four-cylinder engine powered this Clapham, London, company's principal offering, a two-seater light car. 8 hp Chater-Lea twin-cylinder models were also listed.

DUMAS • France 1899-1902

A Paris-built car with a twin-cylinder 2083cc power unit. A 41/2 hp three-wheeler was also built.

DUMONT • France 1912-1913

A shortlived friction-drive 1335cc single-cylinder voiturette built at Asniéres (Seine), and also sold by Gregoire.

DUNALISTAIR • England 1925-1926

Only four examples of this Nottingham-built car were made. A 14 hp Meadows engine and gearbox were used.

DUNKLEY • England 1896-1925

Dunkley of Birmingham was best known as a pram manufacturer, but from 1896 built a series of gas-propelled cars of curious design. These went into full production in 1901, equipped with take-off pipes so that they could refill from any convenient street lamp. They were built for four or five years. In 1911 Dunkley built a cyclecar called the Alvechurch, after the street in which the factory was located. In 1923 it introduced a design which beat even the gas cars for eccentricity, the motorpram, powered by the Pramotor power pack. It resembled a scooter, with the front wheel replaced by the pram. Top of the range was the "Saloon Pramotor" which, at 135 guineas, cost more than a Model T Ford. A 750cc version appeared in 1924, the year before production ended.

8 hp Duo cyclecar, 1914

DUNN • USA 1914-1918

A $295 15 hp vee-four roadster from Ogdensburg, NY; "a wonder of speed and handling."

DUO • England 1912-1914

The original Duo cyclecar was a 964cc vee-twin. In 1914 a three-car range, 747cc single, 1085cc twin, and 1093cc four, replaced it.

DUPLEX • USA 1908-1911

Two cylinders, two flywheels, two friction drives, two propeller shafts and two crown wheels and pinions earned this Chicago-built 18/20 hp car its name.

DUPLEX • England 1919-1921

The first Manchester-built Duplex had a 10 hp sleeve-valve engine with two parallel rows of four cylinders. Production models used a 11.2-liter Coventry-Climax.

DUPONT • USA 1915

The DuPont car of 1915 was the former Sphinx under a different company and name (see Sphinx.) This DuPont bore no relationship to the later DuPont car built from 1920 to 1932.

DUPONT • USA 1920-1932

Wealthy industrialist E Paul DuPont's company built just 537 luxury cars, starting with a 4.1-liter sv own-make four, followed by proprietary sixes; notably by Wisconsin and Herschell-Spillman. The best-known DuPont was the Model G Speedster, with a 5.3-liter Continental straight-eight, bullnosed radiator grille and Woodlite headlamps. Its top speed was 114 mph. The ultimate DuPont cars were assembled in the Indian motorcycle factory.

1903 Duryea Power Surrey

DUPRESSOIR • France 1900-1914

Paul Dupressoir of Maubeuge (Nord) built chassis and components. He began production in 1899 with De Dion-engined tricycles and quadricycles, as well as a "motor forecarriage" for converting "small carts" into motorcars. The company"s original car was a single-cylinder voiturette with de Dion or Aster power unit but, in 1905, the "Rolling" models of 6 to 24 hp were introduced. Production was delayed by a fire which destroyed the factory in June 1905. Shown at the 1905 Paris Salon were two "Rollings," a special taxicab chassis of 12/14 hp and a 16 hp touring car.

DURANT • USA 1921-1932

Sister marque to Eagle, Flint, Locomobile, Princeton, Rugby, and Star in Billy Durant's "Second Empire," the Durant had an ohv four-cylinder engine and a tubular "backbone" reinforcing its chassis. Production peaked early, reaching 55,000 in 1922 and falling thereafter. An Anstead-engined six was listed in 1922-23. Production reached a hiatus in 1927, restarting in 1928 with a redesigned range of four- and six-cylinder models. Two sizes were offered in 1930, and Continental engines were used in the 1931 Durants. Sales fell to 7,270 that year, and the firm collapsed early in 1932. Canadian Durants were sold as "Frontenacs."

DURKOPP • Germany 1898-1927

A producer of bicycles, sewing-machines, and, later, motorcycles and ball-bearings, Dürkopp of Bielefeld in Westphalia built its first cars on Panhard & Levassor lines. They were known in England under the "Watsonia" trademark, in other countries as "Canello-Dürkopp" cars. Many different models came into being, with two-, four-, six- and even eight-cylinder engines. There was a "six" already in 1904, and an eight-cylinder prototype in 1905; also four-cylinder cars from 14 hp to 100 hp, and even three-cylinder models built under Belgian Dasse license. There were

Kaiserpreis racing cars with 7450cc engines, big fours of 13,077cc (150mm bore and 185mm stroke) and also small 1560cc four-cylinder versions. The famous 2540cc P10 four-cylinder (built from 1914 to 1922) and the 2080cc P8 developing 32 hp at 2500rpm preceded the last Dürkopp passenger car, the 3006cc six-cylinder P12.

DUROCAR • USA 1907-1909

Los Angeles was the home of this car, which had a horizontal 26 hp twin engine beneath the seat.

DURYEA • USA 1893-1916

"A carriage, not a machine" was the proud slogan of America's first production car. The brothers Charles and Frank Duryea built their first "Power Wagon" in 1893 and, following a quarrel, Frank began production in Springfield, Illinois, in 1895. Thirteen Benz-like cars were built in 1896, and two of them ran in the 1896 London-Brighton Emancipation Day run, making Duryea America's first exporter, too. But the company folded in 1898 and Charles took over, producing – from around 1900 – baroque three- and four-wheelers with "one-hand control." (the two gears were selected by moving the steering tiller – whose grip was also a hand throttle - back and forth) and transverse three-cylinder engines with desaxé cranks. These ingenious machines were also license-built in England from 1904-1907, and in Belgium. From 1908 the American company (which had moved to Reading, Pa., in 1903) produced the crude Buggyaut high-wheeler, with two-speed friction drive selected by moving the whole engine in the frame. By 1916 the three-wheeled friction-drive Duryea Gem cyclecar was being built by Cresson-Morris of Philadelphia.

DUTTON • England 1970 to date

From its humble beginnings on a Sussex pig farm, Tim Woolley's low-budget sports car company has gone from strength to strength. From the P1 to Malaga the simple Lotus Seven style machines have followed the same format. Hundreds of kits have now been sold.

DUX • Germany 1905-1926

Dux originated from the Polyphon-Werke at Leipzig, which originally built the American Oldsmobile under license as the "Polymobile." Dux produced a variety of sturdy cars designed by Gustav Schürmann, which included 1546cc, 2038cc, and 2597cc sv four-cylinder models, including sports cars. Two models dominated production to the end, when Dux was bought by Presto. These were a 4680cc four-cylinder developing 50 bhp at 1500 rpm and a 4440cc six-cylinder.

1972 Dutton B-Type sports

1950 Dyna Veritas cabriolet

D-WAGEN • Germany 1924-1925

Made at the Haselhorst factory of the Berlin-Spandau-based Deutsche Werke, the 1290cc four-cylinder D-Wagen was a four-seater touring car. The principal products were D-Rad motorcycles. After 1925 the factory assembled American Durant and Rugby cars, and was eventually bought by DKW for the manufacture of its two-stroke cars.

DYKE • USA 1901-1904

A L Dyke, the "Gasoline Doctor" of St Louis, began by selling his "Automorettes" in kit form for $350 or complete for $600. He made his own engines of 3 to 10 hp and, from 1906-1907, collaborated in producing the 35 hp DLG.

DYMAXION • USA 1933-1934

A "geodesic" three-wheeler with teardrop styling and rear-mounted Ford V-8, conceived by architect Buckminster Fuller. Only three were made.

DYNA-VERITAS • Germany 1950-1952

Handsome cabriolets using the 744cc flat-twin engine and most other components of the fwd Dyna-Panhard. The producer of Dyna-Veritas cars was Veritas; a factory best known for its larger sports and racing cars.

D'YRSAN • France 1923-1930

Another French three-wheeler, made in Asniéres by the Marquis Siran de Cavanac, using Ruby and SCAP engines of 750cc and 1100cc plus independent front suspension by leaf springs. At the end of production the D'Yrsan works made a few four-wheeled cars with Ruby and SCAP engines, some supercharged for racing. It also made motorcycles.

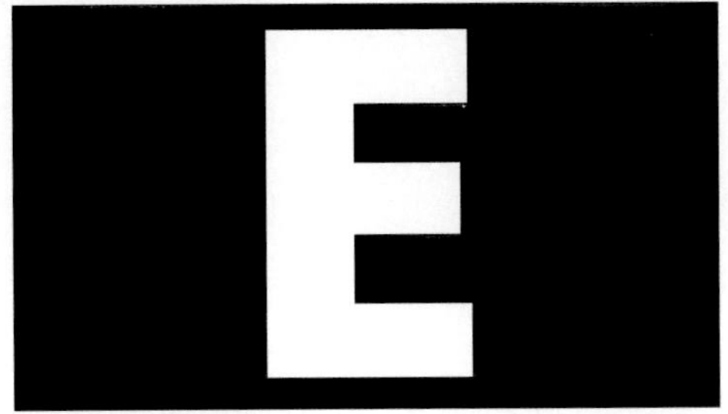

EADIE • England 1898-1900

Eadie of Redditch built motor tricycles and quadricycles with 21.4 hp De Dion engines.

EAGLE • England 1901-1913

Ralph Jackson started building "Ralpho" cycles at Altrincham, Cheshire in 1885 then, in 1899, founded the Century Engineering & Motor Co to build his design of a three-wheeler, the "Century Tandem." He sold the company and the design in 1901 to a London businessman named Begbie, who imported Aster engines into Britain but continued building the tricars in Altrincham under the name Eagle. The two makes even appeared on different stands at the 1904 Crystal Palace Show. Light cars with a similar epicyclic transmission to the Eagle Tandem appeared in 1903; a two-cylinder 9 hp competing in that year's ACGBI reliability trials. There was also a fearsome "Racer" version of the Eagle Tandem, with a 16 hp engine, capable of "over 80 mph." The company was wound up in 1907, but Jackson continued to assemble cars (now called "New Eagle") in a nearby electricity generating station. This continued until 1910, when he founded a garage. In 1913 he produced a prototype cyclecar, the Eagle Runabout, with a vertical twin two-stroke engine and pedal-controlled epicyclic transmission.

EAGLE • England 1913-1914

The Eagle Motor Manufacturing Co, which built a £109 999cc twin and a £175 1131cc four, preceded the Beverley-Barnes.

EAGLE • USA 1915

Three- and five-passenger electric coupés from Detroit.

EAGLE • USA 1923-1924

A brief attempt by Durant to market a car in the $800 price range. Pilot models only were built before the project was dropped. A six-cylinder Continental engine was employed on the Eagle, which had been planned to fill the gap between the Star and the Durant Four.

EAGLE • England 1979 to date

A very pretty, front-engined two-seater sports car with more than a hint of Fiat X1/9, the Eagle has Leyland 1100/1300 subframes bolted to a purpose-built, steel-tube chassis. The body is moulded in glassfiber, has burst-proof doors and a built-in roll-over bar. Alternative power units include Ford Fiesta and Simca.

EAGLE • USA • Canada • Japan 1988 to date

Built in Normal, Illinois, Bramalea, Ontario or Mizushima-Okazaki, Japan, depending on model, the Eagle comes

Eagle Talon TSi

from Diamond-Star Motors, a joint Chrysler-Mitsubishi venture. The first Eagle was the 1988 Premier, a Giugiaro-styled midsize notchback with 3.0-liter V-6 power. Then came the 1989 Summit 1.5-liter compact, available in three- or four-door form. In 1990 Eagle launched the Talon sports coupé with fwd or 4x4 transmisson and, in 1992, came the 1.8-liter Summit Wagon, which combined the merits of car and van, with a sliding side door.

EARL • USA 1905-1909

Earl began with a 15 hp flat-twin car with flitch-plated oak chassis and friction drive. Production started in Milwaukee in January 1906 and, in mid-1907, the company moved to Kenosha, where a 20 hp twin and 22 hp four were announced. By January 1908, 81 Earls had been completed.

EARL • USA 1922-1924

The Earl was simply the continuation of the Briscoe. The Earls, of which some 2,000 units were marketed, were four-cylinder cars with engines of their own design and make. The wheelbase was 112 inches, and the touring car was listed at $1,095.

EASTMAN • USA 1899-1902

H F Eastman of Cleveland, Ohio, built America's first all-steel car, the three-wheeled "Electro Cycle," in 1899. Its battery and electric motor accounted for three-fourths of its weight. A four-wheeled version was built in Detroit.

EASTMEAD-BIGGS • England 1901-1904

With an 8 hp Simms engine, the Eastmead-Biggs had a patent chassis "whereby flexibility is obtained without the use of universal joints." The vehicle was also sold as the "Velomobile."

L'"ECLAIR • France 1907-1908

This Parisian car manufacturer exhibited a 20 hp four at the 1907 Paris Salon.

ECLAIR • France 1920-1925

Made by Lebeau and Cordier in Courbevoie, this tiny cyclecar was powered by a 7/9 hp Anzani 500cc vee-twin and had a two-speed gearbox in the back axle.

ECLIPSE • USA 1900-1903

A three-cylinder shaft-drive steam runabout from Boston.

ECLIPSE • USA 1905

A single-cylinder 1688cc engine powered this epicyclic geared tourer from Milwaukee.

ECLIPSE • England 1906

A coachbuilt 51.2 hp tricar with a vee-twin engine from the maker of the XL-All motorcycle.

ECONOMIC • England 1921-1922

This spindly Economic three-wheeler was propelled by a 200cc twin-cylinder engine, driving by chain to the off-side rear wheel.

ECONOMY • USA 1906-1909

"One of the busiest factories in Joliet, Illinois" built this high-wheeler.

ECONOMY • USA 1917-1921

An assembled six-cylinder automobile, the Economy used a Continental engine and other standard components. It was connected "businesswise" with the Vogue, which was built in the same town of Tiffin, Ohio. The earliest Vogue

1960 Edsel Ranger

models were also frequently described as "Economy-Vogue" cars.

ECONOOM • Holland 1913-1915

Only 85 of these light cars were built in the Amsterdam factory of Hautekeet & Van Asselt, using Ballot engines and MAB chassis imported from France.

EDISMITH • England 1905

Edwin Smith of the Circus Garage, Blackburn, Lancashire, built cars under this name, with Tony Huber and De Dion power units.

EDIT • Italy 1923-1925

Designed by Mascheroni of Milan, the Edit was a cyclecar-like small car with a 10 hp twin-cylinder engine. It was available with a three-seater body and also as a two-seater sports car.

EDMOND • England 1920-1921

A two-cylinder 5/7 hp engine by Coventry-Victor powered the Edmond cyclecar, built by the Shand Motor Company of Lee Green.

EDMUND • England 1920

C Edmund & Co built motorcycles at Chester between 1907 and 1923. In 1920 a shaft-driven cyclecar put in a brief appearance.

EDSEL • USA 1958-1960

Launched in a blaze of publicity to plug the gap between the Lincoln and Mercury lines, the Edsel proved to be Ford's most costly mistake, losing between $250-350 million in its short lifespan. Four series – the low-priced Ranger and Pacer with a 5916cc V-8 and "upper-medium-priced" Corsair and Citation with a 6719cc V-8 – were available in 18 models. Pushbuttons in the steering wheel hub controlled the automatic transmission, standard on the costlier models, and the front-end styling, with its vertical "horsecollar" grille, was controversial. A sales recession coincided with the Edsel's launch, and only 60,000 were sold in the first year, falling to 44,000 in 1959. Completely restyled for 1960, and only offered in the Ranger Series, the Edsel was now basically a Ford with a Pontiac-like grille, and only 2,846 were sold before the division ceased operation.

1958 Edsel Citation

EDWARDS • USA 1912-1914

Forerunner of the Willys-Knight, this New York-built tourer had a 4523cc four-cylinder sleeve-valve engine and an overdrive fourth speed.

EDWARDS • England 1913

This cyclecar had huge airscoops in its hood for cooling its 8 hp Precision vee-twin

EDWARDS • USA 1949-1955

E H Edwards of San Francisco built a sports car endeavouring to combine the best of European and American engineering. A tuned Ford V-8 engine powered the Edwards, which had an aluminum body on a tubular chassis with all-round independent suspension. For racing (where it proved successful) the leather hard top and windshield were removable. Later models used glassfiber bodies and 205 hp Lincoln V-8 engines with GM Hydramatic transmission.

EGG • Switzerland 1898-1919

Rudolf Egg built his first car in 1893 and, between 1896 and 1898, was responsible for the Egg & Egli, a three-speed tricar with a single-cylinder De Dion engine and two-speed belt drive. From 1898 he built Benz-derived four-wheelers at Zurich, but production was halted by a fire in 1905 which destroyed both factory and completed vehicles. In 1914 Egg cars reappeared, based on the Moser voiturette, and in 1918-1919 Moser also built a four-cylinder Zurcher-engined Egg, with a gearbox in the back axle.

EGO • Germany 1921-1927

This marque sprang to fame in 1923, when young Rudolf Caracciola won a race at the Berlin Stadium on an EGO.

1922 Ego 4/14 hp

The EHP of Lenoist/Doré in the 1925 Le Mans

The EGO range included four-cylinder models of 1016cc, 1290cc and 1320cc, the last with ohv.

EHP • France 1921-1929

The Etablissements Henri Précloux made light cars and cyclecars of 903cc, 959cc, and 1094cc. After 1924 it presented a 1203cc CIME-engined version. The company occasionally entered racing events, and built an ohc 1500cc engine for that purpose. The last models had sv CIME six-cylinder engines of 1792cc. They sold very well. EHP were regular entrants at Le Mans from 1925 to 1928.

EHRHARDT • Germany 1905-1924

Gustav Ehrhardt, son of Heinrich Ehrhardt of Wartburg (Dixi) fame, built cars at Zella-St Blasii and at Düsseldorf. These were two- and four-cylinder models of high quality, but also highly priced. The largest was a 7956cc four-cylinder model which, by 1913, had four-wheel brakes. After 1918 the factory built a 40 hp four-cylinder and 55 hp six-cylinder with ohc engines; luxury cars of the highest caliber.

EHRHARDT-SZAWE • Germany 1924-1925

The Szawe was one of the most luxurious cars ever built in Germany. When the Szawe works at Berlin-Reinickendorf closed down, Ehrhardt took over the limited manufacture of the 2570cc 10.50 hp ohc Szawe car, a six-cylinder designed without regard to cost. Even the radiator was made from German silver.

1905 Ekstromer Electric

EISENACH • Germany 1898-1903

Predecessor of the Wartburg, Eisenach mainly built electric cars. The factory adopted the "Wartburg" name soon after production of gasoline cars began.

EJYR • England 1907-1914

In 1907 E J Y R Rutherford of Newbury, Berkshire, built a prototype flash-boilered steam car, and went into production later that year with a three-cylinder 30/40 hp steamer on gasoline-car lines which cost £575 with side-entrance bodywork. After 1908 the cars were known as "Rutherfords", and the price cut to £535. By 1911 the price was down to £400. An improved model with the spiral tube condenser forming the hood sides appeared in 1912, but the Highclere Motor Car Syndicate, which built the cars, went into liquidation soon afterwards.

1898 Cail (SAAC,) immediate forerunner of the Elan

EKSTROMER • England 1905

Ekstromer was a battery manufacturer which also offered a range of electric vehicles, including a light two-seater, said to have a range of 100 miles.

ELAN • France 1898-1900

The original "Elan" had an air-cooled vertical-twin engine and two-seater coachwork by Kellner.

ELCAR • USA 1915-1931

The Elkhart Carriage Co of Elkhart, Indiana, had been in business over 30 years before it produced its first car, the 30/35hp Elkhart of 1905-09. It was followed by the 4.2-liter Sterling (1909-11) and the 1911 Komet. The Elcar appeared in 1915. Two models were offered in the early days, a Lycoming-engined four and a Continental-engined six. A straight-eight, again Continental-engined, appeared in 1925. In 1930 the company became involved with the Reverend Alvah Powell's complex Lever engine, although only four Elcar-Levers were actually built. A lucrative contract supplying El-Fay taxis to a New York operator came to a sudden end when he was gunned down, and a project to market the 1930 Elcar as a revived Mercer for 1931 ended after only two prototypes had been built.

ELCO • USA 1915-1916

A 30 hp touring car from Sidney, Ohio, with a 1852cc Davis power unit.

1919 Elcar Six

ELDREDGE • USA 1903-1906

A light two-seater runabout with left-hand drive, built by the National Sewing Machine Co of Belvedere, Illinois.

ELECTRA KING • USA 1961 to date

Built by Billard & Zarpe of the B & Z Electric Car Co of Long Beach, California, the Electra King had a 45-mile range on a single charge. Powered by a 1 hp DC electric motor and five 6 volt batteries, the car could cruise at 18 mph. In 1972 Robert E McCoy, an electronics engineer, bought the project. Three- and four-wheel versions are currently offered with a choice of four electric motors. Cruising speeds vary from 16 to 29 mph and the range from 18 to 36 miles.

ELECTRICAR • France 1920-1921

An urban car with a 1-2 hp electric engine made by M Couaillet of Paris. It was a single-seater three-wheeler with a single front wheel.

ELECTRIC CARRIAGE AND GARAGE CO • England 1902

Formal electric vehicles (Landaulette, Victoria and Coupé) designed for town use.

ELECTRICIA • France 1901

A tiller-steered electric phaeton designed by Contal.

ELECTRIC MOTIVE POWER • England 1897

A heavy electric phaeton capable of running 20 miles on one charge.

ELECTRIC VEHICLE • USA 1899

These electric cabs were widely used in New York. They pioneered the use of pressed-steel wheels, and had fwd and brakes and rear-wheel steering.

ELECTROGENIA • France 1903-1905

"No breakdowns" was the optimistic promise for this "4 kilowatt" gasoline-electric (known as Champrobert in 1902) from Levallois-Perret.

ELECTROMOBILE • England 1901-1920

This London maker of electric town carriages offered a contract lease scheme as early as 1904. From 1903 the motor was mounted on the rear axle. Design changed little before the First World War. In 1919 a new model, the 8/12hp Elmo electric, with a short hood, appeared.

1920 Elfe Cyclecar

ELECTROMOTION • France 1900-1909

Electric cars with hub motors, built at Neuilly-sur-Seine.

ELECTRON • France 1907-1908

An electric car shown at the 1907 Paris Salon.

L'"ELEGANTE • France 1903-c1907

De Dion-like cars of 4hp to 12hp, built in Paris.

ELFE • France 1920-1925

Made in Levallois by M. Eugène (founder of the Bol d'Or race,) the Elfe started as a cyclecar with passenger accommodation in tandem (the driver being in front) and the 987cc vee-twin Anzani 984cc mounted centrally in the chassis. M. Mauve also made some touring cyclecars with 704cc two-stroke vee-twin Vapor engines.

ELGE • France 1924-1925

A marque created at Bordeaux by Roger Louis Maleyre, a pioneer of aerodynamics. Very low and light, and remarkably streamlined, Elgé cars used CIM engines. Maleyre also built a prototype propeller-driven car which proved to be a one-off design. Total production was about 30 cars.

ELGIN • USA 1916-1925

Starting as a four-cylinder, the Chicago-built Elgin adopted a 2954cc ohv six in 1918, subsequently uprated to 3205cc. The 1922 Elgin six offered a Cutler-Hammer magnetic gearshift.

ELIESON • England 1898

An electric dog-cart with a narrow-tracked front axle.

ELITE • USA 1901

Built by D B Smith of Utica, NY, this steam car and its sister marque, the Saratoga Tourist, were said to be "the handsomest vehicles ever built." The press just called them "singular."

1925 Elgé coupé

1921 Elite 10/38PS

ELITE • Germany 1920-1928

The first Elite was a 3130cc four-cylinder with a sv 45 hp engine. In 1922 Elite introduced a luxurious touring car, the 4600cc six-cylinder developing 70 hp at 2000 rpm. A sporting version raced successfully by Walter Osterreicher had a 90 hp engine. Smaller models had sv six-cylinder engines of 2360cc, others 3128cc power units. In 1927 Elite merged with the Diamant motorcycle works and, in 1928, came under the Opel banner. Opel built motorcycles in the Elite plant, too.

ELIZALDE • Spain 1914-1928

Arturo Elizalde opened a garage in Barcelona in 1909, manufacturing automobile components. Backed by the Biada brothers he began building cars in 1914 and, by 1915, Alfonso XIII had a 20 cv Biada-Elizalde cabriolet in his stable. A 25 cv sports version of this car was marketed as the "Reina Victoria," it was the first Spanish car with four-wheel brakes. In 1920 the 19/30 cv Model 29 was announced, with an ohv 3817cc four-cylinder engine; similar models were built until 1927. But the sensation of

1920 Elizalde 18/20hp Reine Victoria

1906 Elswick 24hp

1920 was the magnificent 50.60 cv straight-eight Tipo 48; one of the first cars of this configuration to go into production. Its 8143cc power unit with four valves per cylinder incorporated a tyre pump which could also be used for vacuum-cleaning the interior of the car. There was also a 5181cc straight-eight Gran Sport version capable of 160km/h (100mph). Elizalde built trucks and aero engines as well as cars.

ELKA • Italy 1912-1914

Driving an Elka, Lucca was sixth in the 1914 Targa Florio. The Elka was really a Laurin & Klement, assembled by a small Italian company which imported components of these Austro-Hungarian cars, forerunners of the Skoda.

ELLEMOBIL • Denmark 1909-1910

In a 1909 catalogue from J C Ellehammer of Copenhagen two different types of car were offered for sale. Both types had air-cooled twin-cylinder engines and friction drive in combination with belt or chain drive. Ellehammer was a famous aviation pioneer and, in 1905, he had built a 11 hp three-cylinder engine for a helicopter, but it was never used for that purpose. In 1913 the engine was modified and put into an experimental car, together with another invention; a hydraulic clutch. There was no production of this car, and few of the earlier models were built.

ELLIOT • USA 1897-1900

Built in Oakland, California, this was a rotund 4 hp motor victoria.

ELMORE • USA 1900-1912

Elmore, of Clyde, Ohio, never built anything except two-stroke-engined cars, starting with a 5 hp 1667cc twin-cylinder runabout with tiller steering and chain drive. A new range of shaft-driven cars with front-mounted two- and four-cylinder engines appeared in 1906, joined the following year by a 24 hp three-cylinder. The company, absorbed by General Motors in 1909, ceased operations three years later, after four-cylinder cars of 30 hp and 50 hp had been completed.

ELSWICK • England 1903-1907

The round-radiatored Elswicks were assembled cars using four-cylinder engines of 13/20 hp and 26/30 hp and a 26/30 hp six.

ELVA • England 1955-1968

Elva was formed by Frank Nichols to build competition cars, but unexpected success led to early thoughts of road versions. Over 2,000 Elvas were eventually made, the most famous of which were the various marks of Courier, and the stillborn Fiore-styled Elva BMW GT160.

L"ELYSEE • France 1903

A "high-class French car" imported into London by Henry Whitlock Ltd.

ELYSEE • France 1921-1925

Made by M Hood in Paris, these were light cars and cyclecars of 779cc, 950cc, and 1995cc.

EMERALD • England 1903-1904

A 4 hp light car from West Norwood, London.

EMERAUDE • France 1913-1914

A friction-drive Buchet-engined cyclecar.

EMERSON • USA 1916-1917

The Emerson was a four-cylinder light car produced in limited numbers only as touring models. In 1918 it became

1908 Empress 16/20hp Roi-des-Belges

the Campbell and was marketed under the latter name through 1919, when the company went out of business.

EMERY • England 1963

Although Paul Emery's name appeared on many successful racing cars, his pretty GT road car was shortlived. Sadly, only four of these Imp-powered, mid-engined two-seaters were built. Their glassfiber bodies were bonded to the neat space-frame chassis for ultimate strength.

EMF • USA 1908-1912

The "million-dollar" Everitt-Metzger-Flanders Co was launched in June 1908. The EMF 30 car, designed by William E Kelley, had a unit engine/gearbox and was planned for an initial production of 12,000 a year at a price of $1,250 for tourer, demi-tonneau, and roadster.

EMILE PILAIN • France 1930-1935

Made in Levallois by Emile Pilain, these were 5 hp light cars with a sv 950cc engine.

EMMS • England 1922-1923

A 10.8 hp 1368cc Coventry-Climax-engined light car from Coventry, the Emms cost £285.

EMPIRE • USA 1901-1902

Built in Sterling, Illinois, the Empire steamer had a vee-twin engine geared to the right-hand rear wheel.

EMPIRE • USA 1910-1919

"The little aristocrat," the four-cylinder Empire 20 was a shaft-drive race-about from Indianapolis. More conventional bodies were later available. The marque announced

1924 Endurance steam car

its 1916 35 hp in April 1915. Final products were a four of 3865cc and a six of 3670cc.

EMPIRE STEAM CAR • USA c. 1925-1927

The three-cylinder compound engined Empire Steamer was designed by Carl Ubelmesser and built by the Gruban Machine & Steel Corporation of New York City. Only one was built, and it was not completed.

EMPRESS • England 1907-1911

Built in Manchester, the Empress had a circular radiator and hood like the Delaunay-Belleville. It had a four-cylinder rotary-valve engine of 18/24 hp; there were also six-cylinder Empress cars of 24/30 hp and 30/36 hp.

EMSCOTE • England 1920-1921

A 961cc vee-twin engine, in unit with a three-speed gearbox, powered these Warwick-built cyclecars with center-pivot front axles.

EMW • Germany 1945-1956

The East German EMW was a slightly modified BMW built at the pre-war Eisenach BMW works, which were nationalized after the Second World War. The engines were similar to the pre-war BMW 326 and 327; and even the BMW emblem was used on this BMW-like car. It was not until 1952 that the name EMW was first used and the body shape changed slightly. The factory also built the AWE sports-racing cars, which were successfully driven by Barth and Rosenhammer.

ENDERS • France 1911-1923

A tiny cyclecar designed by M Violet, with a two-stroke 500cc engine.

ENDURANCE • England 1898-1901

The "New Endurance" car, of similar general design to the Benz, had a rear-mounted horizontal single-cylinder engine and was chiefly notable for its 10-inch water orifice,

1913 Enfield 18.4hp Phaeton

1973 Enfield Electric

designed to be filled straight from a stable-yard bucket; the water tank forming a dummy hood.

ENDURANCE STEAM CAR • USA 1922-1924

The Endurance had its origins with the Coats Steamer. It started in the east, but shifted operations to Los Angeles, California, where a single touring car was made. Endurance then moved to Dayton, Ohio, where one sedan was completed before the firm failed.

ENERGIE • France 1899-1902

The Société l'Energie, of Paris, originally built the Renaux motor tricycle. By 1902 it was making 81.2 hp light cars powered by vertical-twin Buchet engines.

ENFIELD • England 1906-1915

The car-making side of Royal Enfield became a separate entity, the Enfield Autocar Co, in 1906. The first cars to leave the Redditch factory were a shortlived 16/20 hp and a 24/30 hp, both four-cylinders. Enfield was soon acquired by Alldays & Onions, and an Alldays-engined 18/22 hp with a round radiator appeared in November 1907. It had a Hele-Shaw multi-plate clutch, and remained in production until 1910, in which year a new 16 hp was announced. In 1909 came an Enfield version of the 10/12 hp twin-cylinder Alldays, built in the new Enfield factory at Sparkbrook, Birmingham. The largest of the Enfields was the 1909-10 30/35 hp, with a 6107cc power unit. In 1913 there were two Enfield "Autolettes" – an 8 hp twin and a 9hp four; both with Alldays counterparts. The 14.3 hp, 18.4 hp, and 24.9 hp Enfields of 1913-1914 had neat flush-sided torpedo coachwork and detachable wheels.

ENFIELD • England 1973-1976

Over 100 Enfield electric cars were sold, 61 going to the Electricity Council for evaluation. A very good attempt at a mass-production electric vehicle, the Enfield was 8 inches shorter than a Mini. Under its dumpy glassfiber body were Hillman Imp suspension at the front and a live axle at the rear. Power came from a 48V, 6 Kw DC motor fed by eight 12-volt batteries. The maximum speed was 40mph and the range 40 miles.

ENFIELD-ALLDAY • England 1919-1925

The result of a union between the Enfield and Alldays & Onions car companies, the Enfield-Allday was an unconventional device powered by a five-cylinder sv 11.2-liter radial engine designed by A W Reeves and A C Bertelli. It also had a tubular backbone chassis. Orthodoxy triumphed in 1923, however, the 10/20 having a 11.2-liter water-cooled four-cylinder.

ENGELHARDT • Germany 1900-1902

This small, long-forgotten Berlin-based factory built a single-cylinder 61.2 hp vehicle.

ENGER • USA 1909-1917

Starting with a high-wheeled twin-cylinder car, by 1911 Enger of Cincinnati was making a $2,000 four-cylinder 40 hp. In 1915 it announced one of America's first V-12s. The ohv 1916 version of this car could be run as a six by cutting out one bank of cylinders.

ENKA • Czechoslovakia 1928-1929

Made by Kolanda & Spol at Prague, this Novotny-designed 499cc single-cylinder two-stroke two-seater had bodies made by the Aero factory, which was much better equipped for car production than Kolanda. In 1929 Aero took this design for manufacture in its own works. It was the first car to bear the Aero trademark.

ENSIGN, BRITISH ENSIGN • England 1913-1923

Building four-cylinder cars in 1913-1914, the British Ensign company of Willesden, London, introduced an advanced 38.4hp ohc six of 6795cc in 1919. A couple of cars with Crown Magnetic transmission were begun, but were completed only after the firm became bankrupt.

ENTROP • Holland 1909

Before 1909, Entrop of 'sGravenmoer built over 1,500 bicycles, but its car production amounted to only four units.

ENTYRE • USA 1910-1911

A 7.7-liter four from Oregon, Illinois.

ENV • France 1908

This English aero engine company had a French factory at Courbevoie (Seine) where an 8168cc 40 hp V-8 car with electrolytically deposited copper water jackets was also built in 1908. It had a two-speed gearbox and a dual-ratio back axle. The factory later housed the Alda car.

ENZMANN • Switzerland 1957-late 1960s

Enzmann bought new VWs, cut off the bodies and fitted them with elegant glassfiber coachwork produced by a boatyard at Grandson.

EOS • Germany 1922-1923

Made by Rossineck & Co. in Berlin, the small Eos had an 18 hp three-cylinder two-stroke engine. It was raced by the designer Rossineck without great success, as reliability was not its strong point. The car was also known as "Erco, but production was very limited.

1924 Eric Campbell 8/20hp Sports

1919 Essex Speedster

EPALLE • France 1910-1914

Light cars of 8/10 hp (twin) and 10/12, 12/16 and 14/20 hp (fours) from St Etienne.

ERAD • France 1978 to date

Microcar maker from Douai, which even offered a 600cc diesel-engined MG-TC replica.

ERDMANN • Germany 1903-1908

Known as the FEG (which stood for Friedrich Erdmann, Gera) this car had an Erdmann-patented friction drive. The range of models included two- and four-cylinder cars of up to 22 hp. The proprietary engines came from Fafnir, Korting, and Horch.

ERIC • England 1911-1914

The Northampton-built Eric was one of the more substantial cyclecars, with a flat-twin 1088cc engine/gearbox unit mid-mounted in a tubular chassis driving the rear wheel by shaft.

ERIC-CAMPBELL • England 1919-1926

Built originally by aircraft manufacturer Handley Page, the Eric-Campbell was created by Hugh Eric Orr-Ewing and Noel Campbell Macklin, later of Silver Hawk and Invicta fame. A tuned Coventry-Climax engine of 11.2 liters was fitted.

ERIC-LONGDEN • England 1922-1927

Vee-twin JAP engines of 8 or 10 hp powered the Eric-Longden, a rather GN-ish device with shaft drive. Later, in 1922, four-cylinder engines by Alpha and Coventry-Simplex were offered. Eric Longden ran a music-hall before the First World War.

ERIE • USA 1898-1901

Builders of gasoline and steam motor carriages from Anderson, Indiana.

ERIE • USA 1920

This four-cylinder car was assembled in Painsville, Ohio. Reportedly, only one pilot model was completed.

ERNST • Switzerland 1905-c. 1908

Four-cylinder Aster-engined cars of 2438cc and 3547cc with Malicet & Blin chassis, assembled in Geneva by ex-Daimler engineer Gustav Ernst.

ERSKINE • USA 1926-1930

Named after Studebaker's president, Albert R Erskine, the Erskine was advertised as a "European motor car" and such it was, its overseas sales being markedly more successful than those in America. It featured a 2320cc six-cylinder engine, increased in 1928 to 2629cc displacement. By 1930 the Erskine had increased in size and more closely resembled the Studebaker. With a price approaching $1,000 the Erskine was rechristened "Studebaker Six" in May of that year. Mr Erskine committed suicide in 1933.

ESCULAPE • France 1899

"Worked by an improved De Dion-Bouton motor, strengthened by a water current," the two-seater Esculape was said by its maker, the Automobile Union of Paris, to be "fast, silent and vibrationless." It was probably none of these.

ESCULAPEUS • England 1902

This "chainless" voiturette had a 5 hp Ader vee-twin engine and was designed for the use of medical practitioners, with a locker for their bag and full weather protection.

ESHELMAN • USA 1953-1960

The Chester L Eshelman Co of Baltimore, Maryland, manufactured a 54-inch-long, 24-inch wide one-passenger runabout powered by a 70 mpg 3 hp Briggs & Stratton engine. Several gardening attachments were available, including a lawn sweeper, reel mower, and trailer.

ESPANA • Spain 1917-1928

Barcelona textile engineer Felipe Batlló's first car, perversely called the España 2, had a four-cylinder Altos engine of 1847cc. It was followed by the España 3 of 3690cc with a four-cylinder ohv engine and four speeds forward. Only two prototypes were built, one for Batlló's father, the other for Alfonso XIII. España 4 was a 4.5-liter prototype with a 16-valve engine, and a six-cylinder was also built. In 1928 España merged with Ricart.

1973 Excalibur SS 7.4-litre

ESPERIA • Italy 1905-1910

Built by the Societa Automobili Lombarda "Esperia" at Bergamo, the Esperia cars were shaft-driven vehicles of 20 hp and 40 hp with ioe engines.

ESSEX • USA 1918-1932

Hudson"s low-priced ($1,595) and angular Essex line used a 2.9-liter four-cylinder ioe engine. A two-door sedan at $1,295 was added in 1922, making the marque a best-seller. A 2.1-liter six succeeded the four in 1924, and was later uprated to 2.5 liters as the "Super Six." Four-wheel brakes were optional in 1927, and standard the next year. The Challenger 18.2 hp Six of 1930 reinforced the marque's popularity. The 1932 Essex six had a 3.2-liter engine, V-radiator and Startix automatic starter, but was replaced the next year by a new marque, Terraplane.

EUCLID • USA 1907-1908

An air-cooled 20 hp three-cylinder two-stroke engine powered this car from Cleveland, Ohio.

EUCORT • Spain 1940-1953

A bold attempt at producing a "popular car," the Eucort, from Barcelona, had a 764cc twin-cylinder engine. The last new Eucort was the Victoria of 1950, with a 1034cc three-cylinder engine.

EUDELIN • France c. 1905-1908

A Parisian manufacturer which built 14/16 hp and 25/30 hp four-cylinder cars. Eudelin also made an opposed-piston engine with a complex variable-stroke linkage. Eudelin's original power unit was a "double piston engine with a single double-throw crank directly below the combustion chamber."

EUREKA • USA 1900

Ough & Waltenbaugh of San Francisco built this car with a 4408cc rear-inclined three-cylinder engine under the back seat.

EUREKA • France 1906-1909

A single-cylinder voiturette with friction transmission and belt final drive built at La Garenne-Colombes (Seine.) It was fitted with 6 hp De Dion or 12 hp Anzani engines.

EUREKA • USA 1907-1914

A wheel-steered high-wheeler from St Louis, Mo., with a two-cylinder air-cooled engine.

EVANTE • England 1987 to date

Built in a converted bulb warehouse in Lincolnshire, the Evante is a modern interpretation of the glassfiber-bodied Lotus Elan.

EVERITT • USA 1909-1912

After Studebaker took over EMF, Everitt and Metzger built this 30 hp four, which featured a "thiefproof" gear lever lock. It was also built in Canada as the Tudhope.

EVERY DAY • Canada 1911-1913

American-designed two-cylinder high-wheelers from Woodstock, Ontario.

EWING • USA 1908-1910

Designed by Louis Mooers, formerly with Peerless & Moon, the 20 hp Ewing, from Geneva, Ohio, was unusual in being sold with taxicab bodywork. About 100 were built.

EXAU • France 1922-1924

A cyclecar made in Paris by M Kolbac and designed by Jacques Muller (later with BNC) with a sv 870cc SCAP engine.

EXCALIBUR SS • USA 1964 to date

Brooks Steven Excalibur SS, manufactured in Milwaukee, Wisconsin, is loosely based on the 1930 Mercedes SSK. Its 1,500 parts are supplied by 250 manufacturers, and includes Chevrolet Corvette engines. Two models are available, a two-seater roadster and a four-passenger phaeton. Approximately 150 are produced per year, costing $20,000 each.

EXCELSIOR • Belgium 1901-1932

See panel

EXCELSIOR • England 1904-1905

A 41.2 hp tri-car from Bayliss & Thomas of Coventry, which built light cars from 1922.

EXCELSIOR • Switzerland 1905-1907

Designed by Rudolf Egg, the Excelsior was a 6 cv voiturette based closely on the curved-dash Oldsmobile, but with wheel steering. A round-radiatored four-cylinder with a German-made engine appeared in 1906.

EXCELSIOR • France 1907

A cycle and motorcycle maker from Bourgoin (Isère) which also built tricars.

EXCELSIOR-MASCOT • Germany 1911-1922

Only a few of these small cars were made by this Cologne-Nippes factory. They had two- and four-cylinder proprietary engines of 8 hp to 18 hp.

EXOR • Germany 1923

One of the many small post-war German car makers, Exor used a four-cylinder 16 hp proprietary engine.

EXPRESS • Germany 1901-1909

Germany's oldest bicycle manufacturer also built (with some interruptions) cars and, after the Second World War, motorcycles. The cars had 16 hp and 25 hp Fafnir engines. Express became part of the Sachs empire, and the manufacture of motorcycles ceased years ago.

EYSINK • Holland 1903-1919

The Eysink brothers built Holland's first indigenous car in 1897, only a year after the first two cars, a Benz and a Daimler, had arrived in the country. Production did not start in earnest until 1903, with a range of shaft-driven cars, of 10/12 hp, 16/20 hp, and 20/30 hp. A 30/40 hp six was also built. A 6/8 hp light car, announced in 1912, survived until 1919. Peak production of Eysinks was around 50 a year. The firm continued building motorcycles until 1957.

1911 Excelsior tourer

EXCELSIOR • Belgium 1901-1932

For its first few years Excelsior of Brussels built unremarkable light cars with proprietary engines. In 1905 one-, two- and four-cylinder Aster units were fitted. In 1907, however, engineer Arthur de Coninck took over and the company was producing his "Adex" six. Soon after, Belgica was taken over. The classic Edwardian Excelsior, the bi-block 29/30 hp Adex six of 4426cc, appeared in 1911, accompanied by a monobloc 2951cc four. Normally built with sidevalves, these cars had ohv in their sporting incarnations. The six was produced until 1920, when de Coninck launched a new ohc model with his own design of diagonally compensated four-wheel brakes, which was developed into the magnificent ohc Albert ler in 1922. This 5350cc six had triple Zenith carburetors and its cantilever rear springs incorporated anti-roll bars. An improved single-carburetor 30/100 hp version Albert ler, with vacuum servo brakes, appeared in 1926 but, in 1928, Impéria took over Excelsior and production ceased soon after, although a few Albert lers were subsequently assembled from existing parts to special order.

A racing Fafnir with special radiator cowl, 1922

Mk II Fairthorpe TX GT, 1968

FAB • Belgium 1912-1914

Successor to Vivinus, the FAB ("Fabrique Automobile Belge") offered two four-cylinder models, of 2121cc and 3563cc.

FACEL-VEGA • France 1954-1964

Last of the French builders of luxury cars, the Forges et Ateliers de Construction de l'Eure et Loire in Pont-à-Mousson was formerly a body builder for Simca, Ford and Panhard. It started to build complete cars in 1954, using Chrysler V-8 engines of 4.5 liters, and then of 5.8 and 6.3 liters. In 1957 Facel presented a voiture de prestige, the "Excellence." It also made a smaller model, the Facellia, originally fitted with a Facel-built dohc four-cylinder 1600cc engine. This unreliable engine caused great consternation among Facel's customers, and was mainly responsible for the failure of Facel-Vega. In 1962 the 1600cc engine was replaced by the Volvo 1800, but too late to restore confidence.

FADAG • Germany 1921-1925

A Düsseldorf bicycle and motorcycle producer whose cars were designed by Dr Ing George Bergman, Fadag offered four-cylinder models of 16, 18, 25, 30, and 32 hp. An ohc 50 hp with 2650cc Siemens & Halske engine was the only six-cylinder built by Fadag.

FAFAG • Germany 1921-1924

A sporting ohc 976cc four-cylinder built in limited numbers. Fafag's own-make 16-valve engine developed 40 bhp on alcohol fuel in racing form; the top speed was around 82mph. Count Hachenburg was a Fafag racing driver.

FAFNIR • Germany 1908-1926

A leading manufacturer of proprietary motorcycle and car engines, Fafnir of Aachen built four-cylinder cars with own-make ioe engines of 1520-2496cc. Of advanced design, Fafnirs also gained successes in races with such drivers as Caracciola, Uren, Müller, Hirth, and Utermöhle. The ultimate model, built in 1923-1926, had a 1050cc ohv engine developing 50 bhp at 2500rpm. Supercharged racing cars with this engine developed 80 bhp.

FAGEOL • USA 1916-1917, 1921

The Fageol was an enormous automobile produced by a successful firm of commercial vehicle and bus manufacturers in an attempt to seize the super-luxury-car market. The cars, sporting a 142-inch wheelbase, were powered by a six-cylinder ohv Hall-Scott engine with a displacement of 13,514cc. Very few were made. An attempt to market the car as late as 1921 was abortive, the company mounting several bodies on a single chassis in an unsuccessful attempt to win the approval of the affluent.

FAIRFAX • England 1906

The 7/9 hp twin-cylinder Fairfax, built in Chiswick, had "the engines placed well forward under the driver's footboard" and a constant-mesh gearbox simple enough, it was claimed, to be operated by a child.

FAIRTHORPE • England 1952 to date

Following the three-wheeler Atom there has been a succession of unusual glassfiber-bodied sports cars from this unique company.

1961 Facel-Vega Facellia

FAIRY • England 1907

Built by the forerunners of the Douglas Motorcycle Company, the Fairy Tricar had a 6/8 hp flat-twin engine.

F.A.L. • France 1907

Light cars built by Coll'habert et Sénéchal of Saint-Cloud (Seine-et-Oise.)

FAL-CAR • USA 1909-1913

Successor to Reliable Dayton, this was a 35/40 hp four, "trim, classy, speedy, and efficient" with the choice of three body styles.

FALCON • USA 1914

A cyclecar built in Ohio.

FALCON • USA 1922

Built in limited numbers in the Halladay factory, the Falcon was, in a sense, a smaller Halladay with a different design and original name. Using four-cylinder engines of its own make as well as by Rutenber, the Falcon had a 115-inch wheelbase and prices ranged from $1,295 to $1,595.

FALCON • Germany 1922-1926

The first Falcon was a 1459cc four-cylinder with a unit-design 18 hp long-stroke engine, which two years later was uprated to 1520cc. The last car made by Falcon was a 1496cc four-cylinder developing 36 hp at 3600rpm: racing versions had tuned 45 bhp engines and competed in the Avus race in 1922. The works at Ober-Ramstadt were bought in 1927 by Rühr, which built the 1.5-liter Zoller two-stroke racing cars there in 1934-35.

FALCON • England c. 1950-1964

Well-known re-clother of 1950s Fords, Falcon eventually progressed to making complete cars. However, for various reasons neither the 515 or 1000 was a success, and shortly before Falcon's closure the original and very pretty Caribbean Ford 8/10 replacement body was still its most saleable product, over 2,000 being sold.

FALCON-KNIGHT • USA 1927-1928

The Falcon-Knight was a link in the chain of John North Willys' automotive empire and, although technically an independent, it was little more than a companion car to the Willys-Knight 70 and the Whippet Six, with a six-cylinder Knight sleeve-valve engine and a wheelbase of 109½ inches. A complete line of closed and open coachwork was available, and prices ranged from $995 to $1,250. Artilery wooden wheels were standard on all models except the Gray Ghost roadster, the luxury car of the line, which

1962 Falcon Competition sports-racer

sported wire wheels. A unique accessory available on the roadster was a special top to keep the rain off rumble-seat passengers. The last cars were marketed as 1929 models.

FALKE • Germany 1899-1908

Early Falke models were based on French Decauville designs with De Dion engines; later ones had two- and four-cylinder Fafnir engines from 704cc to 1501cc. Production of these cars was on a limited scale.

FANNING • USA 1902-1903

This Chicago company built a "fetching" electric runabout as well as petrol cars.

FARCOT ET OLIVIER • France 1907

A builder of power units for cars and airplanes, this Parisian firm also offered a chassis with "progressive speed change." Taxis were built in some numbers.

FARMACK • USA 1915

An ohc 20 hp four built in Chicago; the two-seater cabriolet cost $1,155. It was succeeded by the similar Drexel (1916-1917,) which also added a dohc 16-valve 3-liter.

FARMAN • France 1902

Henry Farman, later a pioneer aviator, built a light car in 1902, but then joined his brother Dick building "BF" engines of 10, 12, 16, 24, and 45 hp with single-cast cylinders which they supplied to builders of motor cars and launches.

FARMAN • France 1920-1931

After the First World War the Farman brothers decided to build a luxury car in their airplane works. The engine was an ohc straight-six of 6597cc. To this model A6B was later added the NF, with a larger engine of 7069cc. Very few of either were made.

FARNELL • England 1897

Albert Farnell, a Bradford cycle agent, built this 11/4 hp car with tubular chassis, four-speed transmission and independent front suspension. In 1906 Farnell sold the TH 28/36 and 30/40 hp cars.

FARNER • USA 1922-1923

Although the name and specifications were published widely, it is unlikely that the Farner progressed beyond the planning stage. Trade journals of the time listed the car as being powered by a Continental six-engine, and quoted a 115-inch wheelbase together with three available body styles: touring car, coupé, and sedan, with prices ranging from $1,095 to $1,295 fob Streator, Illinois.

FARUS • Brazil 1981 to date

Produces the Quattro plastics-bodied sports coupé in 2.0 and 2.2 liter forms.

FAST • Italy 1919-1923

Designed by Ing Orazi, the Fast had an ohc 2960cc four-cylinder engine. It was an exclusive car built in limited numbers, and disappeared after a short production period.

FASTO • France 1924-1931

One of the few cars made in the Puy de Dome, Fasto started with a 10 hp four-cylinder of 1598cc, followed with another 10 hp of 1693cc, and a 14 hp of 2397cc. In 1930 Fasto offered only a 9 hp four-cylinder of 1616cc.

FAUBER • USA 1914

A low-built cyclecar with steel-faced wood body/chassis unit and an 8/10 hp twin-cylinder engine.

FAUGERE • France 1898-c. 1901

The Faugére was a spidery two-seater powered by a horizontal twin-cylinder engine which could be started from the driver's seat by lever. Top speed was 15mph.

FAUN • Germany 1924-1929

Famous for big trucks and municipal vehicles, Faun of Norimberk succeeded Ansbach, building light cars with ohc four-cylinder engines of 1410cc and 1550cc. The last models had Perrot four-wheel brakes.

FAURE • France 1941-1947

M Faure made a batch of little urban electric cars during the German Occupation.

LE FAVORI • France 1921-1923

A tiny three-wheeled cyclecar made in Paris, with a 987cc twin-cylinder engine.

FAW • China 1991 to date

The First Automobile Works (builders of the Hong-Qi) signed a 25-year contract with VW to build a new factory where Golfs and Jettas are made. In 1989 FAW bought the production line for the Chrysler 2.2-liter engine to power their version of the Audit 100; unfortunately it was incompatible with the German gearbox.

FAY • USA 1921

The Fay was built (or plans were under way for it to be built) as an export venture, but details of its construction are not known.

FD • Belgium 1923-1929

Light cars using 1.1-liter Ruby, 1 1/2-liter CIM, or 2-liter Altos engines.

FEDERAL • USA 1901-1905

A steam carriage built in Brooklyn, with all-steel bodywork.

1931 Farman Sedan

FEDERAL • USA 1907-1909

A wheel-steered high-wheeled motor buggy, originally from Chicago, later from Rockford, Illinois.

FEJES • Hungary 1923-1928

The entire Fejes car was built up from pressed and welded iron sheet, even its 1244cc ohv engine. Plans to produce this Budapest utility vehicle in England as the Ascot were stillborn.

FELBER • Switzerland 1975 to date

This company is based at Morges and builds a Michelotti-styled Lancia-engined roadster, and the FF Ferrari V-12 sports model; one model is the Pontiac Firebird-based Excellence Cabriolet/Coupé.

FELDMANN • Germany 1905-1912

Fafnir supplied the twin-cylinder 804cc engines for Feldmann's "Nixe" voiturette. Other models built from 1908 onwards had ohv 2120cc four-cylinder engines developing 25 bhp and, in a sporting version, 40 bhp.

FEND • Germany 1958-1961

Produced the FMR Tiger, a sporting four-wheeled version of the Messerschmitt cabin-scooter. It had a 493cc twin-cylinder Sachs two-stroke engine developing 19.5 bhp at 5000 rpm, mounted ahead of the rear axle, plus a four-speed gearbox. Only 240 were built.

EL FENIX • Spain 1901-1904

Domingo Tamaro Y Roig, who had worked with La Cuadra, built a few twin-cylinder gasoline-engined cars under this name at Barcelona before joining Turcat-Méry in 1904.

FERGUS • Ireland • USA 1920-1923

The Fergus was the culmination of an earlier (1915) car of the same name built in Ireland by Joseph Ferguson, Senior. At least one car, and probably as many as nine or ten, were practically hand-fashioned at the company's headquarters in Newark, NJ. The car featured a high-revving six-cylinder engine with overhead valves and overhead camshaft, springs housed inside deep frame members and cantilever springs all round. It also boasted complete pressure lubrication. A sedan was priced at $8,500.

FERRARI • Italy 1946 to date

See panel

FERRARI • Italy 1946 to date

The great Enzo Ferrari, closely connected for many years (until the end of 1938) with Alfa Romeo, built a few sports cars bearing his own name and his prancing horse badge, "inherited" from First World War flying ace Francesco Baracca, in 1940, but real car production did not start until after the end of the Second World War. In 1969 Ferrari became part of the Fiat empire, but Enzo Ferrari stayed on as head of his works at Maranello, near Modena. Some Fiat parts were used on his very early sports cars, but when Colombo designed new cars after the war they were a "pure" Ferrari product with dohc 1.5-liter, 2-liter, and 2.5-liter V-12 engines in various stages of tune. After 1950 Lampredi designed 4.5-liter and also 2-liter (four-cylinder) sports and racing cars for Maranello, where V-12s of 4.1 liters, 4.5 liters, and even 4.9 liters were built.

Many superb and powerful sports cars have left the Maranello works over the years, some developing over 400 bhp. Ferraris won Le Mans, as well as many championships all over the world, and built numerous fast cars with V-engines from 6 to 12 cylinders with double ohc valve gear. Recently, Ferrari has adopted flat-12 engines in his Formula 1 racing cars. In 1955 Ferrari took over the 2.5-liter F-1 Lancias, and since 1961 Ferrari competition cars have been rear-engined. There have, however, been many superb front-engined production models, like the 275 GTB with a 300 bhp 3.3-liter V-12 and the 300 bhp 4-liter V-12 330 GT and GTC. Then there have been the 2-liter mid-engined 180 bhp V-6 Dino GT, the 365 GTB 4 with a 4.4-liter 352 bhp V-12, the mid-engined dohc 2.9-liter 352 bhp V-12 and, more recently, the mid-engined dohc 2.9-liter 308 GTB/GTS and the 4.8-liter V-12 400 and 400 GT, successors to the 365 GT; these are coupés with Pininfarina bodywork. Another modern Ferrari, the BB 512, houses an ohc 4.9-liter flat-12 engine.

The Ferrari 400i/412 range appeared in 1979 and kept the V-12 tradition going through the 1980s. It ceased production in 1991 and was replaced by a new 5-liter V-12 model in the early 1990s. Launched in 1982, the 308GTB/GTS was Ferrari's best-selling road car, replaced in 1985 by the larger 328GTB/GTS, in turn supplanted in 1990 by the 348 Series. This grew into the F355 before the new 1999 model 360 Modena arrived with its high-tech alloy body and engine combinations mated to sheer Pininfarina style.The four-seat Mondial model covered different ground, as did the later, limited-edition, F50 road-legal racer with its composite panels and 200 mph top speed. The Testarossa of 1984 was described as "extravagance on four wheels," with a mid-mounted 5-liter flat-12. Launched to celebrate the company's 40th anniversary, the 3-liter V-8 F40 of 1987 was intended to be the ultimate road car, and at 201 mph it was the fastest as well – until the F50 came along. A more subtle, more classic, front-engine V-12 Ferrari returned in the form of the drop-dead gorgeous 456, while the 500 bhp front engined V-12 550 Maranello was a more overtly performance related Ferrari. Ferrari sales soared ever higher and waiting lists of customers got longer. The sign of the prancing horse seems to go from strength to strength.

1947/48 Ferrari 166

The Ferrari Testarossa from the late 1980s was the height of the wide-bodied supercar (above.) Ferrari 250 GTO (left)

FIAT

FIAT • Italy 1899 to date

Giovanni Agnelli, Count Biscaretti di Ruffia and Count di Bricherasio headed the Fabbrica Italiana Automobili Torino, which started business by absorbing Ceirano, on whose payroll was the talented designed Faccioli who created the first Fiat car, with a horizontal twin-cylinder 3½ hp engine. When the directors insisted that Faccioli should design a new model with the engine at the front instead of at the back, Faccioli resigned and was replaced by Enrico, who in 1902 brought out a 1.2-liter four-cylinder model which owed much to the recently introduced Mercedes. The years up to 1914 saw a succession of four-cylinder models of between 1846cc and 10,082cc, as well as sixes of 7408cc and 11,034cc. However, Fiat (known as F.I.A.T. up to the end of 1906) did not essay a popular mass-produced model until 1912, when the 1846cc "Tipo Zero" was launched. Post-war came the Cavalli-designed 501, with a four-cylinder 1.5-liter engine, of which more than 45,000 had been built by 1926. Alongside this, Fiat produced a very few examples of one of their few flops, the hyper-luxury V-12 6.8-litre SuperFiat of 1921-23; the 4.8-litre six-cylinder Tipo 519 was listed until 1929. In 1925 came a more modern light car, the 509, with an ohc 990cc engine, of which over 90,000 were sold up to 1929. The other principal models of the late 1920s were the 1440cc Tipo 514, the 2516cc Tipo 521, and the 3740cc Tipo 525, the latter two being six-cylinder models.

A major step forward came in 1932, with the introduction of the Tipo 508 Ballila (named after a Fascist youth organization), a 995cc ohv four developing 25 bhp in touring form, 36 bhp in its rare and desirable sporting form. It was license-built in Germany by NSU, in Czechoslovakia by Walter and in France by Simca (which also offered a very fast version tuned by Gordini). The backbone-framed 1500 of 1936, with its aerodynamic bodywork and Dubonnet-type ifs, led later that year to the immortal "Topolino" (Mickey Mouse) Tipo 500, with its four-cylinder 570cc engine mounted ahead of the radiator. This tiny two-seater continued almost unchanged until 1948. At the outbreak of war Fiat's best-selling models were the 500 (priced at £120 in England) and the 1100, or Millecento, while the biggest model then available was the 2852cc six, which cost £795 in Britain.

Little of novelty appeared in the immediate post-war years, until the advent of the over-square 1400 four-cylinder in 1950. The last of the Topolini, the ohv 500C, was replaced by the new 633cc rear-engined "600" in 1955; this unit-construction saloon sold a million by 1960. A twin-cylinder "Nuova 500" appeared in 1957, with a 499cc ohv power unit. Over 3 million examples of this model were built before it gave way to the derivative 126 in 1972. In the same vein as the 500 and 600 was the 850, with a rear-mounted four-cylinder in-line engine. In 1966 came one of Fiat's most popular models, the 124, with engines of 1197cc and 1438cc, which formed the basis of big license-production deals, especially in Eastern Bloc countries. A dohc 1608cc four, the 125, appeared in 1967, alongside the 1481cc 1500L, the six-cylinder 1795cc 1800B and 2279cc 2300; the Dino Spyder and Coupé with the 1987cc Ferrari-built dohc Dino V-6 had been launched in 1966.

In 1969 Fiat took over Lancia and Ferrari; Abarth was acquired in 1971. That year Fiat launched the fwd 127, with a 903cc ohv transverse four (a 1049cc version is also available;) the 128 is another fwd model, with 1116cc and 1290cc power units. The successor to the 124, the 131 Mirafiore, was available with 1297cc or 1585cc engines in various stages of tune. There was also a dohc 1995cc Abarth version, with irs and a five-speed gearbox, developing 140 bhp and capable of reaching almost 145 mph in racing guise. A conventional "middle-class" car, the 132 had dohc four-cylinder power units of 1585cc and 1995cc. Fiat also introduced in 1973 a series-production mid-engined sports car, the X1/9, with a 1290cc power unit and Bertone's wedge-styling. The Croma range of 1986 was another attempt at a big saloon by Fiat that just missed the mark. Developed as part of the joint Fiat-Saab "Type 4" alliance, it was accompanied by the elegant and highly popular Uno hatchback range which superseded the modernistic Strada models. Then the Tipo name was reused by Fiat for this mid-range hatchback of the 1980s. This car served as the base for the Tempra saloon.

For the 1990s Fiat put more emphasis on safety, strength and build quality, notably through the best-selling Punto range and the Bravo/Brava models. A dramatically styled 5-cylinder engined coupé model complemented a greater Fiat brand image that was further enhanced by the Barchetta convertible, sadly, for right handed markets, available in left-hand drive only. Again, in a shared alliance, Fiat grew an MPV model (the Ulysse) by sharing body and engine parts with Peugeot-Citroên. A revised Cinquecento known as the Seicento took Fiat back to its baby-car roots in 1998 and made a singularly Italian statement for this Italian company.

1907 Fiat 24 hp with folding canopy (right.) 1899 Fiat 3½ hp victoria (far right)

Fiats have always had character. The Classic 500, with trailer (top,) Bertone's Fiat X19 – mid-engined, tarca topped (middle.) 1960s Fiat styles, 124 Coupe (below left.) 1960s drop head elegance (below right)

1969 Ferves Ranger 500cc

FERRIS • USA 1920-1922

The Ferris is a good example of an expensive, beautifully built assembled automobile. Continental six-cylinder engines were used for all models, the Series C20, C21, 60, and 70 displacements ranging from 4078cc to 5328cc. Disc wheels were used exclusively for the first two years, wire wheels were optional in 1922 and a 130-inch wheelbase was standard. Four open and two closed models comprised the catalog offerings. An estimated 935 cars were produced in three years of manufacturing.

FERVES • Italy 1965-1970

A Fiat-based multipurpose car with a rear-mounted 499cc two-cylinder in-line engine.

FIAL • Italy 1906-1908

This Milanese manufacturer offered a 6/8 hp twin and a 10/12 hp four.

FIAT • Italy 1899 to date

See panel on previous spread

FIAT • USA 1910-1918

This American-financed company built big four-cylinder Fiats under license at Poughkeepsie, New York, in a factory which even had its own foundry. Initially, the 5899cc Type 54 was built; from 1912 a Poughkeepsie-designed "Type 56" was available, with a monobloc 8553cc engine. But the most famous American Fiat was the Type 55, a monstrous 9026cc four whose top speed was only 62 mph. In 1918 Rochester-Duesenberg took over the plant for aero engine manufacture.

FIF • Belgium 1909-1914

Built by Felix Heck, of Etterbeck, near Brussels, the FIF was a voiturette of sporting pretensions.

1938 Fiat 2800 Cabriolet

FILIPINETTI • Switzerland 1967-late 1960s

Motor museum owner and Minister Georges Filipinetti, of the Chateau Grandson, was responsible for these 1600cc VW-powered sports coupÈs styled by Sbarro.

FILTZ • France 1899-c. 1908

Filtz began production with a voiturette powered by a curious power unit with two horizontal pistons each driving separate vertical crankshafts geared together. This power unit was also used by Turgan-Foy, and supplying engines to other manufacturers seems to have been Filtz's main activity, though the firm (from Neuilly-sur-Seine) was still exhibiting its own-make chassis at the 1907 Paris Salon, offering powers of 10 hp to 130 hp, though the cars on display were of 12/16 hp, 20/25 hp, and 35/40 hp.

FIMER • Italy 1948-1949

One of the many mini-cars built after the Second World War, the Fimer had a 246cc two-stroke motorcycle engine in the rear. Few were made.

FINA-SPORT • USA 1953-1954

Perry Fina created the Fina-Sport using a 210 hp Cadillac V-8 engine and Hydramatic transmission on a Ford chassis. Convertible and hardtop styling was by Vignale.

FINLANDIA • Finland 1923

Just two Finlandia cars, large vee-radiatored tourers, were built by coachbuilder P J Heikkila. A fire engine was mounted on the same chassis for use in Helsinki.

1955 Fiat 600

FINLAYSON • Australia 1900-1907

The Finlayson brothers of Tasmania built a successful steam buggy in 1900, then produced nine larger gasoline vehicles, including a bus.

FIREFLY • England 1903

This Croydon, Surrey, firm built 6 hp ("Genuine De Dion engine") and 10 hp cars.

FIRESTONE-COLUMBUS • USA 1907-1915

Starting with high-wheelers, by 1909 this company had progressed to a 26 hp "Mechanical Greyhound" roadster.

FISCHER • Switzerland 1909-1919

Martin Fischer broke away from Turicum at the end of 1908 and began development of a four-cylinder voiturette, still with friction drive. Production began late in 1909 in the former Weidmann factory. After 70 cars had been built Fischer used an ingenious four-speed gearbox in which a pinion on a cardan shaft engaged with internally toothed gears to give direct drive in every ratio. In 1911 Fischer launched a 33cv sleeve-valve four of 2724cc with half-moon-shaped sleeves "rounding off" oval bores; a six-cylinder (4086cc) appeared in 1914. Only two of these were built after the war and Fischer closed down, though the six was built under license in the USA. A 1919 cyclecar with a vee-twin MAG engine and, again, friction drive, proved a shortlived project.

FISSON • France 1895-c. 1898

A two-seater car with a Benz engine.

FISSORE • Italy 1977 to date

Basically a Fiat 127, the Fissore Scout 127 is delivered with a variety of (mainly open) coachwork. The works are at Savigliano.

FL • France 1908-1914

Originally built by H. De la Fresnaye of Paris and Levallois-Perret, the FL light car was produced after 1910 in the Otto works.

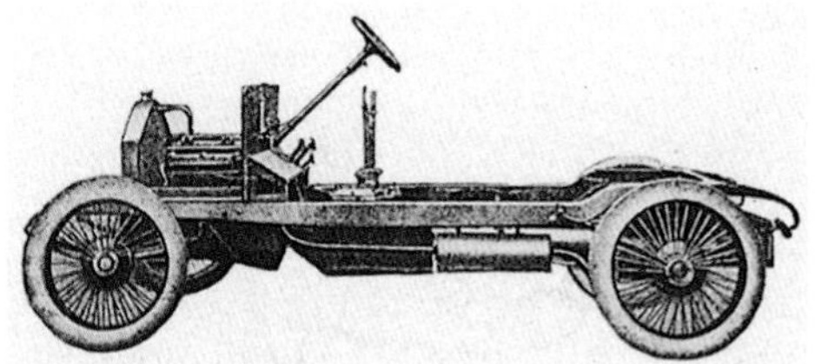

1913 Florio 18 hp chassis

1903 Firefly 8 hp tonneau

FLAC • Denmark 1914-1915

Mammen & Drescher of Jyderup built 25 cars with American 10 hp four-cylinder engines of unknown origin. One or two cars used French engines.

FLAG • Italy 1904-1907

Made on the lines of the English Thornycroft cars, the FLAG had four-cylinder 18 hp and 30 hp and six-cylinder 45 hp 7772cc engines. FLAG also imported Thornycrofts into Italy; hence the close co-operation.

FLAGLER • USA 1914-1915

A $450 cyclecar from Cheboygan, Michigan, the sporty four-cylinder Flagler had shaft drive, not the customary belt.

FLAID • Belgium 1920-1921

This 10/12 hp light car was designed for export to Britain.

FLANDERS • USA 1909-1912

Sister marque to EMF, and sold through Studebaker, this was a 2450cc four, initially offered with two speeds, later with three.

LA FLECHE • France 1912-1913

An 8 hp friction-driven cyclecar from Guders Jack, Paris.

FLETCHER • England 1966-1967

Norman Fletcher Ltd was a boatbuilder by trade, but filled in a quiet period of production in 1966 with its version of the recently terminated Ogle SX1000. John Handley enjoyed success with a racing version, but only four cars saw the light of day.

FLINT • USA 1923-1927

Billy Durant's Flint Six (designed by Zeder, Skelton, and Breer under Walter Chrysler's leadership) was named for America's "Carriage Capital." though it was also built in Long Island City, NY, and Bridgeport, Connecticut. Four-wheel hydraulic brakes were fitted from 1925, except on the low-priced junior model.

FLORENTIA • Italy 1903-1912

Once a well-known make, who also exported cars to England. They had 4396cc, 5425cc, and 9847cc four-cylinder and 6594cc six-cylinder engines. There were also 16 hp and 24 hp four-cylinder models, some built under French Rochet-Schneider license. In later years the Florence-based factory built marine engines. Its designers included such famous men as Cattaneo, who afterwards headed the Isotta-Fraschini design department, and Antonio Chiribiri, who later built fast sporting cars.

FLORIO • Italy 1913

The forerunner of Beccaria cars, this marque was inspired by Cav. Vincenzo Florio, the famous Sicilian pioneer and founder of the Targa Florio. The model made was an 18 hp four-cylinder of 2951cc. Its price in England was £385. There were also a few racing cars made privately by Florio in Sicily.

FN • Belgium 1899-1939

This famous Liége armament factory began production with a twin-cylinder, two-speed voiturette, but by 1906 was building the Rochet-Schneider under license. In 1908 an FN-designed 2-liter appeared, followed by a range of well-engineered light cars of 1245 to 1500cc. Though cars of up to 3800cc were built during the 1920s, the best-known vintage FN was the ohv 1300cc, which was available with front-wheel brakes. This model, and its 1400cc and 1625cc derivatives, enjoyed a number of sporting successes, and remained in production until 1933. A 3.2-liter straight-eight was current from 1930 to 1935, and the 2-liter "Baudouin" model replaced the old 1625cc. There was also an aerodynamic saloon, the "Prince Albert," with either 2.2-liter or 3.8-liter engines. Production effectively ceased in 1935.

FONCK • France 1921-1925

First World War flying ace René Fonck made these luxury cars in the Fraysse Unieux factory. The engines of the Fonck were designed by engineer Gadoux and built by CIME. They were ohc units, available in four-cylinder (2614cc) and eight-cylinder (5228cc) form. Later, Fonck produced a smaller ohc eight of 3303cc. Customers were offered an unlimited guarantee.

FONDU • Belgium 1906-c. 1912

The first Fondu, a pair-cast 24/30 hp four of 4.8 liters, was the pattern for the Russo-Baltique. Fondu, of Vilvorde, Brussels, later offered monobloc fours of 1.7 and 2.1 liters, a 1.1-liter light car appearing in 1912.

FONLUPT • France 1920-1922

At its Levallois works, Fonlupt made a small number of the 1539cc four-cylinder 10 hp Sport and the 10 hp 2155cc Ville, also a four-cylinder. There was also an eight-cylinder of 4310cc. All these engines had ohc.

FORD • USA 1903 to date

See panel overleaf

FORD • Europe 1911 to date

See panel overleaf

FORD • Australia 1960 to date

Ford Australia was originally established in 1925 to assemble Model T Fords with local bodies. The company's manu facturing capacity steadily grew, and in 1960 a locally

FORD • USA 1903 to date

Henry Ford's ambition of "building a car for the great multitude" was reflected in his early twin-cylinder A, C, and F models, though his backers forced him to build higher-priced, less-successful models (the 4-cylinder B and the 6-cylinder K.) His first major success came with the modestly priced 15 hp Model N (1906,) which paved the way for the immortal Model T of 1908-1927, the "car that put the world on wheels." Some 16.5 million were built in its 19-year lifespan. Its successor, Model A, retained Ford's transverse suspension but was much more conventional than the eccentric T, which up to its demise retained a two-speed epicyclic transmission and rear-wheel brakes only. Model A, the first production car with a safety glass windscreen, had four-wheel brakes and a three-speed sliding gearbox; a million were sold in ithe car's first 16 months, an all-time record still unbroken. It was followed by the 1932 AB and its more glamorous derivative, the 18F V-8, "Ford's last mechanical triumph."

The flathead V-8 was Ford's mainstay in the 1930s, with progressive styling and mechanical updates, and the 1942 range was the basis of post-war production, though 1946 cars shared Mercury's 3916cc V-8 instead of using the pre-war 3621cc unit. A milestone was the 1949 line, the first Ford to feature ifs (rear suspension was semi-elliptic, another break with tradition.) Three-speed Fordamatic transmission appeared in 1951, which year also saw the special edition V-8 Crestliner, succeeded by the Victoria hardtop. In 1952 a short-stroke six of 3654cc, to remain Ford's basic unit until 1964, appeared, and the "Y-block" ohv V-8 of 3917cc followed in 1954. All-new styling, wraparound windscreens and bright two-tone paint dispelled Ford's traditionally conservative image on 1955 models, which included the immortal two-passenger Thunderbird "personal car," an instant success. Also included in the 1955 line-up were the Fairlane Sunliner Convertible and the Crown Victoria, whose Skyliner hardtop featured a transparent Plexiglas roof over the front seat. This hothouse roof gave way to the complex Skyliner retractable hardtop, offered from 1957-1959, with total sales of 48,000. The restyled 1957 models, Custom and Custom 300, Fairlane and

1925 Ford Model T Touring (USA) (above,) 1980 Ford LTD four-door sedan (USA) (right)

1957 saw the last of the two-seater Ford Thunderbirds, after which Ford produced a much larger, less sporty four-seater version

Fairlane 500, offered a bewildering array of engines from 4457cc to 5113cc in a 21-model line-up. Introduced for 1959 were the Galaxies. The most successful of the compacts, the 2360cc six-cylinder Falcon, appeared in 1960, and a new intermediate Fairlane range, with a 2786cc six or 3622cc V-8, was launched in 1962.

One of the most successful of all Ford models, the Mustang, appeared in 1964. This 2 + 2 personal sports car was powered by the 2786cc six as standard, with three V-8s up to 4736cc optional. The millionth Mustang was sold in 1966, in which year the fwd Bronco was added to the range, as was the Torino, with engines from 3277cc to 6391cc. In 1967 came the top-of-the-range LTD, based on the Galaxie; by 1969 the Galaxie/LTD range totalled 21 models. The 1969 six-

1960s Ford Mustang (far right.) 1965 Mustang

cylinder Maverick was Ford's smallest model until the advent of the Pinto two years later. Disc brakes were standardized throughout the range in 1974, when Ford offered cars with engines varying from 2294cc to a 7538cc V-8 standard in the T-Bird, and optional in the Torino, LTD and the new Mercedes-inspired Elite. The 1976 line-up was the Pinto, Maverick, Torino, Granada, Bronco, Mustang II, Thunderbird, Elite, and the mighty LTD, which was 18 ft 7 in long, with most power options as standard. In 1978 the Fairmont replaced the Maverick. Promoted as a "European-style automobile," it was powered by engines from 2294cc to 4949cc. The Fiesta 1600 was imported from Europe, and a T-Bird-based LTD II appeared alongside the old LTD, which was downsized to 17 ft 5 in for 1979. This left the 18 ft 3 in LTD II as the biggest Ford, with four-wheel disc brakes standard and 4949cc V-8 power, the 6555cc and 7538cc engines being dropped in the interests of fuel economy.

The fwd 1980 Escort was designed to the same parameters as the European Escort but had only one small gasket in common. Its 1990 replacement had Ford bodywork on a Mazda platform. The 1983 Tempo was a 2.3-litre fwd notchback with aero styling, a bold step for the conservative US industry that paid off handsomely. The aero look was taken further with the Taurus large car, with 2.5-liter 1-4 or 3.0 liter V6 transverse engines driving the front wheels.

The 1988 Probe, originally intended as a new Mustang, is a sports coupé built at a former Ford factory now operated by Mazda in Flat Rock, Michigan. It was later imported into the British Ford market as a Capri replacement.

For the 1990s Ford made the most of its links with Mazda to badge engineer a successive range of small compact type cars, while its large-car sector was revived by the new Thunderbird, Mustang, and Explorer models. In the mid-range an American version of the European type Mondeo platform is marketed by Ford as the Contour model and as a Mercury variant. Just above it in the model range, the popular Taurus went from strength to strength as well, helping Ford survive the recession. In 1999 a retrostyled Thunderbird was announced as American car design, and Ford design, entered a new, more confident era.

MUSTANG

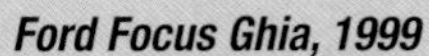

Ford Focus Ghia, 1999

FORD • Europe 1911 to date

The first Ford factory outside America opened in a former tramcar works at Trafford Park, Manchester, in October 1911, assembling Model Ts from imported components. Apart from local coachwork in 1912-1914 and the use (at extra cost!) of a 14.9 hp engine built at Ford's Cork plant, instead of the 24 hp engine, in the Model A from 1928, cars followed the American pattern until February 1932, when the first "European" small Ford, the Dearborn designed 8 hp Model Y of 933cc, was exhibited at Ford's Albert Hall Show after a gestation period of only five months. Improved, it entered production at Ford's new Dagenham, Essex, factory the following August, and formed the basis of Ford light car design until the 1950s. It was also built at Asniéres (Paris), Barcelona and Cologne. In 1934 came the 1172cc Model C Ten, ancestor of the Prefect (1939-1953.) The Model Y became the first and only £100 saloon car in September 1935; its 1940 development, the Anglia, was produced until 1953, when its 10 hp export variant became the Popular, built in the former Doncaster Briggs Bodies plant until 1959. Dagenham built its first 30 hp V-8 in 1935, soon also offering a 22 hp version similar to the Matford Alsace. This provided the coachwork for the 1947-1952 30 hp Pilot V-8. The first unit-constructed ohv Fords with ifs, the Consul four and Zephyr six, appeared in 1950, with convertible models and a deluxe six, the Zephyr Zodiac, available from 1953. That year unit-constructed 1172cc side-valve 100 E models of the Anglia and Prefect appeared.

In 1959 came the lively 105E Anglia, with an ohv 997cc engine and reverse-rake rear window. Transitional models, the 1961 Consul Classic and Capri, heralded the MkI Cortina of 1962, which sold over a million before it was replaced in 1967 by a MkII version. There was even a Lotus version of the MkI and MkII Cortinas. The Corsair line adopted V-4 engines in 1965, followed by a V-4 and V-6 Zephyr and Zodiac MkIVs from spring 1966. In 1966-1970 Ford's Advanced Vehicle Operations at Slough built 101 examples of the spectacular road-racing GT40. The Halewood, Merseyside, plant introduced the Escort in 1968 to replace the Anglia; 1100cc and 1300cc engines were standard, with a 1558cc twin-cam engine fitted to the sporting version. The sporting Escort, in both MkI and MkII versions, became the most successful individual model in the history of motor sport, its victory in the 1970 World Cup Rally giving birth to the 1600cc pushrod-engined Mexico. The 1979 line-up consisted of the Fiesta (announced in 1976,) the Escort, the Capri (MkIII versions of a "personalised" model announced in 1969, but then imported from Cologne, as was the big-car Granada range) and a MkIV Cortina.

Since the 1970s Ford has marketed the same range across Europe, and builds cars in England, Belgium, France, Germany, and Spain. The last models to bear unique names in different countries were the MkIV "TC" Cortina and Taunus, though they were virtually identical otherwise. The TC was succeeded in 1982 by the aerodynamic rwd Sierra, the performance derivative of which, the biplane-spoilered XR4i of 1983, looked stunning but failed to sell in the expected volume. Its 1985 replacement, the XR4x4, was the first Ford with permanent four-wheel drive. Also in 1985 came the dramatic Sierra Cosworth, initially as a 5,000-off homologation special (the RS500 was an even more dramatic follow-on, of which just 500 were made) and, since 1988, as a production-line model in highly civilized 4x4 guise, using the notchback shell of the Sierra Sapphire launched in 1987. The fwd replacement Sierra, codename CDW27, was launched at the 1992 Paris Salon. The old Granada was replaced by the hatchback Scorpio (Granada in Britain) in 1985, but a notchback was several years coming and the estate did not appear until 1992. It was controversially restyled in 1994 and died in 1988. The fwd Escort hatchback of 1980 was joined by the notchback Orion in 1983 and the Escort/Orion range was facelifted in 1986.

A new Escort/Orion range with controversial styling was launched in 1990, and the high-performance RS2000 followed in 1991. The original Fiesta was replaced by an all-new (and slightly larger) Fiesta in 1989; it pioneered the optional CTX continuously variable transmission. Subsequent model variants saw the Fiesta and Escort gain more curvacious styling and more modern engines, replacing the ancient iron-block engines that had soldiered on for years. A Yamaha tuned 1,25-liter engine sparkled in the revised Fiesta, and a new range of Zetec engines with 16-valve technology did likewise across the ranges.

Ford produced its own fwd off-road vehicle in a shared operation with Nissan, whose Terrano model was rebadged with Ford Maverick labelling. With the 1993 launch of the Mondeo to replace the Sierra, Ford UK entered a new era in which its bread-and-butter saloons offered handling, safety, looks and trim that won many sales. It evolved into a V-6 model and furthered Ford's "world car" theme, being available in various guises in other markets. The competence of the new Mondeo was further underlined by the striking design of the new Ford baby hatchback, the Ka, which shocked the press and public alike with its advanced and daring design. They were rocked again by the nimble two-door Puma coupé and yet again by the radical, almost Citroënesque, Focus model, which sported wild curves and leading-edge design themes. Further leading-edge design was offered in the shape of the US-built Cougar, a large coupé with either the 2.0-liter or 2.5-liter Duratec V-6 engine. The Focus did more than replace the Escort, it showed that Ford could lead and take risks (not always what you might expect from Ford, the company that brought us the Cortina and defined bland middle-class values for three decades.) In 1999 Ford's cars served these sectors and went beyond in their excellence of design and driving.

The Ford Capri, beloved by many and an irreplaceable icon (above.) 1999 – Ford Puma, a smash hit in Europe (below)

The Galaxy model MPV Ford

manufactured version of the Ford Falcon was launched with a six-cylinder engine. Subsequent models have progressively grown away from US influence and, since 1965, the Falcon range has been unique to Australia. The 1978 models were offered in five body styles (sedan coupé, wagon, utility, and van), with 6-cylinder and V-8 engines. Ford Australia followed tradition in designing a new Falcon, launched in 1987 and available in notchback or estate forms. The 1989 Capri sports car was a sporting convertible loosely derived from the 1983 Ghia Barchetta show car and sold in the USA under the Mercury label. From 1989 Ford became involved in a model-sharing programme with Nissan under a government quota scheme. Despite this dilution the 1990s Ford Falcons have remained truly unique in their Australian design and specification, as has the large model known as the Fairlane. Yet while high powered, rwd cars like the quintessential Falcon and Fairmount/Fairlane and LTDs are the heart of Ford's Australian brand, Ford Australia has also badge engineered Mazda based models for local consumption, notably the Laser, Telestar, and Ghia styled Capri convertible. A traditional battle between the Ford Australia cars and those of the GM sourced Holden brand has raged, and it is as strong today as ever.

FORD • Germany 1925 to date

From 1925 Ford assembled cars at Berlin-Plözensee and in 1931 opened a new factory at Cologne, where the first cars were made to American designs. They included the 933cc Koln (model 19-Y) and the 3285cc four-cylinder Rheinland, which was really a rebodied Model B. V-8 Fords were imported until 1934, then built at Cologne, using the 3618cc engine, and from 1939 Cologne also offered the smaller 2228cc V-8. The 1172cc Eifel (based on the English Model C-20 10 hp) of 1935-1939 was a bestseller. The post-war 1172cc Taunus, nicknamed "Bückel" (hunchback,) a developed version of the 1939 Taunus, appeared in 1948, and was superseded in 1952 by an improved and modernized Taunus 12M, developing 38 bhp at 4,250 rpm. The 15M, with a 1498cc ohv engine, appeared in 1955. New in 1957 was the 1698cc 17M, followed by 1758cc versions. A new Taunus with 1183cc and 1498cc engines appeared after 1962; this range had V-4 power units and fwd. A 1280cc version, and also larger models with V-engines, were added in 1966 and 1967, while V-motors (including ohv V-6 1998cc and 2293cc engines) were also included in the range of fwd German Fords. Sixes of 2550cc were added in 1969, while 1968 saw the introduction of the 1098cc in-line four-cylinder Escort.

A new 1285cc four-cylinder in-line Taunus appeared in 1970, followed in 1974 by a 1576cc version; the 1981cc Taunus still had the V-6 motor. The first Capris of 1969 had in-line and V-engines of 1288 to 2637cc, thus heralding a move toward total European rationalization (apart from some engine variations) of the Ford range. It was superseded by the improved Capri II in 1974, followed in turn by the four-headlamp Capri III in 1977. A new Consul/Granada range appeared in 1972: the 1978 Granada, built only in Germany, was the flagship of Ford's European range. In 1979 Ford's German factories also built the Fiesta, Escort, Taunus, (identical with the British Cortina) and the Capri. The last Capri, a 280, was built in December 1986. In the 1990s Ford's German (and Belgian) plants turned out many versions of Ford cars for the company's pan-European operations.

FORD • France 1947-1954

Ford-France resumed production post-war in a purpose-built plant at Poissy (Seine,) but the car they introduced, the 2158cc V-8 Védette, an American-styled full-width fastback with ifs, was sadly out of tune with post-war demands for economy. Elegant Facel-bodied Cométe versions were available from 1952, but two years later Ford sold Poissy to Simca, which continued to build the V-8 as the Simca Védette.

1968 Le Mans race-winning Ford GT 40 (top,) The Ford Cougar (above)

FOX • USA 1921-1923

Designed by Ansley W Fox (designer of the famous Fox shotgun favoured by President Theodore Roosevelt on his big game expeditions,) the Fox car threatened the Franklin for a time in its bid for supremacy among American air-cooled motor cars of the period. A larger and considerably faster car than the Franklin, the Fox was also considerably more expensive. Using a 4398cc six-cylinder engine of the company"s own design, the Fox was popular with bootleggers during America"s "Great Experiment" of Prohibition. Unlike the Franklin, the Fox was not prone to overheating. Production was small, however, and relatively few Fox sedans, coupés and phaetons were seen on the highway. Prices ranged from $3,900 to $4,900.

FOY-STEELE • England 1913-1916

A handsome bullnosed radiator adorned this Coventry-Simplex-engined 12 hp sold by ex-racer Charles Jarrott, a co-founder of the Automobile Association. "Foy" steel alloy was used in its chassis; hence the name.

FRAMO • Germany 1932-1937

Closely connected with DKW at Zschopau, Framo was owned by J S Rasmussen (founder of DKW), but did not join the Auto Union. Framo was a large accessory factory which also built the 198cc and 298cc Piccolo cars with

The 24-valve Scorpio model Cosworth

1908 Franklin 18 hp

modified DKW two-stroke engines. There were also three-wheeled Framo models, with two-stroke engines up to 596cc.

FRANCO • Italy 1905-1912

Attilio Franco was a small producer at Sesto San Giovanni which became known when Cariolato's Franco won the 1910 Targa Florio 295 km (184.8 miles) in Sicily, in front of the Sigma driven by De Prosperis. The engine of the Franco cars was a 6.8-liter 28/40 hp four-cylinder.

FRANCON • France 1922-1925

This firm, which specialised in making stationary and marine engines, built light cars with a two-stroke engine, first of 458cc, then of 622cc and 664cc, with friction drive.

FRANKLIN • USA 1902-1934

Every Franklin ever built had air-cooling, most had full-elliptic suspension and, until 1927, all had wooden chassis. The first cars to leave the company's Syracuse, New York, factory had transverse four-cylinder engines with overhead valves; a model with a conventionally disposed engine of four or six cylinders under a circular hood appeared in 1905, and from 1907 featured automatic ignition advance and retard. A new bonnet design and full pressure lubrication were 1912 improvements. In 1915 a Franklin was driven 860 miles across America in bottom gear without overheating; that year's Franklins were probably the first American production cars with aluminum pistons. In 1922 the Renault-style hood was replaced by a sloping dummy radiator; 1925 saw the handsome De Causse-styled Series LL, which included an electric primer for its carburetor. However, four-wheel brakes did not appear until 1927, when the 26 hp Airman model was announced; Atlantic flyer Charles Lindbergh had four of this model. Custom bodies designed by Ray Dietrich proliferated on Franklin cars in the late 1920s, but failed to arrest falling sales. By 1932 the wooden chassis had been phased out; that year a 95 mph Dietrich-styled V-12 appeared, but failed to sell, and the last Franklin, the Olympic, was a Reo in all but power unit.

FRAYER-MILLER • USA 1904-1910

Famous air-cooled cars from Ohio; a 24 hp four and 6522cc six were the principal offerings.

FRAZER • USA 1946-1951

Billed as Kaiser-Frazer's luxury offering, the Frazer was powered by a 3703cc "Supersonic" sv six, designed by Continental but built by K-F. Two models were offered, a four-door sedan and top-of-the-range Manhattan, with interior trim rivalling Cadillac and Lincoln. A convertible was available from 1949, and 1951 models included the dual-purpose Vagabond with rear hatch and fold-down back seat. A total of 151,983 Frazers was built before production of Frazer (and Kaiser) cars ended.

FRAZER NASH • England 1924-1960

Archie Frazer-Nash's highly individual chain-driven sports car was a logical extension of the earlier GN, with which it shared a similar transmission layout. This had a dog-clutch gear change, separate chains for each of the three forward speeds, and a solid rear axle. Quarter-elliptic springs were another inheritance. A variety of proprietary engines was fitted. Initially a Powerplus was listed, though this was succeeded by the 1$^1/_2$-liter side-valve Anzani unit. This, in turn, was replaced by the ohv Meadows. From 1934 an ohc 1$^1/_2$-liter four-cylinder power unit was also fitted, latterly known as the Gough (for its designer, Albert Gough.) This particular engine was fitted to the Shelsley and TT Replica models, though in the former instance yet another engine variant was available, the dohc 1667cc six-cylinder Blackburne.

In 1929 H J Aldington took over the company, and in 1934 began importing the German BMW car. Clearly the days of the archaic chain-drive cars were numbered, though a trickle continued to be made up until 1939. By contrast, the post-war Frazer Nash was a far more sophisticated product, using as its power unit the pre-war 2-liter BMW 328 engine, jointly developed by the Bristol Aeroplane Co and the Aldington brothers. This was mounted in a tubular chassis with transverse leaf independent front suspension and torsion bar rear suspension. In 1948 the High Speed Model appeared, and from that derived the Le Mans Replica (following a 3rd placing in the 1949 24-hour classic.) A win in the 1951 Targa Florio made the Frazer Nash the only British car to have won victory laurels on the twisting Sicilian circuit. Latter-day "Nashes" were fitted with BMW V-6 2.6-liter engines, though the capacity was later increased to 3.2 liters. The marque"s last appearance was at the 1959 Motor Show, production ceasing the following year.

FREDONIA • USA 1902-1904

The 9 hp Fredonia, from Youngstown, Ohio, had a curious single-cylinder valveless engine with a pre-compression chamber to force the fuel-air mixture into the combustion chamber.

FREIA • Germany 1922-1927

Designed and raced by Ernst Schuh, the Freia was an underslung limited-production sports car, with 1320cc or 1472cc sv four-cylinder engines. The factory was at Greiz.

FREJUS • Italy 1909-1924

Made by Diatto at Turin, the Fréjus was a small car initially built under license from Clément-Bayard of France. An own-design small car with a 1350cc four-cylinder engine followed.

FREMONT • USA 1921-1922

The Fremont was intended for export, but whether any cars were actually built and sent abroad is unknown. Specifications called for a six-cylinder Falls engine and standard components throughout. According to promotional literature, the cars had cycle-type fenders, door steps and horizontal louvres on the hood, an unusual mode of design as early as 1921-1922. Fremont also built a truck under the Fremont emblem, and All-American trucks were assembled at the Fremont factory in Fremont, Ohio.

FRICK • England 1904-1906

Alfred Dougill of Leeds built a number of rear-engined cars from 1896-1899; he also made the Lawson Motor Wheel for converting horse-carriages and the 1900-1904 Loidis. The Frick had friction transmission, the principal model being an 8/10 hp twin of 2190cc. A 7 hp single (1095cc) and 12/18 hp three-cylinder (3285cc) were also listed. A handwheel on the steering column operated dual friction wheels "through a system of compound levers."

FRIEDMAN • USA 1900-1903

"The equal of any $1,200 gasoline automobile," the Chicago-built $750 Friedman Road Wagon was a typical gas buggy, with a 6 hp flat-twin four-stroke engine and tiller steering.

FRIEND • USA 1920-1922

A small-production light automobile, the Friend was successor to the Olympian and was produced in small quantities. Using its own-make four-cylinder engine and with

a wheelbase of 112 inches, Friend offered a roadster touring car, coupé, and sedan, with prices from $1,285.

FRITCHLE • USA 1904-1917

In 1905 this electric car maker listed a $2,500 "Torpedo Roadster" with Renault-type hood

FROGEYE • England 1985 to date

Recreates the "Frogeye" Austin-Healey Sprite, using a galvinised chassis and glassfiber bodywork.

FRONTENAC • USA 1906-1912

During 1906 the Abendroth & Root Company of Newburgh, NY, built an initial batch of 40 to 50 touring cars using a 40 hp pair-cast four of 5877cc, carried in a pressed-steel subframe.

FRONTENAC • USA 1922-1924

There is much natural confusion over the "Frontenac" name, as it has been used frequently, both in the USA and Canada. The Frontenac Motors Co/Frontenac Motors Corp produced two distinct automobiles in 1922 and 1924 respectively. In 1922 it announced a 3225cc four-cylinder car with wire wheels. The car never survived the prototype phase. In 1924 a highly attractive eight-cylinder sleeve-valve sport phaeton was shown. This car, with a 5864cc displacement, featured wire wheels and four-wheel hydraulic brakes. Like its 1922 predecessor, it was designed by Louis Chevrolet and appeared only in prototype form.

FRONTMOBILE • USA 1917-1918

An early attempt to build a fwd "Safety Motor," the Frontmobile came from New Jersey. A sharply dropped chassis behind the engine gave a very low build, there was a complex push-pull gear mechanism, and suspension (cantilever at the front, transverse full-elliptic at the rear) was just weird.

FRP • USA 1914-1918

Designed by Finley Robertson Porter, the FRP is historically important as being the second car designed by Porter, the first having been the T-head Mercer. The FRP, of which an estimated nine units were made, boasted a 170 bhp engine and a $5,000-and-up chassis with coachwork available either from Holbrook or M Armstrong. A Mercedes-type vee-radiator was distinctive, and the car was by far the most powerful automobile in America in the stock car category of the time. The FRP was the lineal predecessor of the Porter car of 1919-1922.

1925 Frazer Nash Super Sports in the Six-Hour Trial at Brooklands

FSO • Poland 1951 to date

Successor to Polski-Fiat, it initially built the Russian Pobieda as the "Warszawa." In 1968 the union with Fiat was renewed and FSO began building the FSO 125P, with old 1300/1500 Fiat running gear and newer 124 bodywork. It survived until 1991. Since 1978 FSO has also built the Polonez, restyled in 1986. A further restyle has produced the Caro. A Citroên diesel engine became an option in 1992.

FUCHS • Austria 1921-1922

This was an ephemeral sports car, made by the Inzersdorfer Industrie Werke. It had a sv 1180cc four-cylinder engine and was designed by Hans Fuchs, who also raced his products along with his works drivers Littman and Teutscher.

FULDAMOBIL • Germany 1950-1960

Single-cylinder Ilo and Sachs engines powered this light three-wheeler, fitted first with a composite wood/alloy body, with all-steel construction from 1953 and bodied in glassfiber from 1957.

FULLER • USA 1909-1911

This Jackson, Mich., factory built both high-wheelers and conventional cars. Its 1910 Model 30 roadster had a two-speed epicyclic gear and sold for $1,065.

FULMINA • Germany 1913-1926

The Hofmann-designed Fulmina-cars were made in limited numbers at Friedrichsfeld, near Mannheim. They had sv four-cylinder engines of 2595cc and 4212cc.

FUTURA • England 1971

The Futura was dreamt up by Jem Cars, makers of the Mini-Jem. Based on a VW floor-pan, the car featured a highly eye-catching body, the nose of which hinged sideways to allow entry from the front. However, development of the Futura drained the company"s resources to the point of liquidation.

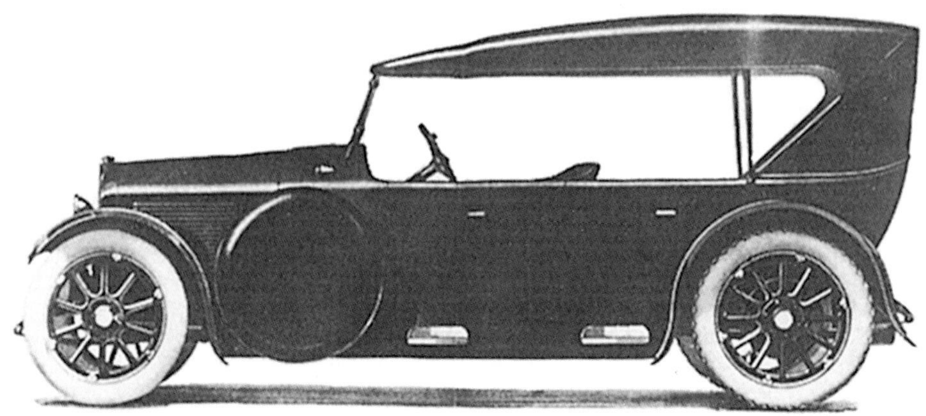

1922 Fremont Six phaeton

GABRIEL • France 1912-1914

Four-cylinder cars of 9/12 hp, 13/18 hp, and 20/30 hp, built in Paris.

GADABOUT • USA 1913-1915

Looking like a mobile wastepaper basket, this four-cylinder cyclecar from Newark, NJ, had a body woven from "waterproof reeds."

GAETH • USA 1902-1911

"The best $3,500 car on the market," the 6423cc 35/ 40 hp 1909 Gaeth was a powerful four-cylinder from Cleveland, Ohio. It succeeded a 25/30 hp horizontal three-cylinder.

GAGGENAU • Germany 1905-1911

Known also as SAF (Süddeutsche Automobil Fabrik,) Theodor Bergmann's works had, in Josef Vollmer, one of Germany's leading designers of the era. It built the 567cc single-cylinder Lilliput, followed by four-cylinder cars of 4991cc and 8830cc. Gaggenau also built high-efficiency racing cars and, eventually, aero engines. Gaggenaus were superb, low-built cars which won many sporting events. Otto Hieronymus was one of their designer-driver aces. Georg Wyss eventually bought the works and concentrated production on commercials, though he also continued to manufacture cars, which he, too, drove in sporting events. There was a close co-operation with Benz at Mannheim, and in 1910 Benz bought the Gaggenau factory.

GAINSBOROUGH • England 1902-1904

The 16 hp Gainsborough car had a horizontally opposed engine with only one double-ended piston to each pair of cylinders, acting on connecting rods outside the cylinders.

GALBA • France 1929-1931

Another Violet-designed small car built in Courbevoie, with a two-stroke 564cc engine.

GALE • USA 1904-1910

Starting with a typical single-cylinder gas buggy, with wheel steering and a dummy hood, the Western Tool Works of Galesburg, Illinois, had progressed by 1907 to a 24/26 hp model which, the company boasted, "climbs hills like a squirrel and eats up the road like an express train.". Gale cars were distinguished by their tilting bodies, for easy access to the mechanism.

1907 Targa Floria Gaggenau

GALLIA • France 1903-1908

Elegant electric carriages from Paris, capable of 16 mph. The company also made Dixi petrol cars under the name "Régina."

GALLIOT • France 1908

A tandem two-seater sporting voiturette designed by Norbert Galliot, with either a single- or three-cylinder mid-mounted engine; a kind of proto-cyclecar!

GALLOWAY • Scotland 1921-1928

Arrol-Johnston's light car, the Galloway had a 1460cc four-cylinder engine and three-speed gearbox. This 10.5 hp model was designed by T C Pullinger and lasted until 1925, being replaced by a 12 hp model with a pushrod overhead valve engine. Originally based at Tongland in Kirkcudbright, production was transferred to Heathall, Dumfries, in 1923.

GALT • Canada 1911-1913

Based on the US Alpena, the Canada Tourist and Roadster used the same 30 hp and 25 hp Hazard engines. In 1912 the Galt became Canada's first car to feature electric starting.

GALT • Canada 1913-1927

Starting by assembling ten cars from components left by the defunct Galt company, this new firm used the profits to develop two gasoline-electrics, but gave up trying to find backers in 1927. One of these cars often provided emergency electric power for the local cinema.

GAMAGE • England 1900-1915

Gamages was a well-known London department store which sold a wide range of cars and motor tricycles under its own name, though most of these vehicles were certainly Continental imports. The 1903 Gamage (with either 7 hp Aster or 6 hp De Dion power unit) was, for instance, very similar in appearance to the Regal. In 1915 a Chapuis-Dornier-engined light car was offered.

GAMMA • France 1921-1922

This minor manufacturer from Courbevoie listed three different models, of 1131cc, 1593cc, and 2297cc, with Ballot and Altos engines. The first Gamma (or Gamma-Hebe) was apparently built in 1914.

GAR • France 1922-1931

M Gardahaut started by making a vee-twin cyclecar in Clichy, but quickly turned to sports cars with various proprietary engines: 1100cc Ruby, SCAP, and Chapuis-Dornier, and 1500cc SCAP. More interesting were his own-make ohc 733cc four and an ohc eight of 1374cc, often supercharged for racing.

GARANZINI • Italy 1924-1926

Racing motorcyclist and motorcycle manufacturer Oreste Garanzini also built a few cars with ohv 1194cc four-cylinder proprietary engines.

GARBATY • Germany 1924-1927

Garbaty"s factory at Mainz built a few ohv four-cylinder cars powered by a 1205cc engine developing 25 bhp at 2500 rpm.

GARDNER • USA 1919-1931

Formerly the St Louis Chevrolet assembly plant, the Gardner carriage works introduced a Lycoming-engined 3153cc "Light Four" in 1919. Six- and eight-cylinder models appeared in 1924, and the marque's sole offering from 1926-1929 was a 4273cc eight with expanding hydraulic four-wheel brakes and centralized door locking. A new six appeared in 1929; a fwd prototype was exhibited in 1930.

1904 Garrard Tricar

1898 Gautier Wehrlé, driven by M Wehrlé

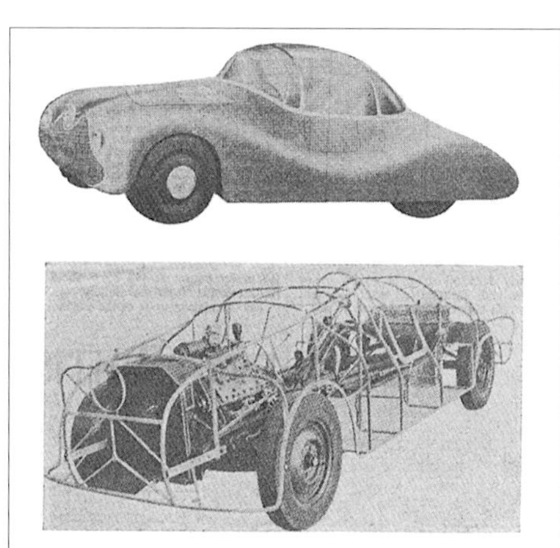

The 1948 Gatford 4-litre Sports Roadster

GAREAU • Canada 1910

Only three of these 35 hp worm-drive fours were built, as the Montreal firm could not raise enough working capital.

GARFORD • USA 1908-1912, 1916

Garford of Elyria, Ohio, which built trucks from 1902 and from 1905 supplied the chassis for Studebaker, Rainier, and Cleveland cars, decided late in 1907 to build a car under its own name. This was a 6098cc 40 hp four with shaft drive and geared-up fourth speed. It built Willys-Knights from 1913-1915, but made a brief reappearance in 1916.

GARRARD • England 1904

A "Suspended Tri-car" from the makers of the Clément-Garrard motorcycle.

GARRARD & BLUMFIELD • ENGLAND 1894-1896

A "neat and well-fitted" electric carriage manufactured in Coventry.

GAS-AU-LEC • USA 1905-1906

The 40-45 hp Gas-au-Lec gasoline-electric from Peabody, Mass., had a copper-jacketed four-cylinder engine with electromagnetically-operated inlet valves.

GASLIGHT • USA 1960-c. 1961

An odd replica of the 1902 Rambler powered by a single-cylinder 4 hp air-cooled engine and selling at around $1,495.

GASMOBILE • USA 1900-1903

Starting with "strictly high grade motor carriages," by 1902 the Automobile Company of America was building a 35 hp "luxurious and Frenchified" phaeton selling at $6,000. In November 1901 Gasmobile exhibited (and sold) a six-cylinder tonneau at the New York Show.

GATFORD • Netherlands 1948-1950

Also known as the "Gatso," this Mercury V-8-engined aero-styled coupé was sponsored by rally driver Maurice Gatsonides; triple headlights and clear plastic "cockpit" were features.

GATTER • Czechoslovakia 1929-1932

There were eight Gatter brothers. Two worked for Austro-Daimler, and subsequently created the small Gatter two-seater with a wooden frame and an air-cooled 344cc Villiers two-stroke engine. Few were built.

LA GAULOISE • France 1907

This firm from Issy-les-Moulineaux (Seine) built single- and four-cylinder voiturettes.

GAUTIER • France 1902-c. 1907

Ch Gautier of Courbevoie, Seine, (formerly of Gautier Wehrlé) built chassis, with or without power units, which could be finished by motor agents who would claim the result as "entirely their own manufacture." Gautier also offered a "Popular" three-seater car that "defies competition." Gautier was the sole agent for Malicet & Blinchassis and components. In 1904 it announced a four-cylinder Mutel-engined light car, "silent and cheap." A landaulette demi-luxe and double phaeton were shown at the 1907 Paris Salon.

GAUTIER WEHRLE • France 1894-1904

Known from 1898 as the "Société Continental d"Automobiles," this company began by making bodies for Serpollet. Its twin-cylinder gasoline cars of 1896 had handlebar steering, shaft drive and independent rear suspension, the rear wheels being driven through universally jointed cardan shafts, the first time this method of transmission had been seen on a car.

GAYLORD • USA 1910-1912

The Gaylord "Utility Car" had a 3295cc four-cylinder Oswald engine and could be converted into a pick-up by removing the rear seats. A demi-tonneau was also listed.

GAYLORD • USA • Germany 1955-1956

Manufactured in Germany by Spohn, and styled by Brooks Stevens, the Gaylord featured a retractable hardtop. Only five were built, three powered by Cadillac and two by Chrysler engines. Priced from $10,000 to $17,500, standard equipment included vacuum and electric power

Front-wheel-drive Georges Irat sports, 1935

Geha electric phaeton, c. 1913

brakes, PAS, automatic transmission, leather seating, and radio.

GAZ • Russia 1930 to date

License-production of Ford Model A cars and trucks began in Moscow in 1929, but was soon transferred to the new Molotov car works near Nijhni Novgorod (later Gorky,) built with Ford technological aid in an attempt to "fill the Russians full of capitalism." This Gorky Automobil Zavod began building "Russki-Fords" in 1930, and was still using the Model A engine in Jeep-like vehicles long after the war. The GAZA was supplanted by the GAZ M-1 in 1936. This had a Russian-designed grille and transmission, but a 1933 Ford body. A 3.5-liter six-cylinder version, GAZ M-11, appeared in 1938, forming the basis for wartime command cars. A new 2.1-liter model, the "Pobieda" (Victory,) designed by Andrei Litzgart, was built from 1946; it had unit construction and independent front suspension, and a fwd version, M-72, appeared in 1955. In 1958 the Pobieda was supplanted by the M-21 Volga, with a 2.5-liter engine. From 1950-57 the Gorky Works also built the straight-eight ZIM luxury model for middle-ranking Communist officials; this was replaced by the "Chaika" (Seagull) based on the vulgar Packard Patrician. The 1978 Chaika was favoured by President Brezhnev. A Mk II Volga appeared in 1968. Today the antiquated Volga GAZ 24 series survives. The "modern" Volga GAZ 3102 has a new cylinder head and a grille like a manhole cover. The Chaika is as dead as Lenin and will be replaced by the Volga GAZ 3105. A 1990 plan to replace the Volga with license-built Ford Scorpios failed because the Americans wanted money up front.

GEARLESS • USA 1907-1909

Big friction-drive cars of up to 75 hp (known as "Olympic" from 1909), built in Rochester, NY.

A Georges Richard 8 hp in the 1900 1,000 Miles Trial

GEARLESS STEAM CAR • USA 1921-1923

Gearless was one of several companies which attempted to market a successful steam automobile in the early 1920s, and succeeded better than many other contenders for the same market. Featuring two separate two-cylinder, double-acting, side-valve steam engines, the Gearless sported wire or wood wheels. Four Gearless officers were charged with mail fraud and the company failed. At least eight cars, open models, and possibly as many as 15 or 20, were manufactured and sold before operations ceased in 1923.

GEERING • England 1899-1904

A crude paraffin-fuelled car with a 3 hp twin-cylinder engine, built in Rolvenden, Kent.

GEHA • Germany 1910-1923

Electric fwd three-wheelers from Harhorn of Berlin, part of the Elite group from 1917.

GEIJER • Norway 1926-1930

A/S C. Geijer & Co of Oslo was essentially a coachbuilding company, but assembled about 20 cars out of parts imported from the USA. Both four- and eight-cylinder cars with hydraulic brakes were built. The frames were manufactured in Norway and, in a more sound economic climate, it is quite possible that the company could have enjoyed success, as the product was robust and reasonably cheap.

GELRIA • Holland 1899-1906

Gelria, from Arnhem, began with a front-engined single-cylinder 4 hp car with chain drive. A 6 hp twin appeared in 1901, but only a few cars were built after 1902.

GEM • France 1907-1909

Racing driver Léonce Girardot ("the eternal second,") formerly of CGV, headed this Parisian company and designed the 20-24 hp gasoline-electric car which it produced. The later models used Knight sleeve-valve engines.

GENERAL • England 1902-1905

This South London firm built mainly 61 hp and 12 hp cars with Aster or Buchet engines, though 30 hp (Simms) and 40 hp (Buchet) models were offered towards the end of its activities. A 40 hp racer with an aggressively pointed snout was built in 1902.

GENERAL ELECTRIC • USA 1898-1899

Built in Philadelphia, these electric vehicles followed horse-carriage practice in design and construction, "the company believing that any radical changes should come by degrees to avoid public aversion to riding in objectionably conspicuous vehicles."

A Georges Roy Berline Grand Luxe, 1914

GENESTIN • France 1926-1929

Even though relying largely on local custom, the Genestin (made in Fourmies, in the north of France) was very successful. Genestin cars had various proprietary engines, mainly SCAP and CIME units of 1100cc and 1500cc, and also an 1808cc straight-eight, sometimes supercharged for racing.

GENEVA • USA 1901-1903

Built in Geneva, Ohio, this was a typical Locomobile-type steamer whose makers announced an initial production of 100 vehicles.

GENTRY • England 1974 to date

For those who cannot afford a real MG TF, the RMB Gentry offers some consolation. Based very obviously on the Abingdon car, the Gentry body is designed to clothe a Herald/Vitesse chassis, though a purpose-built model is available. Over 200 Gentrys have been made.

GEORGES IRAT • France 1921-1946

Georges Irat made very nice cars in the vintage period, starting by making its own engine, an ohv 1990cc four-cylinder, which gave way to a 2985cc six-cylinder in 1926. It turned to Lycoming engines with six and eight cylinders in 1929, when it moved from Chatou to Neuilly. Having been partly taken over by Ruby in 1934, it then moved to the Ruby works in Levallois, where it made a very successful fwd Ruby-engined roadster, followed by a fwd Citroén-engined roadster. Though a prototype was presented after the war, it was never put into production.

GEORGES-RICHARD; RICHARD-BRASIER • France 1897-1905

The first Georges-Richards were crude copies of the Benz, with alarming chain-and-sprocket steering and belt drive, but by 1900 the Ivry-Port factory was offering the Belgian Vivinus built under license, and in 1901 a shaft-drive voiturette appeared. The designer Brasier joined the company in 1902 and produced larger Richard-Brasier cars on conventional lines, mostly with chain drive, culminating in the excellent racing cars which won the Gordon Bennett Trophy for France in 1904 and 1905. Georges Richard left in 1905 to build the Unic, and the marque became plain "Brasier."

GEORGES ROY • France 1906-1929

Built in Bordeaux, Georges Roy cars always had medium to large power units. Starting with an 1140cc single, a 2941cc twin, and a 4561 four, Georges Roy added a massive six of 10,179cc in 1907, one of no fewer than 16 models launched in seven years. In the 1911 catalog three basic models were listed, two four-cylinders (12 and 16 hp) and a 20 hp six. In 1925 the company offered only one chassis, a 10 hp, and three de luxe coachwork options: tourer, "Caddy" two-seater, and interior drive. Light trucks were also offered.

GEORGE WHITE • USA 1909

These 14 hp twin-cylinder shaft-driven high-wheelers came from Rock Island, Illinois.

GEP • France 1913-1914

An 8 hp Anzani-engined light car from Gennevilliers.

GERALD • England 1920

The Gerald cyclecar used chain- and belt-drive, power coming from an 8 hp JAP engine mounted lengthwise in the chassis.

GERALD • France 1920-1923

SCAP-engined 1481cc cars made in Clichy.

GERMAIN • Belgium 1897-1914

Germain of Monceau-sur-Sambre began by building the "Daimler-Belge" under license from Cannstatt. From 1901 cars of "improved Panhard" pattern were offered. The first German "Standard" appeared in 1903; it was a 2917cc chain-drive 18 hp L-head with separate cylinders, and was soon joined by similar 3810cc, 5734cc, and 9811cc. In 1905 came the 28 hp shaft-driven "Chainless" with T-headed cylinders and a distinctive oval radiator. The 3834cc six of 1907 had a ball-bearing crank; there was also a 60 hp six of 8822cc and a monstrous chain-drive "80 hp" four of 12,454cc. The 1912 range had full pressure lubrication and included an ohc 15 hp and a 20 hp Knight sleeve-valve model.

GERONIMO • USA 1917-1920

Named for the famous American Indian chief, the Geronimo was one of the few makes to hail from Oklahoma. With a factory at Enid, the Geronimo began life as a four-cylinder automobile, but a year after its entry into the automobile spectrum adopted a Lycoming six and used it until the end of production. Geronimo never built any closed models; several hundred (perhaps even 1,000) cars were built before the company went to the happy hunting grounds.

GFG • Germany c. 1990 to date

Builds the 3.0-liter Elisar (styled like a 540K Mercedes) and the 5.0-liter Bancroft Roadster.

1972 Gilbern Invader Mk III

GHIA • Italy 1966-1968

This famous coachbuilder, then owned by Alessandro de Tomaso, built the 450/SS, a very sporting cabriolet with 235 bhp V-8 4500cc Plymouth Barracuda engine. Few were built.

GIAUR • Italy 1949-1954

Sports and racing cars with partly modified Fiat 746cc engines and Fiat chassis components were Giaur's main offering. There were also models from 498cc up to 1098cc. One of the directors of Giaur was racing driver Taraschi.

GIBBONS • England 1921-1926

The belt-driven Gibbons was built at Chadwell Heath, Essex, and offered with three engine variants: 349cc Precision and 488cc Blackburne (both single-cylinder) and 688cc Coventry-Victor twin.

GIBSON • USA 1899

A tiller-steered Stanhope powered by a 12 hp carbonic acid gas engine said to weigh 32 lb.

GIDEON • Denmark 1913-1919

The first Gideon cars, from Horsens, were presented at the end of 1913 and were available in three sizes, all with four-cylinder engines. Passenger car engines developed 9.7 hp and were entirely Danish-made. The only imported parts were carburetors and magnetos. Although 129 vehicles were produced, only 17 were passenger cars.

GILBERN • Wales 1958-1977

There have been some chequered careers in the motor industry, but that of Gilbern probably caps them all. The production of some fine cars was interspersed with changes in management and an almost constant threat of liquidation. The last car, the glassfiber-bodied, Ford-

1905 Gilburt 6hp light car

powered Mk 111 Invader, was a sturdy, well-equipped GT car that, marketed by the right hands, could well have saved Wales' only longstanding car manufacturer from the history books.

GILBERT • England 1899-1901

Gilbert & Son of Birmingham devised a two-stroke engine with two cylinders of different capacities.

GILBURT • England 1904-1906

A light 6 hp twin-cylinder car with a tubular chassis and chain drive.

GILCHRIST • Scotland 1920-1923

An ohv version of the 11.9 hp Hotchkiss engine used in the Morris powered this light car from Govan, Glasgow. Total Gilchrist output was around 20.

GILLET • England 1926-1927

A £100 car that used an 8 hp four-cylinder ohv engine and had just enough room for two adults and two offspring.

GILLET-FOREST • France 1901-c. 1908

This firm, with its factory at St Cloud near Paris, built 8 hp and 10 hp cars, including a Traveller's Brougham with cupboards for samples and a 10 hp Duc-Tonneau, perhaps the first car to have a heater as standard equipment. The company last exhibited at the 1907 Paris Salon.

GINETTA • England 1967 to date

The highly enthusiastic Walklett Brothers produced a variety of competition and road cars over the years, the most successful of which has been the rear-engined, Imp-powered G15, over 500 of which were made. But in 1979, back in their original factory, they were primarily concerned with refurbishing G15s and developing their new open-topped glassfiber sports car, the G23, which was powered by the Ford 2.8-liter fuel-injection engine. Launched in 1988, the G32 had a mid-mounted 1.6-liter Ford engine; a turborcharger was available. In 1989 the Walkletts sold out to a Sheffield consortium. The 1990 G33 was a V-8 3.5-liter roadster.

GIRLING • England 1911-1914

Apart from a JAP-engined prototype, the three-wheeled Girling cyclecars were powered by a single-cylinder 3 3/4 x 3 3/4 inch engine of the company's own make. Friction drive was employed. In 1911-1913 110 Girlings were shipped to Australia. Albert Girling later devised the famous Girling braking system.

GITANE • England 1962

The first six Gitanes had rear-mounted Mini-Cooper engines tuned to 83 bhp, and a claimed top speed of 130mph. Plans to develop a light-alloy Gitane engine were stillborn.

The GKN FFF100 coupé. 1972

The 1962 Gitane prototype

1973 Ginetta G21

GJG • USA 1909-1911

Assembled from imported components, including a "Renault-type" 40 hp four-cylinder engine, the GJG was available with either "cruiser torpedo" or "pirate runabout" coachwork.

GKN FFF100 • England 1972

Commissioned by GKN, the FFF100 was built to test the performance and durability of some of the company"s components, including the Maxaret anti-lock braking system and the Ferguson 4wd system. It was a formidable beast, with a William Towns-styled glassfiber body hiding a modified Jensen 4wd chassis, powered by a much modified 7-liter Chrysler engine of some 600 bhp. The car recorded 100 mph in 6.5 sec and 100 mph and back to rest in a mere 11.5 sec.

GLADIATOR • France 1896-1920

Aucoc and Darracq's Gladiator cycle company was acquired by British capital in 1896, and began building spidery, handlebar-steered 4 hp voiturettes in its Pré-St-Gervais factory. Wheel steering and Aster engines of 2 1/2 hp and 3 1/2 hp were used from 1899. By 1901 a 6 1/2 hp Aster-engined Gladiator was available, joined later that year by a 12 hp twin, still Aster engined, with an armored wood chassis. The 1902 range went from a 3 1/2 hp quadricycle to four-cylinder cars. By 1903 fours of 2.1 liters and 2.7 liters of Gladiator's own make were available; the range was very similar to the sister marque, Clément. The 1906 line-up was complex, to the extent that models sold in France had armored wood chassis, while models for the British market had pressed-steel frames! That year, Gladiator"s first six, a 5.5-liter, appeared. From 1908-1909 Gladiators were supposedly also built in Birmingham by Austin. In 1909 Vinot & Deguingand took over, and from then on only the radiators distinguished the two marques (though Gladiator built no more sixes). At the end of 1911 Gladiator offered a 10/12 hp, a 15.9 hp, and a 25/30 hp of 1693cc, 2212cc, and 4166cc respectively. A 15/20 hp of 2614cc was added in 1913, but no new models appeared before production ended in 1920.

GLAS • Germany 1955-1966

Old-established manufacturer of agricultural machinery, from 1951 to 1954 Glas built the Goggo scooter, and from 1955 to 1969 the small Goggomobil with 247cc, 296cc, and 395cc two-cylinder two-stroke engines. In 1958 appeared the first "real" Glas cars with 584cc and 688cc ohv flat-twin engines. Bigger models with ohc four-cylinder in-line engines of 992cc, 1189cc, 1290cc, and 1682cc followed. The last Glas-built cars had ohc 2580cc and 2982cc V-8 engines, beautiful sporting four-seater coupé bodywork by Frua, and De Dion rear axles. Unfortunately these superb cars led the company into financial difficulties. Glas could not afford to spend millions of

1902 12 hp Gladiator rear-entrance tonneau

1966 Glas 1700 four-door saloon

Deutschmarks on the more up-to-date equipment needed for economical production of these high-class luxury cars. In 1966 BMW took over the Glas works at Dingolfing.

GLASSIC • USA 1966 to date

Jack Faircloth and his son built a glassfiber replica Model A Ford using International Harvester components and a four-cylinder Scout engine. Production moved to West Palm Beach, Florida, in 1972, when Fred Pro bought the project. Available as a roadster or phaeton with Ford automatic transmission and powered by a 210 hp Ford V-8 engine, the Glassic (now renamed Replicar) cost $14,950 in 1979.

GLEASON • USA 1909-1914

4A high-wheeler succeeding the "Kansas City."

GLEN • Canada 1921-1922

A three-cylinder cyclecar from Toronto with a Rolls-Royce-like radiator.

GLIDE • USA 1903-1920

The 1903 Glidemobile, designed by O Y Bartholomew, was a single-cylinder 1930cc tiller-steered runabout, joined by a 12 hp twin in 1904. This had a spring-mounted motor subframe and steel-spoked artillery wheels. A 30 hp four-cylinder Glide appeared in 1906, and a 45 hp Rutenber-engined six in 1907. In 1911 a 5806cc single-cast four was listed, and in 1912 came a monobloc 36 hp four at $1550. The year 1916 saw the last new Glide, the 6-40, which continued unchanged, except for an increase in engine bore, until production ended in 1920.

GLOBE • England 1913-1916

Built by sanitary engineers Tuke and Bell, the "torpedo two-seater" Globe cyclecar was propelled by a single-cylinder 1039cc Aster engine. The clutch pedal moved the back axle forward, first slackening the driving belt then forcing the driving pulley against a brake block.

GLOBE FOUR • USA 1921-1922

A conventional assembled car of the time, the Globe Four used a four-cylinder Supreme engine. Production was limited to roadsters and touring models.

GLORIA (GLORIETTE) • Austria 1933-1936

Offered for 3,600 Austrian schillings in 1936, the two-seater Gloriette, designed by former Delta-Gnom motorcycle designer Hans Pitzek, was a modern little car. It had a backbone-chassis and an ohv 795cc four-cylinder engine. Lack of money prevented production on a large scale. Pitzek lacked sufficient facilities, although he was backed by leading Vienna car-dealer and racing driver Bernhard Kandl.

GLOVER • USA 1908

The Glover, from Chicago, was driven by a fifth wheel in the center of the car, which could be forced down on to the road for extra traction.

GLOVER • USA 1920-1921

Like a number of other automobiles made in the United States at the time, the Glover was built exclusively for export, to the order of Glover's Motors Ltd of Leeds, Yorkshire. In all probability the Glover was little more than a Seneca car built in Fostoria, Ohio, equipped with a Rolls-Royce-shaped radiator. The four-cylinder Glover used a Leroi engine. Wheelbase was 114 inches and wire wheels were standard.

GM • France 1924-1928

Gendron et Michelot made some very good CIME-engined cars, a 1099cc four-cylinder and a 1500cc six, in its Paris works.

GMCC • England • France 1903

The General Motor Car Company of London and Paris offered an unlikely car range consisting of a 6 hp Light

A GM in Le Mans trim, 1925

1920 GN on the Brooklands Test Hill

French-built GN-Salmson, 1921

Runabout (120 guineas) and a 40 hp, four-speed touring car weighing $19\frac{1}{2}$ cwt costing 1,500 guineas.

GN • England 1910-1925

H R Godfrey and Archie Frazer-Nash's cyclecar originally used 1100cc JAP and Antoine vee-twins, but by 1911 they were able to offer an engine of their own manufacture. Transmission was by belts and chains, though chain and dog clutch layout was later standardized. After the First World War a new steel chassis replaced the original ash one, and sporting variants were offered, the tuned Legére and Vitesse with a 1087cc overhead camshaft engine, the latter being a revived 1913 GP model. Godfrey and Frazer-Nash left in 1922, the GN rather losing its cutting edge as four-cylinder watercooled engines were offered. Power units by DFP and Anzani were among those used, though only a handful were made.

GN • France 1919-1922

After the First World War the Salmson company in Boulogne-sur-Seine entered the automobile industry by making a cyclecar of British GN design. The vee-twin engine was of 1086cc. It sold very well, and paved the way for proper Salmson cars two years later.

GOBRON-BRILLIE • France 1898-1930

Gobron and Brillié started at Boulogne-sur-Seine building rear-engined cars. Brillié left the association in 1903, but his name remained until the war. From the early days Gobron-Brillié cars were equipped with a very strange engine with two pistons working in the same cylinder, the explosion taking place between them. M Guichard, the designer, claimed that this engine was able to work with any fuel, including brandy or whisky! In 1904 a racing Gobron was the first car to exceed 100 mph. Until 1906 most production cars had tubular frames and twin-cylinder engines of 2290cc or four-cylinder units of 4580cc. The company also made more classic engines with side valves. In 1911 Gobron-Brillié introduced two big cars with inlet over exhaust engines of 8165cc and 9123cc. After the war Gobron-Brillié restarted with the fantastic 35 cv six-cylinder of 7490cc, still with the two pistons per cylinder and, to add some more complications, sleeve valves! More reliable were the few 1495cc Chapuis Dornier-engined cars presented in 1922. At the end Gobron-Brillié tried to sell 1327cc and 1500cc cars in small numbers, the latter under the name of "Turbo-Sport" with a Cozette supercharger.

Dureste on a Gobron-Brillié in the 1907 Coupé de la Presse

GN-GIOVANELLI • France 1922-1923

When Salmson stopped building GNs, a Parisian agent, M Giovanelli, decided to build more cars using the remaining parts. Instead of the vee-twin, he fitted the ohc four-cylinder Nova engine of 950cc.

GNOM • Czechoslovakia 1921-1924

Wealthy hat-manufacturer and racing driver Fritz Hückel built various sporting Gnom cars and helped to found the Nordmührische Automobil Gesellschaft, where a few small two-seater 5 hp cars on Opel Laubfrosch lines were built, using Opel engines.

GNOME • France 1907

These were 12 hp and 18/24 hp cars built by a famous Paris engine manufacturer.

GNOME (NOMAD) • England 1925-1926

Devoid of suspension, and with integral steel/plywood body/chassis, this 343cc friction-driven Villiers-engined cyclecar from London was understandably shortlived.

GNOME ET RHONE • France 1919-1920

This well-known aero engine company presented a 40 hp ohc six-cylinder car of 6000cc just after the war, but was more successful in making motorcycles.

GOBRON-BRILLIE • France 1898-1930

See panel

GODET • France 1919

The Godet Triauto was an 8/10 hp two-seater three-wheeler. Though M. Godet showed at the 1919 Salon, he built only one car.

GODIVA • England 1900-1901

Payne & Bates of Coventry, which built the Stonebow, also offered a similar vehicle under the name Godiva, with a twin-cylinder 9 hp engine. Two- and four-cylinder models of 7 hp-25 hp were listed in 1901. Some Internationals were later built.

GOGGOMOBIL • Australia 1958-1961

Essentially a local version of the German product, the Australian Goggomobil had a glassfiber body and imported components. Produced as a sedan, coupé, and two-seater sports car, the diminutive design was powered by a twin-cylinder two-stroke engine developing 17 bhp. With an overall weight of only 8 cwt, the car accelerated strongly and could reach 55 mph. More than 5,000 were produced, but the arrival of the Morris Mini made the car uncompetitive.

GOLIATH • Germany 1950-1963

Borgward had produced three-wheeled Goliath vans since 1931. In 1950 Goliath cars with 688cc two-cylinder two-stroke engines were offered; 886cc versions with fuel injection developed up to 50 bhp, and a 1093cc version with an ohv flat-four engine gave 55 bhp at 5000 rpm. All Goliath cars had fwd and the engines ahead of the front axle.

GOODCHILD • England 1913-1915

A 10 hp, 1327cc light car sold by T B Goodchild of London.

GOODSPEED • USA 1922

The Goodspeed was a spin-off of the Commonwealth; an attempt to keep the make afloat under a new name, geared strictly for the luxury market. Two sporting open phaetons were built, and displayed at the auto shows in New York and Chicago. A 5178cc six-cylinder own-make engine was used. Wire wheels were fitted and wheelbase was

An Australian-built Goggomobil, 1958

124 inches. The venture failed. Commonwealth's taxicab line became the Checker, which exists to the present day.

GOODYEAR • England c. 1922

Model T Ford engine, gearbox, and axles formed the basis of the Goodyear, the remainder being British. Even the engine was mildly tuned!

GORDANO • England 1947-1949

The Gordano, which took its name from Clapton-in-Gordano in Somerset, never progressed beyond the prototype stage. Construction consisted of a box-section chassis capped with light-alloy bodywork. Suspension was fully independent, with damping variable from the driving seat. Power came from a Wolseley engine. Sadly, Joe Fry, one of the designers, lost his life in a racing accident and no more was heard of the project.

GORDINI • France 1936-1957

"Le Sorcier" Gordini started his career by making "specials" evolved from Simca and Fiat, both sports-racing two-seaters and monoposti. It was only in 1951 that he made the first proper Gordini, using his own engines. He made 1500cc 2-liter and 3-liter racing cars, but his 2.3-liter sports car presented at the 1952 Paris Show never reached the public. Confined to motor racing, he closed his works in 1957 and joined Renault as a consultant engineer. He was responsible for creating the Dauphine "Gordini" and Renault 8 "Gordini."

GORDON • England 1912-1917

Later to achieve fame as a maker of shock absorbers, Gordon Armstrong of Beverley, East Riding, Yorkshire, built

1947 Gordano

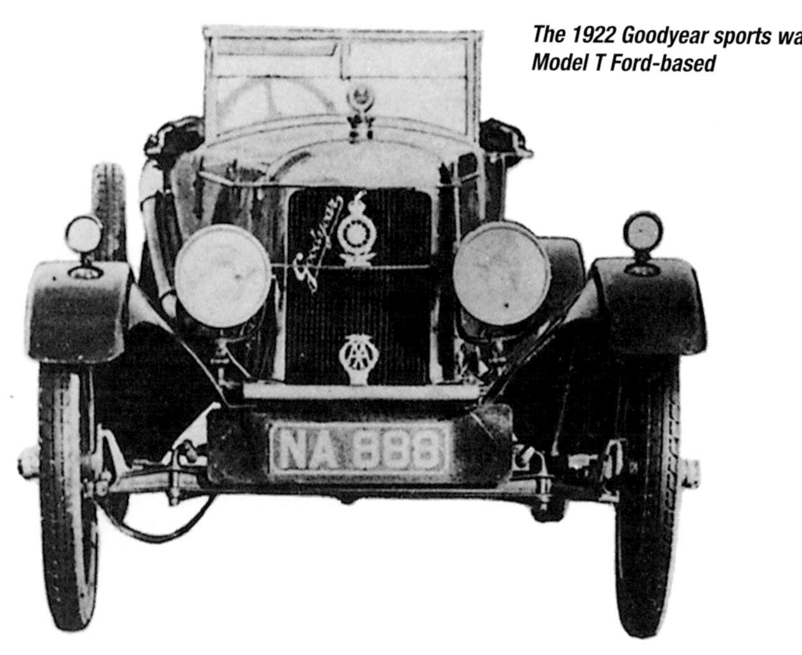

The 1922 Goodyear sports was Model T Ford-based

The Gordon cyclecar, 1912

a range of vee-twin JAP-engined cyclecars with cantilever suspension and the odd feature of supplementary coil ignition on one cylinder only (normal ignition was by magneto) to assist starting. The tubular chassis and body frame were integral.

GORDON • England 1954-1958

A sub-utility three-wheeler built by a subsidiary of Vernons Football Pools, the Gordon had a 197cc Villiers two-stroke engine driving the right-hand rear wheel only.

GORDON-KEEBLE • England 1964-1969

The Gordon-Keeble was arguably ahead of its time, and only 100 or so of these fine cars were built. With its origins in the even shorter-lived Gordon GT of the late 1950s, the Gordon-Keeble featured a multi-tubular chassis topped with a handsome Bertone-designed body. The car's power came from a 5.3-liter Chevrolet Corvette engine of some 300 bhp.

GORDON MINIATURE • England 1903-1904

Sold at 125 guineas complete, the spidery Gordon Miniature was built by a firm of motor and cycle agents in the Seven Sisters Road, London.

GORET • France 1898

The radial three-cylinder engine of this voiturette operated on a "six-stroke" cycle ("intake and mixing,", "compression," "explosion," "exhaust," "intake of scavenging air," "exhaust of scavenging air.")

GORM • Denmark 1917

Karl J Schmidt of Copenhagen produced only 16 cars. Of these, 14 had four-cylinder (probably JAP) engines and two had Perkins engines. Drive was through friction transmission and chain. These cars were also known as AFG (Automobil Fabrik Gorm.)

1966 Gordon-Keeble coupé

1898 Goujon 3¹/2cv **vis-á-vis**

1967 GP Centron

GOTTSCHALK • Germany 1900-1901

Gottschalk, the predecessor of the Berlin Motorwagen-Fabrik, built a limited number of 4 hp cars with De Dion engines.

GOUJON • France 1896-1901

A four-seater voiturette with an air-cooled 3¹/2 hp single-cylinder engine.

GP • England 1967 to date

A strong survivor of the UK "Buggy" era, GP has been responsible for a variety of fascinating products, including the Centron GT car, the fixed-head, four-seat Ranchero, and an ever-improving range of buggies, now sold mainly to Arabs. All these cars have featured well-finished, stylish glassfiber bodies for fitting to VW mechanicals.

GPM • England 1984

The Typhoon 1000 SEC coupé was a spectacular reskinning of the Mercedes 500SEC, with gull-wing doors.

GRACIELA • Argentina 1960-1961

Developed from a Peronist "people"s car," the 1954-1955 Justicialista (built only in prototype form,) this three-cylinder Wartburg-engined saloon was built in a government aircraft factory at Cordoba.

GRACILE • France 1906-1907

There were four models of the Gracile: a 10/12 hp two-cylinder, a 12/14 hp four-cylinder, an 18/24 hp four, and a 30 hp four with dual ignition.

GRADE • Germany 1921-1928

An aviation pioneer and two-stroke engine designer and manufacturer, Hans Grade produced engines, motorcycles, cars and airplanes. His cars had bodywork on aircraft principles. The two-stroke engines were of deflector-type three-port design; they were vertical twins of 808cc and 980cc.

GRÄF & STIFT • Austria 1907-1938

This was the "Rolls-Royce of Austria." Stift was earlier connected with the manufacture of Celeritas cars. After he founded the Gräf & Stift factory in 1902 he built cars for five years on behalf of Arnold Spitz. In 1907 the first Gräf & Stift car appeared. It was the ambition of Willy Stift to build big cars of the highest quality regardless of cost, while the Gräf brothers, Karl, Franz and Heinrich, were the technical experts behind this ambitious venture. In 1897 the Gräfs built a voiturette with the engine in the rear, but it was never manufactured commercially. After 1908

1930 Gräf and Stift SP 6-liter limousine

production concentrated on big 4240cc, 5880cc, 7320cc, and even 7684cc four-cylinder models. A new, smaller model of 1940cc appeared in 1922; there was also a new ohc 7745cc six-cylinder capable of 90 mph. The last Gräf & Stift cars were a 3895cc six and the fantastic SP8 with an ohc 5988cc eight-cylinder engine, which developed 125 bhp at 3000 rpm. Armbruster, Kellner, Jech, and other coachbuilders created superb bodies on these cars. The factory also produced trucks during the First World War, and in the 1920s some interesting sports-racing cars with ohc 7070cc and 7745cc six-cylinder engines. In addition its own designs, the Vienna factory also built Ford, Citroên, and Minor cars under license. The Gräfford was a Gräf & Stift-built Ford V-8 of the mid-1930s.

GRAHAM • USA 1903

The Chicago-built Graham Roadster was available with a choice of electric or gasoline engines at a price of $850.

GRAHAM-PAIGE • USA 1928-1940

See panel

GRAHAM-PAIGE • USA 1928-1940

The three Graham brothers took over Paige in 1928, and continued the old Lycoming-engined 8-85 Straight-away Eight alongside three Continental sixes of 3128cc, 3666cc, and 4740cc. These were, briefly, also built by a Graham branch factory in Berlin. Graham-Paige was the 12th largest US car company in 1928, but from then on its market share fell. The 1932 Blue Streak range, with vee-grille, pontoon wings and rear axle slotted through the chassis to keep the height down, was a trend-setter, but did not help sales. Nor did the adoption of a centrifugal supercharger on the 1934 4350cc Custom Eight. This formed the basis for an English sports sedan version, the Bertelli-bodied Graham British Special of 1935-36. From 1936 Graham-Paige concentrated on six-cylinders of 2780cc and 3679cc, known as Crusader and Cavalier, and the superseded Special Six body dies were sold to Nissan (builders of the Datsun,) which also used Graham engines. A new supercharged Graham-Paige appeared in 1937, followed in 1938 by the controversial "shark-nosed" 3.5-liter six, a range of surpassing ugliness, with the option of "Vacumatic" gear-shift and overdrive. The firm"s last model, the Graham Hollywood, used Cord 810/812 body dies and a Hupmobile chassis. In 1945 the moribund Graham-Paige company was absorbed by Kaiser-Frazer.

1930 Graham-Paige

1923 Grade cyclecar

1910 Great Western 40 roadster

GRAHAME-WHITE • England 1920-1924

A 31/2 hp 348cc single-cylinder engine with kickstart propelled the Buckboard cyclecar, though later a water-cooled 1100cc Dorman was used.

GRAMM • Canada 1913

Twin-cylinder, belt-drive cyclecars built in Walkerville, Ontario.

GRAND • England 1903

Sold by the Motor Vehicle Engineering Company, which also marketed Ader cars under the name "Pegasus," the 10 hp and 16 hp Grand cars were probably French imports.

GRAND NATIONAL • England 1900

After 25 years as cycle manufacturers, H F Copland & Co of SE London went "earnestly in for the Motor Industry" with a 2¾ hp De Dion-engined "Motor Quad."

GRANT • USA 1913-1922

The first Grant automobiles were four-cylinder cars, but by 1915 the make changed to sixes and this policy was retained until the end of the line, a Walker engine being used. The wheelbase was 116 inches, and several thousand Grant Sixes were manufactured before the company ceased production. The 1525cc Grant four was sold in England as the Whiting-Grant.

GRANTA • England 1906

From the same maker as the Westminster, the 28-34 hp car had four separately cast cylinders, "seven point suspension" and shaft drive.

GRAY • USA 1922-1926

The Gray was an inexpensive car which attempted to seize the part of the market dominated by the Model T Ford, presumably aimed at the owner who liked economy but preferred conventional transmission. Featuring a four-cylinder engine of the company"s own design, a 100- to 104-inch wheelbase and a complete line of open and closed body styles, the car did relatively well for a time, 1923 production reaching 30,000 units. Four-wheel brakes were added for 1926, the last year of production. Prices ranged from $490 up.

GRAY-DORT • Canada 1915-1925

This was the US Dort built under license by a carriage and sledge-building company of Chatham, Ontario, using the four-cylinder Lycoming engine until the end of production. The 1922 Gray-Dort Special had, it was claimed, the first factory-fitted automatic reversing lamp.

GRAY LIGHT CAR • USA 1920

Only one Gray was built. This Colorado product, a two-passenger roadster, had a twin-cylinder Harley-Davidson motorcycle engine.

GREAT EAGLE • USA 1910-1918

Big 5.8-liter four-cylinder cars from Columbus, Ohio.

1907 Grégorie 7 hp in the Coupe des Voiturettes

GREAT SOUTHERN • USA 1910-1914

This Birmingham, Alabama, firm made 30 hp and 50 hp fours, in two- and five-seat open models.

GREAT WESTERN • USA 1908-1916

"The Car that awoke Motordom" came from Peru, Indiana. Initially a twin and a 50 hp four were offered, but by 1910 a 40 hp four was the standard model, priced at only $1,600 but "able to go and come back where many cars fear to tread."

GREEN • England 1906

Gustavus Green was a famous manufacturer of engines for everything from motorcycles to airships. Some of his power units incorporated radiators in their water jackets. In 1906 he showed a 26/30 hp chassis with "many novel features" at the Agricultural Hall Exhibition.

GREGOIRE • France 1903-1923

Starting, briefly, with an 8 hp single, 12 hp twin and 20 hp four, Grégoire of Poissy, near Paris, soon switched to building refined voiturettes, the most famous being the 1905 8 hp twin, built until 1912. There was also a 15 hp four. An 18/24 hp six appeared in 1909. In 1912 Grégoire marketed the Dumont (q.v.) under the name Grégoire-Dumont. In 1911-1912 Grégoire experimented with overhead camshafts and hemispherical combustion chambers; it also produced some aerodynamic two-seaters and saloons, mostly on the 3217cc 16/20 hp chassis, which was also encumbered with extraordinary double and triple berline bodies with switchback roof and four-pane side windows. The sporting 14/20 hp of 1913 formed the basis of post-war production, acquiring ohv in 1921; production ended in 1923. The 1919 Grégoire-Campbell was, in fact, a Bignan-Sport built in the Grégoire factory, and the last "Grégoire" was actually built by Hinstin at Maubeuge, with an 1100cc CIME engine. Britons knew it as the "Little Greg."

GREGOIRE • France 1945-c. 1962

J A Grégoire, pioneer of the fwd with the Tracta, presented some cars under his own name after the war. In 1945 a 600cc flat-twin prototype evolved into the "Dyna" Panhard. The 2-liter flat-four of 1947 was made by Hotchkiss under the name of Hotchkiss-Grégoire; from this were developed some Chapron-bodied roadsters sold under Grégoire"s own name. More recently, Grégoire has presented an electric car prototype.

GREYHOUND • England 1904-1905

A three-speed tricar with $3^1/_2$ hp Antoine or 3 hp Fafnir engine, built in Ashford, Middlesex.

1926 Grofri (Amilcar) 20 PS

1920 Griffon 987cc cyclecar

GRICE • England 1927

The Grice was powered by a rear-mounted 680cc air-cooled JAP engine and was a three-wheeler. Made by GWK of Maidenhead, it never went into production.

GRIDI • Germany 1923-1924

A basic car with an 865cc single-cylinder engine and a two-seater body, the Gridi was built in very small numbers.

GRIFFIN • England 1976 to date

A "poor man"s Reliant Scimitar GTE," the Griffin has the unlikely base of the Morris Minor van. The professionally laminated body is well conceived, however, and features a removable estate hardtop.

GRIFFITH • USA 1964-1967

The Griffith used glassfiber bodies (shipped from England) on a tubular frame. Amazing acceleration was provided by 200 hp Ford V-8 engines. Selling at $4,800, a total of 285 Griffiths was built.

GRIFFON • France 1906-1924

A well-established bicycle and motorcycle manufacturer in Courbevoie, Griffon first made cars in 1906 with single-cylinder Aster and Buchet engines. In 1920, after many years of interruption, it produced a cyclecar. This had a vee-twin Anzani engine of 987cc, and was of true motorcycle inspiration.

GRISWOLD • USA 1907

The Griswold from Detroit was a friction-drive twin-cylinder model.

GRIVEL • France 1897

A tubular-framed quadricycle with a rear-mounted vertical-twin air-cooled engine.

GROFRI • Austria 1924-1927

Like the German Pluto, the Austrian Grofri was built under Amilcar license. These sporting cars used sv 903cc and 1074cc four-cylinder engines; some racing versions had Roots-type superchargers. Bernhard Kandl, Karl Sarg and opera-singer Käthe Rantzau were prominent competition drivers of Grofris.

GROSE • England 1899-1900

These were Northampton-built versions of the Benz.

GROSVENOR • England 1908

A 40 hp four-cylinder of 7433cc, the Grosvenor had a brazen laurel wreath attached to its radiator honeycomb.

GROUESY • France 1923-1924

A tiny belt-driven sports-racing cyclecar made in Sartrouville with a 985cc vee-twin.

GROUP SIX • England 1972-1975

John Mitchell"s substitute for a dreamed-of road-going McLaren, the Group Six kit car featured a sporting, self-colored glassfiber body for adding to the traditional VW mechanicals.

Guédon, 1895, ancestor of the Decauville voiturette

GROUT • USA 1898-1913

Better known as builders of steam carriages (sold in England as "Westons,") Grout Brothers of Orange, Mass., also built twin-cylinder gasoline-engined "automobile carriages," which were among the first cars to be equipped with an electric lighting outfit powered by a dynamo. The 1903 Grout came complete with cowcatcher. W L Grout was originally the maker of the "New Home" sewing machine, produced at the rate of one a minute. He and his two sons owned the entire $250,000 capital of the company, which employed 123 workers in 1905. Gasoline cars followed the steamers in 1905, until the end of production in 1913. The 1909 Grout was a 35 hp four-cylinder, with shaft- or chain-drive optional.

GRP • France 1924-1930

Made in Paris by Georges and René Pol, the GRP normally appeared in the form of taxis and commercial vehicles with 1693cc and 1892cc engines.

GS • England 1976 to date

Built by GS cars of Bristol, the GS Europa is basically a reclothed Lotus Europa with attractive glassfiber body featuring flying buttresses for improved vision at the rear.

GSM • England 1960-1961

There were big plans for the GSM Delta. Well sorted suspension hung on a stiff ladder chassis ensured good roadholding, while a light body and the facility of Ford engines in various states of tune ensured good performance. However, the car was more successful on the race tracks than the road, and only 35 or so open cars and a couple of the intended fastback were completed.

GTO • England 1987 to date

A well-engineered replica of the Ford GT40.

1902 Grout (Weston) steamer filling its boiler

GUEDON • France 1897

This voiturette, built at Bordeaux by naval architect Guédon and Cornilleau, is believed to have been the first car with direct drive. The driver could start it without leaving his seat by turning a handwheel mounted on his right. Decauville put this design into production as the "Voiturelle."

GUERRAZ • France 1901

A range of voiturettes with C-spring rear suspension and 1357cc Bolide engines.

GUERRY ET BOURGUIGNON • France 1907

A "tri-voiturette" built by a Parisian cycle company.

LE GUI • France 1906-1914

A voiturette with a double-dropped chassis, a four-cylinder 1593cc engine and a four-speed gearbox, was the first Le Gui ("little fellow.") By 1908, fours of 1.8-3.1 liters and a 5.5-liter six were available. From 1911 10 hp (1726cc) and 15 hp (2650cc) fours were available, the 15 hp being cut to 2121cc for 1912.

GUILICK • France 1914-1930

A maker of proprietary chassis in Maubeuge which normally supplied other car "manufacturers," Guilick also occasionally issued motor cars under its own name with various proprietary engines: CIME, Ruby, Ballot, SCAP, and Altos units from 1100cc to 2000cc.

GURGEL • Brazil 1966 to date

Since 1969 Gurgel has made VW-based off-road vehicles. In 1989 it launched the BR-800 two-seat runabout with a Fiat twin-engine.

GURIK (GEA) • Sweden 1905-1909

Gustaf L M Ericsson worked as an apprentice at the Franklin Company in the USA. When he returned to Sweden in 1904 he started building stationary engines and boat engines in Stockholm. Plans were laid for a large six-cylinder car and one prototype was built. The engine was built up from three German Fafnir twin-cylinder engines. The car was nicknamed Ormen Lange (Long Snake, after a common name for Viking ships), but there was no production. At the automobile exhibition in Stockholm in 1907 the company exhibited both imported cars and cars built at the factory. These were called Gurik and came in two sizes, 12/14 hp and 16/20 hp, both with four-cylinder engines. It is not known whether the engines were bought from outside suppliers or built in Sweden. Probably very few cars were produced, though one is preserved.

GUTBROD • Germany 1933-1954

Founded 1926 as the Standard motorcycle factory, Gutbrod built, from 1933 to 1935, the Ganz-designed "Standard-Superior," a rear-engined car with 398cc and 498cc engines. The more advanced "Gutbrod-Superior" entered the market in 1950, and 7,726 of these cars were made. Most had 593cc two-stroke twin-cylinder engines. A similar 663cc version was offered latterly, the final models having fuel injection.

1975 Guyson

GUY • France 1904-1907

The Guy (built by J Lamy of Paris) was a two-speed voiturette with a 7 hp four-cylinder engine.

GUY • Canada 1911

A 30 hp of high quality built by a carriage and hearse maker of Oshawa, Ontario.

GUY • England 1919-1925

Guy Motors of Wolverhampton, a commercial vehicle maker since 1914, went into the luxury car market in 1919 with its 4-liter V-8 with detachable heads and side valves. This 20 hp car was joined in 1922 by a model with a conventional 2- or 2.5-liter in-line four-cylinder engine. These failed to attract a market, and after 1929 the company reverted exclusively to commercial vehicle production, though in 1929 it acquired Star, another Wolverhampton motor manufacturer.

GUYOT SPECIALE • France 1924-1931

Racing driver Albert Guyot made a few racing cars with Burt-McCollum sleeve-valve engines. He also made some touring cars with 3500cc six-cylinder and 5200cc eight-cylinder American Continental engines.

GUYSON • England 1975

Named after the Guyson shot-blasting concern which sponsored its manufacture, the Guyson E12 was a rebodied Jaguar E Type. Moving far away from the E Type"s own curvaceous lines, the William Towns-designed replacement panels were remarkable for their flatness. Only two cars were made, one for Jim Thompson, director of Guyson, and one for Towns himself.

GWALIA • Wales 1922

This 9 hp Alpha-engined car from Cardiff had an odd suspension by bellcranks and coil springs.

GWK • England 1911-1931

See panel

GWYNNE • England 1922-1929

A manufacturer of centrifugal pumps, Gwynne Engineering first produced the Albert car (for which it had made engines) and from 1923 the cars were known as Gwynne-Alberts. The Gwynne Eight of the same year was a different confection, having an ohv 950cc four-cylinder engine designed by Spaniard Arturo Elizalde. Later a larger engine, a 1247cc Ten, became available, together with a 1021cc sports Eight.

GWK • England 1911-1931

The GWK, made by Grice, Wood, and Keiller, was a friction-drive cyclecar using a two-cylinder rear-mounted Coventry-Simplex engine. Production was centerd at Datchet, Buckinghamshire, but transferred to Maidenhead in 1914. The original engine was briefly retained after the First World War, though soon replaced by a Coventry-Climax four-cylinder of 1368cc. Engine power was again increased in 1924, when a 1.5-liter power unit was fitted. Grice had left the concern in 1920 to make the similar Unit, and although GWK had gone out of production in 1926 he tried to resurrect the concern in 1930.

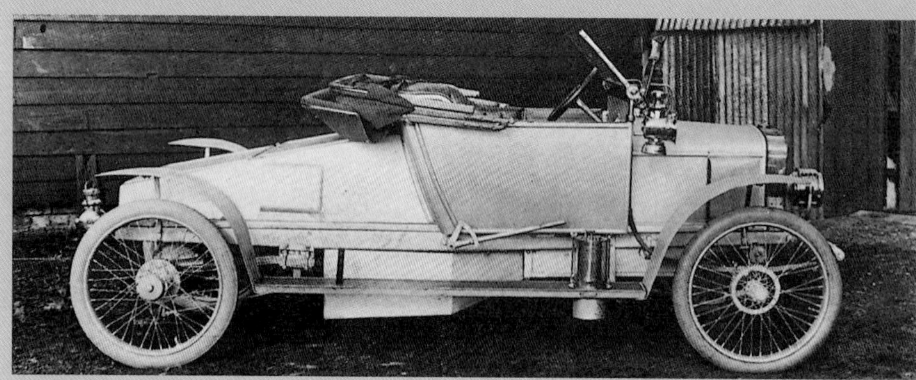

1913 GWK 8 hp two-seater. . .

. . . and its friction-drive chassis

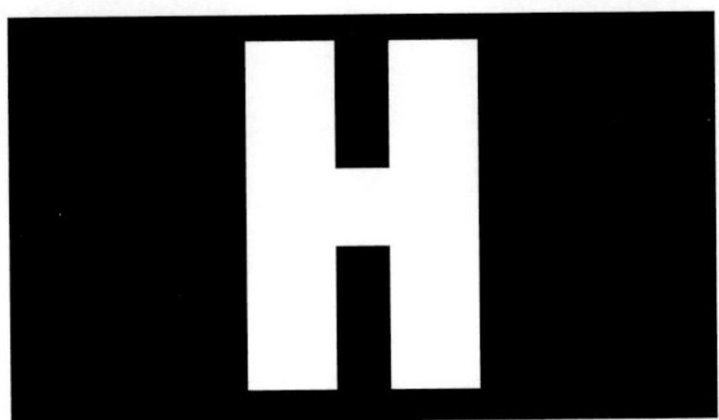

HAASE • USA 1904-1905

Tiller-steered twin-cylinder cars of 6 hp and 8 hp from Milwaukee.

HACKETT • USA 1916-1919

"A prideful car, distinctively different," the $888 Hackett "Ultra Four" was built in Jackson, Mich., as successor to the Argo. In 1920 it was reborn as the Lorraine.

HAG (HAG-GASTELL) • Germany 1922-1927

Cars of advanced design with ohc 1305cc four-cylinder engines. When the Darmstadt HAG factory closed down in 1925, production was resumed at the Gebr. Gastell railroad-carriage works at Mainz-Mombach, where sports-racing cars with 1496cc engines were also built in small numbers. Harry Stumpf-Lekisch was the leading Hag-Gastell racing driver.

HAGEA • Germany 1922-1924

A little-known 1017cc four-cylinder Steudel-engined car with friction drive.

HAL • USA 1916-1918

H A Lozier, brother of E. R. Lozier, left the Lozier company in 1913 to build the HAL Twelve, which had a 6383cc V-12 engine with cylinders cast in threes. Prices ranged from $3,600 for the tourer to $5,000 for the Limousine and Town Car.

HALL • England 1918-1919

An unusual device, the Hall was built by H E Hall and Company of Tonbridge, Kent, with a 20.6 hp horizontal eight-cylinder engine. A Talbot radiator and Studebaker rear axle were incorporated. Only two Halls were made.

HALLADAY • USA 1905-1922

The first dozen years of manufacture of these cars designed by L P Halladay was centered on Streator, Illinois. The cars were subsequently made in Lexington, Attica and Newark, Ohio. For a small-production assembled car the Halladay was singularly long-lived, nearly all using a Rutenber engine. Four-cylinder models were phased out permanently in 1914 in favour of sixes. Control of the Halladay was gained by Albert Barley who, in 1916, three years after his acquisition of the company, introduced the Roamer. Barley sold Halladay in 1917 to concentrate his attention on the Roamer, and the Halladay survived as a manufacturing entity through 1921. Although 1922 models were built, they were probably pilot models only. In addition, a handful of smaller Falcon cars was made by Halladay until production was terminated early in 1922.

1924 HAG 1305cc touring car

1913 11.9hp Hampton two-seater

HALLAMSHIRE • England 1900-1907

The early cars built by Durham, Churchill & Co of Sheffield, used a "friction clutch change speed and reverse gear," apparently an epicyclic transmission adapted from a marine unit. In 1902 the range consisted of a 7 hp and 14 hp, while in 1905 there were a 5/8 hp and a 10/16 hp. The last year of car production was 1907, when an Aster-engined 14/18 hp was offered, still with the same two-speed transmission. Thereafter the company concentrated on its "Churchill" commercial vehicles.

HALL & MARTIN • England 1905

A 10/12 hp car with twin-cylinder Aster engine and armored wood chassis, built in Croydon, Surrey.

HAMLIN-HOLMES, HAMLIN USA 1919-1929

This company attempted to perfect and market a fwd car between 1919 and 1929. Approximately one experimental model per year was completed in this span of years, none looking exactly like another. A production model, announced in 1923, failed to get beyond the experimental stage. One racing version of the car did manage to get into the Indianapolis 500 race in 1926. The name was simplified to "Hamlin" for 1930. The 1930 Hamlin was very similar in design and appearance to the fwd Gardner of the same year. While the Gardner prototype was actually built, there is some doubt concerning the Hamlin.

HAMMER • USA 1905-1906

Like its counterpart, the Sommer, this was a 12 hp twin-cylinder light car, though Hammer did bring out a 24 hp four-cylinder in 1906. The two marques had cloned off the 1902-1904 Hammer-Sommer.

HAMMOND • England 1919-1920

The Hammond, made in Finchley, London, had a long-stroke 2243cc engine and was designed to sell at about £400. Very few were built.

HAMMOND MOUTER • France 1912-1913

A cycle builder of Paris which offered two voiturette models, both four-cylinders, one of 1888cc, the other of 2474cc.

HAMPTON • England 1911-1933

Starting life in Hampton-in-Arden, Warwickshire, the Hampton then moved to King"s Norton, Birmingham, and finally to Stroud in Gloucestershire. The 1912 Hammond was the 12/16 model, with a 1726cc four-cylinder engine, while two years later a shortlived twin-cylinder two-stroke was announced and cyclecars powered by Precision or Chapuis-Dornier engines were offered. A Dorman 1496cc engine was fitted to the 10/16 of 1919; this was later increased to 1795cc. From 1923 Meadows engines were used, and in 1928 a six-cylinder model, the 15/45, appeared at the same time as a new 9 hp car. An excursion into unreality came in 1930 with an order, at the height of the Depression, for 100 straight-eight engines and chassis from the German Röhr concern. The subsequent model was offered with the 2262cc straight-eight, mounted in its own or in a Hampton chassis.

HANDLEY-KNIGHT, HANDLEY • USA 1921-1923

The Handley-Knight was one of a handful of American automobiles which used the Knight sleeve-valve engine, a four-cylinder type being used on this make. Early in 1923 the Knight engine was discontinued, the name was abbreviated to Handley and prices were sharply reduced. Successor to the Handley-Knight, the 1923 Model 6-40 Handley used a six-cylinder Falls engine and a pointed radiator, whereas the 6-60 retained the conventional flat radiator and featured a six-cylinder Midwest motor. Like the earlier Handley-Knights, the cars were distinguished by small handles or loops on the headlights and, despite the fact that Reo also boasted this feature, the Handley slogan was "If it carries handles, it"s a Handley." Checker Cab bought out the make in May 1923.

HANDS • England 1922-1924

After G W Hands had produced the Calthorpe light car he produced a vehicle under his own name with a 1100cc Dorman four-cylinder engine. It was joined in 1924 by a 15 hp ohc six, later to emerge as a Calthorpe after Hands returned to his own company.

HANOMAG • Germany 1924-1939

The little 499cc Hanomag, with its rear-mounted 10 hp single-cylinder watercooled engine, was the first true German "people's car," popularly known as the "Kommisbrot" ("army loaf.") It had an all-enveloping body; a lever between the two seats acted as starter. A cheap but well-made car which performed well in rough and hilly country, it was even raced with success and competed in many long-distance events. A more conventional 745cc Hanomag four-cylinder superseded the Kommisbrot. Further Hanomag cars had ohv four-cylinder 896cc, 1089cc, 1299cc, and 1494cc engines. From 1934 to 1939 an ohv 2241cc six-cylinder was offered and a diesel-engined 1910cc four-cylinder was available from 1937 to 1939. Hanomag also built cars for the German Wehrmacht during the war, but did not re-enter car manufacture after 1945.

HANOVER • USA 1921-1924, 1927?

Hanover was an export-line cyclecar built in Hanover, Pennsylvania. Approximately 800 to 900 of the air-cooled, twin-cylinder Hanover roadsters were marketed. Some six watercooled cars were reportedly produced during the 1927 calendar year.

HANSA • Germany 1905-1939

Founded by August Sparkhorst and Dr Robert Allmers at Varel, Hansa bought the Westphalia car works at Bielefeld in 1913 and the next year merged with Hansa-Lloyd of Bremen. Early Hansa cars were much influenced by French products, mainly the Alcyon voiturette. There were De Dion-engined 720cc single-cylinder models, called "HAG," also available in 1050cc versions, as well as a 1360cc twin-cylinder. Fafnir supplied 1410cc four-cylinder engines to Hansa, which also produced sports cars, including an ohv 2494cc model. From 1910 onwards Hansa built RAF cars under license. The pre-First World War range also included 1550cc, 1796cc, 2080cc, and other models up to a 3815cc four-cylinder 55 bhp model. In 1920 Hansa, Hansa-Lloyd, NAG, and Brennabor formed the "Gemeinschaft Deutscher Automobilfabriken" (GDA.) Between the two wars Hansa offered sv 2063cc four-cylinder 36 hp models and Continental-engined six- and eight-cylinder versions of 3262cc and 3996cc respectively. There was even a 4324cc model with one of these USA-made eight-cylinder engines. All of these cars were made at the Varel works, while the Bremen-built Hansa cars, available from 1930 onwards, had sv 2098cc and 3253cc four-cylinder engines, a 2577cc six-cylinder as well as ohv models with 1088cc and 1640cc own-make engines. New 3485cc and 1962cc ohv six-cylinder models appeared in 1936 and 1937; the last car, already called "Borgward," was the 2247cc six-cylinder, built in 1939. The rear-engined 498cc twin-cylinder two-stroke built in 1934-35 also belongs to the complicated Hansa story. An earlier version with a similar 348cc engine was produced in small numbers only.

1938 Hanomag 1½-liter

The sole surviving Hanzer, a 1902 5hp

HANSA-LLOYD • Germany 1914-1929

Three 4082cc four-cylinder Hansa-Lloyd cars gained renown in the 1914 Alpine-Trial. Improved versions of this model with 50 hp at 1700 rpm appeared on the market in 1921. Another model with 4500cc, called "Treff-Ass," boasted 65 bhp at 2400 rpm and was followed in 1926 by a big ohc eight-cylinder of 5220cc which developed 100 bhp at 3000 rpm. This excellent big car was the last Hansa-Lloyd. After 1930 only trucks were built, in conjunction with NAG.

HANSON • USA 1917-1923

One of the few cars built in the southern United States, the Hanson was an assembled car using a Continental engine and other standardized components. Several hundred units were produced and, like other southern-built assembled automobiles, notably Anderson, the car enjoyed sales outside its own region. Both open and closed models were sold.

HANZER • France 1900-1902

Hanzer of Petit-Ivry built a range of 5 cv and 61/2 cv single and 9 cv twins, all with crocodile hoods; one example survives. From 1902 the cars were sold as "Durey-Sohy."

HARDING • Canada 1911-191

2A 20 hp four on Hupmobile lines built in London, Ontario.

HARDING • England • France 1912

Aeronautical engineer H J Harding, who built monoplanes closely based on the BlÈriot XI, also made a 9 hp JAP-engined "quadcar" in his Paris workshop.

HARDING • USA 1915

The Harding, built in Cleveland, Ohio, was one of the first 12-cylinder cars on the American market. Unfortunately, only one touring car was made before operations ground to a halt.

1928 Hansa-Lloyd ohc 5220cc straight-eight four-door sedan

1913 Hansa 15.9hp sporting tourer 'Type E'

HARDMAN • England 1906„

"Specially built for British Roads," the Hardman cars emanated from Liverpool. The range consisted of 18/20 hp, 25/30 hp and 40/50 hp models.

HARDY • England 1905-1906

A 6 hp Stevens-engined tricar "fitted with an appliance preventing side roll whilst turning a corner," supplied as a chassis and kit of parts "to complete to customer's own satisfaction."

HARISCOTT • England 1920-1921

This obscure sports car from Bradford, Yorkshire, used a 11/2-liter side-valve Coventry-Climax engine. It was so called because the makers were Harrison, Scott and Co.

HARPER RUNABOUT • England 1922-1926

Built in the Avro airplane factory at Manchester, this was a three-wheeled, single-seat, £100 runabout with a single-cylinder 269cc Villiers engine (giving 90-100 mpg) and integral body-chassis construction.

HARRIGAN • USA 1922

The Harrigan Six was an assembled car; the prototype was apparently built in Cleveland, Ohio. Plans called for a factory either in Jersey City or Hoboken, New Jersey. The car used a Continental engine; the touring model was priced at $1,490. The Rolls-Royce-shaped radiator did not lie flush with the hood, but rose above it in the style of the McFarlan.

HARRINGTON • England 1901-1902

A four-seater 7 hp single-cylinder "Panhard system" car offered by London coachbuilder Offord.

HARRISON • USA 1904-1907

The 1906 Harrison, from Grand Rapids, Michigan, had a four-cylinder engine which could run in either direction, thanks to two sets of exhaust cams controlled by the driver. Inlet valves, perhaps mercifully, were designed to be automatic. The cylinders could also be made to fire in pairs "for greater power on hills." An acetylene-powered self-starting system and four-speed constant-mesh transmission were also featured.

HARRIS SIX • USA 1923

An ambitious local project. No cars were actually produced at the Menasha, Wisconsin, plant of the Harris Six until a bankruptcy court ordered as many cars as possible be manufactured and sold from existing parts. Probably fewer than ten were manufactured, disc-wheeled sport phaetons

1923 Harris Six 4078cc sport phaeton

powered by Waukesha or Continental engines. Wheelbase was 120 inches and price was $1,485.

HARROUN • USA 1917-1922

The Harroun, built in Wayne, Michigan, honored the name of Ray Harroun, who won the first Indianapolis "500" in 1911 at the wheel of a Marmon Wasp. This was a low-priced automobile with its own make of four-cylinder engine, selling in the $1,200 price bracket.

HART • England 1900-1903

Ernest W Hart, of Luton and London, was a motor agent who also marketed electric carriages. The 1900 La Toujours contente, with a 21/2 hp Löhner-Porsche electric motor in each hub, was the first 4wd motor car. In 1903 Hart offered a 40 hp gasoline-electric.

HARTNETT • Australia 1949-1955

Designed by French engineer Jean Grégoire (and similar to the British Kendall), the Hartnett was a fwd design which made extensive use of aluminum. It had four-wheel independent suspension, rack-and-pinion steering and an air-cooled horizontally-opposed engine. Plans were made to sell 10,000 a year, but serious difficulties arose when an outside contractor failed to deliver body panels. Some 120 rolling chassis had been completed when Hartnett took the contractor to court. These chassis were fitted with hand-built timber station wagon bodies. Hartnett won a protracted law suit, but the project died.

1915 Harvard two-seater

HARVARD • USA 1915-1920

This was a two-passenger roadster, marketed for export only and manufactured first in Troy, New York, then in Hudson Falls, New York, and eventually in Hyattsville, Maryland. Harvards were all built with right-hand drive; most, if not all, were produced for the New Zealand market. A hidden compartment for the spare wheel in the rear deck was an innovation. A four-cylinder Model motor was used throughout the car"s six-year production.

HASBROUCK • USA 1899-1901

Stephen Augustus Hasbrouck designed a very complex "convertible compound explosive engine" in 1899. His Hasbrouck Motor Company of New York built launches and yachts with "gasoline motive power", and also fitted its power units to carriages which could be "operated by any intelligent person... its speed is gauged from one mile per hour to as fast as one may care to go."

HATAZ • Germany 1921-1925

One of the better small German cars, the 972cc Hataz had a Steudel-made four-cylinder sv engine. Sports versions were available with a similar ohv unit and two-seater bodywork.

HATFIELD • USA 1917-1924

An assembled car, the Hatfield"s only probable claim to fame was its 1917 suburban car, forerunner of today's station wagon. The earlier models used a four-cylinder G. B. & S. engine, later models using both four- and six-cylinder engines by Herschell-Spillman.

HAUTIER • France 1899-1905

"Young engineer" Hautier designed this marque"s "EspÈrance" engines which followed an 1899 electric car. The 1902 models not only had electric lighting, but also an underslung circular radiator beneath a conventional hood. Catalogs that year included a cut-out model of the 1903 four-cylinder; first prize for the best finished model was a new Fr 9,000 twin-cylinder Hautier! Hautier's ultimate range consisted of 20 hp and 30 hp models with frames pressed from a single sheet of steel and constant-mesh gearboxes.

HAVERS • USA 1908-1914

Powerful six-cylinders from Port Huron, Michigan; 1914 models had a 55 hp engine of 6178cc.

1948 Healey Westland two-seater

HAWK • USA 1920

Only one pilot model was built by the Hawk Motor Co of Detroit. This featured disc wheels and a five-passenger touring body.

HAY • USA 1899-1900

Walter Hay, of New Haven, Connecticut, claimed this 6 hp four-cylinder 4212cc Stanhope phaeton would run "without oil or water." It operated on an "eight-stroke" cycle, with two out of four revolutions occupied in "cooling and purifying" the cylinders.

HAY-BERG • USA 1906-1908

Assembled cars from Milwaukee, using an ohv air-cooled 20 hp Carrico four-cylinder engine of 3925cc.

HAYES • England 1904

A "newly invented Balanced Engine and new Ratio Velocity Gear" were this car's main features.

HAYNES, HAYNES-APPERSON USA 1898-1925

Elwood Haynes of Kokomo, Indiana, the inventor of stainless steel, made his first car in 1894, and for many years claimed it as America"s first motor vehicle. However, production did not begin until 1898, when Haynes teamed up with the Apperson brothers, building boxy cars with tiller steering and a rear-mounted flat-twin engine. The Appersons broke away in 1902 to set up on their own, though the cars were still called "Haynes-Appersons" two years later. Wheel steering appeared in 1903; these were among the first left-hand-drive American cars. Haynes cars adopted a front-engine position in 1904, though still using a 12 hp flat-twin. A five-seater aluminum-bodied Roi-des-Belges cost $2,550. A vertical-four engine of 35/40 hp appeared in 1905, last year of the flat-twins. Only big pair-cast fours were available between 1906-1914, in which year the company's first six appeared. This was the Model 27, with electric gear-shift and a pair-cast engine of 7763cc. A 60 (V-12 appeared two years later, with two monobloc cylinders giving a swept volume of 5909cc. The "Light Twelve" remained in production until 1921. The last Haynes was the Model 60, a 5219cc six, available with roadster, tourer, or sedan bodywork.

HB • USA 1908-1909

A 10 hp high-wheeler built by H Brothers of Chicago.

HCE • England 1912-1913

An underslung cyclecar with 6 hp Buckingham engine.

1921 Haynes roadster

c. 1901 Hautier "La Silencieuse" 8hp twin

1927 HE Six at Brooklands

HCS • USA 1920-1925

Harry C Stutz left his Stutz Motor Car Co in Indianapolis in 1919 to head a new concern in the same city, the first HCS automobiles being introduced for 1920. A relatively expensive machine, the HCS resembled the Hispano-Suiza and was highly regarded by sporting car aficionados. The cars were powered by a four-cylinder Weidely engine; in 1924 this was augmented by a Midwest six. The Weidely four was dropped for 1925, the last year of HCS passenger-car production. The company remained in business as a taxicab manufacturer into 1927.

HE • England 1920-1931

Financed by Herbert Merton and designed by R J Sully, the HE was built in Reading, Berkshire, by the Herbert Engineering Co. The first model was a sv 1795cc four, though it was soon succeeded by the 14/20 of 1920. Two years later a sporting model, the 14/40, appeared. A six-cylinder model, a 15.7 hp of 2.3 liters, was added in the 1927 season. The four was dropped in 1928 and a 1.5-liter six appeared in 1930, a few being sold in supercharged form, though it featured quarter-elliptic springs all round, a sign of the times!

HEADLAND • England 1898-c. 1900

Front-wheel-drive electric broughams and phaetons "of not unpleasing appearance."

HEALEY • England 1946-1953, 1989 to date

A highly accomplished driver and experienced engineer, Donald Healey formed plans for the production of a car bearing his name while in the employ of Humber. He had already left his stamp at Triumph, being responsible for the birth of both the Gloria and Dolomite. Production of both the Elliot (closed) and Westland (open) grand touring Healeys began in October 1946. Later, yet more sporting models were produced, the Nash-Healeys finishing with distinction at Le Mans and the Healey Silverstones finding great favour with the club racers at home. The Nash was the most widely produced of the Warwick-built Healeys, 253 being made altogether, as against 105 Silverstones.The Healey Mk IV is a 3500cc Rover V-8-powered recreation of the Austin Healey 3000.

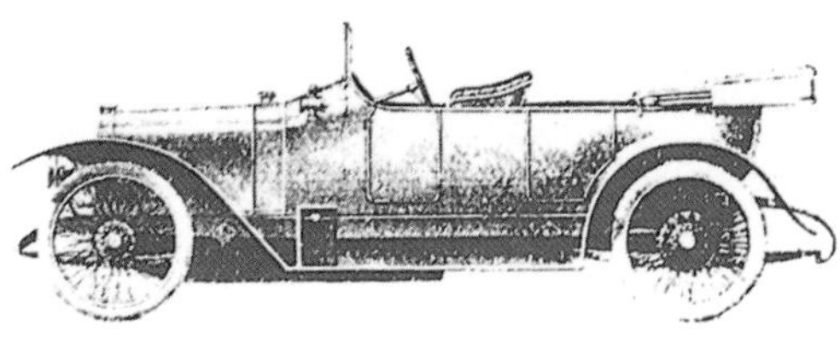

1919 10/12hp Hédéa tourer

HEBE • Spain 1920

A 6/8 cv cyclecar built in Barcelona. Unusually for this type of vehicle, saloon bodies were offered.

HEDEA • France 1912-1924

Made in Paris by M Accary (and sometimes sold under his own name), these were medium-sized cars with 1795cc Chapuis-Dornier engines.

HEIFNER • USA 1920-1922

Located first in Chester, Penn., and later in Geneva, Ohio, the Heifner was developed into a few pilot models at best and just drawing-board plans at least. Announced were six-cylinder models featuring a Continental engine in 1920 and 1921 and a Wisconsin four for 1922. The six-cylinder models, in touring car form, were listed at $3,595.

HEILMANN • France 1897-1900

Monstrously complex, the Heilman (from Le Havre) had a twin-cylinder opposed-piston engine driving a dynamo which powered hub motors. In 1899 this maker of electric locomotives offered a four-wheeled electric avant-train to convert horse carriages.

HEIM • Germany 1921-1926

Made by former Benz engineer and racing driver Franz Heim, these 20 hp, 30 hp and 40 hp touring cars had own-make four-cylinder engines of 1569cc, 2009cc, and 2100cc with side valves; 1924 saw the introduction of an ohc 2385cc six-cylinder. Production of Heim cars was limited, especially of an ohc 1960cc sports six-cylinder which was built in 1925-1926.

HEINE-VELOX • USA 1906-1909, 1921-1922

The initial phase of the car carrying this name was a conventional four-cylinder type built by the Heine-Velox Motor Co of San Francisco, California. The second line of automobiles, enormous and highly expensive machines, was produced by the Heine-Velox Engineering Co of the same city. These later cars rode on a wheelbase of 148 inches and used a modified Weidley V-12 engine with 6383cc displacement. Hydraulic four-wheel brakes were included and both open and closed models were built. Price of the five-passenger touring model was $17,000, making it America"s most expensive motor car at the time.

HEINIS • France 1925-1930

Made in Neuilly by M Heinis, these cars were offered with various engines, from an ohc 799cc four designed by Heinis, through various proprietary 1100cc, 1170cc, 1690cc, and 1947cc units to a 5000cc Lycoming eight.

HEINKEL • Germany 1955-1958

Formerly famous for its military aircraft, Heinkel built three-wheeled 174cc "bubble cars." From 1957 a four-wheeled minicar with ohv 198cc and 204cc single-cylinder engines was also available. In 1958 Heinkel sold the design and production equipment to Ireland and England respectively.

HELBE • France 1905-1907

The Helbé ("LB," for Levêcque and Bodenreider, its constructor) was an assembled light car using De Dion engines of 4.5 hp, 6 hp, and 8 hp and Delage components.

HELIOS (NORDEN) • Sweden 1901-1906

Söderälje Verstäder built railroad rolling stock, but started importing Kuhlstein, NAG, Protos and Ducommun cars from Germany. Any of these cars could probably have been sold under the Helios name in 1901-02. From 1902 the American Northern car was assembled and marketed as Norden. The venture was not profitable and production ceased in 1906.

HELIOS • Switzerland 1906-c. 1907

A shortlived marque from Zurich whose 18/24cv shaft-drive cars were built in the Weidmann factory.

HELIOS • Germany 1924-1926

A small car with a watercooled 972cc flat-twin MI (afterwards Mehne) engine.

HELVETIA • France 1898-c. 1900

Built at Combs-la-Ville (Seine et Marne) by Swiss engineer Jacques Fischer-Hinnen, this was a light electric car. A Helvétia was the first car seen in Prague.

HENDERSON • USA 1912-1915

"More car for less money" was the slogan of this Indianapolis-built 4.6-liter four featuring electric lighting and starting. The sons of the company"s founder made the famous Henderson four-cylinder motorcycle.

HENNEY • USA 1920-1930

The majority of passenger automobiles built by this funeral car manufacturer were formal sedans built either as emergency ambulances, invalid cars or automobiles to accommodate mourners at funerals, and used the conventional ambulance/hearse chassis. A handful of disc-wheeled sport phaetons was destined for West Coast sales in 1920, and in 1930 the company built four convertible sedans featuring long chassis and wire wheels. All four units were sold to funeral directors and were priced at $5,000.

HENOU • France 1923

For one year M Henou of Paris sold some 1843cc cars made by Guilick in Maubeuge.

HENRIOD • Switzerland 1896-c. 1899

Fritz Henriod of Bienne built a steam tricycle in 1888; in 1893 he built a single-cylinder car on Peugeot lines. Production began with a rear-engined 4cv car, shown at the Exposition Nationale in Geneva in 1896, in which year Fritz was joined by his young brother Charles-Edouard. In 1896, too, came a car with rear-mounted flat-twin engine and a transmission consisting of a crown-wheel with three concentric sets of teeth engaged by a sliding pinion. In 1898 Charles-Edouard broke away to set up in France, and Swiss production ended.

HENRIOD • France • 1898-c. 1911

Charles-Edouard Henriod began production at Neuilly-sur-Seine with cars similar to the last Swiss-built Henriods, with flat-twin air-cooled engines mounted at the front of the chassis. Seven models were offered. Among Charles-Edouard"s later inventions was a "valveless" engine which Darracq built under license (and which almost ruined the company). "All the elements of mystery" were contained

1920 Henney Sport Phaeton

in the 1909 Henriod 30/40 hp chassis, which had an air-cooled engine. There was no visible gearbox, the propeller shaft running direct from clutch to rear axle. In fact, the clutch contained a three-speed epicyclic transmission operated by pedal. "No fewer than seven pedals figure on the footboard," commented a press report. "They are not in line, however, three of them being double, with a rocking motion, so that the heel and toe may work one or other of a pair. It must be conceded that the simplicity of the transmission is somewhat discounted by the intricacy of control". The marque survived until at least 1911, building a four-cylinder "valveless" 2614cc car with friction drive to the design of one G Aubrespy.

HENRY • USA 1910-1912

"Built to sell on its merits," the Henry 35 came from Muskegon, Wisconsin.

HENRY BAUCHET • France 1903

A 5/8 cv twin-cylinder light car from Rethel (Ardennes) sold direct to the public, possibly succeeding l'Ardennais.

HENRY-DUBRAY • France 1901

A 5 cv three-seater voiturette from Paris, noted for its "softness in rolling."

HENRY J • USA 1951-1954

The Kaiser-Frazer Company introduced the Henry J in 1951 in an attempt to bolster its sagging fortunes. An ugly compact car designed by American Metal Products, with additional styling by Howard Darrin, the Henry J was powered by Willys-built L-head four- and six-cylinder engines. Although it was available only as a two-door, four-passenger fastback coupé, 82,000 cars were sold. Sales had slumped by the end of 1952, when a new model, the Vagabond, was introduced. Willys merged with Kaiser in 1953 and the Henry J was dropped in 1954, after 120,000 had been sold.

HENSCHEL • Germany 1900-1906

There was no connection between this Berlin machine factory and the famous Henschel locomotive works. They produced electrically driven cars and a small 6 hp gasoline car in limited numbers.

HERALD • France 1901-1906

Hérald secured one of the biggest fleet orders of its day, to supply 100 chassis for "motor hansoms" for London; 14 hp, 18 hp, and 24 hp models were available. Queen Wilhelmina of the Netherlands had a 24 hp Hérald limousine in 1905.

1951 Henry J – "functional beauty without frills"

HERALD • Germany 1903-1906

An "unlucky" car, because the Herald, built by Otto Weiss & Co of Berlin, had so much in common with the 1140cc single-cylinder Maurer-Union that Weiss lost a court action and had to cease car manufacture.

HERBERT • England 1916-1917

An 11.9 hp SUP engine powered this Hampton-like light car assembled in London by Herbert Smith.

HERCULES • Switzerland 1900-c. 1902

Hercules cars, built in Menziken (Argovie,) were heavy wagonettes with single-cylinder 6 cv and four-cylinder 12 cv engines. From 1902 onwards trucks only were built.

1905 Hermes 50hp tourer

1916 11.9hp Herbert Coupé

HERDTLE & BRUNEAU • France 1905

Certainly the smallest four-wheeled passenger vehicles ever were the motorized roller skates produced by this motorcycle maker. Each skate had a 1 hp motor; the controls were fixed to the skater's belt and linked to the skates by flexible cables. Top speed was claimed to be a brakeless 106mph. Hardly surprisingly, motor skating failed to catch on as a pastime.

HERES • France 1910

A four-cylinder 2413cc car with cone clutch and live axle, built in Paris.

HERFF-BROOKS • USA 1914-1916

A 40 hp four and 50 hp six, selling at $1,100 and $1,375, were manufactured in this company"s "one great plant in Indianapolis." A 25 hp, selling at $765, was added for 1915.

HERING • Germany c. 1900-1903

Hering, maker of construction equipment and steam piledrivers at Ronnebourg, offered a range of two- and four-cylinder cars with crocodile hoods and armored-wood chassis.

HERMES • England 1903

Built by the Autocar Construction Co, the 25 hp Hermes was developed from the Accles-Turrell and had a "sliding body," giving easy access to the four-cylinder horizontal slow-speed engine and transmission.

HERMES • Germany 1904-1907

The Hermès (or Hermès-Simplex,) was designed by Ettore Bugatti and built by E E C Mathis at Graffenstaden in Alsace. There were 45 hp (7433cc) and 60 hp (8261cc) four-cylinder models, as well as a limited number of 25 hp and some 90 hp (12,064cc) racing versions. They competed in many events; drivers included Bugatti, Gustav Langen, Emile Mathis, De Vizcaya, and Robert Dunlop.

HERMES (HISA) • Italy • Belgium 1905-1909

This Belgo-Italian factory had works at Liège and Naples. Racing driver and financier Baron de Crawhez was behind these 4192cc four-cylinder cars, which were of up-to-date design and excellent quality. Production was on a limited scale only. There was no connection between this factory and the Bugatti-designed Hermès-Simplex.

1899 Hertel 2½hp

HERMON • England 1936

The Hermon featured André Girling coil-spring independent front suspension and was closely modelled on the 1.5-liter British Salmson.

HERON • England 1924-1926

The Heron was unusual in having an 11.9 hp Dorman engine mounted transversely amidships with chain drive to the rear axle and a Consuta copper-sewn plywood body built by flying-boat manufacturer S E Saunders. Later cars had a conventionally mounted engine of 10.8 hp.

HERON • England 1960-1964

Heron Plastics had been involved in reclothing Austin Sevens at one time, and the body for the Heron Europa was in fact a widened, generally modified version of one of those early designs. Underneath lay a Ford nestling in a backbone chassis. In 1962 the kit was a mere £580. Following early promise and a flirtation with Monteverdi, Heron scrapped the project after 12 years.

HERRESHOFF • USA 1909-1914

This Detroit company built a conventional four-cylinder model, which sold at $950 in roadster form with a mother-in-law seat. The 30 hp Herreshoff chassis "gave an impression of originality which is dissipated, almost wholly, by detail consideration." It had a 30 hp 2199cc engine.

HERRESHOFF • USA 1914

The work of yacht designer Charles Frederick Herreshoff, this 16 hp light car was built in Troy, NY. It was seemingly unconnected with the Detroit Herreshoff.

1901 Hewison-Bell dogcart

HERSOT HELICE • France 1920-1924

Better known as a brake manufacturer in Limours, Hersot made some unusual cars with propellers, like airplanes.

HERTEL • USA 1895-1900

"One of the lightest hydro-carbon motor vehicles on the market," the 1899 Hertel, built by the Oakman Motor Vehicle Co of Greenfield, Massachusetts, scaled 500 lb in running order. The independently sprung front wheels were carried in cycle forks, and a single lever not only controlled the friction drive (by vee-pulleys on to a "driving rim" inside each rear wheel,) brake, and throttle, but was also used to start the twin-cylinder 2.5 hp engine.

HERTZ • USA 1925-1927

The first car made purely for rental, the Hertz was the ancestor of today"s Hertz rental car system. Under Yellow Cab aegis it first appeared in 1925 as a successor to the Ambassador D-1 and survived in both open and closed models until late 1927. It featured the Continental six-cylinder engines, disc-wheels, Buick-shaped radiator, and 114-inch wheelbase.

HEWETT • England 1905

A 24 hp four-cylinder tonneau "suitable for private use or traveller"s business."

HEWINSON-BELL • England c. 1900

Six of these crude Benz copies with wheel-steering were apparently built in the Southampton area.

HEWITT • USA 1906-1907

Hewitt used the same design of "pedals-to-push" gearing as its related marque, the English Adams, and used identical 10 hp horizontal single and 7423cc V-8 engines, though there was also a pair-cast four with an optional sliding gear change.

HEWITT-LINDSTROM • USA 1900-1901

Chicago builder of electric vehicles ranging from light Stanhopes to stagecoaches.

HEXE • Germany 1905-1907

Built in Hamburg, the Hexe ("Witch") was patterned on the Nagant; fours of 18/20 hp, 24/30 hp, and 40/45 hp, and a 35/40 hp six were available.

HEYMANN • USA 1898-1902

A tiller-steered two-seater from Melrose, Mass.

HFG • England 1920-1921

Using a 9 hp flat-twin engine mounted transversely on the near side of the car, the HFG was a shortlived essay by C Portass and Son of Sheffield.

HH • Germany 1906-1907

A long-forgotten producer of cars known as "Ferna," with engines from 10 hp to 28 hp; most had Fafnir four-cylinder engines.

HIDLEY STEAM CAR • USA 1901

Definitely one, and perhaps as many as four, Hidley automobiles were made. The center of operations was Troy, New York.

1908 25hp Hillman-Coatalen Roi-des-Belges

1920 Speed Model Hillman 10hp

HIGHGATE, HMC • England 1903-1904

The 1903 HMC Popular had a choice of 6.5 hp Aster or De Dion engines, and sold at 170 guineas, while the 1904 Highgate light car ("only 125 guineas") had a 6 hp De Dion.

HIGHLANDER • USA 1920-1921

Sometimes listed as "Hylander," this assembled car used a Continental six-cylinder engine. It was built in 1920 and 1921 by Midwest Motors, with the former Stafford Car factory of Kansas City, Missouri, as headquarters. With a 120/125-inch wheelbase, the touring car was listed at $1,975.

HILDEBRAND • Germany 1922-1924

Assembled a few three-seater cars with 15 hp Steudel four-cylinder engines.

HILL & STANIER • England 1914

A 6 hp cyclecar built in Newcastle-upon-Tyne.

HILLE • Germany 1898

A copy of the De Dion tricycle with a 1.25 hp air-cooled engine.

HILLEN • Holland c. 1913

An ephemeral marque from Jutphaas.

HILLMAN • England 1907-1976

William Hillman, a cycle manufacturer of 10 years' standing, commissioned Louis Coatalen to design his first car for the 1907 Tourist Trophy. The 24 hp four-cylinder model was eliminated following a crash. Coatalen left to work wonders at Sunbeam, and Hillman settled down to producing modest and unspectacular models. These included a 9.7-liter six-cylinder car and a 6.4-liter four, though at the other extreme a 9 hp 1357cc car was more successful, spanning the war years and finally being discontinued in 1925, by which time it had grown to 1.6 liters. A 14 hp model came out in 1926, and two years later the company was taken over by the Rootes brothers; a 2.6-liter straight-eight was an uncharacteristic offering for the marque. A landmark for Hillman came in 1932 with the appearance of the 1185cc Minx, while the sporting market was offered the 1933 Aero Minx. There were some six-cylinder models, but by 1939 production was rationalized and only the four-cylinder Minx and 14 hp models were offered.

The Minx soldiered on after the war, and for 1949 received full-width bodywork and the following year a 1265cc engine. Overhead valves came late to the Minx, 1955 seeing their adoption with a 1390cc engine. The faithful Minx remained in production until 1970, by which time it was powered by a 1775cc engine. The company"s entry into the small-car market came with the Imp of 1963, which had a rear-mounted 875cc all-aluminum ohc engine and all-independent suspension, though it never achieved the hoped-for sales. The American Chrysler Corporation attained a majority interest in Rootes in 1964, and one outcome of this takeover was the 1294cc Avenger of 1970.

1955 1390cc Hillman Minx

It was no surprise when the Hillman name ceased to appear in 1976, being replaced by the Chrysler trademark. In 1978 Chrysler's British operations were acquired by the French Peugeot-Citroȉn group as part of its takeover of Chrysler-Europe.

HILTON • USA 1921

A curiosity in that it was only available in coupé form, the 114-inch-wheelbase Hilton sold at $2,375. Head office was at Philadelphia, with the factory at Riverton, New Jersey. All Hiltons had a four-cylinder Herschell-Spillman engine and wire wheels.

HINDUSTAN • India 1942 to date

Morris-based cars built in Hooghly, West Bengal, starting with the Hindustan 10. The current Ambassador range was introduced in 1957, based on the contemporary Morris-Oxford. The current Hindustan Mk IV, with 1.5-liter gasoline or diesel engines, dates from 1979. Hindustan also makes the Contessa, based on the 1972 Vauxhall Victor, with 1.8-liter Isuzu power since 1986.

HINES • USA 1907-1910

William R Hines of the National Screw and Tack Co of Cleveland, Ohio, built his first car in 1902, and soon became an advocate of two-stroke engines. The first production Hines was completed in April 1907; it used an over-square four-cylinder two-stroke engine of 4170cc. A three-cylinder engine was also built.

HINO • Japan 1953-1967

Formerly building only commercials, Hino began assembling the Renault 4 cv under license in 1953, introducing its own design, the rear-engined 893cc Contessa 900, in 1961. The line was revised by Michelotti in 1964, with cars up to 1300. Hino merged with Toyota in 1967.

HINSTIN • France 1921-1926

Made both by M Hinstin in the SUP works in Mezières and by Guilick in Maubeuge, these were light cyclecars with 1099cc CIME and 1094cc Ruby engines. Some light cars with 1500cc SCAP engines were also offered.

HISPANO ALEMAN • Spain 1979 to date

Built two sports cars, one similar to the Malorca but with Ford Fiesta 1300cc engine, the other a BMW-powered BMW 328 replica.

HISPANO-SUIZA • Spain 1904-1938

See panel

HISPANO-SUIZA • France 1911-1938

See panel

HISPANO-GUADALAJARA • Spain 1918-1923

Hispano-designed vehicles, mostly military trucks, were produced in the Guadalajara factory, which operated independently from Barcelona until 1923. Some 8/10 hp light cars were built, also known simply as "La Hispano."

HISPARCO • Spain 1924-1929

Carlos Perez del Arco designed this Madrid-built 6/8 hp sporting light car. Four-wheel brakes, three-speed gearbox and a four-cylinder 961cc engine were features of the specification. About 100 Hisparcos were built, some being sold through a Parisian agency.

HITCHON-WELLER • England 1904-1906

Fitted with the Hitchon Patent Change-Speed Gear, this 9 hp light car was built in Accrington, Lancashire. Later models were known as "Globe," and a 14 hp White & Poppe engine became available.

HL • France 1911-1924

Designed by H L A Hainsselin, the HL ("Europe"s reply to America") was a bullnosed four-cylinder with coil-spring independent front suspension, close-fitting cycle wings and a two-speed gearbox in unit with the back axle. Two engine sizes were available, 2121cc and 3092cc. Also sold as Hainsselin, this marque offered a 2413cc four of similar design post-war.

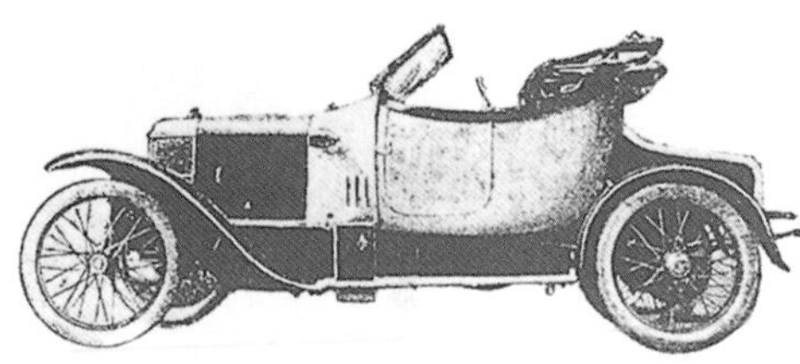

1913 HL 2121cc two-seater

1910 Hobbie Accessible high-wheeler

HMC • England 1913

An 8 hp Chater-Lea-engined cyclecar from Hendon.

HOBBIE ACCESSIBLE • USA 1908-1909

The Hobbie was one of many high-wheeled cars being sold at the time. Featuring a twin-cylinder air-cooled engine, it had tiller steering and solid tires. It was one of the relatively few Iowa-built cars, the factory being located in Hampton.

HOFFMAN • USA 1901-1904

A "general utility car" from a firm of bicycle builders in Cleveland, Ohio, the 8 hp Hoffman became the Royal Tourist in 1904.

HISPANO-SUIZA • Spain 1904-1938

Succeeding Castro, Fabrica La Hispano-Suiza de Automovils recorded its Swiss designer, Marc Birkigt, in its title; production was, again, in Barcelona. At first the Castro four was continued under the Hispano-Suiza name. Then, in late 1906, two pair-cast fours of 3.8 and 7.4 liters were introduced, followed by two big sixes in 1907. Already the young King Alfonso XIII had a Hispano in his stable, the first of some 30 he would own. A racing Hispano built for the 1910 Coupe des Voiturettes sired the famous 3620cc Alfonso XIII sports model (Queen Ena of Spain gave her husband one for his birthday.) By 1912 a Paris factory was in operation, and it was here that the famous 6.5-liter ohc H6 of 1919 was principally built, though Barcelona did turn out a limited number as the T41 (T56 8-liter from 1928; the T49 used the same chassis but a 3750cc six-cylinder engine. In the 1920s Barcelona also built the ohv T30 4.7-liter (1914-1924) and T16 3089cc (1921-1924;) the 2500cc T48 was built for the government public services. Between 1932 and 1943 Barcelona built a series of six-cylinder models, the last of which was the T60RL, introduced in 1934, a depressing machine with servo-assisted Lockheed hydraulic brakes and central gear change.

HISPANO-SUIZA • France 1911-1938

To satisfy its fashionable French clientele, Hispano-Suiza opened a Parisian assembly plant at Levallois-Perret in 1911, moving to larger premises at Bois-Colombes in 1914. It was the French factory which produced the immortal 32 cv H6B in 1919, with its ohc light-alloy engine of 6597cc, joined in 1924 by the even more exciting Boulogne sports derivative of 7983cc. The H6B was built under license by Skoda of Czechoslovakia from 1924-1927. In 1930 Hispano took over Ballot, which built the 4580cc Junior six-cylinder, and in 1931 loftily ignoring the Depression, the company brought out the magnificent Type 68 V-12 of 9425cc, later developed into the 11,310cc Type 68 bis. A six-cylinder version, the K6, succeeded the Junior in 1934. Post-war, the French factory built a fwd prototype using a Ford V-8 engine, which never reached production.

An H6B Hispano-Suiza tourer c.1923 (top,) c.1922 Hispano-Suiza H6B Torpédo Scaphandrier (above,) 15.9hp Hispano-Suiza, 1914, in racing trim (left)

HOFSTETTER • Brazil 1982 to date

Since 1984 this Sao Paulo-based company has built a VW Santana-powered mid-engined sports car in tiny numbers.

HOLCAR • England 1897-1905

Michael Holroyd-Smith, an inventor "determined to break away from the conventional," first made a high-built phaeton with tiller steering and massive unsprung chassis, the body being carried on full-elliptic springs. Holroyd-Smith's 1901 car had a 90(vee twin, and transmission by "employing cones with a specially-devised linked belt." The United Kingdom Inventions Association (Telegrams "Ghostology") of London offered the Holcar, designed by Holroyd-Smith, as well as a "rotary steam motor" in 1903.

HOLDEN • Australia 1948-

After 18 years of assembling Vauxhall and Chevrolet models, General Motors Holden launched Australia"s first mass-produced car in 1948. The light six-cylinder four-door sedan, which was typically American in concept and powered by a 60 hp engine, was an immediate success. More than 4 million Holdens have since been sold. The 1978 range consisted of sedans, waggons, and panel vans, with a choice of six-cylinder and V-8 engines. In 1969 GMH also launched a smaller car called the Torana. Originally based on the Vauxhall Viva, it grew in size and is now produced with a 1.9-liter four-cylinder or a larger six-cylinder unit. The larger Holden was produced in several levels of trim, and in an extended-wheelbase version known as the Statesman.

Holden has always been a GM brand, but in the 1980s and 1990s it was allowed a greater degree of independence. It sold Nissan sourced cars labelled with its own traditional brand names, such as Astra and Barina. The 1990s Holden sedans were all based on the shared GN Omega and Vectra ranges from Europe. In Australia, however, the huge distances and local preferences resulted in all of these cars being fitted with much larger-capacity engines, making them unique to that market. They were US sourced V-6 3.8 liter and V-8 5.7 liter engines shoehorned into engine bays originally designed for smaller powerplants. Although the cars are visually similar to their European counterparts, the Australian design studios and engineering units have tweaked them with new styling themes grafted on to large sedan models, named Calais, Acclaim, and Caprice.

HOLDSWORTH • England 1903-1904

There were three models of the Birmingham-built Holdsworth, a chain-driven 4.5 hp, a 6.5 hp Aster-engined shaft-drive model, and a 6 hp twin with "patent transmission by connecting rods; pedal starting gear; twenty different speeds either forward or reverse."

1978 Holden Kingswood Sedan

1903 Holley Motorette

HOLLAND • USA 1901-c1905

Built cars of 1.25 hp to 12 hp, with one and two cylinders.

HOLLEY • USA 1899-1904

George H Holley of Bradford, Pennsylvania, built tiller-steered three- and four-wheeler cars.

HOLLIER • USA 1915-1921

Built by the Lewis Spring & Axle Co of Chelsea, Michigan, the Hollier was initially available with an own-design V-8 engine. A smaller model with Falls six-cylinder engine was introduced for 1917 and, later, Continental sixes were substituted. All Hollier automobiles were open models.

HOLMES • USA 1918-1923

The Holmes was a well-built, highly regarded, relatively expensive automobile which ranked second to Franklin in air-cooled car sales at the time. Using an ohv six-cylinder engine of the company's own design and make, and with a wheelbase of 126 inches, the Holmes line constituted both open and closed models. A planned four-cylinder did not materialize. In six years of business Holmes manufactured an estimated 2,700 cars.

HOLSMAN • USA 1902 • 1909

The Holsman Automobile Co of Chicago claimed to be the "oldest, largest and most practical manufacturers of carriage automobiles in the world" (all demonstrably untrue,) and built spindly belt-drive high-wheelers with a minimum of mechanical refinement.

HOL-TAN • USA 1908

Moon of St Louis built this European-styled four for Lancia agents Hollander & Tangeman of New York.

HOLYOKE • USA 1899-1903

A gas-engine maker of Holyoke, Mass., which turned to making complete motor vehicles. Matheson took over the factory.

HOMER LAUGHLIN • USA 1916-c. 1918

This was a V-8 with the odd combination of friction transmission and fwd, the friction disc being linked to the front axle by twin chains.

HONDA • Japan 1962 to date

See panel

HONG-QI • China 1959 to date

The Hong-Qi ("Red Flag") prestige limousine is built by the Number One Automobile Plant in Changchun, Manchuria. The first model, Hong-Qi 72, appeared as a prototype in 1958, and was produced in small numbers until 1966, when the Ca 770 series was launched. Powered by a 5652cc V-8, it is said to be capable of 118mph. In 1958 the same factory introduced the 1.5-liter Dong Feng ("East Wind.") Standard color, appropriately, was red.

HOOPER • England 1987 to date

The Hooper Empress was a Bentley Turbo R based luxury car that sold for £275,000. The Emperor, a stretched Silver Spirit, cost up to £400,000.

HORCH • Germany 1899-1939

August Horch, one of Germany"s pioneer car manufacturers, produced 5 hp and 10 hp twin-cylinder cars. In 1902 he moved to Reichenbach and in 1903 designed a 20 hp four-cylinder car with shaft drive. A 22 hp version appeared in 1904, after Horch had again moved production, to a new factory at Zwickau in Saxony. In 1905 a 40 hp 5800cc Horch went into production, and 1907 saw the

HONDA • Japan 1962 to date

Under the guidance of its founder, Soichiro Honda, an engineer with metalworking in his genes, this Japanese company flourished in the early post-war years, firstly as a maker of fine motorcycles, and secondly, in the 1960s, as a maker of precisely engineered small cars. Even today, with its executive-class cars, sports cars, and off-roaders, Honda still excels at minimalist motoring, producing micro cars for its home market. The quintessential Civic range has, however, outgrown its roots as a city car. The last real city car produced by Honda for non-Japanese market consumption was the tall-bodied Jazz model.

From the 1950s onwards Honda made best-selling motorcycles and became the world"s biggest motorcycle manufacturer, a title it holds to this day. Honda unveiled its first car, the twin-ohc S500 Sports, at the 1962 Tokyo show; 360cc and 500cc engines were available, and before long there was an 800cc version too. In 1966 sedans of 360cc and 600cc were introduced, and in 1969 came the Honda 1300, with single ohc and front-wheel drive.

In 1965 Honda entered grand prix racing, and won its first race soon after. Through this exposure the firm learned about double-wishbone suspension and high-revving yet smooth engines, both traits later becoming design hallmarks on most Honda cars.

A stratified-charge engine, the CVCC, was available in the 1973 Civic. A larger model, the Accord, came next, with a 1600cc engine. This was the subject of controversial negotiations in 1979 whereby BL (formerly British Leyland) planned to build it as a "Triumph" model in Coventry as a stop-gap until their LC10 mid-range model became available in the early 1980s. In the end Honda shared its Ballade model with Triumph as the Acclaim model, a stop-gap affair. Triumph died and Rover took over, with Honda eventually taking a share in the events. At that time Rover benefited from being able to use Honda"s smooth-as-silk 2.7-liter V6 engine. In 1982 Honda began building cars in the USA. The Today, launched in 1985, is a 546cc monobox city car, and the 1.3-liter City minicar dates from 1986. The Civic three- and four-door models arrived in 1986; redesigned Civics were revealed in 1991, powered by 16-valve ohc engines of 1.4, 1.5, and 1.6 liters (or the dohc VTEC 1.6-liter with variable valve timing in the VTi.) The VTEC is also used in the CRX "hot hatch." The Concerto range was built in

Honda"s own supercar, the NSX (above,) 1960s Roots the S800 (left)

four- and five-door models with a range of 16-valve 1.6 liter engines. The 2.0/2.2-liter Accord range included the 2.2-liter Aerodeck sports estate car. The new-generation Prelude sports coupé, with all-wheel steering effect geometry, was launched in 1987 to replace the old 1982 model, and was joined in 1990 by the Legend, an all-new luxury car with a 2.7 and then 3.2-liter V6 engine.

Also new in 1990 was the handsome NSX mid-engined sports coupé with V6 3.0 liter VTEC power unit, constructed from a combined aluminum monocoque and offering Ferrari style, Porsche pace, and Honda reliability. It was, perhaps, the first real top-drawer supercar to emerge from Japan, its mid-engined handling and build quality making it a serious competitor for those who looked beneath its badge imagery.

With a short model cycle of around four years, the successive 1990"s incarnations of the Accord, Prelude, and Legend came thick and fast. Ultra-reliable, but also perceived as rather bland, they nevertheless carved a niche in their respective markets and, with the addition of some overseas, European and US design input, emerged as not just competent cars, but characterful ones. This trait is best exemplified by the 1999 model Accord, notably in its race-tuned Type R variant, over which the motoring press raved.

The 1990s Hondas built upon the company's reputation for fine build quality and precise design, and added to that a greater emphasis on safety and style. The firm's involvement in Formula One racing also asisted its image makers.

In America, Honda labelled its upper range cars models as a brand named Acura. Now built in the USA too, they have taken a massive market share and are extremely popular, notably through the Integra and Accord models.

In Europe, Honda set up a manufacturing plant in Swindon, UK, and left its Rover alliance behind. The new Accord, CRV. and HRV lifestyle models and a new two-seat soft-top sportster were all set to take the European market by storm. Building upon a world car theme, Honda tweaked its American and European models to look different but to share engines and underpinnings, thus saving on development costs.

Honda has emerged as the class act of the Japanese motor manufacturers, and has made in-roads into the sales of the likes of BMW, Mercedes, and others. The breadth of the company's product coverage now underlines its true achievement.

1992 Honda CRX Hardtop

Horch 850 5-liter straight-eight cabriolet, 1934

first six-cylinder model, a 7800 65 hp, on the market. Very successful in sporting events, Horch cars soon became extremely popular and production continued to rise. New models included ioe four-cylinder cars of 1588, 2080cc, 2608cc, 3175cc, 4700cc, and 6395cc, and an 8440cc four-cylinder ioe version was built in small numbers. There were also Horch cars with sleeve-valve engines, made under Knight license. In 1909 August Horch left the works and Georg Paulmann took over the design of Horch cars, which now also included a 2582cc model, a small car for that period and therefore called "Pony."

After the war Horch built cars including 8/24 hp, 10 / 30 hp, 15/45 hp, 18/55 hp, 25/60 hp, and 33/80 hp models, all exhibited by the Zwickau factory at the 1921 Berlin Show. Quantity production came in 1924 with a 10/50 hp ohc four-cylinder model of 2630cc, which succeeded a sv 2630cc four-cylinder; 1926 saw the first 3132cc dohc straight-eight in production, followed by a 3378cc version. A capacity increase to 3950cc brought 80 hp at 3200 rpm, but from 1931 onwards there were also new single-ohc straight-eight Horch cars, designed by Fritz Fiedler, with engines from 3 to 5 liters. Another new car in the early 1930s was the sv 6021cc V-12 Horch with a 120 hp engine and ZF-Aphon four-speed gearbox. Most Horch cars belonged to the luxury class and often had exclusive bodywork by Gläser, Neuss, Armbruster, and other leading coachbuilders. The year 1933 saw the introduction of new sv V-8 models of 3004cc, 3227cc, 3517cc, and 3823cc. There was also the 850, with an ohc 4946cc straight-eight motor, which developed 100 bhp at 3400 rpm, while a "hotter" version, the 951A, developed 120 bhp at the same rpm. Less demanding customers got V-8s of 3517cc and 3823cc. In Zwickau from 1933 to 1939 Horch built the rear-engined, Ferdinand Porsche designed, Auto Union Grand Prix racing cars. Horch built high-class, beautiful cars until the war, but in 1945 the original Auto-Union became defunct. The name "Horch" is still waiting for a rebirth in Germany. To be correct, in 1946 there was the rebirth of a Horch in East Germany, at Zwickau, but as the name Horch belongs to the West German Auto Union, the East Germans had to drop it and call the new car "Sachsenring" instead.

1915 Horstmann coupé

HORLEY • England 1904-1907

The 8 hp MMC-engined "Hundred Guinea" Horley of 1904-1906, also known as the "No-Name," was one of the first cars to approach a £100 price tag. Uprated to 9 hp in 1906, it was replaced next year by a 904cc twin at £121.

HORNET • England 1905-1906

The Hornet, sold by Horner & Sons of London, was a cheap car (£131 complete) with a massive 24 hp 3078cc twin-cylinder engine. There was also a 48.6 hp four of 6158cc at £263. Coyly, the company advertised these as "9 hp" and "18 hp."

HORSE-SHOE • France 1908

Built by Glaenzer & Cie of Paris, the Horse-Shoe was available in two models, a one-cylinder 8 hp and a 12 hp twin. Both had radiator surrounds in the shape of a horseshoe, complete with nails.

HORSTMANN • England 1914-1929

The original Horstmann had a 1-liter four-cylinder engine with detachable cylinder head and horizontal overhead valves, though the gearbox was tucked away in the rear axle. After the war the company offered 1368cc or 1498cc Coventry-Climax engines, and in 1921 the Horstman (the Germanic final "n" was tactfully dropped) power unit was dispensed with. Sydney Horstmann also pursued a racing program, and tests were conducted at Brooklands with a supercharged side-valve Anzani power unit. Sports and Super Sports models were offered, being slightly modified racing types. The 1.5-liter Anzani power unit was standardized in 1923, and in 1924 an 1100cc Coventry-Climax engine was offered. Technical advances included front-wheel brakes on racing cars in 1921, the aforementioned supercharging two years later and Lockheed hydraulic brakes in 1925. In the final year of production the 11 hp Anzani and 9/25 hp models were available.

HOTCHKISS • France 1903-1954

See panel

HOTCHKISS • England 1920

A British offshoot of the famous French company, the Coventry firm is usually remembered as building engines for William Morris's famous "Bullnose" model. However, it did experiment with a car of its own with a 1080cc vee-twin ohv engine, but this never went into production.

HOUK • USA 1917

A shortlived beetle-backed phaeton from a famous maker of wire wheels.

HOULBERG • Denmark 1919-1920

The maximum weight allowed on smaller Danish minor roads was 9 cwt, and that law bred a special type of car. One was the Houlberg, first produced in Odense in 1913. The car had a four-cylinder 5/12 hp Ballot engine, shaft drive and hand- and footbrake on the rear wheels. It is possible that an even smaller model with a Dutch Eysinck engine was built. In total 25-30 cars were made.

HOUPT • USA 1909-1912

Racing drivers Harry S Houpt and Montague Roberts were behind this high-speed marque from Bristol, Connecticut. A 40 hp four of 9344cc and a 60 hp six (14,016cc) were available, and the cars were entered for many sporting events.

HOWARD • USA 1903-1905

The Howard company started operations in Troy, New York, but moved to Yonkers, New York, shortly thereafter. An expensive automobile, the 25/30 hp touring-car was listed at $5,000 and closed models (listed as "available") at a considerably higher figure.

HOTCHKISS • France 1903-1954

Connecticut Yankee Benjamin Hotchkiss established his arms factory at St-Denis, 3 miles north of Paris, in the 1870s. The slack period of peace was filled by making motor components, and the company"s first car appeared in 1903, though a factory fire nearly halted the project permanently. This round-radiatored 17 cv four was followed in 1906 by a 7.4-liter six. A quality light car, the 2.2-liter 12/16 hp, appeared in 1912, and the next year a five-car range of three fours (12/16, 16/20, and 20/30 hp) and two sixes (20/30 and 40/50 hp) was cataloged. Post-war, Hotchkiss essayed a super-luxury car, the 6.6-liter Type AK, with ohv operated by a miniature crankshaft, but only one was built. From 1923-1928 the refined 2.2-liter Type AM was the company"s sole offering, gaining pushrod ohv by 1926. In 1928 came a new six, the AM 80, which formed the basis for all subsequent Hotchkiss sixes and was offered until 1923 with torque-tube transmission instead of the traditional "Hotchkiss drive" by open propeller shaft. In 1933 came the sporting AM80S 3.5-liter, based on the car which won the 1932 Monte Carlo Rally (an event which Hotchkiss also won in 1933, 1934, 1939, 1949, and 1950.) The sporting Paris-Nice of 1934 commemorated a sporting victory by A 1937 merger with Amilcar produced the Grégoire-designed Amilcar-Compound, which never saw serious production, and after the Armistice the pre-war 686 model was reintroduced, joined in 1949 by a new 13 cv four. From 1952 the 2-liter fwd flat-four Hotchkiss-Grégoire was built in small numbers alongside the 3.5-liter (which had acquired ifs in 1949.) There was a temporary merger with Peugeot, a permanent one with Delahaye, and in 1954 the company ceased producing cars in favor of commercial vehicles and license-built Jeeps.

1905 17cv Hotchkiss

1950 Hotchkiss-Grégoire

1913 Hotchkiss 40/50hp six, with touring body by Gill of London

HOWETT • England 1912-1913

A vee-twin cyclecar with "eccentric steering."

HP • England 1926-1929

This 500cc motorcycle-engined three-wheeled cyclecar, built by Hilton-Peacey Motors of Woking, Surrey, sold for only £65.

HPS • England 1903-1904

A 6 hp De Dion-engined light car on Panhard lines, said to be capable of 35mph, was the Hyde Park Motor Stores' first offering. Two- and four-cylinder models were listed in 1904.

HRG • England 1936-1956

So called because of the involvement of E A Halford, G H Robins and H R Godfrey (of GN fame,) the HRG was a spiritual successor to the Frazer Nash, though with a shaft-driven rear axle instead of chains. Initially the 4ED 1496cc Meadows ohv engine was used, but in 1939 an 1100cc single overhead camshaft Singer engine was fitted, to be followed shortly by a 1.5-liter power unit from the same manufacturer when supplies of the Meadows engine dried up. After the war the 1496cc Aerodynamic model made a brief appearance, though this was soon dropped in favor of the traditional chunky 1930s-style bodywork. A final fling came in 1955, when an all-independent-suspension disc-braked model with twin overhead camshaft was announced but never proceeded with.

1949 HRG 1500

HUASCAR • France 1930-1932

Made in Courbevoie in close relationship with Deguingand and Galba, these cars were Violet-designed, with a water-cooled twin-cylinder two-stroke engine of 627cc.

HUBBARD • England 1904-1905

A 4.5 hp coachbuilt tricar with front-wheel brakes, built in Coventry.

HUDLASS • England 1897-1902

In 1896 Felix Hudlass, aged 21, spent an inheritance (intended for his training as a doctor) on equipping a motor works, even though he had never seen a car. His first car, with a vertical-twin monobloc engine at the front and two-speed belt drive, appeared the following year, but after a few months was dismantled. Parts were incorporated in a second car which followed Benz lines, with a horizontal single-cylinder engine of 2813cc mounted at the rear. About 20 of this type were built between 1897 and 1899. By 1902 Hudlass was building 6 hp and 10 hp single-cylinder cars, and 12 hp and 20 hp twins with front engines, but a fire at his coachbuilders destroyed much of his stock. As he was not insured he sold out, and joined Weller Brothers of Norwood, which went into liquidation in 1903. Hudlass was chief engineer of the Royal Automobile Club (formerly the ACGBI) from then until he retired in 1947.

HUDSON • USA 1901-1902

A light tiller-steered steamer from Hudson, Michigan.

HUDSON • USA 1909-1957

Detroit store magnate J L Hudson gave his name to this marque, of which the first offering, a 2534cc four of unremarkable design (by Howard Coffin), proved an instant success, pushing Hudson to seventeenth place in the US sales league by the end of 1910. The first Hudson six, the 6-liter Model 6-54, arrived in 1912; two years later Hudson was claiming to be the biggest manufacturer of sixes in the world. The four, by now of 4324cc, was dropped in 1916, and a one-model policy adopted with the 4730cc Super-Six, available in a wide range of body styles and classy enough for President Hoover to order a landaulette. From 1927-1930 the Super-Six engine had inlet over exhaust valves, but after that nothing except side valves were used on any Hudson. Hudson-Essex group sales were third biggest in the USA in 1929, but tailed off after that, despite the introduction of a new straight-eight in 1930. The six was phased out the next year, but the eight was to remain in production until 1954. In 1932 six eight-wheeled tourers were built for the Japanese Government. From 1934-1938, after the demise of Essex, Hudson and Terraplane had much in common, and in 1935 the "Electric Hand" electric gear shift became optional; 1936 saw the "safety engineered chassis" with hydraulic brakes backed up by an emergency mechanical system.

Hudson emerged from the war with a continuation of its 1942 models, but broke new ground with the unit-construction Step-Down design of 1948, offered in five series, from the low-priced Pacemaker to the high-priced Commodore Eight. Engines were a 4293cc six and a 4162cc V-8. The Hornet series used the old L-head six of 5047cc, and from 1951-1954 this model was virtually invincible in stock car racing. Sales had peaked in 1950, however, and Hudson lacked the finance to re-tool. The 1953 compact Jet was abandoned when Hudson merged with Nash to form American Motors in 1954. After that, Hudson shared Nash's body-shell; top of the line was the Hornet Custom Hollywood, with Packard V-8 power (replaced in 1956 by the new 180 bhp AMC V-8). The smaller Wasp used Hudson's old 3310cc six.

1916 Hudson Six-40 town car in fashionable Grosse Point, Michigan

1956 Hudson Hornet V-8 hardtop

HUDSON • England 1975

A one-off electric town car built by John Hudson of Doncaster, the Hudson was capable of 40mph and had a range of 28 miles. Its power came from 3 cwt of lead-acid batteries.

HUFFIT • France 1914

An "absolute cyclecar" with "sporting Alfonso XIII" body, powered by a 1206cc Clement-Bayard twin.

HUFFMAN • USA 1920-1925

The Huffman was an assembled car built in Elkhart, Indiana, offered as line of models, all featuring a Continental six-cylinder engine throughout its solid but rather dull history. A 120-inch wheelbase was featured. The "K" series, introduced in 1923, was built until 1925, the last Huffmans being equipped with disc wheels and four-wheel brakes.

HUGOT • France 1897-1905

A voiturette driven by rear-mounted 2.25 hp De Dion or Aster single-cylinder engines. A few 697cc single-cylinder voiturettes appeared in 1905.

HUMBER • England 1898-1976

See panel overleaf

HUMPHRIS • England 1908-1909

The Humphris Patent Gear was a final drive using a disc with four concentric rings of holes. Pegs on the drive shaft

gave the different ratios, with direct drive in every gear: "guaranteed saving of 20 per cent in power." Four-cylinder engines of 10/12 hp and 12/16 hp were used.

HUNGERFORD • USA 1929

The Hungerford, or Hungerford Rocket, was America's first successful rocket automobile and the first to be licensed for operation on public highways. Built by two eccentric clairvoyant brothers in Elmira, New York, the Hungerford was based on a 1921 Chevrolet chassis with a special rocket hookup and pumps built by the Gould Pump Co of Seneca Falls, New York. The car never progressed beyond the prototype stage, but the one pilot model survives to this day. The Hungerford had to be brought to a halt before being converted to rocket propulsion, or vice versa. Teardrop styling was used, not unlike the Dymaxion.

HUNTER • USA 1920-1921

Little is known of the Hunter car of Harrisburg, Pa. At least one car is known to have been completed, a six-cylinder touring car with 121-inch wheelbase and an announced price of $2,250.

HUPMOBILE • USA 1908-1940

Bobby Hupp and E A Nelson designed the original Hupmobile, a 2.8-liter Detroit-built runabout with two-speed transmission. Selling at $750, it was an instant success, and by 1913 production was up to 12,000. A development of this model was still in production in 1925, when it was joined by America"s first low-priced straight-eight, with contracting Lockheed hydraulic brakes. A 3.2-liter six replaced the four in 1926. In 1929 Hupmobile took over Chandler and built its lower-priced range in their Cleveland factory. The handsome Hupmobiles of 1932-1933 were followed by an aerodynamic range, with a three-panel D-shaped windshield (a proposed fwd model was stillborn.) By 1936 the range had been trimmed to a 4-liter six and a 5-liter eight; cast aluminum wheels were standard. In the summer of that year production was suspended for several months: the revived eights had automatic overdrive. Hupmobile"s last venture was a rear-wheel-drive adaptation of the Cord 810/812. That having failed, the company abandoned car production and moved into car spares, kitchen equipment, and electronics.

HUPP-YEATS • USA 1911-1916

The Hupp-Yeats electric coach was a costly luxury vehicle selling at up to $5,000. "Richest imported tapestries and leathers." and goldplated fittings were this marque"s distinctive features.

1914 Hurlincar

HURLINCAR • England 1913-1916

Hurlin & Co was a motor agent ("two doors from the Hackney Empire") which built an 8 hp JAP-engined cyclecar in 1913, followed the next year by a vee-radiatored 10 hp four-cylinder light car.

HURST • England 1896-1907

George Hurst, "Autocar Builder," claimed his 1903 12 hp two-cylinder and 24 hp four-cylinder were "manufactured throughout" in his Holloway workshop. In 1906 Hurst was offering a 15/18 hp four-cylinder and a massive 30 hp six-cylinder of 5638cc. By 1907 this had been enlarged to 40 hp and 5883cc and was known as the Hurmid, as Hurst was now in partnership with a man called Middleton.

HURTU • France 1896-1929

The Conpagnie des Cycles et Automobiles Hurtu started making pushbikes and motorcycles, and entered the automobile field as subcontractor for Bollée. In 1900 it built the first true Hurtu cars, with single-cylinder De Dion and Aster engines. In 1907 Hurtu had three basic models, the 14 cv (1244cc) and 24 cv (4502cc) four-cylinders, and the 8 cv single-cylinder of 942cc. After 1912 the single-cylinder was abandoned and all Hurtus had four cylinders. Until 1914 the principal lines were the 10 hp of 1693cc and the 12 hp of 1767cc. The company resumed production after the war with the 12 hp, but the most significant Hurtu models in the vintage period were the 12/14 cv (2358cc) and the 10/16 Sport (2001cc) with ohv. The last new model, of 1328cc, appeared in 1925.

HUSTLER • Antigua 1976 to date

A multipurpose low-cost "fun car" with Hillman Imp power, built by Chrysler agent Arawak Motors at the rate of four per week.

1915 Hupmobile 15/18hp four

1933 Hupmobile Six Three-Window Coupé

1904 Humber 5hp Olympia Tricar

HUMBER • England 1898-1976

Thomas Humber's bicycle business was established in Coventry in 1868. It was therefore no surprise that the company's first vehicles to be powered by internal-combustion engines were tricycles and quadricycles. These led to the Humberette of 1903, with a tubular frame and a single-cylinder 5 hp engine. By 1905 the range of Humbers included two- and four-cylinder cars ranging from the 5 hp to a 10/12 hp four. A three-cylinder 9 hp put in a brief appearance in 1903-1904, but from 1905 the two-cylinder cars were dropped, the range consisting of 10/12 and 16/20 models, with a 15 hp appearing in 1907. It was back to twins in 1908, and 1913 saw the Humberette name revived for an air-cooled vee-twin 8 hp (later examples were watercooled). Mention should be made of the team of cars F T Burgess designed for the 1914 Tourist Trophy race. These used four-cylinder 3.3-litre twin overhead camshaft engines, but suffered teething troubles in the race and failed to show their mettle.

The post-war years saw the company establish a reputation for itself by producing solid, well-mannered cars. Side-valve engines were favoured up until 1922, but after this date overhead inlet/side exhaust engines appeared, the 8/18 of 1923 being a typical example. Other excellent fours, a 9/20 and 14/40 hp, consolidated the company's position by 1927, that year also seeing the appearance of a fashionable six, the 20/55 hp model. However, 1930 saw the takeover of the company by the Rootes brothers and the appearance of two more sixes, the 2.1-litre 16/50 and 3.5-litre Snipe. The final departure of the overhead inlet/side exhaust engine came in 1932, Humber settling down to its traditional role of providing cars for the upper middle classes. The following year came the 1.7-litre four-cylinder 12 hp, though by the end of the decade the company was only

1913 8hp vee-twin Humberette cyclecar

1915 11hp Humber two-seater

1936 Humber Snipe (left), 1953 six-cylinder Humber Super Snipe (below),

producing six-cylinder models, the 4.1-litre Super Snipe and its variants being made during the Second World War.

After the war, production of these side-valve sixes continued, the Snipe and 4.1-litre Pullman range being augmented by a 2-litre four-cylinder engine of Hillman origins in the Hawk. Overhead valves did not appear on the Super Snipe and Pullman until the 1953 season, while the Hawk did not acquire them for another year; 1959 saw the re-emergence of the Super Snipe (it having been dropped for a short time) with a 2.7-litre engine, though this was later upped to 3 litres. The ailing Rootes Group was taken over by the Chrysler Corporation in 1964, the Sceptre of that year being a more luxurious version of the Hillman Minx with a four-cylinder engine of 1.7-litre capacity. This was the only upholder of the Humber name, the restyled Sceptre being phased out in 1976.

c. 1921 15.9hp Humber tourer

HUMBER

HUSTLER • England 1978 to date

Arising out of an association between stylist William Towns and Jensen Special Products, the Hustler utility vehicle was by 1979 under construction in the old Jensen works at West Bromwich. The Hustler had an immensely strong, welded box-section steel frame with an integral roll-over cage to which replaceable glassfibre body panels were bolted. The engine and running gear came from the Mini.

HUTTON • England 1900-1905

Jack Hutton began production in Northallerton, Yorkshire, with rear-engined belt-drive voiturettes, but a move south to Thames Ditton, Surrey, saw the introduction of conventional bi-block four-cylinder shaft-drive cars of 12 hp and 20 hp. In 1904 came a one-off curiosity, with an F-head bi-block engine whose pushrod ohv had variable lift controlled by a lever on the steering wheel. It was fitted with the Barber infinitely variable automatic transmission and hydraulic brakes, but was probably never completed. Hutton then concentrated on his Mercedes agency. The "Hutton" cars built for the 1908 Tourist Trophy were actually four-cylinder cars built by Napier.

HYDROCAR • USA 1901-c. 1902

A twin-cylinder 4 hp model built by Colonel Pope"s American Bicycle Company of New York. Early models had hub-center steering.

HYDROMOTOR • USA 1917

Plans were announced for the Automobile Boat Co of Seattle to manufacture William Mazzei"s Continental-engined amphibious car. With a streamlined body, it was said to be capable of 60 mph on land, 25 mph on water.

HYLER-WHITE • England 1899

T Hyler-White designed a curious opposed-piston engine with two crankshafts geared together. He also designed the "English Mechanic" steam and gasoline cars which could be built from plans published in The English Mechanic & World of Science (and reprinted in Horseless Age.) Two such cars survive.

HYUNDAI • Korea 1975 to date

See panel

HYUNDAI/Korea 1974 to date

Like many Asian car makers, Hyundai's roots can be found in the production of license-built versions of western marques. This the company did from the end of the 1960s until it became a car maker in its own right in the early 1970s. British influence had been strong in Hyundai's early days, and this manifested itself in the company"s management structure and modus operandi under its then British director.

Like Proton of Malaysia, Hyundai equipped its early models with Mitsubishi engines, and the first true Korean produced Hyundai was thus powered. Incredibly, it boasted Ital Design styling penned by Guigario. Named Pony, it was a cleanly styled car with a good basic all-round performance. It might not have been wildly advanced, but it was not supposed to be; even more importantly, it was neither backward looking nor obselete before its time.

The Hyundai Pony 1200cc was exhibited in mock-up form at the 1974 Turin Show, and went into production the following year at a plant near the southern tip of the Korean peninsula, part of the largest heavy industry combine in South Korea, run by the Chung family. The Pony was aimed at developing markets, but there was also hope that it might make some small mark in western markets. Of an annual production run of some 90,000 vehicles, around 13,000 were scheduled for export. An annual output of 300,000 was the target for the mid-1980s from a new factory. By this time the Pony had been revized, and then a completely new model, with more modern styling and front-wheel drive, was introduced.

This car built up the name that Hyundai had created for g sound, value-for-money cars, and set firm foundations fo company in the United States and Canada, where Hyu remains a firm favorite to this day. The elegant yet mec ically obsolete Stellar sedan model also sold well to those realistic expectations of what the car was intended to b styling resembled that of the Maserati Quattroporte, bu mechanicals were more Ford Cortina, and later on it m morphozed into Hyundai's foray into the executive car lea in the form of the Sonata. The S Coupé model with bocharged engine sold well in the USA and Britain, but still a step behind the mainstream.

In 1990 the company's fortunes allowed it to introc new models. These included the up-to-the-minute stylir the Accent range of mid-sized hatchbacks, and created stunning shape of the Hyundai Coupé. This car, advertise a sort of mini-Ferrari, certainly had the style to go wit claims, and its 16-valve engine and tenacious handling v Hyundai"s own. Widely liked, the curvy Coupé sold well opened buyers' eyes to the even curvier Lantra saloon estate ranges.

Hyundai's story illustrates the strength of the Korean makers and underlines the rapid advancement and achi ment of the country, not least in establishing itself in Ar ica and Europe. Despite the economic downturn in the rim, the rise of the Korean car makers, perhaps best il trated by Hyundai, teaches many lessons to less efficient less nimble car makers.

1999 The new Hyundai models illustrated the growing strength of the korean car industry

1999 The Hyundai Coupé 2.0 SE

1999 The Hyundai Accent 1.3 Siena 3-Door

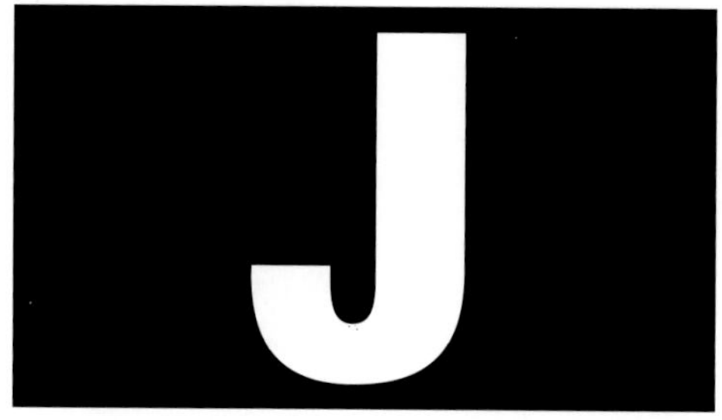

1910 Jackson (US) Model 40 tourer

JACKSON • England 1899-1915

R Reynold Jackson's first offering was a belt-drive "doctor's carriage" with a 3.5 hp De Dion engine. After breaking with Mytholm in 1900, Jackson went to London and sold American Buckmobile, Century, and Covert cars until 1903, when he brought out cars of his own assembly, with 6 hp or 9 hp De Dion engines in Lacoste & Battmann chassis. Singles were the main offering until 1909, though some of these had surprisingly long strokes; the 1909 Demon racer, with an aggressively pointed hood, had an engine of 4 x 8 inch (1809cc). Four-cylinder models of 14 hp and 17.5 hp appeared in 1909, a Chapuis-Dornier-engined light car and a JAP-engined three-wheeler in 1913.

JACK SPORT • France 1925-1930

Built in Paris by M Corbeau (also a maker of motorcycles,) the Jack Sport was a 410cc single-cylinder cyclecar.

JACQUET FLYER • USA 1921

A high-priced sporting car, the Jacquet Flyer had a wheelbase of 124 inches, and wire wheels were standard. It was powered by a four-cylinder Wisconsin engine and a two-passenger roadster constituted its sole model. Few were made.

JAG • England 1950-1956

Sports cars with Ford V-8 and 1172cc Ten engines.

JAGUAR • England 1945 to date

See panel

JAMES & BROWNE • England 1901-1910

Though T B Browne was an early and enthusiastic owner of a Panhard, the first cars built by his company used horizontal power units. The 1902 model had a 9 hp twin-cylinder engine and four-speed transmission, while an 18 hp four appeared a year later. A feature of these cars was a six-seater aluminum tonneau body. There was also a "hoodless" landaulette with underfloor power unit in 1903, aimed at superseding the electric carriage. In 1905 the company announced an 8 hp hoodless light car, while from 1906 luxury vertical-engined fours and sixes were sold under the name "Vertex."

9 hp James & Browne phaeton, 1902

JAMESON • England 1973 to date

Surrey engineer Paul Jameson has been responsible for two remarkable cars. The first, a glassfiber-bodied, front-engined two-seater, was powered by a 750 bhp Meteor tank engine, until the car was all but destroyed by fire. More exciting still, however, is an open two-seater with mid-mounted, blown Merlin engine giving some 1760 bhp. It is a six-wheeler with both rear axles driven.

JAMIESON • USA 1902

A tiller-steered two-seater with a twin-cylinder 7 hp engine and chain drive.

JAN • Denmark 1915-1918

The Copenhagen-built Jan type A had a four-cylinder engine of 1328cc and a three-speed gearbox. The cars were of entirely Danish construction and sported a handsome pointed radiator of hammered copper; 42 Type A Jans were built. The six-cylinder type E came after the war, but only two were built.

The Rolls-Royce Merlin-engined 1976 Jameson Mk II

JANEMIAN • France 1920-1923

Built in Biévres, Essonne, by M Janémian, these were rear-engined cars with chain drive. The 1096cc vee-twin was later enlarged to 1395cc.

JANOIR • France 1921-1922

A maker of motorcycles and sidecars in Saint-Ouen, Seine, M Janoir also assembled some 965cc flat-twin-engined cyclecars.

JANSSEN • Germany c. 1981 to date

Powerful, expensive sports cars loosely based on classic originals, such as the SS100.

JANVIER • France 1924-1926

Well-known manufacturer of proprietary and stationary engines, Janvier et Sabin of Chatillon-sous-Bagneux made cars with 11 hp (1994cc) and 15 hp (2982cc) engines. It also built a 5-litre racing car in 1925.

JAP • England 1904-1905

This most famous of proprietary power-unit makers built a "novel and new pattern tricar" in its Tottenham works. It had side-by-side bucket seats and a front-mounted 4.5 hp JAP.

JAPPIC • England 1925

This single-seater cyclecar by coachbuilder Jarvis of Wimbledon was chain driven and powered by 500cc or 350cc JAP engines. Hence the name!

JAR • England 1913-1915

A vee-twin Precision engine powered this light car sold by J A Ryley of Birmingham. Its "big car" styling was spoilt by a starting crank protruding beneath the nearside running board.

JAWA • Czechoslovakia 1934-1939

With 684cc twin-cylinder two-stroke engines and fwd, the Jawa was built under DKW (Auto Union) license and was similar to the "Meisterklasse." A smaller 615cc model was introduced in 1937: a 1990cc version never went into quantity production.

JAXON (JACKSON) • USA 1903-1923

"Our steam cars are strong, simple and ride like a Pullman," claimed the Jackson Automobile Co of Jackson, Mich., which built tiller-steered steamers similar in design to the Locomobile. It also offered a 6 hp gasoline car under the Jaxon nameplate. Literacy later prevailed and, under

JAGUAR • England 1945 to date

The name Jaguar first appeared in 1935, when it adorned a magnificent two-seater roadster introduced by the Swallow Sidecar Company at the London Motor Show. However, it was not until 1945 that William Lyons (later Sir William) founded Jaguar Cars Ltd. Jaguar has made countless contributions to motoring history, not least by way of the XK roadsters, which took the road and track by storm when introduced in 1948, its five Le Mans wins achieved by the subsequent C and D type sports-racing cars, and the unparalleled value for money offered by the now legendary E Type. However, while the achievements of the Jaguar sports cars are most easily recalled, the sedans were just as successful in their own way. The first Jaguars were difficult to distinguish from their SS labelled counterparts; however, the first all-new sedan, the Mk V, carried the legend a stage further. It is now hard to imagine, but the subsequent, even bigger Mks VII, VIII, and IX were very successful competition as well as road cars. So too were the nimbler Mks I and II, perhaps the best sporting sedans of their time. By the advent of the Mk X in 1962, however, the emphasis was more on refinement, a quality that was the hallmark of XJ series.

Launched in 1968, the XJ6 luxury sedan kept Jaguar alive through its ill-fated union with British Leyland in all its forms and beyond its return to the private sector in 1984, a year before the death of Sir William Lyons. An all-new XJ6 (with the AJ6 power unit that succeeded the faithful XK engine) appeared in 1986. It still had Jaguar's traditional good looks, though the styling was bland in comparison with the "old" body, which continued in production to accommodate the V12 engine. Originally launched in 1975, the Malcolm Sayer styled XJ-S sports car was the first Jaguar with the 3.6-liter AJ6 engine (from 1983) and was subtly restyled in 1991. Ford bought Jaguar for $2.4 billion in 1989, and one of its first acts was to kill off the planned "F-type" sports car ("overweight and over schedule.") The XJ-S was facelifted in 1991, gaining the 4.0-liter AJ6 engine.

At this time the wild curves of the XJ220 arrived. Based on a Keith Helfet concept car design, it went into limited

1946 Jaguar $3^{1}/_{2}$-litre saloon

Jaguar XJ - the essential 'Lyons' line

production and although a stunning icon, it was not the future for Jaguar. Ford's influence saw the creation of the new Jaguar coupé, not just to replace the XJS, but also to take the Jaguar legend into the 21st century. This car, the XK, and the 320 bhp supercharged XK8 sport version, boasted futuristic but typical Jaguar styling and proved a huge success.

Alongside it, Ford's influence improved Jaguar's resources and build quality, culminating in the new smaller Jaguar model, the S type of 1999. This car, with its V-6 3-liter engine and traditional wood-and-leather interior, aped the style of the classic 1960s Mk II sedans and allowed Jaguar to compete in the lucrative middle-range executive car sector. A V-8 4.0 liter is also planned. Beside these two new models, the third incarnation of the XJ40 model, the new XJ of 1986, saw it evolve into a completely overhauled variant with new engines, new interiors and a traditional round-headlamped, curved style. It is also available as an XJR sporting model with a supercharged V-8 engine allied to unmistakably British styling. Having weathered production and quality problems in the 1980s, the new, revitalized Jaguars are superbly designed and finished cars that will, like all of Jaguar's cars, stand the test of time.

Early S-type Mk1(above.)
E-type Jaguar (below).

XK roadsters - 50 years apart (above.) New S-type of 1999 with forebears (below)

Jeep, wrangler ancestry

1990's Jeep

the name "Jackson" the company remained in business until 1923, building large, conventional cars with a sporty image. An ohc engine was offered in 1910, in unit with the gear. The 1914 range included the "Sultanic" six and "Majestic" and "Olympic" fours.

JBR • Spain 1923

A Barcelona dentist, José Bonniquet Riera, was behind this sporting cyclecar which won the 750cc class in the 1923 Armangué Trophy race. He later created the ephemeral 6/8 cv 969cc STORM, also built in Barcelona.

JBS • England 1913-1915

A twin-cylinder 8 hp JAP-engined shaft-drive cyclecar built by J. Bagshaw & Sons of Batley, Yorkshire. The 1915 models used a 10 hp four-cylinder engine.

JEAN-BART • France 1907-1908

Successor to the Prosper-Lambert, the Jean-Bart company built shaft-driven cars of 9 hp (single cylinder), and 16 hp and 40 hp fours.

JEAN GRAS • France 1924-1927

Jean Gras of Issy-les-Moulineaux, Seine, offered 1.2-liter fours and 1.5-liter sixes built in the Philos factory at Lyon.

JEANTAUD • France 1893-1906

Charles Jeantaud, a Parisian coachbuilder, built his first electric carriage in 1881. His output of electric vehicles included the first car to set up a land speed record, 39.24 mph, driven by the Comte de Chasseloup-Laubat, as well as coupés and hansom cabs in which the driver sat high up at the rear. Some Jeantauds had an ingenious bevel-gear fwd layout. In 1902-1904 Jeantaud offered a range of gasoline-engined cars which looked like Panhards of circa 1898!

JEECY-VEA • Belgium 1925-1926

A limited-production light car from a famous Brussels motorcycle factory. Power was by a 750cc Coventry-Climax flat-twin.

JEEP • USA 1963 to date

The Jeep found fame during the Second World War, and was the sole product of Willys-Overland after 1956. It was only recognized as a make in its own right after 1963, when it was taken over by Kaiser Corp. The range consisted of 2 and 4wd station wagons and an updated version of the wartime vehicle. Four- or six-cylinder engines were available, and in 1965 a 5.4-liter Rambler V-8 was offered. Having acquired Jeep in 1970, American Motors expanded the range for 1971 with the luxurious Jeepster series in station wagon, convertible, and roadster forms. Engine options included a 145 hp six-cylinder and the 230 hp V-8, also offered in the Wagoneer. Almost all of the mechanical components were redesigned in 1972, and by 1979 the range was a far cry from the famous wartime vehicle.

JEFFERY • USA 1914-1917

Succeeding Rambler, these were conventional fours and sixes; the firm was renamed "Nash" after Charles W. Nash took over in 1917.

JEFFREY • England 1968-1975

Road-going developments of the successful Jeffrey racers, the J4 and J5 were neat front-engined Lotus Seven-style roadsters with glassfiber and aluminum bodies adorning tubular space frames. Power came from a range of Ford

The Jensen brothers with their 1937 sports tourer

engines. Performance was good, thanks to an all-up-weight of around 10 cwt.

JEM SPECIAL • USA 1922

Little is known of this make, but it is assumed to have been a one-of-a-type car built by or for John E Meyer of New York City. Powered by a Continental six-cylinder engine, the Jem Special had a 128-inch wheelbase. Plans for further manufacture and sales came to nothing.

c. 1900 Jenatzy electric 'dog-phaeton'

1914 Jennings (1098cc Dorman twin)

JENATZY • France 1898-1903

Belgian racing driver Camille Jenatzy was the first man to exceed 62 mph, on a streamlined electric racing car, La Jamaise Contente, of his own design. But the normal Jenatzy electrics, built by the Société Générale des Transports Automobiles of France, were square-rigged machines capable of only 7 mph.

JENKINS • USA 1901-1906

Builder of steam and gasoline cars, Jenkins of Washington, DC, achieved fame in 1901 with the "Littlest Automobile Ever," a 3 ft-long electric victoria "guaranteed to run for 2,000 hours," made for Chiquita, the 26-inch-high "Cuban Midget" who appeared at that year's Pan-American Exposition.

JENKINS • USA 1907-1912

A 6546cc four from Rochester, NY.

JENNINGS • England 1914-1915

Built by the Jennings-Chalmers Light Car Company of Birmingham, this was a neat 1094cc Dorman-engined two-seater.

JENSEN • England 1936-1976

Body stylists Richard and Alan Jensen's first car was a 3.6-liter Ford V-8-powered model fitted with a two-speed

1948 Jensen Saloon

1905 JP 16/20 hp tulip-seat tonneau

Jensen Interceptor Convertible, 1969

Columbia rear axle. Other engine options were available, including the 2.2-liter Ford V-8 and straight-eight Nash units. Although a Meadows-engined 3.8-liter straight-eight was planned for post-war production, it failed to materialize and a 4-liter Austin six was substituted. This engine was used to power the Interceptor of 1950, and also for the glassfiber 541 saloon of 1964. The company reverted to American engines for the 1963 CV8 (in this instance a 5.9-liter Chrysler V-8,) while 1967 saw the announcement of the FF. The engine was now 6.3 liters, but the really sensational aspect of the car was the Ferguson 4wd layout used in conjunction with the Dunlop Maxaret anti-lock braking system.

In 1968 Jensen was taken over by merchant bankers William Brandt from the Norcros Group, which had acquired the company in 1959. An outcome of this move was that Kjell Qvale became president and Donald Healey chairman of the reconstructed company. Consequently, when Jensen announced its new sports car in 1972, it was under the name of Jensen-Healey. The engine was a Lotus-built 2-liter twin-cam 16-valve four-cylinder based on the Vauxhall single cam block. Regrettably the model failed to live up to expectations and, although a GT was announced in 1975, the company ceased production the following year.

JEWEL • USA 1906-1909

A two-stroke runabout from Massillon, Ohio. In 1909 the products of the Forest City Motor Car Company were renamed Jewel-Keeton.

JEWEL • England 1919-1938

John E Wood Ltd of Bradford, Yorkshire, assembled cars to bespoke order for local customers. The 1922 Jewel was a 9 hp Coventry-Climax-engined 1088cc four-cylinder selling at £255. Meadows engines were used from 1924.

JEWETT • USA 1922-1926

Named for Paige's president, H M Jewett, the Jewett was to all intents and purposes a smaller and cheaper version of the Paige. The six-cylinder engines were of Jewett's own make or by Continental; in all an estimated 40,000 cars were manufactured. In 1926 the Jewett was continued under the Paige emblem.

JG SPORT • France 1922-1923

A small cyclecar made by M Janvier, with 970cc Ruby engine and chain drive.

JIMINI • England 1975 to date

This strange-looking four- or six-wheeled Mini-based utility vehicle is one of several kits filling the gap left by the moribund Mini-Moke. About ten Jiminis are made per month.

JL • England 1920

A 1.5-liter four-cylinder Decolonge engine powered the JL, a plywood-bodied light car from London's East Dulwich.

JMB • England 1933-1935

These three-wheelers could be had with two- or four-seater coachwork. A 497cc single-cylinder engine was fitted and final drive was, predictably, by chain.

JOEL-ROSENTHAL • England 1899-c. 1902

A London-built electric carriage with a separate 2 hp engine for each rear wheel.

JOHNARD • England 1975 to date

Johnard manufacture the Donington, a Bentley Special based on the old Mk VI and available with either V-8 or six-cylinder Bentley engines. Made by restoration experts, the Doningtons feature exquisitely finished glassfiber bodies with aluminum hoods and wings.

JOHN O"GAUNT • England 1901-1904

Built by William Atkinson & Sons of Lancaster, the 4 hp John O'Gaunt was "made to meet the requirements of people who do not require a high-priced car."

JOHNSON • USA 1905-1912

Beginning with steamers, by 1907 this Milwaukee company was offering a range of three gasoline cars, the biggest a 50 hp.

JONES • USA 1915-1920

A 3848cc Lycoming-engined six built in Wichita, which sold for $1,150; factory capacity was 100 cars a month. From 1917 a Continental Six was fitted.

JONES-CORBIN • USA 1902-1907

The De Dion-engined Jones-Corbin from Philadelphia had double-chain drive and a honeycomb radiator. An 8 hp Runabout and a 9 hp Tonneau were offered, priced at $1,000 and $1,500 respectively.

JONSSON • Sweden 1921

Alfred Jonssons Motorfabrik of Lidköping specialized in marine engines, but experimented in 1902 with a twin-cylinder car. A more ambitious venture was the planned production of ten cars in 1921, to be followed by series production. Everything was made at the factory except the electrical system, fuel pump, instruments and tires. The engine was a watercooled side-valve of little more than 2 liters capacity. Only one car was built, with an aluminum touring body.

JORDAN • USA 1916-1931

Ex-journalist and advertising man Edward S Jordan was given $300,000 to prove that the car market had not reached saturation point. The Jordan, a well-designed assembled car built in Cleveland, Ohio, always used Continental power units, initially a 4966cc six. By 1921 the "Playboy" model was in the range, subject of one of the most famous advertisements in motoring history. Hydraulic four-wheel brakes were fitted from 1924, and in 1925 a 4408cc straight-eight was introduced. For 1927 "the first truly fine American small car" offered a "custom" range of 3259cc sixes with worm drive, including the "Blue Boy" sports touring and "Tom Boy" collapsible cabriolet, and

Junior R Phaeton

A tiler-steered 1913 Jowett 6 hp twin

1950 Jowett Jupiter Sports

the "Air Line" 4380cc eight, still featuring a "Playboy" coupé. Last new Jordan was the 5277cc Speedway Eight of 1930, with sporting coachwork and streamlined "Woodlite" headlamps.

JOSWIN • Germany 1920-1924

Designer Josef Winsch modified war-surplus Mercedes six-cylinder, 12 spark plug aero engines of 6462cc and 7269cc to power these big luxury cars built at his Berlin-Halensee works.

JOUFFRET • France 1920-1926

Made in Suresnes and then in Colombes, Seine, by M Demeester, these cars were sometimes sold under his own name. They used 1172cc and 1616cc ohv engines from Ruby and SCAP. In 1923 Jouffret took over Sidea, and produced Sidea-Jouffret cars.

JOUSSET • France 1924-1928

Made in Bellac, Haute Vienne, by M Jousset, these were CIME-engined sports and touring cars of 1099cc and 1496cc.

JOUVIE • France 1913-1914

A JAP-engined cyclecar from Paris.

JOWETT •England 1906-1954

Benjamin and William Jowett's light two-seater of 1910 was powered by an 816cc flat-twin engine, the basic layout remaining in production until 1954. It was the outcome of some years of experimentation, but having found their successful formula the Jowett brothers saw little reason to alter their specification. After the First World War the Jowett's engine was increased to 907cc, and a four-seater, the Long Four, appeared in 1923, to be joined by a sedan-version in 1926. Front-wheel brakes finally appeared on most Jowetts in 1929, about five years after the rest of the industry! The faithful flat-twin was gradually refined, having received detachable heads in 1929. It was again increased in capacity to 946cc for 1937. Also, from 1925 it had powered the reliable Bradford van and continued to do so after the Second World War until Jowett ceased production in 1954, by which time it had been stretched to 1008cc. Not that the twin had everything its own way. In 1936 the Ten was announced, powered by an 1166cc flat-four engine. This engine configuration was used to power the Javelin of 1947, a modern design by Gerald Palmer, with bodywork inspired by the Lincoln Zephyr. Suspension was by torsion bar and road holding was excellent. Unfortunately, early cars were unreliable, which was particularly damaging on the export market. A sports car with a space-frame chassis, the Jupiter, designed by Eberan von Eberhorst, appeared in 1950. It ran at Le Mans in 1950-1952. Production of all models ceased in 1954.

JP • France 1905

The Prunello brother of Puteaux near Paris, offered a range of Gnome-engined cars, shaft-driven 10/12 hp two-cylinder and 16/20 hp four-cylinder models and a 24/30 hp four-cylinder with chain drive.

J-P WIMILLE • France 1948-1949

A rear-mounted 22 hp Ford V-8 powered the production versions of this aerodynamic sedan designed by racing driver Jean-Pierre Wimille. Production was no more than 20.

JUHO • Germany 1922

This motorcycle producer tried his luck, unsuccessfully, with a small 400cc two-stroke.

JULES • Canada 1911

This 30 hp four from Toronto had the strange feature of a horn button in the centre of the brake pedal. Only two were built.

JULIAN • USA 1925

Only one car was completed by Julian Brown of Syracuse, New York. It featured a five-passenger coupé body with the steering wheel mounted in the center, and a 60 hp radial engine mounted at the rear. The one car made had a custom body by Fleetwood; projected price of the 125-inch-wheelbase Julian was $2,500.

JULIEN • France 1920-1926

A tiny cyclecar from Blois, Loir-et-Cher, with a 174cc single and two-speed gearbox.

JULIEN • France 1946-1950

A small town car made in Paris by M Julien, using a 325cc four-stroke and chain drive.

JUNIOR • Italy 1905-1910

Giovanni Ceirano built his Junior cars with 12/14 hp twin- and four-cylinder engines of 3920cc and 6367cc. Also known as "FJTA."

JUNIOR R • USA 1924

Only one car bearing this name was produced by General Motors for John J Raskob Jr, son of the then president of the corporation. It consisted of components from Chevrolet, Oakland and Cadillac. The one-off touring car had disc wheels and a 111-inch wheelbase.

JUWEL • Belgium 1923-1927

Optimistic plans for mass-production of an 1100cc tourer having run aground, Juwel introduced an abortive fwd sports car in 1926.

JUZAN • France 1897

A light quadricycle on De Dion lines.

KAC • Denmark 1914-1917

Probably at least four KAC cars were built by the Dansk Motor & Maskinfabrik, Copenhagen. They were of the typical Danish "minor roads" type.

KAISER • Germany 1910-1913

Identical to the Braun, the Kaiser was built at the Justus Christian Braun fire-engine company's Premier works at Nürnburg. There was limited production of cars with 18 hp to 70 hp engines, some supplied by Fafnir of Aachen.

KAISER • USA 1946-1955

See panel.

KAISER-DARRIN • USA 1954

Kaiser stylist Howard Darrin designed a glassfiber-bodied sports car based on a Henry J chassis with sliding doors and landau top. Powered by a 90 hp six-cylinder Willys F-head engine, it had a top speed of 100 mph. Marketed by Henry Kaiser, only 435 examples were built. Darrin purchased the last 100 vehicles, fitted more powerful Cadillac engines and sold the cars from his Los Angeles showroom.

KAMPER • Germany 1905-1906

Makers of proprietary engines, Kämper also built 8 hp four-cylinder cars of simple design.

KAN • Czechoslovakia 1911-1914

KAN built cars, designed by Alois Nejedly, with own-make watercooled one-, two-, and four-cylinder sv engines. Yearly production was 80 cars, of which the 1326cc four-cylinder two-seater was the best seller.

KANSAS CITY • USA 1905-1909

A 35 hp flat-twin with two forward speeds, the Kansas City car was said to be built on "six years of practical experience," and to be "artistic in detail."

KAPI • Spain 1950-1955

A 2 cv single-cylinder two-stroke engine powered this light three-wheeled runabout from Barcelona.

KARMINSKI • England 1902

The hood of the 7 hp Karminski came to a "torpedo point." In 1902 this Bradford-based firm said it could not supply its similar 12 hp model "owing to a contract by a Russian firm for a great quantity."

1916 Kearns Model L 12 hp four

Kerry also marketed tricars under their name; this is a 1905/6 Kerry Tricar Basket Forecarriage

KEARNS • USA 1908-1916

Starting with the high-wheeled twin-cylinder Eureka buggy, this firm from Beavertown, Pennsylvania, progressed to trucks in 1910 and a 12 hp light car, Model L, in 1915, as well as the 1914 LuLu cyclecar.

KEETON • USA 1908-1914

Similar in appearance to the Renault, with a dashboard radiator and coal-scuttle hood, the Keeton (Croxton-Keeton in 1909-10) was advertised as "an European type – at an American price." The 1913 Keeton range, with a 48 hp six-cylinder engine, was available in three models, Riverside touring, Meadowbrook roadster, and Tuxedo coupé, at prices from $2,750 to $3,000 (including a "lamp for changing tires at night.") Keetons were built in Canada from 1913-1915.

KELLER • USA 1948-1949

Successor to the Bobbi-Kar, George D. Keller Motors of Huntsville, Alabama, manufactured the Keller Chief and Super Chief. These cars had 49 hp Hercules or Continental four-cylinder engines, all-round independent suspension and Goodrich's Torsilastic rubber torsion bars. They were available as a convertible with rear-mounted engine or as a station wagon with front engine. (A double bed was an option on the station wagon.. Only 18 examples were ever manufactured in 1949, but the station wagon was produced in Antwerp, Belgium, in 1954-1955, as the PLM.

KELLNER • France 1896

A 3.5 hp horizontal twin-cylinder engine propelled this belt-driven three-seater.

KELSEY • USA 1921-1924

C W Kelsey was a pioneer among American motor car builders, having built his first car, the Auto Tri, in 1898. He subsequently built the Spartan and the three-wheeled Motorette. Former sales manager of Maxwell, he formed his Kelsey Motor Car Co in 1921 for the purpose of building friction-driven cars (Metz was then the only car of this type still being made in the USA.) Both four- and six-cylinder models were featured between 1921 and 1923. In 1923 a four with a conventional transmission was added to the line and, in 1924, was the only Kelsey available. Kelsey also manufactured taxicabs.

KELVIN • Scotland 1904-1906

A 16 hp car built by the Bergius Car & Engine Company of Glasgow; only 14 were built.

KENDALL • England 1912-1913

An ephemeral worm-driven cyclecar from Sparkhill, Birmingham, the Kendall was available with either 945cc or 1042cc vee-twin power units.

KENDALL • England 1945-1946

An ill-fated attempt to build a "people's car" based on the 954cc Gregoire flat-twin, sponsored by Denis Kendall MP, which failed after only a few cars had been built.

KENMORE • USA 1909-1911

Sold direct from its Chicago factory, the Kenmore was a pneumatic-tired high-wheeler with detachable rear seat (ideal for "farmers, salesmen, poultrymen, dairymen.".

KENNEDY • Canada 1909-1910

Starting as a high-wheeler, by 1910 this 18 hp with a De Tamble flat-twin engine had normal wheels and tires.

KENNEDY • England 1914-1916

A 1346cc own-make four powered this sporting belt-drive two-seater from Leicester.

Kaiser

KAISER • USA 1946-1955

Millionaire shipbuilder Henry J Kaiser and Joe Frazer of Graham-Paige commissioned Howard "Dutch" Darrin to design two cars, the Kaiser and the Frazer, in the hope of breaking the Big Three's stranglehold on the US auto industry. A prototype of 1946 incorporated advanced engineering ideas, but conventional mechanics were used in the first production models. The Kaiser had a box-section frame, coil-spring independent front suspension and live rear axle; it was powered by a Continental six-cylinder L-head engine. The cars proved to be very popular, and by 1949 the range included a station-wagon-cum-sedan and a convertible with a power-operated hardtop. Attractively restyled in 1951 with lower lines and more glass, one of the Kaiser's safety features was the unique heart-shaped windshield which popped out of its socket if struck with more than 35 lb force. Kaiser sales reached twelfth place in the USA. Though no Frazers were produced, four Kaiser models, Manhattan, DeLuxe, Virginian, and Special, were manufactured in 1952. Top of the range was the Kaiser Hardtop Dragon, introduced in 1953, featuring Hydramatic transmission, gold-plated exterior trim, and a luxury interior. Sales then dropped, and in 1953 Kaiser merged with Willys. A supercharger was offered as an option on the six-cylinder engine, but sales still continued to decrease. Production then moved to Argentina, where the marque was known as the Carabela.

1951 Kaiser with safety windshield

1954 Kaiser DKF-161 with glassfiber body

KENSINGTON • USA 1899-1904

A light electric carriage, "the successor of the horse," powered by a "patented storage battery" and built in Buffalo, New York.

KENSINGTON • England 1903

A 10 hp twin and 20 hp four, probably French imports, were sold under this name, as was the Mildé electric.

KENTER • Germany 1923-1925

Kenter offered two models; a sv four with a 1060cc Steudel engine and an Atos-engined model of 1305cc.

KENT"S PACEMAKER • USA 1900

Colonial of Boston offered this steamer, which had one front steering-wheel and three rear wheels, the center one of which drove, and an outer pair which could be raised to allow the machine to "coast like a bicycle."

KENWORTHY • USA 1920-1922

Kenworthy and Duesenberg share the honor of being the first production cars in the USA to feature four-wheel brakes and a straight-eight engine. In the case of Kenworthy this was the company's widely touted "Line-o-Eight," although the make could be obtained also with four- or six-cylinder engines (Rochester-Duesenberg and Continental respectively.) The Kenworthy was a sporting car featuring either wire or disc wheels. Probably fewer than 200 cars were built in all.

KERRY • England 1905-1907

Motor factors East London Rubber Company sold 10/12 hp Tony Huber and Thames cars under this name (in the 1930s an open sports Model Y Ford was also called the "Kerry.")

KESSLER • USA 1921-1922

Using its own-make four-cylinder engine, the Kessler was otherwise an assembled tourer with wooden artillery wheels.

KESS-LINE 8 • USA 1922

A spin-off of Kessler, probably only one phaeton was made on the Kess-Line chassis. This featured a 119-inch wheelbase, an own-make eight-cylinder engine and wire wheels.

KESTREL • England 1914

A typical 10 hp light car of its day, save for the friction drive. Few were built.

KEVAH • France 1920-1924

A small cyclecar built by Muller, Allen-Sommer, and Robert at La Garenne Colombes, Seine, the Kevah had vee-twin 1100cc Train or MAG engines and was well made. In 1923 a four-cylinder 898cc sv Chapuis-Dornier-powered Kevah with three-speed gearbox appeared.

KEYSTONE • USA 1899-1900

Based at Lebanon, Pa., this company, predecessor of Searchmont, offered in 1899 a steam car with small three-cylinder radial engines built into each rear hub.

KEYSTONE • USA 1915

Using a Rutenber 55 hp six, the 1914 Keystone was designed by Chas C Snodgrass and built in Pittsburgh.

1925 Kissel straight-edge Speedster

KIA • Korea 1986 to date

Founded in 1944 to build bicycles, Kia began car manufacture 42 years later in an all-new 178-acre plant and sold 530,000 cars worldwide in 1990. An additional 7,400- acre plant will bring annual production capacity to 950,000 cars in 1995 and put Kia in the world top ten by the year 2000. Kia started with the 1324cc Pride, based on a Japanese Mazda design, and in 1991 added the 1.5-litre Sephia ("Mentor" in some markets) sedan and convertible to the range, along with the 2.0-liter dohc Sportage 4x4 leisure vehicle. A special version of the latter, built by Karmann in Europe, has become Kia"s top-of-the-range success, finding a niche by offering both fwd and a small, easy-to-drive body.

KIEFT • England 1950-1961

Best known for his 500cc racers, Cyril Kieft introduced a Gordon Bedson-designed sports-racer in 1953; MG, Bristol and Coventry-Climax engines were used.

1960 8½ hp single-cylinder King Midget

KING • USA 1910-1924

Charles Brady King built Detroit's first car in 1895-1896, and worked for Northern from 1902-1908. His 1910 "Silent" 36 hp was a unit-constructed 5400cc model incorporating 14 patented features, including a pressed-steel front axle. In 1914 the first King V-8 appeared; two years later, eight-cylinder models were the firm's sole offering.

KING MIDGET • USA 1946-1969

A two-passenger steel and aluminum small car, the Midget first appeared in kit form. One-cylinder 8.5 hp Wisconsin engines were used until 1966, when they were then replaced by the 9.5 hp Kohler unit. Styling resembled the Jeep and was mounted on a perforated girder chassis with all-round independent suspension and a unique two-speed and reverse automatic transmission. Over 5,000 King Midgets were manufactured before the Athens, Ohio, plant closed in 1969.

KINGSBURY JUNIOR • England 1920-1927

The Kingsbury Junior was powered by a flat-twin 1021cc Koh-i-noor engine. The power unit hailed from Scotland and was also used in the Rob Roy car.

KISSEL USA 1906-1931

"Every Inch a Car," the Kissel Kar, from Hartford, Wisconsin, began as a pair-cast 26 hp four-cylinder of 4952cc, increased to 5517cc for 1908. Apart from accessories, the entire car was made in the Kissel factory. A six of 8276cc appeared in 1909, and by 1912 the range consisted of fours of 30 hp, 40 hp, and 50 hp, and the 60 hp six; prices ranged from $1,300 – $3,000. By 1913 electric lighting and starting were standard. In 1917 a new range, the "100 Point Six," with a monobloc 4078cc, available as tourer, sedan, or staggered-door all-year Sedane, made its debut, as did a short-lived V-12 Conover T. Silver

1950 Kleinschnittger 123cc two-seater

developed a "Silver Special Speedster" six, and the 4660cc "Custom-built Speedster" of 1919 was a direct development of this. Painted chrome yellow, it was named "Gold Bug" as the result of a $5 contest in the *Milwaukee Journal*, whose editor owned one of the first of this model. There were "Custom-built" tourings, "urban-sedans," "coach-sedans," and coupés, too. A Lycoming eight appeared in 1924. In 1929 came the "White Eagle" speedster, with six- or eight-cylinder engine and internally expanding hydraulic brakes. Plans to revive Kissel to build a Lever-engined car in 1933 came to nothing.

KITTO • USA 1903

The Kitto Mobile Light Car was available with either an 1107cc 8 hp vertical twin or an 8 hp horizontal power unit.

KLAUS • France 1894-1899

A three-wheeled belt-drive tricycle, the Lyon-built Klaus incorporated a "dead-man's handle" engine cut-out in the steering tiller.

KLEIBER • USA 1924-1929

The Kleiber was an assembled car produced by a well-known West Coast truck manufacturer. The cars were strictly assembled affairs, using proven components throughout, and were sold in small numbers on the Pacific Coast. Continental engines were used on the six-cylinder Kleibers until 1929, when a Continental eight was substituted. Two sedans marked the company's entire passenger-car output in this last year of production.

KLEINSCHNITTGER • Germany 1950-1957

A 123cc Ilo single-cylinder two-stroke engine powered this basic car built by ex-employees of East German factories who had emigrated to West Germany.

KLINE KAR • USA 1910-1923

The Kline Kar was initially built in York, Pennsylvania, operations moving to Richmond, Virginia, in 1913. Although the company initially used engines of its own design and manufacture, the product gradually took on the aspect of an assembled car. Continental engines were used during the company"s last years.

KLINGENBERG • Germany 1898-1900

Designed by Georg Klingenberg, a professor of the Berlin-Charlottenburg High School, this pioneer car did not go into serious production until NAG took over the design. The cars made by Klingenberg were (more or less) prototypes.

KLINK • USA 1907-1909

A 30 hp four of 4417cc built in Dansville, NY.

KNAP • Belgium • France 1898-c1909

A three-wheeled voiturette built in Liége with a 4 hp engine was Georgia Knap"s first production car. He returned to Troyes (France) and built prototypes with up to six cylinders before settling on a single-cylinder, four-wheeled voiturette in 1904.

KNICKERBOCKER • USA 1901-1903

This was the gasoline car line built by the makers of the Ward-Leonard Electric.

1929 Kleiber six-cylinder sedan

KNIGHT JUNIOR • England 1914

A bullnosed 11 hp two-seater with a 1743cc engine built by Knight Brothers of Chelmsford, Essex, for motor agents Friswells of London. It sold for £185 complete.

KNIGHT OF THE ROAD • England 1902

A single-cylinder 5 hp voiturette for commercial travellers.

KNIGHT OF THE ROAD • England 1913-1914

From the same maker as the Knight Junior, this was a 15.9 hp 2654cc four-cylinder sold exclusively by Friswells at 350 guineas.

KNOLLER • Germany 1924

Produced a 980cc four-cylinder car in small numbers.

KNOX • USA 1900-1915

The "waterless" Knox was designed by H. A. Knox and built in the old Waltham Watch Tool Factory at Springfield, Mass. The first experimental Knox cars appeared in 1895-97. Production did not begin until 1899, initially by the Overman cycle company, the Knox company not being founded until 1901. These were three-wheelers with the famous air-cooled "porcupine" engine, with pegs instead of fins on the cylinder. In 1903 a hydraulic damper was incorporated in the tiller steering. The "`waterless" Knox was built to special order until 1908, but by then big four-wheeled cars with four-cylinder engines cooled by water were the company's staple product.

KOCH • France 1897-1901

Paraffin-powered cars with a 6 hp opposed-piston engine.

KOCO • Germany 1921-1926

The GN-like Koco was a cyclecar with chain drive and an own-make twin-cylinder 1020cc engine with air- or water-cooled horizontal cylinders. A second version had a sv 1303cc four-cylinder engine and often competed, with streamlined bodywork, in races.

KODIAK • Germany 1987

The prototype of this £70,000 gull-winged 170 mph two-seater supercar had 5.4-liter Chevrolet power; production versions were due to use Mercedes V-8s.

KOEHLER • USA 1909-1915

"The swellest-looking automobile it has been your good fortune to see," the Koehler 40 of 4649cc first appeared in 1909 at the low price of $1,650, with "Montclair Torpedo de Luxe" body.

KOMET • USA 1911

A four-cylinder car built by Sterling of Elkhart.

KOMET • Germany 1922-1924

The predecessor of the smaller Kenter, the Komet had a 1060cc Steudel engine.

KOMNICK • Germany 1907-1927

Strong cars for the bad roads in the north-eastern part of Germany were the forte of this Elbing machine works. Early models had the radiator behind the engine like the contemporary Renaults. Komnick produced cars from 1520cc to 5536cc in the early days, and an own-make ohc 2100cc four-cylinder from 1923 to 1927. Komnick also produced heavy trucks and agricultural machinery.

KONDOR • Germany 1900-1902

A bicycle works which produced 5 hp two-seater cars.

KORN ET LATIL • France 1901-1902

A fwd voiturette with Aster engine of 3.5 hp (later 6 hp) designed by Latil, later well known for his fwd commercial vehicles.

KORTE • England 1902-c. 1905

Built in Leeds, the chain-driven 12 hp Korte had two cylinders, four speeds and an "electric indicator showing stoppage in circulation."

KORTING • Germany 1922-1924

Körting's limited production was of two models, sv four-cylinders of 1569cc and 2085cc with Basse & Selve engines.

1910 Knox Tonneauett

KOUGAR • England 1977 to date

Traces of the Healey Silverstone and various Frazer Nashes can be seen in the beautifully finished, Jaguar-powered Kougar. Based on "S" Type mechanicals, the lightweight Kougar has stunning performance as well as classic looks.

KRC • England 1922-1924

Made by White, Holmes & Co of Hammersmith, London, the KRC was a light car initially powered by a 10 hp vee-twin Blackburne engine. Later options included four-cylinder units by Coventry-Climax or Janvier.

KRIEGER • France 1898-1909

One of the best-known electric carriages, the Krieger had hub motors on both front wheels, giving speeds up to 12 mph. The normal Krieger body style was a formal coupé. This make used to undertake long runs on one charge to obtain publicity. Gasoline-electrics appeared in 1904, and were produced, intermittently, using Richard-Brasier engines.

KRIT • USA 1909-1916

Kenneth Krittenden was behind this four-cylinder popular car, the basic design of remained much the same throughout its production life (save for an underslung model introduced in 1911.) Like Ford, KRIT used vanadium steel for chassis components. Unkind critics claimed the name stood for "keeps right in town."

KROBOTH (FAVORIT) • Czechoslovakia 1930-1933

This Sternberk-built 498cc single-cylinder car was designed by Gustav Kroboth, who made scooters after 1945 in Germany. Originally called Favorit, the marque was financed by Grohmann, a wool manufacturer, but few cars left the works before Grohmann lost interest in car manufacture.

1915 3622cc KRIT tourer

KUHLSTEIN-VOLLMER • Germany 1898-1902

A power pack with a four-stroke engine which replaced the front wheels, axles, and springs of horse-drawn vehicles to convert them into motor carriages; "virtually a motor horse, to be harnessed to any vehicle at will." In 1900 a rear-engined 5 hp twin-cylinder gasoline model was announced. A twin-cylinder gasoline car with three-speed "belt, pinion, and chain" transmission (clutch and speed change operated by a single lever) appeared in mid-1901..

KUHN • Germany 1927-1929

These were slightly modified Opel cars with Kühn-built bodywork. The best-known Kühn car was the 1916cc six-cylinder.

KUNISUE • Japan 1910

A few of these 8 hp twin-cylinder tourers were built in Tokyo. The radiator was a "Japanese copy" of the Argyll pattern.

KURTIS • USA 1949-1955

Frank Kurtis, well known for his racing car designs, introduced his own, distinctive two-passenger Kurtis Sports in 1949. Bodies were of glassfiber and steel on Ford running gear. About 36 Kurtis cars had been built when Muntz Motors took over the design, marketing it as the Muntz Jet. In 1954 Kurtis produced a road version of his Indianapolis racing car. This 500-S model could be ordered with various engines including Mercury"s V-8. Also available was the 500-KK tubular chassis, to which buyers could add their own bodywork. Production ended after 18 model 500-Ms had been built. These had glassfiber bodies, torsion-bar suspension,and four-cylinder ohv supercharged engines.

KURTZ AUTOMATIC • USA 1921-1923

A Cleveland, Ohio, product, the Kurtz featured a preselector gear-change mechanism on the steering column; otherwise it was a typical assembled car, using a six-cylinder Herschell-Spillman engine. The Kurtz car was made in limited numbers, but it was highly regarded and sold well.

KYMA • England 1903-1905

The New Kyma Car Company of Peckham built 6 hp twin-cylinder three-wheelers and four-cylinder light cars.

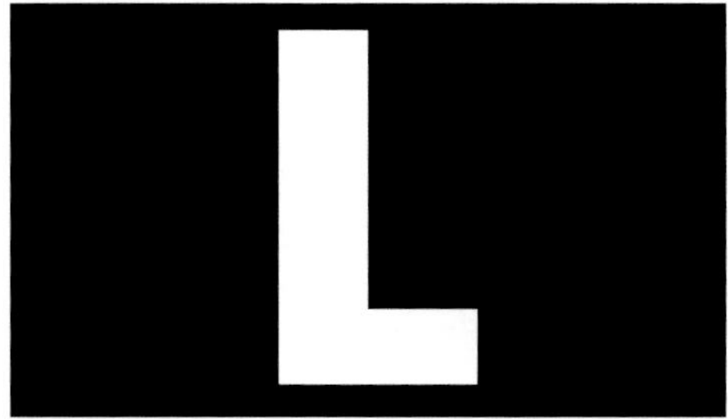

LABOR • France **1907-1912**

Built for cycle manufacturer de Cléves et Chevalier of Neuilly-sur-Seine, in the Weyher et Richemond works. The most popular Labor was the 20/30 hp four.

LACOSTE & BATTMANN France 1897-1913

Builder of chassis and components, Lacoste & Battmann, of Levallois, Seine, rarely marketed cars under its own name, but supplied them to erstwhile "manufacturers," e.g. Gamage, Napoléon, Speedwell, and Jackson. De Dion and Aster engines were used. The last offering was the Aster-engined 1.8-litre Simplicia.

1987 Lada Samara 1300/1500GL

LADA (ZHIGULI) • Russia 1970 to date

Built in the Togliattigrad works (established with Fiat aid,) the Zhiguli car is known outside Russia as the Lada. It is based on the obsolete Fiat 124, with engines of 1200cc to 1600cc. In 1978 a 4wd model the Niva, appeared on Western markets. The 1987 Samara was a fwd hatchback, available with ohc power units of 1.1, 1.3, and 1.5 liters, though the traditional Riva range still makes up the bulk of production.

LADAS • England 1906-1908

J Bowen of Albert Street, Didsbury, Lancashire, showed this 7 hp two-seater, named after a Derby winner, at the 1906 Manchester Motor Show.

LAD"S CAR • USA 1912-1914

"More a real working toy than a go-anywhere motor car," this 3 hp single-seater was made by the Niagara Motor Co of Niagara Falls, NY.

LAETITIA • France 1922-1923

Cyclecar with a 1000cc Anzani air-cooled engine, made in Asniéres, Seine, by M Conelli.

LAFAYETTE • USA 1920-1924

The LaFayette was designed by D McCall White, who was responsible for the Cadillac V-8 of 1915. The LaFayette, itself a V-8, combined luxury and breeding with endurance and excellent craftsmanship. An expensive car, with prices in the $4,000 – $7,000 range, the powerful LaFayette (which was fast as well as luxurious), had an engine developing 100 bhp and thermostatically-controlled radiator shutters, a novelty in its time. LaFayette was absorbed by Nash Motors in 1923, and for a time was continued as Nash's luxury line.

LAFER • Brazil 1972 to date

The Lafer brothers of Sao Paulo built their first "replicar" based on the MG-TD in October 1972, and by 1975 were building 350 cars annually. Apart from the VW-powered "MP" replicar, they offer the modern-styled "LL" 4097cc six-cylinder sports coupé.

LAFITTE • France 1893-c. 1898

A famous Bordeaux coachbuilder, Henri Lafitte built a few cars, starting in 1893. One, with a De Dion engine, competed in the 1898 Bordeaux-Biarritz race.

LAFITTE • France 1923-1928

Curious cyclecar from Genevilliers, Seine, with 736cc sv three-cylinder radial engine, later enlarged to 895cc. Instead of a gearbox there was a strange friction device; the engine pivoted to obtain the different ratios. Most Lafittes were sold as delivery vans.

1962 Lagonda Rapide

A 2-litre Lagonda tourer, 1928

1978 Aston Martin Lagonda

LA FORZA • USA 1989-1990

A luxury sport/utility car that failed through lack of finance.

LAGONDA • England 1906-1963, 1978 to date

Wilbur Gunn, an American of Scots descent, began by building twin-cylinder tricars in the greenhouse of his home in Staines, Middlesex. By 1907 the tricars had been superseded by four wheels, with four-cylinder 20 hp and six-cylinder 30 hp models being offered; much of the production went to Russia. In 1913 Gunn scrapped his previous models and decided to adopt just one line, an 1100cc 11.1 hp car with unit-construction gearbox and transverse front suspension, a marketing policy and design clearly inspired by the Ford Model T. Another progressive feature was the integral body/chassis construction. After the First World War the 11.1 became the 11.9, so that in 1920 Lagonda was clearly chasing the same market as Morris. As the 1920s progressed Lagonda gave up the unequal struggle, chancing its luck in the sports car field, and 1927 saw the appearance of the 2-liter dohc Speed Model; a pushrod 2-liter later appeared. From 1934 the Meadows six-cylinder 4.5-liter engine was fitted, this engine powering the company"s winning car at Le Mans in 1935. The twin-cam 1100cc Rapier also appeared in 1934, but the following year the company went broke and was purchased by solicitor Alan Good for £67,000.

The Rapier was hived off, and Good brought in W. O. Bentley as technical director. The range was refined and the Meadows engine quietened, but the V-12 of 1937 was Bentley's design (though the inspiration and much of the detail of this short-stroke 4.5-liter engine came from ex-Rolls-Royce engineer Stewart Tresilian.)

Lagonda was sold to the David Brown group after the Second World War, this 1947 deal allowing Brown to fit a Bentley-designed dohc 2.6-liter six-cylinder engine to the Aston Martin DB2 of 1950. The Lagonda marque name reappeared in 1961. The Rapide was DB-engined, but production ceased in 1963. An Aston Martin-based Lagonda sedan of grand proportions with elaborate electronic controls and sharp edged William Towns styling began to reach private owners in 1978. After a revision of its looks, with a smoother edge to the styling, it died and the name remains part of the Aston Martin stable.

Lamborghini's Miura; fast, exotic and perhaps from another planet - the classic 1970s supercar

M Lambert with a 1953 Lambert 1100cc sports

LAHAUSSOIS • France 1907

An obscure manufacturer of Paris, which offered both chassis and complete cars.

LAMBERT • USA 1905-1916

In 1891 John Lambert of Ohio City built, and attempted to market, America's first gasoline car, a three-wheeler with a four-stroke single-cylinder engine. He built a number of prototypes powered by his Buckeye gas engines in 1898-1901, and began full-scale manufacture in 1902 with the Union car, a tiller-steered four-wheeler with friction drive. About 300 cars are thought to have been built before the Lambert Automobile Company was formed, taking over Union"s Anderson, Indiana, factory. By 1910 production of the friction-drive Lambert cars was said to be running at 3,000 a year; trucks and tractors were also built. Apart from engines of its own make, Lambert used Rutenber, Buda, Atlas, Continental, Trebbert, and Davis engines. The company manufactured armaments and military fire engines during the First World War, and decided to diversify after the Armistice.

LAMBERT • England 1912

Built in Thetford, Norfolk, the Lambert was a three-wheeled cyclecar with a distinctive oval radiator.

LAMBERT • France 1926-1954

This small firm started in Macon, Saone-et-Loire, building 1100cc Ruby-engined cars with all-round independent suspension by leaf springs under the marque name "Sans Chocs." Lambert later moved to Reims, Marne, and built these sports/touring cars there until the war. After the war Lambert moved to Giromagny, Belfort, where it built fwd Ruby-engined cars.

LAMBERT & WEST • England 1913

An 8 hp cyclecar from Putney, London, designed by Warren-Lambert.

LAMBERT-HERBERT • England 1913-1914

This 1244cc light car was backed by motor agent and racing driver Percy Lambert, but his death at Brooklands in 1913 while trying to beat his own 100 miles in an hour record, ended the project.

LAMBORGHINI • Italy 1963 to date

Tractor manufacturer Ferruccio Lamborghini built his first cars as a hobby, using modified Fiat parts. When he saw a demand for big, exclusive sports cars, he founded his Bologna car factory. Among his creations was the 3939cc V-12 Miura of 1966 with a rear transverse engine. The ultimate Miura, the SV, was available in very small numbers and was regarded as one of the great super cars. A smaller mid-engined model, the 2463cc eight-cylinder Urraco P250, launched in 1970, was a 2+2 seater like the dohc Jarama; the Espada 400 GT was a four-seater with Bertone bodywork. Development brought the 385bhp Miura P400 SV. The ultimate Urraco could be supplied with V-8 engines to 1994cc, 2463cc, or 2996cc, with power

LANCHESTER • England 1895-1956

The Lanchester brothers built the first truly all-British car in 1895. Underpowered, it was rebuilt the next year with a balanced air-cooled power unit (two cylinders, two counter-rotating cranks, six connecting rods,) and with Frederick Lanchester's famous wick carburetor. One valve per cylinder was both inlet and exhaust, thanks to a concentric "crossover" disc valve. The experimental cars set the pattern for production vehicles, which began to leave the Lanchester Engine Company's Armourer Mills, Birmingham, factory in 1900. There was no hood, the driver sitting well forward behind a hinged leather dashboard, steering with a right-hand tiller. Cantilever springs had the same periodicity as a walking man; final drive was by Lanchester worm; compound epicyclic gearing gave three forward speeds.

The first Lanchesters had 4035cc twin-cylinder air-cooled engines and incorporated a disc brake in the transmission. A watercooled version appeared in 1902, a larger "18 hp" model in 1904. Rudyard Kipling, an early owner, reflected his enthusiasm for the car in his short stories. Also in 1904 came the first four-cylinder, the over-square "20 hp" of 2471cc. Though in engineering terms Lanchesters were a long way ahead of their contemporaries (they pioneered the rigorous interchangeability of parts,) their very unorthodoxy created sales resistance, so in 1907 wheel steering became available. A "38 hp" six of 3295cc joined the 28 hp; it was to solve problems of six-cylinder vibration that Frederick Lanchester devised his famous crankshaft damper. Youngest brother George Lanchester took over as chief engineer, and in 1914 produced a thoroughly conventional long-hoodted "Sporting Forty" 5560cc sv six, with half-elliptic front springs.

A similar chassis was used on the 6178cc ohv Forty of 1919. Though it was so different from the pre-war Lanchesters, the new Forty was a worthy rival to the Rolls-Royce 40/50 hp; it was joined in 1924 by an ohc 2982cc "21 hp" six. A 4440cc straight-eight was launched at the 1928 Southport Rally, again with ohc. This proved to be the last "real" Lanchester, for in 1931 the company was acquired by Daimler and Lanchesters became merely re-radiatored Daimlers. The 1932 "Ten" was still in production in the late 1940s, updated with independent front suspension; 1952 saw a "14," the chassis of which was used on the six-cylinder Daimler-engined, Hooper-bodied Dauphin; 1956 saw the short-lived Sprite 1.6-litre with Hobbs automatic transmission.

40 hp Lanchester sedan, c. 1924

1939 Lanchester 14 Roadrider De Luxe

1979 Lamborghini Countach

up to 260 bhp. The Jarama 400GTS model housed an improved 3939cc V-12 engine developing 365 bhp, while the mid-engined Lamborghini Countach LP 400/400S, a Bertone coupé, housed a similar 375 bhp motor and had a top speed of 301.187.5 mph.

Lamborghini was sold in 1972 to a Swiss group, which continued production on a smaller scale. Ownership passed to Chrysler in 1987.The extraordinary Lamborghini fwd off-road vehicle LM002 found a ready market despite its boxy styling; a complete contrast to the low, swooping style of Lamborghini"s road cars. In 1990 the Countach, after many revisions, was replaced by the 500 bhp, 4x4 200 mph Diablo. The Diablo evolved into a roadster and a VT model with nearly 500 bhp on tap. Thus powered it was the world"s fastest car, and this too evolved into further model variants, the ultimate being the 1998 SVR model.

LAMMAS-GRAHAM • England 1936-1938

A supercharged six-cylinder Graham engine powered this rather traditional-looking car built at Sunbury-on-Thames, Surrey. The American power unit was of 3.7 liters capacity and produced 128 bhp. Only chassis were produced, body-builders including Abbott, Bertelli, and Carlton.

LAMPLOUGH-ALBANY • England 1902-1905

A remarkably ugly steam car with gasoline car styling and tiller steering. Mr Lamplough built his first steamer (with shaft-driven live axle!) in 1896. A gasoline car was also marketed under the "Albany" name.

LANCAMOBILE • USA 1899-1901

James H Lancaster of New York designed this "car of the explosive motor power class of the phaeton style, with a vis-á-vis foreseat." It was said to be "compact and speedy."

LANCHESTER • England 1895-1956

See panel

LANCIA • Italy 1906 to date

See panel overleaf

Lamborghini Countach

1903 Lamplough-Albany steam car

LANDA • Spain 1922-1935

Built in Madrid, the Landa had a curious two-stroke engine. Two- and four-cylinders were the normal production; a conventional six-cylinder was sold to the Madrid funeral service.

L & E • USA 1922-1931

Although the car built by Lundelius & Eccleston of Los Angeles, California, was first announced in 1922, it probably was not publicly revealed for another two years. It was an "axleless car," the touring car being powered by a six-cylinder air-cooled engine. Although plans called for a modern factory in Long Beach, Calif., this never materialized, and subsequent production was on a strictly experimental basis. The 1932 model closely resembled a Franklin and was announced in October 1931. This car, probably the last, had four transverse springs both at the front and rear to support the wheels, each rear wheel being driven by a short shaft with two universal joints, the shaft linked to a bevel gear and differential unit hung from cross-members on a frame.

LANDINI • Italy 1919

Initially intended as a cheap way of training pilots, this vee-twin cyclecar was steered by foot, with gears and accelerator operated by the knees. Later models had more conventional controls.

L & P • England 1909-1913

Lloyd & Plaister of Wood Green, London, supplied parts to Dolphin as well as building this 16 hp shaft-drive car and the Vox cyclecar. The company dated back to 1897, when Lloyd had been associated with Hurst, and a few Hurst & Lloyd cars had been built up to 1900, when the partners went their own ways and Lloyd joined with Plaister. Some of the remaining Hurst & Lloyds were sold as "Lloyd & Plaister."

LANDRY & BEYROUX • France 1894-1902

Sometimes known as the MLB, this marque started life with a rear-mounted 4 hp single-cylinder engine, though

LANCIA • Italy 1906 to date

Wealthy soup manufacturer's son Vincenzo Lancia worked for Fiat before founding his own factory at Turin (and continued to race for Fiat until 1908.) His first production model, the 2543cc Alpha, appeared in 1907, and was joined in 1908 by the 3815cc DiAlfa, of which only 23 were made. Lancia ran through the Greek alphabet with the 3117cc Beta (1909), followed by the similar Gamma (1910) and the 4082cc Delta (1911.) The 1912 Eta, also of 4082cc, was the first Lancia with electric lighting. The 4939cc Theta of 1914 was said to be the first European car with standardized electric lighting and starting. A development, the Kappa, with detachable cylinder head, was Lancia's first post-war model, a narrow-angle V-12 with monobloc ohc engine shown in 1919 failing to reach production. The Kappa was followed by the DiKappa and by the ohc V-8 TriKappa, but these were only a prelude to the classic Lambda, which made its public debut in 1922. This had a narrow-angle V-4 engine of 2124cc, sliding-pillar ifs and integral body/chassis construction.

In 1926 the Seventh Series Lambda acquired a 2370cc power unit, enlarged to 2570cc on the Eighth Series of 1928-1929. At the end of 1929 Lancia introduced the more conventional DiLambda, with a 3960cc V-8, and in 1931 replaced the Lambda with the 1925cc ohc V-4 Artena and the 2605cc V-8 Astura (later models were of 2972cc). Unit construction reappeared with the 1196cc Augusta, which proved to have outstanding a road holding and led to Vincenzo Lancia's last classic car, the pillarless Aprilia, introduced just before his death in 1937. A smaller development, the 1091cc Ardea, appeared a little while later. The Aprilia was built until 1950, when the Jano-designed Aurelia was announced, initially with a 1754cc V-6 engine, later enlarged to 1991cc, 2261cc and 2451cc. The Aurelia GT also formed the basis of the sports-racing D23 and D24 models, with 2693cc and 2983cc dohc power units, some supercharged.

In 1953 Gianni Lancia designed the 1091cc Appia V-4, but a couple of years later financial difficulties forced him to sell his company to Fiat. The Flaminia, powered by a development of the 2458cc Aurelia GT engine, succeeded the Aurelia in 1956, but a real sensation was caused in 1961 by the fwd Flavia, designed by Professor Fossia; it had a flat-four engine of 1498cc, increased to 1798cc three years later. The Fulvia, another fwd model, succeeded the Appia as the smallest car in the Lancia range in 1964. By the end of the decade it was available with 1216cc and 1298cc engines. The Beta, first announced in 1972, was available in 1979 with ohc four-cylinder engines of 1297cc, 1585cc, and 1995cc. It was sold alongside the 1999cc and 2484cc Gamma, which had flat-four dohc power units. The Stratos, a limited-production sporting model, had a mid-mounted

1976 Lancia Stratos

20 hp Lancia, 1907

1991 Lancia Dedra Integrale

1925 Lancia Lambda tourer

dohc V-6 developing 190 bhp, and in 1979 won the Monte Carlo Rally for the fifth time.

The Gamma range of elegant sedans and coupés entered the market in 1979 and found a ready market for their characterful personalities. Also launched in 1979, the Guigario styled Delta was a 5-door with engines of 1.3 to 2 liters, the latter being a turbocharged unit reserved for the 1987 Integrale 4x4 model. The fwd Prisma sedan, with 1.3, 1.5, and 1.6-litre engines, appeared in 1982. Diesel and turbodiesel versions followed, and in 1986 a 4x4 2.0-liter version arrived. In 1984 the Thema, with I-4 and V6 engines, succeeded the Gamma. A Ferrari V-8 engine powered the 1986 Lancia Thema 8.32, replaced in 1992 by a derivative of the Thema Turbo 16V. The Y-10 minicar (sold in some markets as an Autobianchi) appeared in 1985, a 4x4 version following in 1986. Next addition to the Lancia range was the Dedra, available with 4x4 transmission from September 1991.

A revised Y model became available in Italy, and boasted dramatic styling in its amazingly short dimensions. Sadly it was denied to the British market, from which Lancia withdrew just as it had licked its image problems and launched a range of top-quality cars. These were best exemplified by the shapely and expertly tailored lines of the Kappa sedan, estate and two-door coupé. For 2000 Lancia replaced the Dedra mid-range sedan with the swoopy styling of the Lybra model.

Lancia remains Italy's premier upper-class brand as a producer of consistently elegant cars. Sadly, the rest of the world is currently denied global access to this fine marque.

Two classic Lancias – the Ferrari-engined Thema, alongside the rare rally-inspired Stratos

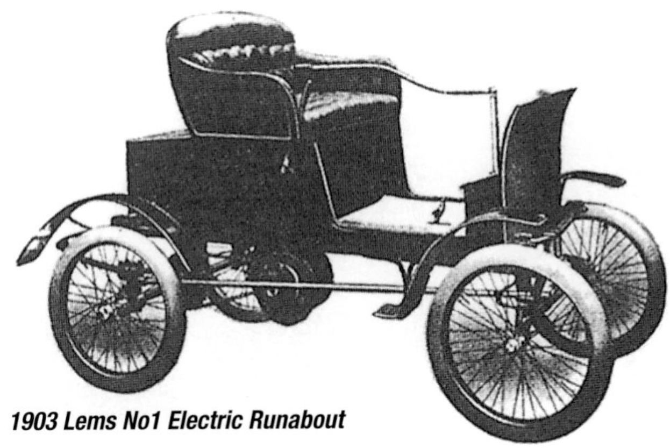

1903 Lems No1 Electric Runabout

LECOY • England 1921-1922

The friction-drive Lecoy, built in Harrow, Middlesex, was powered by an 8 hp JAP vee-twin engine. The front coil springs were an unconventional feature.

LEGROS • France 1900-1913

René Legros of Fecamp (Seine-Inférieure) initially built cars of 4 hp (single-cylinder) under the "La Plus Simple" label, followed by twins of 6 cv and 12 cv. From 1906 he offered two-stroke cars. Two models were available, a 10/12 hp twin and a 20/24 hp four. By 1912 the range had been expanded to two twin-cylinder and two four-cylinder models, still all two-strokes.

LEIDART • England 1936-1938

This Anglo-American model used the ubiquitous Ford V-8 as its power unit. Built in Pontefract, Yorkshire, the Leidart was also available with a Ford 10 supercharged engine.

LEMS • England 1903-1904

The London Electro-Mobile Syndicate offered a two-seater electric runabout ("40 miles on one charge") for 180 guineas.

LENAWEE • USA 1903-1904

A left-hand-drive tonneau with a horizontal single-cylinder engine beneath the front seat.

LENHAM • England 1969 to date

Once known only for its meticulous restorations, the Lenham Motor Company expanded during the 1960s to produce glassfiber panels and accessories for a variety of cars, as well as special bodies for Sprites and Midgets and its own Lenham GT, a futuristic mid-engined vehicle designed primarily for racing. Since 1978 it has made a spartan kit for rejuvenating tired and rusted Healey 100/6s and 3000s. The kit features an aluminum and glassfiber body, special wheels, twin aero screens, plus an outside exhaust and handbrake lever and even vintage-style hood straps.

LENOIR • France 1862-1863

Belgian inventor J J Etienne Lenoir built the first practical "hydrocarbon carriage" in Paris in 1862, and made a number of short, slow journeys with it before selling it to Czar Alexander II

LENOX • USA 1909-1918

The "uncommon" Lenox was, its maker claimed, "the only car built in Boston." Starting with electrics, the company eventually manufactured elegant gasoline cars in its Hyde Park factory.

LEO • France 1897-1898

An early design by Léon Lefévbre, the Léo was a belt-drive car with a Pygmée paraffin engine.

LEO • England 1912-1913

A fwd 8 hp cyclecar sold by Derry & Toms of Kensington, London.

LEO • Germany 1990

Backed by the Japanese Sumitomo group, this was a 750cc microcar.

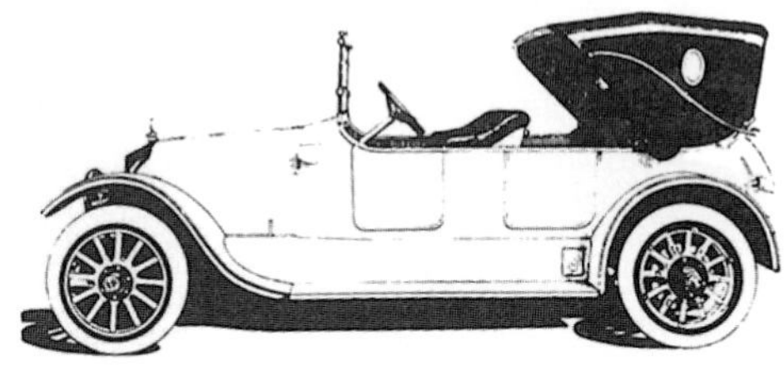

1917 Lenox Victoria

LEON BUAT • France 1901-c. 1908

Buat, of Senlis (Oise,) who began by building 8 cv light cars designed especially for doctors, also offered a De Dion-like voiturette ("La Polaire") in 1902, as well as larger cars with 12 cv twin and 16 cv four-cylinder engines. All power units were supplied by Aster.

LEON LAISNE • France 1920-1937

The Léon-Laisne (Harris-Léon-Laisne from 1927) had tubular chassis side-members housing hydraulically damped coil springs giving all-round independent suspension. Power was by SCAP, CIME or Hotchkiss.

LEON PAULET • France 1921-1927

Made in Marseille, these luxury cars were powered by an ohc six-cylinder 3445cc engine, later enlarged to 3920cc. Very well made, they attracted a lot of local custom. The marque resumed during the war with some small electric cars.

LEON RUBAY • USA 1922-1924

Sometimes erroneously termed "Rubay," this marque was named after Leon Rubay, a coachwork specialist who, like Brewster, had been a carriage builder. Leon Rubay cars were small (118-inch wheelbase) and used an own-make four-cylinder engine. In many ways the Leon Rubay was the same type of car as the contemporary Brewster, although it was cheaper, the sedan selling for $5,200; it featured four-wheel brakes. Very few Leon Rubay automobiles were produced, and the assets of the company passed to Rauch & Lang in 1924. The name Rubay is more commonly associated with bodies than with the specific make.

LEPAPE • France 1898-c. 1901

"Elegant and comfortable," the belt-driven Lepape had its twin-cylinder engine at the front, behind glass windows, so that the driver could see it was working properly.

LEROY • Canada 1902-1904

Having built trial-and-error prototypes from 1899, the Good brothers of Berlin (Kitchener), Ontario, took the easy way out by copying the Oldsmobile for their production cars.

LEROY • France 1927-1928

A pioneer of the two-stroke in France, M Leroy created some strange two-stroke engines for experimental purposes. With the assistance of the prolific M Violet he made some sports cars in Courbevoie, Seine, with four-cylinder two-stroke engines.

c. 1900 Lepape with spider seat

LESTER SOLUS • England 1913

An 8 hp JAP-engined single-seat cyclecar.

LEUCHTERS • England 1898

A De Dion-type motor tricycle "made entirely in Leeds."

LEVERE-PORTAL • France 1907

M Levére-Portal entered a 15 hp four-cylinder of his own construction in the touring class at the 1907 Evreux Trials.

LEWIS • USA 1899-1902

"Chicago inventor" George W Lewis established a factory in Philadelphia in 1899 to build "gasolene wagons" with horizontal single-cylinder 4178cc engines and friction drive by "compressed papers".

LEWIS • Australia 1900-1906

After building a single-cylinder buggy in 1900, Vivian Lewis produced a series of lightweight cars as well as a range of motorcycles. Car production ceased in 1906, but the motorcycles were built for several more years.

LEWIS • USA 1913-1916

Designed by René Petard, who also designed the 1913 Mitchell, and backed by William Mitchell Lewis of the Mitchell company, the Lewis (also known as "LPC") was powered by a longstroke six of 5676cc.

LEWIS • England 1923-1924

A MAG 10 hp vee-twin engine powered the Lewis, which was built in London's Abbey Wood. Although a four-cylinder model was announced simultaneously, neither vehicle went into production.

LEXINGTON • USA 1909-1928

Founded in Lexington, Kentucky, this manufacturer of quality assembled cars moved to Indiana within its first year. Only fours were built up to 1915, when the first six-cylinder models appeared, sixes remaining in production for the rest of Lexington's existence. Output peaked at 6,000 in 1920; in 1921 Lexington adopted Ansted power units. The most popular Lexington models were the Lexington tourer and Concord sedan of the early 1920s. The Minute Man Six also traded on War of Independence legend surrounding the battle of Lexington-Concord, though the battle had no connection with the marque"s Kentucky origins. Though Lexington went into receivership in 1923, small-scale output continued for five years.

LEXUS • Japan 1988 to date

Toyota invented a new marque name for its assault on the luxury car market with this impressive Mercedes-like sedan, with all-new dohc 4-liter V-8 engines powering a body shape that was deliberately tuned to appeal to Mercedes and BMW buyers. The Lexus LS400 incorporates styling elements similar to those of several Mercedes and BMW design hallmarks. After making the LS400 a huge success in the USA and UK, the Lexus brand expanded into a more sporting, Guigario styled GS300 model that would appeal to owners of cars like the BMW 5 series. Although tuned to take on the Americans and win, which

Lexus Coupé

A sportier, more youthful Lexus - the GS300

it did, the Lexus brand in LS400 guise was a touch bland. It has now evolved further to appeal to a wider audience, and features the Harrier or RX300, depending on market, a fwd MPV-type vehicle, and new a small Lexus, the IS200, which will tackle the likes of the BMW 3 series and Mercedes C-class cars, especially in their sporting variants. These cars are intended to broaden the marque's base. In America and in Britain Lexus is a success, but in Germany and France it has yet to take off. In 1998 Lexus sold nearly 4,000 cars in the UK alone, while in France it sold only 100. In less than a decade Lexus has grown from nothing to rank as an established, quality brand; no mean achievement, and testament to the ability of the Japanese car industry to learn and move quickly.

LEY • Germany 1906-1929

Designed by Albert Ley, whose brother Rudolf had founded the company at Arnstadt, the first cars bearing the name Ley (also known as Loreley) had 1559cc four-cylinder engines. In 1907 a six-cylinder was in production. Other pre-war models included 1132cc, 1545cc, and 2068cc four-cylinders and a 2599cc six-cylinder. There was a unique six-cylinder Ley (Loreley) with a small five-bearing sv 1559cc engine developing 18 hp at 1800 rpm. Ley returned to production in 1919 with a 3134cc 40 hp six-cylinder car, but afterwards concentrated on four-cylinder models with sv engines of 1530cc, 1990cc and 3070cc. Ley (Loreley) cars had a good reputation for quality and advanced design. Designer-director Gockenbach tested, together with Rudolf Ley and Paul Jaray, Ley cars with Jaray streamlined bodywork; there was also the TO sports model of 1924, which had an ohc 1498cc four-cylinder engine.

LEYLAND • England 1920-1923

Leyland Motors, a commercial-vehicle builder since 1897, decided to enter the luxury car market with the Leyland Eight of 1920. Designed by J. G. Parry-Thomas, it was the first British production straight-eight, and was of 7.3-liters capacity. This magnificent car bristled with individuality, servo-assisted brakes, leaf-valve springs and torsion-bar-assisted suspension being just some of its more unusual features. Unfortunately, at a price of £3,050 there were few takers and only 18 were built. Thomas, however, actively raced tuned examples at Brooklands.

LEYLAND • Australia 1973-1975

Leyland Australia was born out of the merger of the former Austin and Morris (BMC) subsidiary companies. In post-war years they had launched a series of locally designed cars, such as the Austin Lancer, Morris Major, and Austin Freeway, all based on British designs. In 1970 the newly formed Leyland concern decided to compete against Holden and Falcon. Called the P76, the entirely new car proved to be a very large sedan with a 9ft 3in wheelbase, powered by a conventional six-cylinder engine. An optional Rover-based alloy V-8 was also offered. Body styling was by Italian specialist Michelotti. Leyland Australia ran into sales difficulties and the manufacturing facilities were closed during 1975, when the company had just started to build coupé versions of the P76 and six-cylinder versions of the Morris Marina.

LEYAT • France 1913-1925

This very strange car was remarkable for the use of a propeller at the front, and for steering by the rear wheels. Leyats used ABC motorcycle flat-twin engines at the beginning, later supplanted by a radial three-cylinder Anzani.

LIBELLE • Germany 1922-1924

Founded by ex-Daimler employees, this small factory at Sindelfingen built a few 990cc two-seater cars.

LIBERIA • France 1900-1902

The four-seater Libéria "Light Voiture" had a 5 hp water-cooled Aster engine, a three-speed and reverse transmission and chain final drive. It sold in England for £250.

LIBERTY • USA 1916-1924

The Liberty Six had a 3394cc monobloc six, and sold for $1,095. Included in the standard equipment were fitted tools and a clothes brush. The company was bought by Columbia late in 1923.

LIFU • England • USA 1899-1902

Henry Alonzo House, formerly with the Liquid Fuel Engineering Company, of Cowes, Isle of Wight, moved to Bridgeport, Conn., where he showed his paraffin-fired "Lifu" steam carriage in 1899. The Cowes factory could build 30 heavy steam cars and 20 steam launches a year, and in 1899 a Birmingham branch factory was also established in the former Starley & Westwood Cycle Works at Adderley Park. House joined the Automatic Steam Motor Supply Syndicate of New York late in 1899, but the first

American Lifu did not appear until 1901. Lifus were mostly heavy commercials, but a number of tiller-steered 10 hp cars were built.

LIGIER • France 1981 to date

Four-seat 197cc microcars from a famous racing car maker.

1907 Little Wonder Type 4

LILIPUT • Germany 1904-1908

Designed by Willi Seck for Georg Wiss, owner of Suddeutsche Automobil Fabrik (SAF,) the 567cc single-cylinder 4 hp Liliput had friction drive. Plans to build it in large numbers, not only at the Gaggenau works but also at the Schilling arms factory at Suhl (which in the 1920s produced Rennsteig motorcycles), did not materialize.

LILLA • Japan 1923-1925

The Jitsuyo Automobile Company of Osaka built Gorham twin-cylinder light three- and four-wheelers from 1920, then produced the utilitarian Lilla and Lilla Peaton four-cylinder, which had 2-liter watercooled engines.

LINCOLN • Australia 1919-1924

Built in Sydney, New South Wales, the Lincoln Pioneer Six featured a Continental six-cylinder engine and a radiator suggestive of the Packard. Wire wheels could be had at extra cost, although most Lincolns already had them. In 1923 the company was requested to drop its name by the Lincoln Motor Co of Detroit, Mich., but the plea went unheeded and Australia"s Lincoln went out of business a year later. Two examples survive.

LINCOLN • USA 1920 to date

see panel overleaf

LINDCAR • Germany 1921-1925

although early examples of this well-made light car had air-cooled sv fours of 1299cc, most came with water-cooled proprietary fours, either a 1017cc Atos or a 1320cc Steudel.

LINDSAY • England 1904-1908

There were three models of the 1906-1908 Lindsay, built in Woodbridge, Suffolk; a 12 hp, a 20 hp and a 28/30 hp. All had four-cylinder engines and were described as "economical, reliable and powerful." The marque took its name from Lindsay Scott, who had started with 3.5 hp Minerva-engined tricars in 1904.

LINDSTROM • USA 1899

An electric buggy with separate motors driving each rear wheel through a ring gear.

LINGTON • England 1920

The shortlived Lington used a 10 hp vee-twin engine which could be pedal-started from the driver's seat. Shaft drive was employed.

LINON • Belgium 1900-1914

A two-seater lightweight voiturette, powered by a 3 hp De Dion engine with a watercooled cylinder head, began this firm's activities. By 1912 an 8 hp single and fours of 10, 12, 14, 16, 20, and 22 hp were available.

LINSER • Austria c. 1905-1907

Built in Reichenberg, the "pretty little" four-cylinder Linser had separate cylinders and "all the organs of a large car."

LION • England 1905

Built by Milbrowe Smith of Birmingham, this Aster-engined 16/20 hp car had sterling silver-plated brightwork.

LION • USA 1910-1912

Built at Adrian, Michigan, the Lion 40 had a 5312cc four-cylinder engine and came in run-about style as standard.

LION-PEUGEOT • France 1906-1913

Originally an independent venture by Robert Peugeot in the Peugeot cycle factory at Beaulieu-Valentigny (Doubs,) Lion-Peugeot is chiefly remembered for its eccentric long-stroke racing voiturettes, culminating in the 2815cc vee-twin V-5 (80 x 280mm) and 3451cc V-4 (65 x 260mm) of 1910. There were also touring Lion-Peugeots, single-cylinder and vee-twins of up to 1.7 liters and, following the absorption of Lion-Peugeot back into the mainstream company in 1910, a V-4 which appeared in 1911.

LIPSCOMB • England 1903-1905

The English Motor-Car Company of London made 6.5 hp and 8 hp light cars with three-speed transmission and shaft drive, predecessors of the Bayley.

LIPSIA • Germany 1922-1924

Middle-sized cars with 1530cc and 1980cc four-cylinder engines produced in limited numbers.

LIQUID AIR • USA • England 1899-1902

Liquid Air's first factory opened at Boston, Mass., in 1899, claiming that cars could be built to run 100 miles on liquid air. *Horseless Age* called the system "liquid moonshine." The Boston company went into receivership in July 1901. Stock was $1.5 million, assets $7,500, liabilities $4,500. The Liquid Air car, apparently a modified Locomobile steamer, was demonstrated in London (where the company had a depot) by its designer, Hans Knudsen, in 1902. It was claimed to run 40 miles at 12 mph on 18 gallons of liquid air at a shilling a gallon.

LISTER • England 1988 to date

Long known for its racing cars, Lister produced a 500 bhp 7 liter road car derived from the Jaguar XJS: it also announced it was building a short run of Lister-Jaguars, identical to the 1987 model.

LITTLE • USA 1911-1913

The Little Four, from Flint, Mich., was "out of the ruck of American cars." A neat two-seater runabout which sold for 165 guineas in England, it had a bi-block 2128cc four-cylinder engine in unit with a two-speed gearbox. The company was acquired by Chevrolet.

LITTLE MIDLAND • England c. 1905-1922

A 7 hp two-seater which sold for 150 guineas complete in 1905 was the first of this Clitheroe, Lancashire, company's spasmodic offerings. The next was a 7 hp JAP-engined cyclecar produced in 1911; a modified version appeared post-war, built in Blackburn, then in Preston.

LITTLE WONDER • USA 1907

There were four models of this wheel-steered single-cylinder two-stroke gas buggy; an 8 hp two-seater, a "roomier two-seater," a "Doctor's Phaeton" and a 10 hp Stanhope. The Doctor's Phaeton came complete with instrument case.

LIVER • England 1900-1906

Starting life as a Benz derivative, by 1906 the Liverpool-built Liver had become a conventional four-cylinder with pressed-steel chassis and Aster or PF engines.

LLOYD • Germany 1906-1963

Designed by Joseph Vollmer, the first Lloyd cars built by the Bremen-based NAMAG works had 3685cc and 2311cc four-cylinder engines. A 5520cc four-cylinder 50 hp car, plus a 60 hp version, came into production in 1910-1911. As a result of the merger with Hansa-Lloyd and a co-operation with other factories after the First World War, the name Lloyd disappeared until Borgward, now owner of the works, introduced the little 293cc Lloyd twin-cylinder two-stroke in 1950. It was followed by improved 248cc and 286cc versions. Like their successors with four-stroke engines, they had fwd. The four-stroke range with in-line twin-cylinder ohc engines included 596cc models. From 1959 ohv 897cc flat-four engines were available. The Lloyd disappeared with the collapse of the Borgward group.

LLOYD • England 1936-1951

The pre-war Lloyd used a rear-mounted 350cc single-cylinder engine. Post-1945 types had all-independent suspension and were powered by a 650cc two-stroke front-mounted engine, the device being driven by the front wheels.

LM • France 1913

Only two LM automobiles were built, designed by Charles L Lawrance who, with Arthur Moulton and Sidney Breeze, had manufactured the BLM car in Brooklyn, NY, from 1906 to 1909. The engine was a four-cylinder affair which had ohv and peculiar auxiliary ported exhausts as in a two-cycle engine, controlled by a rotary valve.

LMB • England 1960-1962

Leslie Ballamy, famed for his ifs conversions of transverse-sprung Fords, built a series of 100 tubular chassis for Ford or BMC power; some, with Edwards Brothers glassfiber GT bodies, were sold as EB Debonairs.

LMW • Sweden 1923

The Lidköping Mekaniska Verkstads AB planned to build an initial batch of three cars, but only one was built. The

LINCOLN • USA 1920 to date

Named for Henry Leland's boyhood hero, the Lincoln car appeared at the end of 1920, its fine engineering offset by dull coachwork styled by Leland's son-in-law, ex-milliner Angus Woodbridge. Power was by a 5.8-liter V-8, but many of the chassis components were bought-in assemblies. A bill for alleged tax arrears plunged Lincoln into financial crisis, and the company was bought by Ford, the Lelands resigning soon after. Under the control of Edsel Ford the Lincoln soon acquired the elegance to match its engineering. Its rapid acceleration made it a favorite with police and gangsters alike, and a police model with four-wheel brakes (not generally available until 1927) was offered in 1924; that year Calvin Coolidge became the first US President to own a Lincoln. Engine size was increased to 6.3 litres in 1928, and a further engineering innovation came in 1932 with the V-12 KB model, one of only seven V-12 cars in the US market. Sales, however, were disappointing, and in 1936 a new low-priced range, the ultra-streamlined Lincoln-Zephyr styled by John Tjaarda, made its debut. Of 18,994 Lincolns sold that year, 17,715 were Lincoln-Zephyrs. The Lincoln-Zephyr formed the basis of Edsel Ford's classic Lincoln Continental, a low-slung coupé first seen in March 1939.

When America entered the war the Lincoln-Zephyr ceased production for ever, but the Lincoln Continental and the Lincoln continued after the war, still with the

c. 1924 Lincoln phaeton

Clark Gable with his 1948 Lincoln convertible

flathead V-12 of 4998cc, until the Continental was finally dropped in 1948. (It reappeared as a separate marque in 1956). The 1949 models featured new slab-sided styling and a sv V-8 of 5555cc. Completely new designs appeared in 1952, powered by an ohv 5203cc V-8; the Cosmopolitan was the only series listed, and was available in five series, including the Capri coupé and convertible. The all-new 1956 models had a long, low look and a 6030cc V-8; top of the range was now the Premiere. A 1957 facelift produced vertical dual headlamps and sharply pointed tailfins. The "longer, lower, wider"1958 models were over 19 ft long, weighed 4,880 lb and were powered by a 7047cc V-8.

In 1961 came more compact designs reminiscent of the 1956-1957 Continental Mk II, offered only as four-door sedans or convertibles, the latter unique in the industry. The same bodyshell was retained until 1969, Lincoln preferring detail improvement to drastic restyling (though the convertible was dropped in 1967, and 1968 saw the separate Mk III line introduced.) In 1970 came a new Lincoln using many Ford/Mercury chassis components, with styling that was evolutionary rather than dramatic. Its coffin-shaped hood ended in a smaller grille flanked by retractable headlights. Power was by a 7538cc V-8, and the range consisted of a two-door coupé, four-door sedan and the more costly Town Car, soon joined by a Town Coupé. Changes to this range were minimal, though in 1979 a concession to "down-sizing" was made by the adoption of a 6555cc engine. In mid-1977 the Mercury Monarch-based Versailles joined the Lincoln range; its 1979 version had a 4949cc V-8.

The 1979 Town Car had the 4.9-liter V-8. In 1991 this was replaced by a 4.6-liter V-8. The long-in-the-tooth model was available in Basic, Signature, and Cartier series in 1992. The aerodynamic Mk VII with electronically-controlled pneumatic suspension made its debut in 1983, followed in 1987 by a new Continental 3.8-litre with front-wheel drive.

Lincoln's cars were still large, square rigged cars. By the early 1990s, however, the marque realised that it would have to move with the times, and a new, curved, more aerodynamic look was given to even the biggest models in the Lincoln range, notably through the Mk VIII and later Continental models. However, the Lincoln Town Car remained an old fashioned square rigged, chrome-laden car. In the 1997 model year Lincoln launched its own badge engineered version of its Ford masters fwd off-road vehicle. Named Navigator, it represented an unusual move for the prestige maker, yet found many buyers. However, it is for its upmarket Cadillac competing cars that Lincoln remains best known.

A 'dream car' of the mid-1950s, the Lincoln Continental Nineteen Fifty-X (above.) 1979 Lincoln Town Car (left,) 1940s style (below)

"Locomobile"

1901 Locomobile steam car

LOCOMOBILE • USA 1899-1929

Founded to exploit the steam car design of the Stanley brothers, Locomobile of Bridgeport, Connecticut, was soon, if briefly, America's biggest manufacturer, turning out 4,000 cars by 1902. Its frail steam buggy was widely plagiarized, but in 1902 it built its first gasoline car, a four-cylinder model designed by A L Riker. This was so successful that the company gave up steam cars in 1903 and was soon established as a maker of big, expensive gasoline cars, including in 1904 the two-cylinder Type C 9/12 hp and the Type D 18/22 hp, a chain-drive four on Mercedes lines. These were followed by the Type E 15 /20 hp, the 40/45 hp Type F and the 30/35 hp Type H of 1905-1906, as well as a replica of the company's Gordon Bennett racer, a 17.7-litre four. In 1911 came the 8-litre, six-cylinder Model 48 ('the Exclusive Car for Exclusive People,') which lasted until the end of production in 1929. In 1920 Locomobile was briefly linked with Mercer and Crane-Simplex. Then, in 1923, it became part of Billy Durant's final empire. New models, the 1925-1927 Junior Eight and the luxury Model 90, appeared, and the Locomobile plant also built the low-priced Flint Six. The last Locomobile, Model 88, had a 4.9-liter Lycoming engine.

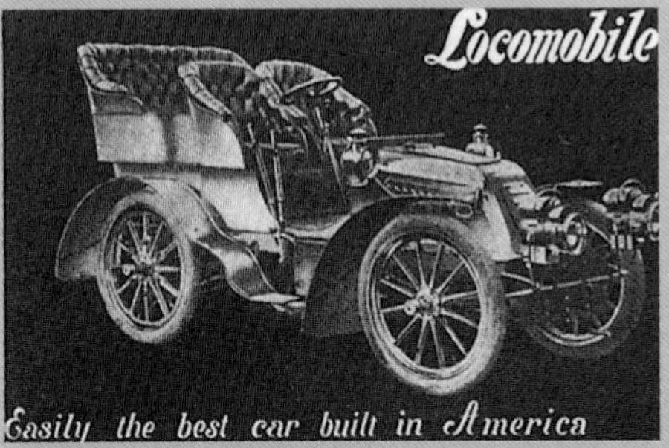

1904 16 hp Locomobile touring car

1928 Locomobile 8-70 straight-eight five-passenger sedan

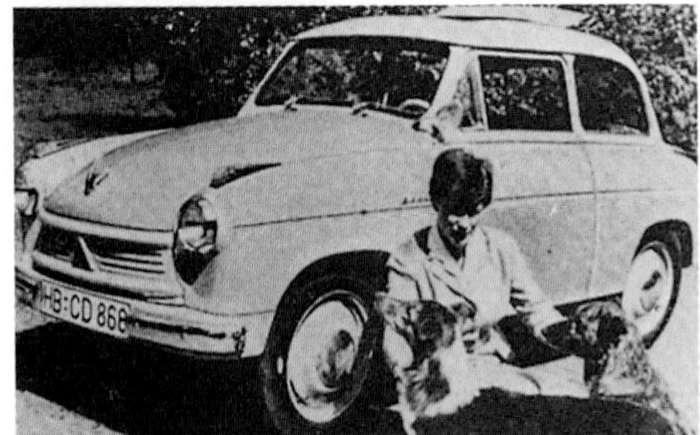

1957 Lloyd Alexander saloon

engine was a French four-cylinder 18 hp CIME with a Cozette carburetor. The gearbox had three forward speeds and the total weight was 1,540lb.

LMX • Italy 1970-1972

A coachbuilder which fitted plastic coupé and cabriolet coachwork on cars equipped with 2293cc Ford V-6 engines. Supercharged 180 bhp versions were also available.

1911 Loeb sporting tourer

LOCKWOOD • England 1921-1922

Produced at Eastbourne, Sussex, the Lockwood was a miniature car intended for use by children.

LOCOMOBILE • USA 1899-1929

see panel

LOEB (LUC) • Germany 1910-1914

Loeb of Berlin was a leading car importer and dealer. Reissig designed its first LUC car, which had 2025cc four-cylinder Knight sleeve-valve engines imported from Daimler at Coventry. Other models of this quality car, known either as Loeb or LUC, had four-cylinder engines of 2612cc, 3052cc and 4084cc. During the First World War Loeb built aero engines, and after the war sold the factory to the Stinnes-owned Dinos company.

LOGAN • USA 1903-1908

A roadster from Chillicothe, Ohio, powered by a 24 hp ohv air-cooled Carrico engine.

LOHNER • Austria 1896-1906

Viennese coachbuilder Jacob Löhner built a few Pygmée-engined gasoline cars before turning to electrics in 1898, in which year Ferdinand Porsche joined the company, designing cars with electric motors incorporated in the front wheel hubs. Gasoline-electrics on this principle were also constructed; in 1906 the patents were sold to Emil Jellinek of Mercedes.

LOIDIS • England 1900-1904

A shaft-driven light car with single-cylinder 9 hp Aster engine; it was named after the ancient Celtic settlement ("Caer Loidis") which was the foundation of its natal town, Leeds. Its maker, Dougill, also imported Lux cars under this name. It subsequently built the Frick.

LOMBARD • France 1927-1929

These sports cars made in Puteaux, Seine, had a wonderful dohc engine of 1093cc. Some of them were supercharged, and did very well in races. In 1929 Lombard presented an ohc straight-eight of 2896cc, which never went into production. The company was taken over by BNC, and some of the racing Lombards had badge engineering inflicted on them.

LOMBARDI • Italy 1969-1971

A two-seater coupé based on a Fiat 850 Special floorpan, with a 47 bhp 843cc four-cylinder engine. Few of these cars were made. The company also rebodied the 903cc Fiat 127 and the 1991cc four-cylinder Lancia.

LONDONIA • England? 1908

Said to be of English origin, but probably imported from the USA, this marque was linked with the mysterious Owen. In 1908 an 8/10 hp twin, 20 hp four, 35 hp four, and 30 hp six were listed, though the same photograph illustrated each in *The Autocar Buyer"s Guide*.

LONDON SIX • Canada 1921-1925

"Canada"s Quality Car" used a 4078cc Herschell-Spillman engine and rode on laminated-wood disc wheels; bodies were initially supplied by an Ontario coffin maker. Plans to use this car as the basis of an automotive empire ended in insolvency for its promoter, William Stansell, after 98 had been built.

LONE STAR • USA 1920-1922

Sold by a truck and tractor firm in San Antonio, Texas, the Lone Star was available either as a four or a six, Lycoming engines being used in both models. The cars were actually built by Piedmont in Lynchburg, Virginia, along with such other assembled marques as Bush, Marshall, Norwalk Six, and Stork Kar.

Lombard dohc 1100cc

The Canadian-built London Six, 1922

LONSDALE • England 1901-1902

Albert Lambourne, who later built the Old Mill car, designed this 463cc single-cylinder car with chain-driven ohc. Three were built in Hove, Sussex.

LOOMIS • USA 1900-1904

A single-cylinder 2.5 hp "park carriage" selling at $450 was this Massachusetts firm's first offering (though Gilbert J Loomis had built his first car, a steamer, in 1896.) By 1901 only flat-twin engines were available, and in 1904 a three-cylinder was offered.

c. 1903 De Dietrich 30 hp

LORD • England 1915

An own-make flat-twin of 1068cc was fitted to this friction-drive light car from Surbiton, Surrey, which retailed at £100.

LA LORRAINE • France 1899-1902

A vis-á-vis built by Charles Schmid of Bar-le-Duc, Meuse, with infinitely variable belt-drive.

LORRAINE • USA 1907-1908

John O Hobbs of Chicago built his first "self-starting" car in 1903; the starter was powered by compressed air. The first Lorraine was completed in May 1907, and used Hobbs's "elastic driving shaft" built up from 24 steel torsion rods; it had electric lighting. Four-cylinder engines of 30 hp and 50 hp were available.

LORRAINE • USA 1920-1922

This assembled car, successor to the Hackett, was manufactured in Grand Rapids, Michigan. A four-cylinder Herschell-Spillman engine was used; a few hundred cars were assembled.

LORRAINE • USA 1920-1923

The Lorraine, produced by the Lorraine Car Co of Richmond, Indiana, had no connection with its Grand Rapids counterpart, but rather was the ambulance and hearse division of the Pilot automobile. Continental motors were used, and small number of limosines was made in addition to hearses and ambulances.

LORRAINE DIETRICH Germany • France 1896-1935

An old-established maker of railway locomotives in Alsace-Lorraine, De Diétrich et Cie started to build motor cars under licence from constructors such as Bollée, Vivinus or Turcat-Méry at its Lunéville and Niederbronn plants. From 1902 Bugatti worked for them as the engineer at

1925 3-litre Lorraine Dietrich

1964 Lost Cause

Niederbronn, where he designed a 5304cc four and a 50 hp racer with the seat behind the rear axle. In 1908 the marque name was changed to Lorraine-Dietrich. In 1909 it had a six-cylinder of 11,460cc, many four-cylinder models, from the small 12 cv of 2120cc to the big 60 cv of 12,053cc, as well as a twin-cylinder 10 cv of 1060cc. The following year a 3619cc six-cylinder 15 hp was introduced. Most of these cars were made right up to the war, excepting the twin-cylinder. After the war, when Alsace became part of France again, Lorraine-Dietrich restarted production with the ohv 12 cv of 2297cc and ohv 15 cv six of 3445cc, as well as the 30 six (6107cc). The 15 cv Lorraine was the backbone of production for many years, and eventually won the Le Mans 24 Hour Race. Before business ceased, Lorraine introduced the sv 20 cv six of 4086cc; it was a complete failure.

LORYC • Spain 1920-1925

Lacy, Ribas y Compana of Palma, Mallorca, gave its name to this sporting cyclecar designed by the Frenchman Albert Ouvrard, formerly with Hispano-Suiza. Ruby, SCAP, and EHP engines imported from France were used.

LOS ANGELES • USA 1914-1915

A four-cylinder watercooled cyclecar manufactured in Compton, California.

LOST CAUSE • USA 1963-1964

Charles Peaslee Farnsley"s "Lost Cause" was basically a Chevrolet Corvair luxuriously modified by the Derham Custom Body works. Equipment included altimeter, mint julep cups and matching luggage.

LOTHIAN • England 1920

The Lothian apparently used a four-cylinder engine available in 10 hp and 11.9 hp variations.

LOTIS • England 1908-1912

Built in the old British Duryea factory at Coventry under the aegis of Henry Sturmey, founding editor of *The Autocar* (and inventor of the Sturmey-Archer hub gear for cycles,) the original Lotis was a front-engined 22 hp four, soon joined by a single-cylinder 8 hp, 10/12 hp, and 12/18 hp vee-twins with Riley engines and a 30/35 hp. Only the twins were built in 1909, and a totally new range (10/ 12 hp twin, 12/18 hp twin (with a different power unit), 16/ 20 hp four, 20/25 hp four) was announced the next year. The range was reshuffled again in 1911 and in 1912, the last year of production.

LOTUS • England 1947 to date

see panel overleaf

LOUET • France 1903-c. 1908

This Parisian firm offered "light cars for luxury or touring," with 25/30 hp and 30/35 hp four-cylinder engines. A six-cylinder had apparently been built in 1903.

LOUIS CHENARD • France 1920-1932

No relation to the "other" Chenard, this Colombes, Seine, works started with a sv 7/9 hp of 1244cc. In 1922 it launched an ohv 10 hp of 1693cc, followed in 1923 by a 7/9 hp Chapuis-Dornier-engined 1093cc and an ohv 10 hp of 1496cc, enlarged to 1525cc in 1925. These models remained until the end.

LOUTZKY • Germany 1900

A two-speed 3.5 hp "neat two-seated carriage" from Berlin. Herr Loutzky also built parcels carriers for the German post office.

LOYD-LORD • England 1923-1924

Although the Loyd-Lord began life with a 1795cc four-cylinder engine, 1924 examples were offered with supercharged two-stroke air-cooled two- and four-cylinder engines of mind-boggling complexity.

1913/14 Lozier seven-passenger tourer

LOZIER • USA 1899-1917

George A Burrell, supervisor of the Lozier Cycle Company's Toledo plant, designed a three-wheeled carriage in 1899. When H. A. Lozier Sr retired from the business in 1900, his son, E. R. Lozier, and Burrell, set up the Lozier Motor Company in Toledo. However, production did not begin until 1905, when Lozier's Plattsburg, NY, factory introduced a pair-cast 40 hp four, selling at $5,500-$6,500 according to body. From 1907 Loziers were shaft driven, yet retained dummy chain-covers to add to their "sporty" image. Best known of the early Loziers was the sporting 7450cc Briarcliff toy tonneau, named after the 1908 Briarcliff Trophy race (in which Lozier was not actually very successful.) There was also a 9085cc pair-cast six version; like the four, it could be specified with Briarcliff, touring or limousine coachwork, at prices from $6,000-$7,000. Other exotic body styles graced Lozier cars: the three-seat "Meadowbrook," seven-passenger "Riverside" touring, and "Knickerbocker Berlin." Production shifted to Detroit in 1910; by 1914, prices were down. The Lozier "77" bi-block 6378cc six cost $3,250 as a tourer, and the "84" monobloc 6044cc four was only $2,100. But the price cuts failed to counter falling sales, and by 1918 "the quality car for quality people" had ceased production.

LOZIER • USA 1922

It is doubtful whether any cars were produced by the Lozier Motors Co of New York City, although two models were quoted; a touring car at $8,500 and a limousine at $10,000. Likewise it is doubtful whether the marque had any connection with the earlier Lozier.

LSD • England 1920-1924

A JAP vee-twin was the motive power of this rather ungainly three-wheeler hailing from Yorkshire. Final drive was by chains.

LT • Sweden 1923

Anders Lindström of Torsby had very advanced mechanical ideas, and his 20 hp fwd car had clean lines, a pointed radiator and was very well made. It is rumored that Lindström was contacted by various sources who wanted to finance production, but he preferred to stay independent. The workshop, deep in the forests of Värmland in the western part of Sweden, burnt down after only three cars of a planned production of 50 were produced, one of them being exported to Norway.

LUCAR • England 1913-1914

A 1094cc light car from Brixton, London, with electric lamps.

LUC COURT • France 1899-1936

The distinctive feature of the early Luc Courts from Lyon was the "demountable chassis" devised by one Lacoin. The front part of the chassis could be detached from the bodywork and rear wheels and attached to a different body and wheels, "the transformation taking place within a few minutes, without tools." The year 1912 saw a three-car range, fours of 2155cc and 3631cc, and a 3233cc six. Post-war, Luc Court built mostly light commercials, plus a few 12 hp and 20 hp cars.

LUCERNA • Switzerland 1907-c. 1909

Garage-owner A H Grivel offered a range of assembled cars, using Aster engines and Malicet & Blin chassis: four-cylinders of 10/14 hp, 14/18 hp, and 20/24 hp, and a 20 /24 hp six.

LUCIA • Switzerland 1903-1908

Designed by Lucien Picker, the Lucia originally appeared as a 905cc four-cylinder with two speeds and shaft drive. From 1904 L Picker, Moccand & Cie built these cars in a new factory at Chene-Bougeries, Geneva. Two models were available in 1905, a 12/16 cv twin and a 24/30 cv four. Picker devised a "squish" cylinder head, akin to the Ricardo head of the 1920s, for these cars. About 100 Lucias were made.

LUDGATE • England 1904-1905

A two-seater "light runabout" with 4 hp watercooled engine and chain drive.

LUFBERY • France 1898-c. 1902

Charles-Edouard Lufbery's rear-engined vee-twin car combined epicyclic gearing with a three-speed belt transmission to give a primitive overdrive.

LULU • USA 1914"

More than a cyclecar", the $398 LuLu (made by Kearns) had a four-cylinder monobloc engine and three-speed gearing.

LURQUIN-COUDERT • France 1907-1914

"Voiturette-tricars" from a Parisian maker of industrial engines. A twin-cylinder ran in the touring class at the 1907 Château-Thierry hill-climb, and vee-twin cyclecars were built from around 1910.

LUTECE • France 1906-1907

A shaft-drive 14 hp four built by G Cochot of Colombes, Seine, and shown at Olympia in 1906. Cochot had sold

1896 Lutzman dogcart

1906 Luc Court landaulette

rear-engined 2.5 hp voiturettes in 1900-1901 under his own name.

LUTIER • France 190

7A four-cylinder car of unknown provenance.

LUTZMANN • Germany 1893-1898

One of the leading German car pioneers, Friedrich Lutzmann built his first car in 1893. From 1896 onwards came a production version with a 2540cc single-cylinder engine, which developed 5 bhp at 300 rpm. This car had a two-speed gearbox, chain drive to the rear wheels and a 23 mph top speed. Opel bought the Lutzmann design and the production equipment in 1898, transferring the operation from Dessau to the Opel bicycle works at Russelsheim.

LUVERNE • USA 1913-1919

In 1915 the "Big Brown Luverne" 38 hp six sold for $2,500 in seven-seater tourer form.

LUWO • Germany 1922-1923

Another car with a 1320cc four-cylinder Steudel engine, built in small quantities in Munich.

LUX • Germany 1897-1902

The early Lux cars, from Ludwigshafen-am-Rhein, had rear-mounted 604cc flat-twin engines. A later version had the power unit in front and a "patent safety clutch."

LUX • Italy 1906-1908

Small four-cylinder cars with own-make 10 hp or 16 hp engines were built in small numbers by this Torinese cycle works.

LUXIOR • France 1912-1914

The four-cylinder Luxior from Vincennes, near Paris, had a 1779cc engine and was one of the earliest light cars to be offered in sedan form. In 1912 Luxior also produced a 1767cc model with "valveless pre-compression engine with super-imposed cylinders."

LYMAN & BURNHAM • USA 1903-1904

Built for Lyman & Burnham of Boston by the Fore River Ship and Engine Co of Quincy, Mass., this 12 hp twin-cylinder car had an odd throttle valve "located in the cylinder casting and surrounding the inlet valve... said to be very sensitive".

LYNX • 1973 to date

Formed by entrepreneurial engineers Chris-Keith Lucas and Guy Black, Lynx was originally involved in racing car preparation and classic car restoration. It then manufactured a remarkably faithful reproduction of the Jaguar D-Type, based on E-type mechanicals and all built in-house. Available in short- and longnose forms and subsequently as an XKSS version, the Lynx D-Type led to bespoke conversions of other luxury cars such as the Jaguar XJ-S, available in convertible and estate forms. Ownership changed in 1992.

LYONS ATLAS • USA 1913-1915

With Knight sleeve-valve engines and worm-drive rear axles, these Indianapolis-built cars were designed by Harry A Knox.

LYS • France 1908-1909

Fernand Marx of Paris produced engines of 8/10 hp, 10 /12 hp and 12/16 hp and components, as well as the complete Lys car.

1973 JPS Lotus Europa

1963 Lotus Elite

1973 Lotus Super Seven Mk IV

Elan - the Lotus of Legend

LOTUS • England 1947 to date

The Lotus legend started in 1947, when talented engineer Anthony Colin Bruce Chapman took to building 750 specials. Public demand for replicas led to the forming of Lotus Engineering in 1952 and, a few years later, the first production Lotus, the 6, since when Lotus has grown out of all recognition. Now many times World Champion Car Constructor, as well as maker of up-market sports and GT cars, not to mention luxury yachts, Chapman has become a legend in his own time as well as a multi-millionaire. The first four Lotuses were all based on the Austin Seven. The Mk 5 never happened, but was to have been a 100 mph sports-racing car. The ubiquitous Mk 7 lives on today, known simply as the Seven and built by Caterham Cars. The next road car was the pretty glass-fiber Elite. This was effectively superseded by the Elan in late 1962, the Plus 2 version of which appeared in 1967. Shortly before, however, in December 1966, Lotus announced its first mid-engined road car, the Europa. Initially Renault-powered, it eventually sported the same Ford-based, twin-cam engine as its stablemates. Following special and expensive derivatives of the Elans and Europas, Lotus finally cut its ties with the enthusiast and launched an executive dream, the Elite, in 1974. With only the badge in common with the original car of the same name, it heralded a new era for the company, which soon afterwards added the Eclat (a coupé version of the Elite) and the mid-engined Esprit to complete its range of fast, sleek rich men's toys.

The Espirit Turbo appeared in 1980. This era saw the Lotus Formula One racing team dominate the grand prix world and achieve triumph alongside tragedy, when Ronnie Petersen was killed driving for the team.

Colin Chapman died of a heart attack with the company in serious financial trouble, and BCA and Toyota bought into it. A proposed V-8 engine was introduced in 1984 in the Giugiaro-designed ETNA prototype, but proved a dead end, the range concentrating on 16-valve 2.2-liter units. In 1986 Lotus became a wholly-owned subsidiary of General Motors. Two years later a Peter Stevens redesigned Espirit appeared, with a 156 mph top speed. In 1989 a new 1588cc front-wheel drive drophead Elan was launched. This proved a great success, but financial troubles and a change of ownership into Italian hands, and then into an agreement with other investors, saw a lack of product continuity. In the end the Malaysian Proton car making group stepped in and remains owner of Lotus.

As part of the previous events, the new Elan later also emerged re-badged and with an Isuzu/GM engine. However, the new alloy-and-composite Elise model was just what the traditional Lotus market wanted, and sold well, its minimalist design and nimble handling getting great press reviews. In 1999 this two-seat soft-top sports car in true Chapman tradition gained a 148 bhp, 1.8-liter Rover K series VVC engine and took on a new lease of performance life as the Elise 111s. The car's light weight and race-bred handling caused a sensation. Stability also allowed Lotus to re-engine a revised Esprit range with its own, new V-8 motor. Finally, after years of almost hitting the target as a true super car, the Esprit, by now two decades old but still looking very modern, managed it. The company also continued its role as a development and research centre, carrying out design and production modification for Isuzu, Vauxhall and others.

The Espirit V8 (below.)
The Espirit - the final, ultimate version of the Espirit model originally designed by Guigario and then skillfully updated by Peter Stevens (left.)

In the Lotus Elise, the company returned to its original themes

R471 AAH

MAB • England 1906-1911

A 16/20 hp car from cycle makers A G Fenn of Mortimer Market, London ("MAB" = Mortimer Auto Bikes.)

MAB • France 1925

Maker of automobile components and chassis, Malicet et Blin in Aubervilliers, Seine, occasionally assembled ohc Anzani-engined cars.

MACDONALD STEAM CAR • USA 1923-1924

The MacDonald Steam Automotive Co of Garfield, Ohio, flourished briefly as a builder (and rebuilder) of steam engines and other parts of existing steam cars. It also advertised a roadster termed the "Steam Bobcat." None was built, although one MacDonald sedan is known to have been made.

MACKENZIE • England 1899

Electric phaetons and dog-carts built in Lambeth, London, and based closely on the Riker.

MAD • France 1919

A range of voiturettes from Levallois-Perret, Seine, shown at the 1919 Paris Salon.

MADELVIC • Scotland 1898-1900

Madelvic electrics were built at Granton, Edinburgh, but the vehicles proved impractical and the company lasted less than two years.

MADISON • USA 1915-1921

Madisons were assembled cars made in Anderson, Indiana, in roadster and touring car form. One model was appropriately called the "Dolly Madison" model, the misspelled first name (it should be "Dollie") designed apparently to honour the wife of the fourth US President, James Madison. Rutenber four-cylinder engines were used throughout (excepting a Herschell-Spillman V-8 which was offered, briefly, in 1916.)

MADOU • France 1922-1926

This strange example of "badge engineering" was a small batch of Marguerite cars sold under the name of Cora Madou, a famous actress of the day, as a special order by her rich boyfriend.

MADOZ • France 1921

Powered by a 175cc two-stroke engine and also known as the "Propulcycle," this light cyclecar was built in Nanterre, Seine.

1921 22hp Maiflower two-seater

MAF • Germany 1908-1922

Air-cooled in-line four-cylinder cars designed by the works owner, Hugo Ruppe (whose father and brothers owned the Piccolo-Apollo car factory.) Hugo Ruppe left MAF in the early 1920s, designed the first DKW two-stroke engines and afterwards built Bekamo motorcycles in Berlin. The MAF was made at Markranstadt, near Leipzig. Pre-1914 models ranged from 1192cc to 1910cc. After the war the range included an 1833cc version, some improved 1230cc pre-war models, and also an ohc 3483cc four-cylinder car. Apollo took over MAF when production ceased.

MAG • Hungary 1911-1934

Built on German lines, the MAG cars were quite heavy and not always in line with the latest developments. Real production, on Hungary"s first moving assembly line, started after the First World War with 1790cc four-cylinder and 2407cc six-cylinder cars, which proved very popular as taxicabs. Udvarda drove one of the "Mago-Six" models in the Monte Carlo Rally.

MAGENTA • England 1972 to date

A cheap, easy-to-build sports car, the Magenta features a rigid ladder frame, and a simple glassfiber body designed to accept an MG 1100 subframe and running gear. Several Magentas have achieved success in rallying, and hundreds of kits have been sold.

MAGNET • England 1903

A range of three cars: 12 hp twin-cylinder and 16 hp and 24 hp fours.

1907 28hp Maja of Graf Hugo Boos

MAGNET • Germany 1921-1924

This Berlin-Weissensee firm produced motorcycles and three-wheelers pre-1914, and in the early 1920s offered a small 789cc four-cylinder car.

MAGNETIC • England 1921-1926

American Entz magnetic transmission was the distinctly novel feature of the Magnetic. Burt McCollum sleeve-valve engines of two capacities were offered, a four-cylinder of 2614cc, and an eight of 5228cc. A 2888cc six-cylinder ohv power unit appeared in 1924.

MAHINDRA • India 1947 to date

This highly successful company started assembly of Willys Jeeps from CKD kits, progressing to manufacture after a 1954 agreement with Willys-overland. The first diesel jeep was launched in 1975 (the company builds Peugeot diesels in a modern engine plant.) Mahindra also has one of India"s most up-to-date vehicle plants, built in 1983 for Nissan.

MAIBOHM • USA 1916-1922

Built initially in Racine, Wisconsin, and later in Sandusky, Ohio, the Maibohm was a conventional assembled car, using a four-cylinder engine up to 1919 and a Falls six from 1918 to 1922, the four being dropped in 1919. Open and closed coachwork was available, and bodies were built by Millspaugh & Irish. The Maibohm became the Courier in 1922.

MAICO • Germany 1956-1958

Still a well-known motorcycle factory, Maico produced an improved version of the little Champion car. The engines, 452cc twin-cylinder two-strokes, were built by Heinkel, the bodywork by Baur of Stuttgart. The engine was behind the driven rear axle, the gearbox in front of it.

MAIFLOWER • England 1919-1921

This Model T Ford-based device was built by army captains M Price and A I Flower. A newly fabricated rear end and alterations to the front transverse suspension were variations on the standard Ford chassis.

MAIL • England 1903

A four-seater 8 hp single-cylinder model and a six-seater 12 hp twin-cylinder coupé were sold by this shortlived company.

MAILLARD • France 1900-c. 1903

Two models of the Maillard were offered, a 6 hp and a 10 hp (uprated to 8 hp and 12 hp in 1901.. These were also license-built in Belgium as Aquilas.

1919 6/12hp Majola

MAISON PARISIENNE • France 1897-c. 1898

M Laboure of La Maison Parisienne assembled Benz cars under license for the French market. Some were sold under the name "l'Eclair." In 1898 the company's engineer, Serex, designed a flat-twin car, still on Benz lines, which ran in the Marseille-Nice Race.

MAJA • Austria 1906-1908

Ferdinand Porsche designed this 4520cc four-cylinder car for the Jellinek-owned Osterreichische Automobil Gesellschaft. The name came from Jellinek's younger daughter; the older one was Mercédès. However, Maja cars, actually built by Austro-Daimler on behalf of Jellinek, failed to gain much popularity. Improved "Maja" models were built by Austro-Daimler until the First World War.

MAJESTIC • France 1926-1930

Big cars made in Paris by MM. Gadoux and Lelong with an ohv straight-eight engine of 2996cc. Few were built.

MAJOLA • France 1911-1928

From 1911-1914 the St Denis, Seine, works only offered one 1327cc model. In 1914 it presented an ohc 984cc 6hp car. In 1921 it announced a 1393cc model. The two latter models remained in production until the end, the ohc car being enlarged to 1086cc in 1922.

MAJOR • France 1920-1921

Once again M Violet was responsible for the design of the Major cyclecar, built in Courbevoie, Seine. Powered by a twin-cylinder two-stroke engine of 1060cc, it featured a friction transmission. It was later sold under the name of Mourre.

MALCOLM • England 1906

The Yukon Motor & Engineering Co of Balham, South London, built "Malcolm" engines with two, four, or six separately cast cylinders. It also made the Malcolm car "in all powers." Its 6/8 hp twin had a pressed steel frame, chain drive and a honeycomb radiator.

MALCOLM • USA 1915

A New York-built 13 hp four of attractive appearance, retailing at $595.

MALCOLM JONES • USA 1914-1915

A four-cylinder watercooled cyclecar from Detroit.

1920 Major sporting cyclecar

MALLALIEU • England 1974 to date

The Mallalieu Bentley Specials owe their name to Derry Mallalieu, a one-time Bugatti racer. Both the Barchetta and Mercia are based on the 1950s Mk 6 chassis. Most are exported to America.

MALLIARY • France 1901

A 6 cv shaft-drive voiturette from Puteaux (Seine.)

MALLORCA • Spain 1975 to date

A Lotus Seven-based sports car with 1438cc or 1756cc Seat engine.

MALVERNIA • England 1897-1913

T C Santler, who claimed to have helped Karl Benz design his first car and to have produced a car in 1887, built two Benz-like cars in his Malvern Link, Worcs., workshops in 1897. Front-engined light cars appeared in 1906 and 1913.

MANCH-ASTER • England 1904-1905

As its name suggested, this 20 hp Aster-engined car was built in Manchester. It was assembled by Bennett & Carlisle, predecessor of Newton & Bennett, which sold the NB car.

MANEXALL • USA 1921

The Manexall was merely the Cyclomobile fitted with a rear deck. To achieve this the wheelbase was increased to 102 inches. Price was $475.

MANIC • Canada 1969-1971

Built in Montreal and Granby, Quebec, this was a glassfiber sports car based on a Renault floorpan.

MANNESMANN • Germany 1923-1929

Made by the Mannesmann brothers at Remscheid, Mannesmann cars had 1289cc four-cylinder 20 hp engines. In 1927 a 2395cc ohv eight of advanced design was built, followed by a Rickenbacker-engined sv 5130cc eight (Rickenbacker engines were then made by the Rasmussen-owned Audi works.) Before building cars the Mannesmanns produced Mulag lorries.

1976 Mallalieu Bentley

1970 Marcos Mantis

MANON • France 1903-c. 1905

A light car with either a 6 hp or 9 hp engine, built by H Chaigneau of Paris and sold in England as the Mohawk-Manon.

MAPLEBAY • USA 1908

An air-cooled 22 hp runabout from Crookston, Minn., with a Reeves four and friction drive.

MARATHON • USA 1908-1915

Built initially in Jackson, Tennessee, Marathon cars were produced in Nashville after 1910. The 1913 range included three big fours: a 2837cc 25 hp, a 4177cc 35 hp, and a 6758cc 45 hp.

MARATHON • USA 1920

The Marathon of Elkhart, Indiana, was no relation to the Nashville Marathon. The Elkhart-built Marathon was strictly an export concern, though if any cars were actually made and/or exported, they were few indeed. The Marathon Company and the Crow-Elkhart Company, another Elkhart concern, were taken over by Century Motors and the Marathon became the Morriss-London.

MARATHON • France 1954-1955

This was a last attempt by Rosengart to re-enter the automobile field, with a 750cc Panhard flat-twin-engined car.

MARAUDER • England 1950-1953

Built mainly from Rover parts, the Marauder was marketed by Wilks Mackie & Co Ltd of Dorridge, Birmingham. The 2103cc Rover engine was installed in a box-section chassis clothed with a handsome touring body. Several were built.

MARBLE-SWIFT • USA 1903-1905

A friction-drive two-seater with a 10 hp twin-cylinder engine, built in Chicago.

MARCA-TRE-SPADE • Italy 1908-1911

Four-cylinder ioe 24 hp cars with four-speed gearboxes, from a famous gunsmith.

MARCHAND • Italy 1898-1909

This cycle and sewing-machine works at Piacenza first built a number of rear-engined Decauville-type cars, then progressed to front-engined cars, mostly four- and six-cylinder models of up to 60 hp.

MARCOS • Wales • England 1959-to date

Between them, Jem *MAR*sh and Frank *COS*tin contrived to build one of the prettiest sports cars of all time, the Marcos Volvo (the same shell was subsequently fitted with a variety of Ford engines.) Marsh alone must take responsibility for the ugly but nonetheless successful Mini-Marcos, and also the Dennis Adams-styled Mantis with which Marcos was forced to close its books after 32 had been built. In 1981 Marsh relaunched the classic Marcos 1800 shape in 1.6, 2.0 and 3.0-litre form, with a new Rover V-8-powered model, the Mantula, appearing in coupé form in 1984 and as an open Spyder in 1986. In 1989 the Mini-Marcos was relaunched. For 1991 came the lower-priced Ford Cortina-based Martini coupé and Spyder. Since then Marcos has moved upmarket, and now offers the choice between Rover based V-8s and a 4.6-litre Ford sourced V-8 unit in its Mantaray model. The Mantis/LM also boasts such units, allied to even wilder styling. The cars now have strengthened chassis, leather trim and a far more professional air to them than their kit-built ancestors.

1907 Marie de Bagneux tricar

MARCUS • England 1919

A cyclecar built by G L Marcus of Golders Green, North London.

MARENDAZ • England 1926-1936

Early Marendaz Specials used sv 1.5-litre Anzani engines, sometimes in supercharged form; for 1932 D. M. K. Marendaz offered a small six of 1900cc. The following year a 2.5-litre car, the 17/97, was announced. For 1935 a new 2-litre six by Coventry-Climax was marketed. Production of these handsome sports cars with flexible external exhaust pipes and Bentley-like radiators was transferred from south-west London to Maidenhead in 1932. Among pre-war drivers was Mrs Alfred Moss, mother of future racing driver Stirling, who actively campaigned an attractive white two-seater.

MARGARIA • France 1910-1912

A 2297cc four-cylinder car shown at the 1910 Paris Salon, the shaft-drive Margaria sold for Fr 5,000 in chassis form. In 1912 M. Margaria teamed up with M Launay to build the SCAP.

MARGUERITE • France 1920-1928

Made by the Marguerite brothers in Courbevoie, Seine, these were light cars with Ruby and SCAP 1093cc engines. They were also sold under the name of Morano-Marguerite, Induco and Madou.

MARIE DE BAGNEUX • France 1907

A single-seat three-wheeler, M. Marie de Bagneux"s belt-driven car weighed 220 lb and had a 1.25 hp De Dion engine.

MARIENFELDE • Germany 1899-1902

Owned by Daimler directors without Gottlieb Daimler"s official consent, Marienfelde offered, among other models, a copy of the 5900cc four-cylinder Daimler. Daimler of Canstatt eventually took over the Marienfelde works and used them for the manufacture of heavy trucks.

MARION • USA 1904-1914

Starting life as a transverse air-cooled 16 hp, by 1906 the Indianapolis Marion had acquired more conventionally positioned power units of 16 hp and 24 hp. The shaft-drive 1907 20 hp four-cylinder Marion had a two-speed

Hassler gear incorporated in the differential unit. An experimental 9455cc V-12 was built in 1908. By 1913 Marions were being built in a former Willys Overland factory, operating a night shift to cope with the flow of orders. "Much better finished and with better style than the average American car around this price", the $1,475 Marion had right-hand steering and central gear and brake levers.

MARION-HANDLEY • USA 1916-1920

An assembled six-cylinder car, the Marion-Handley was a continuation of the earlier Marion automobile. Continental engines were used, except for a few cars at the end of the company's existence, which used a Rutenber. The company was reorganized and became the Handley-Knight, which in turn became the Handley and was finally absorbed by Checker.

MARITIME • Canada 1912-1915

Apart from two prototypes, the Maritime Six was no more than an assembled Palmer-Singer from St John, New Brunswick.

MARLBOROUGH • France • England 1906-1926

Though the chassis and engine of the Marlborough were French, the car was virtually unknown in that country, being assembled for sale in Britain by T B André (later famous as maker of Hartford shock absorbers,) using Malicet et Blin chassis. First shown at Olympia in 1906 in single-cylinder 8 hp form, twin-cylinder 10/12 hp, and four-cylinder 14 hp models by Gauthier & Co (also agent for CCC,) the early Marlboroughs had round radiators and hoods. A change of direction came in 1912 with a near-cyclecar, the vee-radiatored 8 /10 hp of 1094cc, which had grown into a more substantial light car by the outbreak of war. Postwar, a 1087cc CIME-engined version was offered, and there were a few sporting models with British Anzani and Coventry-Climax engines, the latter being a 2-liter six with four-wheel brakes announced in 1925, which never saw production. Some 2,000 Marlboroughs were built.

MARLBOROUGH-THOMAS • England 1923-1924

Only a few of these exciting sports cars were built, T B Andre and J G Parry Thomas producing them from a shed at Brooklands Motor Course. The engine was a dohc 1.5-liter unit; the use of leaf-valve springs was a distinctive Thomas feature.

MARMON • USA 1902-1933

The Nordyke & Marmon Company of Indianapolis dated back to 1851. From 1902 to 1908, Marmon built pressure-lubricated air-cooled V-4s designed by Howard

1923-25 Marmon coupé, bodied by Hume

c1914 Marlborough 10hp two-seater

Marmon, joined in 1908 by a 60 hp V-8. Big fours of 40 /45 hp and 50/ 60 hp were introduced for 1909, and in 1911 the Marmon Wasp six-cylinder racer won the first Indianapolis "500" race. In 1914 two models, the four-cylinder "32" (5213cc) and the six-cylinder "48" (9383cc,) were listed. The advanced "34" ohv six (5565cc) was launched in 1916. A development was still in production eleven years later, alongside the "Little Marmon" 3115cc straight-eight, which heralded an all-eight policy lasting until 1931, when the 8046cc alloy-engined V-16, one of the great American classics, appeared. It was the sole model offered in 1933, though a backbone-chassis V-12 was on the stocks. The Marmon name survived on trucks. From 1929-1931 Marmon offered an eight at less than $1,000, under the Roosevelt marque name.

LA MARNE • USA 1920

The La Marne, successor to the Richard car, was an eight-cylinder automobile with a 128-inch wheelbase and a touring car price of $1,485. Few were produced.

MAROT-GARDON • France 1898-1904

Starting with racing tricycles, by 1900 this firm from Corbie (Somme) had progressed to a 4.5 cv "miniature carriage."

MARQUETTE • USA 1912

Succeeding Welch and Rainier, the Marquette was built in two models, with pair-cast engines of 6435cc and 6757cc, at prices of $3,000 and $4,000 respectively.

MARQUETTE • USA 1929-1931

A small side-valve six priced at $990-$1,060, briefly produced by Buick as a separate marque.

MARQUEZ • France 1930

Streamlined fwd cars of which very few were made, using a straight-eight ohv SCAP engine of 2344cc.

MARR • USA 1903-1904

Marr of Detroit subcontracted an order for 100 Marr Autocars to the Fauber Manufacturing Co of Elgin, Illinois, but the marque died when the Fauber factory burned down in August 1904.

MARRIOTT • England 1901-1902

A 2.75 hp De Dion-engined quadricycle from St Albans, Herts.

MARS • England 1904-1905

A 4 hp White & Poppe engine powered this two-speed tricar from Finchley, North London.

MARS • Germany 1904-1908

Famous for the Mars motorcycles of the 1920s (with 956cc Maybach flat-twin engines,) Mars, of Norimberk-Doos, earlier produced cars with one- and two-cylinder Korting engines and Maurer friction drive.

MARSEEL (MARSEAL) • England 1919-1925

The Coventry-built Marseel was produced by D. M. K. Marendaz and one Seelhaft. A 1.5-liter four-cylinder Coventry-Climax engine was used. In 1923 Seelhaft departed and the spelling was anglicized. The 1.25-liter 11/27 joined the 1.5-liter, while an ohv six of 1750cc also put in a brief appearance.

MARSH • England 1904-1905

A 3.5 hp Tri-Car from Kettering, Northants, the Marsh had the curious option of wheel or side-tiller steering, and could run on gasoline or paraffin.

MARSH • USA 1921-1924

The Marsh was built in Cleveland, and the first models built were powered by a four-cylinder Lycoming engine. Wheelbase was 114 inches. In 1923 this was extended by 3 inches and a six-cylinder Continental engine substituted. At best, Marsh was a hand-to-mouth proposition, and only four fours and two sixes were built before the factory burned down in 1924, destroying two more cars.

Max de Martini's 20hp Martini

MARSHALL • USA 1920-1921

The Marshall has always confused historians, as it was actually a Norwalk sold by a Chicago distributor named Marshall. The Norwalk, in turn, was manufactured by Piedmont and was similar to other Piedmont-built cars like the Lone Star, Stork Kar, Bush, and Alsace. A four-cylinder Lycoming engine was used on all Marshall (and Norwalk Six) cars.

MARSHALL-ARTER • England 1912-1915

Formerly maker of the "QED," Marshall-Arter of Hammersmith, London, manufactured a handsome two-seater with 1244cc Chapuis-Dornier engine.

MARTA • Hungary 1912-1914

To cope with the atrocious Hungarian roads, Marta cars were strong and heavy vehicles, based on Westinghouse designs. Built at Arad (which became part of Romania after the First World War,) Martas were offered with sv four-cylinder engines of 22 hp, 30 hp, and 45 hp, the last with chain drive.

MARTIN • France 1907

A manufacturer of voiturettes at Saint-Germain-en-Laye (Seine-et-Oise.)

MARTIN • Canada 1911

Possibly the only car ever built in a church, this friction-drive high-wheeler sold only two.

MARTIN • USA 1920-1922

The Martin was a motorcycle which attempted to pass itself off in its sales pitch as an economical automobile in the same fashion as Ner-a-Car. It had a twin-cylinder engine and sold for $250. Martin also built a clumsy-looking three-wheeler, the Scootmobile.

MARTIN • USA 1927-1932

Designed by Miles H Carpenter, formerly of Phianna, and built by the M P Moller Company of Hagerstown, Maryland, this midget car underwent tremendous promotion between 1928 and 1932. Produced and promoted by Capt. J V Martin of aviation fame, the $200 Martin failed to excite anyone who could have aided the venture. With a four-cylinder Cleveland motorcycle engine, the disc-wheeled two-passenger Martin coupés (prototypes only) had 60-inch wheelbases. The crate in which the car was to be delivered would become its garage. The promoters also had plans for an export Martin which would be sold abroad under the name "Dart," and the car's 1929 prospectus used the Dart name and insignia. Only two or three prototypes constituted the entire production of this ill-fated venture.

MARTINI • Switzerland 1897-1934

This famous armaments factory also made stationary engines, and in 1897 built a rear-engined twin-cylinder car with tube ignition. Front-engined cars on Panhard lines appeared in 1899, and in 1903 Martini began building Rochet-Schneiders under license in a new factory at St-Blaise, which passed into English control in 1906 and was reacquired by Swiss capital in 1908. Big pair-cast fours were its stock-in-trade, though ohv voiturettes of 1087cc appeared in 1908, and a team ran in that year's Coupe des Voiturettes at Dieppe. A sleeve-valve 25 hp was listed in 1913, and in 1914 came the 2614cc 12 cv Sport, with an ohc engine boasting four valves per cylinder in hemispherical heads. The range was now from a 1357cc four to the 18 cv of 3563cc. In 1921 the first new post-war Martini, the 18/45cc type FN, appeared, and in 1924 the firm was acquired by Swiss engineer Steiger, who brought out a 3.1-liter six in 1926. Two sixes of 15 cv and 20 cv were listed in 1929, but the following year license production of the 2.5-liter Wanderer six began. Martini's last fling was a 4.4-liter monobloc six, type NF, which appeared early in 1931. Total Martini production was around 2,000 cars.

1922 MASE 10hp Sports

MARUTI • India 1980 to date

Builds the 800cc three-cylinder Suzuki Alto minicar under the name "Standard.."

MARVEL • France 1905-1908

Built in Paris, Marvel cars were conventional four-cylinder vehicles of 14 hp to 30 hp. The last model was a 15 hp of 2799cc.

MARYLAND • USA 1900-1901

A solid-tired steam car from Luke, Maryland, with a 12 hp twin-cylinder engine.

MARYLAND • USA 1900-1910

Built by the Sinclair-Scott Company, manufacturer of canning machinery, farm equipment and car components, these ohc 3.3-liters were initially known as "Ariels." Total production was 100 cars.

MASCOT • France 1906

A range of two- and four-cylinder cars from 8 hp to 24 hp, shown at Olympia in 1906.

MASCOTTE • England 1919-1921

A Peters engine of 1645cc initially powered the Mascotte, though later examples used a 1795cc version. Only a few examples of this London-built light car were constructed.

MASE • France 1921-1924

The Manufacture d'Automobiles, d'Outillage et de Cycles de Saint-Etienne made a small batch of sports cyclecars with an interesting 995cc och engine. They were also available with a 1097cc power unit.

MASERATI • Italy 1926 to date

See panel overleaf

MASON • USA 1906-1910

The swiftest and strongest two-cylinder car in America," the 1906 24 hp Mason from Des Moines, Iowa, sold for $1,250 and was Fred Duesenberg"'s first design. In 1910 the cars became known as "Maytags."

MASS • France 1903-1923

Built in Courbevoie, Seine, for the English market, the Mass took its name from its importer, Mr Masser-Horniman (from 1912 it was sold in its homeland under the name of its constructor, Pierron.) Initially there were singles of 4.5 hp and 6 hp, but in 1905 two- and four-cylinder cars

MASERATI • Italy 1926 to date

The Maserati brothers, Alfieri, Bindo, Carlo, Ettore, Ernesto, and Mario, were associated with motor cars from the very early days. Alfieri, Ernesto, and Bindo built two 2-liter Grand Prix cars for Diatto in 1925, then took them over and linered them down to 1.5 liters when Diatto withdrew from racing a year later. The new car, driven by Alfieri, won the 1926 Targa Florio, its first race. Maserati made its name with racing cars with four, six and eight (even 16) cylinders of 1088cc to 4995cc, though road-going cars with detuned racing engines did appear during the 1930s. Even one of the fearsome *sedici cilindri* (two straight-eights mounted in parallel, with the crankshafts geared together) was converted into a road car.

c. 1933 Maserati eight-cylinder sports (above.) Maserati 1970s style, elegance and engineering (below)

In 1937 Omer Orsi took over control, though the Maserati brothers stayed on until 1947, when they left to found OSCA. Racing cars were again the mainstay of the company after the war, most famous being the 250F designed by Giaocchino Colombo in 1953, and raced until 1958 in various forms by drivers including Moss, Hawthorn and Fangio. Then Maserati decided to withdraw from competition, concentrating on a range of expensive sports cars with the six-cylinder 3485cc 300S engine. However, the 1994cc and 2890cc "Birdcage" Maseratis enjoyed some competition success in the early 1960s in private hands.

In 1969 Citroën took over control of Maserati for approximately 1,000 million lire. The Modena factory then built about two-and-a-half cars a day, as well as some 30 engines for the Citroën Maserati SM grand touring model. In 1975 Maserati announced that it was going out of business, but was rescued at the eleventh hour by the De Tomaso group. It currently offers the mid-engined V-6 Merak of 2965cc, and the smaller Merak 2000; a mid-engined 4719cc V-8 Bora; the 4930cc Khamsin V-8; and the dohc 4136cc V-8 Quattroporte, available with coupé or limousine coachwork.

The 4.9-liter Royale luxury sedan appeared in 1976 and is still in production. In 1982 Maserati launched the 2.0-liter V-6 Biturbo sedan, a Spyder convertible following in 1984. Derivatives of this were still the mainstay of production in 1992. From 1984-1988 Chrysler had a minority stake in Maserati; the 1988 TC Coupé was the child of this union. In 1990 Fiat took a 49 per cent share in Maserati. The latest Maserati is the new 162 mph Shamal 3.2-liter, and in late 1993 the mid-engined Chubasco supercar, with a modified Shamal engine, went into production. Good as they were, these were perhaps not pure super cars in the essential Maserati mold, and it was with considerable relief that the new Maserati company, with new directors, new factory and an all-new car, the 3200 GT coupé, arrived in 1998. This car, with its low, long fronted, traditional fastbacked coupé design returns Maserati to the super car fold.

appeared. The 1907 range was most complex, with a 573cc single, 1005cc twin and fours of 3403cc, 4787cc, 5420cc, 6872cc, and the biggest Mass of all, the 30/40 hp of 8015cc. A monobloc 10/12 hp appeared in 1912, and in 1913 came a long-stroke six of 5429cc. The 1914 range were all Ballot-engined, culminating in a 5340cc four, but only a 2800cc 15.9 hp survived the war.

MASSEY-HARRIS • Canada 1900-1902

Canada's first series-production gasoline vehicles, these were tricycles and quadricycles with De Dion engines.

MASTERBILT SIX • USA 1926-1927

Three Masterbilt cars were built in all, a seven-passenger sedan, a two-door sedan and a coupé. An air-cooled car, the Masterbilt had a modified Franklin engine. Built by the Govro-Nelson Co of Detroit, the car was designed by Victor Gorvreau, who had previously been associated with Pan.

1926-27 Masterbilt Six

1910 Mass 15hp two-seater

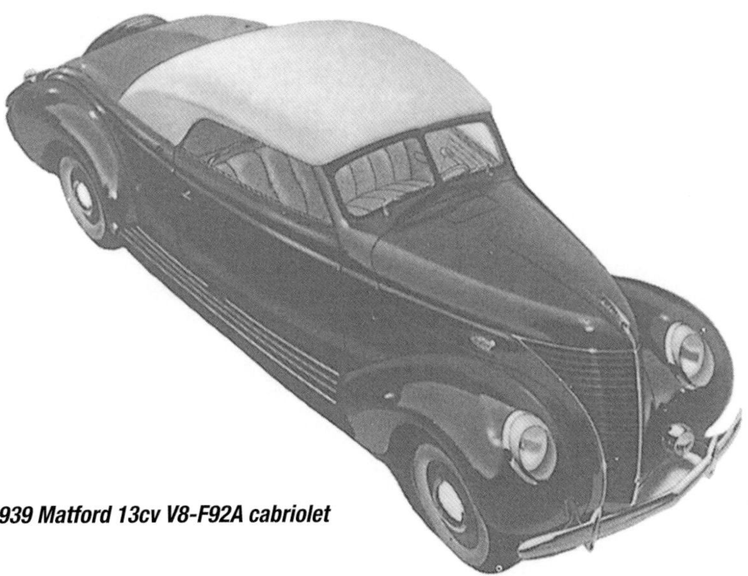

1939 Matford 13cv V8-F92A cabriolet

MATAS, SRC • Spain 1917-1925

The first Matas cyclecars, with front suspension by a transverse spring, had 8/10 hp Dorman engines; soon Continental engines, imported from the USA, were being fitted. The design was subsequently sold to another Barcelona firm, Stevenson, Romagosa y Compana, which built the cars under the name "SRC."

MATCHLESS • England 1906-1907, 1913-1929

This famous motorcycle works at Plumstead, Kent, showed a 6 hp twin-cylinder Fafnir-engined runabout at the 1906 Stanley Show. A three-wheeler cyclecar appeared in 1913 and, post-war, a very few integral-construction cyclecars with fwb and ifs appeared, powered by a flat-twin of 1250cc.

MATFORD • France 1934-1939

Henry Ford needed to expand his French production as his Asniéres, Seine, plant was too small, and Emile Mathis needed finance, so these two individualists struck up an often stormy relationship which resulted in the production of the Ford V-8 at the Mathis plant in Strasbourg under the "Matford" label. Initially the 30 hp V-8 was produced, then, in 1935, Dearborn created the 22 hp "Alsace" engine for France (Dagenham also adopted it.) Matfords were generally better styled than their British counterparts, and some handsome cabriolet models appeared. Mathis broke with Ford in 1939, but plans to transfer V-8 production to a Bordeaux factory were scotched by the outbreak of war.

MATHOMOBILE • Belgium 1980 to date

VW-based plastic-bodied Bugatti T35 replica, with flying helmet and goggles supplied!

MATHESON • USA 1903-1912

The first Mathesons were built in the factory of the recently defunct Holyoke company, but in 1906 the firm moved to Wilkesbarre, Penn. Initially a 24 hp ohv four was listed; by 1906 chain-drive fours of 40/45 hp and 60/65 hp were cataloged at prices ranging from $5,000 to $7,500. Chain drive was featured on most models until 1910 (except the 50 hp six of 1909.) By the end of production only the 5213cc "Silent Six" was available.

MATHIEU • Belgium 1902-1908

Sold in England as the Beckett and Farlow, the Mathieu was claimed to be "simple, reliable, noiseless... can be started without jerk." One-, two-, or four-cylinder engines were offered. At the 1907 Paris Salon, fours of 18/24 hp (3770cc) and 30/40 hp (6902cc) were exhibited.

MATHIS • Germany • France 1905-1950

See panel

MATRA • France 1965 to date

Aerospace group Matra (Mécanique-Aviation-Traction) took over René Bonnet and continued to produce that firm"s sports cars, becoming better known, however, for Formula One racers. When its first own-design road-going car, the Matra 530, with V-4 Ford engine, failed to sell in sufficient numbers, Matra linked with Chrysler at the beginning of the 1970s to develop the Simca 1300-powered Bagheera sports coupé with three-abreast seating.

MAUDSLAY • England 1902-1914, 1923

An offshoot of the famous engineering company founded by Henry Maudslay, this Coventry-based firm began production in 1903 with a 14 hp en bloc three-cylinder car with an overhead camshaft, thought to be the first application of this principle on a production car. A fully pressured lubricated crankshaft was another advanced feature. Standard bodywork included a "convertible omnibus" rear section which lifted off to convert the car to an open tonneau, and the first-ever production shooting-brake, the "All-Round" car, a solid-tired car capable of carrying eleven passengers or "300 head of game, well hung." Early Maudslays had "coalscuttle" hoods, but by 1905 a conventional radiator and bonnet were in use; later that year came the celebrated round radiator and hood which recalled the company's marine boilers. The three-cylinder Maudslay was built until 1906 (a 25 hp version was introduced in 1904, along with two big sixes, exactly double the capacity of the threes.)

MATHIS

MATHIS • Germany • France 1905-1950

Emile Mathis was a leading car dealer in Strasbourg, Alsace, handling Fiat, De Dietrich, and Panhard-Levassor among other makes. The first car marketed under his own name was the Hermés (or Hermés-Simplex,) designed for him by the young Bugatti and built at Grafenstaden. Current for 1905-1906, it was built in 28, 40, and 98 hp forms, all Mercedes-like cars with chain drive. Then designer and racing-driver Esser created cars of 2025cc and 2253cc which were built under license from Stoewer. The first true Mathis appeared in 1913, in the guise of the 951cc (soon enlarged to 1029cc) Babylette. A 1131cc version appeared in 1914, forming the basis of post-war production. Other pre-1914 Mathis included the Baby, with engine and gearbox in unit, built in 1327cc and 1406cc models, plus two sv models of 1850cc and 3453cc and a 4.4-liter Mathis-Knight. The famous London store Harrods sold the Babylette under its own name. Post-war, with Alsace now in France, the small Mathis cars were built at a prodigious rate, and the marque soon became the fourth biggest in its new homeland. In 1921 came the vee-radiatored SB ohv 1.5-liter, developed from an ohc racer, while Mathis countered the 5 cv Citroën with a basic car of 760cc, which had electric lighting but no instruments or differential. Like the other little Mathis it featured a four-speed gearbox. Since 1920 Mathis had been experimenting with small sixes, the first production model, of only 1188cc, appearing in 1923. There was even a 1.7-liter ohc straight-eight in 1925, a depressing and gutless machine.

After producing a bewildering variety of small cars, Mathis pursued a single-model policy in 1927 with the 1.2-liter four-cylinder sv MY, joined the next year by the 1.8-liter Emysix. These stolid machines set the pattern for the early 1930s, though in 1930 there were bigger sixes of 2.4 and 4.1 liters, and 1931 saw two shortlived straight-eights. The larger of these, Type-FOH, was of 3 liters. The more modern Emyquatre, with ifs and synchromesh, appeared in 1933, but its Emyhuit sister had only just appeared when production of Mathis cars was ousted by the Matford. Mathis regained his factory just before the war, and resumed activity in 1946, after an attempt to interest the Americans in plastics-bodied cars. His post-war projects, an Andreau-styled three-wheeler and a 2.8-liter fwd flat-six, failed to reach production. His plant was bought by Citroën in 1954.

c. 1913 Mathis Babylette 8hp

1935 Mathis 'Emyquatre' sedan

1905 Maudslay 15hp phaeton

A four-cylinder range had been announced in 1905, and after 1906 nothing else was made. The 1907 range consisted of a 20/30 hp and a 35 /45 hp, both with four-speed gearboxes with overdrive top. Maudslay"s most famous model was the "Sweet Seventeen" introduced in October 1909, the last production Maudslay. After the war the firm concentrated on commercial vehicles, apart from an advanced 2-liter twin ohc 15/80 hp six with four-wheel brakes, of which three examples would have been shown at Olympia in 1923, had not the show landaulette been destroyed at the coachbuilders. Chassis price was £825, but the decision was taken to shelve the project after prototypes only had been built.

MAURER • Germany 1908-1909, 1923-1924

A complicated story, because Ludwig Maurer, the founder of this factory, also founded Maurer-Union. His 1908 cars had 1520cc two-cylinder engines and friction drive. In 1923 a flat-twin two-stroke car followed a long succession of Maurer motorcycles.

MAURER-UNION • Germany 1900-1908

Ludwig-Maurer"s original design was his famous friction-drive car, built first with 1140cc single-cylinder 6 hp, afterwards 8 hp, engines. There was also a vee-twin version. Four-cylinder cars were under development when the Nürnburg factory went broke. It was bought by C J Braun's

1904 Maxim 24hp and its lift-up body

c. 1915 Maxwell 25hp tourer

1935 Maybach Type SW35 Sport Cabriolet

Kaiser car works (associated with Premier.) Soon afterwards, Maurer's wife Johanna "founded" the new Maurer works on behalf of her husband. Many other car producers copied Maurer designs, especially the friction drive, though only a few, like Mars, actually bothered to pay for the Maurer license.

MAUSER • Germany 1923-1927

A famous rifle and revolver manufacturer, Mauser first built a two-wheeler car, the "Mauser-Einspurauto." In 1923 came an ohv four-wheeler with a 1569cc four-cylinder engine.

MAVERICK • USA 1953-1955

Not to be confused with Ford's model of the same name, the Maverick was a large car with room for only three passengers. It used a Cadillac chassis and engine with a glassfiber body. The floor was of marine plywood, the dashboard was spun copper and the seats were upholstered in plastic. About seven Mavericks were made before production ceased.

MAX • France 1920-1926

A small cyclecar made in Billancourt, Seine, with single-cylinder 350cc or vee-twin 483cc two-stroke engines. The smaller version had a friction transmission and the bigger, a conventional gearbox.

MAXIM • England 1903-1915

Sir Hiram Stevens Maxim of Maxim machine-gun fame built this car, sold in limited numbers only. In 1904 there were two models, a 2281cc 16 hp twin and a 24 hp four. The tonneau body was hinged at the rear so that it could be lifted to inspect the mechanism for service or repair.

MAXIMAG • Switzerland 1922-1928

Motosacoche, founded by the Dufaux brothers, was famed for motorcycles and Mag engines. It built ohc 5 cv four-cylinder voiturette engines of 1904cc from 1914, but did not make a complete car until 1922. The 5 cv Maximag was a sporting two-seater, still of 1094cc, but with side-valves. A four-seater 7 cv (1593cc) appeared shortly after. Some Maximags are believed to have been built in the Motosacoche branch factory in Lyon. Total output was around 200 cars. Some Maximags were built in the Motosacoche branch factory in Lyon using 1093cc Ruby engines from 1925-1927.

MAXWELL-BRISCOE, MAXWELL USA 1904-1925

Jonathan Dixon Maxwell and Ben Briscoe collaborated to create a 1647cc flat-twin runabout, followed by four-cylinder cars of up to 30/40 hp. In 1909 Maxwell-Briscoe was part of the United States Motor group, surviving its collapse in 1912 and producing Mascotte and Mercury models. Low-priced monobloc fours were the staple offerings thereafter. The 1921 "New Good Maxwell" was the prelude to Walter Chrysler's takeover in 1923 and the marque's replacement by the four-cylinder Chrysler two years later.

MAYBACH • Germany 1921-1940

After leaving Mercedes in 1907, Wilhelm Maybach collaborated with Graf Zeppelin to build aero engines, particularly for airships, and his Friedrichshafen factory also made marine engines and motorcycle power units before introducing a sv 5738cc six-cylinder car (the engine was also sold to Spyker in Holland.) First shown in 1921, the Maybach originally featured a two-speed pedal-controlled gearbox; Spohn, Glaser, Armbruster, Erdmann & Rossi, and Voll-Ruhrbeck were among the coachbuilders who clothed this high-quality chassis with exclusive bodywork. An ohv 6995cc engine appeared in the W5 of 1926, available with a schnellgang auxiliary two-speed gearbox. A 6922cc V-12 made its debut in 1929, and was developed into the Zeppelin model of 1930. From 1931 a 7977cc V-12 was also available. Some Zeppelins had the W5 six-cylinder; all had seven-speed gearboxes. The ohc SW series included the 3790cc SW38, current from 1934 to 1940; there were also 3.5-liter and 4.2-liter SW models. Always an expensive car, the Maybach could cost over DM 40,000 in V-12 Zeppelin form with custom coachwork.

MAYFAIR • England 1900

The Sports Motor Car Company of South Kensington, London, offered a range of De Dion-engined voiturettes similar to the Belgian Pieper; they may indeed have been imports. Its 8 hp "Sports Car" was the first car marketed under that title.

MAZDA • Japan 1960 to date

The Toyo Kogyo Cork company, founded in Hiroshima in 1920, built its first three-wheeled truck in 1931. The name "Mazda," the Zoroastrian god of good and light, was derived from that of the company's founder, Mr Matsuda. The first Mazda car, the 360 coupé, appeared in 1960, followed by the 600 (1962,) 800 Sedan (1964,) 1000 (1965,) and 1500 (1966.) Significantly, in 1967 Mazda announced its first rotary-engined model, the R-100, the start of a dedication to the Wankel principle that was to culminate in the first victory in the Le Mans 24 Hour Race by a rotary-engined car (and the first Japanese victory) in 1991. Mazda built its millionth rotary-engined car as early as 1978. A year later Ford acquired 25 per cent of Mazda with funds it had acquired by the sale of the waterfront site of its

Mazda's unique rotary engined RX-7

1967 Mazda L 10A

pre-war factory in Yokohama but could not take out of Japan. This enabled Mazda to gain a foothold in the USA by taking over a redundant Ford factory at Flat Rock, Michigan, where it builds Ford- and Mazda-badged cars.

Mazda's first forward drive car was the 1980 323, a line which has been progressively developed over the years. The current 323 range consists of fastback, hatchback, sedan, and estate models. The smallest 1992 Mazda is the 700cc minicar (Revue,) which in Japan replaces an earlier model also sold as the Ford Festiva. Another joint model is the 626 (alias Ford Telstar.) Mazda's sports cars are particularly attractive. The MX-3 coupé, sold in Japan as the Eunos Presso, is powered by a 1.8-liter V6, the world's smallest. The delightful rwd MX-5 (Eunos Cosmo) launched in 1989 is a return to the pure-bred sports car concept. The RX-7 is the latest rotary-engined Mazda, and the only rotary-engined sports car in the world. The Mazda 929 (Luce in Japan) was replaced in 1991 by the Sentia with 2.5 or 3.0-liter V6 power. Also new in 1991 was the Proceed Marvie 4x4 wagon.

For the 1990s the RX7 (still with the only reliable rotary engine application in the world) was given a sculptural new body design and sold well in America. The pretty little MX-5, or Miata as it was originally known in the USA, was lightly revized and as par to Mazda's tie-up with Ford, the European market was treated to a British-built version of the Ford Fiesta wearing Mazda badges and sporting a three-year warranty, as opposed to Ford's 12-month offering for an identical car! The fastbacked 323 made many sales, and in V-6 form became an unknown gem. Sadly, its 1998 model replacement looked more like an estate than a coupé and many observers were disappointed. The 626 models also evolved more conservatively, and the motoring press felt that Mazda had lost some of its design direction. The top-of-the-range 929 models sold well in America but made a minimal impact in Europe. By opening a new European design centre, Mazda aspires to inject some more locally orientated character into its cars. Despite its link with Ford, the history of fine design and advanced and daring engineering innovation at Mazda counts for much.

Mazda's sporty and smart MPV Concept idea

1993 Mazda RX-7

1922 McCurdy Six

1925 McFarlan SV Coach-Brougham

McCURDY • USA 1922

Only one McCurdy was built by the Hercules Corporation of Evansville, Indiana. The car was named after the president of the corporation. It had a 127-inch wheelbase, a Continental engine and wire wheels.

McFARLAN • USA 1910-1928

The McFarlan automobile was the product of a carriage works which had turned to motor car manufacture and, from the first cars made, the product became larger, more expensive and more prestigious. Several makes of engine were used in those first cars up to 1916, and a large Teetor-Hartley type was adopted in that year. Although many standard components went into the manufacture of the McFarlan, it was never regarded as an assembled car in the usual sense. In the autumn of 1920 the "TV" or Twin-Valve series was introduced, with enormous six-cylinder engines of McFarlan design and manufacture, requiring 18 spark plugs. A complete line of open and closed models commanded prices as high as $10,000 per car. A few fire engines and ambulances were also built on the TV chassis. The engines of this model were similar to those used on the Maxim fire apparatus, built in Middleboro, Mass., and the Maxim Company served as New England distributors for the McFarlan. In 1924 the company introduced the "SV" or Single-Valve six, a considerably less expensive car. It was not a success and was withdrawn in 1926. However, the Eight-in-Line series, which more closely resembled the big six but used a Lycoming eight-cylinder engine, was introduced in 1926 and, like the larger car, was built to the end of production. The 1928 models were sleeker and lower than their forebears, but few were made. Some 235 cars were built in McFarlan's best year; total production was about 2,090.

McGILL • USA 1920-1922

The McGill would have been a strictly conventional and uninteresting assembled car of its time had it not been for its four-wheel drive. It was promoted spasmodically around Fort Worth, Texas, where it was assembled, and the one pilot model probably constituted the entire production. The touring car featured a six-cylinder Continental engine and was to have sold for $2,385.

McINTYRE • USA 1908-1914

Successor to the Kiblinger (1907-1908,) this was a typical high-wheeler with two-cylinder engines of 12/14 hp and 16/18 hp and a four-cylinder 28/32 hp with shaft drive. This company also built the Imp cyclecar.

McKAY • Canada 1910-1914

Based on the US Penn (because the company"s engineer had no engineering experience,) McKays used 30 hp and 40 hp engines. Some 25 cars were built at Kentville, Nova Scotia, and a further 200-odd in a new factory at Amherst.

McKENZIE • England 1914-1927

An expensive four-cylinder light car built in Birmingham, the McKenzie was unusual for its day in having a four-speed gearbox.

McLACHLAN • England 1899

An omnivorous 2.5 hp motor capable of running on "gasoline, paraffin or benzoline" powered this car, available with three or four wheels. "If its performances are as satisfactory as its simplicity is marked," commented The *Autocar*, `it should meet with great success."

McLACHLAN • Canada 1899-1901

Canada's first production gasoline car, a friction-drive model on Benz lines, built in Toronto.

McLAREN • England 1969-1970

Launched in 1997, the McLaren F1 Supercar was born from that Grand Prix team's desire to produce the ultimate road-going race car, under the direction of designer Gordon Murray. The BMW engined V12 6.0-liter car can reach 231mph the fastest supercar speed yet. The F1 has a composite carbonfibre body and can carry three passengers abreast, with the driver central. Equally at home on public roads or the racing circuit, the car has an amazing ($1,000,000) price tag, making it both the fastest and most expensive car in the world.

McLAUGHLIN • Canada 1908-1942

One of Canada's most highly regarded carriage builders, McLaughlin of Oshawa, Ottawa, wanted to build an all-Canadian car to avoid the high tariff on imported cars, but the illness of its designer nullified this plan. Instead it began production of cars based on the four-cylinder Buick, but better-finished. McLaughlin became a wholly-owned subsidiary of General Motors in 1918; its cars were by then based on Oakland and Chevrolet as well as Buick chassis. In 1923 the company was renamed McLaughlin-Buick. Its products were marketed as plain "Buick" in England, where they attracted less import duty than the US version.

MEADOWS • England 1958-1959

Henry Meadows Ltd had long been established as an engine manufacturer when it appeared, somewhat surprisingly, with the Frisky Sport at the 1958 Motor Show. Designed by Gordon Bedson in association with Raymond Flower and Italian coachbuilder Michelotti, the Frisky had a ladder chassis with rubber torsion unit front suspension and a solid axle with motorcycle suspension units at the rear. Power came from a twin-cylinder two-stroke engine driving the closely coupled rear wheels by chain. Maximum speed was said to be 65 mph.

MEDIA • England 1913-1915

Forerunner of the Rhode, the Media (from its makers, Meade and Deakin) first appeared as an 8 hp JAP-engined cyclecar, but in 1914 two light fours, a 1093cc 8/10 hp, and a 1645cc 10/12 hp, both selling at £150, appeared.

MEDICI • England 1904-1906

A 10 hp twin-cylinder Tony Huber engine powered this 180-guinea voiturette built by J J Leonard of 20 Long Acre, London.

Mercèdes

MERCEDES • Germany 1901-1926

Emile Jellinek, Austro-Hungarian Consul at Nice and agent for Daimler cars, which he sold to his wealthy acquaintances, persuaded Wilhelm Maybach to design him lower, lighter and more powerful cars, which Jellinek named after his elder daughter, Mercedes. The first Mercedes, the 35 hp, had a 5913cc four-cylinder engine and combined the most modern design features, pressed-steel chassis, honeycomb radiator and gate gear-change, in a vehicle which finally broke with horse-carriage traditions and set the pattern for quality car design in Europe and America. The name Mercedes, chosen to improve the marque's sales prospects in France, was soon adopted by Daimler for its private cars. Developments of the 35 hp followed, under the name Mercedes Simplex; most famous were the 18/22 hp, the 6780cc 40/45 hp and the mighty 9240cc 60 hp, with overhead inlet valves and 80 mph performance; one of these won the 1903 Gordon Bennett Cup Race in Ireland when the official team of 90 hp cars had been destroyed in a fire which gutted the Cannstatt factory.

Maybach left Mercedes in 1907, his last designs for the company being sixes of 9480cc and 10,178cc. He was succeeded by Paul Daimler. The marque dominated the international racing scene before the First World War; touring models of the period included a wide variety of cars from 1570cc to a 9575cc four, as well as Knight-engined models, the 4055cc Mercedes surviving until 1923. Apart from this, the post-war range included the 7250cc ohc six, which Paul Daimler used for his supercharging experiments in 1921-1922, and two small ohc fours of 1568cc and 2600cc.

Ferdinand Porsche became chief designer in 1923, and shortly before the 1926 amalgamation between Mercedes and Benz he introduced a blown ohc six-cylinder of 6240cc, known as the 24/100/140 from its rated/unblown/blown power outputs. Porsche also created the Type K, developing 110 bhp unblown, 160 bhp blown.

King Edward VII's 24/28hp Mercedes, c.1904

1907 120hp Mercedes of Baron Pierre de Caters (right.)

MEDINGER • England 1913

A 1-liter two-stroke twin powered this sporting cyclecar, designed by Emile Médinger.

MEGY • France 1901-1903

With a primitive "automatic transmission" and clutch and brake operated by moving the steering wheel up and down, the Mégy bore promise of exceptional mechanical derangements.

LE MEHARI • France 1927

M Reynaud of Nouzonville, Ardennes, made this strange cyclecar with two 350cc two-stroke engines, each one driving a belt to one rear wheel.

MELEN • England 1913-1914

A twin-cylinder Alpha engine of 1104cc powered this Birmingham-built light car.

MENARD • Canada 1908-1910

A 16 hp high-wheeler designed by Byron Covert for "Moses" Menard of Windsor, Ontario, Canada's largest wagon dealer.

MENDIP • England 1913-1920

Founded at the time of the Napoleonic Wars, the Cutler"s Green Iron Works of Chewton Mendip, Somerset, made steam and gasoline commercial vehicles before building 1269cc four-cylinder light cars, mainly for local consumption. One survives.

MENEGAULT-BASSET • France 1907

Shown at the 1907 Paris Salon, this was a "simplified automobile with new organs transmitting directly and integrally the motive power to the driving wheels and suppressing the clutch, gearbox, differential, and other organs."

MENON • Italy 1898-1902

Treviso-built, the Menon was an early motor vehicle with a 3.5 hp single-cylinder engine. Production was on a small scale.

MERCEDES • Germany 1901-1926

See panel

MERCEDES-BENZ • Germany 1926 to date

See panel overleaf

MERCEDES-BENZ • Germany 1926 to date

The newly amalgamated Mercedes-Benz group could draw on a wealth of technical experience, Ferdinand Porsche heading a team which included Fritz Nibel and Nallinger (and later Rudolf Uhlenhaut and Max Sailer.) First fruit of the merger was a 1988cc six-cylinder, followed by a 2968cc six, known as the Stuttgart and Mannheim respectively. World famous, though built in limited numbers, were Porsche's supercharged ohc six-cylinder sports cars, the 6250cc K, the 6789cc S and the 7020 SS, SSK, and SSKL. Famous Mercedes of the 1930s were the 3444cc Mannheim six, the 4592cc Nürberg (enlarged to 4918cc in 1932,) the 2560cc Stuttgart and the ostentatious straight-eight Grosser Mercedes, with a supercharged 7655cc ohv engine, built in its initial form from 1930 to 1937 and, with a more modern chassis and swing axles, from 1938. An "economy class" Mercedes, the popular Type 170, with a 1692cc six-cylinder engine and independent front suspension, appeared in 1931, followed in 1933 by the 1962cc Type 200, but the rear-engined "Heckmotor" 130H (a 1308cc four) of 1934-35 enjoyed no lasting success. Sporting

1930 Mercedes-Benz 36/220S supercharged

Mercedes of the 1930s came with supercharged engines of 3796cc, 5018cc, and 5401cc, all straight-eights. The last pre-war 540K developed 115 bhp unsupercharged, 180 bhp with the blower engaged. Backed by the German state propaganda machine, Mercedes racing cars (and Auto Union) won most of the major races of the 1934-1939 era.

Rebuilding after the war took some time, and the first post-war model, the 1697cc 170V sv 4-cylinder, did not appear until 1947. Continuing a line begun before the war, Mercedes brought out a diesel-engined version of this car, the 170D. A breakaway from pre-war design came with the unitary-construction 180 series of 1954, but the classic Mercedes of that decade were without doubt the ohc six-cylinder 300S and 300SL sports models of 2996cc of 1952 onward, most famous in their original gull-wing coupé form. A sports-racing straight-eight derivative, the 300SLR, won many competition victories. The luxury Type 600, with an ohc V-8 of 6330cc, appeared in 1964.

Since 1971 the 6- and 8-cylinder S-class cars, with fuel-injection, have been flagships of the Mercedes fleet, though the diesel-engined models also sell well. The most powerful production Mercedes is the 6834cc ohc V-8 450 SEL model, with a 225 km/h (140 mph) top speed. A milestone was passed at the beginning of 1979, when the cheapest Mercedes model passed the DM 20,000 price tag.

In 1983 the 190 Series "compact executive car" was launched; a million were built in five years. Mercedes' comprehensive mid-range offerings include the 200E, 230E, 250D, 260E, 300E and 300D. The SL sports of 1989 was offered with a choice of three engines and boasted such safety features as a rollbar that deployed

automatically in the event of an accident. In 1991 Mercedes launched the new S Class luxury car range, the 300SE/SEL, 400SE/SEL, 500SE/SEL, and 600SE/ SEL, with engines from 3.2 to 6.0 liters (the latter a V-12) and such pioneering features as a five-speed automatic transmission, heated windshield wipers, servo-assisted doors and the world's first double-glazed side windows.

For the 1990s the Mercedes range, commandingly styled by the M-B design studio under Bruno Sacco, evolved into a leaner looking model line-up with reduced bulk and more curvacious freedom in their lines. The C class, round-headlamped E class and new S class were all exquisitely honed to look futuristic but also to reflect Mercedes' past design iconography. Mercedes entered the small-car market for the first time with its baby sized MPV, the A class, and in doing so created a new type of car with broad appeal. The firm's work on the Smart micro car also did likewise. A new, smaller roadster appeared in the form of the SLK model, and Mercedes also introduced the supercharger across its range via its Kompressor models. A tie-up with the Chrysler Corporation created Daimler-Chrysler, the world's biggest auto maker, with huge future potential in their respective chosen areas of activity. For Mercedes, the stunning 1999 Vision SLR concept car pointed to a future still aimed at the wealth- and image-conscious sectors of the market, yet with a more sporting overtone; fine testament to the firm's past glory on the racetrack.

Classic M-B sedan style (right.) 1956 Mercedes 300 SL coupé-Gullwing (top and middle)

1979 Mercury Marquis Brougham

The L-head Mercer Raceabout, 1922

Film star Raymond Massey with his 1948 Mercury Sedan

MERCER • USA 1910-1925

Succeeding the Roebling-Planche, the Mercer took its name from Mercer County, New Jersey, in which its factory at Trenton was situated. The first Mercers had T-head Beaver engines; a Speedster was the fastest 1910 model. Then chief engineer Finlay Robertson Porter produced a roadgoing adaptation of the Type 30-M racer, the immortal Type 35-R Raceabout, a stark two-seater designed to be "safely and consistently" driven at over 112 km/h (70 mph). It was produced alongside more sedate Mercers, which initially had four speeds against the Raceabout"s three. When Porter left in 1914 to build the FRP he was succeeded by Erik H Delling, who produced the F-head 22/70, which actually boasted a body with sides and a windshield, as well as other effete items such as left-hand drive and central gearshift, and an optional hood. In 1918 Mercer became part of the Hare's Motors Group, with Locomobile and Crane-Simplex. Delling was replaced by A C Schultz, whose Series 4 and 5 Sportsters even had electric starters. A 5.5-liter ohv Rochester-engined development of these was the "Car of Calibre's" sole offering in the last two years.

c.1922 Mercury 10hp on the Brooklands Test Hill

MERCER • USA 1931

The 1931 Mercer was an attempt to revive the earlier Mercer car, and three were built and exhibited. A Continental straight-eight was used and the chassis was built by Elcar. The car was handsomely designed with a slight vee radiator, but the Mercer, and Elcar, failed shortly after the introduction of the new car.

MERCURY • USA 1897

An opposed-twin 4 hp dos-á-dos built on Benz lines, but with chain and pinion transmission.

MERCURY • England 1905

Also known as Ivanhoes, these 24 hp fours were built by a London Weigel agency.

MERCURY • England 1914-1922

The original 12/14 Mercury from Twickenham, Middlesex, had a 1944cc monobloc four-cylinder engine. A 10 hp of 1287cc with cantilever rear springing was shown at Olympia in 1919.

MERCURY • USA 1918-1920

A relatively light car, the Mercury carried a wheelbase of 114 inches and used a Weidely four-cylinder engine. This car had a door situated in the floor to give the driver ready access to the service brake mechanism, but otherwise differed little from the rank and file of assembled cars. Production was small. It was built in Hollis, New York.

MERCURY • USA 1922

Like its Cleveland counterpart of two years earlier, this car, reportedly made in Belfast, New York, was listed as being available, although it was probably never built. Theoretically available either as a four or a six, both engines were supposedly of Mercury"s own manufacture. Price for the three-passenger coupé on the four-cylinder 128-inch wheelbase model was given at $4,875, and $5,625 for the similar body style on the 132-inch wheelbase six-cylinder chassis.

MERCURY • USA 1938 to date

Originally known as Ford-Mercury, this 3.9-liter V-8 model was intended to plug the gap between Ford and Lincoln. The "Ford" was dropped for 1940 when a four-door convertible was introduced; it was not particularly popular. The 1942 models were restyled with a low, wide grille. Post-war, the marque image began a move upmarket with

Mercury Cougar Coupé c.1998

the 1949 models, which had a new 4179cc engine; automatic transmission became available in 1951, and power-assisted steering in 1953. A year later came the first ohv V-8, a 4785cc unit later adopted by the Ford Thunderbird. From 1952 the Monterey name (initially seen on a vinyl-roofed hardtop of 1950) was applied to a new de luxe line. In 1954 came Lincoln-style ball-joint ifs and the Sun Valley, a transparent-roofed hardtop.

Mercurys of the 1956-59 era, notably the 1957 Turnpike Cruiser, were perhaps the most ornate cars of their day. Mercury's first car with other than a V-8 engine was the 1960 Comet compact, an enlarged Ford Falcon with the Ford 2360cc six. The new Ford short-stroke six was also available in the bigger Monterey, and three six-cylinder Mercurys were catalogued for 1962. A year later came the first V-8 Comet. Mercury gained a performance image in 1965 with the 320 bhp Comet Cyclone, and in 1967 came the Mustang-derived Cougar coupé, with a curious "waterfall" grille. The 1969 Marquis Brougham shared the Lincoln Continental"s bodyshell, though its engine displaced 7030cc to the Lincoln's 7538cc. By 1972 economy and rationalization were the keynotes; the latest Comet was little more than an upmarket Ford Maverick, while a small-car line was achieved by importing German Ford Capris. The 1972 range slotted carefully between Ford and Lincoln, the huge 7538cc Grand Marquis retaining Lincoln styling while, at the other end of the scale, the four-cylinder Bobcat paralleled Ford's 1540cc Pinto, and the Monarch was now a de luxe version of the Ford Granada. By 1977 the Marquis offered four-wheel disc brakes, but the Cougar name was now reserved for a more humble replacement. A "brand new European-size compact" for 1978, the Zephyr, was just a rebadged Ford Fairmont. The 1979 line-up embraced the Capri, Zephyr, Monarch, Cougar, and Marquis; the Grand Marquis offered tinted glass and "coach lamps."

By this time Mercury had fallen victim to overkill in the badge-engineering department, yet by the 1990s it had reasserted itself. It still used Ford models, but tweaked them in more than looks alone, often using only the larger engine options, and it also returned to placing its brand in higher specification ground, above mainstream Fords but below the Lincoln range. The sable model and the Mondeo /Contour based Mystique were good all-rounders and heralded better times for the marque. Mercury still offered the traditionally sized large cars that Americans have always loved, and the Mercury Grand Marquis sedan and the Cougar XR coupé more than satisfy American traditional tastes in an age when downsizing and lightening are to the fore.

MERCURY SIMPLEX • England 1904

A light car from the Anglo-French Motor Syndicate of Folkestone, Kent.

MEREDITH • England 1902

John Child Meredith of Birmingham, who also built the Abingdon cars, offered a 10 hp two-cylinder with "a new system of gearing" as well as a "Motor-car, smaller size."

MERKUR • Germany 1984-1990

The XR4Ti (a Sierra XR4 with a flawed American powertrain) and Scorpio represented an ill-starred attempt to sell German Fords to the USA as a new marque.

MERZ • USA 1914

A cyclops-headlamp cyclecar from Indianapolis, designed by racing driver C C Merz.

MESSERSCHMITT • Germany 1958-1961

Aircraft designer Willy Messerschmitt created the three-wheeled Messerschmitt bubble-car (and also the Fend-built FMR four-wheeled Tiger). A 493cc Sachs twin-cylinder two-stroke engine powered the three-wheeler.

MESSIER • France 1926-1930

Established in Montrouge, Seine, the Messier works made some cars chiefly remarkable for their pneumatic *"sans ressorts"* suspension. The engines were 1511cc and

MG • England 1923-1980; 1982 to date

Few marque histories have been as blurred and misquoted as that of the MG. Nobody can state with certainty when the first MGs were produced, though the honour should probably fall to the six Raworth-bodied, two-seater sports cars the founder, Cecil Kimber, commissioned to be built on Morris-Cowley chassis in 1923. At the time Kimber was still Manager of Morris Garages, from where the MG name originated. The Hotchkiss-engined car so often and erroneously referred to as "Number One" did not, in fact, appear for another two years, and was more accurately Kimber's first attempt at building a car solely for competition. The first model to be built in any numbers (about 400) was the 14/28 Super Sport, which came with either two or four seats and open or closed bodies. From then until 1952, when the Nuffield Group (of which MG was a part) amalgamated with the Austin Motor Company to form BMC, the prolific little firm at Abingdon, Berkshire, produced countless sports and sedan cars for both road and track, breaking record upon record on the way. Though they now bore the Leyland stamp, the 1979 MGBs and Midgets nevertheless owed much to their ancestry.

British Leyland closed the Abingdon factory in 1980, after turning down an Aston Martin rescue bid. The MG marque was revived two years later, but only for go-faster versions of BL's family sedans.

True MG enthusiasts were less than happy at seeing the illustrious name tacked on to mildly warmed-over versions of the Austin range, especially in basic Metro and Maestro variants. The marque languished in the doldrums until the MGRV8 emerged. This was a reborn 1960s MGB roadster with a V-8 engine and modified styling. It held the fort until the real new MG arrived in the form of the mid-engined MGF. This nimble and stylish car revived the MG fortunes. It featured a 1.8 version of the acclaimed K series engine and added variable valve timing for instant response and tuned engine performance. The MGF means that a pure MG car is back.

Classic MGs from 1938 and 1960s (above.) 1933 MG Magnette sedan with novel sunshine roof.

The MGA looking as earnest as it was (above.) MG Midget from the 1960s (center-left.) The MGB GT in rubber bumpered guise (center-right.) MGF in profile, with air cooling ducts ahead of the rear wheel arches (below.)

1898 Mildé et Mondos 4cv Mylord electric

MIGNONETTE • France 1900

Built by Wehrlé & Godard-Demarest of Neuilly (Seine,) this 3 hp voiturette had aluminum coachwork and could be started from the driver's seat.

MIGNONETTE LUAP • France 1898-1900

A Bordeaux-built voiturette constructed by Paul Legendre, with a rear-mounted De Dion engine. The steering lever could be fixed in the center with only the driver aboard, or moved to the side when a passenger was carried.

MIKROMOBIL • Germany 1921-1924

The Schorch-designed Mikromobil was a small car with a 7/9 hp air-cooled vee-twin engine. The last version had an 18 hp four.

MILANO • Italy 1906-1907

An unorthodox car with a 28 hp four

MILBURN ELECTRIC • USA 1914-1922

One of the more prominent electric automobiles built in the USA, the Milburn was especially noted for its smooth lines and custom-type craftsmanship. Smaller and more delicate in appearance than such contemporary electrics as Detroit or Rauch & Lang, Milburns were popular and sold well. In 1919 a formal design, similar in appearance to conventional gasoline cars, was introduced. Between 7,000 and 8,000 cars were built. Milburn went out of business after a disastrous fire destroyed its factory in Toledo, Ohio.

MILDE ET MONDOS, MILDE • France 1898-1909

MM Mildé and Mondos built a range of electric vehicles from light tricycles and a clumsy "Mylord" victoria to omnibuses. From 1904 a range of Mildé gasoline-electrics was built under the supervision of Fréderic Gaillardet, formerly of Doctoresse and Diamant, and latterly these were known as Mildé-Gaillardets. The 1908 range was a 12 hp twin and a 22 hp four.

MILLER • USA 1915-1932

Best known for his racing cars (many with fwd) and ohc racing engines, which he built from 1915, Harry Miller of Los Angeles also produced a couple of road cars in 1930-32, including a 400 bhp speedster with a dohc 5096cc V-16 power unit and 4wd, at a reputed cost of $35,000.

MILLER-QUINCY • USA 1922-1924

The Miller-Quincy was a funeral car, a few units of which were built in sedan and limousine form. A Continental six served as motive power, wheels were disc and wheelbase was 130 inches. Price of the seven-passenger sedan was $2,780.

MILLOT • France 1901-1902

Better known as a maker of mobile saw-benches (some now restored as "veteran cars,") Millot of Gray (Haute-Saône) also built 6/8 hp twin-cylinder cars and four-cylinders of 8 hp and 12 hp.

MILLOT • Switzerland 1906-1907

Four models were offered by this Zurich company. Two, a 25/30 cv four and a 35/50 cv six, had shaft drive, and two, a 40/50 cv four and a 70/80 cv six, were chain driven. Prices ranged from Sw Fr 15,000 to Sw Fr 30,000.

1924 30hp Minerva All-Weather Coupé

MILNES • England • Germany 1900-1902

Sometimes known as "CPC" (Cannstatt-Paris-Coventry,) these 8 hp, 12 hp, 16 hp, and 20 hp cars were actually built by the Marienfelde Daimler factory and bodied by tram manufacturer G F Milnes of Wellington, Shropshire. Milnes subsequently sold Cannstatt-Daimlers.

MILTON • Scotland 1920-1921

The friction-drive Milton was built in Edinburgh and engines were made by Alpha or Decolange, of 9 hp and 10 hp respectively.

MILWAUKEE • USA 1899-1902

The 1899 Milwaukee was a typical American steam buggy, and had a twin-cylinder 6/7 hp "marine type engine." The company also supplied components for building steam cars. Its final offering was a 26 hp "Racing and Touring Car" with a semi-flash boiler.

MINERVA • Belgium 1904-1939

Cycle maker Sylvain de Jong of Antwerp built an experimental car before the turn of the 19th century. A Panhard-like prototype appeared in 1902, full-scale production starting two years later with a range of two-, three-, and four-cylinder cars of 1.6, 2.4 and 3.2 liters. There was also a basic single-cylinder model, the 636cc Minervette. Up to 1910 Minerva concentrated on big four-cylinders, including models of 3.8 and 5.9 liters; then it became the first marque in mainland Europe to adopt the Knight sleeve-valve engine, announcing a 38 hp dual-ignition 6.3-liter four (King Albert was an early patron), followed shortly by models of 2.3 and 4.25 liters. By the outbreak of the First World War the 38 hp had grown to 7.4 liters; there was also a 2.3-liter Fourteen. The first post-war model was the 1919 NN 20 hp four, joined in 1921 by a 5.3-liter 30 hp six which acquired four-wheel brakes in 1923. The TT of 1923 had a sleeve-valve engine of under 2 liters and central gear-change. The 30 hp was succeeded by the Type AK 32/34 hp, with a proven sporting image, joined in 1930 by the Type AL straight-eight of 6616cc; but the 1930s saw a gradual decline into oblivion for "the Goddess of Automobiles," which merged with Impéria in 1936.

LA MINERVE • France 1899-1906

"The transmission made by two chains enables any flexion of the frame without producing the unpleasant creaking of the different parts," ran a contemporary description of this 3 cv voiturette from Billancourt (Seine.)

The world's favourite 4WD, the Shogun/Pajero

MINI-JEM • England 1966-1975

Like Mini-Marcos, the Mini-Jem was a direct development of test pilot "Dizzy" Addicott's Dart, a much modified racing Mini-van. Eventually known by the nickname of its original manufacturer, Jeremy Delmar-Morgan, the Jem was a very basic kit designed to accept Mini mechanicals; even the doors and glass had to be fitted by the customer. A change of management produced a far better Mk II version, but after two further close calls the design finally met its end after only 200 or so had been built.

MINIMUS • Germany 1921-1924

The Minimus was a small car available first with a vee-twin and later with a four-cylinder motor.

MINISPRINT • England 1965-1966

Brainchild of Dorset chemist Geoff Thomas, the Minisprint project was masterminded by Neville Trickett and consisted of removing the bodies of unsuspecting Minis, cutting off $1^1/_2$ inches from above and below the waistline, increasing the rake of both front and rear screens and modifying the nose to bring the whole car back into proportion. Over 100 Minisprints were built, most of which were exported.

MINISSIMA • England 1973

One of several design studies produced by the talented William Towns, the Minissima city car was first seen on the BLMC stand at the 1973 London Motor Show and featured a space frame clothed in scanty glassfiber bodywork.

MIRACH • England 1989

A 150 mph open two-seater, the 3.9-liter Mirach had a carbonfiber and glassfiber body on a tubular chassis.

MITCHELL • USA 1903-1923

An old-established carriage builder of Racine, Wisconsin, Mitchell began with a 7 hp runabout with a front-mounted 1419cc engine air-cooled by a rotary blower. A four-cylinder model of similar design appear in 1904, and the option of air- or watercooling was offered a year later. By 1912 Mitchell offered four models of conventional design, fours of 3982cc and 4649cc, and sixes of 5973cc and 6974cc. These were superseded the following year by a new range designed by Frenchman René Petard, which had very long strokes and consisted of "Little Sixes" with the option of 152mm or 180mm-stroke engines (5579cc or 6509cc) and a 9764cc "Big Six." A brief-lived V-8 was built in 1915-1916, and from then on Mitchell sold monobloc sixes of conventional design. The 1920 model had a mildly raked radiator which earned it the nickname "the Drunken Mitchell." Customer reaction, despite a reversion to vertical coolers, was such that Mitchell folded in 1923. Nash bought the factory.

MITSUBISHI • Japan 1917, 1959 to date

Founded in 1870 as a shipping company, this major industrial group built a series of some 20 Fiat-based Model A cars in 1917. It then devoted itself to commercial vehicles until 1960 (the sole exception being the PX-33 diesel of 1934,) when the 360 and 500 mini cars were produced.

The first Mitsubishi Colt appeared in 1962. By 1966 the Colt range comprised a three-cylinder two-stroke and pushrod fours of 1000cc and 1500cc. Also in 1962 the top-of-the-range Debonair six appeared. In 1966 a 356cc model, the Minica, was launched. In 1970 the ohc Colt Galant hardtop and GTO appeared, joined a year later by the Galant Coupé and the 360cc ohc Minica Skipper. Developments of these models were the company"s mainstay during the 1970s, along with the Lancer and Celeste ranges and the three- and five-door 1400 GLX with an eight-speed gearbox. In 1971 Mitsubishi entered into an agreement with Chrysler, whereby the US corporation took 35 per cent of a new joint company, Mit-Chrysler, with Chrylser-Mitsubishi derived cars being sold in the USA. In Britain the marque remained as "Colts" until the generic Mitsubishi name took over, "Colt" becoming a model name in the 1990s.

Mitsibushi Carisma sedan - built at the Dutch Volvo/Mitsibushi plant

Mitsibushi - Japanese supercars

The company's mid-range products such as the Tredia and Corida served it well at mass-market level, yet it was the oddly named Starion coupé that really brought the marque to the attention of serious drivers. The Starion, a superbly styled two-door coupé (later revised with a wider body), featured a 2.6-liter twin turbo engine and a stong body. One-piece door pressings and unusual seats also added to the car's character. Launched to the press and public at various racing circuits, it was the first enthusiasts' sports car from Mitsubishi to hit its target.

The second-generation Lancer appeared in 1979, and the first passenger car turbo diesel was introduced in 1980. The pioneering sixth-generation Galant of 1987 was the first production car with forward and four-wheel steering. In 1992 Mitsubishi launched the 3000GT/GTO sports car, bristling with electronic gadgetry; the most powerful version has twin turbochargers. It entered the supercar territory and took the company into a new league. The 1991 Sigma luxury car (sold as the Debonair in some markets) bristled with advanced technology, including active suspension. In 1995 the FTO model arrived in Japan. The car, a mid-range sporting coupé with adventurous styling and over 200 hp on tap, rivalled the best coupés from Alfa Romeo and BMW in pace and grace.

Through a tie-up with Volvo of Sweden, Mitsubishi has built cars at a joint factory in Holland. Here the new Carisma model, with its revolutionary twin-tuned direct-injection gasoline engine offering a choice between economy and performance, is constructed alongside the Volvo S/V 40 range.

Subsequent Galant and Sigma models have gone upmarket and high tech, with styling that apes certain BMW shapes. Equipped with expensive alloy wheels, ceramic impeller turbocharger vanes and a range of attractive trim options, the cars have become an individualistic emblem among the mainstream Japanese marques. With successful 4wd models like the Shogun/Pajero becoming worldwide best sellers, and world rally championship wins with the Lancer EVO model, Mitsubishi, maker of ships, industrial heavy plant, trucks and infrastructure services, remains a dedicated and enthusiastic motor manufacturer.

MMC • England 1897-1908

The Motor Manufacturing Company was the "flagship" company of H J Lawson"s empire, with the most important concentration of production in his Coventry "Motor Mills." Daimler, in an adjoining building, made engines and chassis on the "English Panhard" system, MMC making the bodies at first. George Iden became chief engineer in 1898, and rear-engined cars designed by him, such as the horizontal-twin 10 hp Hampton Char-a-Banc and 4.5 hp Princess, appeared the following year. MMC also made tricycles and quadricycles with British De Dion engines of 1.75 hp and 2.25 hp. Production of front-engined cars,

mostly on Panhard lines, survived the collapse of Lawson's operation. Ousted from the Motor Mills by Daimler in 1905, MMC moved to Parkside, Coventry. A final move to Clapham, London, in 1907 produced only prototypes of a 35/45 hp six.

MOBILE • USA 1899-1903

John Brisben Walker broke away from Locomobile and built steam cars of identical design in a factory at Philipse-Manor-on-the-Hudson, New York.

MOBILE • England 1903-1908

The 1903 Birmingham-built Mobile was a 6 hp two-seater with a De Dion single-cylinder power unit. Two years later a three-car range was offered: a 20/22 hp four with Aster engine, a twin-cylinder Aster-engined 12/14 hp and an 8 /10 hp, "one of which has been driven from Birmingham to London on top speed."

MODEL • USA 1903-1907

The Model, from Peru, Indiana, had a tilting body for easy access to its underfloor 24 hp engine. By removing the tonneau it could be converted into a "runabout with style" with a flat luggage deck. For 1908 the Model was known as the Star. In 1911 the company built three four-cylinder cars called "Izzers" (not "was-ers!")

MODEL A • USA 1979 to date

Announced in mid-1979, this was an ambitious plan to build 10,000 Pinto-engined replica 1928 Model A Fords in 1978-80, followed by replica 1955 Ford Thunderbirds.

MOHLER & DEGREES • Mexico • USA 1898-c. 1901

A box-like 2 hp car mounted on bicycle wheels, this was Mexico"s first motor car (built by the country"s first cycle manufacturer.) By June 1899 Mohler was selling engines in Mechanicsburg, Pa., and in 1901 the partners were building engines and carriages at Astoria, LI.

MOHS • USA 1967 to date

Bruce Baldwin Mohs designed the Mohs Ostentatienne Opera Sedan manufactured by his company, Mohs Seaplane Corp. of Madison, Wisconsin. It was an extraordinary vehicle with many safety features in addition to the Federal safety requirements. The cantilever roof beams were combined with roll bars, and the absence of side doors (entrance to the four-passenger car was from the rear) allowed full-length arm rests which concealed elbow-height chassis rails for side-collision protection. Bucket seats swung laterally on turns (which kept passenger weight in the seats), and the seats also pivoted horizontally in the event of a head-on crash. An extensive range of standard equipment included a refrigerator, a 24-carat gold inlay walnut grain dash, velvet upholstery and a Holley carburetor conversion unit for butane operation. The automatic transmission was watercooled and the custom-made tyres, filled with nitrogen, had a claimed life of 100,000 miles. Standard power came from a 4982cc V-8 engine, but a 8997cc International Harvester V-8 with five-speed manual box was optional. The Ostentatienne had an overall length of 246 inches and cost $19,600 or $25,000, according to engine size. Mohs introduced another unique vehicle in 1971. This eight-passenger dual-cowl metal-topped convertible, named the Safari-Kar, had rear seats which converted into a bed. Five inches shorter than the Ostentatienne, it cost $12,000.

1924 Mollmobil cyclecar

MOLINE • USA 1904-1919

From East Moline, Illinois, the Moline Automobile Company"s early products included a 12 hp flat-twin selling at $1,000 and a $1,600 four-cylinder. By 1912 it was offering a 25 hp pair-cast four equipped with a self-starter, the Dreadnought "35", still moderately priced at $1,700. Its ultimate offering was the four-cylinder 22.5 hp Moline-Knight sleeve-valve model.

MOLKAMP • Germany 1923-1926

A coachbuilder which took up manufacture of ohc 2650cc six-cylinder cars in the former Primus factory, Mölkamp also built an ohc 1420cc four-cylinder under Ceirano license.

MOLL • Germany 1921-1925

Moll of Chemnitz produced 1595cc and 1960cc four-cylinder cars with Siemens & Halske engines, as well as a simple cyclecar, the 1924 Mollmobil with DKW two-stroke engines. Designed by Görke, the high, narrow Mollmobil first had a 164cc engine, later a 173cc power unit.

MONARCH • USA 1905-1909

A high-wheeled motor buggy with a 3.2-liter four-cylinder engine and epicyclic transmission.

MONARCH • England 1912-1914

An 8 hp cyclecar built by R Walker & Sons of Tyseley, Birmingham, with air- or watercooled Precision engines.

MONARCH • USA 1914-1917

Bobby Hupp was behind this assembled car, which used monobloc four- and six-cylinder Continental engines of 3153cc and 4730cc. Electric lighting and starting were standard. A Herschell-Spillman V-8 was added for 1915.

MONARCH • England 1925-1928

A 13.9 hp Meadows four powered this rare assembled sedan from Birmingham.

MONARCH • Canada 1948-1961

A Canadian Ford product based on the Mercury. It was discontinued for 1958 when the Edsel was introduced, returning in 1959 after the Edsel flopped. As standard Fords became more luxurious, Monarch production ceased.

MONDEX-MAGIC • USA 1914

This New York marque was powered by license-built Fischer slide-valve sixes of 4.2 and 7 liters. Production was doubtless even more limited than its Swiss prototype.

MONET-GOYON • France 1921-1926

This well-known motorcycle manufacturer of Mâcon, Saône-et-Loire, made some awful cyclecars. The Automouche was a three-wheeler powered by a fourth wheel on which an engine was mounted; this power unit was also adaptable to pushbikes. The "Voiturette" Monet was a three-wheeler with an engine mounted on the front wheel. The true Monet-Goyon cyclecar was a four-wheeler with a 350cc Villiers engine. The company also made other three-wheelers with Mag engines of 750cc and 350cc Villiers units.

MONICA • England • France 1969-1976

A highly desirable and fully developed car that never quite went into full-scale production. A prestige four/five-seater with elegant steel body fixed to a strong independent chassis, the Monica was eventually powered by a 5.6-liter Chrysler V-8. Top speed was over 140 mph and the 0-60 mph time was 7.7 secs. Some 30-35 examples were made, 25 of them prototypes. When the limited French production run closed there was talk of Panther being involved; much of the development had occurred in England. Sadly, nothing materialized.

1973 Monica sedan

MONITOR • USA 1915-1922

The Cummins-Monitro Co of Columbus, Ohio, marketed this low-priced ($795-$895) range, with 4-30 and 6-40 power units and "350 parts less than in the average car."

MONITOR • France 1921

A cyclecar made in Suresnes, Seine, with a vee-twin side-valve 748cc engine and offered in single-seater as well as two-seater form.

MONNARD • France 1899

A light four-seater electric dog-cart.

MONOCAR • France 1936-1939

This small single-seater three-wheeler, powered by a 175cc two-stroke engine, was made in Paris.

MONOTRACE • France 1925-1927

This strange vehicle, halfway between motorcycle and car, was built by the Société Francaise du Morgan Monotrace and had a single-cylinder 510cc watercooled engine. Small wheels held up the "car" when it was at rest.

MONROE • USA 1914-1924

A four-cylinder 1969cc engine, in unit with the gearbox, initially powered this roadster, built until 1916 in Flint, thereafter in Pontiac. In 1917 a sedan was introduced; at $1,850 it cost virtually twice as much as the roadster. The marque was acquired by Stratton in 1923, and both were then taken over by Premier.

MONTEVERDI • Switzerland 1967 to date

Basle garage owner Peter Monteverdi began production of his Chrysler V-8 engined 375S luxury model (and the sporting 400SS version) in 1967, joined in 1968 by the long-wheelbase 375L. In 1971 the mid-engined Hai

1924 publicity for the Montier Special

1919 Moore

("Shark") 450SS was unveiled. Limited production of 375 and Hai-based models continues.

MONTIER & GILLET • France 1897

A lumpish tiller-steered steam waggonette with a boiler of curious design.

MONTIER SPECIALE • France 1919-1935

The Montier family, father and sons, made some good specials in Levallois using Ford spares and engines. They often raced their cars.

MOON • USA 1905-1931

Louis P Mooers, late of Peerless, designed the first cars offered by Scots-born Joseph W Moon, who ran a buggy factory in St Louis. The Model A Moon had a 30/35 hp Rutenber four-cylinder engine; by 1912 two four-cylinder models, of 5.2 and 5.6 liters, were made, joined the next year by a six. Continental sixes of 3.6 and 5 liters were offered in 1916, and the marque soon acquired an imitation Rolls-Royce radiator. The 1922 Moons had side-valves instead of ohv, and quarter-elliptic front springs, three-quarter elliptics at the rear. Four-wheel Lockheed hydraulic band brakes were specified in 1924, as were detachable disc wheels with detachable rims. In 1928 Moon offered a 4.4-straight-eight inherited from its defunct alter ego, Diana. This became the Windsor in 1929, in which year Moon became embroiled with the New Era Motors group. Moon built a few Ruxtons before finally waning in 1931.

MOORE • USA 1906-1908

The "ball-bearing car" was a 40 hp four from NY with three spark plugs per cylinder; "safe, speedy, reliable."

MOORE • USA 1916-1921

Approximately 600 Moores were manufactured during the company"s six-year existence. Moore automobiles were four-cylinder cars with G. B. & S. engines and price tags ranging from $550 in their earlier days to nearly $1,200 in the final year of production.

MOOSE JAW STANDARD • Canada 1917

Five local residents bought enough parts from the USA to build 25 Continental-engined luxury cars, but gave up after they each had a car because they could not find buyers for the rest.

MORA • USA 1906-1910

"The ideal gentleman"s car," the Mora was built first in Rochester, NY, then in Newark, NY. A 24 hp roadster was listed initially, joined in 1908 by a 42/50 hp six, available as a tourer or as a "racytype" built in a "limited edition" of 100. In 1907 a 25 hp Mora took the "World"s Sealed Hood Record," covering over 10,000 miles.

MORELAND • USA 1920-1924

A Moreland passenger car was announced in November, 1919, by the Moreland Motor Truck Co of Los Angeles, California, which said operations would begin shortly at Burbank. Whether prototypes were ever made is not known. A "DeLuxe" sedan was announced in 1924, but plans failed to materialize. The company ceased production of trucks in 1941.

MOREL & GERARD • France 1897

A quadricycle of basic design, virtually two bicycles linked by parallel cross-members carrying a single-cylinder engine.

MORENY • France 1907-1908

A manufacturer of cars and chassis of Montmartre, Paris. The 14/18 hp Moreny had a four-cylinder engine of 2413cc.

MORETTE • England 1903-1905

B. E. Dickinson of Birmingham built this bathchair-like three-wheeler with 2.5 hp or 4 hp engine driving the front wheel by friction roller.

MORETTI • Italy 1945 to date

Moretti first produced motorcycles, but soon concentrated on exclusive small cars with 350cc, 596cc and 746cc two- and four-cylinder engines with single- or twin-overhead camshafts and special bodywork. There were also Moretti cars with Fiat and Fiat-Abarth parts, and some very "hot" racing versions. A reorganization in 1962 led to a concentration of special bodywork and prototypes.

1930 Montier sedan based in the Model A Ford

1920 Moon 23.6hp tourer

Moretti's current models are Fiat-based and include the 126 "Minimaxi" and the 127 "Midimaxi" with 903cc and 1049cc engines and multipurpose bodywork.

MORGAN • England 1904-1905

Better known as a coachbuilder, Morgan offered an 8 hp Electric Motor Phaeton in 1904. In 1905 Morgan announced the 24 hp "all-British" chassis, powered by a Mutel engine. At a chassis price of £750 (with formal coachwork adding another £250) it proved too costly, and only a handful were built before Morgan became agent for the German Adler and consequently abandoned motor car production altogether.

MORGAN • England 1910 to date

The prototype Morgan three-wheeler was built in 1908-09 in the school workshops at Malvern College. H F S Morgan, with the help of Mr Stephenson-Peach, the engineering master, produced a design that in layout remained in production until 1950, while the independent front suspension is, in essence, still in use on current models. Production started in 1910, the car having a tubular chassis frame and sliding-pillar front suspension. Power was provided by an 1100cc air-cooled vee-twin JAP engine, which

The classic, timeless time-warp that is the Morgan 4/4

MORRIS • England 1913 to 1984

Oxford cycle and motor agent William Morris sold his first car, the two-seater Morris-Oxford, in 1913. Costing £180, it was powered by a 1017cc engine by White and Poppe, with the gearbox in unit. Rear axle was by E G Wrigley, wheels by Sankey and bodywork by Raworth of Oxford. It was, in effect, an assembled job, but a good one. The Oxford was joined in 1915 by the 1496cc engined Cowley with engine/gearbox by the Continental Motors Company of Detroit, USA. Production began again in earnest after the First World War, with copies of the US engine being manufactured by Hotchkiss of Coventry. One major difference between the two engines was that the Coventry-built model had a cork clutch that ran in oil, one of the few contributions Morris made to detailed engine design! The "Bullnose" Oxfords and the more austere Cowleys were destined to become the best-selling British cars of the decade. In 1921 Morris made a sensational series of price cuts and never looked back. In 1923 an 1802cc engine was offered as an option in the Oxford, this being standardized from 1924. Both models remained in production until 1926, though the peak production year was 1925, when 54,151 cars were built, representing 41 per cent of new car production in Britain. The 1927 season saw the appearance of the less inspiring "Flatnose" models, though the 2.5-liter Empire model failed to woo the export market for which it had been designed. Although a few sixes had been made earlier, it was not until 1928 that Morris adopted this engine configuration in a big way with an ohc 2.5-liter car, a reminder that Wolseley, a firm adherent to this engine layout, had been purchased the previous year.

Morris's entry into the small-car market came in 1929 with the ohc 847cc Minor (also of Wolseley parentage.) The ohc engine was dropped from the Minor in 1931 (though it had been successfully used in the MG Midget,) being replaced by a simple side-valve unit, the two-seater version selling for £100. Lockheed hydraulic brakes first appeared on the six-cylinder Morrises of 1930, and during the following four years the whole range was converted. The early 1930s were poor years for Morris, and 1933 witnessed the appearance of the 1.3-liter 10/4. Morris hit the production jackpot again with his 918cc Series 1 Eight of 1935, a season in which, incidentally, he offered no fewer than 32 different models! The Eight continued in production until 1938, by which time 250,000 had been built, making it the best-selling car of the decade. It was replaced for the 1939 season by the Series E Eight with completely new bodywork and faired-in headlamps. Although the Eight was Cowley's best-seller, the Morris range at this time boasted four other models, ranging from the 10/4 to the 3.5-liter 25. All, with the exception of the Eight, had ohv engines. The year 1939 was also significant for Morris in that the Series M 1140cc Ten marked the company's first foray into integral construction.

The immediate post-war years saw the reappearance of the pre-war Eight and Ten, though a major landmark came in 1948 with the announcement of the Issigonis-designed Minor, initially powered by the 916cc Series E engine, which featured torsion bar ifs, rack-and-pinion steering and 14-inch road wheels. It remained in production until 1971 and was the first British car to top a million sales. The ohv Austin 803cc engine from the A30 was fitted from 1953 and the capacity progressively increased to 1098cc. The sv 1476cc Oxford and series MS Six, powered by an ohc 2.2-liter engine, also appeared at the same time as the Minor and shared similarly styled bodywork. The creation of the British Motor Corporation in 1952 by the merging of the Austin and Morris companies inevitably resulted in rationalization, with the Cowley and more powerful Oxford receiving ohv Longbridge engines in 1954, the former 1200cc model appearing the same year.

By 1959 the appearance of the Farina-bodied 1.5-liter sedan meant that the differences between the Cowley and Longbridge products were less marked. The sensational Issigonis-designed forward 848cc Mini of the same year was sold under the Mini Minor name tag, while a logical progression was the best-selling 1100 of 1963, both models later being available under the Austin banner. The year 1968 saw the swallowing of BMC by Leyland Motors to form British Leyland. A result of this new corporation was the Marina model of 1971, with a conventional engine and gearbox layout and rear-wheel drive, 1.3 and 1.8-liter engine options being available. The following year came the forward 2200 model. For 1979 the range consisted of 14 variations on the Marina theme. The Marina was updated as a stop-gap car by Ital Design, who facelifted its styling, but the ancient mechanicals remained the same. Controversially known as the "Ital," it was the last genuine Morris car, and signalled the end of the marque.

William Cooper's one-off 1919 wooden-bodied sports Morris-Cowley (left.) 1917 Morris-Cowley two-seater (above.)

1926 Morris-Oxford touring car (top.) Morris Minor in pick-up form (center.) Mini Cooper, the ultimate rally winning icon reflecting Mr Cooper's input (right)

Auguste Pons' 1907 Pekin-Paris Mototri-Contal, whose mudguards became an emergency bridge

MOTOR CARRIER • England 1904

A 6 hp "pleasure car" which could be converted into an 8 cwt goods vehicle.

MOTORETTE • USA 1910-1911

The three-wheeled Motorette was designed and manufactured in Hartford, Connecticut, by automotive pioneer C W Kelsey (see Auto Tri, Kelsey, Pilgrim, and Spartan,) and as many as 300 might have been made. The car sported two front wheels and a rear wheel, and steering was by tiller. Initially air-cooled, the later cars were equipped with radiators. A tendency to roll on turns led Kelsey to develop the anti-sway bar. Price of the Motorette passenger-car model was $385, delivery-van price being slightly higher. A special rickshaw body was developed for sales in Japan, where a number of Motorettes were exported. They also enjoyed sales throughout the USA as well as in Denmark, Mexico, Canada, and Australia.

MOTORLAND MIDGET • England 1908

"Designed to supersede the tricar," the 7/8 hp single-cylinder Motorland Midget had a two-speed transmission and could attain 30-40 mpg.

MOTOTRI CONTAL • France 1907-1908

The high point of this company's existence was the entry of one of its three-wheelers in the 1907 Peking-Paris Race (though it failed to get very far.) More elaborate than most tricars, the Paris-built Mototri Contal featured "Roi-des-Belges" coachwork on its more costly models. Delivery tricycles were also made.

1924 Mourre cyclecar

LA MOUCHE • France 1898-1902

A De Dion-engined voiturette built by Teste et Moret of Lyon-Vaise (Rhône.)

MOURRE • France 1920-1923

Antoine Mourre started by building a six-cylinder 25 hp car named "Pan American." In 1921 he decided to make the Major cyclecar under license, with Violet two-stroke engines (later with a 950cc Fivet four-cylinder four-stroke engine.) These cars were sometimes sold under the "Jack Enders" name.

MOUTETTE • France 1922-1925

Made in Paris by M M Van der Eyken, Hurian, and Vigy, these cars had 1327cc and 1328cc Altos engines, as well as 1495cc SCAP and 1093cc Ruby engines.

MOVEO • England 1931-1932

A 2973cc Meadows engine, available with supercharger if required, powered the Moveo, an ill-timed essay from Bolton, Lancashire. Other Meadows-engined options were listed, but none was built.

MOYER • USA 1911-1915

Initially offered with four- or six-cylinder engines, this car from Syracuse, New York, was later only available with a 5047cc four-cylinder engine.

MP • France 1908-1909

An imported French make sold by J E H Monypenny of London, the MP was a 30 hp four-cylinder of 5123cc with a shouldered radiator reminiscent of the De Dietrich. A 16 hp four of 2011cc and a 45 hp six of 9784cc were also available.

MPM • USA 1914-1915

A 44 hp eight-cylinder from Mount Pleasant, Michigan; hence the name!

MS • France 1922-1925

MM Morain and Sylvestre started in Courbevoie, Seine, making a 961cc Chapuis-Dornier-engined light car. The company changed hands in 1924, and was taken over by M M Martin and Blanco of Suresnes, Seine, who added a 1093cc model.

c.1898 Mueller-Benz Trap

1918 Murray Eight Model 70T Town Car

1924 Murray-Mac six-cylinder

MSL • England 1911-1912

Assembled from imported French components by Motor Showrooms Ltd, these were a 10/14 hp of 1847cc and a 12/16 hp of 2121cc.

MUELLER • USA 1895-1900

Mueller, of Decatur, Illinois, imported the Benz into the USA from an early date and, indeed, competed with one in the 1895 *Chicago Times-Herald* race. The company later turned to manufacture of an "improved" version of the Benz, with a tubular chassis which carried the cooling water from the single-cylinder engine at the rear to a tubular radiator on the front of the dashboard. Belt drive gave three speeds forward and reverse, and the standard bodywork was a four-seat *dos-á-dos*.

MULLNER • Austria 1913

A cyclecar with a 6 hp Zedel engine and chain drive.

MULTIPLEX • USA 1912-1914

Only 14 examples of this well-designed 50 hp four-cylinder car were made by this Berwick, Pennsylvania, manufacturer, selling at $3,600. A second Multiplex, a sports car with ifs and F-head Willys engine, appeared in 1954, but only three were built.

MUNTZ JET • USA 1950-1954

In 1950 Earl "Madman" Muntz, a zany character and astute businessman, purchased the tools and dies of the Kurtis Sports car and set up Muntz Motors to produce cars, first at Evansville, Ind., then in Chicago. The car was redesigned by Frank Kurtis and Sam Hanks, who lengthened the wheelbase to allow the installation of a rear seat. Numerous detail improvements went into the chassis and body, and production got under way in Illinois. Named the Muntz Jet, the first 28 cars used Cadillac 160 hp engines; later cars used 5195cc Lincoln V-8s with Hydramatic transspeed was a claimed 125 mph. Muntz was reputed to have lost around $400,000 on the 394 handbuilt cars he produced.

MURRAY • USA 1920-1921

This car with a six-cylinder Continental engine was built by the Murray Motor Car Co of Newark, New Jersey, and was a continuation of the earlier Murray Eight. John McCarthy subsequently took over the make and moved operations to the Boston area. As many as five or six of the Newark Murrays were sold.

MURRAY EIGHT • USA 1916-1918

Built in Pittsburgh, Pennsylvania, the Murray was a highly regarded and excellently built automobile at a reasonable price. Boasting such niceties as an electric clock as standard equipment and a slanting windshield, the car was distinguished by a Rolls-Royce-shaped radiator and precision coachwork, especially on its limousine and town-car models.

MURRAY SIX • USA 1921-1928

Also known as the "Murray-Mac" (after its owner, John McCarthy,, very few of these cars were produced, probably six or less. Most, if not all, were assembled largely from existing parts. Beaver and (probably) Continental engines were used, and the five-passenger touring car was listed at $5,000. Assembly was in Atlantic, Mass., near Boston. Around 1928 McCarthy built a handsome roadster in an effort to show and promote his venture, but he found no takers and the car remained his personal transportation for many years.

MUSTAD • Norway • France 1917

Clarin Mustad of Oslo, an automobile pioneer in Norway, built sleeve-valve engines in 1909. In 1917 he built a prototype six-wheeled car with supplementary steering on the forward rear axle. The car had a four-cylinder engine, later replaced by a six-cylinder one, both built by the factory. The car was used up to the Second World War, but was rebuilt in 1927. Mustad planned to sell the license rights to Unic in France, but neither this, nor trials of the design as Paris buses, came to anything. However, a Duclair firm offered 7086cc Clarin Mustad six-wheelers until 1922.

MWD • Germany 1911-1913

Identical with "Der Dessauer" cars, MWD stood for "Motoren-Werke-Dessau." Production concentrated around a sv 2100cc four-cylinder model.

MWF • Austria 1905-1907

When Wyner of Vienna closed down, MWF of Simmering continued the production of Wyner cars under its trademark. It built cars from 9 hp to 40 hp, but concentrated on the smaller models. Manufacture was on a limited scale.

MYRON • Czechoslovakia 1934

A beautiful 796cc twin-cylinder two-stroke car built at Zlin (now Gottwaldov), the Myron attracted many orders when exhibited at the Prague Motor Show, but was never produced. The reason was simple; the exhibited car, offered for less than 10,000 Kcs, had a specially built body by Fischer of Brno which had cost 21,000 Kcs to produce!

MYTHOLM • England 1900-1902

Thomas Potter and J W Brown's Mytholm Cycle Works at Hipperholme, Halifax, built a three-wheeled car in 1897, followed by a four-wheeled prototype. They joined forces with R Reynold Jackson in 1899, building some Jackson cars, but after Jackson's departure for London in 1900 a number of Mytholm cars were built. Chain driven, with steering-column gear-change, they had a 1357cc single-cylinder engine.

NACIONAL PESCARA • Spain 1929-1932

Raul, Marquis de Pescara, built a number of sporting 2948cc ohv straight-eights. A 3.9-liter straight-ten was also proposed in 1931.

NACIONAL RG • Spain 1948

Cuban engineer and aviator Ramon Girona built two-seat airplanes in his Barcelona factory, as well as streamlined twin-cylinder 740cc light cars with sedan or cabriolet coachwork.

NACIONAL SITGES • Spain 1933-1937

Built at Sitges, site of a Brooklands-inspired racetrack, the Nacional Sitges was a conventional four-cylinder sedan of 1235cc. From mid-1936, for political reasons, the marque was known as "Popular Sitjes."

NAG • Germany 1902-1934

See panel

NAGANT • Belgium 1899-1927

Starting with license-built Gobron-Brilliés, Liégeois arms manufacturers Léon and Maurice Nagant then launched a 6872cc chain-driven 35/40 hp four of conventional design in 1906, followed in late 1907 by a 4589cc 20/30 hp. The 1908 season saw a 14 hp "for the man of moderate means." The 35/40 hp was discontinued in 1911, and in 1912 a new 10/12 hp appeared. Post-war production began in 1920 with a 16 hp four, shortly followed by an ohv sporting four of 1954cc with Adex four-wheel brakes. A supercharged Nagant was shown at the 1927 Brussels Show alongside the last production model, a sv six. Soon after, Impéria swallowed Nagant.

NAMELESS • England 1908-1909

British-built all through," the Nameless was a low-priced (£290) 14 hp four from Hendon.

NAMI • Russia 1927

An air-cooled flat-twin powered this little four-seater, planned as the first mass-produced Soviet car. About 300 were built.

NANCEENE • France 1900-c. 1903

Built cars and trucks on Gobron-Brillié lines.

NAPIER • England 1900-1924

See panel overleaf

NAG • Germany 1902-1934

NAG, successor to AAG, initially continued the cars created by Prof Klingenberg. His successor, Joseph Vollmer, designed two- and four-cylinder 10 hp and 20 hp cars, as well as commercial vehicles. A variety of models followed, including 5185cc and 7956cc four-cylinders and even an 1866cc twin-cylinder car. A 1570cc four-cylinder model (the 'Puck,' as well as 2071cc, 2579cc, and 8384cc NAGs, were later produced. The marque was favoured by the Kaiserin. The last NAG before the First World War was a 2579cc four-cylinder. During the war NAG built the 200 hp Benz aero engine under license. In 1919 it became a member of the GDA car production group together with Brennabor, Hansa and Hansa-Lloyd. In 1920 NAG resumed car production with a sv 2536cc four-cylinder car, soon launching a sports version which won many races. An ohv 2640cc four-cylinder went into production in 1923, joined by six-cylinder models of 3075cc and 3594cc from 1926 onwards. A joint venture with Protos, which NAG took over that year, these ohv sixes were called NAG-Protos. In 1927 NAG took over Preston and Dux. Designer Paul Henze joined the Berlin NAG works in 1929 and created the 1930-1932 ohv 3963cc six-cylinder and the ohv V-8 of 4499cc. Together with Bussein, Henze also designed a fwd version of the big V-8 car in 1932. The last NAG was the fwd Type 220 built from 1933 onward, with a 1468cc flat-four engine, developed by Bussein for Voran. Only a few had been built before NAG decided to concentrate on commercial vehicles, and merged with Büssing.

1912 18hp NAG sports two-seater

1921 NAG 10/40hp Sportwagen

1908 30/40hp Nagant tourer

NAPOLEON • France 1903

A Lacoste et Battmann-based 5 hp car sold by Bernard Neave of Richmond, Surrey.

NAPOLEON • USA 1916-1917

An L-head 30 hp four from Napoleon, Ohio.

NAPTHOLETTE • France 1899

A light 2.5 hp car on Decauville lines with a body that could be "removed in an instant and another one substituted."

NARDI • Italy 1947-1963

Enrico Nardi created small racing and sports cars, using 498cc and 746cc BMW motorcycle engine components. He later employed modified Fiat and Lancia engines. An ex-Ferrari employee, he was an excellent engine tuner. Some of his racing cars had Giannini-designed 746cc dohc four-cylinder engines. His factory also produced tuning equipment for Fiat and other makes.

NARDINI • France 1914

An attractive light car designed to be sold on the English market by M Nardini. Altos engines of 1244cc and 1779cc were used, and the chassis was reportedly very similar to that of the SUP.

NASH • USA 1917-1957

See panel overleaf

EL NASR • Egypt 1959 to date

This company, with a factory at Helwan, offered license-built versions of the Fiat 128 and 125 in 1979.

NATIONAL • USA 1899-1900

At least five Nationals, with 2.5 hp, 5 hp or 8 hp twins, were built in St Louis in 1899.

NATIONAL • USA 1900-1924

"Electrically-propelled pleasure vehicles" occupied this Indianapolis firm until 1904, when it introduced a round-radiatored petrol car with a 4649cc four-cylinder Rutenber engine, dropping "Electrobiles" altogether in 1905. A year later came a six-cylinder model, but powerful big fours really established National, which claimed its 7320cc 40 hp as "the fastest stock car built." The 1912 Speedway Roadster commemorated the marque's victory in the Indianapolis "500" race that year. By 1913 electric starting and lighting were standard, as was an engine-driven tyre pump. The 1914 models had left-hand drive, and in 1915 a new model with a 4966cc Continental Red Seal six was launched, joined for 1916 by a 6064cc V-12 of National"s own manufacture, listed until 1919. In 1920 came the 30 hp Sextet six, which ran until the end of production. A 1922 merger with Jackson and Dixie Flyer led to some cars of these marques appearing as "Nationals."

NATIONAL • England 1902-1906

A tricar with a 4 hp MMC engine, the Manchester-built National had a coachbuilt body and wheel-steering.

NATIONAL • England 1904-1912

Rose Brothers, a maker of tobacco wrapping machinery, built these cars of conventional design, with two, three, and four cylinders, though a 15/17 hp five-cylinder was reportedly shown in 1904.

1914 Nardini 1779cc chassis

NAVARRE • USA 1921

A C Schulz, builder of the Navarre, had been associated with both Locomobile and Marmon, and plans had been made to build a quality luxury car. Only one car was made, a five-passenger sedan. This featured an own-make engine (a six) and a price tag of $6,000.

NAW • Germany 1908-1919

Producers of NAW, Colibri and Sperber cars at Hameln Weser, the works were bought by Selve.

NAZZARO • Italy 1912-1922

Felice Nazzaro, closely connected with Vincenzo Florio and Fiat as a very successful racing driver and technician, built these 20/30 hp cars with 4396cc four-cylinder engines. A smaller 12 hp car of 2092cc was made for British agents Newton & Bennett. The Nazzaro cars built for the 1919 French Grand Prix, with ohv four-cylinder 16-valve power

NAPIER

NAPIER • England 1900-1924

Montague Napier's Lambeth works was famed for precision engineering long before its association with motor cars. The prototype Napier, a 2471cc vertical twin, successfully competed in the 1900 1,000 Miles' Trial; a 4942cc four appeared later that year, notable for a one-piece aluminum cylinder block with pressed-in iron liners and three atmospheric inlet valves per cylinder. From the start Napier cars were sold and promoted by the forceful S F Edge. Napier pursued an active racing policy which won the 1902 Gordon Bennett Trophy for Britain, and Napier Green became the official British racing livery.

In 1903 Napier launched the first series-production six-cylinder car, the 4942cc 18 hp. Initially, periodic vibration caused crankshaft whip and even breakage, which Edge euphemized as "power rattle," but the overall smoothness and flexibility of the six proved strong selling points, and by 1906 there was a range of two sixes of 40 hp (5001cc) and 60 hp (7753cc) and two fours of 18 hp (3160cc) and 45 hp (5309cc). The next year a 9653cc 60 hp driven by Edge averaged 65.9 mph for 24 hours on the new Brooklands race track, a record which stood for 18 years. Biggest production Napier was the 90 hp, introduced in 1907, which had a swept volume of 14,565cc. A complex range of two-, four-, and six-cylinder models was replaced by only five models for 1912; a 15 hp four and sixes of 30, 40, 45, 65, and 90 hp. The First World War saw Napier building aero engines, including the famous "broad-arrow" Lion 12-cylinder designed by A J Rowledge, who was also responsible for the post-war Napier, a light-alloy ohc 6227cc 40/50 hp six. Only 187 were built, out of a total of 4,258 Napier private cars. A 1931 bid to acquire Bentley was thwarted by Rolls-Royce.

The original Napier car, in the 1900 1000 Miles Trial

c.1913 30hp Napier touring car

units, retired with engine troubles. Nazzaro left the works in 1916 and eventually returned to Fiat. His successors produced a few 3480cc cars.

NB • Scotland 1909-1912

Successor to the Drummond, the North British was a 10 hp twin of 1652cc which sold for £200.

NB • Italy 1910-1915

This was a "semi-Italian" car, as the design and the finances came from the UK car dealers Newton & Bennett. There was reportedly a technical co-operation with Nazzaro, as both works were at Turin and Newton & Bennett imported Nazzaros. The four-cylinder NB cars had 2155cc engines.

NEANDER • Germany 1937-1939

Designer Ernst Neumann-Neander produced unorthodox motorcycles in the late 1920s, and afterwards created various small three- and four-wheeled cars, which never went into serious production. Between 1937 and 1939 he built a range of 1000cc sports-racing cars with JAP or Harley-Davidson vee-twin engines.

NEC • England 1905-1920

A famous "hoodless" car with all seats within the wheelbase, the NEC, built by the New Engine Company of Acton, London, had a horizontal power unit. There was originally a 30 hp four-cylinder, joined in 1906 by a 15 hp twin. The 30 hp, oddly enough, could be had with either two- or four-speed transmissions. For 1908 the 15 hp was bored out to create a 20 hp, and a 40 hp four of similar cylinder dimensions was offered alongside the 30 hp. Both the 30 hp and 40 hp were still theoretically available after the war, but these were almost certainly unsold 1914 models. The brothers J G and G F Mort, who owned NEC, also produced Roots-supercharged two-stroke aero engines as early as 1910.

NECKAR • Germany 1955-1968

Made by NSU-Fiat at Heilbronn, the Neckar was really a Fiat 103 design with an ohv 1089cc four-cylinder engine. After 1966 the factory became independent from NSU, and concentrated on Fiat products.

LA NEF • France 1899-1914

A three-wheeled car built at Agen by Lacroix et de Laville, La Nef had a wooden chassis and tiller steering. According to the model, De Dion engines of 2.75 hp to 8 hp were used. Robust and easily driven, it was known as "the country doctor's car." Production was around 200.

1951 Nash Healey sports

NASH • USA 1917-1957

Charles W Nash rose to become President of General Motors in 1912, but his ambition was to build a car under his own name. He therefore resigned and bought the Jeffery company in 1916, phasing out its name in favour of "Nash" a year later. The first Nash car, an ohv 4-liter six, appeared in autumn 1917; it was joined by an ohv 2.5-liter four late in 1921, as Nash recovered from the 1920 recession. LaFayette and Mitchell were acquired in 1922 and 1924 respectively, but the Mitchell's successor, Ajax, proved a flop. The Model 328 of 1928 was said to be "America's cheapest seven-bearing six," helping to boost sales to 138,137, a record that stood until 1949. The 1930 range covered 32 variants, including the all-new Twin-Ignition Eight of 3920cc, as well as the Single Six and Twin-Ignition Sixes, both of 3378cc; the Eight featured a starter operated by the clutch pedal. To counter sliding sales Nash boosted its model range to 25 "First Series" body styles and 28 "Second Series" in 1932, and launched a "Big Six," giving it two sixes and two eights. Apart from GM, it was the only US manufacturer to show a profit that year. The 1934 models had revized styling, with spatted wings, raked tails and rear-mounted spare wheels, and a low-priced LaFayette line was added. In 1934 the millionth Nash was built; drastic rationalization the next year brought the range down to two six-cylinder body styles and four eight-cylinder styles, with swept-tail "Aeroform design." The 1936 models had the option of conventional-styled models with a trunk, and a rear seat which converted into a double bed. That same year's models also included the low-priced sv 400 six, of 3037cc or 3779cc, and the ohv Ambassador Six and Eight models. In 1937 Nash merged with Kelvinator refrigerators; a year later came "Weather Eye" conditioned air heating and ventilation, and vacuum-operated gearboxes. The 1940 models had a tall, narrow grille, curved inwards at the foot, and there was a limited edition of around 50 Nash Special convertibles styled by Count Alexis de Sakhnoffsky. The 1941 models featured an integral body/chassis, hailed as an American first; the new 2.8-liter "600" six was claimed to cover 600 miles on one 20-gallon tankful of gasoline.

After the war Nash was quickly back in car production, the 1945 vehicles being carry-overs from 1942. An interesting 1946 model was the Ambassador Suburban Sedan, with wooden side panels. Airflyte styling distinguished the 1949 models, though enclosed wheels all round made tire changing almost impossible. All models employed unitary construction; seat belts were optional, and the front seatback dropped down to convert the interior into a double bed (mattress and curtains were options.)

Nash's best year was 1950, when it launched the first successful post-war compact, the Rambler, with the old sv six; Nash sales that season reached 175,722. The old 600 was replaced by the Statesman. A meeting on the *Queen Elizabeth* between Nash president George Mason and Donald Healey led to the English-built Nash-Healey, powered by a tuned Ambassador six, offered between 1951 and 1954. In 1954 Nash took over Hudson to form American Motors, with George Romney at the helm. Romney was not interested in full-size cars, and concentrated AMC's efforts on the Rambler. A 1955 restyling saw the option of Packard's 5244cc V-8 in the Ambassador, while 1956 saw the Ambassador with AMC"s new 4097cc V-8. Sales fell to 9,474 in 1957, despite flamboyant styling with dual vertical headlamps, and Nash was finally phased out.

1932 Nash Six Convertible Victoria

1950 Nash Ambassador Super Sedan

1926 Nash Advanced Six Sedan with auxiliary Gruss air-springs

1904 Nesselsdorfer 12hp phaeton

NEGRE & RUFFIN • France 1896-1897

"Though the engine may be efficient enough to propel the vehicle," said a press description of the V-4 steam power unit used on this car, "it is doubtful whether the system is all that is required by buyers." In 1897 M. Négre offered a steam car with cylinders in "X" formation.

NELSON • USA 1917-1922

The Nelson was designed along European lines by Emil A Nelson, who had previously been affiliated with Oldsmobile, Packard, and Hupmobile. A relatively small car, the Nelson featured an ohc four-cylinder aircraft-type engine of its own make. Although production was limited, an estimated 350 to 400 cars had been produced by the end of 1920. Any 1921-1922 Nelsons were presumably assembled from parts in hand. Most Nelsons were touring models, although some roadsters and sedans were built in earlier days, probably to special order.

NESSELSDORFER • Czechoslovakia 1897-1923

This pioneer factory completed its first "President" motor car on 21 May 1898. From 1923 onwards Nesselsdorf (now Koprivnice) built cars which became known as "Tatra." Its most famous designer was Hans Ledwinka, who created some excellent cars, including the ohc 5328cc six-cylinder Type "U," which was made from 1914 to 1923, when Ledwinka's famous twin-cylinder Tatra came into being.

NEUSTADT-PERRY • USA 1903-1907

This "combination car" from St Louis was furnished engineless so that the buyer could fit steam or gasoline power to choice.

NEW BRITISH • England 1921-1923

The chain-driven New British used friction transmission and was powered by a 10 hp vee-twin Blackburne, either air- or watercooled.

NEW CENTURY • England 1903

Made by old-established carriage builder Henry Whitlock Ltd in 7.5 hp, 12 hp, 16 hp, and 20 hp models.

NEW COURIER • England 1898-1900

The New Courier Cycle Company of Wolverhampton built carrier tricycles and two-seater motor tricycles "with patent starting gears." Its 1900 three-wheeled "Motorette" could be converted into a tradesman's box tricycle by removing the front seat.

NEW ENGLAND • USA 1898-1900

A tiller-steered two-cylinder steamer built at Waltham, Mass.

NEW ERA • USA 1915-1917

The "Simplicity 16" was a $660 tourer built at Joliet, NY.

NEWEY ASTER, NEWEY • England 1907, 1913-1923

Newey of Birmingham and Leamington claimed to operate the biggest garage in the Midlands. It was an agent for Siddeley, Star, and De Dion, and in 1907 also built its own models with 10/12 hp, 20/22 hp, and 24/30 hp Aster power units. With a 1324cc Aster engine, the 1913-1923 Newey was a well-built light car with rotund two-seat coachwork.

NEW HUDSON • England 1913-1924

Built by a famous Birmingham motorcycle factory, the pre-war New Hudson was a 4.5 hp four-wheeled cyclecar. A vee-twin MAG engine powered the post-war three-wheeler.

NEWMOBILE • England 1906-1907

"Specially designed to meet the requirements of the medical profession," the Newmobile was one of the first cars to feature unit construction of engine and gearbox. The constant mesh gears were engaged by a series of cone clutches.

NEW ORLEANS • England 1900-1910

The "Orleans" recalls Bourbon connections with Twickenham, Middlesex, where this marque was made. The first New Orleans model was a 3.5 hp license-built version of the Belgian Vivinus (there was also a 6 hp two-cylinder on similar lines,) but by 1902 a four-cylinder 14 hp and 8 hp and 9 hp light cars were available. A 22 hp four appeared in 1906, a year after the company had become simply "Orleans," the novelty presumably having worn off. By 1909 a 30/40 hp four and a 35/45 hp six were listed.

NEW YORK SIX • USA 1928-1929

Sold by the New York Motors Corporation of Baltimore, Maryland, this car was actually built by the George W Davis Motor Co of Richmond, Indiana, and, with the Davis Eight, featured the unique Parkmobile, a jacking mechanism with small wheels allowing the car to be maneuvred sideways in and out of parking spots. The car had a Continental engine and resembled Reo's Wolverine. Few were built.

NIAGARA • USA 1915-1916

Gustav H Poppenberg, who owned the biggest piano warehouse in Buffalo, NY, backed this 36 hp four with "motor yacht line" coachwork.

NICLAUSSE • France 1906-1914

Better known as a maker of "unexplodable boilers," J & A Niclausse of Paris introduced a 30 hp four-cylinder shaft-drive car in 1905, which remained current (though later uprated to 35 hp) throughout the marque"s life. A 20 hp four appeared in 1908, followed by a 12/16 hp.

NIMROD • England 1899-1900

A De Dion-engined "Roadster Motor Tricycle" built by a Bristol cycle manufacturer.

NISSAN • Japan 1931 to date
(see also Datsun)

See panel overleaf

NIXE • Germany 1905-1908

Voiturettes made by Feldman of Soest (Westphalia,) Nixe cars had ioe 804cc twin-cylinder Fafnir engines.

NOEL • France 1920-1925

Light cyclecars from Brienne-le-Château, Aube; one was a tandem two-seater with a 1089cc Anzani vee-twin engine. Noel also made a more conventional Ruby-engined 902cc cyclecar.

NOEL BENET • France 1900

This fwd car from Offrainville, Seine-Maritime, powered by a single-cylinder De Dion engine, had front-wheel braking through the differential.

NOMA • USA 1919-1923

An assembled car with sporting lines, the Noma used a six-cylinder Continental engine (a Beaver powerplant was also available). Low-slung and wire-wheeled, the Noma used step plates in place of running boards. An oval radiator was a distinctive feature, reminiscent of the Brewster or Phianna. Although most of the several hundred Nomas produced were open models, a number of closed cars was also built.

1920 New Hudson three-wheeled cyclecar

NORDEC • England 1949

General engineers (they even offered model-aircraft engines,) the North Downs Engineering Co of Whyteleafe, Surrey, made the LMB ifs conversion for Fords and the Marshall-Nordec supercharger. These were both incorporated in this Ford Ten-powered sports car, built in limited numbers.

NORDENFELDT • France 1906-1910

The Nordenfeldt first appeared in 1906 with a 24/30 hp Bariquand & Marre four-cylinder engine. Originally sold in England by racing driver Clifford Earp, the Nordenfeldt is something of a mystery car, for its actual maker is unknown. Four-cylinder models of 12, 16, 20, 30/35, and 40/45 hp were listed during the Nordenfeldt's five-year production span.

NORFOLK • England 1904-1905

A Blackburn & Co of Cleckheaton, Yorks., built about a dozen twin-cylinder cars of 1458cc and 1701cc.

NORIS • Germany 1902-1905

Made at Nürnburg, the Noris was a small car with one-, two-, and four-cylinder proprietary engines up to 24 hp.

NORMA • England 1914-1915

A 10 hp four-cylinder light car with a 1460cc power unit, which sold for £178 complete.

NORSK • Norway 1907-1911

The first car from this Oslo firm was a single-cylinder 8 hp car with four-speed gearbox, which was presented in the spring of 1908. The second type of car had a twin-cylinder engine. Altogether around 10 cars were built.

NORTHERN • USA 1902-1909

Designed by Charles Brady King, the original Northern cars were typical gas buggies on Oldsmobile lines (King worked for Olds from 1900-1902) with one- and two-cylinder engines. A folding steering column was a feature. In 1904 came the flat-twin "Silent Northern," with a huge U-shaped silencer some 10 ft long and an epicyclic transmission controlled by a steering column lever. The 1906 ohv four-cylinder Northern had compressed-air-operated brakes, clutch, and fuel feed. The company was absorbed by EMF in 1909.

NORTHERN • England 1908-1910

There were two models of the Northern, from Cleckheaton, Yorkshire, a 10 hp twin of 1759cc and a 20 hp four of 3518cc.

NORTH-LUCAS • England 1923

Ralph Lucas (of Valveless) and O D North collaborated to design this all-independent suspension car with unit-construction body/chassis and rear-mounted five-cylinder radial engine, built in the KLG spark plug factory.

NORTH STAR • England 1920-1921

This cyclecar, built in Lee Green, London, used a 4 hp single-cylinder Blackburne engine. It was belt driven and cost £159.

NORTHWAY • USA 1921-1922

Northway was a subsidiary of the Northway Engine Company, part of General Motors, which manufactured commercial vehicles as well as engines for other makes of car, including Oakland and Oldsmobile. Northway featured, naturally, a Northway engine for 1921, in which year a touring car sold for $4,200. For some reason the make opted for a Herschell-Spillman engine in 1922; few (if any) of these were sold.

1975 datsun 240Z

NISSAN (formerly Datsun) • Japan
1931 to date

Nissan is the current-generation name for the range of cars previously marketed worldwide under the Datsun banner. The name Nissan comes from the heavy-industries group that encompassed the Datsun car making group. Datsun undertook its name change in the early 1980s, and has since moved from being a small-time importer of bread-and-butter-type, basic small cars and sedans to become a producer of highly respected hatchbacks, sedans, sports cars, MPV wagons, and 4wd leviathans.

The group's origins go back to Japan in 1914-1926, when the original founders started the DAT car maker as the predecessor of Datsun. DAT (from its founders, Den, Aoyama, and Takeuchi) built cars on a small scale. The 2.0-liter four-cylinder DAT 31 of 1915 was followed by the 2.3-liter DAT 41 of 1916-26. In 1926 DAT merged with the makers of the Lila car; between 1927-1931 only trucks were built under the DAT name. Then the company became DATSUN as part of the giant Nissan industrial group. Officially formed in 1931, Datsun was founded in Yokohama, though after the war production centered on the Tokyo area. Its main product during the 1930s (during which period the Nissan company name was adopted) was an Austin Seven-based 750cc model (a proposal to build the 10 hp Ford under license came to nothing.) Big cars based on the Graham-Paige appeared in 1937. Post-war, production resumed in 1947 with models again derived from Austin designs. Then, in 1955, the 110 sedan appeared; its 1959 derivative, the 310, was the first of the Bluebird line. Also in 1959 the first Datsun 2000 appeared. A prestige model for the home market, the President, appeared in 1964, followed two years later by the Datsun 1000. In 1966 Datsun merged with Prince Motors, and important new models followed: the 510 Bluebird, of 1967, with 1300cc and 1600cc ohc engines; and the 1800 Laurel of 1968. The Fairlady soft-top of 1969, an MGB lookalike, and the 240Z sports six-cylinder, which was to win the East African Safari Rally twice, both proclaimed Datsun's sporting aspirations. The Z cars, sportsters with attractive styling and good reliability, wiped ailing British makes like the MGB off the face of the American market and established Datsun as a known name in what was to become its most improtant market, the United States.

The 1000 was replaced by the 1200, and a new fwd model, the 100A Cherry, was launched, finding its greatest favor in export markets. By the mid-1970s a comprehensive range included the Cherry, 120Y Sunny, 140J/160J Violet, Bluebirds of 1.6 to 2 liters, ohc 2-liter Laurel, 260Z Sport,s and the 3-liter straight-six and 4-liter V8 President. In a weird incarnation, the 1980s Nissan Cherry was sold both as a Cherry "Europe" model and as an Alfa Romeo badged car with an Alfa engine, known as the "Arna." The unfortunately named Japanese market model, the Cedric, did not follow suit, and along with other big Datsun models it remained a Far Easetern oddity.

By the mid-1980s the reliable but bland image of the cars was causing the maker's star to fade slightly, and a rush of new models arrived from that period and on through the 1990s, by then under the Nissan name. The over-ornate styling was ditched in favour of sleeker, more western-shaped cars. The Z cars returned to their purer, less overweight, roots, and the 200ZX and Porsche-rivalling 300ZX put the marque back on target. Nissan set up a manufacturing plant in Britain (at Washington, Sunderland) and first produced the last of the Bluebirds and then the highly succesful Micra hatchback and Primera executive car ranges. This move complemented Nissan's earlier move of buying a 35 per cent shareholding in Spanish car making concern Motor Iberico, from which Nissan built up its 4wd production base. This 4wd segment was expanded beyond the venerable Patrol model and encompassed a joint deal with Ford, whereby the two makers shared a basic 4wd car design and

badged them separately, the Nissan version being named Terrano and built in Spain. Other model highlights included the bahn-storming Skyline GT-R road-legal sedan-shaped coupé racer with advanced electronic engineering and four-wheel drive, tied to a 300 bhp twin-turbo engine.

Further overseas expansion took place, Nissan setting up plants in America (Symrna, Tennessee) from which it took on the US domestic market with US-built cars. As the 1990s progressed, Nissan, Japan's second biggest car maker and the world"s number six car producer, entered a period of uncertainty. It survived this, and its recent moves have included relaunching the true spirit of the Z-cars through a retrostyled new model first premiered at the 1999 Detroit Auto show. One of the heavyweights, Nissan is learning to become a nimble footed player on the world stage.

Nissan Patrol - big foot of the 4wd brigade (top,) 300ZX, Nissan's own supercar (center,) Terrano, a 4wd shared with Ford and built in Spain (left,) Almera, people carrier (above)

NSU • Germany 1905-1929, 1958-1977

Neckarsulmer motorcycles and bicycles were already well-known when this company started building Belgian Pipe cars under license. In 1906 it began production of a Pfaender-designed car with a 1420cc four-cylinder engine, followed by models of up to 2608cc. A vertical-twin voiturette of 1105cc appeared in 1909, a year which also saw the arrival of one of the most popular NSU cars of the period, the 1132cc four-cylinder, produced until 1913; there was also a 1550cc version. The biggest pre-war NSU was a 3300cc four. Introduced in 1913, the 1232cc 5/15 PS was still in production in 1926. Other models of the 1920s had four-cylinder engines of 2100cc and 3610cc, and sixes of 1567cc and 1781cc. Production was shifted to Heilbronn in 1927, but ceased when this had to be sold to Fiat. In 1934-1935, however, the Neckarsulm factory produced some VW-like prototypes, with assistance from its English designer, Walter Moore. But car production was not resumed until 1958, with the 583cc ohc vertical-twin Prinz, followed by an improved 598cc version. Meanwhile, NSU had sold its entire motorcycle production set-up to Yugoslavia. In 1963 NSU created a sensation with the introduction of the first quantity-production Wankel-engined car, the Spider, developing 50 bhp from the equivalent of 500cc; it was built until 1967. The 1964 four-cylinder ohc 996cc Prinz was followed by models of 1085cc and 1177cc. Successor to the Spider was the elegant Ro80 sedan, produced for nearly a decade, despite some durability problems with early examples of its rotary power unit.

1913 8/24hp four-cylinder NSU

1908 NSU 10/20 PS phaeton

1976 NSU Ro80 with the Wankel rotary engine

NORWALK • USA 1911-1922

From Martinsburg, West Virginia, the 1911 Norwalk was a sporty car with an underslung chassis, riding on 40-inch wheels. It cost $3,100. After 1916 a conventional chassis was used.

NOTA • England 1972

The Nota Fang was a basic little rear-engined alloy- and glassfibre-bodied sports car with steel space frame; it had sold successfully in Australia before coming to the UK. Excellent performance from a choice of BMC A series engines was not enough to sell more than a handful of Notas in Britain.

NOVA • England 1971-1990

The futuristic Nova had a glassfibre shell with overtones of the Lamborghini Miura and Ford GT40, on a VW Beetle chassis.

NSU • Germany 1905-1929, 1958-1977

See panel

NSU-FIAT (NECKAR) • Germany 1929-1973

NSU had to sell its new Heilbronn factory to Fiat in 1929; Fiat cars assembled there were initially sold as NSU, later as NSU-Fiat cars. Best known were the 570cc (500) and 1089cc models. After the Second World War the works assembled the twin-cylinder 570cc, 479cc, and 499cc Weinsberg and the 633cc and 767cc four-cylinder Jagst models. The cars were known as "Neckars" after NSU resumed production in 1958. The factory is now the home of the German Fiat AG, which merely imports Fiats (as well as Russian and Polish Fiat-license cars).

NUG • Germany 1921-1925

A small car produced in small numbers, the Niebaum-designed 960cc ioe four-cylinder NUG was one of the better cars of this period.

NYBERG • USA 1912-1914

Biggest of the Indiana-built Nybergs was a 5441cc six-cylinder seven-passenger tourer.

NYMPH • England 1975-1978

Designed by Bohanna Stables, the originators of the AC 3000, the Nymph was an open four-seat runabout of glassfibre monocoque construction; 34 of these Imp-powered machines were built.

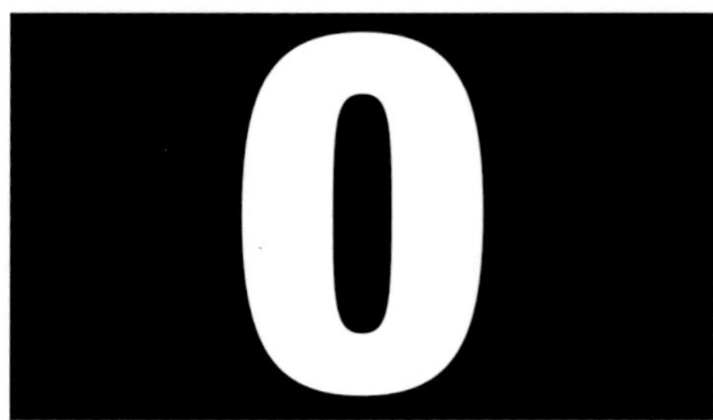

1921-1922 Ogren Sedan

OAKLAND • USA 1907-1932

The first car to leave Oakland's Pontiac, Mich., factory was a 20 hp twin, designed by Alanson Brush (and had his typical hallmark, an engine that cranked anti-clockwise.) It had an epicyclic gear-change incorporated in the back axle. In 1909 Oakland became part of General Motors and introduced its first four. By 1912 fours of 3 and 4 litres were offered, followed in 1913 by a 5999cc 40 hp six, both having vee radiators. A 5.5-liter V-8 appeared in 1916, as did an ohv 15/20 hp six of 2955cc, which soon became Oakland's sole model. It was succeeded in late 1923 by a 3038cc side-valve six with centralized chassis lubrication from the engine pump, and four-wheel brakes. It was also the first Ducco-finished car. But the introduction of a sister marque, Pontia, in 1926, hit Oakland sales. A 1930 V-8, based on the Viking, was the last Oakland.

OBUS • France 1907-1908

A Souriau of Montoire (Loire-et-Cher) built this voiturette.

OCENASEK • Czechoslovakia 1906-1907

A rotary air-cooled 16 hp eight-cylinder built in Prague, probably only in prototype form.

OCTO • France 1920-1928

M Vienne, maker of the Carteret cyclecar, also made bigger cars in Courbevoie, Seine, under the "Octo" name. The first model was a Ballot-engined 10 hp of 1592cc. In 1921 it was followed by a cyclecar with the 902cc Ruby engine. From 1923 to the end of production Octo made only light touring and sports cars with 969cc Ruby engines.

ODENSE MOBIL • Denmark 1905

Two Odense Mobil cars were built, but probably were only Oldsmobiles with more comfortable bodies. It is not known if mechanical changes were also made.

ODETTI • Italy 1922-1924

Early Odetti cars had twin-cylinder two-stroke engines. Production was limited. One model had an interesting "streamlined" two-seater racing body, another was an open four-seater with a four-cylinder 12 hp engine.

OFELDT • USA 1899-1901

August W Ofeldt, the Brooklyn steam and naphtha launch builder, offered tiller-steered carriages with vee-formation compound engines. In 1901 he offered an X-formation four-cylinder compound power unit.

1929 Oakland All-American 6

OFFORD • England 1896

Well-known Kensington, London, coachbuilder which also built an electric dog-cart.

OGLE • England 1960 to date

David Ogle's first attractive replacement body was for the Riley 1.5. The subsequent Ogle Mini, later known as the Ogle SX1000, was a more commercial project, however, and 66 were completed before the manufacturing rights were sold to Norman Fletcher following Ogle's untimely death. Before he died Ogle had designed the Daimler Dart-based SX250, which later became the prototype Reliant GT. Subsequently his company built the Triplex GTS, the prototype Scimitar GTE and Ogle Aston Martin. This was renamed the Sotheby Special after Aston Martin had decided against putting it into production.

OGREN • USA 1914-1923

A high-quality assembled car designed by Hugo W Ogren, who had already created a number of successful racers and other cars under various marques. All Ogrens were six-cylinder cars with Beaver and Continental engines. No production statistics are available, but after output had been increased in 1920 the figure may have reached 400 units. Prices ranged from $3,500 to about $5,700. An attempt to reorganize Ogren and move operations to Chicago under the name "Commander" failed, with only one Commander touring car (actually an Ogren with a reworked emblem) displayed. The last Ogren cars were sold in 1923, but these were left-over 1921 and 1922 units.

1924 Oldfield sedan

1962 Ogle Mini

OHB • USA 1904

O'Halloran Brothers of London, which imported the Crestmobile into Britain, disguised its cruder features under English-built bodywork and sold it as its own make.

OHIO • USA 1909-1913

A shaft-drive 40 hp four from Cincinnati.

OHIO • USA 1910-1918

Expensive electric broughams built in Toledo.

OHTA • Japan 1934-1957

This Tokyo firm built a prototype in 1922, but production began in 1934 with a sv 736cc four, reminiscent of the contemporary Model C Ford (then assembled in Yokohama.) This model was built until 1939. Post-war, a range of small fours was offered until Kurogane swallowed Ohta in 1957 and halted car production.

OKEY • USA 1907-1908

A two-stroke three-cylinder 2.6-liter runabout built by Perry Okey of Columbus, Ohio.

OLDFIELD • USA 1924

Only a single Oldfield, a three-passenger coupé, was ever constructed. Built by the Kimball Truck Company for the Oldfield Motors Corporation of Los Angeles, the enterprise was headed by world-famous racing car driver Berna Eli "Barney" Oldfield, who had been heading the Oldfield Tire Company. The car sported four-wheel brakes, balloon tyres, and was equipped with a six-cylinder Wisconsin engine. Barney Oldfield drove the car to Indianapolis in May 1924 to promote sales; on his return to the West Coast the Wisconsin motor was removed and an eight substituted. The project petered out at this point after the Kimball Truck plant, Oldfield, and an apathetic public collectively lost interest in the venture.

OLDSMOBILE • USA 1896 to date

See panel

OLTCIT • Romania 1981 to date

A joint venture between the Romanian government and Citroën to build the Citroën Visa. The factory never reached its projected output of 130,000 cars a year, and in 1990 was accused by the new regime of owing the state 8.7 billion French francs.

OLYMPIAN • USA 1917-1921

A small-production assembled car, the Olympian sported a four-cylinder engine of its own make, touring cars and four-passenger roadsters being the only models available. The Olympian became the Friend car in 1920, and Olympians sold in 1921 were 1920 leftovers.

OM • Italy 1918-1934

Successor to Züst, OM built some excellent sporting cars until this old-established machine factory, founded in 1899, became part of the Fiat empire. OM at first took over the existing 4170cc Züst-design; its own cars had 1496cc, 1991cc, 2216cc, and, eventually, 2325cc four- and six-cylinder engines. Some had ohv heads; a few boasted Roots-type superchargers. OM won the first Mille Miglia in 1927.

RF Oats in a 2-litre OM at Brooklands, c. 1926

1904 Curved-Dash Oldsmobile

c. 1923 Oldsmobile

OLDSMOBILE • USA 1896 to date

Olds built few cars until 1899, when copper and lumber magnate S L Smith bought the company to give his two sons a lucrative hobby. Original plans were for a $1,250 luxury car with pneumatic clutch and electric starter, but it failed to sell and Ransom Olds then designed the immortal single-cylinder tiller-steered Curved-Dash Oldsmobile, which made its debut in 1901. By 1904 production of the "Merry Oldsmobile" had reached 5,000; that year Ransom Olds left the company, soon to found Reo. By 1905 flat-twin and wheel-steered variants of the Oldsmobile were available; the next year saw a vertical-twin two-stroke, the 20/24 hp "Double-Action" Model L, and the company's first four, the 26/28 hp Model S. A 7,400cc six was introduced in 1908, when the ailing company was acquired by General Motors. In 1910 came a colossal 11,469cc six, so tall that it needed two-tier running boards! By 1912 the biggest Olds was "only" 6997cc. An efficient 4-liter V-8 with aluminum pistons arrived in 1916, surviving until 1923. From 1921-1923 an ohv four with the same 2.8-liter engine as Chevrolet was available. A one-model policy prevailed until 1929, with a 2774cc six with Buick-like radiator; from 1927 it boasted fwb and chromium plating. The low-priced Viking V-8 was offered from 1929-1931. A new 3933cc straight-eight appeared in 1932, and 1935 saw the controversial "turret-top" styling. A reputation for technical innovation was maintained with the option of GM's first production automatic transmission in 1938, though it reportedly "didn't become reliable" until 1940.

The pre-war sixes and eights were continued for the first three post-war seasons. Even in 1948 three-fourths of cars sold had the Hydramatic transmission. Along with Cadillac, the top of the range Olds 98 received GM's first new post-war body in 1948, with its split curved windshield and wraparound rear window, but a new power unit did not materialize until the next year. This was Gilbert Burrell's short-stroke ohv 4965cc Rocket V-8, initially developing 135 bhp and giving 240 bhp by 1965. "Autronic Eye" automatic headlamp dipping came in 1953; 1958 saw quad headlamps, exaggerated tailfins, and a short-lived air-springing option. The 1961 F85 compact had an aluminum V-8 of 3523cc; sporting derivatives included the 185 bhp Cutlass range and the 1963 Jetfire, available with turbocharger. Bigger Oldsmobiles used 6457cc V-8s from 280 to 345 bhp.

In 1964 the F85's V-8 had been replaced by the more economical Buick V-6, and there was a range of full-size Jetstar eights of 5407cc, also aimed at economy. The Toronado sports coupé of 1966 was the first successful fwd automatic (with drum brakes, as originally specified, it proved too fast for its chassis.) Its 6965cc V-8 (7456cc from 1968) drove the front wheels through silent-tooth chains. By 1971 Oldsmobile was still listing three lines of convertible (Cutlass Supreme, 442, Delta 88) and all but the cheapest models had front disc brakes. A compact model, the 1973 Omega, was the equivalent of the Pontiac Ventura, with which it had a 4097cc six and 5736cc V-8 in common. The 1975 Starfire had Chevrolet, Pontiac, and Buick sister models; that year's Delta Royale was Oldsmobile's last convertible. Five-speed transmissions were available on 1976 Starfires and Omegas, and the Cutlass claimed to be America's best-selling model, with 515,000 registrations. An important technical breakthrough of 1978 was an optional 5.7-litre diesel engine. An all-new, scaled-down Toronado headed the 1979 range.

For the 1980s, cost sharing was the name of the US auto makers' game, and Oldsmobile was no exception. Thus a rash of GM parts-bin-sourced, badge engineered cars came to the fore. As with so many other famous

1953 Oldsmobile Ninety-Eight sedan

American marques, it was a mistake that would leave the door wide open for Japanese makers to come in with up-to-the-minute, individual designs. GM fought back in fine style with the clean lines of the Aurora, which had overtones of European styling and looked very sleek and purposeful. It was joined by a range of cars including the LSS and Intruige, all of which were at the forefront of the advance, the leap, that American cars had to make in their improve-or-die situations. Through the Aurora and its siblings, Oldsmobile thrived once again and rejoined the list of American greats.

Oldsmobile's Omega was one of its 1980 "X-cars,"designed to incorporate "European" characteristics

The OldsmobileToronado featured "revolutionary" front-wheel drive

1925 Le Mans Oméga-Six

1914 Omnium light car

OMAHA • USA 1912-1913

An underslung chassis was used on the 3818cc four-cylinder Omaha.

OMEGA • France 1900

Tubular-framed voiturettes of 3 cv or 5.5 cv, built by the Kreutzberger brothers of Paris, who supplied folding push-bikes to the French Army.

OMEGA • Germany 1921-1922

Predecessor of the Omikron, the sv 796cc four-cylinder Omega was a basic cyclecar, built in small numbers.

OMEGA • England 1925-1927

In 1926 this 980cc JAP-engined three-wheeler from a Coventry motorcycle maker took six world class speed records, covering over 297 miles in six hours.

OMEGA-SIX • France 1922-1930

Very few Oméga-Six cars left the Boulogne-sur-Seine works. They had engines designed by the engineer Gadoux. One was an ohc six-cylinder of 2915cc, the other a 1991cc six.

OMIKRON • Germany 1922-1925

Omikron took over where Omega at Berlin-Charlottenburg left off. It built a Pingel-designed 960cc four-cylinder with Steudel sv engine, and also a sporting ohc 1042cc two-seater model.

OMNIA • Holland 1900-1911

This Voorburg firm built a range of two-, three-, and four-cylinder models from 10 hp to 55 hp. After 1910 the 18 hp Spyker was built under license. No more than 100 Omnias of all kinds were produced.

OMNIMOBIL • Germany 1904-1910

Fafnir of Aachen, which had built the 1902 Aachener, supplied a 353cc single-cylinder engine (and, later, two- and four-cylinder units) along with nearly all the necessary components for building complete cars. These Omnimobil sets led to a couple of new "makes" from enterprising assemblers. Complete Fafnir cars were available from 1908.

OMNIUM • England 1913-1914

Initially a £135 twin-cylinder "miniature car". A 1094cc four was launched in January 1914.

ONE OF THE BEST • England 1905

A 9 hp light car built by a jack manufacturer named Adams of Tunbridge Wells, Kent.

ONLY • USA 1909-1913

An early production sports car, the Only took its name from its huge ohv 3380cc single-cylinder engine, with a bore of 130mm and a stroke of 254mm. Guaranteed top speed was 60mph.

ONNASCH • Germany 1924-1925

Small cars with sv 746cc MI (later Mehne) flat-twin engines.

OPEL • Germany 1898 to date

See panel

1905 One of the Best Voiturette

1907 40 hp Opel owned by Victor Leon

OPEL • Germany 1898 to date

Adam Opel, founder of the Opel cycle and sewing machine works at Russelsheim, died in 1895. His sons bought Lutzmann and produced the first Opel car, "System Lutzmann," in 1898. In 1900 they started importing Renaults and also Darracqs (for which they acquired the production license.) From 1902 Opel-designed cars (initially twin-cylinder 1884cc models) were offered alongside Opel-Darracqs of up to 8008cc. The Opel range was always very wide, and by 1914 four-cylinder models from 1392cc to 10,200cc were offered, the latter having a 100 hp three-valve ioe engine and four-speed gearbox. In the 1920s young Fritz Opel won races on Opel motorcycles and Opel cars, and in 1928 drove the first Opel racing car powered by rockets at the Avus race track. Models built in the early 1920s included 1984cc and 3430cc fours and a six-cylinder 5598cc model.

After installing a moving assembly line in 1924, Opel built the Citroën 5cv-like 951cc four-cylinder "Laubfrosch" in large numbers. Priced at 4000 Gold Marks, it sold well. A 1016cc 14hp model followed, while other models included excellent sixes of 1735cc, 1924cc, 3540cc, and 4170cc. From 1929 Opel also offered the eight-cylinder 5972cc Regent, built on American lines; understandably so, because General Motors of Detroit had taken control of Opel in 1928. New small Opel fours appeared, including the 1074cc Kadett and 1488cc Olympia. The Kadett became a best-seller. Among six-cylinder Opels were the 2473cc Super-Six and Kapitän and the 3626cc Admiral, all with ohv engines. When the Second World War broke out, Opel was the leading European car manufacturer, selling the small versions in large numbers; some 107,000 Kadetts were built from 1937 to 1941.

The first Opel car after the war was the pre-war Olympia, now with an ohv 1488cc four-cylinder engine,

which entered production in 1947. The first new 2473cc six-cylinder Kapitän arrived in 1948. Other models included the Rekord and the 1200. The year 1962 saw a new, modern Kadett with a 993cc four-cylinder engine. New 1963 Rekord models had 1488cc and 1680cc ohv four-cylinder motors. Later, four-cylinder engines up to 1897cc and six-cylinder power units of 2586cc were available in the Rekord. Six-cylinder Kapitäns and Admirals had engines up to 2784cc, while other big Opel cars, including the Diplomat, housed Chevrolet-built V-8 motors. The 1979 Opel range consisted of Kadett, Ascona, Manta, Rekord, Commodore, and Senator/Monza models, with a variety of engines from 1196cc to 2969cc. The Ascona medium sedan made its debut in 1981. The Corsa minicar appeared in 2- and 3-door forms in 1982, with 4- and 5-door versions appearing in 1985. A new Kadett was launched in 1984. The Omega succeeded the Rekord in 1986, and a new Senator was launched in 1987. In 1988 the Vectra replaced the Ascona in the key C/D sector. The Astra replaced the Kadett in 1991. The Calibra sports coupé is claimed to be the world's most aerodynamic production car, with a drag factor of only 0.26. The Vectra in German Opel guise was as popular as the British version, which for once kept the same name. Both cars were given facelifts in 1999 and continued the styling themes started by the swoopy, Mk 2 Cavalier/Ascona. The Omega models came in the mid-1990s and also scored a success, notably in their higher powered versions.

1991 Opel Calibra Turbo

1979 Opel Monza

GM's Capri rival - the Manta

1898 4 hp Orient Express

OPES • Italy 1948-1949

A fwd "People's car" with a three-cylinder radial engine of 748cc, built in small numbers.

OPPERMANN • England 1896-1907

Carl Oppermann, whose works were in Clerkenwell, London, built both front- and rear-wheel-drive electrics. He claimed his 1902 electric broughams and landaulettes could run 50 miles on one charge.

OPUS • England 1966-1968

One of stylist Neville Trickett's more lighthearted designs, the Opus was a hot-rod, loosely inspired by the Model T Ford and using Ford Anglia components.

OREL • France 1905-1914

From Argenteuil (Seine-et-Oise,) Orel offered 8/10 hp twin-cylinder and 12/14 hp four-cylinder cars, with chain or shaft drive.

ORIAL • France 1920-1923

The Office de Représentation Industrielle et Automobile in Lyon was mainly a motorcycle manufacturer, but also made some Senechal-inspired cyclecars with sv 902cc Ruby engines.

ORIENT • USA 1899-1909

The Waltham Manufacturing Company of Massachussets was a famed cycle builder before it introduced a De Dion Bouton-engined tricycle, which could be converted into a quadricycle by removing the front wheel and forks and replacing them with a frame carrying two wheels and a seat. Steam cars were also built from 1897-1999. In 1900 came a light wheelsteered car, the Victoriette, and a tiller-steered Runabout. Aster engines were used. In 1902 the company introduced the Orient Buckboard, a lightweight two-seater relying on the spring in its wooden plank flooring for suspension.

ORIENT EXPRESS • Germany 1896-1903

Designed by Josef Vollmer, the single-cylinder 1922cc Orient Express, built at Theodor Bergmann"s Gaggenau works, was similar to the early Benz but had four-speed belt drive, ten handles, and one pedal (which worked the warning bell.) Improved versions had two- and four-cylinder power units of up to 16 hp.

ORION • Switzerland 1900-1910

Orion of Zürich began production with six front-engined single-cylinder vis-á-vis cars, then concentrated on making trucks.

ORIX • Spain 1952

Powered by a 610cc flat-twin engine, the Orix looked very like the VW Beetle.

ORPINGTON • England 1920-1924

The Orpington was a truly assembled car containing Model T Ford components, a 1.5-liter Coventry-Simplex engine and Moss gearbox.

ORSON • USA 1909

"One hundred men interested in financial, railroad and industrial affairs" organized this company to build cars for themselves ("and later for the general trade.") Its showrooms were, appropriately, on Wall Street.

ORYX • Germany 1907-1922

Successor to BMF, the Berlin-based Oryx works produced 1555cc four-cylinder cars, was taken over in 1909 by Dürkopp and afterwards built an 1830cc four-cylinder car. Enlarged to 2080cc, the last Oryx was built at the Dürkopp works.

OSCA • Italy 1947-1967

The Maserati brothers sold their works to the Orsi family in 1937, but stayed on until 1947, when they left and founded a new factory, OSCA. The first design was a 4472cc V-12 racing engine for existing 1.5-liter Maseratis. OSCA built 1093cc and 1350cc four-cylinder, as well as 1987cc six-cylinder, sports and racing cars with ohc and dohc engines; there was also a 1490cc six-cylinder. In the late 1950s a fast 749cc "Four" was added, capable of 115 mph. Some of the last 1492cc dohc machines could reach 145 mph, the 1987cc version nearly 162mph. In 1966 the Maseratis retired and sold everything to MV-Agusta.

OSMOND • England 1899-1900

A Birmingham-built motor quadricycle.

OSTERFIELD • England 1907-1909

Despite its Germanic name, the Osterfield, "for the man of moderate means," was built by Douglas S Cox of South Norwood, London. There were three models, a 2596cc four, a 3893cc six, and a straight-eight of 5191cc, at a chassis price of £850.

OTAV • Italy 1901-1914

Max Türkheimer was a pioneer of the Italian motor industry. He built motorcycles and cars, and imported British Ariel machines. He had been commercially connected with

Ariel since 1897, so his early products used various Ariel-built parts. His cars had single-cylinder and, later, four-cylinder 2786cc engines. A versatile man, Türkheimer was also involved with the Torino-built Junior cars.

OTOMO • Japan 1924-1927

Having built two experimental Ales cars in 1921, Junya Toyokawa produced an air-cooled 944cc light car, joined in 1926 by a 24 hp model.

OTRO FORD • Spain 1922-1924

As its name cheekily implied ("Another Ford,") this was a Model T Ford-based marque in the same mold as the English Maiflower.

OTTO • France 1901-1914

Starting with a 10 hp horizontal-engined twin and a vertical-engined 20 hp four, Otto of Paris offered, in 1902, two 10 hp models, a twin and a four-cylinder. In 1907 a 30cv model was shown at the Salon de l'Automobile, and in 1910 the company took over the FL, built under Serex license, with a 12 hp four-cylinder 2011cc engine. An 18 hp six appeared two years later.

OTTO • USA 1910-1912

"Highest grade at any price," the Philadelphia-built Otto sold for $2,000. Fours of 4.2 to 5.1 liters were offered.

OTTO • Germany 1923-1925

Designed by Gustav Otto, son of Nikolaus Otto, the famous inventor of four-stroke gas engines, the luxurious 4.9-liter Otto car was built in small numbers. The Munich factory produced Flottweg bicycle engines and motorcycles between the wars. It was later bought by BMW.

OURS • France 1906-1909

Round-radiatored cars built in Paris; the motto was "Perfection–Solidity–Economy." The 1908 range consisted of a 10/12 hp twin-cylinder, a 14/16 hp three-cylinder, a 20/24 hp four-cylinder, and a 30/35 hp six-cylinder.

OUZOU • France 1900-1901

Soncin-engined 4 hp and 6 hp voiturettes from Paris.

OVERHOLT • USA 1908-1909

A four-seater motor buggy with friction drive, built in Galesburg, Illinois.

c. 1905 OTAV voiturette rebuilt as a cyclecar in 1912

O-WE-GO • USA 1914

A tandem-seat $385 cyclecar from Owego, NY.

OWEN • England 1895-c. 1936

Originally a mechanical and marine engineering company, Owen, whose works were said to be in Birmingham, claimed to have built a 5 hp single-cylinder car with five-speed chain-and-belt transmission as early as 1895. Its showroom was at Carrick House, Comeragh Road, London W14. Production was, at best, spasmodic. Indeed, there is some speculation whether the company built any cars at all! It was (it claimed) principally a maker of engines, gear boxes, axles, brakes, and wheels for the motor trade. In 1920 it listed the 2994cc 20 hp (with only one forward speed!) and the 40 hp Owen Dynamic, a 3216cc gasoline-electric. Other marques associated with Owen were the Twentieth Century Voiturette (1901), Parisia, Londonia, Twentieth Century, and Owen"s Gearless (1905-1906), as well as Orleans, Atalanta, Italian,a and Owen"s Petelecta. Owen"s cars could well have been rebadged examples of other makes. A 1921 5302cc V-8 seems to have originated in America, and the last Owen was the 60 hp of 1925 (listed until 1936 in some sources,) with a 7634cc straight-eight.

1912 Oryx 18/24 hp phaeton

OWEN • USA 1910-1914

Noted for its high 42-inch pneumatic-tired wheels, the 50 hp Owen had a 5912cc four-cylinder engine and left-hand drive.

OWEN MAGNETIC (CROWN MAGNETIC) • USA 1914-c. 1921

Ray M Owen of Baker Raulang devised a magnetic transmission based on the Entz system used in oil-engined battleships; it was used in a 38 hp six-cylinder luxury car. Design rights to this "Car of a Thousand Speeds" were sold to J L Crown, who began production at Wilkes-Barre, Pa., in 1920. He brought a Crown Magnetic to England soon after, and the Owen transmission was fitted to a few Minervas, two Ensigns, and a few Magnetics. But the Crown Magnetic proved too complex and expensive; steep hills could cause "magnetic drag" which brought the 2.5 tonne (50 cwt) car to a standstill, and production ceased.

OWEN-SCHOENECK • USA 1915-1916

A 5.2-liter Herschell-Spillman-powered four from Chicago.

OXFORD • England 1899

A 21/4 hp light belt-driven three-wheeler sold in Oxford Street, London.

OXFORD • Canada 1914-1915

The six Pontbriand brothers, plus two cousins, ran Oxford Car & Foundries Ltd of Maisonneuve, Montreal, which built four pair cast sixes to the design of H M Potter.

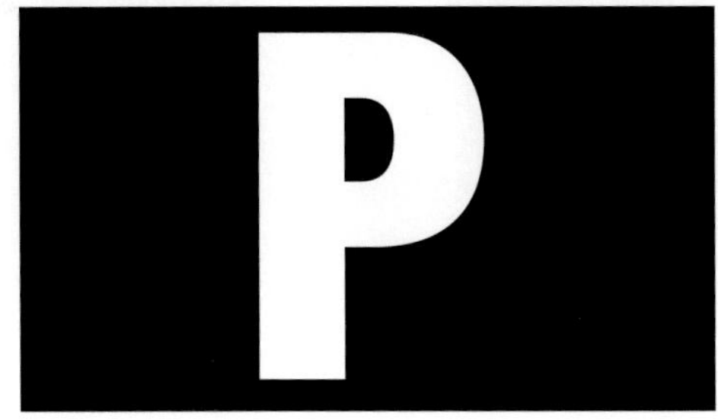

PACKARD • USA 1899-1958

See panel

PADUS • Italy 1906-1908

Voiturettes with 6 hp (single) and 10 hp (twin) engines, built in Turin.

PAGANI • Italy 1999 to date

This new name in Italian car manufacturing intends to turn out a two-seat super car named Zonda, with a 400 bhp Mercedes V-12 powerplant. The car uses carbonfiber composite construction with subframes in steel. Top speed is 190 mph and 0-60 mph in 4 sec is the target. A mid-engined, rear-driven layout with race-car-type styling gives this car true supercar potential.

PAGE • USA 1905-1907

A twin-cylinder air-cooled runabout from Providence, RI.

PAGE • USA 1921-1924

The Pagé (or Victor Pagé) "Aero-Type Four" automobile, despite a total production of five units, commanded a good deal of attention in the American automotive press in the early 1920s. Photographs were published of a well-advanced-in-design car, available as a four-passenger roadster or a four-passenger coupé. These cars were built by Major Victor W Pagé, a former textbook writer on automotive subjects, flying instructor in the American Expeditionary Force during the First World War, and editor of *Scientific American* magazine. The cars had an air-cooled four-cylinder engine and were displayed at the 1922 New York Automobile Show, but failed to go any further. Pagé built a smaller air-cooled car, the Utility.

PAIGE, PAIGE-DETROIT • USA 1908-1927

The 25 hp Paige-Detroit of 1908 had a 2172cc three-cylinder two-stroke engine in unit with a two-speed gearbox. In 1908-1909 302 cars were built, after which four-cylinder four-stroke engines were adopted. The 2896cc "25," current until 1914, was succeeded by the 4118cc "36." From 1915 only sixes, a Rutenber of 3771cc and a Continental of 4967cc, were used. In 1916 a moving assembly line was installed in the plant. From 1921 the "Most Beautiful Car in America" had an elegant plated radiator like a shouldered Bentley cooler; this looked especially well on the handsome Daytona roadster of 1922-1926. The 1927 range consisted of three sixes and an eight. Next year the marque became "Graham-Paige." From 1923-1926 Paige built the Jewett.

French advertising for the 1919 Paige Six

PAKYAN • Iran 1974 to date

Chrysler UK Hunters exported in kit form for assembly by Iran National.

PALLADIUM • France • England 1912-1925

"A remarkably good car at a remarkably low price," the Palladium was originally built in France for sale in England. There were three models, with Chapuis-Dornier engines, a 1725cc 10/12 hp, a 2121cc 12/22 hp, and a 2651cc 15/20 hp. Two new models were added in 1913, an 18/30 hp (3664cc) and an eight-cylinder 20/28 hp of 3451cc, twice the capacity of the 10/18 hp four. That year Palladium production was switched to Twickenham. A complete *volte-face* came in 1919 with a chain-driven flat-twin-engined cyclecar of 1331cc. It was replaced in 1922 by a 1496cc four-cylinder 12 hp with a Dorman engine. A sports version was listed from 1923.

PALMER • USA 1899-1900

This marine engineering company of Mianus, Connecticut, sold engines and components and built at least one complete motor car.

PALMER-SINGER • USA 1908-1914

"Built in small quantities and sold to the select few," Palmer-Singers (built by the sole agents for Simplex) were initially available in "Four-Thirty" (4185cc) and "Six-Sixty" (9583cc) forms. A dashboard-radiatored 28/30 hp "Skimabout" was listed in 1908. Fast and powerful, Palmer-Singers achieved some sporting success, however, when failure loomed the company tried desperately to rekindle public interest by announcing its 1915 range in 1913.

PALMERSTON, PALM • England 1921-1923

A 688cc Coventry Victor-engined light car built by the Palmerston Motor Company of Boscombe, Hants. The later Palm was a 9 hp.

PAN • USA 1917-1922

The Pan takes an important place in American automotive history as a car built in what became one of the greatest automobile swindles in history from the viewpoint of stock sales. The builder of the car was Samuel Conner Pandolfo, who founded "Pan-Town-on-the-Mississippi," today St Cloud. An ambitious promoter, he built the town and everything in it, including what was probably the first motel. The Pan factory was a model of modern efficiency, and the promotional catalogue for the car was probably the most elaborate ever printed in automotive history. The Pan featured a four-cylinder motor and body styles were restricted to open models. Seats were collapsible to form a double bed. Before the Federal Government stepped in to investigate the Pan stock maneuvres, which ultimately sent Sam Pandolfo to prison, about 737 cars had been manufactured.

PAN-AMERICAN • USA 1918-1922

"The American Beauty Car," built in Decatur, Illinois, was distinguished by a white-painted radiator shell; it was

PACKARD

1928 Packard Eight 526 convertible coupé

PACKARD • USA 1899-1958

Convinced that he could build a better car than the new Winton he had just bought, electrical equipment manufacturer James Ward Packard began production of single-cylinder cars with automatic ignition advance at Warren, Ohio, in November 1899. His company was taken over in 1901 by Detroit businessman Henry B Joy, under whose aegis the first Packard four, designed by the Frenchman Charles Schmidt, appeared in 1903, the year the factory moved to Detroit. Schmidt's 1904 Model L four-cylinder was the first to bear Packard's distinctive yoked radiator. The firm's first six appeared in 1912, confirming Packard's reputation as a maker of high-priced luxury cars.

In 1916, inspired by the pioneering aero engines designed by Sunbeam in Britain, engineer Jesse G Vincent produced the V-12 Packard Twin-Six for the 1916 model year; this 6950cc model accounted for almost half that year's sales and was current until 1923, by which time 35,046 had been built. US President Warren Gamaliel Harding was the first to ride to his inauguration by car, in a Twin-Six. A 4395cc Single-Six appeared in 1921, followed in June 1923 by the Twin-Six replacement, the Single Eight of 5681cc, with four-wheel brakes and four-speed transmission. This model gave Packard supremacy in the luxury car market, and was produced in various Series designations.

1903 Packard 12 hp single-cylinder tonneau

The six was dropped in 1928. That year limited production of a Speedster Eight based on the new Sixth Series began, lasting into the Seventh Series, but only 220 of this performance model were built in all. Eights remained the company's mainstay during the 1930s (though 5744 examples of a new Vincent-designed 7298cc V-12, again designated Twin-Six, were made up to 1939). A moderately priced Packard Eight, the 120, had the marque's first ifs, and sold for only $990 in its cheapest form; its appearance in 1935 was followed two years later by a six, which boosted production to an all-time record of 109,518 in 1937. The luxury eights, the Senior Series 160 and 180, ran through until the war, when, in a gesture of US-Soviet goodwill, their body dies were sold to Russia, resulting in the 1945 ZIS-110 series.

This meant that Packard had no luxury car immediately post-war to compete with Lincoln and Cadillac, relying on a warmed-over version of its 1941-introduced Clipper series, ranging from the 4015cc Clipper 6 to the DeLuxe Clipper and Super and Custom range, with eights of 4621cc and 5834cc. Unfortunate slab-sided styling based on the old body earned 1948 Packards the nickname 'Pregnant Elephant'. Three series, Eight, Super Eight, and Custom Eight, with either 4720cc or 5359cc engines were offered, the six being relegated to taxis and export models. Sales reached a post-war peak of 104,593 in 1948, then began to fall. Packard's own automatic, the Ultra-matic Drive, appeared in spring 1949.

The first all-new post-war Packards arrived in 1951; this 'Twenty-fourth Series' consisted of the 200, 200 DeLuxe, 250, 300, and 400. The 4720cc engine was standard on the Clipper 200, 250, and 300; the high-priced 400 Patrician had the 5359cc engine (optional on other models) as standard. A new president, James J Nance, was determined to revive the ailing company and return to luxury cars, so the low-priced Clipper became a separate marque, and in 1953 some Derham-bodied Patricians and a series of 750 Caribbean convertibles were produced. In June 1954 Packard bought Studebaker, which was in dire financial straits; three months later came revolutionary new 1955 Packards, cleverly reskinned on the old body, with a brand-new 5801cc V-8 and 'Torsion-Level' suspension linking all four wheels. 'Twin-Ultramatic' transmission was a standard feature.

Production rose to almost 70,000, but the millstone of Studebaker dragged Packard down. The Curtiss-Wright Corporation took the group over as a tax loss, and the last true Packards appeared in 1956, a new Executive model attempting to bridge the gap between Clipper and Packard lines. The 1957-1958 Packards were no more than Studebakers using leftover Packard components; the bizarre Hawk (of which only 588 were built) had a wide-mouthed glassfiber snout.

1951 Packard Patrician 400, with Ultramatic transmission

1895 Peugeot 3 1/2 hp vis-á-vis

The Peugeot 201 team in the 1933 Tour de France

1948 Peugeot 203 Berline grand luxe

1991 Peugeot 106 XN

PEUGEOT • France 1889 to date

Armand Peugeot built his first steam car in 1889, and from 1891 made Daimler-engined cars with rear engines in tubular chassis; they sold very well for the era. In 1896 Peugeot started to make his own engines. In 1902 the 758cc "Bébé" was presented, and two years later Peugeot offered cars from 1.7 liters to 7.1 liters. Its first six-cylinder, a 10.4-liter, appeared in 1908, followed the next year by a smaller six of 3317cc. In 1912 Bugatti designed a new 855cc four-cylinder "Bébé," and the same year Peugeot also made a V-4 of 1725cc. At that period the dohc Peugeot racers designed by Ernest Henry were victorious in many events, including the French Grand Prix and the Indianapolis 500. At the outbreak of the war Peugeot's staple products were the model 153 12cv of 2613cc and the 7cv of 1452cc.

After the war Peugeot resumed production with these two models, to which were added the 10cv of 1525cc and the 25cv six of 5954cc. The popular 667cc "Quadrilette" was introduced in 1920, giving way in 1923 to the 5cv, this model being enlarged in 1925 to 719cc. During the 1920s there also was the sleeve-valve six. The basic model was the 201 of 1100cc, which lasted for 10 years before giving way to the 1500cc 301. The last of the pre-war Peugeot six-cylinders, the 601, appeared in 1936; a year later came the streamlined Peugeot 402 which lasted until the war, alongside the 302 and 202. During the Occupation Peugeot experimented with the electric-powered VLV.

Post-war production restarted with the 202, and in 1947 Peugeot presented the 1.3-liter 203. The next step was the 403 of 1955, with a 1500cc engine. The 404 came in 1960, with a 1600cc engine. All these cars were also available in diesel form. A small car, the 1100cc 204, was launched in 1965, to be replaced in 1969 by the 304 with a 1300cc engine. The 504 was born in 1968. In the 1970s Peugeot took control first of Citroën, then of Chrysler Europe. The 104 small hatchback of 1973 shared engines, transmissions and floorplans with such cars as Citroën LNA and Visa, Renault 14, and Peugeot 205. The 604 of 1975 used the V-6 "PRV" (Peugeot-Renault-Volvo) joint engine. In 1983 Peugeot launched the highly-successful 205 minicar, and the 309 of 1986 used a stretched 205 floorplan.

A new flagship model, the 505, was also launched in 1986. The year 1988 saw the arrival of the 405 range. The 106 small car made its debut in 1991, powered by engines ranging from 954cc to 1360cc. A top-of-the-range 605 model appeared, and was followed by the new 406, a 405 replacement. The 306 range competed admirably with other mainstream hatchbacks, and its tuned performance GTI version was seen by the motoring press as the best of its genre. Then followed a Peugeot MPV, the 806, which shared its pressings with the Fiat and Citroën MPVs of the same alliance. In styling and performance terms the 406 Coupé marked a return to form for Peugeot, and sold in large numbers. Its Ferrari-like style, performance and value for money drew many buyers from more expensive coupé marques. The new 106 was revised but it failed to cover the fact that, after the death of the Peugeot 205, once dubbed "car of the decade" by a leading magazine, there was a gap in the Peugeot range. This was ably filled in 1999 by the new 206 car, a design of chic sophistication with much-improved levels of safety, security, and engineering.

The 1990s saw the expansion of the MPV or "people mover" sector. This is the Peugeot 806 model (above.) Peugeot's long line of soft-tops with Pininfarina styling continued with the elegant 306 Cabrio (left.) 1999 saw the 205 replacement, the 206, here seen in rally trim (bottom)

model with drainpipe exhaust, geared to 40 mph at 1,000 rpm, was listed. Mr Pick subsequently turned to greengrocery.

PICKARD • USA 1908-1912

The three Pickard brothers, from Brockton, Mass., built their first car, a 5 hp single, in 1903. The 1908 Pickard had an ohv four-cylinder air-cooled 25 hp engine and a composite oak/steel chassis.

PIC-PIC • Switzerland 1905-1924

Hydraulic engineering company Piccard-Pictet of Geneva began building cars designed by Marc Birkigt (and very similar to the recently introduced Hispano-Suiza) for the Société d'Automobiles á Genéve. While the marque was known as SAG in Switzerland until 1910, in export markets it always seems to have been "Pic-Pic." The first cars were shaft-driven pair-cast 20/24 hp and 35/40 hp fours, a 5655cc six appearing in 1907. In 1910-1912 Pic-Pics of 14/18 hp and 18/22 hp were introduced. Single-sleeve-valve engines appeared in 1912, and front-wheel brakes and hydraulic shock absorbers were used on the firm"s 1914 Grand Prix cars, which introduced the handsome shouldered vee radiator used on the post-war Pic-Pics (one of the GP cars was rebodied as a coupé by London Improved Coachbuilders of Lupus Street, London). The firm was reformed after a financial crash in 1919 and taken over in 1921 by the Ateliers de Charmilles, which sold off the car-building activities to a group of financiers. But the 3-liter sleeve-valve shown at the 1924 Geneva Salon proved to be the last of the Pic-Pics.

PIEDMONT • USA 1917-1922

Although the Piedmont was a relatively successful small-production assembled car in its own right, it is far better known for its manufacture of cars for other firms (Alsace, Bush, Norwalk, Lone Star, Marshall, and Stork Kar). Piedmont cars were available in open and closed models, powered by four-cylinder Lycoming or six-cylinder Continental engines.

PIEPER • Belgium 1899-1903

Piéper was a cycle maker of Liége whose first two-seater voiturette appeared in 1899. "Once seen, always admired," the Piéper had either a 3.5 hp single or 6 hp twin-cylinder engine with belt drive, and was aimed at the lady motorist.

PIERCE-ARROW • USA 1901-1938

See panel

1908 Pic-Pic racing car converted to road use

1905 7 hp Pick

PIERCE-RACINE • USA 1901-1911

A J Pierce of Racine built his first gas engine in 1884. The Pierce company claimed to have built its first car in 1894 and the second in 1899. In 1901 20 8 hp "detachable seat surreys" were sold at $800 each, and in 1903 some 150 twin-cylinder cars were sold. The first four-cylinder Pierce came in 1905; fours of 30 hp (3678cc) and 40 hp (5738cc) were produced. Case took over the company in 1911, and continued manufacturing the cars under its own name.

PIERRE ROY • France 1902-1909

No connection with its contemporary, the Georges Roy, this car from Montrouge (Seine) started life as a 10/12 hp twin-cylinder shaft-drive car on Renault lines, with lateral radiators and a crocodile hood. Pierre Roy drove one of his creations to a class victory in the 1903 Dourdan speed trial. Later, four-cylinder cars of 14/20 hp and 24/30 hp were offered. At the 1908 Paris Salon 10/14 hp four-cylinder cars were exhibited.

PIGGINS • USA 1909

The "Practical" Piggins was a big six of 36 hp or 50 hp from Racine, Wisconsin.

PIGGOTT • England 1899-1901

Manufactured a motor quadricycle with the option of tube or electric ignition.

PILAIN • France 1894-1898

Francois Pilain worked for Serpollet, then moved to Lyon to build Serpollet steam three-wheelers under license at La Buire. He set up on his own in 1893, building his first tiller-steered phaeton early in 1894. In 1898 he joined Vermorel as Director General, with his nephew, Emile Pilain, as assistant.

PILAIN (SLIM-PILAIN) • France 1902-1920

Made in Lyon by Francois Pilain, these cars had initially two- and four-cylinder engines. In 1903 the twin-cylinder was dropped. Pilain's four-cylinder models were the 20 cv of 5701cc and the 40cv of 8621cc. The year 1909 saw the introduction of the 12/15cv of 2120cc, which continued until 1920. A 15/18cv six 2389cc was announced in 1913, alongside a long-stroke (3 1/4 x 7inch) 18/24cv four of 4199cc. After the war Pilain's most significant models were the 11cv of 1725cc, the 15 cv of 1888cc, and the 15cv of 2484cc, made under the name of SLIM-Pilain, for the Ste. Lyonnaise d'Industrie Mécanique et Automobile, whose factory Pilain had taken over in 1920. The finest cars made by Pilain were the ohc 3817cc and the 4268 12 hp, with four overhead valves per cylinder controlled by two camshafts in the crankcase. A particuarly distinctive feature of this marque for many years was a pneumatic starter.

PILGRIM • England 1906-1914

The twin-cylinder 11.9 hp Pilgrim, built by the Pilgrims' Way Motor Company of Farnham, Surrey, had a Renault-type hood and, unusually, featured fwd.

PILGRIM OF PROVIDENCE • USA 1911

A prototype which C W Kelsey had planned to construct in Providence, RI, but built at his factory in Hartford. A four-cylinder car of conventional design, it was scrapped when the Motorette failed and the factory was closed.

PILOT • England 1910-1914

"A £150 car and course of instruction FREE" was the prize offered in a monthly competition run by Motor Schools Limited, owner of Pilot Motors. Alternatively, you could buy a Pilot, a 10.5 hp two-seater with five-speed friction drive.

PILOT • USA 1911-1924

Big Teetor six-cylinder engines of 55 hp and 75 hp powered the 1914 Pilots, "champions of the road and hills." In 1921-1924 Herschell-Spillman sixes of 4078cc were also available.

PIERCE-ARROW • USA 1901-1938

George N Pierce began business in Buffalo, NY, in 1865, making birdcages and squirrel cages, and progressed to shaft-drive cycles via cycle spokes. His company built an unsuccessful steam car in 1900, followed by a De Dion-engined quadricycle. Its first production model, the De Dion-engined Motorette, was designed by Yorkshireman David Fergusson, who came over with Pennington in 1899. Later in 1902 came a 15 hp twin, the Arrow, and in 1904 Fergusson introduced a Mercedes-inspired 24/28 hp, the 3770cc Great Arrow. Next year 30 hp and 40 hp Great Arrows were added, and Pierce-Arrow won the 1,000-mile Glidden Tour reliability trial for the first of four times in succession. From 1905, cast aluminum body panels were used, and the first Pierce (the marque adopted the name Pierce-Arrow in 1909) six-cylinder made its debut in the 1906 Glidden Tour.

By 1910 only sixes were available, the biggest being the gargantuan "66" of 11,700cc (uprated to 13,514cc in 1912, making it America"s biggest-ever production car; 1,638 were built in ten years.) The marque's distinctive fender headlamps appeared with the 1913 "Second Series," which also ended annual model changes. The 1918 "Fifth Series" 47 hp had pair-cast cylinders and four valves per cylinder, but was soon replaced by a revised monobloc version. In 1920 Pierce-Arrow finally dropped right-hand steering. For 1925 a "cheap" model, the Series 80, the first four-wheel-braked Pierce-Arrow, was introduced. The Series 81, which replaced it in 1928, had unfortunate Art Deco styling by James R Way, and sales suffered, precipitating an ill-starred merger with Studebaker.

The new 5998cc straight-eight of 1929 was an excellent car, and 8,000 were sold in its first year, but by 1932 sales had crumbled to 2,692, despite an exciting new V-12 (a prototype set up a new 24-hour record, broken in 1933 by a production V-12 at 117 mph. An ultra-streamlined "Silver Arrow" was built for the Chicago World's Fair in 1933, shortly after a consortium of Buffalo businessmen had bought Pierce-Arrow back from Studebaker. The outstanding 1936 range, Model 1601 eight, and Models 1602 and 1603 twelves, failed to halt the sales slide.

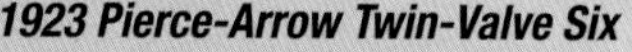

1923 Pierce-Arrow Twin-Valve Six

1929 Pierce-Arrow straight-eight

PILOT • Germany 1921-1925

Of advanced design, the 1098cc Pilot had an ohc 16-valve unit-design engine and was made by a railway carriage factory. Production was limited, and the car became known mainly in south-west Germany.

PINEDE • France 1898

A light 3cv twin-cylinder voiturette selling at Fr 4,000-6,000.

PINNACE • England 1912-1913

Forerunner of the Norma, this JAP-engined cyclecar was shaped like a ship's pinnace, with a sharp bow!

PIONEER • USA 1907-1911

High-wheeled shaft-drive runabouts (20 hp two-cylinder, 28/30 hp four) from El Reno, Oklahoma.

PIONEER • USA 1915

The Pioneer was a 14 hp four from Troy, NY.

PIPE • Belgium 1898-1914

One of Belgium's best-engineered cars, the Ghent-built Pipe began the century as a 6 hp twin on Panhard lines, joined in 1902 by a 15 hp four. A few gasoline-electrics were built in 1904-1905, but the 1904 Paris Salon saw the introduction of pushrod ohv in a hemispherical head, on four-cylinder cars of 3770cc and 8302cc. There was an apparent gap in production in 1908-1910, though Pipe built some V-8 airship engines during that period. The 1910-1911 model was a small side-valve, and long-stroke side-valve fours saw the marque through to the end of private-car construction.

PIPER • England 1967-1976

Well over 120 Ford-powered, glassfiber-bodied Pipers were built during the life of this company, many of which still survive today. Though not particularly successful, the

1907 50/60 hp Pipe

1968 Piper GTT

mid-engined GTR race version looked fantastic. Later plans to market replicas on VW chassis did not get far.

PITT • England 1902-1904

The Pitt Yorkshire Machine Company of Liversedge built these "Durable and perfect" 5 hp, 9 hp, and 12 hp crocodile-hooded cars.

PITTSBURGH • USA 1899

A 3 hp twin-cylinder "gasolene runabout" with a top speed of 18 mph, predecessor to Autocar.

PITTSBURGH SIX • USA 1908-1910

"Simple, powerful and efficient," the 70 hp Pittsburgh Six car had a side-valve engine of 9147cc and shaft drive. A "small" 40/45 hp (6570cc) six was added for 1910.

PIVOT • France 1904-1908

The 1905 Pivot, from Puteaux (Seine), had a 24/30 hp power unit with "three double cylinders, three pistons, six compression chambers, cranks set at 120 degrees." The 1908 16/20 hp, and 24/30 hp were conventional four-cylinder cars.

PLANET • England 1904-1907

Built a range of shaft-driven cars with engines of 6 hp to 24 hp.

PLASS • USA 1897

Reuben Plass, who claimed to have built his first car in the 1860s, offered this rear-engined phaeton with an L-shaped tiller for steering with hand or foot.

PLASSON • France 1910

The 2413cc four-cylinder Plasson, built in Montmartre, ran on paraffin. The maker claimed it was the "sole paraffin motor sold at the same price as a gasoline motor."

LA PLATA • France? 1906

The 8/10 hp La Plata had a twin-cylinder Aster Engine, and though it was probably an import from France, had Sheffield-built coachwork.

PLAYBOY • USA 1946-1951

War prevented production until 1946, although an experimental Playboy had been running in 1940. It was a practical little car with an overall length of 155 inches. Height was a mere 54 inches and the car featured an all-metal folding top which stowed away behind the three-passenger seat. Powered by a 40 hp four-cylinder Hercules engine, it used a Warner Gear automatic transmission and self-adjusting brakes. The unitary body was undercoated and the Playboy sold for $985. Louis Horwitz, president of the Playboy Motor Car Corp, had expected annual production to be 100,000, but only 90-100 cars were built in Tonawanda, NY.

PLUTO • Germany 1924-1927

Made by the gigantic Ehrhardt group at the Zella-Mehlis/St Blasii works, the Pluto was a French Amilcar built under license, with 970cc, 1054cc and 1111cc four-cylinder sv engines. Supercharged racing versions were also built which, driven by Gockenbach, Mederer, Friedrich and von Einem, won many sporting events.

PLYMOUTH • USA 1910-1911

A heavy friction-driven 50 hp from Plymouth, Ohio, mostly built with commercial bodywork, though at least one tourer appeared.

PLYMOUTH • USA 1928 to date

See panel

PM • Belgium 1922-1924

A 1795cc Peters engine powered this light car from Liége, which had business ties with Carrow of England.

PLYMOUTH • USA 1928 to date

Chrysler "went into the low-priced field with the throttle wide open" with the 1928 Plymouth Four, demand exceeding supply to such an extent that a second factory had to be built by 1929. The 1930 Plymouth U sedan cost the same as comparable Ford and Chevrolet models, and offered a radio as an option. The all-new 1931 Plymouth PA, with eight different body styles, was followed by the PB of 1932, and the marque"s first six, the PD, costing only $495. The 1933 models featured an automatic clutch which operated every time the throttle was released. On 10 August 1934 production reached the first million. Unlike Chrysler and DeSoto, Plymouth never produced an Airflow model; its styling emphasized safety features such as padded seatbacks and recessed controls, though one odd 1936 model, convertible from sedan to ambulance to hearse "in a matter of seconds," seemed to be carrying things too far. Sealed-beam headlamps were standardized on 1940 models, and the 1942 Plymouth 14C had full-width styling.

A development of this, the 15S, formed the basis of post-war production up to 1949, when all-new styling in three series was introduced: the P17 DeLuxe and P18 and P18 Special DeLuxe, all with the same 3569cc sv six. Some export markets knew the Special DeLuxe as the "DeSoto Diplomat" or "Dodge Kingsway." Conservative styling lost Plymouth its third place in sales to Buick, so the 1955 cars were longer and lower, with a new 4621cc Hy-Fire V-8, unique to Plymouth. (The sv six was finally replaced in 1960.) Sales rose to a record 742,991 in 1955, but the third place in sales was not regained until 1957, when Virgil Exner"s FlightSweep styling appeared, with more glass, less chrome and taller tailfins than the opposition. The Fury performance model had a potent V-8 of 5211cc, optional on other models, and Plymouths adopted the Chrysler group"s torsion-bar front suspension. A new 5736cc V-8 appeared in 1958, but production fell to half the 1957 level, due to poor quality control.

The 1960 models had engines up to 6276cc, new styling and unitary construction; fins were bigger than ever, though they were to vanish a year later. A brand new compact, the Valiant, with the new Slant Six of 3687cc, was launched, but Plymouth again lost third place, this time to AMC's Rambler. New and unusual styling graced the 1962 big Plymouths; models included the Belvedere and Fury I, II and III. The Belvedere Satellite performance model offered a 6981cc V-8 of 425 bhp. The Barracuda fastback appeared in 1964, and was totally redesigned in 1967, with the Slant Six as standard. That year 38 models and a staggering variety of engine options were offered. The Belvedere intermediate formed the basis for the

1931 Plymouth PA sedan (left)
Plymouth Fury (below)

performance GTX, as well as for the 1968 Road Runner (its horn sounded like the cartoon character from which it took its name!,) claimed to be the world's fastest coupé with a top speed of up to 160 mph. A limited-edition "Super Bird" Road Runner (1200 were built) was even faster. The 1970 Duster, with 3244cc Slant Six or 5572cc V-8, was known as the "pocket Road Runner." Top of the 1971 range was the Sport Fury with Brougham luxury interior, as the 1966-launched VIP had been dropped, as indeed had the Belvedere, replaced by the Satellite Coupé, Custom and Sebring. The "Plymouth Cricket" was an imported Chrysler-UK Avenger.

By 1975 cars like the Road Runner, Satellite, and Barracuda had disappeared, victims of the 1973 oil crisis, while the Fury came in three sizes, "intermediate, large and full-size," Valiant and Duster still being offered. A new line of compacts, the Volare, appeared in 1976, completely supplanting the Fury line by 1978. For 1979 the Volare was the biggest Plymouth, with standard engines up to a 5211cc V-8 and models including a Road Runner; a Police Package offered a 5899cc V-8 and 120 mph top speed. New was the fwd 1716cc Horizon with all-round independent suspension, while the Sapporo and Arrow were Mitsubishi imports.

The fwd 2.2-liter Reliant compact debuted in 1980 and the Caravelle, with similar engine, followed in 1984. The 1987 Sundance, with engines from 2.2 to 3.0 liters, was a hatchback that looked like a notchback. The 1992 Duster was a 3.0-liter performance derivative. For 1989 Plymouth launched the Japanese-built Colt hatchback "supermini," and in 1989 came the mid-size Acclaim sedan car. In 1990 the Laser 2+2 sports coupé was launched, a 4x4 version appearing in 1992. The 1991 Voyager is a multi-purpose vehicle with fwd or 4x4 transmissions; the 1992 Colt Vista is a five-passenger "monobox" wagon with optional 4x4 transmission. In the 1990s Plymouth drew its new-model ranger from its Chrysler roots, yet it also sold imported cars via its links with Mitsubishi and developed a new range of cars under the Diamond Star label. The biggest success in the Plymouth range turned out to be its giant MPV, named the Voyager, which is also available on the European market under Chrysler badging. The Plymouth Prowler concept car took Americans back to their 1950s stock car roots when it was first shown, and despite its wild styling, complete with running boards and tapered nose, it went into series production and found a ready market.

PMC • USA 1908-1909

A 12 hp high-wheeled buggy built by the C. S. Peets Mfg Co of New York.

PODEUS • Germany 1911-1914

The Podeus machine works at Wismar produced two models: 2248cc and 2536cc sv fours.

POLSKI-FIAT • Poland 1948 to date

Originally assembling the Russian Gaz Pobieda under license as the Warszawa, this state-owned company began building the Fiat 125 P under license in 1968. The modern Polonez uses Polski-Fiat 125 running gear, and there is also a Polski-Fiat 126 P.

POLYMOBIL • Germany 1904-1909

Based on the Curved-Dash Oldsmobile, the 1563cc three-seater Polymobile "Gazelle" was made by the manufacturer of the Polyphon, a coin-in-the-slot clockwork musical box which was the remote ancestor of the juke box. A twin-cylinder version of 1356cc appeared in 1908; a four-cylinder 20 hp was built in small numbers.

LA PONETTE • France 1909-1925

This very small car builder started in 1909 with a single-cylinder 697cc car which looked like a small Renault. In 1911 it was followed by a four-cylinder 1592cc Ballot-engined car which remained in production until 1920. Some minor models were also made, with various proprietary engines until the Société des Automobiles la Ponette, from Chevreuse, Yvelines, collapsed in 1925.

PONSARD-ANSALONI • France 1898

Also known as "Brulé," this was a power-pack conversion for horse-carriages, with a twin-cylinder Roser-Mazurier engine.

PONTIAC • USA 1907-1908

Another of the legion American high-wheelers, this twin-cylinder had friction drive.

PONTIAC • USA 1926 to date

See panel

PONTS-MOTEURS • France 1912-1913

A twin-cylinder 1081cc power pack, built in Paris for transforming horse vehicles into motor vehicles "in a few hours, without modification."

PONTIAC • USA 1926 to date

"The chief of the sixes" was designed by Ben H Anibal as a low-priced running mate for Oakland; it was so successful that it ousted the older marque entirely. Indeed, it was (and is) the only marque created (rather than acquired) by General Motors to last more than a couple of seasons. The original sv 3064cc six lasted until 1930, when a Marquette-based 3277cc ohv six appeared. The last Oakland, an Olds Viking-based V-8 of 4104cc, became a Pontiac for 1932, but failed to last, and was quickly succeeded by America's first under-$600 straight-eight, a 3654cc unit which even briefly supplanted the six. "Knee-action" ifs was introduced in 1934, as were "turret-top" bodies. For 1935 "Silver Streak" styling was launched as "the most beautiful thing on wheels"; the British importer, Kaye Don, offered English-built coupé versions. A new look came with the 1941 Torpedo range, sold alongside the Streamliner and Streamliner Chieftain. The first post-war redesign came in 1949, with fastback (Streamline) and notchback (Chieftain) bodies, but that year's Canadian Pontiacs were basically Chevrolets with Pontiac grilles.

The first Catalina hardtops appeared in 1950, dual-range Hydramatic transmission in 1952, wraparound rear windows and power steering in 1953. The sv eight was replaced by an ohv V-8 of 4703cc in 1955, and the sixes relegated to Canadian production. Only 3,700 sporting Safari station wagons were built. There was a brief flirtation with fuel injection in 1958, while the wide-track Pontiacs of 1959 had extravagant tailfins as well as a "tail grille" matching the front-end styling. A more compact model, the unit-construction Tempest, appeared in 1961, with an oversquare four of 3179cc and swing-axle irs and manual or automatic transaxle. It was replaced by a more conventional Tempest by 1964, though its "Le Mans" version sired the legendary GTO, with 6555cc or 7456cc V-8 power, and offering 125 mph for $3000 in 1966, when over 95,000 GTOs were sold. Almost as fast, if less sporting, was the 1963 Grand Prix, and by 1968 there was a family of small sporting coupés, the Firebirds, with a small ohc six (replaced in 1970 by a pushrod unit, also used on the 1971 Ventura compact.)

For 1973, low, wide lines rather than high performance characterized Pontiac's new intermediates, the Grand Ams two- and four-door hardtops. Fastest cars were now the Trans Ams coupés, and disc front brakes were standard on all but the Ventura and the cheapest Firebirds. The inevitable sub-compact, the Astre, appeared in 1975, evolving into the Sunbird (with optional five-speed manual gearbox) a year later. The Ventura range now included a hatchback, and big cars offered V-8s of 5 liters as standard, with 5.7 and 6.6-liter units optional. The immensely complex 1979 range included the Sunbird, with a choice of two four-cylinder Pontiac engines, Buick's V-6, or Chevrolet's 5162cc V-8; Firebird sport coupés up to 6604cc; the Phoenix intermediate; the Le Mans range; and full-size Pontiacs, only available with automatic transmission.

1935 Pontiac 28 hp six-cylinder

Pontiac's version of the GM J-car was the 1981 Sunbird, still in production a decade later. The 1983 Fiero was a two-seat sports coupé with plastic bodywork. In 1984 a new Grand Am coupé appeared, a sedan following in 1985; a turbo engine was offered in 1987. The Firebird was redesigned in 1990. For 1991 the Grand Am was rebodied and given a new range of engines. The Bonneville also had new bodywork, shared with Buick LeSabre and Oldsmobile 88 Royale. A return to a more sporting image came in the late 1980s and early 1990s, when Plymouth launched a series of two-door coupé types, from the small Sunfire through to the mid-range Grand Am and onwards to the curvacious Grand Prix GT coupé of 1998. The Firebird made a return with a V-8 engine and muscular looking styling. The purposeful looks of the Pontiac Bonneville with its V-6 3.8-liter engine and fine handling made it a big sedan to be reckoned with, and it sold very well against stiff European competition. Through such cars, Pontiac further defined its sporting heritage.

1946 Pontiac Six Station Wagon

Pontiac Fiero Mk2

1992 Pontiac Grand-Am

1999 Pontiac GTO at the Detroit Motor Show

1920 Porter Town Car

POPE-HARTFORD • USA 1903-1914

Chain-drive 10 hp single-cylinder two- and four-seaters were the first cars offered in this mid-priced range from the Pope group, though a 16 hp shaft-driven twin with flitch-plated wooden chassis was available in 1905. The Model F of 1906 had a 28/30 hp four, and sold for $2,500; standard color scheme was purple lake. By 1912 the range had become complex; seven models were available on the 36 hp four-cylinder chassis and seven on the 44.6 hp six, including "pony tonneaux" and "Front Door Roadsters." Such uncoordinated marketing policies led to the fall of Colonel Pope's cycle and car empire in 1913.

POPE-TOLEDO • USA 1903-1909

The luxury range in Colonel Pope's line-up, "the silent mile-a-minute car" succeeded the Toledo Steamer, though all its products had four-cylinder gasoline engines. Prices initially ranged from $3,500 for the 20 hp to $7,500 for the 60 hp racer. A peaked radiator shell was a distinguishing feature of the Pope-Toledo. The last Pope-Toledos were big 50 hp fours of 6500cc, selling at $4,250. The company was taken over in 1909 and production of Pope-Toledos ceased. John Willys bought the plant for Overland.

POPE-TRIBUNE • USA 1904-1907

This was Colonel Pope's economy line. The initial models were chain-drive 10 hp single-cylinder runabouts, followed in 1905 by a 12 hp front-engined twin with shaft drive.

POPP • Switzerland 1898

Lorenz Popp of Basle offered two models of twin-cylinder car, financed by the Benz agent for Switzerland. Hardly surprisingly, these were largely Benz-inspired. Inlet valves were automatic, but a chain-driven overhead camshaft actuated the exhaust valves.

POPULAIRE • France 1899

A light rear-engined voiturette with three-seater bodywork.

PORON • France 1898

A rear-engined opposed-piston "motorcycle" with friction drive and tiller-steering.

PORTER • USA 1900-1901

"The only perfect automobile," the Porter steam Stanhope from Boston, Massachusetts, sold for $750, and was "controlled by one lever only, as in times of danger several levers are confusing."

PORTER • USA 1919-1922

Successor to the FRP, the Porter was one of the most costly automobiles in the USA, some models costing upwards of $10,000. Using an ohv four-cylinder engine of its own design and make, the Porter, with a displacement of 6516cc, produced 140 hbp at 2600rpm, making it the most powerful car in America at that time. The car had a 142-inch wheelbase and the option of wire or wood wheels. A total of 34 Porter motor cars was constructed; coachwork was provided by Brewster, Holbrook, Demarest, and Blue Ribbon.

PORTHOS • France 1906-1914

This Billancourt firm began with a 24/30 hp four, joined for 1908 by fours of 14/18 hp and 40 hp and sixes of 40/50 hp (6842cc) and 60 hp (8143cc). A straight-eight Grand Prix racer of 10,857cc found no production parallels, and in 1909 production was suspended until 1912. Then 16 hp and 24 hp fours, and 20 hp and 30 hp sixes were offered, joined in 1914 by a 10 hp.

PORSCHE Austria • Germany 1948 to date

See panel overleaf

PORTLAND • France • England 1913

Claiming dual nationality, the Portland was sold in two models, a £95 6/8 hp one-cylinder two-seater and a 10 hp four-cylinder (£145). The firm's telegraphic address was "Skidlessly."

POWELL SPORTSWAGON • USA 1955-1956

Made in Compton, Calif., by the Powell Corp, the Sportswagon was based on 1940/1950 Plymouth mechanical components. Bodies were made of metal and glassfiber. Models included station wagons and pickups.

1933 Praga Lady Sedan

Chassis of the 1906 Premier (England) 20/24 hp four

POWERDRIVE • England 1956-1958

One of the better-looking post-Suez economy cars, the Powerdrive had a three-abreast aluminum body and 322cc Anzani engine. It later reappeared as the Coronet.

PRADO • USA 1920-1922

Using an 8237cc Curtiss OX-5 aircraft engine converted for passenger-car use and similar to the V-8 powerplants used on Curtiss and Wharton cars, the Prado sported disc wheels. Available in chassis form or "open types," an estimated nine were built. Chassis price was $9,000.

PRAGA • Austria • Czechoslovakia 1907-1947

This leading Bohemian engineering works' first products were based on French Renault and Charron designs. After the war, when its Prague base had become part of Czechoslovakia, Praga became the new country's leading producer. A range of sv fours was produced during the 1920s, including the 850cc and 994cc Piccolo models, the Alfa (1243cc,) the Mignon (2300cc,) and the Grand (3800cc.) By the end of the decade the Alfa and Mignon had become sixes of 1790cc and 2636cc respectively, and the Grand a straight-eight of 3585cc. In the early 1930s new models appeared; the 995cc Baby, the 1450cc Lady, and the 1660cc Super-Piccolo, most of these designed by Frantisek Kec. The immediately pre-war range consisted of two light fours, the 1128cc Piccolo and 1660cc Lady, and two sixes, the 2492cc Alfa 23 and the 3485cc Golden, the latter having a six-speed gearbox. Praga cars competed successfully in international trials. A few light cars were built after the end of the war.

LE PRATIC • France 1908-1908

Monobloc-engined cars of 8/10 hp (twin-cylinder) and 16/20 hp (four-cylinders) built in Paris.

PRATT, PRATT-ELKHART • USA 1911-1917

The Elkhart Carriage and Harness Company entered the motor business with a four-cylinder 40 hp model. A 50 hp six appeared later.

PREMIER • USA 1903-1925

"First in rank among motor cars," the Premier from Indianapolis was conventional in design, but always well engineered. Air- or watercooling were optional from 1903-1907, and a transverse air-cooled four was listed in 1904. Big fours and sixes were built, notably the 4-40 and 6-60, with pair-cast cylinders: capacities were 5473cc and 8210cc. In 1913 a convoy of 12 Premiers drove across America; from that year only six-cylinder cars were offered. The Premiers of 1919-21 had the Cutler-Hammer magnetic gear-shift, controlled by a lever on the steering wheel;

1912 Pratt 40 tourer

the monobloc alloy six-cylinder power unit of 4838cc had overhead valves and aluminum pistons.

PREMIER • England 1906-1908, 1911-1913

Though its sponsors claimed that "ceaseless thought and tireless energy" had accompanied the creation of the 20/24 hp Premier of 1906, it was really an imported Marchand from Italy. A 25/30 hp six was also available. This Birmingham company did build a car of its own, later in the same year, with a 10/12 hp two-cylinder Aster engine, which sold for £150 with two seats, £200 with four. By that time, too, it was acknowledging the Marchand's true parentage. A year later the firm was concentrating on its agencies for Humber and Marchand, and on the manufacture of hoods and windshields, and the 10/12 hp was dropped soon after. In 1911-1913 the PMC, a tiller-steered three-wheeled cyclecar with a 6 hp JAP engine, was built by Premier.

PREMIER • Germany 1913-1914

A small two-seater car with a sv four-cylinder 1030cc engine, built at the J C Braun factory at Nürnberg (which also produced Kaiser cars.)

PREMIER • Austria 1913-1914

Basically an English factory which had produced motorcycles since 1908. Since 1911 it had owned a German branch at Nürnburg, which in 1913 moved to Eger (now Cheb,) which became part of Czechoslovakia. The car was a small 4/12 hp four-cylinder whose design came from the Braun works. Few were built.

PREMIER • India 1944 to date

The Premier Padmini, built in Bombay, is based on the obsolete Fiat 1100; over 17,000 were produced in 1977. Since 1985 Premier has also made the Fiat 124-diesel 118 NE, with a Nissan Cherry engine.

PREMOCAR • USA 1921-1923

One of the relatively few American cars built in the Deep South, the Premocar hailed from Birmingham, Alabama. In its first year it offered both four- and six-cylinder models, the former with a Rochester-Duesenberg engine and the latter with a Falls. The four was dropped for 1922, but the six, designated the "6-40" or "Magic Six," was continued through the last year of manufacture. Few Premocars were built.

PRESCOTT • USA 1901-1905

A L Prescott, maker of "Enameline" stove polish, was behind the manufacture of this twin-cylinder tiller-steered steam car.

PRESTO • Germany 1909-1927

This cycle and motorcycle works' first cars had French four-cylinder Delahaye engines. Among the first own-design models was a 6238cc four-cylinder with a long-stroke (4 inches x 8 inches) engine and a smaller 4920cc model. Quantity production led to smaller 2340cc and 2078cc four-cylinder cars. Production of Presto cars increased after the war, when this Chemnitz factory joined the GDA group. Top model was now a 2350cc four-cylinder developing 30 bhp, followed by an improved 40 bhp version in 1925. The last Presto cars were ohv six-cylinders of 2613cc and 3141cc. In 1926 Presto bought the Dux works, and it became part of the NAG group in 1927. NAG sold the Chemnitz work to Auto-Union in 1934.

PRETOT • France 1896-1899

A two-cylinder 5 hp two-wheeled "power pack" for converting horse carriages to horseless carriages, built under Kühlstein-Vollmer patents.

PRIAMUS • Germany 1899-1921

When Priamus at Cologne ran into financial difficulties in 1921 it was taken over by Molkamp. In the early years

Engine of the 1907 Prima 10 hp voiturette

PORSCHE • Austria • Germany 1948 to date

After his post-war release from internment in France, Ferdinand Porsche settled in Gmünd, Austria, where he created the first Porsche cars, with 1086cc VW-based engines and sporting light alloy roadster bodywork. However, he found working conditions at Gmünd too difficult, with shortages in materials, components, and skilled labour. Porsche cars were then relatively cheap, and demand high, so, after building 50 of this original model 356, Porsche moved to Stuttgart-Zuffenhausen in Germany. The rear-engined model 356 appeared in many guises, with engines from 1096cc to 1966cc; coupés, cabriolets, speedsters, and convertibles were offered. It was succeeded by the 1965-1969 Porsche 912, with a light-alloy 1582cc engine, still a flat-four. A year earlier the famous ohc flat-six 1991cc Porsche 911 had made its debut, available from 1969 onward with larger power units, of which the ultimate development was a 2993cc unit. From 1972-1975 the Carrera was available, with a 2687cc flat-six developing 260 bhp; it was concurrent with the 1969-1975 mid-engined Porsche 914, available with fours of 1795cc and 1971cc or the 1991cc six. The 1979 Porsche range consisted of the front-engined 924, with an in-line watercooled four-cylinder engine of 1984cc, the rear-engined 911SC, with the 2993cc flat-six in 180 bhp form, the 911 Turbo, with a 3299cc six equipped with Bosch K-jetronic fuel-injection, and the front-engined 928, with a 4474cc V-8 power unit.

1960 Porsche 356B Coupé

In 1981 Porsche launched the 944, which in its latest 3.0-liter form is capable of almost 150 mph. The 200-off 959 of 1987 was a 200 mph supercar with four-wheel drive adaptable to weather conditions. Just 250 were built. To celebrate the 25th anniversary of the 911, the 3.6-liter Carrera 4 was launched in 1988. The 3.2-liter 911 Carrera was replaced by the 911 Carrera 2 in coupé, Targa and cabriolet forms, with Tiptronic dual-function transmission. A new 911 Turbo appeared in 1990, with an uprated 3.3-liter engine. The later model 928 boasted a tire pressure monitoring system, a world first.

The much loved, air-cooled, rear engined 911, the icon of Porsche, finally bowed out in 1997, its final model being a wild fwd 400 bhp twin-turbo car with extended bodywork and track. It was replaced by a new 911, water-cooled, safe, perhaps more refined, but to some less pure. However, it found a ready crowd of buyers world-wide and certainly continued the 911's styling themes in fine form. The 928 died, as did the 968, into which the original 924-944 had mutated. A new soft-top roadster, the Boxer, arrived in 1996, and with its mid-engined layout, low price but true Porsche style took Porsche back into the more financially accessible realms that the 928 and ultimate 911s had eschewed in the boom years of the 1980s. Porsche had learned from the recession and boom-and-bust economic cycle in Europe and America, and its new models, with their broader range and appeal, will ensure that, while it will always be a maker of supercars, it will also have wider foundations. The company also carries out extensive research and development for other manufacturers at its Weissach R&D centre.

The Porsche 928 GT, a supercar from the 1980s

The sheer enjoyment of Porsche driving is captured as the power is unleashed (left.) The pure lines of the purist's Porsche. The 911 lasted in various forms for three decades (above)

1922 Protos 16/46 hp sporting tourer

Priamus had produced single- and twin-cylinder cars, followed by fours of 1592cc to 3052cc. Production was never on a large scale.

PRIMA, PRIMA-LUX • France 1906-1909

Léon Lefébvre, designer of the Bolide, was behind the Prima marque. A 10 hp single and fours of 15 hp and 20 hp with unit-constructed engine/gearbox were the staple offerings.

PRIMUS • Germany 1899-1904

Kaiser, a famous manufacturer of sewing machines and bicycles, also built three-wheeled vehicles with De Dion-type own-make engines. Small cars with two- and four-cylinder engines up to 12 hp were available from 1902 onwards.

PRIMUS • England 1903

The "noiseless" Primus was built in Brixton, London, and cost 175 guineas in 5 hp form, with 7 hp and 9 hp models also available. It was said to be "very reliable, steady and fast."

PRINCE • Japan 1952-1966

Post-war, the Tachikawa Aircraft Company built Tama electrics, then brought out the 1.5-liter Prince. The ifs-equipped Skyline appeared in 1955, the first Japanese car to be sold in Europe (from 1957.) In 1961 came the 1.9-liter Gloria, later available with engines up to 2.5 liters. The Prince Royal heralded the merger with Nissan (Datsun) and the rationalization of the two ranges.

PRINCEPS • England 1902-1903

A 4.5 hp "Bijou voiturette" from a famous Nottingham motorcycle maker.

PRINCESS • England 1906

The 3261cc Princess, made by the Century Motor Company of Willesden Junction, London, had a magneto and coil ignition.

PRINCESS • USA 1914-1919

This was a coal-scuttle-hooded 1599cc light car built in Detroit. A four-cylinder L-head 1557cc engine was used. A Golden, Belknap & Schwartz-engined 30 hp four, of conventional appearance, was launched for 1915.

PRINCESS • England 1923

Shock absorber manufacturer Streatham Engineering Co Ltd was responsible for the Princess, a light car using an 8.9 hp vee-twin air-cooled engine.

PRINCETON • USA 1923-1924

The Princeton automobile was William C Durant's bid to bridge the gap between his Flint and Locomobile cars. Only two or three were probably ever built, all designated 1924 models. The Princeton was an impressive car for the price, its 128/132-inch wheelbase sedan selling for $2,485. An Ansted six-cylinder engine was employed. Similar in appearance to the Flint, the make was discontinued before production could be started.

PRINETTI & STUCCHI • Italy 1899-1901

The great Ettore Bugatti worked with this company when it built motor tricycles, motorcycles and some twin-cylinder cars. While still very young, he subsequently moved to De Dietrich in Alsace.

PRODHOMME • France 1907-1908

Builders of cars with 18 hp opposed-piston engines á la Gobron-Brillié, Prod'homme's factory was at Ivry-Port (Seine.)

PROGRESS • England c1898-1903

Cycle-maker Progress turned to building a voiturette based on the De Dion. Its final offerings were a 9 hp De Dion-powered car and 6½ hp and 12 hp models with Aster engines, which reappeared in 1904 as the West-Aster.

PROGRESS • England 1934

The three-wheeled Progress from Manchester had a 980cc flat-twin engine. It was manufactured by Haynes Economy Motors Ltd.

PROJECTA • England 1914

A vee-twin JAP engine powered this monocoque-bodied cyclecar from Hendon,

PROSPER LAMBERT • France 1901-190

From Nanterre, Seine, the Prosper Lambert was said to be "most beautiful, most elegant, least expensive." Starting with a single-cylinder De Dion-engined 7 hp model, by 1905, 9 hp, and 12 hp models were available, at prices from Fr 4950 to Fr 7900. In 1907 the marque changed its name to Jean-Bart.

PROTON • Malaysia 1985 to date

A 70/30 joint venture between the Malaysian government and Mitsubishi, this rapidly-growing company produces a range of 12 fwd models in two body styles, all with Mitsubishi I-4 12-valve engines of 1.3 or 1.5-liter capacity. In the 1990s the company was still using Mitsubushi engines, and also had access to recently replaced Mitsubishi model ranges that it facelifted into a Proton badged style. An ever expanding range of worthy but hardly world-leading cars has emerged and found a ready market in the value-for-money sector. A top-of-the-range 133bhp coupé was added in 1997, but despite its name the car was a boxy two-door sedan-type design. Proton now owns Lotus.

PROTOS • Germany 1899-1926

Mrs Lilli Sternberg was a well-known pioneer motorist, and her husband, Alfred, founded the Protos factory in Berlin. His first design, a 749cc single-cylinder voiturette, was followed by his three-cylinder "Kompensengin." From 1904 Protos, already finding favor as Berlin taxicabs, were available with four-cylinder engines of up to 45 hp. A 100 hp six-cylinder racer was built in 1905; though it did not enter production, it paved the way for a 45 hp six. That year, too, Sternberg sold Protos to Siemens-Schuckert and Crown Prinz Wilhelm bought a six-cylinder Protos. A wide variety of Protos cars, from 1501cc to a five-bearing 6838cc six, were built up to the outbreak of war. The first models to appear after 1918 were an ohv 2612cc four and the sv 4137cc "16/46." Then came a sv 2596 four, which was the basis of all Protos production up to 1926, when NAG took control. After the takeover some NAG models were sold as "NAG-Protos."

1907 Puch 12/18 hp four-cylinder

PRUNEL • France 1900-1907

Prunel, whose factory was at Puteaux, Seine, offered a four-car range in 1903, consisting of the "Apollo" single-cylinder 6 hp, which, like the slightly larger 9 hp, had a De Dion engine, and two Aster-engined cars, a 12 hp twin and 16 hp four. By 1905 it was offering a 24/30 hp four of 4942cc, but by 1906 was concentrating principally on the manufacture of large commercial vehicles. The Prunels were also connected with Gnôme, Gracile, and JP cars, and the 1912-1914 Phénix. Prunel cars were sold in England by a gunpowder and ammunition manufacturing works in Hendon.

PTV • Spain 1956-1962

Automoviles Utilitarios SA of Manresa built 1250 of these minicars, powered by a 246cc single-cylinder two-stroke engine of the company's own make, before turning to the production of dumper trucks.

PUBLIX • USA 1947-1948

The Publix was a three-wheeled convertible with the single wheel at the front. Its aluminum body was attached to an aluminum tube frame. The engines (also of aluminum) ranged from 1.7 to 10.4 hp. The overall length was 72 inches and weight varied from 150 to 250 lb.

PUCH • Austria 1906-1923

Puch was already a well-known manufacturer of bicycles and motorcycles when he engaged the well-known German designer Slevogt to produce a prototype. Tests were also carried out with French cars before the first Puch car, a well-conceived 7 hp voiturette, made its bow. Puch's Graz factory followed this with a 25 hp four, both models achieving some sporting success. A 9 hp twin was added to the range then, in 1909, Slevogt designed an ohc 3992cc four. Other Puch models included a sv 1580cc four, another sv four of 4400cc, and the sporting Alpenwagen, with a 40bhp sv four of 3560cc. The final Puch had a 1588cc four-cylinder engine and a four-speed gearbox; it formed the basis of works racers produced in 1921-1922 which gained many successes driven by Kirchner, Weiss and Zsolnay. Car manufacture ceased when Ing Marcinello produced the first of the famous double-piston Puch motorcycles.

1903 Pullman

PULLMAN • USA 1903-1917

Built by the Hardinge Company to A P Broomell's design, the 1903 Pullman was a complex six-wheeler, succeeded by the conventional "York" range in 1905. The 1908 models were a 40 hp four and a 30 hp six. Pullman built cars up to a 60 hp 8603cc six with compressed-air starting (1912,) and from 1915 offered the Cutler-Hammer push-button magnetic gear-change system.

PUMA • Brazil 1964 to date

Founded under the name Luminari, this Sao Paulo company started with the DKW-engined Malzoni, introducing the Puma GT in 1966. It gained VW power in 1968. From 1974 there was also a 4-liter GM-engined Puma GTB. In 1986 the Puma name was acquired by Arancavia, which planned a joint venture with ex-world champion boxer Muhammed Ali to build cars in Brazil for Saudi Arabia, underwritten by Saudi Prince Al-Fasse. The Porsche-powered Ali Stinger was developed for the USA.

PUNGS FINCH • USA 1904-1908

These powerful touring cars were built by a Detroit gas engine factory. For 1908 the Model 35 Runabout of 5808cc and the Model 50 of 6435cc were cataloged: prices ranged from $2,500 to $5,000.

PURITAN • USA 1902-1903

Built in Salem, Massachusetts, the 6 hp Puritan Steamer had a folding steering column for easy access to the driver's seat.

PY • France 1899-1900

Andre Py was manager and designer for the Compagnie des Automobiles du Sud-Ouest, which built this Bolléelike motor tricycle. It had fwd and rear-wheel steering.

PYRAMID • England 1914

A JAP-engined 8 hp cyclecar built by Payne's Engineering of Chiswick, London.

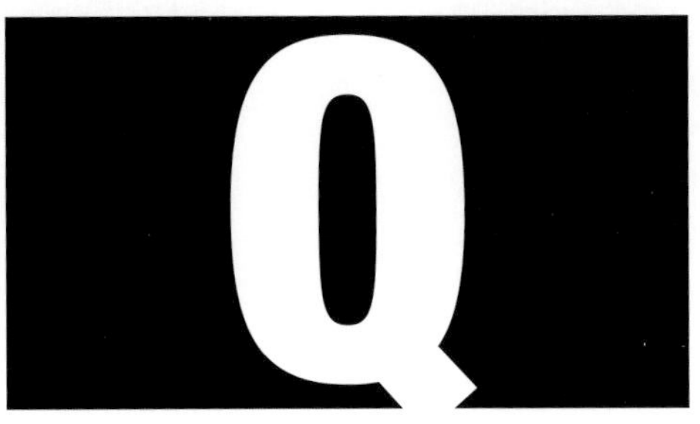

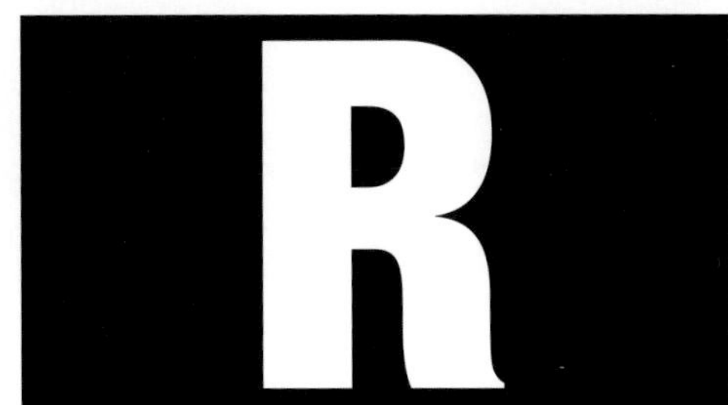

QUADRANT • England 1905-1906

In 1905 Quadrant of Birmingham exhibited a chassis with a four-speed Lloyd "crossed rollers" gearbox, giving direct drive on all speeds.

QUEEN • Canada 1901-1903

A gas buggy from Toronto with a single-cylinder 824cc engine.

QUEEN • England 1904-1905

"The car for the million or the millionaire" was sold by Horner & Sons of Mitre Square, London. 12 hp and 16 hp models were offered, at prices from 235 guineas to 275 guineas.

QUEEN • USA 1904-1907

Chain driven one-, two-, and four-cylinder cars built by Blomstrom, who also made the Gyroscope car. The 1906 Queen was available in three models; 14 hp and 18 hp twins, 26/28 hp four.

QUICK • USA 1899-1900

This otherwise conventional tiller-steered gas buggy was the first American car to have an overhead camshaft power unit. The twin-cylinder engine had a chain-driven ohc and developed a heady 4 bhp at 700 rpm.

QUINBY • USA 1899

Electric carriages "on the Leitner system" with two 2.5 hp motors geared to the rear wheels.

QUO VADIS • France 1921-1923

A cyclecar made in Courbevoie, Seine, with a twin-cylinder Train engine.

1906 Queen (USA) 26/28 hp touring car

RABA • Hungary **1912-1914**

Made by the Hungarian Machine Factory at Raab (Györ,) the Raba was the 3.8-liter 45 hp Praga 'Grand' built under Praga license, in limited numbers. Raba also imported many foreign makes, including Benz, Panhard, and Austro-Daimler.

RABAG • Germany 1922-1925

Rabag built French Bugatti Types 22 and 23 under license. These were ohc 16-valve 1453cc and 1496cc ohc four-cylinder cars. Special racing cars were imported from Molsheim and equipped with Rabag radiators. Rabag did not produce many more than 100 cars in all.

907 Radia voiturette

RADIA • France 1907-1908

It is not known whether this company of Levallois-Perret (Seine) was connected with the Radia (or l'Automotrice) built in Bergerac; at the 1907 Paris Salon three Radias were exhibited, a shaft-driven 14/18 hp four-cylinder voiturette, and cars of 20/30 hp and 30/40 hp.

LA RADIEUSE • France 1907

Voiturettes built at Bayeux (Calvados) by M E Marie and shown at the 1907 Paris Salon.

RADIOR • France 1920-1922

M Chapolard, Rochet-Schneider agent in Bourg-en-Bresse, assembled some 1592cc Ballot-engined cars, sold as Radiors.

RAF • Austria 1907-1913

The Reichenberger Automobil Fabrik was founded by the great pioneer Baron Theodor von Liebig and two wealthy wool-manufacturers, Alfred Ginskey and Oskar Klinger. They built superb, expensive cars to a very high standard. From 1912 onward Knight sleeve-valve engines were built under license; in 1913 Laurin & Klement bought the RAF works. Most RAF cars were big ones, with engines ranging from 30 hp to 70 hp.

1924 Rabag (licence-built Bugatti) sports phaeton

RAGLAN • England 1899

A virtual carbon copy of the Benz, built in Coventry.

RAILTON • England 1933-1949

The Railton was a cheap and fast sporting car, though a Yankee at heart. The work of Reid Railton, it was originally based on the 4-liter Terraplane 8 chassis, though from mid-1934 a Hudson straight-eight of 4.2 liters was used. However, the British coachwork disguised the origins, while the riveted hood was reminiscent of the Invicta, Noel Macklin being concerned with both projects. The Hudson straight-eight engine, despite its crude internals (such as splash-lubricated big ends) gave the Railton a top speed of about 90 mph. Increased costs resulted in a smaller model appearing in 1938, fitted with 2.7- and 3.5-liter sixes, also by Hudson. A baby Railton of the same year was fitted with a Standard engine of 10 hp, however. A handful of cars was made after the Second World War.

RAINIER • USA 1905-1911

The first Rainiers were 22/28 hp and 30/35 hp fours built by Garford. After 1907 this Saginaw, Michigan, company built its own chassis. The last Rainiers were 45/59 hp fours.

RALEIGH • USA 1920-1922

Built first in Bridgeton, New Jersey, and later in Reading, Pennsylvania, the Raleigh was a typical assembled car of its time. Raleighs used Herschell-Spillman six-cylinder engines and had a wheelbase of 122 inches; the five-passenger touring car cost $2,750. Probably fewer than 25

Chassis of the 1907 RAF

cars were made and, although a four-cylinder model was announced in 1921, it was not forthcoming.

RALEIGH • England 1933-1936

The famous Nottingham cycle company built a few four-cylinder cyclecars circa 1916, but true production did not begin until 1933, with the 742cc vee-twin "Safety Seven" three-wheeler, which subsequently became the first Reliant.

RALLY • France 1920-1933

This Colombes, Seine, works started by converting Harley-Davidson sidecar outfits into cyclecars. In 1922 it built proper cyclecars, still with the 987cc Harley-Davidson vee-twin. The same year Rally presented its first four-cylinder-engined car, followed by many with various French proprietary engines (SCAP, Chapuis-Dornier, or Ruby) from 900cc to 1100cc. In 1931 Rally presented cars with modified Salmson chassis and dohc 1300cc Salmson engines.

RALPH LUCAS • England 1901-c. 1908

Lucas's first car was a curious paraffin-powered two-stroke car, with a piston and crankshaft at either end of its single cylinder. The speed of the engine was controlled by a button in the steering wheel, and the coachwork was of pressed steel. The Lucas 1908 two-stroke design was the origin of the Valveless.

RAMBLER • USA 1900-1914, 1950 to date

Thomas B Jeffery, born in Devon in 1845, emigrated to America aged 18. In 1879 he built his first Rambler cycle. His son Charles built two tiller-steered runabouts in 1900, followed by a left-hand-drive wheel-steered car in 1901. Model C of 1902 was the first production model, a crude, spidery single-cylinder buggy with tiller-steering. The 1904-1908 model had a secondary "steering wheel" which operated the throttle. A twin-cylinder, patronized by Teddy Roosevelt, appeared in 1905, and a 40 hp four followed in 1907. Production was limited to 2,500 cars in 1910 "to assure maximum quality," a customer that year traded six cows for a new Rambler. Thomas Jeffery died while visiting Pompeii in 1910. The 1911 models had locking gasoline taps and adjustable steering columns, and electric lighting was standardized in 1913; the cars were renamed Jeffery in 1914. The name was revived in 1950 by Nash Motors and continued after the creation of American Motors in 1954 (see American Motors.)

R & V KNIGHT • USA 1920-1924

Built by the R & V Division of the Root & Vandervoort Engineering Co of East Moline, Illinois, the R & V Knight was successor to the Moline-Knight. A highly regarded make, it was produced at the rate of 500 to 750 units per year, in both four- and six-cylinder models. A full line of open and closed models was available at prices ranging from around $1,650 to $4,000.

1905 Rambler Surrey Type One

1939 Railton 21.6 Fairmile

An 1100cc Rally sports two-seater

RANGER • England 1913-1915

An 8 hp Precision-engined cyclecar from Coventry.

RANGER • USA 1920-1923

Ranger was a limited-production assembled car company specializing in four-cylinder models until 1922, when a six was introduced in addition to the existing line. Some of the roadsters and touring cars on the larger model chassis carried such names as "Pal o"Mine," "Commodore," "Blue Hood," and "Newport" and were distinguished with full sport treatment, including aluminum door steps, cycle fenders and side wind-wings. Prices were as high as $3,500. Few of the sixes were built, however, and the 1923 line would have used the four only, had the company not failed before it could be put into production.

RAOUVAL • France 1899-1902

Similar in design to Léon Lefévbre's Pygmée, the power unit of this car from Anzin (Nord) was an 8 hp twin of 2851cc.

RAPID • Switzerland 1899

This was the Egg & Egli tri-voiturette under a different name. A trailer with two extra seats was available as an option.

RAPID • Italy 1904-1921

Giovanni Ceirano created these cars, which were built with a variety of four-cylinder engines from 2110cc to 9847cc. Most models were of advanced design with four-speed gearboxes and a very sophisticated rear suspension.

RAPID • Switzerland 1946

A backbone chassis was used on these streamlined three-wheelers from a mowing-machine works at Dietikon near Zürich, powered by a rear-mounted opposed-piston MAG engine. Only 36 were built.

LA RAPIDE • England 1919-1920

Built in south-west London, La Rapide was an unusual cyclecar with an air-cooled 8 hp JAP, mounted outside the body, drive being transmitted to the offside rear wheel.

RAPIER • England 1935-1940

Originally a Lagonda design, the Rapier was sold by the Staines company until the firm was placed under receivership in 1935. The model had a dohc 1104cc engine, a progressive layout for a car with a chassis price of £270. The original intention was to produce the engine in an aluminum alloy, but cast iron was eventually used on grounds of cost. The new management under Alan Good did not want the Rapier, so a new company, Rapier Cars Ltd, was formed by designer Tim Ashcroft, W H Oats and N Brocklebank to buy the design and manufacture it under the name of Rapier. It was available in supercharged form from 1936, and in all about 300 examples were made.

1907 Regner voiturette chassis

REGAS • USA 1903-1905

The 12 hp Regas, from Rochester, NY, had a vee-twin engine with air-cooling by slotted tubes "on the Bunsen burner principle." The Regas was one of the first side-entrance four-seaters on the American market.

REGENT • England 1899-1900

A Birmingham cycle company which built a tricycle with an Accles-Turrell engine.

REGENT • Austria 1899-1910

These cars were identical with the Bock & Hollender cars. When the works ceased car manufacture, a new company bought the remains and founded WAF.

REGINA • France 1903-1908

These were license-built Dixi cars of 17, 26, and 40 hp from the Société l'Eléctrique of Paris, which also made the Gallia and Galliette electric cars. It also built cycles, motorcycles, and tricars.

REGINA • France 1921-1925

A small cyclecar made in Paris, this three-wheeler had a single front wheel and was rear-engined with a four-cylinder 902cc Ruby unit.

REGINETTE • France 1920-1921

A Paris-built copy of the Briggs & Stratton Flyer. Only the Briggs & Stratton engine was imported.

REGNER • France 1905-1908

Originally a belt-driven voiturette built in Paris. By 1908 big cars of 12/16 hp and 24/30 hp were also marketed.

REKORD • Germany 1904-1908

Willi Schulz drove a 45 hp Rekord in the 1905 Herkomer Trial; these Berlin-built cars used French components, especially Aster engines and Gladiator chassis.

1976 Renaissance coupé

RELIABLE DAYTON • USA 1906-1909

A "simple and powerful" two-stroke engine of 1104cc powered this $500 high-wheeler with "piano box body."

RELIANT • England 1935 to date

Reliant started its career as a three-wheeler manufacturer; the Robin being the best known of its three-wheeler designs. The Les Bellamy-designed Sabre was its first four-wheeler, with four- and six-cylinder Ford engines. The Ogle-designed Scimitar and its hatchback successor, the GTE, were more popular. In 1975 a four-wheeled derivative of the Robin, the Kitten, appeared. Launched in 1984, the Michelotti-styled SS1 failed to impress. In 1987 Reliant sold the rights to the original Scimitar to Middlebridge Engineering, which built a handful of cars in Nottingham (the Princess Royal bought the first) but went into receivership in 1990. It was acquired by Beans Industries, which had last built a car in 1929. The SS1 was restyled by William Towns as the Scimitar 1800 Ti in 1988, when the US-based Universal Motors Group bought the manufacturing rights. The SS1 died when Reliant folded yet again. Several financial packages to run Reliant came and went, but a brighter future emerged when a British group revived the brand with styling updates and an attempt to sell the workhorse, pick-up versions of the Robin sedan for a wide variety of commercial applications.

REMINGTON • USA 1900-1901

From the famous typewriter company, the four-cylinder Remington ran on a mixture of hydrogen and acetylene.

REMINGTON • USA 1914-1915

A four-cylinder cyclecar with a preselector transmission designed by Philo E Remington, whose grandfather had founded the Remington arms company. A V-8 was used in 1915 cars.

RENAISSANCE • Canada 1976

Le Vicomte Classic coachbuilders of St Sauveur des Monts, Quebec, planned a limited edition of 50 of this 1930s-styled four-seat luxury coupé, powered by a 6559cc Ford V-8. The massive chassis was formed from 6.5-inch steel channel.

RENAULT • France 1898 to date

See panel overleaf

Reliant Scimitar GTE

1907 Reo 18 hp

RENE BONNET • France 1962-1965

After Deutsch left D B, René Bonnet continued to build sports cars with Renault 850 and 1100cc engines, front-engined like the Le Mans or rear-engined like the Djet. He also made some racing cars. When Bonnet was taken over by Matra in 1965, the Champigny, Val-de-Marne, works continued to produce cars for a while under the name of Matra-Bonnet, then as "Matra."

RENEGADE • England 1971 to date

One of the more streamlined VW-based buggies, the Renegade was first seen at the 1971 Racing Car Show.

RENFERT • Germany 1924-1925

A little-known 776cc twin-cylinder two-stroke two-seater, made in small numbers.

RENFREW • Scotland 1904

A 16/20 hp four from Glasgow.

REO • USA 1904-1936

Ransom E Olds retired from Oldsmobile in 1904, but was persuaded to head a new company producing a single-cylinder gas buggy; there was also a twin-cylinder model. An unsuccessful four appeared in 1906. Reo"s next four was, Ransome Olds claimed, "pretty close to finality." He called this "Reo the Fifth" his "farewell car," but went on to produce four- and six-cylinder models, concentrating on the six-cylinder Model T in 1920. This car was underslung at the rear. A new 25 hp Flying Cloud six replaced this car in 1927, also available as the Wolverine. The 1931 season saw a Flying Cloud Eight, as well as the Sakhnoffsky-styled Custom Royale Eight, and in 1933 Reo, which had already pioneered synchromesh, offered a two-speed automatic transmission.

REPUBLIC • USA 1911-1916

A "classy" 35/40 hp whose four-cylinder T-head engine had a desaxé crankshaft.

RESTELLI • Italy 1924-1925

Small producer of advanced four-cylinder cars of sporting appearance, with ohv engines of 1368cc.

REVELATION • France 1922-1923

A cyclecar made in Paris, using Train or Villiers engines. It had a wooden chassis.

1920 ReVere speedster

REVERE • USA 1917-1926

One of America's prestige sporting cars, ReVere cars were powered by four-cylinder Rochester-Duesenberg engines exclusively until 1924, when the Monson, also a four and based on the Rochester-Duesenberg powerplant, was substituted. In that same year a six-cylinder Continental was also available. Several ReVeres were built to special order for heads of state, including King Alfonso XIII of Spain. The last cars of this make were equipped with balloon tires and four-wheel brakes, as well as a rudimentary power-steering system, this being effected by dual steering-wheels, one within the other, which had a lower ratio to expedite parking.

1904 Rex 8 hp tonneau

REVOL • France 1922

Made in Fontenay-aux-Roses, Seine, this cyclecar was available with 990cc Train or 1100cc Anzani engines.

REVOLETTE • England 1905

This was a three-wheeler built by the New Revolution Cycle Company of Birmingham.

REX • England 1901-1914

Starting with a 900cc single-cylinder voiturette, Rex was soon producing a complex range of cars and tricars (Rexette tricars were the main offering from 1903-1906,) and in 1906 three- and four-wheeled Airettes were available. Rex-Simplex 12 hp twin-cylinder cars were current from 1904-1905, followed in 1906 by the 18/22 hp four-cylinder Ast-Rex; in 1906 came the vee-twin AiRex. A model known as the Remo was current between 1905-1907; the 1908-1909 Remo range consisted of round-radiatored fours of 2556cc and 2799cc. Thereafter the company concentrated on motorcycles, apart from a 1912 vee-twin cyclecar and a 1914 1100cc Dorman-engined light car.

REX (REX SIMPLEX) • Germany 1901-1924

Richard & Hering at Ronneburg (Saxony) was a manufacturer of bicycle parts which built cars with De Dion and Fafnir proprietary engines. It built car models from single-

1912 Rex-Simplex touring car

RENAULT • France 1898 to date

Louis Renault made his first car, a De Dion-engined vehicle of 273cc, in 1898, in the back yard of his parents' house. Having received orders from potential customers, he founded Renault Fréres in Billancourt, Seine, with his two brothers Fernand and Marcel. From 1900 Renault fitted 500cc De Dion engines, and then made twin-cylinder models such as the 1060cc 8cv and the 4398cc four-cylinder 20cv. Many of the twin-cylinder Renaults were used as taxis in Paris and London, where they survived for many years. The first six-cylinder Renault, a 50cv 9.5-liter, was presented in 1908. In 1912 Renault Fréres offered no fewer than 15 different models, of which the best was the six-cylinder 40cv of 7539cc. The following year a smaller six-cylinder, the 4523cc 22cv, appeared.

By the outbreak of war Renault had become one of the most important manufacturers of cars in Europe. During the war the Renault taxis became the legendary "Taxis de la Marne" and Renault pioneered the building of light tanks. After the Armistice the twin-cylinder Renaults survived for only a few months in production, as Renault resumed manufacture of most of the pre-war models. In 1923 Renault launched a new model to compete with the 6cv Citroën, the 951cc 6cv "KJ." The same year came the six-cylinder JY of 4222cc, later enlarged to 4766cc. The 40cv still continued, but since the war had been enlarged to 9123cc. In the late 1920s there was also a sv six of 1500cc, and many commercial vehicles. A complete change came in 1929 with the firm"s first straight-eight, the 7100cc "Reinastella," soon followed by the "Nerva." Nevertheless, none of the Renaults of the time, the "Monaquatre," "Monasix," or "Vivaquatre," was modern compared with the products of the marque's arch-rival, Citroën. Renault had only just moved the radiator to the front of the car, having persisted with dashboard radiators for 25 years. The immediate pre-Second World War range was from 951cc to a 5.4-liter straight-eight.

First production Renault, the 1898 1¹/₂ hp

1924 Renault NN tourer

After the war Renault was taken under government control and became the Regie Nationale des Usines Renault. It resumed production with the "Juvaquatre," and later with the rear-engined "4cv" of 760cc, which lasted until 1961. The "Frégate," introduced in 1951, was the last of the front-engined, rear-drive cars made by Renault. The Dauphine came in 1956, and a "Dauphine Gordini" was presented the following year. In 1959 came the Floride, and three years later the 747cc R4 with front-wheel drive. After an attempt to build the American Rambler under license, the 956cc R8 arrived, giving way later to the "R8 S," the "Major" and the "Gordini." The R16 was presented in 1965, followed four years later by the R12 and then the R6 in 1970. The R15 and R17 came in 1971, and then the unsuccessful R12 "Gordini." Latest in the line in recent years are the Rodeo (a sort of plastic Jeep,) the R5 and the sporty R5-Alpine ("Gordini" in the UK,) the R14, R18, R20, and R30.

The 1980s saw Renault overtaken as France's biggest producer by Peugeot-Citroën and an unsuccessful partial takeover of AMC in the USA. They also saw the end of the perennial Renault 4 in 1986, a year after the original 5 had been replaced by the second-generation "Supercinq," with transverse power unit. Other new models were the Fuego (1980,) 9 (1982,) 11 (1983,) 25 (1984,) and 21 (1986.) The trendsetting plastic bodied, steel framed, Espace one-box "people carrier," built by Matra, appeared in 1985. Through several updates it remains the definitive MPV. The 19 replaced the 9 at the end of the decade, and a cabriolet version appeared in

1911 Renault 20/30 hp sedan

Renault Alpine GTA

1991. The new Clio, which superseded the 5 (which nevertheless remained in production) was voted Car of the Year in 1991. Power was by 1.2 and 1.4-liter gasoline and 1.9-liter diesel. In 1991 the 16 valve dohc 1.8-liter Clio 16-V "pocket rocket" replaced the R5 GT Turbo. A "Williams" tuned limited edition version further underlined the Clio's character, allied to a very successful advertising campaign throughout Europe. The Clio Baccara is a luxury small car with leather trim and an electronic four-speed transmission. A 19 cabriolet was added to the range in 1991, and the Renault-badged 2.9-liter turbocharged Alpine A610 went into production in January 1992. However, Renault abandoned its Alpine link in order to launch its own, lightweight, two-seat sportster, the Spyder. With no roof, bare trim, an alloy chassis and grand-prix-type suspension, it was a unique move for Renault.

1992 Renault Espace

The 19 range was superseded by the Megane hatchback range, which brought improved, class-leading standards of safety and a return to style and verve, notably in the coupé versions. Megane also spawned a mini-MPV and a convertible version of the Coupé. The Laguna range covered the middle-market ground for Renault with great success. It featured basic 1.8 engines as well as a 2.0 liter, and a smooth V-6 range topper. This was later evolved into a more sporty model, and offered real performance in a quiet package. Sadly the Safrane executive sedan was, like the 25, another big-car disappointment for Renault. A new Clio with highly individual styling appeared in 1998, reflecting the view of Renault's design director, Patrick le Quement, that Renault should return to individualism and style.

In March 1999 Renault secured an automotive industry coup when it pulled off a deal to buy a 35 per cent share in the giant Nissan company. Nissan, suffering from overcapacity and the Asian recession, took the hard step of allowing in foreign investment. This will give Renault access to a wider market and allow it to reassert itself in America as well as cutting costs in design, development, and engineering fields.

1925 Rhode 9 hp tourer

cylinders of 698cc to four-cylinder cars of 7440cc. Post-war, only fours of 3176cc and 2467cc were built. After Richard & Hering began mass-production of car wheels in 1921, Elite took over production of the larger Rex-Simplex model.

REYONNAH • France 1951-1954

M Hannoyer in Paris made this strange folding car with a 175cc two-stroke Ydral engine.

REYROL (PASSE-PARTOUT) • France 1901-1930

Based at Neuilly until 1906, and at Levallois-Perret, Seine, thereafter, Reyrol started with a 5 hp single-cylinder voiturette, progressing to more substantial vehicles with $4\frac{1}{2}$ hp De Dion and 6 hp Buchet engines by 1905. Armored-wood chassis had been replaced by pressed steel in 1907, in which year three 942cc cars ran in the Coupe des Voiturettes under the marque's alter ego, Passe-Partout. At the 1908 Paris Salon Reyrol showed an 8/12 hp four-cylinder, and in 1910 a 2121cc four was listed. Post-war, cars of 1.5 and 2.3 liters were offered; the type "Passe-Partout" of 1927 had a 1.1-liter Chapuis-Dornier engine and fwd.

RH • France 1920

Raymond Holbet, of Rueil, Seine, made some 10 hp Ballot-engined 1449cc cars.

RH • France 1926-1927

M Hébert of Levallois, Seine, was mainly a builder of chassis, but also made some complete 1098cc CIME-engined cars.

RHEDA • France 1897-1898

A 2.5 hp horizontal engine powered this tricycle carriage built at Saint Cloud.

RHEMAG • Germany 1924-1926

A sporting two-seater with an ohc four-cylinder 1065cc engine and Fulmina-Perrot four-wheel brakes. It had a60 mph top speed and was also available with three- and four-seater bodywork.

RHODE • England 1921-1931

Built by F W Mead and T W Deakin, the Rhode light car used an engine specially manufactured for it. This was a 1087cc four-cylinder with overhead camshaft, an unusual feature for a light car. For 1924 a larger 1232cc engine was offered, and in 1926 it was quietened by the introduction of pushrod ohv, and designated the 11/30 hp. A completely new car, the Hawk, initially powered by an ohc version of the 11/30 hp engine, appeared in 1928; it was subsequently powered by a 1.5-liter Meadows.

RIBBLE • England 1904-c. 1908

Southport-built tricars with 5 hp Forman or 8 hp MMC power units; 10/12 hp and 12/16 hp four-cylinder four-wheelers followed.

RICART, RICART & PEREZ, RICART-ESPANA • Spain 1922-1930

Wilfredo Pelayo Ricart, pioneer aviator and engineer, began production of fast 1500cc four-cylinder ohc 16-valve racing cars in conjunction with Francisco Perez, but the venture lasted only a year. Thereafter Ricart built sporting cars, 1500cc fours and a well-engineered 2401cc six, under his own name. In 1927 a 1601cc fou,r and a 1486cc six were shown at the 1927 Paris Salon. In 1928 Ricart merged with Espana to form Ricart-Espana. Apart from a new 2400cc six, Ricart-Espanas were similar to the Ricarts.

RICHARD • USA 1914-1917

The long-stroke 7362cc engine of the $1,850 Richard, from Cleveland, was rated at only 25 hp, but developed a claimed 96 bhp, which gave the car a 80 mph performance.

RICHARDSON • England 1903-1907

The cars produced by this manufacturer from Saxilby, near Lincoln, consisted of a 6.5 hp Aster-engined single-cylinder two-seater, a 12/14 hp twin and an 18/29 hp four, all with speed controlled by variable-lift inlet valves.

RICHARDSON • England 1919-1922

JAP or Precision vee-twin engines powered this friction-drive cyclecar from Sheffield.

RICHELIEU • USA 1923

Designed by Newton VanZandt (formerly with ReVere,) the Richelieu was similar to the ReVere, although heavier. Like ReVere it used the Rochester-Duesenberg four-cylinder engine. High, rounded radiators, similar to Daniels, distinguished the Richelieu, and open and closed models were offered from $3,950 to $6,000. An estimated 25 to 50 cars were produced in two years of business. In 1923 the Richelieu interests were bought by Salvatore Barbarino, who later built the Barbarino car.

RICHMOND • USA 1908-1914

Air-cooled fours of 22 hp to 30 hp powered these cars from Richmond, Indiana, up to 1911; big watercooled fours were used after that.

RICHMOND • England 1913

A 10/12 hp four-cylinder two-seater with underslung rear axle.

RICKENBACKER • USA 1922-1927

"The car worthy of its name" carried the "Hat-in-the-Ring" insignia of its promoter, Captain Eddie Rickenbacker, top-scoring American First World War air ace. Three years of development by Harry Cummingham, Barney Everett and Walter Flanders were behind the six-cylinder Rickenbacker, with its double flywheels for smooth running and, from 1923, internal expanding four-wheel brakes. This was the first time this feature had been used on a medium-priced American car, and rival manufacturers started a "whisper campaign" about the alleged dangers of too-powerful brakes, fearful that they, too, would have to face the cost of fitting front-wheel brakes. Despite handsome styling, sound engineering and the pioneering use of two-tone paint schemes, the Rickenbacker was unequal to such pressure. After Walter Flanders' accidental death, Captain Eddie called a halt to production.

RICKETTS • USA 1908-1909

Brownell engines with four cylinders (35 hp) and six cylinders (50 hp) powered these touring cars from South Bend, Indiana.

RICKSHAW • England 1975

The brainchild of Roy Haynes of Witham, Essex, the four-seater open-top electric Rickshaw ran on 12 batteries and was capable of covering 50 miles between charges at up to 30 mph.

RIDDLE • USA 1920-1926

A highly respected hearse and ambulance manufacturer, this erstwhile carriage firm started building motorized emergency vehicles of these types on its own chassis in 1916, previously having mounted coachwork on White chassis. In 1920 it began limited manufacture of sedans, either conventionally designed for the use of bearers at funerals, or pillarless on one side to allow passage for wheelchairs. All of these cars were built to special order only and, like the commercial vehicles, used Continental six-cylinder engines.

1921 Riddle invalid car

1905 Richardson 14 hp tonneau

RIDER-LEWIS • USA 1908-1909

"The biggest little car ever built," the 1909 ohc 3707cc Rider-Lewis 30 hp four sold for $1,000. The same firm built the single ohc 4942cc $2500 "Excellent Six" in its Muncie, Indiana, factory.

1900 Riker Electric Victoria

RIDLEY • England 1902-1907

These 3.5 hp and 4.5 hp voiturettes had a two-speed rear axle, incorporating a reverse gear. The company, based in Coventry, was wound up in 1904, and John Ridley worked for Horbick and Arrol-Johnston before starting production again in 1905 in Paisley, Scotland, with 4, 5, 6 and 7 hp cars. The first few chassis were built by Horbick. The new company folded in December 1907.

RIDLEY • England 1914

An 8 hp "carette" from Woodbridge, Suffolk.

RIESS-ROYAL • USA 1921-1922

This was a continuation of the Bell "6-50" with minor differences. Only prototypes were built.

RIKAS • Germany 1922-1923

An unlucky attempt to produce a small 900cc four-cylinder car with inadequate resources.

RIKER • USA 1896-1901

Andrew Riker's company was one of the most famous manufacturers of electric vehicles, built in a wide range of styles and sizes, and all featuring an unusual hub-centre steering layout. Riker's first gasoline car, a 1667cc twin-cylinder, appeared in July 1901; he later designed gasoline cars for Locomobile.

RILEY • England 1898-1969

See panel overleaf

1924 Riley Redwing 11.9 hp four-seater

RILEY • England 1898-1969

Although the first Riley was a neat four-wheeled voiturette with a single-cylinder engine, production vehicles were initially motor tricycles; tricars were made until 1907. Four-wheelers followed, powered by 1034cc vee-twin engines. Capacity was increased to 2 liters from 1908. Although these were still in production by the outbreak of the First World War, a 2.9-liter four was now also available. Post-war Rileys initially used a sv 1.5-liter engine, the Redwing sports version of 1923 being a particularly handsome variant. However, the really sensational model of the 1920s was Percy Riley"s Nine of 1927, particularly the fabric-bodied, high-waisted Monaco sedan, complete with boot (an unusual feature for the date.) The engine was outstanding, an 1100cc four-cylinder with twin camshafts set high in the block, actuating inclined valves by pushrods in a hemispherical head.

This proved a highly tunable layout, without the complexity of overhead camshafts, and remained a feature of Riley engine design up until 1957. In 1928 a touring version of the Nine appeared, and also the low and lively Brooklands model, inspired by J G Parry Thomas. A six-cylinder variant of the Nine theme was inevitable. This, the 1.6-liter Fourteen, came in 1929. The 1930s saw many variants on the four- and six-cylinder engines, the distinctive fastback Kestrel and more conventional Falcon appearing in 1933. Not surprisingly, the Riley engine layout lent itself admirably to competition activities; one instance was successive wins in the BRDC 500 Mile race at Brooklands in 1934/35/36. Sporting models were the 9 hp Imp, the six-cylinder MPH and, later, the 1.5-liter 12/4 four-cylinder engine appeared in 1934 and was produced alongside the faithful Nine. Two years later a 2.5-liter long-stroke four was marketed. Financial storm clouds were gathering, however, and William Morris took over the company in 1938. The new broom saw that only the 1.5- and 2.5-liter cars remained in production, these engines also powering the post-war cars. The 2.5-liter Pathfinder of 1954 retained the classic Riley engine, though this ceased in 1957. Remaining models were merely badge-engineered BMC variants, mainly on the Mini and 1100 theme.

1934 Riley Imp

1962 Riley Elf

1907 Rochet-Schneider 20 hp

RIP • France 1908-1912

Ominously named voiturettes from Rive-de-Gier (Loire,) with transverse coil springs all round, independent rear suspension, and the choice of 5/6 hp single- or 10/12 hp four-cylinder engines.

RITZ • USA 1915

This two-seater 12/15 hp light car built by Driggs-Seabury had a two-speed transmission in the back axle.

RIVIERRE • France 1912-1913

Successor to the Mototri-Contal, this was a four-cylinder 1460cc two-seater torpedo with transmission by "lateral shafts."

ROADABLE • USA 1946-1947

Built in Garland, Texas, by the Southern Aircraft Division, Portable Products Corp., the Roadable could be converted into an airplane in five minutes by the addition of 30 ft wings, tai,l and propeller. A 130 hp six-cylinder air-cooled engine drove the three-wheeled vehicle while the rear-wheel drive was used in conjunction with the propeller for take-off. A top speed of 110 mph in the air, combined with a600-mile range, was claimed.

ROADSTER • USA 1902-1904

"No experiment but a full-grown Automobile," the "8 full horsepower" Roadster from the Flint Automobile Company of Flint, Michigan, was claimed to be a great favourite with physicians. It sold for $950.

ROAMER • USA 1916-1930

Designed externally to resemble the Rolls-Royce, the first Roamers were powered by Continental sixes. Rochester-Duesenberg fours became available in 1921, and remained the power unit until 1925. Thereafter, with a few Continental sixes marketed in 1926, the make used Lycoming eights exclusively. The Roamer was built by Albert C Barley (who had been producing the Halladay car) and was designed by Karl H Martin (who would also design the Deering Magnetic and Kenworthy and build the Wasp.) Production slackened after 1926, and the Roamers found fewer and fewer buyers. Cars sold as 1930 models were actually leftover models from 1929.

ROBE • USA 1923

The Robe was built in Nansemond, Va., by W B Robe, who had built a cyclecar in Portsmouth, Ohio, in 1914, and J D Strong. Using a four-cylinder engine of its "own" manufacture, according to the announcements (but in fact probably a Continental,), the 106-inch wheel-base Robe featured full leaf springs on either side of the body. At least

1923 Robe prototype

one test chassis and one touring car are known to have been built; this may well have been the total production.

ROBERTSON • England 1915-1916

An alarming-looking three-wheeled cyclecar from Manchester, powered by 965cc JAP or Precision vee-twins.

ROBINSON • USA 1900-1904

"Modelled after the best French designs," the Robinson (or "Pope-Robinson") from Boston was available with two- or four-cylinder engines, including a 5000cc "fast touring carriage."

ROBINSON • England 1907

Only three Robinsons were built out of a projected total of six. As the four-cylinder 12 hp engine was cooled by its

1902 10 hp Rochet

own exhaust gases, which passed through a "radiator" before being directed on to the cylinder heads by a copper cowl, this shortfall is perhaps understandable.

ROBINSON & HOLE • England 1906-1907

A four-cylinder 16/20 hp model with gate-change three-speed gearbox and shaft drive, built in Thames Ditton, Surrey.

ROB ROY • Scotland 1922-1926

This cyclecar originally used a 9 hp flat-twin engine, which also powered the Kingsbury Junior. It later graduated to four-cylinder engines by Dorman and Coventry-Climax.

ROCHDALE • England 1952-1968

Stylish glassfiber-bodied fixed-head sports cars, the Rochdales sported a number of engines over the years. Some 400 Olympic Phase 1s and 2s were built. Many have survived and retain an enthusiastic following.

ROCHESTER • USA 1901-1903

A $600 tiller-steered light steam carriage.

ROCHET, ROCHET-PETIT • France 1899-1905

This Parisian company bought the design of its first car, a 6/8 hp "of Daimler type," from Edouard Rossel of Lille, adding a 120 hp in 1900. The 4.5 hp Aster-engined Rochet-Petit appeared in 1902.

ROCHET • France 1907

Tricars and "tri-voiturettes" from Albert (Somme.)

ROCHET FRERES • France 1898-1901

A Lyon-built voiturette with front-mounted De Dion engine.

1933 Rohr 3.3-liter straight-eight

ROCHET-SCHNEIDER • France 1894-1932

This well-known Lyon factory started by making Benz-like cars, then built cars inspired first by Panhard, and subsequently by Mercedes. In 1909 it had nine different models, of which two were six-cylinders, of 30cv (7135cc) and 45cv (10,857cc,) and which were chain driven. In 1914 Rochet-Schneider had six different models, the largest being the 50cv four of 7238cc; there were also two six-cylinders, an 18cv (3619cc) and a 28cv (5228cc,) all with sv. The company made trucks for the army during the war, and resumed production in 1918 with pre-war models like the 14cv, 18cv, and 30cv. The first new car to be made was the 1920 sv six-cylinder of 6126cc. It eventually acquired ohv, and in 1926 was replaced by another six, of 3769cc, enlarged in 1930 to 4561cc. From 1932 Rochet-Schneider switched to building trucks and buses, as its old-fashioned four-cylinder models had become increasingly difficult to sell.

ROCKAWAY • USA 1902-1903

A basic single-cylinder chain-drive runabout from Rockaway, New Jersey, selling for $650.

ROCK FALLS • USA 1917-1926

A manufacturer of funeral cars, Rock Falls produced a limited number of sedans and large limousines. Continental six-cylinder engines were standard throughout, and the eight-passenger limousine was listed at $4,500. Fewer than 50 (probably much fewer) were built per year.

ROCKNE • USA 1931-1933

The smallest of the Studebaker line, the Rockne six made its bow on the automotive scene in 1931, ostensibly to fill the gap previously occupied by the Erskine, which had been withdrawn a year before. It was named after Knute Rockne, football coach at Notre Dame University (located in South Bend, Indiana, like Studebaker.) It was felt that a hero's name would sell cars, Knute Rockne having been employed by Studebaker in addition to his professional activities on the football field. Whether it was the fact that the car had been launched in a Depression year, whether it was that the great Rockne was killed in a plane crash before the car had actually been introduced, or whether the car was somewhat overpriced ($585 to $675) for its size, the Rockne never really caught on. Some 30,000 to 35,000 Rockne cars were sold before the make was quietly phased out in 1933.

1919 Rock Falls sedan

1925 3-liter Rolland-Pilain at Le Mans

ROCKWELL • USA 1909

An 18/20 hp four "specially designed for taxi-meter work."

ROEBLING-PLANCHE • USA 1909-1910

Designed by the French engineer Planche, the Roebling-Planche was built in the Walter factory and financed by the Roebling family, builders of the Brooklyn Bridge. The marque became the Mercer a year later.

ROGER • France 1888-1896

Emile Roger, perhaps the world's first motor agent, assembled Benz cars for the French market, but the venture ended with his death.

ROGER • England 1920-1924

The friction-drive Roger used a 10.8 hp Coventry-Simplex engine. Later, in 1923, the option of shaft drive was available.

ROHR • Germany 1927-1935

Founded by one of Germany's most capable designers, H G Röhr, the factory built very advanced ohv eight-cylinder cars of 2250cc and 3287cc, some of them supercharged. Röhr left in 1930 to join Adler; Porsche's design office at Stuttgart created an improved 100 bhp eight-cylinder Röhr in 1934. An air-cooled ohv flat-four 1486cc Röhr car built under Tatra license had appeared in 1933. The Röhr works at Ober-Ramstadt also built the 1934 Zoller-designed 1496cc two-stroke racing cars.

LE ROITELET • France 1921-1924

A fwd cyclecar made in Paris with a twin-cylinder 749cc engine.

ROLAND • France 1907

Tricars from an Albert (Somme) cycle works.

ROLL • France 1922-1923

Cyclecar made in Paris with a 990cc four-cylinder Ruby engine.

ROLLAND-PILAIN • France 1906-1931

Established in Tours, Rolland-Pilain started in 1906 with a 20 cv four-cylinder model of 2211 cc. In 1910 it experimented with sleeve-valve engines, and introduced a 1500cc model. In 1913 it added a 20cv of 3969cc and a big 60cv of 6902cc. At the outbreak of the war the company was building only the 20cv and the 10cv (1924cc.) It restarted production after the war with these old models, but in 1921 presented the ohv 12cv of 2297cc, with brakes on all four wheels. In 1922 Rolland-Pilain raced a 2000cc straight-eight, and 1924 saw the 2008cc 11 cv ohv four, the best model ever made by the firm. The following year came the 1924cc 10/12cv. At the very end Rolland-Pilain experimented with American Continental engines.

ROLLIN • USA 1923-1925

Designed and built by Rollin White, chief engineer of the White Company, the four-cylinder Rollin was planned as an economical automobile to capture a share of the low-priced market. Its engine was similar to that of the Cletrac tractor (a White subsidiary,) and the first Rollin cars were not only built in the Cleveland Tractor plant but shared the Cletrac emblem. The 112-inch wheelbase, disc-wheeled Rollin was just a bit too high-priced for the market for which it had been intended. Output in 1924, its best

year, was some 6,500 units, but total production probably failed to reach 10,000 before the car was discontinued in 1925.

ROLLO • England 1911-1913

"The best thing in motor cycles, not the poorest in motor cars," the Birmingham-built Rollo was nevertheless a typical cyclecar, with an 8 hp JAP engine and chain-cum-belt drive. There were three models: a tandem seater "for two or more"; a Sociable, "for those who prefer to sit side by side"; and a Mono-car (70 guineas.)

ROLLS-ROYCE • England 1904 to date

See panel overleaf

ROLLS-ROYCE • USA 1920-1931

Rolls-Royce of America, Inc, was formed in Springfield, Mass., in 1920 to build and supply Rolls-Royce cars. Some 50 highly trained craftsmen were moved with their families and possessions to Springfield before operations began there. Between 1921 and 1929 some 2,601 chassis left the Springfield works, both "Silver Ghost" and "New Phantom" models. Eventually the domestic Rolls-Royce became as much an American product as any other domestic car. The 12-volt electrical system was changed to 6-volt and the four-speed transmission was dropped in favour of a three. In 1925 the steering wheel was moved to the left. The "New Phantom" did not appear on the American scene until 1926, the same year Rolls-Royce bought coachbuilder Brewster & Company. Most subsequent Springfield cars carried custom coachwork by this firm. When the "Phantom II" was introduced by Derby the Springfield operation ceased actual new car production owing to lack of finance. However, in 1930-1933 it managed to assemble some 350 additional, now outmoded cars from existing parts. In addition it imported 121 Phantom II chassis and sold them in lefthand drive form and mounted with Brewster coachwork. In 1934 Rolls-Royce of America, Inc, was dissolved and its place taken by the newly organized Springfield Manufacturing Co, which assembled Brewster cars until 1936.

ROLUX • France 1938-1952

Builder of the New-Map motorcycles in Lyon, Martin made some light cars with 125cc and 175cc two-strokes, also sold as "New Map."

ROM CARMEL • Israel 1958 to date

Initially known as the Sabra, based on Reliant designs, from 1966 to 1971 this Haifa company was in partnership with Triumph of Coventry. Late 1970s production was 1,800 glassfiber-bodied cars annually; the four-door Rom 1300 used a Ford Escort engine.

1914 Ronteix, sold in Britain as the Cummikar

ROMER • USA 1921-1922

Built in Danvers, Massachusetts, the Romer was an assembled car using a Continental six-cylinder engine. The five-passenger touring model was priced at $1,975; other body styles including a speedster, roadster, coupé, and two-door sedan, as well as a small truck, were available. Production was limited and passenger-car production was terminated in late 1921 (although truck production continued into the following year.)

RONTEIX • France 1907-1914

Ronteix of Paris built a "suspended voiturette" in 1907, as well as tricars and fore-carriages. Their early cars used a curious multi-ratio crownwheel and pinion like the Sizaire-Naudin, though from 1913 a normal gearbox was fitted. Four-cylinder engines and shaft drive placed the 905cc Ronteix on a higher technical plane than many of its contemporaries.

ROOSEVELT • USA 1929-1931

The Roosevelt, smallest of the Marmon line of cars, was announced on New Year's Day, 1929. Featuring a radiator emblem depicting the head of President Theodore Roosevelt, horizontal hood louvres, and a choice of wire or wood wheels, the Roosevelt was the only American straight-eight costing under $1,000 at the time. In 1930 the Roosevelt-head insignia was dropped and the car was renamed the Marmon-Roosevelt.

ROOTS & VENABLES • England 1895-1904

J D Roots was one of the pioneers of British motoring. All his cars ran on "heavy oil" (paraffin,) which then cost 5½d a gallon, against 11d for "motor spirit." His earliest trials took place on the Continent to avoid the repressive British laws. "The car would have been an instantaneous success," recalled a contemporary, "but for the intensely objectionable smell it gave off when starting and occasionally running."

ROPER-CORBET • England 1911-1913

A four-cylinder 14/16 hp model which sold for £350 complete.

ROSENGART • France 1928-1955

L Rosengart started in Neuilly, Seine, just before the Depression with Austin Sevens built under license. They were very similar to the British models, except that the bodywork was adapted to the French taste. In 1932 the chassis was lengthened, and a small 1100cc six offered. In the years preceding the war Rosengart made some fwd "Supertraction" cars based on the Adler Trumpf and, later, on the Citroën. After the war Rosengart resumed production with some pre-war models and introduced the "Supertrahuit" with Mercury engine, a complete flop. The 1954

1948 Rosengart Supertrahuit ST8

Silver Seraph
Silver Seraph

1999 Rolls-Royce Silver Seraph

Vintage Rover style

ROVER • England 1904 to date

Rover built the first true safety bicycle in 1888, but apart from an early electric tricycle and a De Dion-engined bathchair, did not venture into car production until 1904, when a neat 8 hp model designed by Edmund Lewis appeared, using a great deal of cast aluminum in its construction, particularly in its backbone chassis frame. A more conventional 6 hp appeared the next year, as did two four-cylinder models, the 10/12 and the 16/20, the latter a neat monobloc of 3199cc which won the 1907 Tourist Trophy Race. Sleeve-valve Rovers of 8 hp (single-cylinder 1042cc) and 12 hp (four-cylinder 3764cc) were announced for 1911, in the autumn of which year an excellent 2297cc 12 hp designed by Owen Clegg made its bow. It formed the basis of post-war production, joined by the Rover Eight, a 998cc flat-twin designed by J Y Sangster. These basic models were succeeded by the four-cylinder Nine and the P A Poppe-designed 14/ 45, a 3.4-liter six shown in 1923 having proved unsatisfactory. The ohc 14/45 (uprated to 16/50) did not sell well, and was replaced in 1928 by the 2-liter "Light Six," which formed the basis of 1930s production in capacities up to 2.7 liters. A rear-engined 839cc V-4, the Scarab, with an £85 price tag, failed to reach production in 1931, and thereafter Rover stuck to its solid middle-class image.

1926 Rover 14/40 hp Saloon

In 1948 new ioe 4- and 6-cylinder models, the P3 60 and 75, with ifs for the first time, appeared, as did the 4wd Land-Rover. October 1949 saw the P4 75, with full-width styling and "Cyclops" central headlight; it sired a range which lasted until May 1964. In 1963 came the radically different Rover 2000, available from 1968 with the GM-designed light-alloy 3.5-liter V-8 also found on its luxury P4 stablemate. The 4wd Range Rover, aimed at a more sybaritic market than the Land-Rover, appeared in 1970, and 1976 saw a new Rover 3500, with Ferrari-like styling. It subsequently became available with Rover's in-line sixes as well.

Since the Austin name was dropped in 1989, all the old Austin Rover group cars have been badged as "Rovers" except the indestructible Mini, which had been a marque on its own since 1969, and the Metro, later to be rebadged as the Rover 100. The year 1984 saw the launch of the 213/216, based on the Honda Ballade, as a replacement for the Triumph Acclaim.

Ford tried to buy Rover in 1986, but was thwarted. In 1988 the group was sold to British Aerospace. The then model line-up included the Maestro and Montego (the 2-liter performance models of both are badged "MG,") the 200/400 derived from the Honda Concerto) and the top-of-the-range 800, again designed in conjunction with Honda and available with I-4 power in 820i, Si and SLi trim and with the 2.7-liter Honda V6 in 827Si, and Sterling trim. A new range of Honda based hatchbacks appeared in 214 and 216 guise. They were, in some versions, powered by the excellent new Rover K series engine, and the later models of the 800 also saw new Rover engines installed, notably as the KV6.

During this period the jewel in Rover"s crown, the Land-Rover brand, underwent great change. An all-new Range Rover was introduced to complement the existing Discovery range of lifestyle orientated 4wd cars.

1977 Rover 2600 six-cylinder

1963 Rover 110 Sedan

In 1948 new ioe 4- and 6-cylinder models, the P3 60 and 75, with ifs for the first time, appeared, as did the 4wd Land-Rover. October 1949 saw the P4 75, with full-width styling and "Cyclops" central headlight; it sired a range which lasted until May 1964. In 1963 came the radically different Rover 2000, available from 1968 with the GM-designed light-alloy 3.5-liter V-8 also found on its luxury P4 stablemate. The 4wd Range Rover, aimed at a more sybaritic market than the Land-Rover, appeared in 1970, and 1976 saw a new Rover 3500, with Ferrari-like styling. It subsequently became available with Rover's in-line sixes as well.

Since the Austin name was dropped in 1989, all the old Austin Rover group cars have been badged as "Rovers" except the indestructible Mini, which had been a marque on its own since 1969, and the Metro, later to be rebadged as the Rover 100. The year 1984 saw the launch of the 213/216, based on the Honda Ballade, as a replacement for the Triumph Acclaim.

Ford tried to buy Rover in 1986, but was thwarted. In 1988 the group was sold to British Aerospace. The then model line-up included the Maestro and Montego (the 2-liter performance models of both are badged "MG,") the 200/400 derived from the Honda Concerto) and the top-of-the-range 800, again designed in conjunction with Honda and available with I-4 power in 820i, Si and SLi trim and with the 2.7-

1990s Mk 2 Range Rover 4.6 HSE

1999 Rover 75

XTX 88

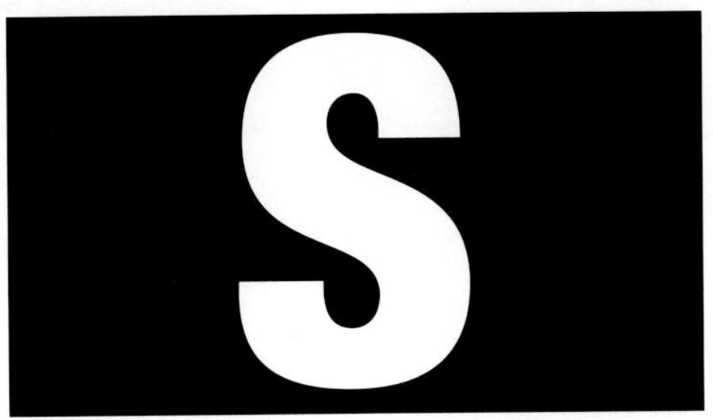

SAAB • Sweden 1949 to date

See panel

SABA • Italy 1926-1928

A Fiat-like car with an ohv four-cylinder 983cc engine in unit with the gearbox, the SABA had a top speed of 45 mph. Very few of these "Stelvio" models reached the market.

SABELLA • England 1906-1914

A T Warne of Leytonstone, London, first showed the single-seat Sabella (designed by Fritz Sabel) at the 1906 Stanley Show. "For doctors, travellers, golfers and professional men," it was a single-seat four-wheeler with a 5 hp twin-cylinder engine whose speed was controlled by varying the valve-lift. It cost £85, and Warne also offered a hand-propelled Sabella for £2.10s. A 10 hp twin-cylinder car appeared in 1907, and a sporting cyclecar designed by Warne in 1912.

SABLATNIG-BEUCHELT Germany 1925-1926

The Sablatnig-designed 1496cc four-cylinder car was one of many shortlived German creations of the early 1920s.

SACHSENRING • Germany 1956-1959

Made by the nationalized Horch works at Zwickau, East Germany, the Sachsenring had an ohv 2407cc six-cylinder engine. Originally known as Horch, the name had to be changed because the Horch title was still owned by the then West German Auto Union.

SAF • Sweden 1921-1922

Svenska Automobilfabriken's idea was to assemble American components into a "Swedish" car at its Bolinäs factory. In 1919 negotiations started with American manufacturers, and in 1921 the first assembled cars left the factory. The engine was a four-cylinder Continental with a three-speed gearbox. Rear springs were cantilevers, and the only body type was a five-seater tourer. Production was planned on a grand scale, but probably only 25 cars were produced. "Rather bad" quality made them hard to sell.

SAFIR • Switzerland 1907-c. 1909

Commercial vehicles mostly were built by the Zürich firm, but it also offered big shaft-driven four-cylinder 30 hp and 50 hp touring cars built under Saurer licence.

SAGE • France 1900-1906

Sage of Paris made a wide variety of two- and four-cylinder touring cars, from 10 hp to 50 hp.

SAAB AUTO AB (Svenska Aeroplan Aktie Bolaget) Trollhattan • Sweden 1949 to date

In 1945 the Svenska Aeroplan AB of Linköping, an established Swedish aircraft maker and industrial fabricator, decided to go into car production. A small team of existing SAAB engineers were gathered together to create the nucleus of a team that worked on the first Saab car. Headed by Gunnar Ljungstrom, who engineered the car and its drivetrain, with body and structural design by Sixten Sason and handling and driving engineered by Rolf Melde, the first Saab car prototype was highly advanced. Noted for its advanced aircraft design, Saab employed much of that technique on its car. It had unitary construction, an aerodynamic body, and the engine was a two-stroke twin of 764cc with a marked resemblance to the pre-war DKW unit. It also incorporated a reinforced passenger cabin that set new standards of safety at a time when safety was hardly considered by car makers.

The car was front-wheel driven and had all-independent suspension. All this came to production years before the mini's front-driven fame, and years before Citroën really went to town with the art of aerodynamic styling. Although such advanced thinking formed the core of Saab's alternative image, it is often overlooked by historians and advertisers.

Initially only a two-door saloon was offered. Cars were shown in 1947, but production started in late 1949. The model name was Saab 92, changed to 92B in 1952 when small body changes were made. The Saab 93 of 1955 had a three-cylinder 748cc engine and coil-spring suspension. Sports models, called Granturismo 750, were also built, mainly for export. The 1959 Saab 95 was a station wagon with an 841cc engine, also used in the 1960 Saab 96 with redesigned rear end. There were also several sports versions. Saab had many rally successes, among them Monte Carlo Rally wins in 1962 and 1963, and the RAC Rallies of 1960 and 1962. The legendary Eric Carlsson was behind the wheel for these successes, and he took the little car to even greater fame in African and American rally events. In 1966 a small glassfibre GT coupé, the Sonett II, was launched, and after a Mk III incarnation was quietly dropped it was, despite the later success of the 99 Turbo, Saab's one and only pure sports car design.

The 1967 Model 96 had the German Ford derived V-4, but the two-stroke engine was still available; the 96 was still being produced in Finland in the 1980s. In 1969 the all-new Sason styled Saab 99 started production. Again aerodynamics and safety played a major theme in the car's design, a highly curved windshield setting a Saab design hallmark. Initially the 99's engine was a Triumph-designed 1.7-litre ohc four, later enlarged to 2 litres. In 1972 full production of the engine started in Saab's Sodertalje plant. Later versions were the 110 bhp fuel-injected EMS and the 140 bhp Turbo of 1977. The 99 Turbo was a milestone car for Saab, and a

1950 Saab 92 saloon

Saab 96

The classic 900 Mk 1; note the curved screen (left.) The Saab revised Saab 900 Mk 2 1999 (below)

milestone car for the motor industry. Other attempts (notably by BMW) to employ the turbocharging concept in a mass-production car did not achieve worldwide success. The well engineered, practical turbo application in the 99 turbo opened the floodgates for all manufacturers to apply the turbocharging concept, and at the same time it gave Saab's image and standing a much needed boost. The 99 turbo model is now a car of classic cult status, and is seen by many as the ultimate embodiment of all that was Saab.

A development of the 99 emerged in the form of the 900 model, which has been available from 1978 in its first-generation and from 1994 in its mark two models. Since then the model name has been supplanted by the 9-3 version of the 900. The original 900 was a long-nosed version of the 99, with mechanical refinements, notably the first use of automatic performance controlling (APC) systems within the ignition and fuel systems. A four-inch extension to the wheelbase provided more room and better crash absorption capacity to met new legislation in the USA.

In the 1980s Saab merged with the Scania group and Saab-Scania (truck) was formed. In 1984 the new Saab 9000 range appeared, jointly developed by Saab and Fiat Auto of Italy. The 9000 shared its underpinnings and floor pan with the Fiat Croma, Lancia Theme, and, less obviously, the Alfa 164. Luckily for Saab its version seemed to hit the mark best, and although the 9000 was not a true Saab it was a success. It had a transverse 2.0-liter 16 valve engine with turbo and non-turbo options. A second-generation version, the 9000 CS, with redesigned bodywork, appeared in 1991, models ranging from the 9000 CS 2.0i to the 9000 CS 2.3 turbo and 9000 CS Carlsson models. The flagship CD range also included a 2.3 Turbo and Carlsson performance models. The car, like the later 9-5, topped the crash safety league polls. Saab also introduced the concept of a light-pressure turbo option in this period, offering a performance boost of lower charge which reduced turbo lag and improved component life.

In 1989 GM snatched a 50 per cent share of Saab from under Fiat's nose and added much needed resources to Saab. Although subsequent Saab models have been based on GM parts-bin components, they have retained an identity of their own, and the 9-5 model, the current flagship, has been very well received. Many hope that Saab will return to its roots and develop a new small car to serve such a market sector and place its financial future on a broader base.

Through its various incarnations, and also through clever marketing, Saab has carved a niche as a supplier of high-quality, safe, yet exciting cars that appeal to the type of person who seeks something different from the mainstream of car imagery. Saab's US market share has grown, and the 9-5 estate, launched to end a 20-year gap for Saab estate/station wagon models, has sold in large numbers worldwide.

1903 St Louis 9 hp tonneau

SAGER • Canada 1911

Though illustrations of this 30 hp four were released, probably no cars, nor the "extensive factory" at Welland, Ontario, were completed.

ST JOE • USA 1908-1909

St Joe took over the bankrupt Shoemaker Automobile Company, founded in Elkhart, Indiana, in 1906, and continued production of "pleasure and commercial cars" under its own name. Leading line was a 40 hp selling at $2,500.

ST LOUIS • USA 1898-1907

The products of "America's pioneer motor car manufacturers," George P Dorris, were also known as "Rigs that Run". The 1899 St Louis "gasoline stanhope," made in the first purpose-built car factory west of the Mississippi, had a 6 hp horizontal-twin engine. The company"s ultimate offering, following a move from St Louis to Peoria, Illinois, was a $2,500 four-cylinder 32/35 hp.

ST LOUIS • USA 1922

The name on this car was changed from Neskov-Mumperow for obvious reasons; however, there is little reason to believe that anything more than pilot models ever appeared. These were sporting cars with advanced lines and used Weidely four-cylinder engines. Price of the four-passenger touring model was $3,500.

SALAMANCA • Spain 1904

A Paris-made single-cylinder 8cv engine and transmission were used to build this wagonette.

SALISBURY • USA 1896

A clumsy four-seater car built by the Horseless Carriage Company of Chicago, Wilber S. Salisbury"s car had a twin-cylinder 3 hp engine and three 48-inch wheels.

SALISBURY • England 1903

The 10 hp twin-cylinder Salisbury (there was also a 7 hp single) offered the advanced feature of a four-speed gearbox.

SALMON • England 1912-1914

From the same factory as the ACE and Baguley, the Salmon was an 11.9 hp four-cylinder model with bulbous coachbuilt body. An 8.1 hp model similar to the ACE was also offered.

1926 Salmson 1100cc Grand Prix sports two-seater

SALMSON • France 1921-1957

A well-known aero engine manufacturer, the Société des Moteurs Salmson started by building the British GN under license. It launched its first Salmson in 1921, and fitted it with a 1086cc engine with four "push-pull-rods," which controlled both the inlet and exhaust valves. At the same time, engineer Petit evolved a racing version with dohc. In 1923 Salmson presented an 8/10 hp of 1194cc, then in 1930 it started the S4 series with a dohc 1500cc engine which was finally developed to 2.3 liters in the last new Salmson models made in 1953. Salmson cars won many sporting events.

SALVA • Italy 1906-c1908

The Societa Anonima Lombarda Vetture Automobili of Milan offered fours of 16/25 hp and 28/45 hp, plus a 60/75 hp six.

SALVADOR • Spain c1918

A cyclecar, with independent front suspension by parallel leaf springs, rack-and-pinion steering, and a vee-twin MAG engine.

SAO • South Africa 1991 to date

Built by SAMCOR in Africa's most-up-to-date car factory in Pretoria, with a capacity of 500 cars a day, the Sao Penzo is a Japanese designed 1.3-liter family car, available as a 5-door hatchback or 4-door sedan.

SAM • Italy 1924-1929

This Leghorn factory was first connected with the three-wheeled Vaghi cyclecar. SAM afterwards built sporting 1056cc two-, three-, and four-seater voiturettes with four-cylinder sv and ohc engines of its own make. Fritz Jackl of Czechoslovakia drove SAM cars in hillclimbs.

Salmson cyclecars (derived from the GN,) 1922

SAMPSON • USA 1904, 1911

The Alden Sampson Company manufactured the chassis for the 1903 Moyea, a license-built 18/22 hp Rochet-Schneider, and continued this car under its own name. The company later became the truck division of the United States Motor Company, but built a number of 35 hp touring cars in 1911, with pair-cast 5734cc four-cylinder engines.

SANCHIS • France 1906-1912

Enrique Sanchis, a Spanish engineer on a government mission to France, built a number of V-4 voiturettes with chassis and body skeleton pressed as one unit, ready for steel panelling to be riveted on.

SANDFORD • France 1922-1939

An Englishman in Paris, Malcolm Stuart Sandford made some lovely Morgan-inspired sporting four-cylinder Ruby-engined three-wheelers from 900cc to 1100cc, some of them supercharged. He also made some flat-twin 950cc Ruby-engined three-wheelers and four-wheelers.

S & M • USA 1913-1914

Strobel & Martin of Detroit built this luxury six-cylinder touring car, which became the Benham in 1914.

S & M SIMPLEX, SIMPLEX • USA 1904-1914

Mercedes agent Smith & Mabley introduced 18 hp and 30 hp luxury cars in 1904 to beat the 40 per cent tax on imported models, but the S & M Simplex was a victim of the 1907 slump. The Simplex name was bought by Herman Broesel, who financed a Mercedes-inspired model designed by Edward Franquist and built from the finest materials available. Best-known was the T-head 50 hp. In 1911 a 38 hp, 7.8-liter shaft-drive model appeared. The 1912-1914 75 hp of 10-liters was probably America"s last big chain-drive car. In 1914 the marque became Crane-Simplex.

SANDRINGHAM • England 1902-1905

"Royal Motor Repairer" Frank Morriss showed a 10 hp car of his own make at the 1903 Cordingley Show in London.

S & S • USA 1924-1930

Successor to the earlier Sayers, this car was a sideline of the Sayers & Scoville Company of Cincinnati, Ohio, builder of Sayers & Scoville hearses. It was available primarily as a pall-bearers' car, large sedan or limousine. Continental six-cylinder engines were used until 1928, when eights of the same make were substituted. The model designations included "Brighton," "Elmwood," "Gotham," and "Lakewood". All were available to the general public.

1923 SARA 1098cc air-cooled two-seater

Sandford three-wheelers in action, c. 1924

1912 chain-driven Simplex

SANDUSKY • USA 1901-1903

"Mud, sand and hills shrink before it" was the optimistic slogan of the Sandusky Runabout from Sandusky, Ohio.

SANFORD • Spain 1902-1903

A four-seater car with an alcohol-powered engine shown at the Madrid "Alcohol Exhibition" in December 1902.

SAN GIORGIO • Italy 1906-1907

Big six-cylinder cars from 25 hp to 60 hp produced under Napier license, using many English components.

SAN GIUSTO • Italy 1922-1924

This very advanced cyclecar, with rear-mounted 738cc four-cylinder engine, central backbone chassis, and independent suspension on all wheels, enjoyed no commercial success.

SANTAX • France 1922-1927

Small cyclecar made in Paris with Anzani single-cylinder engines of 125cc and 500cc.

SANTOS-DUMONT • USA 1902-1904

Named after the famous Brazilian aeronaut, the air-cooled flat-twin Santos-Dumont from Columbus, Ohio, was styled on De Dion Bouton lines and sold for $1,500. A 20 hp flat-four appeared in 1904, selling for $2,000.

SARA • France 1923-1930

The Société des Applications du Refroidissement par Air made some interesting air-cooled cars with four-cylinder 1098cc engines which sold well. However, in 1927 it presented the ill-fated SARA 6, an 1806cc six-cylinder model.

SATURN (GM) • USA 1991 to date

A new American model range exclusively devoted to the value-for-money market sector. Factory based in Spring Hill, Tennessee. Three models, a basic floorpan design and one four-cylinder engine supporting coupé, sedan and estate/station wagon types that all use similar mechanicals and trim. Sold in a direct-selling, no-hassle, fixed-

1915 Saxon Six tourer

1914 SAVA 36/50 hp sports two-seater

price operation, Saturn cars are a new marque under the giant General Motors. Saturn is the first car company to be run by a women (Cynthia Trudell.)

SAURER • Switzerland 1897-c. 1938

The first Saurer gas engines were built in the company's Arbon workshops in 1888; a single-cylinder opposed-piston engine powered the first Saurer car of 1897-1898. Sent to Paris, it formed the basis of the design of the Koch car. Serious production began in 1902, and from 1904 Saurer cars, 24/30 hp fours of 4398cc, had air-braking similar to that used on Rovers, using movable cams which prevented the exhaust valves opening. Also offered in the 1904-1914 period were 30/35 hp (5321cc) and 50/60 hp (9236cc) single-cast fours. Car production was gradually phased out in favour of the trucks for which Saurer is still famous, but in 1934 Saurer began assembly of Chrysler cars.

SAUTEL ET SECHARD • France 1903

A three-wheeled "nouvelle voiturette" from Gentilly, which combined steering, clutch, braking, and gear-changing on the pivoting steering column.

SAUTTER-HARLE • France 1907-1912

Pioneer motoring journalist W F Bradley was an enthusiastic owner of a Sautter-Harlé, built in Paris. The first of this marque were 16/20 hp fours, and a 10/12 hp two-cylinder. In 1910 12 hp and 18 hp fours were also listed.

SAVA • Belgium 1910-1923

The Société Anversoise pour Fabrication des Voitures Automobiles, of Antwerp, began production with an 18 hp, 2011cc monobloc four with a worm-drive back-axle. At the end of 1912 a 1966cc 18/16 hp appeared, with the odd layout of side inlet, overhead exhaust valves, and four or eight sparking plugs. The 1913 range consisted of a 14/18 hp (2474cc) the 18/26 hp (now 2957cc) and a 36/50 hp four, also with eoi head, which sold for £610. The company suffered badly in the First World War, and there was little post-Armistice activity until 1923, when the 1915 model (based on the 1914 Tourist Trophy cars) made a belated appearance, just in time for the firm to be taken over by Minerva.

SAVER • England 1912

A "gearboxless" tandem-seater from Manchester, with 14 hp Hewitt piston-valve engine.

SAVIANO SCAT • USA 1960

Weighing 765 kg (1,700 lb,) the Saviano Scat used body steel twice as thick as that of most cars. A two-door, four-passenger Jeep-type vehicle built on a welded rectangular tube frame, its two rear seats could be folded out of the way to provide extra cargo space. The doors were removable, as was the top, which was available in either steel or canvas. A 25 hp Kohler air-cooled engine provided power.

SAVOY • England 1900

With a water-cooled 3.5 hp De Dion engine, the Savoy voiturette, from the same firm as AMC and Carlton, sold at £198.

SAXON • USA 1913-1923

"The car that makes both ends meet," the Saxon was once one of Detroit's most popular products. The original Saxon was a four-cylinder light car selling for only $395. It was built by a company started by Hugh Chalmers and Harry (no relation to Henry) Ford. It sold well, and in 1915 a $785 Saxon Six was added to the range. By 1916 production was running at 27,800 annually, but the four-cylinder roadster was dropped the following year, and Saxon sales, which had reached tenth place in the US sales league, began to fall off. By 1921 the Saxon, now an ohv four known as the Saxon-Duplex, had become one of the most expensive cars of its type. The inevitable demise followed swiftly.

SAYERS • USA 1917-1923

Produced by a division of Sayers & Scoville, noted for hearses and ambulances, this assembled car was highly regarded from the standpoint of its body workmanship. Continental six-cylinder engines were used throughout its seven-year production. Although open models constituted the greater percentage of Sayers Six cars built, coupés, sedans, and limousines were also available. In 1923 the Sayers was succeeded by the larger and more expensive S&S limo.

SB • Germany 1920-1923

The first little Slaby-Behringer cars were battery-electrics, but there were later cars with 169cc DKW two-stroke single-cylinder engines. Slaby also designed the first DKW cars.

SBARRO • Switzerland 1973 to date

Franco Sbarro is a highly creative designer whose products, all built in small numbers, have varied from classic replicas to high-performance super-cars. The Osmos design features Sbarro's unique "hub-less" wheels.

SCACCHI • Italy 1912-1914

An advanced 3815cc four-cylinder with the engine in unit with a four-speed gearbox, known in the UK as Storero or Caesar.

SCAMP • England 1976 to date

A Mini-based kit car on the lines of the obsolete Mini Moke; the Mk 2 version is offered with gull-wing doors.

SCANIA • Sweden 1901-1911

Maskinfabriks AB Scania of Malmö was formed in 1900 to produce bicycles, but in 1901 the first car was built. The initiative was taken by the manager, Hilding Hessler, and the car was constructed mainly by Anton Svensson and Reinhold Thorssin. The first series was produced in 1902, when six cars were built with German twin-cylinder Kämper engines. One was driven to the Stockholm Automobile Exhibition in 1903, quite a sensation in those days of bad roads. Mostly trucks were built, but passenger cars with one-, two-, or four-cylinders, from 5 hp to 20 hp, were also produced. From 1908 there were new types of engines, from 12 to 45 hp. In 1911 the firm merged with Vabis.

1914 SCAT 22 hp limousine

SCANIA-VABIS • Sweden 1911-1929

After the merger between Scania and Vabis, the new company based in Södertälje mostly used the Vabis-designed four-cylinder engines. Three sizes of engines were mainly built, of 22, 30, and 50 hp. Cars were exported to the other Scandinavian countries, and also to Russia and Australia. The main production was trucks of various sizes, and from 1924 Scania-Vabis concentrated on these, though three or four cars were assembled in 1929 from old model parts, even though the bodies looked fairly modern.

SCAP • France 1912-1929

The Société de Constructions Automobiles de Paris bore no relationship to the maker of proprietary SCAP engines, though some later models used these power units. In its Billancourt, Seine, works, it started by making Ballot-engined cars of 9 hp (1460cc,) 11 hp (1725cc,) and 14 hp (2814cc.) A 20 hp (3810cc) was presented in 1914. After the war it resumed with a 12 hp of 2538cc. In 1923 came a 1098cc SCAP-engined model. In 1925 the company presented a 10 hp (1485cc) model, and a new SCAP-engined car of 1098cc came in 1926.

SCAR • France 1906-1915

The Société de Construction Automobile de Reims first built an 18/20 hp four of 2.5 liters, joined in 1907 by a 4.1-liter four and a 6-liter six. The 1910 models had dashboard radiators, and ranged from a 1.3-liter twin to a 2.4-liter four, and a 3.6-liter six. Long-stroke fours of 2.1, 2.8, and 3.2 liters were the marque's ultimate offerings.

SCARAB • USA 1934-1939

Developed from the prototype Sterkenberg, designed by John Tjaarda (later designer of the Lincoln Zephyr,) this was a limited-production streamline monocoque sedan with a rear-mounted Ford V-8 engine. Designer was aero engineer William B Stout.

1901 12cv Schaudel tonneau

SCARAB • USA 1958-1963

Barbara Hutton's son, Lance Reventlow, built several versions of the Scarab as competition cars. They employed modified components from various production cars, including the Corvette. One Scarab, using a 1958 Corvette 385 hp engine, had phenomenal acceleration and a top speed of almost 161 mph.

SCAT • Italy 1906-1914

Giovanni Ceirano's SCAT was a superb car whose production was partly financed by Newton & Bennett of Manchester. The range included cars with 2722cc, 2949cc, 3052cc, 4710cc and 4483cc four-cylinder engines and four-speed gearboxes. The SCAT was also successful in races; Ceirano won the 1911 and 1914 Targa Florio, Snipe-Pardini the same event in 1912.

SCEPTRE USA 1979 to date

A 6.6-liter Ford V-8 powers this "pseudo-classic" built in Santa Barbara, California. It has outside exhausts and solid silver emblems, and sold (as a limited edition of 250-300) at $50,000 in 1979.

SCH • Belgium 1927-1928

A light cyclecar exhibited by a commercial vehicle maker at the 1927 Brussels Show.

SCHACHT • USA 1901-1913

The first Schachts were flat-twin friction-drive high-wheelers, but a 40 hp four-cylinder model appeared in 1909. After 1913 the company concentrated on trucks.

SCHAUDEL • France 1897-1902

A car built in Bordeaux by a former arms manufacturer who applied the methods of his profession, such as strict interchangeability of components, in its construction. Schaudel was, moreover, inventor of the unit-construction engine/gearbox layout. Manufacture of his designs was taken over by Motobloc from 1902; about 150 Schaudels were built.

SCHAUM • USA 1901-1905

W A Schaum's first engines had twin cylinders with separate cranks geared up to a central driving shaft.

SCHEIBLER • Germany 1901-1907

In 1901 Scheibler of Aachen built a 6 hp car with pivoted floor so that the owner, a paralytic ex-cavalry officer, could be hauled into the vehicle in his wheelchair. This engine

1915 Scripps-Booth Model C

and car factory produced a variety of two- and four-cylinder cars with engines up to 6786cc, as well as a range of commercial vehicles.

SCHILLING • Germany 1905-1906

Suhl in Thuringia was the home of the Schilling arms factory, where 12 hp cars with four-cylinder Fafnir engines were built. They were also known as VCS or Rennsteig cars.

SCHMIDT • France 1910-1911

A manufacturer of St Quentin (Aisne) which exhibited at the 1910 Paris Salon.

SCHULER • USA 1924

The price of the only Schuler model, a small two-passenger vee-twin roadster, was $245. Though it was advertised in the press of its city of manufacture, Milwaukee,, Wisconsin, it is doubtful if many (even any) were actually sold.

SCHULZ • Germany 1904-1906

Limited-production cars with engines up to 28 hp. Schulz, the designer-manufacturer, competed in many sporting events.

SCHURICHT • Germany 1921-1925

A Bavarian manufacturer of small four-cylinder cars with Breuer proprietary sv engines from 12 hp to 20 hp.

1922 Seabrook two-seater

SCHWANEMEYER • Germany 1900-1901

"With motor-gear and axle combined," the Schwanemeyer was the forerunner of Fafnir. Its immediate successor was the Aachener.

SCIMITAR • USA 1956

Brook Stevens Associates built three cars based on Chrysler components: a station wagon with a sliding roof, a convertible, and a town car.

SCIROCCO • England 1961-1963

A stylish replacement body for the Ford Popular, the production Scirocco was a development of the gull-wing-doored Ford 100E-powered car built by Peter Hammond for his own use. Only about ten were made.

SCOOTACAR • England 1957-1964

Longer-lived than many of the breed, this odd tandem-seat bubblecar had three wheels and a Villiers engine, initially of 197cc, later of 324cc.

SCOTSMAN • Scotland 1922-1923

The Glasgow-built Scotsman had an option of three four-cylinder engines, a 10 hp, an 11 hp, or a 45 hp ohc unit.

SCOTSMAN • Scotland 1929-1930

Built in Edinburgh, the second make to bear the name Scotsman used a French six-cylinder air-cooled SARA engine. The well-proven Meadows 4ED was fitted later.

SCOTT • France 1912

A Parisian marque; 15 hp and 24 hp fours of 2120cc and 3780cc were listed.

SCOTT SOCIABLE • England 1921-1925

The Scott Company had been making its famous water-cooled models from 1909, and its Sociable, an offset three-wheeler, was an inevitable development of this work. Power was naturally supplied by the company"s watercooled 578cc twin-cylinder two-stroke engine, drive being transmitted by shaft to the offside rear wheel.

SCOUT • England 1904-1923

Dean and Burden Brothers of Salisbury, Wiltshire, began production with a 6 hp twin and 12 hp four. Scout cars

enjoyed mostly local acclaim, though the company did enter a 14/16 hp in the 1905 Tourist Trophy, and an 18/20 hp the following year. In 1907 production of the two-car range was said to be 100 a year, and in 1908, from a new factory, Scout offered a 12 hp twin, 15 hp fou,r and 30 hp six of 4390cc, enlarged the next year to 5638cc. Post-1909 production seems to have been negligible, though a monobloc 1870cc 10/12 hp appeared in 1910, and a few 15.9 hp cars were assembled by the firm and its successors after the war.

SCRIPPS-BOOTH • USA 1914-1922

The son of an author, James Scripps-Booth was a talented artist who in 1908, aged 20, conceived a gigantic two-wheeled car (supported at low speeds by retractable auxiliary wheels) and completed its design while on his honeymoon in Paris in 1911. Financed by his uncle, a builder of marine engines, he built this "Bi-Autogo" in Detroit in 1912, at a cost of $25,000. It had a 6306cc V-8 engine and weighed 3,200 lb. Predictably, its steering was awesomely heavy, and only the prototype (which survives) was completed. The following year Scripps-Booth built a prototype tandem-seat cyclecar inspired by the Bedelia, which went into production as the "JB Rocket" in January 1914.

The Scripps-Booth Cyclecar Company was sold at the end of 1914 to the Puritan Machine Company of Detroit, which continued production under its own name for a short while. Scripps-Booth then introduced a luxury light car based on European practice and designed by Bill Stout, later to become a famed aeronautical engineer, responsible for the immortal Ford Tri-Motor. The Sterling-engined Scripps-Booth Model C was said to be the first American car to have a horn-button in the centre of the steering wheel. It also had electrically-operated door locks, though these were prone to jam on open models. Scripps-Booth owners included the King of Spain, the Queen of Holland, Winston Churchill, and Count John McCormack, the singer.

In autumn 1916 a new Scripps-Booth, the Model D, appeared, powered by a Ferro V-8 engine designed by Alanson Brush. Roadsters and town cars were available. James Scripps-Booth resigned over company policy in October 1916; sales fell the following year as a result of production difficulties. By the end of 1917 Scripps-Booth had been absorbed by Chevrolet, destined to become part of General Motors in July 1918. Thereafter Scripps-Booth cars were no more than Oaklands with a 40 hp Northway six-cylinder engine, and were phased out in 1922 at Alfred P Sloan"s express order, the plant being turned over to production of Buick sedans. James Scripps-Booth tried to get back into the motor industry in 1923 with a low-slung luxury car called the Da Vinci, with an Argyll single-sleeve-valve engine, but failed to sell his designs (though he claimed that Stutz had pirated them.) In 1930 he built a one-off belt-drive cyclecar, the Da Vinci Pup.

1903 Type VII Searchmont tonneau

1991 Seat Marbella 900 Special

SEABROOK • England 1917-1928

Originally formed in 1896 to make cycle components, Seabrook of London imported the American Regal Underslung before building a four-cylinder light car under its own name, with a monobloc 1796cc four-cylinder engine.

SEAL • England 1912-1924

A curious JAP-engined three-wheeler, resembling a motorcycle combination but steered from the sidecar.

SEARCHMONT • USA 1900-1903

"America's leading automobile," built at Searchmont, Philadelphia. Seven different models were built, with prices up to $2,500. Designer was Lee Sherman Chadwick, and racing driver Charles Fournier headed the company.

SEARS • USA 1908-1912

Mail order king Richard Warren Sears spent some of his company's $50 million annual revenue in putting a flat-twin Motor Buggy on the market late in 1908. It sold for $395 complete, "shipped and crated so as to secure the lowest possible freight rate," but it used an obsolescent formula, and purchasers wanted more than tiller steering and a 25 mph top speed. The introduction of a closed model, the "Cozy Cab," did nothing to increase sales, and by 1912, having lost $80,000 on the automobile division, Sears stopped selling complete cars and turned instead to mail-order accessories and components. In 1952-1953 Sears marketed the Henry J compact as the "Allstate".

SEAT • Spain 1949 to date

Starting life as the Spanish subsidiary of Fiat in 1919 (from 1931 the cars were known as "Fiat-Hispania,") Seat was owned by the Spanish state industry holding company INI from 1949 to 1979, when Fiat took over the majority shareholding. Seat cars were largely based on Fiat prototypes, like the 600, 850, and 1400, though in 1979 Lancia models were introduced with 2-liter Seat engines. Fiat withdrew in 1980, but Seat continued to build Fiat Pandas under the name Marbella. The Ibiza was launched in 1984 and face-lifted in 1991, the year the mid-range Toledo was launched. VW took a controlling stake in SEAT in 1986. Since that time successive Seat models have used VW engines and components. The Mk 2 version of the Ibiza was styled for Seat by Guigario, and was perhaps the last real in-house Seat. It used VW engines and in Cupra Sport trim was that rare thing in the 1990s, a real "hot hatch". The new Toledo range uses VW underpinings, as does the stylish Arosa city car, a longer nosed version of which VW brought out as the Lupo. Seat also had access to the shared design that saw Ford and VW create their own MPV; the Seat version being tagged the Alhambra, in true Spanish style. Far from being bargain-basement cars aimed at value-for-money buyers, Seat's cars have become well finished, well designed, and well built, with good handling. In the new Toledo Mk 2, especially in V-5 form, Seat has a car that ranks at the front of its class.

SECURUS • Germany 1906

A two-speed tricar built in Berlin by Max Ortmann.

SEIDEL-AROP • Germany 1925-1926

The Seidel-designed car was another doomed attempt to produce a good small car using inadequate facilities. It had a sv 1020cc four-cylinder engine.

SEKINE • USA 1923

The Sekine was probably only a prototype, the design of I Sekine, an importer who had plans to build a small car for the Japanese market. Without a differential, the drive was, according to a brochure "taken from a four-cylinder engine, angled at 17˚(from the longitudinal axis of the car to the left rear wheel and thence through fabric universals to the right wheel by the way of a shaft".

SELDEN • USA 1906-1914

George B Selden, who claimed to have invented the motor car in 1877, did not go into production until 1906. His cars were conventional fours of 18/30 hp, selling for $2,000.

1898 Serpollet cab

SELECT • France 1920

Made in Paris, these were V-8-engined cars of which little is known.

SELF • Sweden 1916, 1919, 1922

The two young Weiertz brothers, Per and Hugo, of Swedala, built three different cyclecars in 1916, 1919 and 1922. Some parts were re-used, but engines were changed from a one-cylinder to a four-cylinder and, finally, to a twin-cylinder. The four-cylinder engine was of German manufacture and seems to have been the best.

SELVE • Germany 1919-1929

Basse & Selve was a manufacturer of light-alloy car engines. When Sperber at Hameln was up for sale after the First World War, Walther von Selve bought the works in 1919 and started manufacture of his own Selve cars with, of course, own-make engines. Chief designers were Lehmann, Slevogt and Henze, who created some excellent cars, including 1569cc and 2085cc four-cylinder and 2850cc and 3075cc six-cylinder models.

SENECA • USA 1917-1924

Seneca assembled open models only, half of each year's production being exported. Four-cylinder LeRoi engines were used until 1922, and Lycoming fours thereafter. Several hundred units a year were built; the Glover, built for export to the United Kingdon, was probably also made by this Fostoria, Ohio, concern.

SENECHAL • France 1921-1929

Aviator and racing driver Robert Sénéchal started making cyclecars, using various French proprietary engines, in "Sport" and "Grand Sport" form, with capacities ranging from 900cc to 1100cc. Taken over by Chenard & Walcker, he made the 1500cc "Torpille" Chenard-Sénéchal.

1921 Selve of Frau Hedi Hof

Robert Sénéchal driving a 1922 Sénéchal sports car

SENSAUD DE LAVAUD • France 1926-1928

A strange car with automatic transmission and ifs by rubber in compression, made in Paris by M Sensaud de Lavaud, with an Alpax cast-alloy chassis and a steam-cooled 5475cc six-cylinder American engine. Few were built.

SERENISSIMA • Italy 1965-1966

Count Volpi's dream car, the Serenissima was offered with 3-liter and 3.5-liter dohc V-8 engines, but very few were built. The factory also produced various (not very successful) racing cars. Sasamotor of Modena was responsible for most Serenissima designs.

SERIN • France 1899

A light Bollé-like three-wheeler with a 4 hp horizontal engine.

SERPOLLET • France 1889-1907

Blacksmith's son Léon Serpollet, born in 1858, built his first steam car at the age of 18, but it produced "more soot than motion". He then devised a "flash boiler" for the instantaneous generation of steam, set up shop in Montmartre and built a steam tricycle, which was the only self-propelled vehicle running in Paris in 1887. Three Serpollet steam three-wheelers were built by Peugeot in 1889, but Peugeot's interest soon waned and Serpollet continued on his own, building twin-cylinder steam cars of 4/6 hp with coke-fired boilers and (from 1891) four wheels, though his backers insisted that he concentrate mainly on steam trams and railcars.

In 1898 Serpollet met wealthy American Frank Gardner, who had dabbled in petrol-car construction, and the two went into partnership. Gardner-Serpollet steam cars had a flat-twin engine with paraffin-fired boiler, and from 1900 became more and more like petrol vehicles in their styling. A light 5 hp model appeared that year, and from 1901 an 8 hp V-4 and flat-four engines of 6-9 and 12 hp were adopted. In 1902 a streamlined racing Serpollet, Oeuf de P,ques, was the first car to exceed 75 mph. The end of 1903 saw a 15 hp flat-four and the Serpollet Simplex, a 6 hp voiturette of uncomplicated design. In late 1904 came an improved 15 hp and a big 40 hp, both boasting a clutch and almost automatic engine control. There was, apparently, an eight-cylinder Serpollet for 1906, but Serpollet was already a very sick man. When he died of consumption in February 1907, the company quickly followed him to the grave.

SERVICE • England 1902-1906

Probably a French import, this 7/8 hp car had a twin-cylinder Gnome engine and a pressed-steel chassis. Controls were "simple, and carried out on top of the steering wheel". A 6.5 hp Aster-engined Service with tubular chassis, "perfectly practical and very graceful," competed in the 1905 Small Car Trials.

SETA • England 1976 to date

An extremely futuristic-looking glassfibre sports-car kit based on the ubiquitous VW floorpan, the Seta is one of several latter-day machines to feature gull-wing doors.

SEVEN • England 1973 to date

Caterham Cars had long since marketed the Lotus Seven, and thus logically took over full production of this front-engined, spartan sports car when Chapman's company shed it on its way up market. The glassfibre-bodied S4

Two 1905 Serpollet 15 hp tourers

ceased production in 1974. Now only the prettier, alloy-bodied S3 is made.

SEVERIN • USA 1920-1922

An assembled car, the Severin featured a six-cylinder Continental engine and 122-inch wheelbase, the five-passenger touring car selling for $2,550.

SFA • France 1912

The Société Française d'Automobiles et d'Aviation, of Orléans, offered the BGV monobloc 12 hp four of 1544cc.

SGV • USA 1910-1915

Successor to the Acme, the 25 hp SGV had a monobloc four-cylinder engine of 3167cc.

SHAD-WYCK • USA 1917-1923

A good deal of mystery surrounds this marque, which was under the control of the Shadburne Brothers of Chicago. It seems that the initial spate of cars marketed as Shad-Wycks between 1917 and 1919 were leftover Bour-Davis cars with another emblem! The 1920-1923 line claimed to have two different engines (depending on what chart one read,) Weidely or Rochester-Duesenberg, and it appears that some cars may have actually been made. The Shadburne Brothers were also involved in the final days of the National, Jackson and Dixie Flyer automobiles.

SHANGHAI • China 1960 to date

Appearing in prototype form in 1958, this car was originally produced as the Feng Huang (Phoenix.) After the Cultural Revolution it became the Shanghai SH 760, using a 2.2-liter six-cylinder engine. A new prototype, SH 771, appeared in 1978. In 1984 a 25-year joint venture deal was concluded with VW to produce the Santana; for 1992, the Passat Variant was added. China's leading car maker, Shanghai built 18,500 vehicles in 1990.

SHAPECRAFT • England 1963-1964

Racing driver Barry Wood was the man who persuaded Shapecraft to make a fastback conversion for the Lotus Elan. Altogether some 20 were built, their aluminum roofs and tails being riveted to the glassfiber bodywork. Peter Sellers and Tony Brandon were among the customers.

SHARON • USA 1915

A tandem-seated 12/15 cyclecar (sister marque to Ritz) with friction drive, built by Driggs-Seabury.

SHARP-ARROW • USA 1908-1910

William H Sharp's sporting roadsters were similar in concept to the Mercer, also built in Trenton, NJ. In 1908 a Sharp-Arrow, driven by its designer, won the188-mile Vanderbilt Motor Parkway Garden City Sweepstake Race at an average of over60 mph.

SBARRO • Switzerland 1973 to date

Franco Sbarro is a highly creative designer whose cars, all built in small numbers, have varied from classic replicas to high-performance supercars, often using underpinnings from well-known marques. From the 1970s to the 1990s Sbarro has always presented its styling modifications and complete cars at the Geneva motorshow where, Sbarro has become a legend. All of Sbarro's cars contain a degree of individual design interpretation. His work began with replicas of famous vintage marques, and has culminated in the founding of a Sbarro auto design school. It was Sbarro who created the hubless wheel (mounting the wheel via circumferential bearings rather than in the traditional manner,) which was debuted on the Osmos show car. A series of wild show car concept design specials in the 1980s and 1990s belied the fact that Sbarro's modified and rebodied cars, new vehicles in their own right, often achieved limited series production. One of Sbarro's finest styling achievements was the 1997 lonas, which reinterpreted the classic Lancia Stratos. The 1996 Issima roadster, based on an Alfa Romeo theme, was also a styling hit.

SHAW • USA 1920-1921

The Shaw was a spin-off of the earlier Shaw taxicab interests, and the passenger car introduced for 1920 was a 136-inch-wheelbase automobile using a Rochester-Duesenberg four-cylinder engine. The open touring car was priced at $5,000, the closed cars commanding considerably higher prices. Later a Weidely 12-cylinder engine was used. For a time the Shaw masqueraded under a different name, "Colonial". It later reverted to "Shaw," and shortly thereafter the company was sold to Yellow Cab, which marketed the existing chassis, but with a Continental six-cylinder engine, as the "Ambassador".

SHAWMUT • USA 1905-1909

These 6391cc four-cylinder tourers succeeded the Phelps.

SHEEN • England 1964-1965

The brainchild of Surrey wine merchant, Peter Sheen, the two aluminum-bodied, two-seater Sheen Imperators were based on the Hillman Imp floorpan. Production was planned with glassfiber shells, but the project never got off the ground.

SHEFFIELD-SIMPLEX • England 1906-1922

One of the great Edwardian cars, the round-radiatored Sheffield-Simplex was sponsored by Earl Fitzwilliam and designed by Percy Richardson. It retained the two-pedal

1920 Shad-Wyck Six

control of the Brotherhood-Crocker, and from 1908 to 1913 the 45 hp six of 6982cc was available in "gearboxless" form (with one normal speed and an "emergency box".) One gearboxless 45 hp even went from Land's End to John O'Groats on its single gear. The 1910 h14/20 hp seemed to have an engine based closely on the Renault 14/20; the same year a three-speed 20/30 hp six appeared, and soon a redesigned 30 hp development of this was the company's leading model. But the post-war Sheffield-Simplex was the 45 hp; in its final version its bi-bloc engine was replaced by an anachronistic unit of 7777cc with individually-cast cylinders.

SHELBY • USA 1962-1970

Racing driver Carroll Shelby modified ACs and Mustangs in California. Ford V-8 engines of 4736cc or 6977cc were fitted in British ACs. These fast Shelby Cobras were so popular that 1,100 were sold in three years. Even more successful were the Shelby GTs based on stock Mustang fastbacks. With reassembled bodies and modified suspension and engines (4736cc and 6997cc,) over 14,000 were sold by selected Ford dealers. In 1968 FoMoCo took over the Shelby operation; the Cobra name later appeared on Ford's Torino fastback.

SHEPPEE • England 1912

A 25 hp steam car from a firm better known for steam commercials.

SHERIDAN • USA 1920-1921

Produced in the former Inter-State factory at Muncie, Indiana, the Sheridan was an early General Motors car. Plans called for both a four and a V-8 (although the latter failed to materialize beyond the drawing board.) Designed to fill the gap between the Chevrolet and Oakland, the car used a Northway engine and had a wheelbase of 116 inches. Price of the touring car was $1,800. In 1922 the factory was acquired by William C. Durant, and the Sheridan car, with a longer wheelbase, Ansted engine and new emblem, was continued as the Durant Six.

1909/10 Sheffield-Simplex 45 hp

1917 Silver-Knight, built on a Willys-Knight chassis

SHORT-ASHBY • England 1921-1923

Designed by Victor Ashby and manufactured by aircraft manufacturer Short Brothers, this light car was powered by a French Ruby engine of 970cc.

SHRIVE • England 1969 to date

The first of the production Mk 6 Bentley Specials, the Shrive is distinguished by its neat, cast-aluminum footplates and enormous Lucas P100 headlamps. On the Shrive, the original grille is retained, as is the hood (though in modified form.) The body is glassfiber, the wings are steel.

1921 Sigma 10 hp four-seater

SHW • Germany 1923-1926

Designed by Professor Kamm of Stuttgart, famed for his work on car aerodynamics, the SHW was built by Schwabische Hütten-Werke at Boblingen. It had a sv 1030cc flat-twin engine and fwd. There was not enough money for large-scale production.

SIATA • Italy 1949-1970

This small factory, having concentrated on tuning Fiat cars pre-war, built a wide range of very sporting cars with engines from 494cc to 1990cc from 1949. From 1960 onward there was close co-operation with Abarth. The most popular Siata models had 843cc, 1295cc, 1481cc, and 1579cc engines; one of the last Siatas had a rear-mounted four-cylinder 843cc engine and a two-seater cabriolet body.

SIBLEY • USA 1910-1911

A two-passenger roadster with 30 hp four-cylinder 3622cc engine. The firm was still offering spare parts in 1918.

SICAM • France 1919-1922

Marcel Violet, engineer and pioneer of the two-stroke, created the Société Industrielle de Construction d'Automobiles et de Moteurs in Pantin, Seine, and built proprietary two-stroke engines. He also made some cyclecars powered by his twin-cylinder two-stroke 487cc engine.

SICO • England 1905

The Sandholme Iron Co of Todmorden, Lancashire, built this 18 hp four-cylinder model with an Abbot constant-mesh gearbox.

SIDDELEY, WOLSELEY-SIDDELEY • England 1902-1910

Originally producing little more than modified 12 hp and 18 hp Peugeots assembled in Coventry, Siddeley soon launched a 6 hp single-cylinder model built for the company in Wolseley's Crayford, Kent, factory. In May 1905 Wolseley absorbed the Siddeley Autocar Company and John Davenport Siddeley became manager of the new company, which marketed its cars as Wolseley-Siddeleys, Siddeley-Wolseleys or simply Siddeleys. New models were designed by Charles Rimmington, including a 40 hp which covered a 10,000-mile reliability trial and needed only 1s 10d-worth of replacement parts.

SIDEA • France 1921-1925

The Société Industrielle des Etablissements Automobiles in Charleville-Méziéres, Ardennes, made some cars with 1168cc and 1693cc SCAP engines. Taken over by Jouffret, they were renamed Sidea-Jouffret in 1923.

1923 Sima-Violet team for the Bol d'Or

SIEGEL • Germany 1908-1910

A now-forgotten 9 hp car with a vee-twin motorcycle engine, probably by Fafnir.

SIEMENS-SCHUCKERT • Germany 1907-1910

This big Berlin-based works bought Protos at almost the same time that it entered the market with its own car designs. These included a 1596cc four-cylinder and a 1501cc version, with sv engines made by Korting. Some carried the Protos trademark on the radiator.

SIGMA • Switzerland 1909-1914

The Société Industrielle Genevoise de Mécanique et d"Automobiles, headed by a son of one of the founders of Piccard-Pictet, took over the old Lucia factory and began production of four-cylinder 1470cc cars with round radiators. In 1911 the company became sole licensee for the Knight sleeve-valve engine in Switzerland, introducing two "valveless" models, an 18 hp of 2614cc and a 28 hp of 4576cc. Sigma cars enjoyed a number of sporting successes, including second place in the 1910 Targa Florio.

SIGMA • France 1913-1928

Made in Levallois, Seine, these were initially Ballot and Chapuis-Dornier-engined cars. After the war they had various Ballot, SCAP, and CIME engines from 894cc to 1614cc.

SILENT KNIGHT • USA 1906-1909

Built to promote Charles Yale Knight's sleeve-valve engine, the 40 hp Silent Knight was made in Chicago. Despite testimonials referring to it as "the peer of all other types," the car was not a commercial success.

SILHOUETTE • England 1971 to date

A sleek glassfiber-bodied two-seater sports car, designed to bolt on to the VW "Beetle" floorpan.

SILVA-CORONER • France 1927

Made by M Silva-Coroner, these were ohv straight-eight-engined cars of 2490cc.

SILVER HAWK • England 1920-1921

Noel Macklin, having cut his automotive teeth on the Eric-Campbell, decided to build a sports car based on that design, which he called the Silver Hawk, with a tuned sv 1373cc engine.

SILVER KNIGHT • USA 1917

Conover T Silver of New York built this sporting model, using Willys-Knight chassis.

SILVERTOWN • England 1905-1910

An electric car with coachwork by W & F Thorn; in 1908 a 4wd model was available.

SILVER VOLT • Puerto Rico 1979 to date

An initial run of 300 electric station wagons was to be given a one-year test by "qualified residents" of Fort Lauderdale, Florida, before production of these $14,500 models began. Up to 7,000 were to be built annually from 1980. Its special battery enables the Silver Volt to take an 80 per cent charge in 45 minutes and to reach 70 mph. A $120,000 luxury version was planned.

SIMA-STANDARD • France 1929-1932

When M Violet left the SIMA company, engineer Emile Dombret made some cars using spares from other manufacturers. There were two models, a 5 hp of 855cc and a 7 hp of 1307cc.

SIMA-VIOLET • France 1924-1929

The Société Industrielle de Materiel Automobile of Courbevoie was run by the prolific Marcel Violet, who made a 496cc twin-cylinder two-stroke cyclecar and some two-stroke racing cars, of which the best was a flat-four of 1484cc.

SIMCA • France 1935-1981

See panel overleaf

1938 Simca-Huit Gordini two-seater

1957 Simca Aronde Montlhéry

1978 Simca 1100LX

SIMCA • France 1935-1981

The Société Industrielle de Mécanique et Carrosserie Automobile was founded by Henri Théodore Pigozzi, who started by assembling Fiat cars like the Topolino 500 (sold under the name of Simca 5) and the 508 (Simca 8.) After the war Simca returned with the pre-war models and soon presented the ohv Simca 6. The year 1949 saw the Simca Sport, and in 1950 the 1100 Simca 8 was enlarged to 1200cc. The following year the 1200cc Aronde appeared. Simca had grown to the extent that it could now take over Unic, Ford France, Saurer and Talbot. In 1954 Simca continued production of the Ford V-8 at the newly acquired Poissy factory with the Versailles, Chambord and Présidence. In 1956 it presented the Aronde "Montlhéry," and the Ariane the following year.

In 1958 Chrysler bought its way into the company, and by 1963 a 1100cc five-bearing engine was being used. But a new generation of Simca cars appeared the following year, with the 944cc rear-engined Simca 1000 designed to challenge Renault; a coupé version subsequently appeared. After the end of the Aronde in 1964 came the 1301 and 1501. The first fwd Simca was the 1100 presented in 1968, though the "Sim 4" (a detuned version of the 1100) was unsuccessful. From 1970 Simca was officially known as Chrysler France, and the 1501 gave way to the Chrysler 150 (1639cc) and 180 (1812cc.) The 1601 was presented in 1977 as a Simca-Chrysler.

Simca was acquired by Peugeot in 1978 and the Simca name phased out in favour of Talbot (itself dropped in 1986.)

SIMMS, SIMMS-WELBECK • England 1899-1908

Frederick R Simms was the original importer of Daimler engines into Britain in 1893, and helped to found Daimler of Coventry. With Robert Bosch he devised the low-tension magneto, and in 1899 he developed a motor quadricycle equipped with a quick-firing machine-gun. An armored "war car" was also built to his design by Vickers, Sons & Maxim. His first private vehicle was the strange little "Motor Wheel," steered by its single rear wheel and driven by two front ones. It was capable of "turning turtle on the slightest provocation," which it did several times in the 1900 1,000-Miles Trial. Simms built his own engines, which were used in vacuum carpet cleaners and road rollers, as well as cars and motorcycles. An early project was an ohc "100 hp" power unit for a fire engine. In 1903 the Simms-Welbeck name was adopted, and two four-cylinder models, a 20/25 hp and a 30/35 hp, were introduced. The Simms-Welbeck was the first production car to be equipped with bumpers; sprung pneumatic devices of Simms"s invention. There was a 12/14 hp four as well, and in 1907 came a pair-cast six of 6494cc.

SIMMS • USA 1920-1921

Simms built five-passenger touring cars only, and very few of those. An own-make four-cylinder engine was used and the price was $1,015. The Simms was succeeded by the Innes.

SIMPLEX • Holland 1898-1915

The Simplex Machine en Rijwielfabrieken of Amsterdam was an engineering and cycle-making company. Its first cars were based on the Benz. A front-engined Fafnir-powered voiturette appeared in 1902. Vivinus engines were also used.

SIMPLEX • England 1902

A car built by A Ryall of Frome, Somerset.

SIMPLEX • France 1920-1921

A light car with a horizontal 735cc single-cylinder engine.

SIMPLIC • England 1914

A 5 hp two-seat cyclecar, selling for only £75.

SIMPLICIA • France 1910

This 10/12 hp light car had independent front suspension and a backbone chassis in unit with its Aster engine and gearbox.

SIMPLICITY • USA 1906-1910

"Without gears, therefore without trouble," this was a $3,000 40 hp from Evansville, Indiana.

SIMPLO • USA 1908-1909

A $600 10/12 hp twin-cylinder friction-drive runabout built in St Louis. It had a detachable "mother-in-law" seat.

SIMPSON • Scotland 1897-1904

John Simpson, an engineer from Stirling, built about 20 steam cars of 6 hp, 10 hp, and 12 hp.

SIMSON-SUPRA • Germany 1911-1933

These very sporting cars were built by a well-known armaments factory, Simson & Co of Suhl, in Thuringia. The cars designed by Paul Henze and built after 1924 were especially noteworthy. Earlier models had 1559cc and 2595cc four-cylinder ioe engines; Henze created ohc and dohc 1960cc four-cylinder cars. Single ohc versions developed 40 bhp at 3000 rpm, dohc cars 60-66 bhp at 4000rpm. There was also an ohv 3108cc six-cylinder model in the production, which was always limited as every car was built by hand. The last Simson-Supra was a sv 4673cc straight-eight.

SINGER • England 1905-1970

See panel overleaf

SINCLAIR • England 1985

The strange three-wheeled C5 was an attempt by computer designer Sir Clive Sinclair to create a mass-market single-seat electric town runabout. It was a complete commercial flop, but the undaunted Sinclair announced plans for the C15 four-seater, with putative 80 mph speed and (250-mile range, in 1990.

SINGER • USA 1915-1920

The Singer was the successor to the Palmer-Singer; it featured a six-cylinder Herschell-Spillman engine and a distinctive vee radiator. The last Singers had a V-12 Weidely engine; total production of this luxury marque seems to have been about 1,100.

SINGLE CENTER • USA 1907-1908

"Not a buggy but a racy-looking automobile runabout," this friction-drive 12/15 hp flat-twin-engined high-wheeler came from Evansville, Indiana.

1896 Simms light car

1927 Simson-Supra sports two-seater

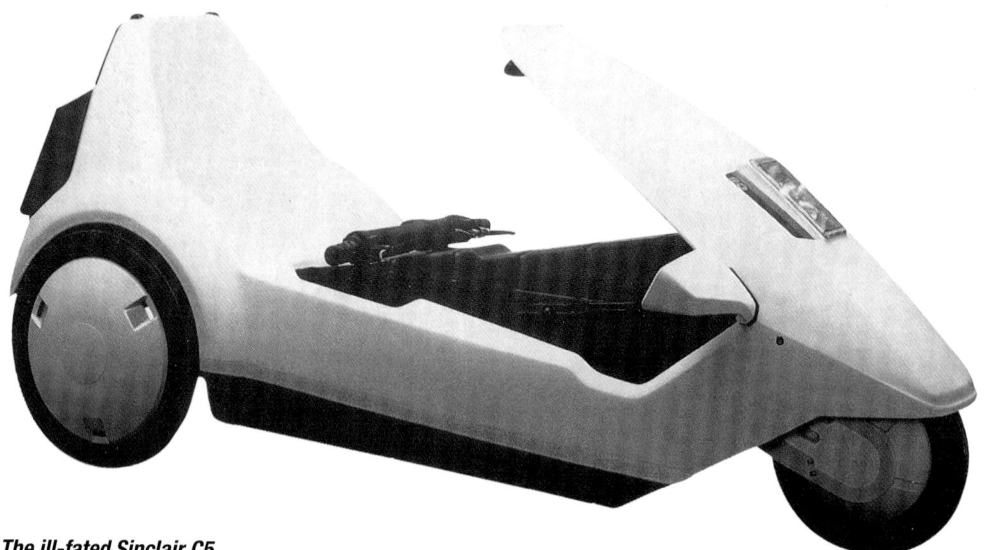

The ill-fated Sinclair C5

SINGER • England 1905-1970

The first Singer car (the firm had made motorcycles from 1900) was made under license from Lea-Francis. It was a 15 hp three-cylinder horizontal-engined device with connecting rods no less than 39 inches long! By 1907 this design had been dropped and replaced by vertical two-, three-, or four-cylinder White and Poppe engines rated at 8 hp, 10 hp, and 12 hp. Two larger models used Aster engines (12/14 hp and 22 hp,) though Singer soon developed its own power unit. In 1912 the popular 10 hp was announced, with rear-axle-mounted gearbox. This was continued after the war, though in 1922 a conventional gearbox position was adopted. The car was redesigned the following year. A bewildering number of models followed, the ohc 848cc Junior of 1927 being very significant. The following year Singer was third in the British car production stakes behind Morris and Austin. By the mid-1930s all models had ohc engines, a particularly appropriate layout for the A G Booth-designed Sports Nine. One of these was placed 13th at Le Mans in 1933 and 7th in 1934, resulting in the model being given the generic title of "Le Mans;" 1100cc and 1.5-liter engines were supplied to HRG for its sports car production.

10 hp Singer Junior tourer, 1926

Pre-war designs were continued after the Second World War until the SM 1500 of 1949, while the 1500 Roadster appeared two years later. The Hunter sedan of 1955 failed to save the company; in 1956 Singer was taken over by the Rootes Group. The Hunter was replaced by the Gazelle (of Hillman Minx lineage.) From then on Singers were upmarket Hillmans, the Chamois of 1965 being an Imp derivative. The 1496cc-engined Gazelle and the 1725cc Vogue also lasted until the marque ceased in 1970.

1934 Singer Le Mans team

SINPAR • France 1907-1914

De Dion-engined voiturettes ("Sinpar" implying "without equal") from Courbevoie, Siene, with 4.5 hp and 8 hp power units. A 1912-1914 8 hp four was identical to the 8 hp Demeester.

SINTZ • USA 1899-1904

The Sintz Gas Engine Company of Grand Rapids, Michigan, built all types of carriage, as well as rail cars and light trams, which were powered by a two-stroke engine of its own manufacture.

LA SIRENE • France 1900-1902

A 5 hp vee-twin with three-speed and reverse gear and tonneau body, built by Fernandez of Paris.

SIRRON • England 1909-1916

Mr Norris was one of the promoters of this light car (hence "Sirron,") which first appeared, built from imported French components, as a 13.9 hp four-cylinder of 1767cc. This was given a longer stroke in 1910 (making it 1944cc,) and joined by a short-lived 16/20 hp of 2723cc in 1911. The following year saw a new 16/20 hp (2554cc) and a 12/16 hp (2212cc.) The sole 1913 Sirron was a 2412cc 14/20 hp, then in 1914 came the 10/12 hp light car with "luxurious full-sized two-seated torpedo body". It had a 1357cc four-cylinder engine and sold for 220 guineas, complete with Koh-i-Noor dynamo lighting set.

SIR VIVAL • USA 1960

This most extraordinary car, manufactured by the Hollow Boring Co of Worcester, Mass., was billed as an experimental safety car. The Sir Vival was built in two sections, hinged in the middle, and both sections were completely surrounded by rubber bumpers. The driver sat in the rear section, higher than the passengers, and turned the car's front section by means of a swivel. Around him was a drum-shaped windshield which provided unobstructed vision and could be rotated and cleaned at the touch of a switch.

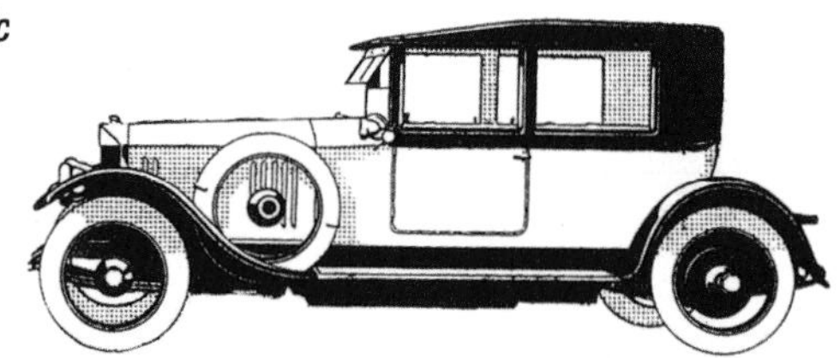
1920 Sizaire-Berwic

SISCART • France 1908-1909

At the 1908 Paris Salon this firm showed a two-seater 8 hp car, a 12 hp "type course" and a side-entrance 12 hp phaeton.

SIVA • Italy 1967-1969

Equipped with Conrero-tuned German 1996cc Ford V-6 engines developing 130 bhp, the Siva Sirio was a beautiful two-seater "Spider" coupé with a tubular chassis frame and a top speed of over 125 mph.

SIVA • England 1969 to date

Neville Trickett's fertile brain has resulted in countless diverse vehicles over the years, many under the Siva banner. These include the futuristic, VW-based S160, the Saluki, the Aston Martin-powered S530, the go-anywhere Llama, and a variety of Edwardian replicas.

1925 Sizaire Frères tourer

SIX • France 1923

A little-known six-cylinder car of 1791cc.

SIXCYL • France 1907-1908

Built in the Bréguet aviation works in Paris under the supervision of Paul Chenu, who also constructed cars under his own name from 1903. There were two six cylinders, a 30/35 hp (6126cc), and a 50/80 hp (8822cc.)

SIZAIRE-BERWICK • France • England 1913-1927

The "poor man's Rolls" was a luxury car designed by Maurice Sizaire and built pre-war at Courbevoie, Seine. It had a 20 hp engine of 4072cc. Its radiator copied the Rolls exactly, but Rolls-Royce sued the company (and settled out of court when it discovered it had omitted to register the radiator design, Sizaire-Berwick thereafter adopting a handsome vee-fronted cooler.) Post-war the engine was uprated to 4.5 liters and, from 1920, the Sizaire-Berwick was also built at Park Royal in England. Austin gained a controlling share in the British operation in 1923 and, until production ceased in 1925, some depressing cars with 12 hp and 20 hp Austin engines were offered. The French operation lasted for two more years, ending with Lycoming-Six power units.

SIZAIRE FRERES • France 1923-1929

Maurice and Georges Sizaire made some interesting cars with independent suspension all-round in their Courbevoie, Seine, works. The first model, an ohv 1996cc four, was made until the end, but they also tried Knight and Hotchkiss engines and experimented with a 3000cc Knight sleeve-valve six.

1974 Siva Llama

1972 Siva V-8 coupé

M Naudin at the wheel of a 1907 Sizaire-Naudin

SIZAIRE-NAUDIN • France 1905-1921

There was little conventional about Maurice and Georges Sizaire's first car, which appeared at the Exposition des Petits Inventeurs in March 1905. It had a single-cylinder 6 hp engine in a wooden chassis with independent front suspension by a transverse spring and sliding pillars, as well as direct drive on all three forward speeds by a triple-ratio pinion engaged with the crown-wheel by a cam device. This design was progressively developed and became more conventional. By the outbreak of war a four of 1593cc was available, and, post-war, a 2.3-liter.

SJR • USA 1915-1916

A small Boston-built four-seater roadster, powered by a four-cylinder Wisconsin engine.

SKODA • Czechoslovakia 1924 to date

The first Skoda was a Marc Birkigt-designed French Hispano-Suiza, built under license at Plzen by this big arms- and machine-works. Soon afterwards Skoda took over the Laurin & Klement car factory at Mladá Boleslav, where it built the 1950cc four-cylinder models 110 and 120 and the 3495cc sleeve-valve six-cylinder models 350 and 360. There were also the 3880cc eight-cylinder 860 and the Type 645 with a 2490cc six-cylinder engine. The four-cylinder Type 430 was a bestseller. During the 1930s the 995cc four-cylinder Popular and the 1380cc Rapid had excellent sales. Another good model was the six-cylinder 2480cc Superb. The last pre-war range included the sv 995cc Popular and the ohv 1089cc Popular. The Rapid now had a modern ohv 1560cc engine and the Superb an ohv 3140cc six-cylinder motor.

After 1945 Skoda resumed production with a revised Popular, the Skoda 1100, and the 3.1-liter Superb. From 1950-1954 Skoda built the 2.0-liter Tatraplan. In 1952 came the Skoda 1200; this was replaced in 1970 by the Skoda 440 Spartak, developed into the S445, Octavia and Octavia Combi. A new factory at Mladiá Boleslav began production of the first chassisless, rear-engined Skoda, and 1000MB, in 1964. It was developed into the 1100MB, Skoda 100,110, and 110R Coupé. Fire damaged the plant in 1969, but by 1973 production was over 630 cars a day. In 1977 came the LS (Estelle,) developed into the Super Estelle and Estelle Two. In 1989 the 4wd Favorit succeeded the Estelle and production of the rear-engined Skodas was halted. In 1990 VW took a major stake in Skoda, but insisted that it would retain the marque name. VW"s first move was to re-engineer the Favorit, and, suitably improved, it emerged as the Felica model. So good was this car that it stopped for ever the British market"s perception of Skodas as joke cars, from a time past. In Europe a different perception of Skoda was apparent and the success of the Felica in Europe encouraged VW and Skoda to press ahead with a new, larger model. This arrived in 1998 in the form of the Octavia, a striking styled, five-door hatchback with strong and reliable VW engines and underpinings. Once again it was an excellent car at a good price. It offered 1.6, 1.8 petrol powerplants and a 1.9 diesel engine.

1976 Skoda Estelle

1989 Skoda Favorit 136 LS

The Skoda Fabia, 2000 (below,)
Skoda Octavia hatchback SLX 1.8, 1999 (right)

SKELTON • USA 1920-1922

An assembled car, the Skelton used a four-cylinder Lycoming engine and other proven standard components. Skelton cars were built by the Standard Car Company of St Louis, Missouri, a tramcar and railway carriage company of high renown, which pre-1911 had built the American Mors and later the Standard six.

SKENE • USA 1900-1901

The twin-cylinder 5 hp Skene steamer, from Springfield, Mass., was undistinguished in design, despite its maker"s claim of "many points of superiority".

SKEOCH • England 1921

This cyclecar used a 348cc single-cylinder Precision engine. A two-speed Burman gearbox was fitted, and final drive was by chain.

SKIRROW • England 1936-1939

These midget racing cars, produced by Harry Skirrow of London, used a 1000cc JAP engine with chain drive to all four wheels.

SKODA • Czechoslovakia 1924 to date

See panel

SLM • Switzerland 1899, 1935

This locomotive works at Winterthur built an opposed-piston voiturette in 1899 before turning to steam trucks. In 1935 it made three SLM-Pescara sports cars to the design of the Spanish Marquis de Pescara. A V-16 of 3.6 liters, the SLM-Pescara, was capable of 103 mph.

SLR • England 1963-1965

"Sprinzel Lawrencetune Racing" brought together two keen racing protagonists of the 1960s for the purpose of beating Porsche at its own racing game. Though essentially competition machines, the three SLRs, one based on a Triumph TR4 chassis, the others on Morgan hardware, did see road use and would undoubtedly have sold well had they gone into production. Each was fitted with a beautiful alloy body styled by Rolls-Royce man Chris Spender and built by Williams and Pritchard.

SM • England 1904-1905

George J Shave was formerly works manager of Locomobile's British works in Kensington, London. With Irving J Morse he devised a flash boiler with completely automatic control. The SM car, built by the successors to Locomobile, had a four-cylinder monobloc single-cylinder engine which developed 8.5 hp, capable of 40 mph; a 20 hp model was also available.

1907 Sizaire-Naudin 7 hp two-seater (see page 421)

1903 Soames

SMB • Italy 1906-1908

A small-production 3140cc four-cylinder car built with a four-speed gearbox in unit with the engine.

SMITH • USA 1905-1911

Starting life as plain Smith, by 1907 this marque from Topeka, Kansas, had become the Great Smith, "World's Greatest $2500 Car". It was a conventional four-cylinder with full-elliptic springs and "magnificent upholstery".

SMITH & CO • Denmark c. 1903

No technical details are known about this car, except that it had a single-cylinder engine in front and tiller steering. The prototype was built by one of the employees of Smith & Co A/S, Odense, but the directors decided not to go into car manufacturing.

SMITH & DOWSE • England 1900

Motor engineers and repairers at Isleworth, Middlesex, Smith and Dowse built cars to special order.

SMITH FLYER • USA 1917-c. 1920

Motoring at its most basic, the Milwaukee-built Smith Flyer consisted of four cycle wheels linked by planks, which served as both floor and suspension. Two bucket seats were the sole bodywork; power was supplied by a Smith Motor Wheel (a power-pack attachment for pedal cycles) mounted at the rear. A "clutch" pedal merely lifted this fifth wheel off the road. In winter the wheels could be replaced by ski-runners. From 1920 to 1923 the "Flyer" was built by Briggs & Stratton. A 12v electric, the "Auto Red Bug," lasted from 1923 to 1928.

SNA • Switzerland 1903-1914

Fritz Henriod designed the air-cooled cars of the Société Neuch,teloise d'Automobiles. First models had flat-twin engines of 6/8 cv, 10/12 cv and 18/20 cv at the front, under a hood shaped like an upturned boat. Some SNAs had electric headlamps. In 1907 came a 25/30 cv of 4942cc, with four cylinders in line, cooled by twin fans; it resembled the contemporary CGV in external appearance, and six chassis were fitted with Charles-Edouard Henriod's friction drive. The 25/30 cv lasted until the end of production.

SNYDER • USA 1906-1908

A flat-twin 10/12 hp engine powered this high-wheeled buggy from Dansville, Illinois.

SOAMES • England 1903-1906

One of the first cars to have a flexibly-mounted engine to minimize vibration, the Soames also had a three-speed, constant-mesh gearbox.

SOCIETE GENERALE DES VOITURES AUTOMOBILES • France 1900

Built by the Compagnie Francaise de Moteurs á Gaz. This was probably the first company to offer diesel engines in addition to two- and four-cylinder petrol-engined cars.

SODERBLOM • Sweden 1903

Söderbloms Gjuteri & Mekaniska Verkstad of Eskilstuna normally produced trucks, but one passenger car was built to special order. It had a watercooled 10 hp twin-cylinder engine, a two-speed gearbox and chain drive. The body was a five-seater tourer.

rumors circulated that the body was a fire risk, the timber was sheathed in steel. The Southern Cross was powered by a locally-made flat-four engine of unknown capacity. It developed 55 bhp, giving a brisk performance for the day. Open and closed models were produced. Two cars were built using an Australian-developed torque-converter in place of the conventional clutch. The total number of production vehicles is uncertain, but is believed to have been about 10. None survives. Kingsford Smith was in the process of raising additional capital for the project when he was killed attempting a new England-Australia air record.

SOLANET • France 1921

A rear-engined V-8 car made by Count Solanet. It seems that only one was built.

SOLIDOR • Germany 1905-1907

Berlin-assembled Passy-Thellier cars were marketed under this name.

SOLOMOBIL • Germany 1921-1923

Built at Chemnitz, the Hugo Mitzenheim-designed Solomobil was a three-wheeler. Solomobil later produced a cyclecar with four wheels and a sv 12 hp vee-twin engine.

SOMEA • Belgium 1920-1921

Paul Bastien, later of Metallurgique and Stutz, designed the 2-liter ohc SOMEA, launched at the 1920 Brussels Show. Only prototypes were built of this successor to the ALP.

SOMMER • USA 1904-1907

An offshoot of the 1902-1904 Hammer-Sommer, the Sommer had a 12 hp twin under the seat and, at first, a "coal scuttle" hood.

SONCIN • France 1900-1902

A two-seater 4.5 hp voiturette, forerunner of Grégoire.

SORIANO-PEDROSO • France 1919-1924

Made in Biarritz by two Spaniards, the Marques de Pedroso and Senor Soriano, these were initially Ballot-engined 1131cc and 1590cc cars. Then Soriano-Pedroso built a 902cc Ruby-engined cyclecar and a straight-eight prototype; however, its main product was marine engines.

1912 15 hp SPA tourer

1978 Spartan sports two-seater

SOUTHERN • USA 1909

Built in Jackson, Tennessee, the sporty Southern Roadster sold for $1,500.

SOUTHERN • USA 1921-1922

Two Southern cars, both tourers, are known to have been built, one probably in 1920 and the other a year later. These had Herschell-Spillman engines and Rolls-Royce-shaped radiators. Prices were quoted as $2,375 and $2,995 respectively.

SOUTHERN CROSS • Australia 1931-1935

A most unusual car, financed by flying pioneer Sir Charles Kingsford Smith, the Southern Cross featured a monocoque chassis body made from laminated plywood. When

SOVEREIGN • USA 1906-1907

Built on European lines, this was a chain-driven four-cylinder touring car of 7633cc, with an eight-seat aluminum Roi-des-Belges body.

SPA • Italy 1906-1928

Matteo Ceirano designed and constructed the SPA at Torino. Among the SPA cars were a 1526cc twin-cylinder and four-cylinder models from 2615cc to 7598cc. There were also two six-cylinder models of 5100cc and 11,536cc. After the war the range of models included 2680cc four-cylinder and 4380cc six-cylinder models. A sporting version of the six had a dohc 24-valve head; even this advanced car could not prevent the end of SPA after the war. Fiat took over SPA in 1925, and production became centered on trucks. In pre-war days Ciuppa won the 1909 Targa Florio on a SPA.

SPAG • France 1927-1928

Made in Asniéres, Seine, by M M Simille and Pequignot, these were 1100cc Ruby and 1500cc SCAP-engined sports cars.

SPARKS • USA 1899-1900

This San Franciscan company offered a twin-cylinder 4 hp car with belt drive to all four wheels for "less than $700". A prospectus was issued, but it might have been just a stock promotion fraud.

SPARTAN • USA 1911

Built at the Motorette works in Hartford, Connecticut, by C W Kelsey, the Spartan never went into production. Conventional in most aspects, it featured front doors, a novelty in 1911.

SPARTAN • England 1973 to date

Jim McIntyre built the first Spartan after years of repairing sports cars. Traditional in approach and touch and resilient, Spartans have been powered by countless

engines, from the Ford Mexico to the Rover V-8. Initially a Triumph chassis was used, but this was replaced by a purpose-built unit.

SPATZ • Germany 1956-1958

Based on a design by racing driver Egon Brutsch, the red, rear-engined Spatz had first a 198cc Sachs two-stroke engine, then a 246cc Victoria two-stroke. Originally made by Friedrich of Traunreuth (Bavaria,) the Spatz was later built by Victoria at Nuremberg. Total output was around 1,500 cars. It was a small open two-seater with mini-wheels. The Nuremberg-built version bore the Victoria trademark.

SPAULDING • USA 1910-1916

From Grinnell, Iowa, the Spaulding 30 was available with epicyclic or sliding gear-change.

SPEEDSPORT • Belgium 1924-1927

A sports car assembled in Brussels from Model T Ford components.

SPEEDWELL • England 1900-1908

Speedwell was chiefly a motor agent, but also marketed cars under its own name. In 1904 there were three Speedwells, single-cylinders14/16 hp and 24/30 hp appeared for 1905, and late in 1906 a 25 hp four was available, with a handsome circular radiator and a double rear-axle, with separate load-carrying and driving members. For 1907 a 45 hp six was listed, and in 1908, the last year of production, came a 45/50 hp six.

SPEEDWELL • USA 1907-1914

"The surprise of the Automobile World," the first Speedwells, designed by George Loomis, were a 40/45 hp four and a six, built next door to the Wright Brothers" aircraft works at Dayton, Ohio. About 25 cars were built in the first year, after which the six was dropped, production rising to 100 in 1908, 400 in 1909. Later Speedwells had 6899cc six-cylinder engines; a double rotary-valve engine was offered from 1913 in addition to an engine with conventional valves.

SPEEDY • England 1905-1906

Jackson Brothers & Lord of Salford, Lancashire, built this 4 hp tricar, which was unusual in having the passenger seated at the rear in a "comfortable and cosy seat".

1908 Speedwell (GB) 24 hp Roi-des-Belges

1913 Sperber 1545cc tourer

SPEEDY • England 1920-1921

A cyclecar built in Peckham, South London, the Speedy used an 8 hp air-cooled vee-twin engine. Drive was by chain and belt. It was hoped to mass-produce the Speedy, but these heady ambitions were never realized.

SPENCER • USA 1921-1922

A small car using a four-cylinder engine of the company's own make, the five-passenger touring car sold for $850 and rode on wooden artillery wheels. Few of these 104-inch wheelbase Spencers were built.

SPERBER • Germany 1911-1919

The 500-man workforce of NAW of Hameln (builder of the Colibri) also built the small Sperber cars with sv 1330cc, 1545cc, and 1592cc four-cylinder engines. Production was not resumed after the war, and Selve bought the NAW works for the production of Selve cars in 1919.

SPERLING • USA 1921-1923

The Sperling was an export automobile, and therefore had right-hand steering. It featured a four-cylinder Supreme engine and slightly pointed radiator. Both open and closed cars were available, the five-passenger touring model being listed at $980.

SP HIGHWAYMAN • England 1974-197

Built by established restorer Hooe Garage of Sussex, the SPs were the brainchild of Bugattiman Jack Perkins. The first was open, the second closed in by a unique tinted glass roof. Both featured Rover power and clever negative-roll front suspension.

SPHINX • France 1912-1925

Made in Courbevoie and then in Asniéres, Seine, by M M Forster and Terrier, these were cyclecars with 1399cc twin Forster engines. They were also available with the 6 hp single-cylinder Aster. After the war the company also made a four-cylinder 1327cc Altos-engined car.

SPHINX • USA 1914-1915

The Sphinx was built as a five-passenger touring car; an estimated 250 to 300 units were produced of this sole model. A four-cylinder Lycoming engine was employed, and wood or wire wheels were available. It has been stated

SP Highwayman, 1974

1914 Sphinx (US) 2932cc tourer

that the advent of the 1916 Overland (a car similar to the Sphinx but giving better performance for less price) was responsible for the demise of this marque. The Sphinx Motor Car Co of York, Pa., was succeeded by the DuPont Motor Car Co, which briefly continued the Sphinx under the DuPont name, an estimated 40 to 50 being sold later in 1915.

SPHINX • Germany 1921-1925

A more-or-less home-made small car with a sv four-cylinder engine of 1320cc.

SPIDOS • France 1921-1925

Made in Lyon, this was a 902cc Ruby-engined cyclecar.

SPINELL • Germany 1924-1926

Equipped with an ohv 496cc Kuhne single-cylinder motorcycle engine, the Spinell was just another chain-driven cyclecar.

SPITZ • Austria 1901-1907

Originally a car dealer, Spitz entered car manufacture (at the Gräf & Stift works in Vienna) with a 4wd design. Otto Hieronymus, famous as a designer and racing driver, later designed a 24 hp four-cylinder car which won many races. Production versions included 16 hp, 20 hp, and 24 hp models.

SPO • France 1908-1911

The Société Franáise du Petit Outillage was a manufacturer of engines and components at Clichy (Seine.) It also built complete chassis.

SPORTS JUNIOR • England 1920-1921

This was a 10 hp two-seater with a four-cylinder Peters engine and detachable disc wheels.

SPRINGFIELD • USA 1908-1911

Springfield built in limited numbers (1910 production was 100 cars,) but for 1911 offered a "made-to-order car for 300 exacting people," though the main choice offered seemed to be in the color scheme. This shaft-drive car sold for $2,500 with "touring or torpedo body".

SPRINGUEL • Belgium 1907-1910

Springuel of Liége, which merged with Impéria in 1910, built a 24 hp pair-cast four. It was manufactured in small numbers.

SPYKER • Holland 1900-1925

The Spijker brothers, carriage-builders based at Trompenburg, built a two-cylinder car in 1900. As early as 1903 they completed the construction of a one-off 4wd, four-wheel-brake, six-cylinder racer designed by the Belgian Laviolette, though a small number of 40 hp 4wd tourers were subsequently completed. That year a 16 hp twin and a 20/24 hp four were introduced. In 1904 the company introduced the "Dustless" chassis, with liberal under-shielding to minimize dust-raising on unmade roads. The entire output of four-cylinder cars for 1904-1906 was exported to England (there were also many twin-cylinder Spyker taxis in London.) An 80/100 hp Spyker won the Pekin-Paris race in 1907, the last year of Spijker family involvement, while from 1909 all models were fitted with worm-driven transverse camshafts for smooth running. The post-war Spyker C4, with a 5741cc Maybach engine and French chassis, was designed by aero engineer Fritz Koolhoven; a curious airplane-styled "Aerocoque" sports, with vestigial tail surfaces, was listed. Over-expansion during the war proved Spyker's downfall. Attempts to market Mathis 1.2-liters as Spykers, and to assemble American trucks, failed to delay the inevitable demise.

1913 Spyker 20 hp landaulette

1937 SS Jaguar 2½-liter coupé

SQUIRE • England 1934-1936

Adrian Squire built his visually exciting sports cars at a small garage at the top of Remenham Hill, near Henley-on-Thames. Powered by a potent supercharged 1.5-liter R1 Anzani engine, the Squire had a preselector gearbox for good acceleration. Available in two chassis lengths, with bodywork by Vanden Plas or Ranalah, the Squire was one of the best-looking British sports cars of its day. Unfortunately there were snags. Prices began at £1,195 and the engines proved unreliable unless regularly maintained. Even the announcement of a cheaper two-seater, with body by Markham of Reading, failed to attract buyers, and only seven cars were built during the two years of production. However, another two cars were subsequently built up by Val Zethrin, owner of one of the two long-chassis examples. The Squire made brief appearances at Brooklands in 1935, driven by Luis Fontes, who managed to finish only once, being placed in a Mountain Handicap race at the track.

1939 SS100 Sports two-seater

1935 Squire raced by Luis Fontes

SS • England 1932-1945

The forerunner of Jaguar Cars, this company was founded in 1934, though William Lyons and William Walmsley had been making motorcycle sidecars from 1921. They graduated to producing distinctive bodies on Austin, Morris and Standard chassis. The SS1 of 1932 sprang from the Swallow-bodied Standard 16, having a low coupé body and long hood and costing just £310, the engine being a conventional 2054cc six-cylinder Standard unit. In addition, the SS11 used the 1052cc Standard Little Nine engine. The first sports car was the 2.5-liter 90 of 1935, with stylish two-seater bodywork. A good-looking four-door sports sedan was named the Jaguar and, although the 2.7-liter engine had Standard origins, it had been much improved by Harry Weslake and W M Heynes. Particularly handsome was the two-seater SS100 of 1936, powered by a 2.5-liter engine, also Standard-based. A new 3.5-liter power unit was used not only in the sedan and drophead coupé for 1938 but, more significantly, in the 100. In this more powerful form it cost only £445, yet was capable of the magic 100 mph. After the Second World War the company was renamed Jaguar Cars, in view of the by then sinister associations of the company's original initials.

SSANYONG • Korea 1954-1999 (brand taken under Daewoo flag)

Although strangely named to western tastes, this Korean company has a surprisingly long history. Like its other Korean counterparts, its car division started life building its own versions of recently retired western marque's models. Supported by its industrial work and construction interests, the company built a jeep-type vehicle for many years. In the 1980s it became involved with Mercedes, which took shares in the company and started to supply engines.

1920 Stabilia 12-15 torpedo

1929 Standard Nine Teignmouth fabric sedan

SsanYong entered the 4wd market with a joint alliance designed five-door Range Rover/Shogun-type rival. Called the Musso, it was available with a Mercedes diesel engine and was styled by a British team. Latterly a petrol engine was available and a luxury trimmed Musso 2.3 GX model sold very well. The Korando model was a two-door, 4wd car that resembled an updated original Jeep. The firm achieved success, notably in the British 4wd agricultural and leisure market. In 1999, in the midst of the Asian economic crisis, SsanYong's model range ceased to be when it was swallowed up by Daewoo, which immediately relaunched the Musso and Korando with new badges and grilles under the Daewoo brand name.

STABILIA • France 1907-1930

Vrard, the inventor of the Stabilia, worked with Léon Bollée from 1896, then with De Dion. He showed his first car at the 1904 Paris Salon, though serious production did not begin until 1907. The "uncapsizable" Stabilia was underslung at front and rear, giving a very low build. A pair-cast 2.2-liter four-cylinder engine was used initially, and various small fours were subsequently offered. Though bizarre suspension mediums like coil springs in tension were adopted from time to time, the basic layout of the Stabilia remained constant.

STACK • England 1921-1925

A 766cc vee-twin engine was used in the Stack, made in East Croydon, Surrey. Transmission was by friction discs with chain final drive.

STAFFORD • England 1920-1921

An assembled car with an ohv 1790cc Dorman engine.

STAG • England 1913-1914

A 5/6 hp cyclecar built in Sherwood, Nottinghamshire.

STAIGER • Germany 1924-1926

Made by Autostaiger of Stuttgart, this was yet another small 12 hp car with a sv four-cylinder engine.

STAINES-SIMPLEX • England 1906

With a Renault-style dashboard radiator and hood, the Staines-Simplex (or SSS) first appeared as a 16/18 hp four. An 8/10 hp twin was introduced in September 1908. Production was spasmodic, apparently only taking place when the chauffeurs employed by the Staines Motor Company had nothing else to do.

STALLION • USA 1979

Silver Classic Coachcraft of California build this glassfiber-bodied car based on the design of Shelby"s AC Cobra. The Stallion is powered by 4949cc Ford V-8 engines.

STANDARD • England 1903-1963

Standard cars were so called because they were assembled from standardized patterns and interchangeable parts. The company was founded by R W Maudslay (whose cousin designed the Maudslay car, also made in Coventry.) The first production Standards were fitted with oversquare single- and twin-cylinder engines, though by 1906 two six-cylinder models were listed. A 12 hp four appeared in about 1909, and a 9.5 hp Rhyl was marketed for 1913. The post-war era saw an enlarged version of the Rhyl, the SLS, appear, to become the 11.6 hp SLO of 1921. A six-cylinder model, the 2.2-liter, was marketed for 1927; the following year the Popular Nine appeared, with a fabric body and worm-driven rear-axle. In 1929 Captain John

Black became Standard's managing director, and two years later the company was offering a Big Nine and 16 hp and 20 hp sixes, while a Little Nine appeared in 1932. A Ten came in 1934 and in 1936 the Flying Standard range was introduced in 12 hp, 16 hp, and 20 hp variants. A short-lived 2.7-liter V-8 was a feature of the 1937 season. By contrast, the 1-liter Eight was popular in 1939. Standard bought the bankrupt Triumph company in 1945, and the first true new model of the post-war era was the Vanguard of 1948, with a 2.1-liter wet liner four-cylinder engine. The company's small car was the 803cc Eight of 1954, later joined by a larger Ten, the engine and independent front suspension being transferred to the Triumph Herald of 1959. A takeover of the company by Leyland Motors took place in 1961, the Triumph marque becoming the flagship of the group. The last Standards, which were phased out in May 1963, were the 2138cc Ensign and Vanguard Six, the engine of which was used in the Triumph 2000. As a marque name Standard ceased to exist; what once had been a complimentary title had become debased.

1957 Standard Vanguard III

STANDARD • USA 1904-c. 1908

Successor to the "US Long Distance," this was a 25 hp four with wooden side-entrance coachwork, retailing at $3,500.

STANDARD • Italy 1906-1908

The Fabbrica Automobili Standard of Torino built a 10/14 hp four-cylinder car, also sold as FAS.

STANDARD • Germany 1911-1912

Equipped with unreliable and not fully-developed Henroid rotary-valve engines, these four-cylinder cars made at Berlin-Charlottenburg did not gain many friends or customers.

STANDARD • USA 1912-1923

The Standard Steel Company of Pittsburgh was among the first companies to offer a V-8, from 1916. Its 80 hp engine had a swept volume of 5217cc. Standard Steel, builder of rairoad carriages, also made First World War armored cars.

STANDARD • Germany 1933-1935, 1950-1954

This famous motorcycle factory, owned by Wilhelm Gutbrod, first built the Josef Ganz-designed Standard-Superior with a 494cc twin-cylinder two-stroke vertical-engine in the back. A second version had a 396cc motor of similar design. Gutbrod-Superior cars with twin-cylinder two-stroke engines of 593cc and 663cc were made from 1950 to 1954.

1934 Standard (German) coupé

STANDARD • India 1961 to date

Built a Triumph with body work changes, such as four doors, and called it the Gazelle. Since 1990 has concentrated on the 2000, a 2-liter version of the old Rover SDI.

STANDARD SIX • USA 1909-1910

After building Mors cars under license as "American Mors" from 1906, this St Louis company built an ohv 50 hp six of 6965cc under its own name.

STANDARD STEAM CAR • USA 1920-1921

The Standard, also known as the Scott-Newcomb, featured a Rolls-Royce-shaped condenser and closely resembled the Roamer gasoline car in appearance. The twin-cylinder horizontal steam engine used kerosene for fuel and, it was claimed, raised a full head of steam within one minute! One touring car is known to have been built; as many as five cars of this type have been reported, though this is unverified.

STANDISH • USA 1924-1925

Only two Standish cars were built by the Luxor Cab Mfg Co of Framingham, Mass., a division of the M P Moller Co (builder of the Dagmar automobile.) Resembling both the Dagmar and the Luxor, the Standish carried a pointed radiator later used by the Elysee truck, another Moller product. It had a Continental six and a 124-inch wheelbase.

STANGUELLINI • Italy 1946-1965

Known in pre-war days as a tuner of Fiats (mainly the Ballila,) Vittorio Stanguellini also built after the war many sporting cars with 741cc and 1089cc Fiat engines, in most cases with dohc. His bigger engines developed 90 bhp, some even over 100 bhp. He also built rear-engined Fiat-powered Formula Junior cars.

STANHOPE • England 1919-1925

This three-wheeler from Leeds was belt-driven, power coming from an 8 hp JAP vee-twin. Although the car was known as the Bramham from 1922 to 1924, it re-emerged as the Stanhope in 1925.

1920 Stanhope fwd three-wheel two-seater

1904 7 hp Star three-seater

STANLEY • USA 1899-1927

See panel

STANWOOD • USA 1920-1922

A typical assembled car with a Continental six-cylinder engine, the Stanwood offered a line of open and closed body styles.

STAR • England 1897-1932

Edward Lisle's Wolverhampton-based Star Engineering Company built cycles from 1883, and built its first 3.5 hp Benz-based car in 1897. A two-cylinder version appeared in 1900, followed a year later by a Panhard-type 7 hp vertical twin. Mercedes provided the inspiration for the 1903 12/16 hp four, joined by a 3261cc version in late 1905. Star's first six, the 6227cc 30 hp, was listed from 1906 to 1911. A new 15 hp of 2862cc appeared in 1909, and was replaced in 1912 by the famous 15.9 four of 3016cc; in 1914 this model and the 3817cc 20.1 hp were offered with streamline torpedo coachwork and bullnose radiators. The 15.9 hp and 20.1 hp survived until 1921, when they were supplanted by a sv 11.9 hp of 1795cc, which became a 1945cc 12/25 in 1924; the similar 12/40 hp Sports had front-wheel brakes and pushrod ohv. A six-cylinder version was known as the 18/40 hp. Two years later came two new models, the 2120cc ohv 14/40 hp four and the 3181cc 20/60 hp six. In 1928 Star was taken over by Guy, and the range cut to two sixes, the 18/50 hp and the 20/60 hp. These were redesigned in 1930 as the Comet and Planet, with four-wheel hydraulic jacking and

STANLEY • USA 1899-1927

Identical twins F E and F O Stanley sold their photographic dry plate business to Kodak and began building steam cars as a hobby in 1897. They received so many orders that they began building a batch of 200 steam buggies, but a consortium bought them out for $250,000 to build their design as the Locomobile, and they then developed an improved model with twin-cylinder engine geared direct to the back axle. This went into production in 1901. The fire-tube boiler was eventually shifted to the front under the famous "coffin nose" hood. In 1906 a racing Stanley Steamer, its body developed in a windtunnel, exceeded 127 mph at Ormond Beach, Daytona, Florida. The production 1907 Gentleman's Speedy Roadster could reach over 75 mph. A foot-and-mouth disease epidemic in the Stanley's New England home area in 1914 caused the removal of many roadside horse-troughs, so the cars had to be fitted with condensers in 1915. Development costs cut production that year to 126, compared with 743 in 1914, though it rose to 500 in 1917, the last year in which the Stanley brothers were involved. Prescott Warren controlled Stanley until 1924, but the marque never recovered from the post-war slump. The company was taken over by the Steam Vehicle Corporation of America of Allentown, Pa., but it is unlikely that it built any further Stanleys before it ceased trading in 1927.

1910 Stanley Model 71 20 hp tourer

1909 Star 12 hp two-seater

1931 Star Planet Coupé

servo brakes, offering "1941 motoring luxury and economy," but production was suspended in March 1932.

STAR • Italy 1905-1921

Yet another enterprise belonging to the Giovanni Ceirano, Star had nothing in common with the British Star car, but was virtually identical with the Ceirano-designed and -built Rapid cars, except for minor differences in the shape of the bodywork, the radiator, and other small items.

STAR • USA 1908

An ephemeral marque built by Model, of Peru, Indiana, which offered a chain-drive twin and a shaft-drive four.

STAR • USA 1922-1928

Billy Durant's Star, originally built in Elizabeth, NJ, was an assembled car with a 2137cc Continental monobloc four. Selling at only $490, it was intended to rival the Model T Ford, and by 1923 the marque was seventh in popularity in America. A six was added to the range in 1926, with a sv 2774cc engine. During 1927 front-wheel brakes were added, and in 1928 the six was renamed "Durant Model 55". The marque, known as "Rugby" outside the USA, was a casualty of the collapse of Durant's "Second Empire".

STARLING • England 1905-1909

Edward Lisle Jr ran the Star Cycle Company of Wolverhampton, which in 1905 produced the 6 hp single-cylinder Starling; it sold for only £110 in two-seater form. In 1907 a 10 hp twin was introduced.

STARLITE • USA 1959

Kish Industries of Lansing, Michigan, designed the 148-inch- long Starlite. The car had sports car styling and was powered by an electric motor. Two body styles were planned, but nothing came of the project.

START • Czechoslovakia 1921-1931

The first Petrásek-designed Start had an 1105cc twin-cylinder engine, another (four-seater) model a sv 1459cc four-cylinder engine. The last Start was an air-cooled twin cylinder of modern design, but few were built.

STATUS • England 1970-1974

The rear-engined Status Minipower, originally known as the Symbol, was the brainchild of ex-Lotus man Brian Luff (who was also involved in the Clan project.) Featuring a glassfiber-clad spaceframe chassis, it was light and manageable. Twenty chassis were built, but only eight complete kits sold before production ceased in 1974. One of several proposed body designs formed the basis for the 365, another Status product.

STAUNAU • Germany 1950-1951

The fwd Staunau, powered by 398cc or 746cc Ilo two-stroke twin-cylinder engines, was probably one of the worst small cars ever made after the Second World War.

STAVER • USA 1907-1914

The first Staver cars were 18/20 hp high-wheelers, but after two years the company was building conventional four-cylinder models, available with touring or torpedo coachwork. The 1914 Staver 65 was a 7413cc monobloc six.

STEAMOBILE • USA 1900-1902

A 7/9 hp twin-cylinder steam buggy from Keene, New Hampshire, designed by one Locke.

STEARNS • USA 1898-1930

The first cars built by Frank B Stearns of Cleveland, Ohio, were single-cylinder gas buggies with tiller steering, replaced by wheel steering on the 4083cc model of 1900. Plans in 1901 to build ten cars a day were greeted with press scepticism. A front-engined twin appeared in 1902, priced at $3,000. A 36 hp four on Mercedes lines appeared in 1904, developing into the 1906 40/45 hp four with cast aluminum body panels. This was soon joined by the 45/90 hp six of 12,913cc, reckoned to be the fastest stock car of its day. In 1909 came a 15/30 hp, "The Ultimate Car," and 1914 saw two Knight sleeve-valve-engined models, the 5.1-liter four and 6.8-liter six; a V-8 joined the range

1929 Stearns-Knight Model 8 Coupé

1925 Steiger sports two-seater

1908 Stella 16/20 hp – "a perfect gem"

in 1917. Frank Stearns retired in 1919, and in 1925 Willys Overland took over (though it retained the Stearns hallmark of a white line round the inside edge of the radiator shell.) The last Stearns Knights of 1929-1930 were a 27.3 hp six and a 6.3-liter straight-eight.

STEARNS • USA 1900-1904

A twin-cylinder steam carriage with side-tiller steering from Syracuse, NY.

STECO • USA 1914

A streamlined 10 hp tandem-seat cyclecar of aggressive appearance, from Chicago. Independent front suspension was featured.

STEEL • France 1907

An obscure marque built by Lochner, Willem, et Cie of Meudon (Seine-et-Oise,) the Steel had a 2043cc four-cylinder 13/15 hp engine.

STEIGER • Germany 1920-1926

Superb Paul Henze-designed four-cylinder cars with ohc 2604cc (later 2824cc) long-stroke engines, which were also built as sports cars with neat two-seater bodywork, and gained many successes. Steigers were handmade and expensive. Noll of Düsseldorf, known also as a Bugatti driver, supplied Steiger parts after the works (at Burgrieden, near Laupheim) closed.

STEINMETZ • USA 1920-1927

Said to be the only electric car produced south of the Mason-Dixon line, the Steinmetz, from Baltimore, Maryland, was named for the crippled "Electrical Wizard," Charles Steinmetz (who drove a Detroit Electric.)

STELA • France 1941-1948

Electric cars made in Villeurbanne, Rhône, during the Second World War; most of them were delivery vans.

STELKA • Czechoslovakia 1920-1922

A machine works at Primbram, which started light car manufacture with very limited technical and commercial possibilities. The Stelka, designed by Rudolf Stelsovsky, the owner of the factory, was a 1080cc twin-cylinder with a high, narrow body.

STELLA • Switzerland 1906-1913

Successors to the CIEM, Stella cars were distinguished by a round radiator and used a conventional transmission. Initially a 3-liter 10cv was built, followed by other four-cylinder models of 14/16cv, 18/20cv, and 24/30cv.

1917 Ams-Sterling roadster

1924 Sterling-Knight

STELLITE • England 1913-1919

The 1100cc Stellite was built by Electric Ordnance and Accessories of Birmingham, a Wolseley offshoot. The chassis of this £157 car was of flitch-plated wood, and up to 1915 only two speeds were available.

STEPHENS • England 1898-1900

R Stephens, a Clevedon, Somerset, cycle engineer, built about a dozen 8 hp twin-cylinder cars with belt and chain drive and independent suspension, the prototype survives.

STEPHENS • USA 1916-1924

An offshoot of the Moline Plow Company, the Stephens was always built as a six-cylinder, the "Salient Six," of 3671cc, with ohv from 1918, after which the company switched from Continental engines to its own-make power units.

STERLING • England 1987 to date

Quality problems have dogged this venture by Rover into the USA with a rebadged Rover 2.5 liter (2.7 liter from 1989) which used chassis and drive-train from the Honda Acura.

STERLING • USA 1917-1923

The Ams-Sterling of 1917 was a roadster with an ohv 2081cc LeRoi four-cylinder engine. Later models also used a Herschell-Spillman six.

STERLING-KNIGHT • USA 1921, 1923-1926

Sterling-Knight started in Cleveland, Ohio, with 1921 models, but suspended production that year owing to lack of capital. After reorganization, with a factory in Warren, Ohio, production started anew in 1923 and continued until mid-1926. The cars featured a Knight-type six-cylinder engine and bodies by Phillips. Between 425 and 450 were built.

STEUDEL • Germany 1903-1909

Best known as a producer of car and marine engines, Steudel in its early years built small two- and four-cylinder cars with proprietary engines made by De Dion, Aster and Fafnir, of up to 16 hp.

STEVENS • England 1976-1978

Already involved in the manufacture of custom-built delivery vans, Tony Stevens ventured into the realm of sports car manufacture with the two-seater Sienna in 1976. Based on the Reliant Kitten, the Sienna was capable of 60 mpg. Despite interest from Reliant, the project never got off the ground.

The "Distinctive" Stewart Six, 1913

1936 Steyr 22PS streamline sedan

STEVENS-DURYEA • USA 1900-1927

J Frank Duryea, having quarrelled with his brother Charles, joined Stevens Arms & Tools of Chicopee Falls, Mass., which began production in the Overman factory of a 6 hp horizontal-twin Victoria Stanhope with tiller steering, joined in 1905 by a 20 hp four of conventional appearance. In 1905 came the 9.6-liter Big Six with three-point suspension of its engine gearbox unit. From 1907 the company concentrated on big sixes. The last new model was the 1915 Model D 7.7-liter. Frank Duryea sold his share in the company that year, and production was suspended until 1920, when the Model D was revived; as Model E. Later, in 1923, the marque was taken over by Ray M. Owen (of Owen Magnetic,) and the plant built Raulang electric cars and coachwork. Few Stevens-Duryeas were built after 1924.

STEWART • USA 1915-1916

The Stewart, like the Renault, sported a sloping hood and had its radiator mounted at the rear of the engine. Roadsters and touring cars were available, and a Continental six-cylinder engine was used. Price of the touring model was $1,950. The Stewart Company is better known for its commercial vehicles, which were manufactured from 1912 to 1942.

STEWART • USA 1922-1923

The petrol-powered Stewart was successor to the Stewart-Coats Steamer, which itself was connected with the Coats Steam Car. Stewart offered three models, a four (using a Herschell-Spillman engine) and two sixes, the "Royal Palm" which featured a Rutenber, and a larger model powered by what purported to be an engine of Stewart"s own design. It is thought that no more than a single pilot model of each type (if that) made up the total production.

STEWART-COATS • USA 1922

An offshoot of the Coats Steam Car, operations were located in Columbus and Bowling Green, Ohio. Only a pilot model was made.

The Steyr-built Mercedes 4wd G

STEYR • Austria 1920 to date

Hans Ledwinka, famous creator of Nesselsdorf and Tatra cars, joined the Steyr armaments works in 1917. Its first car appeared on the market in 1920 with a 12/40 hp six-cylinder ohc engine of 3325cc; a sv 1814cc four-cylinder model followed. The Six underwent much development until 1929, Ledwinka returning to Tatra in 1923. In 1926 a smaller six-cylinder model of 1560cc appeared, followed by yet another ohc version, this time of 4014cc. The first models had pointed radiators, later cars flat coolers; most engines used a single overhead-camshaft. The range of models also included ohv 2078cc sixes and also the ohv 1990cc Steyr 120S. In 1929-30 Ferdinand Porsche designed a new luxurious Steyr, the straight-eight "Austria," which never went into production.

In 1934 the factory merged with the Puch combine, of which Austro-Daimler was part; that was the end of Austro-Daimler cars. The first small Steyr was the Type 100 of 1934, with a sv 1385cc four-cylinder engine; in 1937 came the 1498cc Type 200, which was also available (as Type 220) with an ohv 2260cc power unit. The 1158cc Steyr 55 of 1938 was small and very streamlined. It had a sv flat-four engine and was the successor to the Type 50 984cc of 1936. From 1949 onward Steyr assembled Fiat cars from Austria; from 1957 onward it built the Fiat 500 as the Steyr-Puch 500 with an own-make flat twin-cylinder engine, built mainly at the Graz (Puch) factory. Steyr was also connected with the assembly of Opel cars in the mid-1930s. In 1979 it began manufacture of 4wd vehicles for Mercedes.

STILSON • USA 1907-1910

Stilson offered big Herschell-Spillman-engined sixes with an early form of hydraulically controlled clutch.

STIMSON • England 1972 to date

A six-wheeled, mini-powered, open-topped, go-anywhere vehicle with fully independent suspension. Available complete or in kit form.

STIMULA • France 1907-1914

This company, from St Chamond, Loire, offered an 8 hp single, as well as fours from 10/12 hp to h16/20 hp.

STIRLING • Scotland 1897-1903

Stirling, of Hamilton, Lanarkshire, an old-established coachbuilder, built its first 4 hp Stirling-Daimler in January 1897, on Coventy-Daimler lines. Until 1900 it built its own dog-cart and waggonette bodies on Coventry-Daimler chassis, and then imported the archaic Clément-Panhard voiturette, which it sold as the Clement-Stirling or Stirling-Panhard. After 1903 the company manufactured only trucks.

STIRLING • USA 1920-1921

An assembled car, the Newark, New Jersey-built Stirling had a six-cylinder Continental engine; the five-passenger touring car was priced at $2,350. Only six Stirling cars were built.

STODDARD-DAYTON • USA 1904-1913

The first examples of this highly-regarded marque from Dayton had 4605cc Rutenber engines; sixes were available from 1907. Stoddard-Dayton became part of the US Motor Company, and went down when that failed. The final range consisted of three fours, the 3707cc "Savoy," the 4766cc "Stratford" and the 5808cc "Saybrook," and a massive Knight sleeve-valve six of 8691cc.

1930 Stoewer fwd sedan

STOEWER • Germany 1899-1939

Emil and Bernhard Stoewer were pioneers of the German car industry. They owned an iron works at Stettin (now in Poland) and produced first De Dion-engined three-wheelers and then rear-engined 2080cc twin-cylinder cars. Other twin-cylinder models had 1526cc and 2280cc power units. The first four-cylinder Stoewer was of 3052cc; 1906 saw a new 5880cc four-cylinder and even an 8829cc six-cylinder. Four-cylinder models of 1501cc and 2544cc followed. In 1910 Stoewer cars were built under license by Mathis of Strasbourg. An ohv 11,160cc six-cylinder, which had a modified Loutzky-designed aero engine, was built soon after the First World War, in which Stoewer had produced the aero engines under Argus license to use up surplus parts. A racing version of this was successfully driven by works driver Emil Kordewan. A smaller racing car of 2490cc had a four-cylinder ohc engine and streamlined bodywork. Production after 1918 included 1570cc, 2120cc, and 2292cc four-cylinder models and sv six-cylinder cars with 3107cc and 3383cc engines. The year 1928 saw the introduction of 1997cc and 2462cc straight-eight models. There was also the 3974cc eight-cylinder Gigant (also available in a 3633cc version,) while the Marschall had eight cylinders displacing 2963cc. The last big Stoewer was the beautiful 4905cc 100 hp straight-eight Repräsentant. Stoewer was for many years a typical family business, with the founder-owners and their families taking an active part. Unfortunately the factory ran into financial difficulties and, after a reorganization in the early 1930s, the founders left the works.

Economic reasons led to the manufacture of cheaper cars in the 1930s. The first, in 1931, was an 1188cc V-4 with fwd. The Greif-Junior was built under Tatra license, with an ohv air-cooled 1474cc flat-four engine from 1936 to 1939. Own-design engines were used in 1354cc, 1460cc, and 2390cc four-cylinder models, the ohv six-cylinder 3585cc Arcona and the 2488cc V-8 Greif. During the Second World War Stoewer supplied cars to the German forces, but the works were not rebuilt after extensive damage in an air raid.

STOKVIS • Holland c. 1913

Built by W J Stokvis of Arnhem, the Stokvis is believed to have been a prototype only.

STOLLE • Germany 1925

An advanced design, the ohc 1494cc four-cylinder Stolle sports car developed 40 bhp, and was the work of famous motorcycle designer Martin Stolle of BMW, Victoria, and D-Rad fame. Only a few Stolle cars had been built when Hugo Stinnes, who was backing the venture, died suddenly; Vorster & Stolle, the Munich-based factory, had to close.

1913 2016cc Knight-engined Stoneleigh torpedo

1925 Stolle

STONEBOW • England 1900-1902

Named for an ancient gateway near the premises of its begetter, R M Wright of Lincoln. The Stonebow dog-cart, available with 5 hp or 7 hp engine, was probably built by Payne & Bates of Coventry, makers of the Godiva.

STONELEIGH • England 1912-1914, 1922-1924

A 12 hp four-cylinder model, the Stoneleigh had a conventionally-mounted radiator, unlike its sister marque, Siddeley-Deasy, which used a dashboard cooler. The post-war Stoneleigh light car had a vee-twin 1-liter power unit, reputedly designed to use war-surplus aero-engine cylinders.

STORCK • USA 1901-1903

Selling at $725-800, this was a light steam runabout assembled by cycle agent Frank Storck of Red Bank, NJ.

STORERO • Italy 1912-1919

Storero of Turin produced a 4396cc 20/30hp and a 6280cc 24/80 hp version. Designer was Cesare Scacchi.

STOREY • England 1920-1930

Although early examples of the marque used proprietary engines (Coventry-Simplex and Chapuis-Dornier,) at the end of 1920 engines of Storey Motors" own manufacture were used in 10, 12, 15.9, and 20 hp forms. The earlier cars were fitted with rear-axle-mounted gearboxes, but the unit reverted to a more conventional position with these later power units. The company was reconstituted in 1921, production being transferred from Tonbridge, Kent, to Clapham Park, London. Initially, Storey engines were fitted, though later on Meadows power units were featured. Another reconstruction in 1925 saw three models listed: 10/25 and 14/40 fours plus a 17/70 six-cylinder, though production by this stage had been reduced to a trickle.

STORK KAR • USA 1919-1921

A typical assembled car, with a four-cylinder Lycoming engine, the Stork Kar was identical to a number of others of its type, including the Norwalk and the Marshall (which is hardly surprising, as all of these were made by Piedmont.) The Stork Kar differed only in featuring right-hand steering for the export market.

STOTT • England 1903

Made in Manchester, the Stott was built to individual order with either 9 hp single-cylinder or 12 hp twin-cylinder power units.

STOUT • USA 1946

William Bushnell Stout was once credited with "more technical innovations than any man since Edison". He designed a car which had neither axles nor chassis, the wheels simply being attached to the body. Suspension was by compressed air cylinders and the engine was rear-mounted. It was one of the earliest cars to use glassfiber extensively. Stout built these 137-inch-wheelbase cars as experimental exercises, but the Consolidated-Vultee Aircraft Corp held the rights to manufacture.

STRADA • England 1974-1975

Though exhibited at the London motor show in 1974, the mid-engined Strada never went into serious production. Its striking mid-engined glassfiber-bodied design nevertheless caused quite a stir.

1914 Straker-Squire 15/20 hp Standard Limousine

STRAKER-SQUIRE • England 1906-1926

Starting with license-production of the French Cornilleau St Beuve 25 hp, Sidney Straker & Squire of Bristol (builder of steam "lurries" from 1901,) progressed to the 16/20 hp "Car for the Connoisseur" in 1907 (a sister company built the 12/14 hp Shamrock.) Roy Fedden designed the 15 hp Straker-Squire of 1908, the marque's most successful model. During the First World War Straker Squire built Rolls-Royce Eagle aero engines; the general lines of this power unit were used in the post-war model which appeared in prototype form in 1918. Produced at Edmonton, North London, this 24/80 hp Straker-Squire had an ohc 4-liter engine with six separately-cast cylinders, but this "Aeroplane of the Road" didn"t reach production until 1921, and the old 15 hp had to be revived as a stop-gap. A 1460cc Dorman-engined sports appeared in 1923, too late to save the company from receivership in 1924.

1924 Straker-Squire 24/80 hp

STRATHMORE • USA 1899-1912

In the optimistic tone of its day, this Boston, Mass., firm advertised "motor vehicles built to order–carriages, coaches, runabouts". These were illustrated by a dramatic picture of a nine-seated stagecoach-like vehicle, apparently steam-powered, careering along with no visible means of control.

STRATTON • USA 1922-1923

The Stratton (sometimes spelled "Strattan") was absorbed by Premier before more than one or two prototypes were built. Because of its new parent company, the name occasionally crops up as "Premier-Stratton" or "Stratton-Premier" in automobile trade journals of the time. The car had an own-make four-cylinder engine. Price of the touring car was $575.

STREATHAM • England 1902

These were 6 hp single- and 8 hp twin-cylinder cars, the brakes of which could be "made to act backwards as well as forwards".

STRINGER • USA 1901

A four-cylinder steamer from Marion, Ohio.

STRINGER-WINCO • England 1921-1932

The Stringer-Winco light car used a four-cylinder 1088cc Alpha engine. In 1922 the company produced the Stringer Type S or Stringer-Smith, using an 11.9 hp Meadows engine. Alpha engines of 9 hp and 11 hp featured in later models.

STROMMEN • Norway 1933-1940

The Strommen factory built advanced buses with unitary construction and assembled American Dodge cars. Some of the special long-wheelbase versions were known simply as Strommen, though they were Dodge-based.

STUART • England 1906-1907

A de luxe version of the Starling, the Stuart was a 7 hp twin-cylinder shaft-drive car, available with two-, three-, or four-seater bodywork.

STUDEBAKER • USA 1902-1964

See panel overleaf

STURGES • USA 1895

A crude four-seater electric carriage, built in Chicago.

STURTEVANT • USA 1904-1908

From 1905 this 7800cc four-cylinder roadster from Boston used a primitive automatic transmission.

STUTZ • USA 1911-1935

Harry Stutz of Indianapolis built a racing car in five weeks, to prove the quality of his gearbox rear-axle unit, and entered it in the first Indianapolis 500-mile race in 1900. It finished 11th, earning the slogan "the car that made good in a day". Production of Stutz cars, powered by 6.3-liter Wisconsin engines, began soon after. In 1914 came the archetypal Stutz, the stark Bearcat speedster, promoted by the racing successes of the "White Squadron" Stutz team, with highly non-standard 16-valve 4851cc

STUDEBAKER • USA 1902-1964

Founded as a wagon builder in 1854 in South Bend, Indiana, Studebaker was the "largest vehicle house in the world" by 1875. Turn-of-the-century orders for automobile chassis led to the building of 20 Studebaker electrics in 1902. The first gasoline Studebakers (actually built by Garford) appeared in 1904, joined by a cheaper range (built by EMF) in 1908. Studebaker and EMF merged in 1910 as the Studebaker Corporation, and the Garford, EMF and Flanders models were all phased out. A two-car line, the 3146cc four and 4736cc six, appeared in 1914, the four being replaced by a new 3392cc Light Six in 1920, when a Big Six of 5810cc was also available alongside the old Special Six. A straight-eight, the President, was launched in 1928, and the sixes renamed Dictator and Commander, acquiring smaller eights in 1929. From 1928 to 1933, when it was declared bankrupt, Studebaker owned Pierce-Arrow. The receivers sold this off, dropped the President 8 and launched new sixes using the engine from the discontinued Rockne to put Studebaker back in business.

Raymond Loewy was hired as styling consultant in 1936, the embarrassingly named "Dictator" was toppled in 1938, and a new small six, the 2687cc Champion, appeared in the 1939 model year, pushing sales in both 1940 and 1941 over the 100,000 mark. Studebaker was one of the first companies to launch brand-new post-war models, in May 1946. Styling was by Loewy, with front fenders blending into the body and a full-width grille combining to earn this range, Champion and Commander, with 2786cc or 3704 sv sixes, the "coming or going?" nickname. The 1950 models had a cyclops headlamp, and Studebaker"s first V-8, a 3802cc unit, appeared in 1951. New Studebakers, the 2769cc Champion six, the V-8 Commander and the Land Cruiser, appeared in 1953, with classic styling by Robert E Bourke, chief designer of the Loewy studios; chromium plate and a wraparound windshield impaired its looks in 1955, after the Packard takeover.

The Loewy studios produced a neat reskinning of the existing body to produce the 1956 Flight Hawk (3032cc six,) Power Hawk (3671cc V-8,) Sky Hawk (4244cc V-8) and Golden Hawk (5768cc Packard V-8.) However, sales continued to fall, unchecked by the launch of the frugal Scotsman, powered by the old sv six. There was a disastrous facelift in 1958, with grafted-on dual headlamps and tailfins, though the compact Lark of 1959 (readied for production by stylist Duncan McRae in just ten months) reversed the slipping sales to some extent; the only other 1959 Studebaker was the 4736cc Silver Hawk V-8. A wider Lark range was available in 1962, and midway through the year the distinctive glassfiber-bodied Avanti sport coupé was announced. Power was by the 4736cc V-8, with optional supercharger, in which form an Avanti took 29 stock car records. But the Avanti, the elegant Lark and the Hawk GT of 1962-1964 came too late to avert new financial difficulties which resulted in production being transferred to Canada in 1964, where Studebaker struggled along fitfully until 1966.

Studebaker 25/30 hp six-cylinder tourer, c. 1915

1923 Studebaker Big Six Four-Seat Speedster

1956 Studebaker Silver Hawk

1963 Studebaker Lark convertible

Wisconsin engines. A 1916 Bearcat broke the trans-America record, taking 11 days 7½ hours for the trip. In 1919 Harry Stutz left to build the HCS, and the company came under the control of steel tycoon Charles Schwab, whereupon Stutz began building its own four- and six-cylinder engines. The last Bearcat was the 4.7-liter Speedway Six of 1924.

Frederick E Moscovics acquired Stutz in 1925 and brought in Belgian designer Paul Bastien, late of Métallurgique, whose ohc 4.7-liter Safety Stutz Vertical Eight was an extremely low-built car, boasting four-wheel hydraulic brakes and wire-mesh safety glass. A Stutz Black Hawk Speedster finished second in the 1928 Le Mans 24 Hour Race. The Black Hawk six of 1929 ranks as a separate marque. In 1931 came a revived Bearcat with the twin ohc DV 32 power unit and a guaranteed 160 km/h (100 mph) top speed. From 1928 to 1938 Stutz offered a rear-engined light van, the Pak-Age-Car, but car production ceased in 1935.

STUTZ • USA 1970 to date

The Stutz Blackhawk is not a facsimile of the original classic, but a modern luxury car styled by Virgil Exner. The Stutz Motor Company of America took the Stutz name because it epitomized the best money could buy. The new Stutz is hand-assembled in Italy by Carrozzeria of Modena, using a Pontiac V-8 and modified Pontiac chassis.

STUYVESANT • USA 1911-1912

A big, costly ($4,200) 9.4-liter six from Sandusky, Ohio.

SUBARU/Japan 1958 to date

Part of the former Nakajima Aircraft Company, Fuji Sangyo was organized in 1945, then re-formed in 1950 by order of the occupying Allied forces into 12 smaller companies, of which five became Fuji Heavy Industries in 1953, building scooters, railway rolling stock and aircraft power units. They joined the Nissan heavy industries company in 1968. Their first car, the 360, with a rear-mounted two-stroke engine, appeared in 1966, and in 1968 came the 997cc front-engined, front-wheel-drive FE, with all-round independent suspension. A 1088cc version appeared in 1970, followed a year later by a 1300cc model. Although it was an established name in its home Japanese market in the 1960s and 1970s, it was not until the 1980s that the brand became a significant marque in the USA, Britain and, latterly, Europe. The company made its first inroads into these markets by selling small pick-up trucks, notably to the agricultural sector. By carving itself a niche and extolling its brand icon as a supplier of full-time 4wd cars, notably estates/station wagons, Subaru made its wider name. By going rallying and winning the world rally championship, Subaru earned worldwide headlines and a high profile. The 200 bhp 4wd Imprezza model in road-going rally-type specification became a cult car and sales success overnight.

The earlier Subaru line-up saw models such as the Leone series; the 1978 models used 1361cc and 1595cc engines and the Complex range included two 4wd models. The Rex minicar range had a low-emissions 544cc four-stroke engine. A new Rex appeared in 1981, and two years later a 4 x 4 Rex was launched, with a turbo engine on offer from 1984. A constantly variable transmission was introduced in 1987. The Justy, launched as a prototype in 1983, was available in 1992 with 1.1 and 1.2-liter engines and selectable 4x4 transmission. In a complicated deal, the later Justy model emerged as a reworked Suzuki Swift, with 4wd added, and the car is built in Hungary rather than in Japan. Subaru is said to be the world's largest producer of 4x4 passenger cars. The rally-going flat-four Legacy

Subaru Legacy 4wd Estate/Wagon

1928 Stutz Black Hawk Special, an attempt to take the world land speed record

1991 The restyled Subaru Legacy, rallying version

1933 Stutz Super Bearcat

Subaru Imprezza 4wd Turbo Sedan, 1990

has permanent 4wd; in 1991 it was restyled and given new power units, including a high-performance 2.0-liter 4 CAM Turbo engine. A new SVX sports coupé was outlined for 1992, and it showed a new, more advanced style for the company.

Throughout the 1990s Subaru retained its individuality, sticking to its flat-four engine design and perfecting the four-wheel-drive technology that had become its trademark. In the USA the company greatly extended its market share, and further rally success and a range of cars that extended its remit, such as the Forester model of 1998, created a 4wd, sport utility range of wide appeal. In Europe the Legacy turbo estate became a firm favourite within the estate/shooting brake market. Despite being seen earlier as a smaller, niched car maker, Subaru has established itself as a growing marque with firm foundations.

SUBURBAN • USA 1911-1912

A De Schaum venture, the Suburban Limited was a 4261cc six, available in three styles.

SUCCESS • USA 1906-1909

A crude high-wheeler buggy with the single-cylinder two-stroke engine mounted on the side of the body, the Success, from St Louis, Missouri, was claimed to cover 100 miles per gallon. With iron-tyred wheels it sold for $250. John C. Higdon, head of the Success Auto-Buggy Manufacturing Co, had built his first horseless carriage in 1896.

SUERE • France 1905-1931

Established in Paris, Suére started with a 763cc single-cylinder car, replaced by a four-cylinder 1592cc Ballot-powered model in 1913. After the war it presented a 1413cc sv V-8. In 1921 there was an 1874cc four-cylinder Ballot-engined car, followed in 1925 by an Altos-engined 1990cc six. After that, Suére made cars with SCAP and CIME proprietary engines from 1500cc to 2000cc.

SULTAN • France • USA 1903-1910

Sultan cars were built by Martin & Lethimonnier of Paris. Martin, who had experience of American manufacturing methods, was the designer; he also designed an "excellent hydraulic clutch". Robust and elegant, Sultan cars had the cylinders cast separately, with brass water-jackets. The 1907 range consisted of 6/9 hp, 9/12 hp, 13/18 hp, and 20/30 hp models; that year, too, a 7897cc car was built for (and failed to start in) the Kaiserpreis. In August 1907 Martin drove one of his cars (they were also known as Martin-Lethimonniers) in the Criterium de France. On the outskirts of Bordeaux he collided with another competitor in a Peugeot and was killed, together with his works driver, Villemain. It was doubtless Martin's American connections which brought about the creation of the Sultan Motors Corporation of Springfield, Mass., a branch of the Otis Elevator Company, which began building Sultans for the American market in 1906. Like the French company, it went out of business in 1910.

SUMINOE • Japan 1954-1955

A Tokyo bodybuilder made this spindly "Flying Feather" two-seater powered by a rear-mounted 350cc twin-cylinder engine.

SUMMIT • Australia 1922-1926

Advertised as a "New Wonder Car," the conventionally designed Summit tourer was unusual in several ways. It was very well equipped, down to a radio and electric stop lights (in 1922,) and came with a full 12 months' warranty. The power unit was a four-cylinder Lycoming engine of 3.4 liters. An unusual mechanical feature was the use of triplex combination springs running the full length of the chassis frame. It is not known how many cars were built, but only one survives.

SUN • Germany 1906-1908

Founded in Berlin by Paul and Emil Jeannin, Sun produced big and expensive cars with four-cylinder engines from 22 hp to 75 hp. Paul Jeannin was a designer with Argus in earlier years. Most cars had shaft-drive, some models retained chain-drive.

Suzuki 4wd the Vitara

SUN • USA 1921-1924

The Sun Runabout, from Toledo, had a 22 hp ohv Cameron air-cooled engine.

SUNBEAM, SUNBEAM-TALBOT • England 1899-1976

See panel

SUP • France 1919-1922

The Société Usines de Paquis, from Méziéres (Ardennes) showed 10 hp cars at the 1919 Paris Salon. The marque was closely linked with Hinstin.

SUPER • France 1912-1914

Levíque of Ruby built this belt-drive tandem-seat cyclecar, with single- or twin-cylinder motorcycle engines.

SUPERIOR • Germany 1905-1906

This bicycle manufacturer assembled Fafnir-built Omnimobil components, fitted 6 hp twincylinder 704cc engines, and called the result "Superior".

Suzuki Cappuccino

SUPERIOR • Canada 1911-1912

A four-cylinder 25 hp engine powered this assembled car from the Ontario oil town of Petrolia.

SURREY • England 1921-1930

This assembled light car from Putney, London, used some Model T Ford parts and a Coventry-Climax engine. Later, Meadows engines of 9.8 hp and 11.8 hp were available.

SURRIDGE • England 1912-1913

The Surridge Cyclar was a cyclecar produced by a firm of accessory factors from Camberwell, London. It had a twin-cylinder 978cc Fafnir engine and a five-speed friction transmission.

SUZUKI • Japan 1955 to date

Founded in 1909 as Suzuki Shokkuki Seisakusho, this famous Hamamatsu motorcycle firm did not enter the car

1906 Sunbeam 16 hp six-cylinder tourer

1913 12/16 hp Sunbeam tourer

SUNBEAM, SUNBEAM-TALBOT • England
1899-1976

Like many of its contemporaries, Sunbeam was bicycle manufacturer which went into the motor business. Its first car, the Sunbeam-Mabley, was a strange device, looking rather like a Victorian sofa on wheels, powered by a single-cylinder 326cc engine. More conventional were the Thomas Pullinger-designed models based on the French Berliet car. These 12 hp Sunbeams were solidly-made fours, produced between 1902 and 1905. Six-cylinder engines put in a brief appearance between 1904 and 1907. In 1909 the Breton designer Louis Coatalen joined the Wolverhampton company; he was responsible for the cars which achieved a sensational 1-2-3 victory for the marque in the Coupe de l'Auto race of 1912. This was with a modified version of the sv 3-liter 12/16 hp model, which remained in production until 1921. The Sunbeam, Talbot, Darracq combine was created in 1920. The 16 hp and 24 hp Sunbeam models received ohv in 1922, while a six-cylinder car, the 16/50hp, joined the range in 1924. A magnificent dohc 3-liter six-cylinder was announced for 1924 and made in small numbers until 1930. The company's racing programme was maintained, the marque's outstanding victory being Segrave's win in the 1923 French Grand Prix, the first British GP victory. He repeated his success at the following year's San Sebastian event. Sunbeams maintained their careful, well-engineered designs into the 1930s, a new model being the 2.9-liter Speed model of 1933 (though the Dawn of the following year, with its ohv 1.6-liter four-cylinder engine, was hardly in the Coatalen traditions.)

1955 Sunbeam Alpine

The collapse of the unwieldy STD combine in 1935 saw a takeover by the Rootes Group. Consequently there were no Sunbeams in 1938 and the name was combined with Talbot to create the Sunbeam-Talbot of 1939. Sunbeam-Talbots were merely luxury versions of Hillman and Humber models. The Sunbeam name did not reappear in its own right until 1953, with the announcement of the Sunbeam Alpine, a two-seater variant of the Sunbeam Talbot 90. Three years later came the Hillman Minx-based Rapier, starting with a 1.4-liter engine, later increased to 1.5 liters. On the sports car front, further versions of the Alpine theme followed; in 1964 came the Tiger, basically an Alpine fitted with a 4.3 liter Ford V-8. An exercise in badge engineering was the Sunbeam Stiletto, a coupé version of the Hillman Imp, though the fastback Rapier of 1968 was a distinctive offering. "Sunbeam" was used as a model name for the front-engined Chrysler of 1977, a far cry from its Grand Prix ancestry.

1925 Sunbeam 20/60 hp six-cylinder tourer

1963 Sunbeam Alpine GT Coupé

Sunbeam enthusiast Bob Baxter in a Sunbeam Alpine Roadster, with Talbot Sedan post-war classic behind

1903 Swift 6 hp two-seater

1929 10 hp Swift Migrant Sun or Shade Sedan

field until 1955, with the Suzulite 360 utility car. The fwd Fronte 360 appeared in 1967, followed a year later by the Fronte 500. As well as an updated version of the Fronte, Suzuki now also offers the Jimmy, a light (539cc, three-cylinder) 4wd utility model. In 1982 Suzuki launched the 4x4 SJ series (Samurai) powered by a 1.3 liter ohc I-4 engine. Suzuki has factories in Canada, Taiwan, and Spain as well as Japan. Launched in 1982, the 3-cylinder Alto gained 4wd in 1984. A turbocharger was available from 1987. In 1988 Suzuki launched the Vitara 5-door, with the Vitara JLX SE Estate following in 1991. The Swift (Cultus) line dates back to 1983: the Swift 1.6 had permanent 4wd. From 1993 the Swift was also built in Hungary.

SVELTE • France 1906-1907

A range of cars from 16 hp to 50 hp, built by a well-known small-arms and bicycle works of St Etienne (Loire.)

SVP • France 1905-1906

An 8 hp two-seater with belt intermediate transmission.

SWALLOW • England 1922

Two models of Swallow were built. One had a twin-cylinder Blackburne engine and the other a four-cylinder Dorman. A two-speed epicyclic gearbox featured in both instances.

SWALLOW DORETTI • England 1954-1955

Built by a Walsall coachbuilding company descended from Swallow Sidecars (parent of SS cars,) this sports car used Triumph TR2 engine and drive-train in a tubular chassis with elegant two-seat bodywork.

SWAN • France 1922-1923

"Four cylinders, four speeds, four seats" was the slogan promoting M Bloch's Altos-engined light cars, of 1328cc, 1359cc, and 1779cc, from Neuilly (Seine.)

SWEANY • USA 1895

Dr F L Sweany's steam carriage, built by the Chas. S Caffrey Company of Camden, NJ, was driven by four 3 hp motors, one for each wheel. It failed to reach production.

SWIFT • England 1900-1931

Swift of Coventry had made sewing machines and bicycles long before it went into the car business; its first car used the famous De Dion Bouton engine. Although early examples were probably made from assembled French parts, in 1904 a Swift-designed voiturette was announced, though it still had a 4.5 hp De Dion engine. Other proprietary engines by Simms and Aster featured on some later models, though the 1906 10 hp was significant in having a Swift-designed engine. Although this was a twin, a four-cylinder 10 hp car appeared in 1912. After the war the company unfortunately became embroiled in the ill-fated Harper Bean combine, which did little to aid its finances. Post-war models included the aforementioned Ten and a new Twelve, which appeared in 1920. The Ten was modernized in 1923 with a detachable cylinder head and unit construction engine and gearbox, the Twelve later receiving a similar facelift. A 17.9 hp 18/50 hp arrived in 1925. A new Ten appeared later in 1930 and in 1931, the last year of production, the cheap 8 hp Cadet at £149 did not sell in large enough numbers to save the old-established concern.

SYRENA • Poland 1956 to date

The Syrena is a three-cylinder two-stroke of 842cc built by Fabryka Samochodow Osobowych in Warsaw. It has changed little since its introduction.

SZAWE • Germany 1921-1924

Szawes were expensively-built luxury cars designed by Georg Bergmann for Szabo & Wechselmann, a Berlin coachbuilder. The range included a sv 2536cc four-cylinder with an engine and chassis built for Szawe by NAG. Szawe's masterpiece was the ohc 2570cc six-cylinder with fully-enclosed valve-gear. Szawe production was limited; the last cars were made by the Ehrhardt works until production came to an end in 1924.

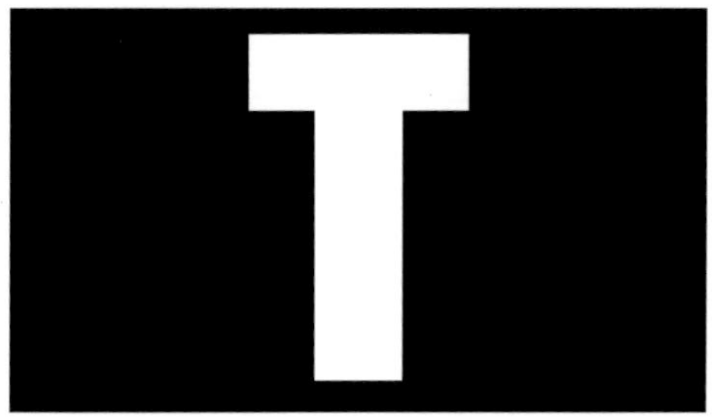

TAGA (La Ford Francisée) Torpédo Sport Luxe

TAG • Switzerland 1978

Shown at the 1978 Paris Salon, the TAG "Function Car" was a Cadillac-based six-wheeler incorporating a telecommunications center. The price was around £120,000, depending whether or not the car was bullet-proofed.

TAGA • France 1921

A Model T Ford-based car from Courbevoie, Seine, with Rolls-Royce-like radiator.

TAINE • France 1907-1909

An obscure four-cylinder light car from Asniéres (Seine,) also sold as "La Joyeuse."

TAKURI • Japan 1907-1909

Japan's first production gasoline car, the Takura was built in Tokyo to the design of Komano-suke Uchiyama. About a dozen of these 1875cc flat-twins were built.

TALBOT • England 1903-1938, **1979 to date**

See panel

TALBOT (TALBOT-LAGO) • France 1920-1959, **1979 to date**

Known as Darracq to 1920, Talbot of Suresnes, Seine, was acquired that year by the British Sunbeam-Talbot combine. For some years cars were made on both sides of the Channel under the joint names of Talbot Darracq. This led to some confusion, for they were sold from France as Talbot and from England as Darracq. The same confusion happened with the firm's racing cars. The first models to leave the Suresnes factory after the merger were the 18/20, the four-cylinder ohv 10cv (1505cc) and 12/14cv (2950cc) as well as the 4594cc V-8, discontinued in 1923. The four-cylinder models were built until 1926. In 1927 came the excellent six-cylinder Talbots, available in three versions; 2687cc, 2915cc and the 3027cc sports model. In 1930 Talbot presented a straight-eight of 3800cc, of which very few were made.

1913 25 hp Talbot (London) sports two-seater

1919 Talbot 25/50 hp limousine-landaulette

1914 publicity for the London-built Talbot

1930 Talbot (London) six-cylinder 75 sedan

TALBOT • England 1903-1938, **1979 to date**

The origins of the Talbot go back to 1903, when a syndicate, financed by the Earl of Shrewsbury and Talbot, was formed to build French Cléments for the English market. They were initially known as Clement-Talbots, though the French connection was gradually dropped and the Talbot slowly emerged as a marque in its own right. As befitted the times, a variety of models was offered, from an 11 hp twin to a mighty 50 hp four-cylinder. The year 1906 saw the first of the truly British Talbots, a 3.8-liter 20 hp car. This and the 12/16 were fairly fleet of foot and established a competitive reputation for themselves. By 1914 the range included a six-cylinder model and a 4.5-liter 25 hp car, later known as the 25/50.

Although the company became enmeshed in the Sunbeam-Talbot-Darracq combine after the First World War, Georges Roesch, an outstanding Swiss engineer who had joined Talbot in 1916, was responsible for the 10/23 of 1923, which complemented some of the models of the pre-war range. Roesch's next car was the pushrod ohv 1666cc 14/45, a refined and well-engineered six with significantly light valve gear, offered alongside the older 20/60 model in 1927 and 1928, though it was the company's sole model for the following two years. From this sprang the 75 and 90 variants for 1931, while the following year the 3-liter 105 with new six-cylinder engine appeared, remaining in production until 1937. The ultimate development of this theme came with the 110 of 1935, having a larger bore than the 105, giving 3.5 liters.

These fast, quiet and reliable cars lent themselves naturally to sporting activities, 3rd and 4th places being attained at the Le Mans 24 Hour Race in 1930, with class wins at the Irish Grand Prix, the Ulster Tourist Trophy race and the Brooklands 500 Mile event. The 105 similarly lent itself to the racing circuits, chalking up a 3rd place at Le Mans in 1932. Unfortunately, at the end of 1932 the factory association with the Tolworth concern of Fox and Nicholl (which prepared these splendid machines for the circuits) came to an end, though this did not prevent a team of 105s from attaining a joint win (with the Adler team) in the 1934 Alpine Rally, an event they had also won in 1932.

Tragically, in 1935 the Rootes Group took control of Clement-Talbot. A concern with a background of sales, rather than engineering, was hardly likely to look sympathetically on Roesch and his intelligently created cars, and in 1936 a Rootes Talbot Ten, with Hillman Minx ancestry, appeared. In 1938 the marque was renamed Sunbeam-Talbot. In 1979 new owner Peugeot renamed the old Chrysler UK marques Talbot, but the Talbot Alpine, Solara, Horizon, and Samba models were replaced by Peugeot ones in 1986..

A Tamplin cyclecar taking part in a 1922 trial

1898 Tauzin twin-cylinder

c. 1904 Tarrant tonneau

In 1935 the old French factory saw the arrival of brilliant engineer Anthony Lago, who modified the six to create the Talbot-Lago Special engine of 4000cc. After the war Talbot-Lago had a great racing history with the wonderful 4483cc ohv six-cylinders. Its "Record" models sold very well. In 1955 Talbot-Lago presented a 2500cc coupé with Maserati engine, and a "Baby" 2.7-liter. BMW 2.6-liter engines were then used, and the last of the line had Simca power. Post-takeover Talbot models included the Horizon (1978,) Solara (1979,) Tagora (1981,) and Samba (1981) before Peugeot dropped the marque.

TAM • France 1914-1926

The Société des Travaux Automobiles et Mécaniques started in Boulogne, Seine, with a 12 hp 1874cc car. In 1920 it presented 8/10 hp Altos-engined 1328cc cars and 12 hp Decolange-engined cars of 2001cc.

TAMM • Germany 1922

A friction-driven light car with an air-cooled 678cc vee-twin motorcycle engine.

TAMPLIN • England 1919-1927

Captain Carden, who had also been responsible for the Carden of pre-war days, also created the Tamplin, which used a JAP vee-twin engine, drive being by chain and belt. Independent front suspension was a progressive feature, although tandem seating, a la Bédelia, must have had its drawbacks. A conventional two-seater layout came in 1922; later examples were fitted with Blackburne engines.

TANKETTE • England 1920

The Tankette was a strange device, a diminutive three-wheeler driven by a 2.75 hp single-cylinder two-stroke Union engine.

TARKINGTON • USA 1923

Reputedly designed by the brother of American novelist Booth Tarkington (as was the abortive Canadian Brock automobile,) this was a relatively expensive car which never reached the market. Featuring a 126-inch wheelbase and a six-cylinder engine of its own make, the first pilot models were built in 1923, although the company had been organized three years earlier.

TARRANT • Australia 1897-1907

Colonel Harley Tarrant made the first serious attempt to produce gasoline-driven cars for general sale in Australia. His first model had a 6 hp Benz engine, but the later cars were fitted with locally made two- and four-cylinder units. Despite success in local motor sport, Tarrant cars failed to sell well, as the limited production made them very expensive. It is doubtful if Tarrant sold more than 16 cars. Two survive.

TATE • Canada 1912-1914

The Windsor-built "aristocrat of electrics" used Tate's powerful "Bifunctional" batteries. A full range, from roadsters to coupés, was offered.

TATIN • France 1898-1899

A steam-driven tricycle of simple design was Tatin's first offering, followed by a gawky tiller-steered, three-wheeled steam carriage, built by the Société Européenne d'Automobile of Paris.

TATRA • Czechoslovakia 1923 to date

See panel

TAUNTON • Belgium 1914-1922

Backed by British capital, this Liége company does not seem to have started production until 1921, when an 1800cc four-cylinder was introduced.

TAUNUS • Germany 1907-1909

Ex-Adler employees founded this small company to manufacture a small 12hp car with a twin-cylinder engine.

TAURINIA • Italy 1902-c. 1908

Named for the ancient tribe who founded Torino, this factory offered a 12 hp and a 14/20 hp, both four-cylinders.

TAUZIN • France 1898

A twin-cylinder voiturette with direct drive on all three speeds, by triple crown-wheels and pinions controlled by levers on the steering column.

TAYLOR, GUE • England 1904

A three-wheeled chassis sold complete, apart from the power unit, which was left to the buyer"s discretion. This company later made Veloce motorcycles (the origin of Velocette).

TAYLOR • England 1923-1924

Built by Taylor Motors of Newcastle-upon-Tyne, the Taylor was an assembled car fitted with a 14 hp Meadows engine and gearbox.

TB • England 1920-1924

One of the more attractive three-wheelers, the TB (Thomson Brothers) had an air-cooled 980cc twin-cylinder engine and Bugatti-style dummy radiator.

TECO • Germany 1924-1925

A motorcycle producer at Stettin (now Poland,) which also built an ohv Selve-engined 1501cc four-cylinder car of sporting appearance and advanced design.

TEMPERINO • Italy 1919-1925

The Temperino was a small car with a rotund body and a sv vee-twin 746cc engine, which was later superseded by an ohv 1096cc version. Production was on a small scale.

TEMPLAR • USA 1918-1925

Billed as the "Superfine Small Car," the Cleveland-built Templar was a four-cylinder ohv sports model capable of some 45 mph. Its price of $2,685 included a gradient meter, compass and a 1-A Junior Autographic Kodak camera.

TEMPLE-CROWSLEY • England 1906-1907

A tricar built in London with wheel-steering bucket seats and 5 hp Peugeot engine.

TEMPLE-WESTCOTT • USA 1921-1922

Virtually nothing has been discovered about this elusive make, other than the fact that a six-cylinder engine was used and an estimated 10 to 20 cars were built. The car is frequently erroneously listed as "Temple-Woodgate."

TEMPO • Germany 1933-1935

Tempo, after building commercial three-wheelers for many years, introduced a small car the Pony, with a 198cc Ilo two-stroke engine in the 1930s. There was also the Tempo-Front T 6 and a Combi, which could be used as a delivery van as well as a private car. There were 596cc twin-cylinder versions as well, but few were built or sold.

TATRA • Czechoslovakia 1923 to 1999

Tatra succeeded Nesselsdorfer in 1923, and designer Hans Ledwinka revolutionized existing design principles by creating a frameless car with a large-diameter backbone tube in place of a conventional chassis. The air-cooled engine was a 1056cc flat twin, mounted transversely above the front axle. This Tatra 11 was succeeded by the improved model 12, which was built until 1930. They were very sturdy cars, and were also successful in races. A watercooled 2-liter six appeared in 1926. The 1.72-liter Type 30 flat-four superseded the two-cylinder versions in 1930. It, too, was air-cooled and had the engine transversely mounted. The water-cooled 2.3-liter Type 31 followed the earlier 2-liter six-cylinder in 1927, while the 1160cc Type 57 of the early 1930s was a new small air-cooled four-cylinder; the 1690cc Type 75 was similar in layout. In the early 1930s two water-cooled ohv luxury models appeared, one with a 3850cc six-cylinder engine, the other a 5990cc V-12. Few of these expensive models were built. In 1934 Ledwinka, never short of unorthodox ideas, created another interesting car, the Tatra 77. It had an air-cooled V-8 engine of 2970cc mounted in the rear. The body was aerodynamic, with a central box-type frame. Only air-cooled cars were being made by Tatra when the war broke out. These were all four-cylinder models, the 52 (1910cc,) the 57 (1260cc,) and the 97 (1760cc,) the last being rear-engined and the others having flat-four engines in front. The rear-engined 2960cc model 87 was the successor to the Tatra 77. All now had ohv engines, except the model 52.

After the war Tatra first produced improved versions of the rear-engined cars with 2472cc V-8 engines, but concentrated more and more on big trucks. From 1949-51 it built successful sports cars and racing monoposti with rear air-cooled engines which, driven by Vermirovsky, Soyka, and Pavlicek, proved successful. From 1955 different versions of the rear-engined Tatra 603 appeared, followed by the improved 613; most of these cars were supplied only to governments in Eastern Europe. Production was now on a small scale. The 1998 613 had a dohc V-8 engine of 3495cc, mounted above the rear axle and giving 165bhp at 5200 rpm. It could attain 120 mph. In early 1999 Tatra ceased to build cars and returned to making trucks.

Tatra 613

1920 TB three-wheeled cyclecar

TENTING • France 1896-1899

M Tenting was an early protagonist of the infinitely variable friction drive. His opposed twin-cylinder engine used a primitive form of fuel injection.

TERRAPLANE • USA 1932-1937

This 2.6-liter sv six replaced the Essex; it was joined in 1933 by a straight-eight of 4 liters, which was the basis for the original Railtons. A swept-back grille and ifs characterized the 1934 models, which had the 3.5-liter Hudson six (export models retained the 2.6-liter engine.) Hydraulic brakes were added in 1936.

TERROT • France 1912-1914

Better known as cycle and motorcycle builder, Terrot of Dijon also built 10 hp light cars with 1460cc four-cylinder monobloc engines.

T ET M • France 1920-1922

Pushbike maker Tremblay et Malencon made some single-cylinder 500cc cyclecars with belt drive.

TEXAN • USA 1918-1922

The Texan was as assembled a car as one could imagine, even the prototype being an Elcar with a new emblem.

1911 10/12cv Terrot 1593cc four-cylinder bodied by Py-Laroche of Dijon (M Py-Laroche seated at the rear)

Texans featured Lycoming four-cylinder engines and were built as open models only, the five-passenger touring car selling for $1,495. Although standard components were featured, oversize tyres were provided, ostensibly to make the car suitable for service in the Texas oil fields. An estimated 2,000 cars and 1,000 trucks were manufactured.

TEXMOBILE • USA 1920-1922

Centered in Dallas, Texas, where it was built by Little Motors Kar Co, the Texmobile was also billed as the "Little Kar." With a wheelbase of 102 inches, the four-cylinder Texmobile sold in touring car form for $750. Very few were marketed.

TH • Spain 1915-1922

Talleres Hereter of Barcelona, founded in 1905 to make spares and accessories for motor cars, began building light cars to the designs of the brothers Claudio and Carlos Baradat in 1915, initially under the name "Ideal." In 1918 an improved design, the 15 cv "TH," with a four-cylinder 2121 cc monobloc engine in unit with its gearbox, appeared. The company also built aero and marine power units.

THAMES • England 1906-1911

The Thames Ironworks, Shipbuilding and Engineering Company of Greenwich, London, built commercials before launching a 45 hp six and a 40/45 hp four at the 1906 Olympia Show. Few cars seem to have been built until 1908, when a worm-drive twin of 1961 cc and a four of 3922cc were offered alongside sixes of 6981cc, 7778cc, 9653cc, and a monstrous 80 hp of 12,931cc. By the end of 1910 (after an apparent pause in production in 1909) more modest cars, an 8 hp single of 1296cc and a 15 hp four of 2413cc, were the staple offerings. The 15 hp was available with four-wheel brakes.

1913 5501cc Théophile Schneider Type Sport

THEOPHILE SCHNEIDER • France 1910-1931

Leaving Rochet-Schneider, Théophile Schneider formed Automobiles Théophile Schneider in Besancon, Doubs, in 1910. He made four-cylinders of 12cv (1693cc,) 18 cv (3685cc,) and 25cv (5195cc) as well as a six-cylinder 15cv of 3180cc. For a long time Théophile Schneiders remained old-fashioned, with the radiator behind the engine a la Renault." In 1912 a new model, the 14/16cv of 2993cc, was added, and all these cars were made until the war. When the factory resumed production post-war it was still building these pre-war models, but with the radiator at the front. Most of the post-war production was based on the 14/16cv, of which a six-cylinder version, the 4489cc 20 cv, was also built. In 1926 came a smaller car, the 7 cv with a 1172cc engine. This was the last new model to be made by this firm, which also built trucks.

THIEULIN • France 1907-1908

A light four-cylinder from Besançon (Doubs.) Seven were built: one survives.

THOLOME • France 1920-1922

A cyclecar made in St Ouen, Seine, by M Tholomé, with a wooden chassis and 902cc Ruby engine. Tholomé moved to Levallois, Seine, and later fitted a 1093cc Ruby engine. A cheaper version with a vee-twin Train engine of 748cc was also available.

THOMAS • USA 1902-c. 1919

Edwin Ross Thomas bought the moribund Globe Cycle Company of Buffalo, New York, in 1900, producing his first cars, light single- and twin-cylinders, in 1902. A crocodile-hooded 24 hp three-cylinder appeared in 1903, acquiring a conventional hood and the name Thomas-Flyer the next year. The 1905 range consisted of fours of 40 hp and 50 hp and a 60 hp six; the following year the Thomas-Flyer range was on European lines, reputedly a carbon copy of the contemporary Richard-Brasier. In 1907 a total of 700 cars and 400 taxicabs was built; a 1907 Thomas-Flyer 60 hp four won the 20,000- mile New York-Paris race in 1908. Sales peaked with 1,908 cars in 1909, but the poor reliability record of the company's first shaft-drive

The 1907 Thomas-Flyer which won the 1908 New York-Paris Race

model, the Model L Flyabout, caused a sales downturn to 913 in 1910, in which year E R Thomas (who had never learned to drive) sold the company to a New York banking company. Even so, it went into receivership in August 1912, and its assets were auctioned off in 1913. Theoretically, Thomas-Flyers were available to special order until 1919.

THOMAS • England 1903

A weird two-seater three-wheeler on cycle lines, with a single-cylinder engine slung between the front wheels.

THOMAS • USA 1906-1908

A joint venture by employees of Olds and the E R Thomas Company of Buffalo, the Thomas-Detroit was a shaft-driven 40 hp four designed by Howard Coffin and available as a runabout or touring car. It was succeeded by the Chalmers-Detroit.

THOMOND • Ireland 1925-1926

Only prototypes of this ohv 1750cc four-cylinder from Dublin were built.

THOMPSON • USA 1901-1902

An electric runabout from Plainfield, NJ.

THOMSON • Australia 1896-1905

Herbert Thomson built one of Australia's first cars, a lightweight 5 hp steamer. Work commenced in 1896; two years later the car was being driven extensively, with Thomson undertaking the longest car journeys of the day. He took orders for 150 cars but delivered only 12. One is known to survive. The four-wheeled phaeton seated six people. Its frame was built mainly of timber, with large-diameter wheels fitted with Dunlop pneumatic tyres. Steering was by side-lever. The vertical compound engine had tandem cylinders and ran at speeds up to 1000 rpm.

THOMSON • USA 1898-1902

Professor Elihu Thomson devised a four-cylinder steam carriage with a hydraulic steering lock incorporated in the tiller.

THOMSON • France 1913-1928

Thomas of Bordeaux assembled these cars from bought-in components. They had a distinctive vee-shaped radiator.

THOR • England 1904-c. 1906

The Simms-engined 6/8 hp Thor, built in Leicester, had a special cross-spring suspension, "rendering pneumatic tyres, with all their troubles, unnecessary."

THOR • England 1906-1923

Simpson Taylor, of Buckingham Palace Road, London, claimed to have built cars from 1906, fitting American engines from 1913. In 1920 the company stated that it was building three 2255cc four-cylinder cars a week.

THORN ET HOGAN • France 1901-1902

This Anglo-French concern offered cars on Panhard lines: a 12 hp started in the Paris-Berlin race of 1901.

THORNYCROFT • England 1903-1913

Thornycroft, builder of steam launches and trucks, entered the private car market in 1903 with gasoline models of 1814cc (twin-cylinder) and 3626cc (four,) the larger model having a dynamo fitted. The 1905 range was of more modern appearance, and new models of 18 hp and 30 hp

1898 Thomson (Australia)

1919 Thor landaulette

(four-cylinder) and a 45 hp six were announced in 1907. The six was discontinued by 1911, and in 1912-13 only the 18 hp was available.

THRIGE • Denmark 1909-1918

Thomas B Thrige AS of Odense built the first gasoline-engined Thrige car in 1910, but an electric ltruck had been built in 1909. In 1911 production started with cars using Ballot or Daimler sleeve-valve engines. Fifty cars of a very light type (so they could be used on the minor roads in Denmark, where cars over 990 lb were forbidden) were built, with four-cylinder 4/12 hp Ballot engines. The gearbox had three speeds, but there was no differential. Most parts came from France, including frame, axles, engine, and steering. Other models in 1914 were the 8/22 hp, also with a four-cylinder Ballot engine, and the 13/35 with a four-cylinder Daimler-Knight engine. Main production was trucks, taxis, and buses.

THRUPP & MABERLY • England 1896

Another famous carriage builder which produced electric vehicles. An electric Victoria was built for the Queen of Spain to the design of a Spanish engineer named Julien.

THULIN • Sweden 1920-1928

After the First World War, Thulinverken (of Landskrona) felt that the future for its airplanes and aero engines might not be too good, and decided to start building cars. It bought the license rights for the German AGA car, but AGA had bought its license rights from FN in Belgium. The engine was a watercooled four-cylinder of 20 hp. The radiator was sharply pointed in the German fashion, and the body was also in typically German style. All parts were made in Sweden, except carburetor, instruments, tires, and electrical system. There were plans for 1,000 cars, but only 300 were built before production stopped in 1924. A few years later the Weiertz brothers (see Self) were engaged to produce an entirely new and advanced car, the low-built Type B. The engine was an ohv 1.7-liter four-cylinder unit, and the car had four-wheel brakes. In 1927 a few pilot cars were built. Unfortunately, American cars were cheap in Sweden at that time and Volvo had just started production, so the promising Type B was killed in its infancy. Around 10 cars were built, one presumably with a six-cylinder Hupmobile engine.

THURLOW • England 1920-1921

The Thurlow three-wheeler, built in Wimbledon, London, used a 10 hp vee-twin Precision engine and three-speed Sturmey Archer gearbox.

1907 Thornycroft 45 hp tourer

1935 Tornax Sportwagen

TICI • England 1972

Stylist William Towns's idea of the city car, the diminutive Tici had its track equal to the wheelbase. The car was powered by a rear-mounted Mini engine.

TIDAHOLM • Sweden 1906-1913

Trucks were built by Tidaholms Bruks AB from 1903, and a few of these were apparently converted to some very crude kind of passenger car. Three or four ordinary passenger cars were built, probably in 1911-12. One was exported to St Petersburg in Russia. Tidaholm then concentrated on trucks and buses until 1933, when production ceased.

LE TIGRE • France 1920

Made in Asniéres, Seine, Tigres were 10/12 hp Altos-engined cars of 1327cc.

TIMEIRE • Ireland 1970

Tim Conroy's Mini Special never reached its scheduled production. With an aluminum alloy fastback body, the prototype spent much of its time in competition before being pensioned off in 1973.

TINCHER • USA 1903-1909

Big, powerful cars (up to 90 hp, six-cylinder) initially from Chicago, latterly from South Bend, Indiana.

TINY • England 1913-1915

A substantially made cyclecar with an 8 hp vee twin JAP engine, tubular chassis and shaft drive, the "torpedo"-bodied Tiny was built in Esholt, Yorkshire, by Nanson, Barker & Company, which later produced the Airedale.

TISSANDIER • France 1896

A two-seater car which ran in the 1896 Paris-Marseille Race.

TJORVEN • Sweden 1969

In 1964 Kalmar Verkstad and the Swedish Post Office started planning together for a small vehicle suited to local post distribution. The result was a small DAF-engined van with a sliding door on the driver's side. Production began in 1967; 1,000 were ordered, using DAF 44 parts and glassfibre bodies. In 1969 the "Tjorven" (a name derived from a popular children's book) was presented. It was supposed to be a combination of passenger car and van, and had removable seats. The engine was a Renault R8, and most parts came from the DAF 55. Due to a financial crisis no cars were produced.

TOKYO • Japan 1911-1912

A 3656cc four-cylinder model built in conjunction with Kunisue, Tokyo, in a small series.

TOLEDO • USA 1900-1904

A steam carriage powered by a vertical-twin engine with generally robust construction, built by one of Colonel Pope's companies.

TOLOSA • France 1919-1927

Made in Toulouse, Tolosas were assembled from US Army surplus Model T Ford parts.

TOM POUCE • France 1920-1924

MM Blanc and Guillon started to make cyclecars in Puteaux, Seine, after the war, with twin-cylinder two-stroke SICAM engines of 731cc and four-cylinder 1093cc Ruby and 1592cc Ballot power units. The marque moved to Dommartin, Somme, in 1923 with a new owner, M Ernault, who built the last Tom Pouces with 723cc Lemaitre & Gerard engines.

TONY • France 1920-1921

Tony Bouley, maker of sidecars in Paris, built some cyclecars with various motorcycle and proprietary engines.

1935 8 hp Tracford fwd saloon

1961 Trabant saloon

1932 Tracta 3-litre saloon

TONY HUBER • France 1902-1906

From Billancourt, Seine, the Tony Huber Company sold engines as well as complete cars. In 1906 it listed an 8 hp two-cylinder, a 16 hp four, and a 25 hp four with copper water jackets.

TORBENSON • USA 1902-1908

In 1906 this Bloomfield, NJ, company was offering air-cooled three- and six-cylinder cars of 14 hp and 28 hp.

TORNADO • England 1957-1963

The ugly Typhoon, some 400 of which were sold, was replaced by the short-lived Tempest, which in turn was superseded by the Talisman, without doubt Tornado's most important model. Now collectors' items, nearly 200 of these Ford-powered glassfiber-bodied four-seaters were made.

TORNAX • Germany 1934-1937

Built by a well-known motorcycle factory at Wuppertal-Langerfeld, the Karpe-designed Tornax was one of the better little German sports cars. It had fwd and was powered by a mildly tuned 684cc DKW Meisterklasse twin-cylinder two-stroke engine.

TORO • Philippines 1974 to date

A 1300cc VW engine powers this sporty 2+2 coupé from Manilla.

TORPEDO • England 1909

Cycle maker F Hopper of Barton-on-Humber offered this range for one year only. The 6 hp single and 10 hp twins were based on the contemporary Starling, and there was also a 10 hp four.

TORPILLE • France 1913-1924

Made in Saumur, the first Torpilles were 1328cc Altos-engined cars. After the war production was resumed, along with new 1592cc Ballot-engined and 1693cc SCAP-engined models.

TOURAINE • USA 1912-1915

Forerunner of the Vim Motor Truck Company, Touraine followed a one-model policy with a T-head engine of 4343cc and two-, five-, and seven-seat touring coachwork.

TOURAND • France 1900-1908

Originally manufactured with a 6 hp twin-cylinder engine, the Tourand was produced spasmodically. The Suresnes, Seine, factory offered cars of up to 80 hp. The first Tourands had 6 hp twin-cylinder Crozet engines.

TOUREY • France 1898

Jules Tourey's 4 hp "Petit Duc" was built very much on Benz lines.

TOURIST • USA 1902-1909

Built in Los Angeles, the Tourist Range consisted of friction-drive twins and fours with conventional gearboxes.

TOWARD & PHILIPSON • England 1897

A coke-fired six-seater steam wagonette with a three-stage tubular boiler.

TOYOTA • Japan 1935 to date

See panel

TRABANT • Germany (East) 1958 onwards

A product of the nationalized East German car industry, all Trabants had fwd and two-stroke twin-cylinder in-line engines. Introduced with 499cc engines, from 1963 they used 594cc power units. They were air-cooled, with a rotary inlet-valve and were built at Zwickau in Saxony. Bodywork was in resin-reinforced papier maché! In 1990 the "Trabi" had a heart transplant, a VW Polo engine replacing the noxious two-stroke, but it finally expired a year later.

TRACFORD • France 1934-1936

Made in Gennevilliers, Seine, this was an attempt by Louis Carle, a Ford-France director, to convert the Model Y Ford into a fwd model.

TRACTA • France 1926-1934

A pioneer of fwd, engineer J A Grégoire made some excellent sports and touring cars in Asniéres, Seine. He used such proprietary engines as the SCAP 1100cc and 1600cc (sometimes supercharged) and a 2.7-liter Continental; later a 3000cc Hotchkiss engine was used. Grégoire often raced the Tractas in endurance events.

TRACTION AERIENNE • France 1921-c. 1926

Another propeller-driven car like the Layat, this Neuilly, Seine, marque offered a saloon steered by the front wheels. It was also sold as the Eolia.

TRACTOBILE • USA 1900-1902

A steam avant-train attachment for horse-carriages, with a "Battery of Patent Unit Boilers" and small two-cylinder engines acting on each front wheel. It was a venture apparently promoted by the egregious Mr Pennington.

TRAIN • France 1924

Famous maker of proprietary engines for the motorcycle and automobile industry, the Train factory of Courbevoie, Seine, made 350cc single-cylinder cyclecars, with friction transmission.

TOYOTA • Japan 1935 to date

The Toyota Loom Company built its first car, the Chrysler Airflow-like A-1 45 hp six, in May 1935. Developments of this, available in tourer and sedan variants, were offered until the Second World War. The first post-war model, the 27 bhp SA two-door Toyopet sedan, appeared in 1947. In 1954 came the 1453cc ohv Crown, and in 1957 the Corona 1000cc was introduced, succeeded in 1965 by the New Corona two-door hardtop, designed to fill a gap in the US market. In 1959 Toyota opened its Motomachi plant, producing Crown and Corona models, and in 1961 came the 700cc Publica. The next year Toyota built its millionth vehicle and began exporting to Europe. The two-millionth vehicle came in 1965. In 1967 the Century model appeared, the Corona gained 1.5- and 1.6-liter engines, and the Crown acquired six-cylinder and V-8 power units. The Corona Mk II was launched in 1968, and in 1969 the Corolla model became the first Toyota to reach a million units. Celica and Carina models were launched from the new Tsutsumi plant in December 1970, while two new Toyotas, the Starlet and a redesigned Corona, appeared in 1973. The 1979 range included the 993cc and 1166cc Starlet, the 1588cc Carina saloon and estate, the Celica, available in 1588cc and 1968cc models, and the 1968cc Cressida; the biggest Toyota was the 2563cc Crown luxury model. The fifth-generation Corolla of 1983 was the first with transverse engines and fwd.

In 1984 Toyota entered the sports car market with the MR2, and currently has a large and complex range befitting its status as the second-biggest car manufacturer in the world. Among the current models are the Camry, Carina, Corolla, and Starlet sedans as werll as the Supra, Celica, and MR2 sports cars. Toyota has 41 factories in 20 countries. In 1991 it built its 70-millionth vehicle, a Vista 2000GT Hardtop. The company retained its position as the world's number one car maker throughout the 1990s, and brought forth a whole new series of cars. The Lexus division, separately marketed, took Toyota upmarket with great success, while the revized Celica,

1970s style Celica Liftback (above,) Toyota 2000 supercar (below)

Toyota MR2 (above,) Toyota Land Cruiser 4wd (center,) Toyota Celica Cabrio (below)

MR2 and Supras continued to evolve. The best-selling, ever-perennial Corolla grew into subsequent versions and in 1997 took on a radical new "designer" face with its bug-eyed look. A range of pick-up trucks, a new small coupé named Paseo, the large Previa MPV, and new versions of the ubiquitious Land Cruiser emerged. The Carina family/middle-management range was modified into the Avensis range and a small, urban-style-orientated 4wd type known as the RAV 4 neatly created an off-road, recreational vehicle niche for the firm. The traditional top-of-the-range Camry model headed the sub-Lexus strata of Toyota's globally encompassing range. A new hatchback design named Yaris was announced in early 1999, and with its tall body, pert styling, and large interior space was heralded as rivalling the new Clio, 206, and Polo. The press agreed, and the Yaris was assured a great future; another hit for Toyota.

1965 TVR Trident

1926 Trojan tourer

TRIBELHORN • Switzerland 1899-1919

Production of Tribelhorn electrics began in earnest in 1902. Three- and four-wheeled cars were offered. After 1919 only light utility vans were built.

TRIBET • France 1909-1914

The first cars built by Tribet, of Villeneuve-la-Garenne (Seine,) were an 8/10 hp and a 12/16 hp. At Olympia in 1910 a 12 hp Cabriolette of 1539cc, selling for £325, was shown.

TRIBUNE • USA 1913-1914

An open tourer powered by a 4-liter Buda engine.

TRIDENT • England • France 1919-1920

A fwd tandem-seated three-wheeler of odd design, with the 8 hp engine on one side of the single front wheel. Prototypes were built in France, but production was planned to take place in England (though it probably never got under way.)

TRIDENT • England 1966-1978

Once a TVR prototype based on the Healey 3000 chassis, the Trident was another of Fiore's striking designs. Available with 4.7-liter V-8, Ford V-6, and Triumph 2.5-liter engines, during its life the Trident notched up over 200 sales, some 50 per cent of which went abroad.

TRIOULEYRE • France 1896-1898

A horizontal-engined car on Benz lines. Two Triouleyres started in the 1896 Paris-Marseille.

TRIPPEL • Germany 1934-1965

During the war Hanns Trippel built amphibious cars in the occupied Bugatti works at Molsheim. These cars were similar to those he had produced in pre-war days with Adler and Opel engines at his small Homburg/Saar workshops. His post-war amphibians had 1147cc Triumph Herald four-cylinder engines. Trippel also designed the Amphicar.

TRITON • England 1963

A Surrey businessman planned to produce the Triton in quantity. As it turned out, the original David Johnson-Webb road-racer remains unique. Its round-tube space-frame

1949 Tucker sedan

1924 Turcat-Méry 15cv

chassis was topped by a two-seater body and powered by the evergreen BMC "B" Series engine.

TRIUMPH • USA 1906-c. 1910

"The self-starting car–you merely push a lever and the motor responds," the Chicago-built Triumph sold for $2,250-$2,500.

TRIUMPH • England 1923 to date

See panel overleaf

TROIKA • France 1897-c. 1901

Daniel Augé's Troïka voiturette had a 7 hp twin-cylinder horizontal Cyclope engine with hot-tube ignition, and was "remarkable for the power and simplicity of its mechanism." A more conventional car was subsequently marketed under the Augé or Cyclope names.

TROJAN • England 1922-1936, 1961-1965

The Trojan was an ingenious utility car designed by Leslie Hounsfield. It was powered by a 1.5-liter horizontal two-stroke twin-cylinder engine, while transmission was by two-speed epicyclic gearbox and double chains to a solid rear axle. A punt-type chassis was used, and long cantilever springs were fitted. Solid tires were another unusual feature for the day. Although originally built by Leyland, the manufacture was taken over by Trojan Ltd in 1928. This change of manufacture resulted in the new RE model, which retained the same clever engine and transmission layout, but mounted at the rear of the car. Production was reduced to a trickle in the 1930s, though commercial versions of the design continued to sell well. The Mastra was announced for the 1936 season, with a 2.2-liter six-cylinder two-stroke engine; but it did not go into production. Passenger cars did not feature again until 1962, when the company manufactured the Heinkel "bubble car" under license, after production had ceased in Germany.

TROLL • Norway 1956

Although Troll Plastik & Bilindustri, of Lunde, planned a first series of 15 small cars with glassfiber two-seater coupé bodies, only five were built. Twin-cylinder two-stroke engines and drive line were bought from the German Gutbrod company.

TUAR • France 1914-1925

M Morin of Thouars, Deux-Sévres, made cars using such proprietary engines as CIME, Fivet, Chapuis-Dornier, and Ruby.

TRUFFAULT • France 1907-1908

A belt-driven single-cylinder voiturette with combined chassis/body frame and weird coil-spring suspension, built in Paris.

TRUMBULL • USA 1913-1915

This was a friction-drive four-cylinder light car, built by the American Cyclecar Company of Bridgeport, Connecticut.

TRUNER • England 1913

A vee-twin JAP engine powered this chain-driven cyclecar.

TUCKER • USA 1946-1948

Preston Tucker's 122 mph dream car, designed with the aid of Alex Tremulis, was truly ahead of its time. It was powered by a rear-mounted Franklin flat-six helicopter engine converted to sealed-system watercooling, and had many safety features: all-round disc brakes, pop-out windshield, and padded dash. Suspension was independent all-round, and transmission was normally four-speed manual with preselector or electric shift, though some cars had "Tuckermatic" transmissions with only 30 basic parts. Tucker had produced 51 cars in a former Dodge aircraft plant in Chicago before he was taken to court by the Securities Exchange Commission on allegations of stock fraud. Though he was exonerated in 1950, it was too late to resurrect the Tucker car, and Preston Tucker died in 1956 while negotiating to build a small car in Brazil. Of the 51 Tuckers built, 49 still survive.

Chassis of the 1907 Truffault voiturette

TUDHOPE • Canada 1906-1913

Originally a high-wheeler, based on the McIntire from Indianapolis. After a 1909 fire destroyed the firm's Orillia, Ontario, factory, a new start was made with an EMF-based four-cylinder. New four- and six-cylinder models appeared in 1912, but the company failed a year later. Reorganized, it built a similar design under the name "Fisher" until war work halted car production in 1914.

TRIUMPH • England 1923 to 1984

Although Triumph had been making motorcycles since 1903, it did not build its first car until 1923, this being the 10/20, a 1.4-liter model. Two years later it was replaced by the 1900cc 13/30 (best remembered for being fitted with Lockheed external contracting hydraulic brakes.) The year 1928 saw the appearance of the 832cc Super Seven, while 1931 marked the arrival of the Scorpion, powered by a fashionably small six-cylinder engine of 1.2 liters. A Coventry-Climax overheard inlet/side exhaust engine was featured in the Super Nine of 1932, joined the following year by the Ten. The sporting front was not neglected, and in 1934 came the Gloria, available with either 1100cc four-cylinder, or 1500cc six-cylinder engines, again by Coventry-Climax. A fabulous extravagance was the supercharged dohc 2-liter Dolomite, an unashamed copy of a contemporary Alfa Romeo; it found few buyers. By 1937 Triumph-made ohv engines were supplementing the Coventry-Climax units, the range by this time embracing the 1.5-liter Gloria and four- and six-cylinder versions of the Dolomite, the name of the twin-cam eight thus being perpetuated.

Financial solvency had been a constant problem, and the company was placed under receivership in 1939. It was not until 1945 that Triumph was snapped up by Sir John Black's Standard Motor Company. For Triumph's first post-war model, an 1800cc ohv engine made for the 1.5-liter Jaguar was fitted to the razor-edge 1800 sedan and Roadster, the latter being the last series-production car to be fitted with a dickey seat. However, it was not long before a new engine appeared, this being Standard's wetliner four, fitted to the range from 1949. In 2.1-liter form it powered the TR2 sports car of 1953, the first model of a long and distinguished line. It was used in all the TR variants until the TR5 of 1967, being replaced by a 2.5-liter six. By contrast, sedan car production did not get into its stride until the 948cc Herald of 1959, the razor-edge Renown (the renamed 1800 sedan) having been phased out in 1955. In 1962 a six-cylinder version of the Herald, the Vitesse, was announced, while the Spitfire sports two-seater was another derivative. The sporting theme was further perpetuated by the 2-liter GT6 of 1967.

Standard-Triumph had been taken over by Leyland Motors in 1961, resulting in a rapid expansion of the range. The 2000 saloon of 1964 was followed by a 2.5 PI derivative and the fwd 1300 in 1966, while sporting laurels were upheld by the TR6 of 1969, replaced by the wedge-shaped TR7 of 1976. The 3-liter Stag of 1970 lasted until 1977, while the Dolomite of 1972 and the ohc 2-liter Dolomite Sprint offered sports car performance in the guise of a family sedan. In 1979 a convertible TR7 was launched, but the TR7 and the US market TR8 were killed off in 1981, a year after the Spitfire. The Triumph name was retained on the Acclaim (based on the Honda Ballad), but this was produced for less than three years. Its Honda Civic-based successor was badged as a Rover. In 1984 this illustrious name disappeared, and with it went what many regarded as part of England.

1936 Triumph Gloria Southern Cross Sports

Triumph Herald saloon

Still-born proposal based on the production model Triumph Stag

Triumph TR2a (top,) TR4 (center,) and 1978 TR7 (below)

TULSA • USA 1917-1923

One of the few cars to be built in Oklahoma, the Tulsa was a strictly assembled product using Herschell-Spillman four- and six-cylinder engines. Only open cars were made; advertising emphasized the ruggedness of the cars and their suitability for working in the vicinity of Oklahoma oil wells.

TURBO • Switzerland 1921

With a five-cylinder radial engine of 1546cc and a triangulated girder chassis, the Turbo, from Zurich-Oerlikon, was a shortlived venture.

TURBO • Germany 1923-1924

S W Müller had little luck with his advanced five-cylinder radial-engined Turbo cars, with ohv 1546cc and 1980cc engines. After he failed at Oerlikon in Switzerland, he fared no better in Stuttgart, Germany. The Turbo had a tubular frame with coil-spring suspension, but was never fully developed. A 1980cc racing version had a special 75 bhp engine.

TURCAT-MERY • France 1896-1928

Automobiles Turcat-Méry of Marseille made its first cars in 1896, using Panhard and Daimler engines until 1901, when its designs were taken up by De Diétrich. In 1907 Turcat-Méry offered a big six-cylinder of 10,200cc. In 1908 it listed a 28cv (6333cc,) 18cv (3053cc,) and 14cv (2412cc) among many other models. After the war the company made a 3015cc 15 cv in 1922, followed in 1923 by the 2978cc 15cv. The following year a 2993cc 15cv was added. In 1925 Turcat-Méry presented an ohc 12cv of 2388cc. After 1926 the firm was forced to fit proprietary engines to survive. These included the SCAP and CIME 1500cc and 1700cc and some SCAP eight-cylinders, of which very few were made.

TURGAN-FOY • France 1899-1910

Powered by a vertical-crank 4.5 hp twin-cylinder Filtz engine, the original Turgan-Foy had four-speed belt-and-pinion drive. From 1902 conventional engines of 16 hp, 24 hp and even 60 hp were used.

TURICUM • Switzerland 1904-c. 1918

Martin Fischer's first voiturettes, built in a former skittle-alley in Zürich, were single-seaters with pedal-operated steering and friction drive, but production vehicles, from a new factory in Uster, had wheel-steering and two seats. The name "Turicum" is the Latin form of Zürich. The first four-cylinder Turicums appeared in 1908, still with friction drive. About 1,000 cars had been built when production ceased.

TURINELLI & PEZZA • Italy 1899

A fwd electric carriage from Milano.

TURNER • England 1906-1907, 1911-1930

This Wolverhampton company concentrated on the Turner-Miesse steam car until 1906, when it produced the Seymour-Turner for Seymours of London. This had a 4.1-liter four-cylinder engine and shaft drive. Steam took over again, however, and it was not until 1911 that the Turner cyclecar appeared, having an 1100cc vee-twin engine. A Ten also appeared the following year, and at the same time a 2.1-liter Fifteen was announced. The company did not get into its post-war stride until 1922, offering 1.8-liter and 2.3-liter models, though for 1923 a 1.5-liter Dorman engine was adopted. In the latter half of the 1920s only the 12 hp car was made, production ceasing in 1930.

TURNER • England 1954-1966

A simple ladder-frame chassis and attractive lightweight glassfiber body were the key to the success of the early Turners. Although remembered best as competition cars, subsequent Turners continued to offer excellent performance from modest power outputs.

TVR • England 1954 to date

See panel

TWOMBLY • USA 1910-1911

W Irving Twombly spent six years and $250,000 developing a car with a flat-four engine with no connecting rods and only two double-ended pistons. Engine and transmission could be exchanged inside five minutes, and the bodywork could be altered from "completely enclosed, heated and ventilated limousine, to open car in less time than it took to open the hood of a landaulette."

TWOMBLY • USA 1913-1915

An underslung tandem-seated cyclecar with a four-cylinder 15 hp water cooled engine, built by Driggs-Seabury.

TYNE • England 1904

A 12 hp two-cylinder model, sold by W Galloway & Co of Gateshead-on-Tyne, British agent for the Stanley Steamer.

TYSELEY • England 1913

The Bowden Brake Company of Birmingham marketed this 8 hp twin-cylinder shaft-drive cyclecar, which sold for 160 guineas.

TVR • England 1954 to date

TVR has survived the car kit era, countless management upheavals and a major fire to become a respected manufacturer. The MkI lasted until 1960, followed by the MkII (1960-1962) and MkIII (1960-1963.) Then came the Griffith 200 (1964) and 400 (1965,) followed by the 200V8 (1966,) Tuscan SE, and Vixen 1600 (1967,) Vixen S2 (1968,) Tuscan V6 (1969,) 1600M (1972-1973,) 2500 (1970-1973,) and 2500M, and 3000M (1972.) The Turbo appeared in 1975, and the Taimar in 1976. The more angular Tasmin range appeared in 1978; its current descendant is the 'brutal' 400 series. The TVR S series, launched in 1986, uses the classic TVR body shape taken from the original molds.

In 1990 TVR showed the new Griffith model, which went into production in 1991. Combining stunning good looks with the use of high-tech materials, such as Kevlar and carbonfiber, to keep weight down, the Griffith is powered by Rover-based V-8 engines of 4.0 or 4.3 liters and has a top speed approaching 150 mph. Also launched in 1991 were the 25-off Limited Edition 400 SE and an rhd version of the TVR 8S, previously sold only for export. After relying on modified Rover V8 engines, TVR designed its own and put this 4.2-liter, 75 V-8 into production in 1997. By then the sleek Griffith and traditional Chimaera ranges had secured for TVR many new buyers and a greater market share than ever before. The four-seat Cerbera further widened TVR's range in 1998. All of these cars boasted 0-60 mph times of around 5 to 6sec and top speeds in excess of 150 mph. For 1999 the Cerbera developed into a Speed Six model with more raw more power from TVR's new straight-six engine. A name from the past emerged when TVR announced a new Tuscan for the 2000 model year. This features the 6-cylinder engine, radical styling with stacked headlamps, and wild curves. With a full orderbook and 750 staff, the new TVR, purveyor of true supercars, is a far cry from its origins and past difficulties.

TVR Griffith 500 (left.) TVR's first four-seater (below)

ULMANN • Germany 1903-1904

Berlin-based Oldsmobile importer Edmund Ulmann also produced a few De Dion-engined 12 hp cars.

ULTIMA • France 1912-1914

This Lavallois-Perret, Seine, manufacturer offered single- and four-cylinder voiturettes of 954cc and 2121cc, with six-speed friction drive, built under Turicum licence.

ULTRAMOBIL • Germany 1904-1908

A single-cylinder 1590cc runabout, produced by outside companies under Olds licence for the Deutsche Ultramobil GmbH at Berlin-Halensee.

UNDERBERG • France 1899-1909

Built in Nantes, Loire-Atlantique, this was a belt-driven voiturette with a single-cylinder 3 hp Gaillardet engine until 1901, when a 6/8 hp twin and 12/16 hp and 24/ 80 hp fours were available. They were sometimes known as the "Salvator."

UNIC • France 1904-1939

See panel

UNICAR • England 1956-1959

A glassfiber coupé powered by rear-mounted twin-cylinder two-stroke Excelsior engines of 225cc and 328cc, the Opperman Unicar sold for under £400.

UNION • Germany 1920-1922

A small 1151cc two-cylinder car, built by Union-Werke AG in Mannheim. After the marque's demise (it was also known as Bravo) the works were taken over by Rabag for license production of Bugattis.

UNION • USA 1921

An assembled make, the Union reached only the prototype stage. It was mounted on a 118-inch wheelbase and used a Continental six-cylinder engine and other standard components. The touring car was to have sold for $2,850. Headquarters of the Union were at Eaton, Ohio.

UNIPOWER • England 1966-1970

Undoubtedly one of the best of the Mini-based specials, the Unipower GT featured a very strong two-seater glassfiber body, bonded to a complex spaceframe powered from the rear by any suitable Mini engine. About 75 GTs were built, over half of which were exported.

1899 Underberg voiturette with Gaillardet engine

UNIQUE • England 1915-1916

A twin-cylinder own-make engine of 1034cc powered this cyclecar from Clapham, London.

UNIT • England 1920-1923

A rear-mounted flat-twin 1100cc engine powered the Unit No 1, a friction-drive light car promoted by Grice, late of GWK. In 1923 a front-mounted Coventry-Climax four was used.

UNITED • USA 1920

Built by the United Engine Co of Greensburg, Indiana, the United failed to develop beyond the prototype stage. A touring car of 121-inch wheelbase was announced for $1,850. A Herschell-Spillman four-cylinder engine was used.

UNITED STATES • USA 1899

The United States Automobile Company of Attleboro, Mass., built an electric car in which both the field and armature of the motor, which was mounted on the rear axle, revolved.

UPTON • USA 1900-1907

From a 3.5 hp De Dion-powered runabout, this firm progressed to the big 1904 Beverly four whose headlamps turned with the steering.

URECAR • England 1923

An 8.9 hp four-cylinder Dorman engine powered the Urecar; it seems possible that only one was made.

URRIC • France 1905-1906

A "well-conceived" voiturette, shown at the 1905 Paris Salon.

US • USA 1907-1908

A "12 hp and over" four-cylinder air-cooled engine of 1767cc powered this two-seater run-about from Upper Sandusky, Ohio.

1958 Opperman Unicar 328cc twin-cylinder

1920 Unit No 1 two-seater

UNIC • France 1904-1939

When Georges Richard left the Richard-Brasier concern in 1904 he founded Unic in Puteaux, Seine, starting with a twin-cylinder engined 10cv of 1797cc. He added another model, the 2615cc 14cv four, the following year. The 1943cc 12cv (later enlarged to 2120cc) was sold mainly as a taxi and survived in production for nearly 20 years. Also notable were the 1909 4085cc six-cylinder and the 1914 4523cc. After the war Unic's bread-and-butter model was the 1847cc four, along with the 12cv taxis. Unic also specialized in building trucks of all sizes. A 1997cc sports model was presented in 1923, and the firm also offered sleeve-valve-engined cars, but without great success. In the 1930s Unic marketed two eight-cylinder models and an ohv 3-litre six-cylinder. Unic was eventually taken over by Simca, which wanted a commercial vehicle department. It survives in this guise.

1905 Georges-Richard Unic 10cv tourer

1924 Unic 12 hp Type L sedan

c. 1905 publicity for the Unic

1919 Utilis cyclecar

US AUTOMOBILE • USA 1899-1901

A 3 hp electric carriage with three speeds forward and two back.

US CONTINENTAL • USA 1946

This company built the Fulton Airphibian, an aluminum-bodied car with independent suspension and aircraft-sized wheels. It was powered by a six-cylinder 165 hp engine, and fabric-covered wings and rear fuselage could be easily attached to convert it into an airplane.

US LONG DISTANCE • USA 1901-1905

The US Long Distance car was similar in appearance to the Curved-Dash Olds, but had left-hand steering by side tiller. In 1903 a conventional 25 hp four-cylinder five-seater 'Standard Tourist' appeared, and by 1905 the marque name had been changed to 'Standard.'

UTERMOHLE • Germany 1903-1905

This Cologne coachbuilder and car-importer also constructed a 16 hp Peugeot-engined four-cylinder car which was imported into England by Corben and Sons of London.

UTILE-SIMPLEX • England 1904

A single-cylinder two-speed four-seat car from Kew, which cost £150 complete.

1922 Utility Four range – and entire production

UTILIS • France 1923-1925

M Lafarge made this tiny cyclecar in Courbevoie, Seine, using a wooden chassis and two-stroke Train engine of 350cc.

UTILITAS • Germany 1920-1922

Only 440 lb in weight, this little car had a sv 785cc four-cylinder engine of advanced design. The Berlin factory also built cyclecars with one- and two-cylinder engines.

UTILITAIRE • France 1907-1909

An 8 hp belt-driven light car built in Paris and shown at the 1907 Salon. In 1908 two-stroke one- and three-cylinder models were listed.

UTILITY • USA 1921-1922

The Utility Four was built by Major Victor W. Pagé as a companion car to his 'Aero-Type Four' cars, which were displayed at the New York Auto Show in 1922. The Utility boasted a four-cylinder air-cooled engine, similar in design to the Aero-Type line, and four prototypes were made; a touring car, a roadster, a small pickup truck, and a station wagon. Price for all models was planned at $1,450.

VABIS • Sweden 1897-1911

Vagnfabriksaktiebolaget i Södertälje, Södertälje, was a subsidiary of Surahammars Bruk, a maker of railway rolling stock. In 1896 Gustaf Eriksson was employed by Surahammars Bruk to find out if car production was worthwhile. He built two experimental cars in 1897 and 1898, but they were not very successful. In 1903 the company exhibited cars in Stockholm and a 12 hp tonneau in Paris. Cars with four-cylinder (probably also twin-cylinder) engines were built until 1911, when Vabis merged with Scania.

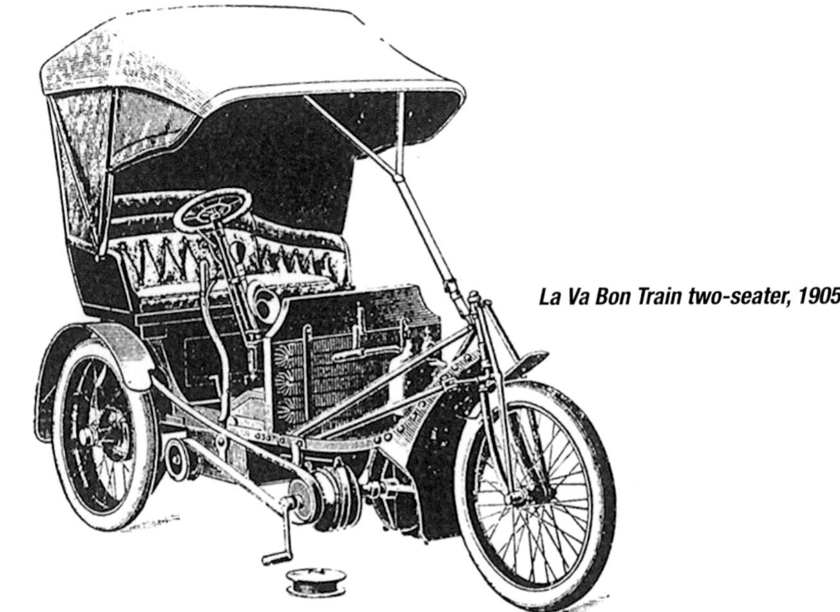

La Va Bon Train two-seater, 1905

LA VA BON TRAIN • France 1904-1914

Larroumet and Lagarde, of Agen, Lot-et-Garonne, built this three-wheeler, the name meaning "goes like blazes." With an iron chassis, wheel-steering, and a 6 hp De Dion engine, between 50 and 100 La Va Bon Train cars are thought to have been built.

VAGHI • Italy 1920-1924

Originally a three-wheeler, the last Vaghis had a 546cc twin-cylinder engine and four wheels. There was a close connection with the SAM.

VAILLANT • France 1922-1924

A cyclecar made in Lyon with a Chapuis-Dornier engine of 961cc or 1350cc.

VAJA • Czechoslovakia 1929-1930

A sporting cyclecar, driven by a sv 746cc air-cooled flat-twin Itar engine. Weighing 792 lb, it could reach 40 mph, but with the optional sv 996cc JAP vee-twin engine could attain a heady 48 mph.

VAL • England 1913-1914

An 8 hp cyclecar with friction drive, from Birmingham.

VALE • England 1932-1936

Built in London's Maida Vale, the Vale Special was initially powered by an 832cc Triumph engine. These cars were nearly all two-seaters, though the Tourette, a four-seater, was offered in 1933. In 1934 it was announced that larger engines would be fitted; these were Coventry-Climax fours and sixes of 1098cc and 1476cc respectively. A supercharged six-cylinder racing car was built in 1935 for Ian Connell, though production of all cars ceased the following year.

VALENTIA • France 1907-1908

"Tricars of all powers" built by Saunier of Vernon (Eure.)

1897 Vallée racer 'La Pantoufle'

VALLEE • France 1895-1901

A Le Mans, Sarthe, cycle builder, Vallée first constructed a 4 hp flat-twin car on cycle lines. By 1898 twins of up to 7 hp were available. His oddest offering was the 1899 "Pantoufle" ("Slipper") racing car, which had a 7603cc horizontal four-cylinder engine and a wide driving belt, and took its name from its streamlined nose, shaped like a Turkish slipper.

VALVELESS • England 1908-1915

The Valveless was the successor to the Ralph Lucas Valveless, and marked the entry of the David Brown group into motor manufacture. It had a 25 hp duplex two-stroke engine with "only six working parts" (two pistons, two conrods, and two crankshafts, which were geared together and counter-rotated.)

VAN • USA 1910-1911

A 22 hp ohv four-cylinder engine powered this roadster from Grand Haven, Michigan.

VANDEN PLAS • England 1960 to date

Founded as the British branch of the famous Belgian coachbuilding firm, Vanden Plas was acquired by Austin after the Second World War and provided custom coachwork on the bigger Austin chassis. It became a separate marque in 1960 with the de luxe Austin Princess. In 1964 there was also the Vanden Plas 1100. The 1965 Princess R used a Rolls-Royce military engine of 3.9 liters. The latest Vanden Plas, the 1500, is a de luxe Austin Allegro. Vanden Plas also carried out coachwork for Daimler and Jaguar at its Park Royal, London, factory, but early in 1979 it was announced that the works were to be closed and activities transferred to Jaguar in Coventry.

VANDY • England 1920-1921

Built by members of the Vandervell family (of CAV motor accessories), the 23.5 hp Vandy was assembled from American components, including a 3772cc Rutenber engine.

VAN GINK • Holland 1899-c1903

With two separate rear-mounted 2.5 hp engines, the Van Gink was a tubular-framed voiturette from an Amsterdam cycle maker.

VAN WAGONER • USA 1899-1900

"Built on a simple plan that does away with several levers and push-buttons", the Van Wagoner, from Syracuse, NY, could be "controlled with one hand." From 1900-1903 it was built as the "Syracuse."

VAPOMOBILE • England 1902-1904

This Nottingham-based manufacturer made (or assembled) steam cars of various designs.

1902 Vapomobile steam car rotund phaeton

VAR • Austria 1923-1926

Gianni Varrone, half-Swiss, half-Viennese, worked with Nesselsdorf and Austro-Daimler before setting up his own factory at Hard (Voralberg.) His voiturette had a wooden chassis/body and a curious flat-twin two-stroke engine with double-ended pistons and external connecting rods acting on the ends of the gudgeon pins, which protruded through a slot in the cylinder walls. Only prototypes were built.

VARLEY-WOODS • England 1918-1921

The Varley-Woods was so called because of the involvement of Ernest Vernon Varley Grossmith and John Robert Woods in the project. The former had been concerned with canned soups and mouth-organ manufacture, while the latter was a Near East river trader. Built by Turners of Wolverhampton, the Varley-Woods was a good-looking car with a Rolls-Royce-type radiator and polished aluminum hood. A 1795cc Dorman engine was used, this interesting power unit having an aluminum block and ohc. But from mid-1920 a more conventional 14.3 hp Tylor was fitted.

VATE • France 1908-1909

Three models, an 8 hp single-cylinder, a 10 hp twin, and a 15 hp four, were built by this firm from Puteaux, all with electric transmissions.

VAUXHALL • England 1903 to date

See panel

VAUZELLE • France 1902-1908

Emile Vauzelle originally marketed an Aster-engined 5 hp voiturette under the name Vauzelle-Morel, though in the marque's latter days its cars and voiturettes were known simply as "Vauzelle." A 12 hp 1815cc four was offered in 1907-1908.

VECHET • Czechoslovakia 1911-1914

Small cars of sporting appearance. The first model was a watercooled twin-cylinder of 1004cc, the second (and last) a 2111cc four-cylinder with a three-seater body. Production of these neat cars was on a small scale.

VECTOR • USA 1991 to date

A constant motor show exhibit since the mid-1970s, the twin-turbo 6 liter Chevy-powered Vector supercar finally went into production in 1992.

1913 Vauxhall 25 hp Prince Henry tourer

VAUXHALL • England 1903 to date

The first Vauxhall of 1903 was an American-inspired 5.5 cwt runabout with a transverse 5 hp horizontal engine, chain drive and tiller steering. A 6 hp version came out the next year, boasting the luxury of a reverse gear! In 1905 the company moved from London's Vauxhall to Luton, Bedfordshire, bringing out no fewer than three models of three-cylinder cars (this time with vertical engines.) These cars were successfully used in trials and hillclimbs, but an entry in the 1905 Tourist Trophy proved abortive, despite the use of a six-speed gearbox. Although demand continued, a more conventional shaft-driven car, the 18/20 four-cylinder model, proved extremely successful, leading to the demise of the earlier types. A 3-liter Vauxhall put up a sterling performance in the German Prince Henry Trials in 1910 and 1911. The engine capacity was increased to 4 liters and the car named the Prince Henry in recognition of the achievement. From this emerged the most famous of all Vauxhalls, the 30/98. For this, works manager L H Pomeroy increased the engine capacity to 4.5 liters in 1913. A few examples were made before the First World War, though it was again available in 1919. Designated the E-Type, it received a new ohv 4.2-liter engine and front-wheel brakes in 1922, thereafter being known as the OE.

The company had been one of the few to continue manufacture throughout the war, the D-Type being made for the Services. In 1922 the cheaper 14/40 appeared and the D-Type was granted overhead valves. In December 1925 the American General Motors took over, though it was not until three years later that the first GM-inspired Vauxhalls appeared, the 20/.60 with overhead valves, coil ignition, and central gear-change. The 2-liter Cadet of 1931 was a cheap six announced the following year, offering a synchromesh gearbox and beating Rolls-Royce to the post. Two other lighter sixes, the 12 and 14, were introduced in 1933, though at the other end of the range the company offered a 3.2-liter six in 1934, this "Big Six" surviving until 1937, when it was replaced by the independent suspension 25 hp model. Unitary construction on the four-cylinder 10 of 1938 gave Vauxhall another technical first in Britain. Priced at £158, though

1961 Vauxhall Velox PA 2 1/4 litre six-cylinder sedan

1992 Vauxhall Astra GT

only having a three-speed gearbox, it offered 40 mpg. The following year all models were fitted with hydraulic brakes, one being the newly introduced J model, a 14 hp car with a 1781cc six-cylinder engine, costing a competitive £220.

The post-war era saw the four-cylinder 10 and 12 and the six-cylinder 14 offered, though by 1948 all had been phased out and replaced by the 1442cc Wyvern and the 2275cc Velox, using four- and six-cylinder engines respectively. These L-Type models featured completely new styling, with a markedly transatlantic front end and faired-in headlights. A steering-column gearchange was another feature imported from America. In 1952 both models were restyled, with short-stroke engines replacing the original power units. Three years later a luxury version of the six, the Cresta, appeared, costing £844. These E-Type models remained in production until 1957, the year that saw the introduction of the four-cylinder 1.5-liter Victor with its distinctive wraparound windshield, the six being similarly equipped in 1958. By 1962 the Victor had been restyled, the Velox and Cresta receiving similar treatment the following year. In 1964 more powerful engines were introduced, the Victor now displacing 1.6 liters, while the six was increased to 3.3 liters.

Vauxhall made a major departure from previous practice in 1964 by announcing a new small car, the 1057cc Viva. It was restyled for 1967 and again in 1970, this HC variant being offered in 1159cc and 1256cc forms. A completely new Victor appeared for 1968 in 1.6- and 2-liter variants, having inclined ohc engines, the camshaft being driven by a neoprene belt, the first occasion that this feature was offered on a production car in Britain. The faithful 3.3-liter six was fitted into a similar bodyshell, and named the Ventora.

It was "all change" again in 1971, the Victors being upped to 1800cc and 2300cc and sporting chunkier bodywork also shared with the Ventora. The Victor engine, though of 1600cc, was also offered in the Viva bodyshell.

Classic Vauxhalls from a classic 1970s era. This is the Viva range (above.) Vauxhall's coupé, the Tigra (left)

A coupé version, the Firenza, appeared in 1971, with a choice of 1256cc, 1600cc, and 2300cc engines. However, in 1973 the entire Viva/Firenza range was overhauled, the Viva being retained for the smallest-capacity engines, the 1800 and 2300 being called Magnums. In 1975 a new model, the Chevette, was launched, a good-looking coupé with hatchback tailgate, powered by the 1256cc Viva engine, and available in 10 variants in 1979. Early in 1979 new Opel-based luxury models, the Carlton and Royale, were announced. The Cavalier, a 1300 /1600/1900cc mid-sized sedan originally imported from Belgium, was by that time made in Britain. The last Viva was built in mid-1979.

Vauxhall and Opel became totally integrated in the 1980s, though some mid-decade Opel specialty cars, such as the Manta GTE of 1985 and Monza GSE, were sold under their original marque name. The Spanish-built 1983 Nova, Vauxhall's first minicar, was the same as the Opel Corsa. The all-new Astra hatchback of 1984 was an Opel Kadett by any other name; the 1985 Belmont was a notchback derivative. Late in 1986 came a new Carlton executive saloon, an Astra convertible following in 1987. In 1988 came a thoroughly-modern Cavalier in two body styles and 22 model variants, including a 4x4 2.0-liter version. In 1991 Vauxhall entered the off-road leisure vehicle market with the Frontera, while an all-new Astra made its debut in 1992 in hatchback sedan and estate versions. The Vectra sedan and hatch range took over from the Cavalier and competed successfully against the Mondeo, styling being the Vectra's strong point. The Calibra range of coupés also sold well, especially in the gap in the market left by the demise of the Ford Capri, which was not filled by the Probe. A new small coupé named Tigra debued in 1993. The company shared the Omega with its Opel partner, and in estate form this sold well in the UK. It also became a popular company car. The high powered MV6 version found favor with several police forces as a high-speed pursuit car. In 1998 a new Astra arrived with new engines, new specifications, and advanced styling and crash safety levels. With 1.4, 1.6 and 1.8 engines in a range of styles and trim levels it heads the hatchback class, alongside the new VW Golf. A brief affair with the US sourced Sintra MPV showed Vauxhall how overcrowded the MPV market was, and in 1999 it was dropped, to be replaced by an Astra based MPV.

1950 Veritas sports saloon

1918 Velie Sport Car

1903 Miniature Velox

VEDOVELLI & PRIESTLEY • France 1899

A three-wheeled electric carriage which was steered by slowing the speed of rotation of the wheel on the inside of the curve.

VEERAC • USA 1913

"Valveless, Explosion Every Revolution, Air Cooled" summed up this two-cylinder 1655cc two-stroke from Anoka, Minnesota.

VEHEL • France 1899-1901

Available with 6 hp single or 8 hp twin power units, the Véhel was built by M & A Dulac of Paris.

VELIE • USA 1909-1928

W L Velie, of Moline, Illinois, had built up to 25,000 carriages annually for over 40 years before producing the Velie "30" early in 1909. It had a four-cylinder 3295cc American & British engine, and its price of $1,750 was based on projected sales of 10,000 in 1910. The 1915 season saw the 40 hp "Biltwell Model 22" Continental-engined six at $1065, and for 1917 the "Greater Velie Biltwell" was launched. Marque popularity in Shreveport, Louisiana, was such that a suburb of the town was named Velie in 1916. The four-seat "Sport Car" of 1918 had a long-stroke 4966cc six with triple external exhausts and a Victoria hood of impractical but elegant design. For the 1920s Velies became cheaper and more angular, the company making its own 3335cc ohv six-cylinder power unit from 1922. Some 1927-1928 models had a Lycoming straight-eight.

VELOX • England 1902-1904

Velox of Coventry claimed to be "one of the pioneers of the English motor trade;" its 1903 12 hp was a tubular-framed four-cylinder shaft-drive car. It also made the curious low-slung Baby Velox voiturette, one of which survives.

VELOX • Austria 1906-1910

A single-cylinder 10 hp car with the engine mounted below the driver's seat. Many of these cars were used as taxicabs, while others were exported (mainly to Russia.) Velox operated these cabs on many routes in and around Prague, which was then still in the Austro-Hungarian Empire. After car production ceased, Velox imported cars and parts and for some time operated the biggest garage in town.

VENTURI •France 1990 to date

A new name in supercar manufacturing, Venturi is a French based concern making the Atlantic 300 mid-engined V-6 sportscar featuring a composite and steel braced body, electric steering rack, and superb handling. The elegant and clean lined body has shades of Pininfarina and Ferrari influence. It sells in exclusive numbers to a discerning number of well heeled buyers, for whom fuel costs and depreciation are not a concern.

VERITAS • Germany 1946-1952

Founded by ex-German motorcycle racing champion Ernst Loof and some ex-BMW employees, Veritas first built sports and racing cars with the pre-war 1971cc BMW 328 six-cylinder engines. It also produced a few coupés and cabriolets with this engine, as well as with ohc 1899cc six-cylinder Heinkel motors. In conjunction with the French Panhard factory, Dyna-Veritas cars with ohv 744cc flat-twin Panhard engines were also built in small numbers. Lack of sufficient funds eventually led to the demise of this make, which also produced Meteor 2-liter FII racing cars. Successful Veritas racing drivers included Kling, Pietsch, Ulmen, Helfrich, Lang, and Hirt.

VERMOREL • France 1904-1930

The first Vermorel cars, designed by Pilain, were horizontal twins of 2598cc, but serious production did not begin until 1908 with a pair-cast four of 1874cc, soon uprated to 2064cc. In 1912 a 3308cc four appeared, and a 1642cc light car was added at the end of the year. Though various sporting models were produced throughout the 1920s, the post-war mainstay of this Villefranche-sur-Saône, Rhône, factory was a four-cylinder 12 cv with dual rear springing.

The 1900 fwd Victoria Combination (2 1/4 hp De Dion engine), sold in Britain as the 'Eureka Voiturette'

1904 twin-cylinder 2597cc Vermorel

c. 1899 Victor steam Stanhope

VERNON • USA 1920-1921

The Vernon succeeded the Able, which had been in business since 1917. With its own make of engine, the Vernon line featured a V-8 and a four; touring car prices were reported as being $1,695 and $845 respectively. Production was limited.

VESPA • France 1958-1961

The Ateliers de Construction de Motos et Accessoires, established in Fourchambault, Niévre, made the twin-cylinder two-stroke 400cc Vespa car under license.

VESTA • England 1903

A 7 hp "car set" for home assembly, sold by Danny Citröen of Holborn Viaduct, London.

VICEROY • England 1915

An 1162cc light car built in Nottingham.

VICI • England 1906-1907

A 12/16 hp four-cylinder engine powered this assembled car from north-west London.

VICKSTOW • England 1913

Vickers and Bristow of London assembled the chassis of this £125 two-seater from bought-in components, mostly American. It had a 1968cc monobloc engine and a "particularly smart" bullnose radiator.

VICTOR • USA 1899-1904

A. H. Overman, of Chicopee Falls, Mass., built the Victor steam and gasoline cars. The 1899 Victor had a vertical twin-cylinder engine, and incorporated a curious anti-theft device; a spring lever under the seat locked the throttle when the driver rose to leave the car.

VICTOR • England 1915-1921

The Tyler Apparatus Company of London built this vee-radiatored cyclecar with 965cc Precision engine and belt drive.

VICTORIA • Germany 1900-1909, 1956-1958

Well known as a motorcycle manufacturer, Victoria of Nürnburg built single-, twin-, and four-cylinder cars, using De Dion, Aster and Fafnir proprietary engines with capacities ranging from 482cc to 2680cc. From 1909 to 1956 it concentrated on two-wheelers, and entered car manufacture again with the Spatz.

VICTORIA • Spain 1904-1905, 1917-1923

Named after Queen Victoria Eugenie, the 1904 Madrid-built Victoria was available as a twin-cylinder 4cv or a four-cylinder 18cv. In 1917 the same company, the Garage Franco-Espagnol, began production of a neat ohv 950cc four-cylinder light car. About 100 were built before the London-based Gwynne company took over the design.

VICTORIA • England 1907

A 10/12 hp four-cylinder side-entrance phaeton from Godalming, Surrey.

VICTORIA COMBINATION • France 1899-1901

The Société Parisienne produced this curious tiller-steered two-seater, which used what amounted to the rear end of a De Dion tricycle as a fwd unit. It was also known as the "Eureka" ("with the little friction clutch.") More conventional Duc-Spider and Duc-Tonneau cars followed, with Aster engines.

1914 Violet-Bogey 10 hp two-seater

1923 Vinot 12/25 hp Special Three-Quarter Coupé

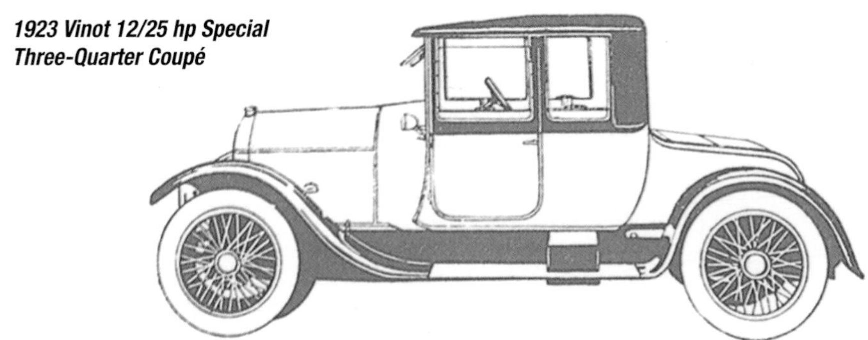

VICTORIAN • Canada 1900

A flat-twin prototype built by a Nova Scotian furniture manufacturer.

VICTRIX • France 1903

Successors to the 1902 Farman, Victrix cars were 6 hp single-cylinder voiturettes. Victrix engines of 12 hp and 24 hp were also made, but the cars in which they were used were sold as "FAC."

VICTRIX • France 1919-c. 1924

A 15 hp, from Paris, "of entirely French construction."

VIKING • USA 1919-1930

Built by Olds, this was a lower-priced version of the La Salle, distinguished by a 4244cc V-8 with chain-driven camshaft between the blocks.

VIKING • Isle of Man • England 1965-1967

Some 20 Viking Minisprints were built. The car featured a square-tube chassis to which the fastback glassfiber bodies were attached. All mechanical parts were from the Mini.

VILAIN • France 1900-1905

The Vilain, from Paris 16e, had an underfloor horizontal single-cylinder engine and two-speed chain drive.

VILLARD • France 1925-1935

When the Colombe cyclecar ceased production the design was taken over by M Villard in Janville, Eure et Loir, who made it under his own name. These small three-wheelers had a two-stroke Harissard engine of 346cc.

VINCKE • Belgium 1894-c. 1905

Belgium's first car manufacturer, Vincke, built heavy, Panhard-like vehicles at its Malines factory. In 1903 a model known as the Vincke-Halcrow was sold in England.

VINCO • England 1904-1905

A 3.5 hp Fafnir-engined tricar made in Peterborough.

VINDELICA • Germany 1899

This make, sold in England as the PTS, showed a four-wheeled motor carriage at the 1899 National Cycle Show in London. The car cost £160; the hood was an extra £20. The company also made tricycles, including an expensive (£950) "Tricycle and Goods Truck."

VINET • France 1900-1904

Aimed especially at "doctors, architects, businessmen and commercial travellers", these low-built crocodile-hooded voiturettes had Aster engines and "combined every desire of the most exacting sportsmen."

VINEX • England 1903

An obscure marque sold by Robert Ramsbottom of Manchester.

VINOT-DEGUINGAND • France 1901-1925

Vinot-Deguingand of Puteaux and Nanterre, Seine, started with 1500cc twin-cylinders, then made four-cylinder models of 12cv (2211cc) and 18cv (3685cc.) In 1911 it added a 50cv six of 8101cc to the range. Vinot took over Gladiator in 1909, and its cars were often sold under that name, and vice versa. The 1912 9cv of 1693cc was continued after the war alongside new models like the 12cv of 2613cc and the 10cv (1847cc.) When Vinot failed, its works were bought by Donnet; the Deguingand name was resurrected in 1928 for the limited production of a Violet-designed cyclecar.

VIOLET-BOGEY • France 1912-1914

Marcel Violet, prolific designer of curious two-strokes, also designed this lively twin-cylinder four-stroke cyclecar of 1.1 liters, with friction transmission and overhead inlet valves.

VIOLETTE • France 1909-1914

Built by Franc & Cie of Levallois-Perret, Seine, La Violette was a crude cyclecar designed by Marcel Violet. It had friction transmission, chain final drive and an armored-

Rudolf Valentino in his 1924 Voisin C5 tourer

wood chassis. Single and twin-cylinder engines were initially available, though a more conventional four-cylinder light car appeared in 1914.

VIPEN • England 1898-c. 1904

Probably Continental imports, the early cars offered by this Hull cycle manufacturer resembled the contemporary Panhards.

VIQUEOT • USA • France 1905

Chassis of 28/32 hp and 40/45 hp were built at Puteaux (Seine) for this marque and shipped to Long Island City for bodies to be fitted for the American market.

VIRATELLE • France 1922-1926

Made in Lyon by the Société Anonyme des Motocyclettes et Automobiles Viratelle, these were small 350cc-engined cyclecars.

VIRGINIA • USA 1923

The Virginia automobile was the result of a corporation change in what had been formerly Piedmont; any automobiles bearing the Virginia nameplate were simply Piedmont cars with the new name.

VIRUS • France 1930-1935

The Virus, made in Paris by the Garage Renouvier, was a fwd cyclecar with a 350cc two-stroke engine.

VIVINUS • Belgium 1899-1912

The original Vivinus was a single-cylinder belt-driven voiturette, also manufactured under license by New Orleans in England, Georges Richard in France, and De Dietrich in Alsace-Lorraine. A twin-cylinder derivative appeared in 1900. Vivinus, whose factory was at Schaerbeek, Brussels, brought out a shaft-drive 15/18 hp four, later offering twins and sixes on similar lines. The final range consisted of three fours, a 10/12 hp, a 16/20 hp, and a 24/30 hp.

VOGTLAND • Germany 1910-1912

Small 12 hp and 20 hp cars with proprietary engines and many other bought-in parts.

VOGUE • USA 1920-1923

The Vogue was an assembled car closely affiliated with the Economy and built in Tiffin, Ohio. Two six-cylinder models were marketed throughout the Vogue"s four years of production, the 6-55 (powered by a Herschell-Spillman engine) and the Continental-powered 6-66, touring models of which sold for $2,285 and $2,485 respectively. Several hundred cars were probably built.

VOISIN • France 1919-1939

Aviation pioneer Gabriel Voisin was forced to convert his Issy-les-Moulineaux, Seine, works after the war because there were no more orders for airplanes. He decided to build cars but, being a strong individualist, his cars were far from conventional, and all used sleeve-valve engines. The first car built by Voisin was a 18/23cv of 3969cc, which was continued for nearly ten years. A 7238cc V-12 was exhibited as early as 1921; that year saw the launch of the 1244cc C4 four-cylinder model. In 1927 Voisin presented some attractive six-cylinder models, the best of which was the 13cv of 2300cc. In 1930 came the 4800cc Diane and the Simoun 5.8-liter six. There was also the Sirocco V-12. In the 1930s some Minerva models were built under license without great success. The year 1936 saw a strange 6-liter straight-twelve, which remained a prototype. At the very end Voisin was forced to use the American Graham 3500cc engine, the sole exception to the sleeve-valves. Gabriel Voisin made many of the bodies for his cars; it is said that he was helped in their design by architect Le Corbusier. These controversial bodies may not have been fashionable, but they certainly attracted a good deal of attention. Voisin's engineering drew heavily on aircraft practice, and he always made great use of light alloy. After the Second World War Voisin made the tiny Biscooter for Spain.

VOLKSWAGEN • Germany 1938 to date

See panel overleaf

VOITUCAR • England 1900

With a 4.5 hp MMC-De Dion engine, the Voitucar was a two-seater ("best English carriage building") with an additional "Emergency Seat for two more."

VOLKSROD • England 1967 to date

Along with the various GP models, the Volksrod VW-based glassfiber buggies were by far the best of an otherwise indifferent breed. Short- and long-wheelbase versions sold for a little over £300 in early 1979.

VOLPE • Italy 1947-1949

An ambitious mini-car with a rear-mounted 123cc flat-twin two-stroke engine and a sporting open two-seater body, the Volpe was not a best-seller. The former aircraft factory at Piacenza soon ceased production of this little car.

The Porsche Type 60 which evolved into the Volkswagen Beetle, the most successful car in motoring history

VOLKSWAGEN • Germany 1938 to date

Ferdinand Porsche designed the prototypes of his "Volkswagen" (people's car) at the behest of the Nazi party in 1934-1936, and a series of 30 pilot cars was constructed in 1937 by Daimler-Benz. In 1938 Adolf Hitler laid the cornerstone of the Volkswagen factory at Wolfsburg, but though the cars were known as the KdF-Wagen (Kraft durch Freude: Strength through Joy) and theoretically available on subscription, no cars were released to the public before the war. Various military VWs appeared with a rear air-cooled flat-four engine of 1131 cc, this power unit being used on the post-war models which began to be produced by loyal employees in the bomb-flattened ruins of the Wolfsburg factory.

Both an Allied investigation team and Henry Ford II dismissed the VW (nicknamed Kuäfer: Beetle) as having no commercial future, but it went on to become the most successful car in motoring history, outselling even the Model T Ford. Over the years the Beetle acquired more powerful engines of 1192cc (1954,) 1285cc, (1965,) 1493cc (1966,) and 1584cc (1970.) The first break with tradition was the VW 1500 of 1961; engines of up to 1795cc were subsequently adopted on this model. Then VW acquired NSU, and with it the new K70 with a front-mounted ohc water-cooled vertical four of 1594cc, and this was produced as a VW from 1970 to 1974. In 1973 VW introduced the Passat, with engines of 1297cc to 1471cc, followed a year later by the Scirocco of 1093cc to 1457cc, and the Golf with a 1093cc engine. In 1975 came the highly successful Polo minicar with an 895cc engine; 1093cc and 1272cc versions were subsequently offered, and a version with a conventional trunk instead of the hatchback was introduced under the name Derby.

The Golf is now available with engines up to 1588cc, and is built (as the Rabbit) in Pennsylvania, with such success that US-built VW sales actually outstripped American Motors in the sales league in December 1978, only a few months after the factory had gone into operation. The Golf is also offered with a 1471cc ohc diesel engine. At the 1979 Geneva Show a Cabriolet version was launched. The VW Polo hatchback and Derby notchback appeared in 1981, and in 1985 a low-volume supercharged version, the G40, was introduced. The Scirocco was another 1981 introduction. A new-look Golf hatchback was launched in 1983; a year later its notchback derivative, the Jetta, was launched. A new Passat appeared in 1988; from 1991 it was available with VW's first six-cylinder engine, the 2.8-liter VR6. A Golf III was launched in 1991, the Jetta following in 1992.

VW has a factory in Brazil where the Gol, Voyage and Parati make up the "BX" range. The VW-Brazil Apollo was a rebadged Ford Verona.

In the 1990s Volkswagen underwent a stunning series of changes. Always a provider of basic bread-and-butter-type cars, such as the Passat and Golf, as well as sports cars like the Scirocco and the later Corrado coupé, the firm was hardly seen as a leader in the field of advanced design. Yet in the space of a few model cycles VWs mainstream cars served not only its traditional buyers but also set new design parameters for the marque and the industry. The Mk 4 Golf looked evolutionary, not revolutionary, yet it had very high levels of trim and build quality that set new class standards. A completely new Polo range with 1.0, 1.4, and 1.6-liter engines was launched in 1996 and went straight to the top of its class as the definitive small car, where it remained for a long time. The new Passat range was revolutionary in its "hooped roof" styling and advanced engineering, the turbocharged direct-injection diesel engine providing class leading economy allied

1978 VW 1303 Convertible

1978 VW Passat (left,) VW Golf GTI Mark III in black (below,) the 1999 VW Beetle RSI (bottom)

to strong mid-range performance. A five-cylinder V5 engine and a 4wd option complement this car's abilities.

For many, the highlight of VW's design-led charge was the launch of the new Beetle. Built in Mexico and shipped into America and Europe, it created much exposure for VW with its throwback styling and sporting Rsi variants. In 1999 the new Lupo city car arrived. It drew on VW partner Seat's experience, and was just one example of the new VW's breadth of capability. Through being part of the giant VW/Audi conglomerate, where floorpans, engines, and subassemblies could be mixed and matched throughout model ranges, greatly reducing costs, and through buying Skoda, Bentley, Seat, and Bugatti, VW has amassed for itself an enviable collection of brand legends with which to complement its own past, as well as its more recent achievements.

VOLVO AUTO AB • Sweden 1927 to date

The name Volvo derives from the Latin word meaning "to roll." It was perhaps fortuitous that when the first production Volvo did indeed attempt to roll out of the factory, it was, reputedly, in reverse gear! The first Volvo left the Gothenburg factory on the morning of 14 April 1927. But planning had started in 1924 when Assar Gabrielsson and Gustaf Larson discussed assembling a car suited to Swedish roads from components commissioned from Swedish firms. The SKF ball-bearing company provided backing, and ten prototypes were built and tested in 1926. The car had a 1.9-liter single-valve four-cylinder engine and was American-inspired. This was no wonder, as at least two of the designers had worked in the USA, and the car was tested by a Swedish-born Hupmobile employee, later employed by Volvo to develop its six-cylinder cars. Some 1,000 examples of the OV4 tourer and the PV4 closed sedan were sold in two years. In 1929 a 3.1-liter six (PV651) on American lines appeared. The PV652, almost the same car but with hydraulic brakes, came in 1930 and was developed until 1936. The PV36 Carioca of 1935 looked like a Chrysler Airflow and had ifs and an all-steel body. It was not a success, and was followed by the more conventional PV51/52 at the end of 1936. Volvo produced nearly 2,000 cars in 1937, although only 56 were exported. Commercial vehicles were still much more important. In 1938 the more streamlined PV53-56 appeared, a development of the earlier model. It was produced in small numbers during the war, often being sold with a wood-burning gas-producer unit on a small trailer. The PV60 went into production in 1947, though prototypes were tested in 1942. It was to be the last six-cylinder Volvo for many years. The experimental PV40 developed just before the war was a small rear-engined car with an eight-cylinder radial engine and unit body construction, but production problems caused it to be abandoned.

1935 Volvo TR703 saloon

Volvo 264 GLE saloon

1960 Volvo P1800 sports coupé

Planning started for the more conventional PV444, with a four-cylinder 1.4-liter ohv engine, ifs, rear coil-suspension and unit body construction. The car was shown in 1944, but lack of body steel meant that production did not started until 1947. The car was redesigned in 1958 and called the PV544. The five-bearing 1.8-liter B18-engine appeared on the 1962 model. Around half a million were built. In 1956 the 120 or 122 appeared (there were many variations, and in Sweden the model was called Amazon), with a totally new body, but many mechanical components shared with the older model. Before it was dropped in 1970, 600,000 had been built. A sports car with glass-fiber body, the P1900, was built in 1956/57, but it was underpowered and unsuccessful. Its successor was the P1800, a two-seater coupé with the B18 engine. Pressed Steel in Scotland built the bodies, and the cars were assembled by Jensen. The first cars came from England in 1961, three years after the car had been exhibited in New York, which caused some embarrassment in Gothenburg. Production was slow and assembly was moved to Gothenburg in 1963. The Swedish-built cars were called P1800S, and in 1966 and 1969 the engine output was increased. The 1800E had electronic fuel injection and 130 bhp, enough for 110 mph. In 1971 a 2+2 (1800ES) with glass rear hatchback door was produced; 39,414 cars of various types of this sports car were built before production ended in 1973. The 100-series (the first model was the 144, which meant 1 = 100-series, 4 = four-cylinder, and 4 = four-door) was introduced in 1966 and had many safety features, which set the standard for years to come. The B18 engine was used, but in 1969 came the 2-liter B20 engine, with fuel injection on one model in 1971. The line was redesigned in 1973 and given new ohc engines. In 1968 came the six-cylinder 164 with the 3-liter B30 engine; later, co-operation with Renault and Peugeot resulted in a new V-6 engine. In 1974 Volvo bought the Dutch DAF factory and introduced the Volvo 66 in 1975, a DAF with safety features added. In 1976 came the Volvo 343, a new car with a De Dion rear axle, four-cylinder engine and belt transmission. It was then made available with an ordinary gearbox and became an unexpected sales success, notably in Britain, where the fuel-injected GLT model offered high power and good old-fashioned rear-wheel-drive handling. Although it was a small car it had big-car safety standards, and in crash safety terms exceeded its medium sized hatchback sector competitors. The 240 series of cars took over from the 140 series, as a longer-nosed, restyled development, and in estate/shooting brake form made Volvo's name for such cars. In 1977 Volvo launched the limited-edition 262 Coupé made by Bertone; a proposed merger with Saab-Scania was dropped. Volvo's first turbo model, the 240 Turbo, appeared in 1980. The US-influenced, angular 740/760 executive car range was introduced in 1982; its last development was the 940/960/ V90 range. Volvo Holland launched the sporty 480 in 1985 and the 440 in 1988. A 480 cabriolet concept appeared in 1991. That year, Volvo announced that it was entering the upper middle class with the transverse five-cylinder-engined 850.

The 850 started a revolution at Volvo. While it was traditionally Volvo in being safe and a superb estate/station wagon, it handled far better than previous Volvos. Although still square-rigged in styling terms, it introduced a softening of the Volvo "tank" or square-edged image. Subsequently it was revised as the V80 and S80 models. After that, 1997 saw the curvaceous and elegant S/V40 range of smaller sized Volvos and 1999 saw the S80 model. The C70 coupé Volvo"s first in years, was a smash hit and sold well in America, notably to the Hollywood set, who loved its curved yet subtle looks. These models reflected the design input from a revitalized Volvo design unit headed

The Volvo 850 R which, in estate form, found favor with police forces as a high-speed pursuit vehicle

by Englishman Peter Horbury, who was brought in and tasked by the Volvo management with reviving the image and extend its appeal. In the super-safe, superb-handling, swift and curvaceous S80 he produced a car that was forward thinking yet also harked back to Volvo's past without being a retro design pastiche

With its high-quality image, safety reputation and huge brand loyalty in America, Britain, and Europe, Volvo became a success, and many were surprised when the company"s board recommended acceptance of a surprise cash offer for the entire Volvo car company from the giant Ford conglomerate in 1999.

The V40 kept the regular Volvo grille design

VOODOO • England 1971-1975

Started as a private venture, the Voodoo first appeared on the *Daily Telegraph* stand at the 1971 Motor Show. The center of the sleek, glassfiber body was bonded to the purpose-built chassis, while the nose and rear sections were bolted in place. Power came from a rear-mounted Hillman Imp unit.

VORAN • Germany 1926-1929

Belonging to NAG, Voran's Berlin factory first built motorcycles, then small sv 1076cc four-cylinder cars with Amilcar engines license-built by Pluto. A 30 hp model had a 1461cc four-cylinder motor. These fwd cars were designed by Richard Bussien.

VOUSEMOI • France 1904

Vousémoi ("vous et moi": "you and I") cars were available with either 10 hp twin or 16/20 hp four-cylinder Gnome engines.

VOX • England 1912-1915

From the same maker as the L & P, this was a two-stroke 6/9 hp cyclecar of flimsy appearance.

VULCAN • England 1902-1928

The first Vulcan was a belt-driven single cylinder model, the result of two years' experimentation by the Hampson brothers, Thomson and Joseph. A 10 hp twin followed, with 12 hp and 16 hp cars appearing in 1905. By the outbreak of the First World War a wide range of models had been built, most between 2 and 3 liters capacity. The postwar years were plagued by financial difficulties, caused to some extent by the firm's involvement with the Harper Bean combine. A 3.5-liter V-8 appeared briefly in 1919; by 1922 Howard sleeve-valve engines were being considered but failed to materialize. Dorman engines were fitted to the 1.8-liter 12 and 2.6-liter 16/20, though the 20 hp used Vulcan's own 3.3-liter engine. From 1923 the company established a link with Lea-Francis, with Vulcan being responsible for some Lea-Francis engines and L-F making parts for Vulcan. Dealer resources were also pooled. But the Vulcan 12 of 1925 had a Dorman engine, even though it looked much like a Lea-Francis! Private car production was gradually run down, and from 1928 only commercial vehicles were produced.

VULCAN • USA 1913-1914

"Like a thunderbolt from a clear sky", the $750 Vulcan Speedster was a light car from Painesville, Ohio. Ambitious production plans for this "truly remarkable car" (an $850 five-seater was also offered) came to nothing.

VULPES • France 1908-1910

Vulpes of Paris built an 8 hp single as well as fours up to 30/40 hp. In 1906 it listed a 12/15 hp and 20/24 hp featuring the circular radiator with raised header tank that distinguished the Vulpés. De Dion single- and Janus four-cylinder engines were used; the marque even had Grand Prix aspirations.

1931 5879cc Walter Royal 12-cylinder cabriolet

WADDINGTON • England 1903

A 6.5 hp voiturette built in Middlesbrough with De Dion or Aster power unit.

WAF • Austria 1910-1927

Owned by Dr Zachariades, WAF built cars on a limited scale in the former Bock & Hollander works. It offered four-six-, and, eventually, eight-cylinder models as well, which, driven by Zachariades, also competed in sporting events. Among smaller models, the 2.8-liter four-cylinder was a very good car for connoisseurs, as it was (like all WAF models) very expensive.

WAGGENHALS • USA 1913-1915

A 24 hp three-wheeler with chain drive to the rear wheel; a van version was built for the US Post Office.

WAHL • USA 1913-1914

This Chicago firm (the name means "choice" in German) offered 3261cc cars without nameplates for enterprising "manufacturers" to sell as their own creation.

WALKER • USA 1900-1901

A two/four-seater steam carriage named after Orrin P Walker, president of the Marlboro (Mass) Automobile & Carriage Co.

WALL • England 1911

Built by the maker of the Roc motorcycle, this curious machine resembled a wide sidecar mounted on a three-wheeled chassis, the single front wheel being controlled by a long tiller.

WALTER • Czechoslovakia 1913-1937

Founded by Josef Walter, this Jinonice-based factory built motorcycles and three-wheelers before it began production of cars of the highest calibre. Aero-engine manufacture was introduced in the 1920s. Walter originally built 18 hp, 25 hp, and 30 hp four-cylinder cars; in the 1920s it offered 1540cc light cars with sv and ohv engines and a sv 2120cc four-cylinder model. Later versions had ohv engines of 1945cc and 1540cc. A beautiful 2990cc six-cylinder was added in 1929, soon followed by a 3.3-liter version. Many bodies were made by such famous coach-builders as Sodomka, Jech, Brozik, Aero (Weymann), Uhlik, and others. A 5879cc V-12 Walter, the "Royal," was the most expensive and luxurious car made by the factory. It was built between 1931 and 1934 in small numbers. Even a bus with a 7354cc V-12 engine appeared on the market in 1931. More popular was the 1438cc four-cylinder Bijou; the six-cylinder Standard 3-liter and Super 3.3-liter touring cars also sold well. From 1933 Walter built 995cc and 1089cc Fiats with ohv four-cylinder engines under license. During the 1920s racing cars were made for Walter works-driver Jindrich Knapp. Walter cars also won many big trials and rallies, often driven by the then owners, the Kumpera family. The factory, now nationalized, still produces aero engines.

1926 Wanderer

1914 Warren-Lambert

WALTHAM • USA 1898-1901

A typical tiller-steered steam runabout. Though the prototype was built in the Waltham Manufacturing Company"s Orient cycle factory, there was no other connection.

WALTHAM • USA 1922

Successor to the friction-drive Metz, the Waltham had a conventional transmission. Featuring a Rutenber six-cylinder engine, the Waltham offered a full line of body types with prices beginning at $2,450 for the touring car. Relatively few cars were built, and most of those were open models.

WALTON • England 1904

Built at Great Sankey, Warrington, Lancashire, this was a 5 hp twin-cylinder forecarriage with a watercooled power unit.

WANDERER • Germany 1911-1939

Wanderer built superb tools, bicycles, motorcycles, and cars. Its first Wanderer cars had ioe 1145cc and ohv 1220cc four-cylinder engines with two- and three-seater bodywork. Improved versions of the 1220cc car were built until 1925. New in 1924 was an ohv 1550cc four-cylinder, followed in 1926 by a 1940cc version. The first six-cylinder Wanderer, displacing 2540cc, appeared in 1928, and 1930 brought a 2995cc sports car into the Wanderer range. Together with DKW, Horch, and Audi, Wanderer became a member of the newly founded Auto-Union in 1932. This brought a new shape to these excellent cars, and the 1692cc four-cylinder of 1933-1934 resembled the DKW. The Wanderer works at Siegmar and Schonau in Saxony later built a range of six-cylinder models with the W 50 of 1936-1939 as one of the top versions. Its ohv 2257cc engine developed 50bhp at 3500rpm. Other models were the sv four-cylinder 1767cc W 24 and the sv six-cylinder 2632cc W 23.

WARE STEAM WAGON • USA 1861-1867

Although not an automobile in the true sense, the Ware Steam Wagon was not a "one-off" but a make in its own right, several having been built by Elijah Ware of Bayonne, New Jersey. In addition, a Ware was probably the first self-propelled vehicle made in the USA to be exported. In 1866 a Ware Steam Wagon was exported to Rustico, Prince Edward Island (now a province of Canada but then a British Crown Colony,) having been ordered by the local Catholic priest, a Father Belcourt.

WARFIELD • England 1903

A paraffin-fired four-cylinder steam car with a flash boiler.

1964 Wartburg saloon

WARNE • England 1913-1915

An 8 hp JAP-engined cyclecar from Letchworth, Hertfordshire.

WARP 8 • Wales c. 1976

Masterminded by Welsh school teacher Owen Williams, the exotic-looking Warp 8 had a glassfiber body bonded to a VW floorpan. Power came from a modified Porsche 1600 unit.

WARREN-DETROIT • USA 1909-1914

A monobloc 3707cc four-cylinder engine powered the Warren-Detroit 30; the "12-40" had a 4416cc power unit.

WARREN-LAMBERT • England 1913-1922

A twin-cylinder Warren-Lambert light car, built in Richmond, Surrey, climbed the 1:2.5 gradient of Nailsworth Ladder four up in 1914, a feat repeated by the post-war four-cylinder model in 1920. Touring 1920 Warren-Lamberts had a 1330cc engine; the Sports model had a 1498cc power unit.

WARTBURG • Germany 1898-1904

The Fahrzeugfabrik Eisenach was founded by Henrich Ehrhardt's arms factory to build Wartburg cars at Eisenach in Thuringia under French Decauville license. From 1903 onwards the works became an independent car factory. The first cars had air- or watercooled ioe 479cc twin-cylinder engines of 4 hp, 5 hp, 8.5 hp, and 10 hp. Later four-cylinder models were up to 3140cc. Former Scheibler and

1972 Wartburg Knight

Cudell designer Willi Seck joined Eisenach in 1903 and created new cars, which became known as Dixi. BMW took over the Dixi works in 1928, and produced the Austin Seven under license in 1929-31, calling it the BMW "Wartburg."

WARTBURG • Germany 1956 to date

This three-cylinder two-stroke car, built by the nationalized (former Wartburg, Dixi ,and BMW) works at Eisenach in Thuringia, has fwd. Originally with a 900cc engine, from 1957 on power output was increased from 37 bhp to 50 bhp. In 1962 a 991cc engine was specified. The 1979 version of the Wartburg still used this three-cylinder unit.

WARWICK • England 1960-1962

Bernie Rodgers left Peerless to produce this Triumph TR development of his design. A 3.5-liter Buick V-8 was also offered in 1961.

WASHINGTON • USA 1909-1911

Built by the Carter Motor Car Corporation, of Washington, DC, (former maker of the Carter Twin Engine) the Washington car was guaranteed for five years. Embarrassingly, it only survived in production for two.

WASHINGTON • USA 1921-1924

Built in Eaton, Ohio, the Washington was a typical assembled car of its time, featuring two six-cylinder models in 1921 and 1922, using Falls and Continental engines. The Falls engine was dropped for 1923; the last gasoline Washingtons were built that year and used the Continental powerplant. For 1924 a steam car was announced and one pilot model was built. An estimated 65 units constituted the entire production of this make.

WASHINGTON • USA 1923

This car was announced but never built. Operations were centred on Washington, Penn. This car had no connection with the contemporary Washington from Eaton, Ohio.

WASP • England 1907-1908

The Wasp was a 3064cc shaft-driven six-cylinder model selling at £500 complete.

WASP • USA 1920-1925

Built by Karl H Martin of Bennington, Vermont, formerly the designer of the Roamer, Deering Magnetic, and Kenworthy automobiles, the Wasp appeared as a four-cylinder car between 1920 and 1924 and as a six afterward,

1960 Warwick GT

1924 Wasp Victoria

1899 Waverly electric runabout

using Wisconsin and Continental engines exclusively. Relatively high-priced (the fours selling for $5,500 each,) the entire output of 18 Wasp cars carried Victoria coachwork. Elaborate plans for a complete line of other open styles, as well as a complete line of formal closed cars, did not materialize. Mr Martin, a devout Episcopalian (Anglican,) had designed and cast a handsome St Christopher Medal during the First World War which had proved popular with US Armed Forces; all Wasp automobiles carried one of these medals on the dashboard as standard equipment.

WASSE • England 1903

Wasse cars in 8 hp and 16 hp forms were shown at the 1903 Crystal Palace Show.

WATROUS • USA 1905-1907

Better known for its fire-engines, this Elmira (NY) firm also built 12 hp two-cylinder light cars, priced from $400.

WATTEL & MORTIER • France 1921-1923

A six-cylinder car made in Paris with a sleeve-valve engine of 2655cc.

WAVERLEY • England 1910-1931

The first Waverleys used a 9 hp vee-twin JAP engine with a rear-mounted gearbox. This was later joined by a 10 hp four-cylinder and 15 hp car, with engines by Chapuis-Dornier. After the First World War One the 12 was the staple model. From 1922 a 10 hp Coventry-Climax-engined 1.5-liter was announced, and renamed the 11 hp two years later. A new 12 with a sleeve-valve engine was marketed in 1924, while a 16 hp model with Coventry-Climax engine appeared in 1925. A £100 car was an offering in 1925, with a watercooled flat-twin 900cc engine, but there appear to have been few takers.

WAVERLY • USA 1898-1916

Waverly Electrics were built by the Indiana Bicycle Company (a Pope firm) of Indianapolis. Among the vehicles offered was a 2.5 hp brougham fitted with an electric heater. The marque survived until 1916, building shaft-drive electrics.

WAYLAND • England 1901

A tricar whose manufacturer is unknown.

WAYNE • USA 1904-1908

The "Reliable Wayne," from Detroit, was available with either a 16 hp flat-twin engine or a vertical four-cylinder 24/28 hp power unit. The company's final offering was a 30 hp four selling for $2,500 fully equipped: "nothing to buy but the license"

WEARWELL • England 1899-1900

Two separate mid-mounted 4.5 hp De Dion engines powered this Wolverhampton-built voiturette with a triangulated tubular chassis.

WEBB • England 1922-1923

A stylish 9 hp Alpha-engined 1088cc four-seater from Stourport, Worcestershire.

WEBER • Switzerland 1899-1906

J Weber & Cie of Uster (Zürich) was a textile machinery manufacturer which built Rapid trivoiturettes under license, before turning to 2642cc single-cylinder cars with infinitely variable belt drive by expanding pulleys.

1913 Waverley 15 hp all-weather coupé

WEGMANN • Germany 1925-1926

A small car with a 1016cc four-cylinder Steudel engine, built by a railway carriage producer at Kassel

WEIDMANN • Switzerland 1905-1908

Also known as "Brunau," this Zürich marque had its unit engine/gearbox mounted on a subframe. Monobloc fours of 14/18 hp and 20/24 hp were offered.

WEIGEL • England 1906-1910

Danny Weigel was an ebullient motor agent and one of the prime movers in the establishment of the Clement-Talbot company in 1903. The cars he brought out under his own name in 1906 were suspiciously similar to the contemporary Itala. At first a 7433cc 40 hp was offered, followed in 1907 by a 60 hp six of 11,150cc, and a 4562cc 25 hp. That same year Weigel built the first British straight-eight Grand Prix car, using two 40 hp engines coupled end-to-end. The company was re-formed in 1907, moving in London from Islington to Notting Hill, where a 2850cc 20 hp was announced for 1910, but Weigel was taken over by Crowdy soon after.

WEISS • Germany 1902-1906

"Every speed without gears" was the slogan of Weiss cars, made in Berlin. They had friction drive and own-make two-and cylinder engines from 6 hp to 14 hp. Otto Weiss & Co also supplied engines to other manufacturers.

WEISS-MANFRED • Hungary 1927-1931

A sv 875cc four-cylinder car which gained fame when its creator, Ing Victor Szmick, finished second in the 1929 Monte-Carlo Rally behind a 4718cc Graham Paige. Early Weiss-Manfred models, from a big machine and arms factory in Budapest, had 746cc engines.

WELCH • USA 1903-1911

Former cycle builders of Chelsea, Michigan, the Welch brothers began serious production in 1904 in Pontiac. Their first car, a twin-cylinder 20 hp, had ohv in hemispherical heads. A 36 hp four appeared around 1906, with an overhead camshaft and an odd three-speed constant-mesh transmission with a separate hand clutch for each speed. A six was built in 1907-1908. In 1911 General Motors took over Welch, merged it with Rainier and created the Marquette.

WELDOER • Canada 1913

A twin-cylinder friction-drive cyclecar from Kitchener, Ontario, built by the Welker-Doerr Company.

WELER • France 1920-1923

Another cyclecar made by M Violet in Levallois, Seine, with a twin-cylinder 1060cc two-stroke engine with rotary valves. It was also available with 500cc and 1380cc engines.

1920 Weler cyclecar

WELLER • England 1902-1904

The Weller brothers of West Norwood, London, built a 20 hp four-cylinder with inlet valves whose time and degree of opening could be controlled by the driver. A 10 hp two-cylinder and a 1.75 hp motorcycle were also offered. Weller was the founder of AC.

WELLINGTON • England 1900-1901

Motor agent Frank Wellington built this rear-engined 2.5 hp single-cylinder voiturette.

WENDAX • Germany 1950-1951

One of the really bad cars, built soon after the Second World War with insufficient technical and financial facilities. It had a 746cc two-cylinder Ilo two-stroke engine and was handbuilt in limited numbers. Production ceased after the reputation of this primitive car worsened.

WENKELMOBIL • Germany 1904-1907

Early Wenkel-designed cars with one- and two-cylinder proprietary engines, supplied by De Dion, Fafnir and others.

WERNER • France 1906-1914

One of the great names in motorcycle manufacture, Werner Fréres also built a 5 hp twin-cylinder tricar and a 7/9 hp based on the Sizaire-Naudin. A 10/14 hp four was added for 1908, and in 1912 four-cylinder models of 1833cc, 3016cc, and 4072cc were listed, with attractive sloping radiators.

WEST, WEST-ASTER • England 1904-1912

West of Coventry built a range of cars, all with Aster engines. In 1906 it offered a 15 hp 16/20 hp, and 20/22 hp, all with four-cylinders; the following year a six was

1902 Weller 20 hp tonneau

1913 Westfalia limousine

1907 Westinghouse in the Coupé de la Presse

announced, with separate cylinders and a lubrication system worked by exhaust pressure. It had a curious gear-change, in which the lever had only two fore-and-aft positions, yet managed to control a three-speed and reverse gearbox (noisily, one imagines). From 1908 chassis were made for other firms.

WESTCAR • England 1922-1926

The Westcar was the brainchild of Major Charles Prescott-Westcar, and was built by the Strode Engineering Works of Herne, Kent. The Westcar used an 11.9 hp four-cylinder engine by Dorman; the same company also built the Heron.

WESTCOTT • USA 1910-1925

The first Westcotts had 45/50 hp Rutenber four-cylinder engines and sold for $2,000-$2,250. For 1915 the range consisted of three fours and a Northway-engined six. The 1917 Springfield Touring Sedan had foldaway window glasses so that it became a "hard-top" tourer. By 1920 Westcotts were being exported to Europe, despite their limited production. The 1921 range consisted of two monobloc sixes, the 3670cc "C-38" and the 4966cc "C-48." The last production Westcott had a 4078cc six; hydraulic four-wheeled brakes were offered in 1925.

WESTFALIA • Germany 1907-1914

A still extant producer of dairy apparatus, Ramesohl & Schmidt at Oelde (and for some time also at Bielefeld) built excellent cars with De Dion and Fafnir one- and two-cylinder engines. A 1570cc four-cylinder was made from 1909 to 1914; two other contemporary models had 1945cc and 2125cc engines. The biggest Westfalia car had a sv 2536cc four-cylinder engine. The four-cylinder engines were of Westfalia's own design and manufacture.

WESTFIELD • USA 1902-1903

These were "complete automobiles ready for power," though the company did also build some steam- and petrol-engined cars.

WESTFIELD • England 1982 to date

Westfield is a small British car manufacturer which started off building kit-car versions of the original Chapman inspired Lotus Seven-style open two-seater. The car is very much in the mold of the original 7, but now has the company's own distinct styling and engineering differences to differentiate between marques. Westfield has sold over 6,000 cars in the last decade. Now fully Type approved, Westfield's models have grown from the current 1.6 and 1.8-liter, Ford engined cars, through to the FW400 model with carbonfiber bodywork. This is powered by a Rover 4.0-liter V8 engine and can reach 0-60mph in 3.1 seconds. The Seight V8 model comes in Club and Euro variants with prices of over £20,000. You can still buy a Westfield in kit form that requires 120 hours of DIY labour, and many buyers enjoy this option. Whether kit or factory built, the cars are popular with wind-in-the-hair traditionalists looking for quintessential seat-of-the-pants driving enjoyment.??

WESTINGHOUSE • France 1904-1912

The Le Havre factory of the American Westinghouse Electric company produced these cars. The 1908 range consisted of a 20/30 hp shaft-driven four of 4084cc and a 35/ 40 hp chain-driven four of 6333 cc, with hydraulic shock absorbers of surprisingly modern appearance.

WESTLAKE • England 1907

Sold by Hubert Bowes Lyon of Dorney Peach, Taplow, Maidenhead, the Westlake was a two-seater six-cylinder voiturette with a "generally racy appearance." It sold for 190 guineas in air-cooled form, 225 guineas with water-cooling. A two-speed epicyclic gear and a two-throw crankshaft were features of its design.

WESTLAND • England 1906-1907

A 10/12 hp Aster-engined model "built to order" by Fred W. Baker's Stourbridge Motor and Carriage Works.

WESTMINSTER • England 1906-1908

The 20 hp Westminster, with a four-cylinder (3402cc) engine, was available with either shaft drive ("for high-class town work") or chain drive ("for country work and touring

WESTWOOD • England 1920-1926

An 11.9 hp Dorman-engined light car was this Wigan company's first model, followed in 1924 by a similar car with 14 hp Meadows power.

WEYHER ET RICHEMOND • France 1905-1910

Two "well-known Austrian engineers," Friedmann and Knoller, designed the 15 cv Weyher et Richemond steam car, built at Pantin, near Paris. It had a flash boiler fired by paraffin, and was styled on gasoline car lines, with the boiler at the front under a well-ventilated hood. The chassis price was 15,000 francs, and there were internal-expanding brakes on all four wheels, almost certainly the first time this feature had been offered on a production

car. Gasoline cars were this firm's later products and a six-cylinder model, as well as 16/20 hp and 28/32 hp fours, was shown at the 1907 Paris Salon.

WHARTON • USA 1921-1922

An ambitious enterprise which achieved very little, Wharton, of Dallas, Texas, announced three different models, a four, six, and an eight. Whether any of the fours or sixes were actually built is speculative, although at least one of the large eight-cylinder cars, a roadster, is known to have been built. This was powered by a converted Curtiss OX-5 aero engine with an 8226cc displacement, developing 104 bhp at 1900 rpm. Wharton was better known as a manufacturer of tractors.

WHERWELL • England 1920-1921

A 7 hp flat-twin Coventry-Victor engine was used in the Wherwell, which had friction transmission and chain drive. Only three examples were built.

WHITE • USA 1900-1918

See panel

WHITEHEAD • England 1921

The Whitehead, which had a wooden chassis, used a 1498cc Coventry-Simplex engine and Moss gearbox. Only about 16 examples were built.

WHITEHEAD-THANET • England 1920-1921

This company planned to assemble 100,000 cars a year, using a British 16/20 hp engine in an American chassis, but probably did not build even one.

WHITEHURST-HOMER • England 1905-1906

A 3.5 hp tricar built in Longsight, Manchester.

WHITGIFT • England 1913

An 8 hp vee-twin JAP engine powered this chain-drive cyclecar from Croydon, Surrey, named for a famous Elizabethan inhabitant of the town.

WHITING • USA 1910-1912

Built in Flint, Michigan, the Whiting 40 hp had overhead exhaust valves, while the 20 hp had an L-head engine.

WHITLOCK • England 1903-c. 1930

Royal coachbuilder Henry Whitlock & Company dated from 1778, and was a motor car agent by 1903, when it offered a range of the Whitlock-Century vehicles. Its first genuine

WHITE

WHITE • USA 1900-1918

The "Incomparable" White steam car was designed by Rollin H.White of the White Sewing Machine Company of Cleveland, Ohio. It first appeared as a typical steam buggy, distinguished only by its "semi-flash" boiler, which ensured virtually automatic control. In the first full year of production, 1901, White sold 193 runabouts, and in 1903 it introduced a 10 hp wheel-steered tonneau with a double-acting compound engine under a hood with frontal condenser. Chassis was of armored wood. A 15 hp model of more substantial construction appeared in late 1904, capable of 50 mph, and in 1907 came the more powerful Model L 20 hp and 30 hp Model K. All these models had a two-speed back axle and clutch mechanism, but improved design meant that these features were omitted from the 1909 20 hp Model O and 40 hp Model M, which had Joy valve gear of simpler design than the Stevenson Link motion used on the earlier cars. The contracting market for steam cars led White to introduce a Delahaye-based gasoline model in 1910, production of steamers ceasing in 1911. From 1912, a 60 hp six was available, and White listed 12 models, becoming the third biggest American luxury car manufacturer. A 32-valve four appeared in 1917, but White relinquished car production for commercials the next year. There were, however, some notable exceptions to the rule, including a large special sedan built in 1920 for a Philadelphia sportsman and a series of special coupés, constructed on the taxicab chassis, for salesmen of the Coca-Cola Company. Two special sedans were made to special order for a Boston physician in 1924 and 1935. The latter of these was mounted on White's light truck chassis and carried custom coachwork by Bender of Cleveland, Ohio.

1905 15 hp White steamer

1904 10 hp White steam car

1924 White sedan

c. 1925 Wills Sainte Claire Grey Goose two-seater roadster

1931 Wikov seven-passenger sedan

production models were the 1904 Whitlock-Asters, twins of 10 hp and 12 hp with armored-wood chassis, and fours of 14 hp and 20 hp with pressed-steel frames. At the 1906 Olympia Show Whitlock exhibited fours of 12/14 hp (chain drive) and 18/22 hp (shaft drive,) but production ceased soon after. In 1914 Whitlock was taken over by motor agent J A Lawton, who announced two new four-cylinder models, a 2413cc 12/16 hp and a 4398cc 20/30 hp; these were sold as Lawtons in 1914, Whitlocks in 1915. Post-war the firm was known as Lawton-Goodman, but did not reintroduce the Whitlock car until 1922, in the guise of a light car with a 1496 Coventry-Climax engine. At £375 in two-seater form this proved too expensive to compete with cars like the Morris-Cowley, so in 1923 came the 14 hp, a Bentley-like car with a 1753cc ohv Coventry-Climax six (bored out in late 1925 to create the 1911cc 16/50 hp) moderately priced at £495 with sports bodywork. In 1926 came an ohv twin-carburetor Meadows-engined six, the 2972cc 20/70 hp, increased in late 1927 to 3301cc. Production probably ended late in 1930, though the marque was listed for some years after. Lawton-Goodman continue as a commercial bodybuilder.

WHITNEY • USA 1895-1899

George E Whitney of Boston, Mass., built a number of experimental steamers (a horizontal-engined 1896 twin-cylinder model survives) and founded the Whitney Motor Wagon Company. After the Stanley brothers sold their design to John Brisben Walker for $250,000 they built Whitney steamers under the name Stanley-Whitney (or McKay, from a sewing machine company owned by Francis E Stanley) until 1902.

WHITNEY • USA 1898-1905

R S Whitney of Brunswick, Maine, built three twin-cylinder steam cars in 1898-1905, after having made bicycles at nearby Lisbon Falls for some years. The first two, completed in 1899 and 1902, resembled the contemporary Locomobile: the third was built of riveted 1 1/6 inch steel plates cut out with a cold chisel.

WHITWOOD • England 1934-1936

The Whitwood was a tandem two-seater two-wheeler, complete with stabilizing wheels! A variety of engines was available, from a 150cc two-stroke to a 1000cc vee-twin JAP.

WIGAN-BARLOW • England 1922-1923

Made, surprisingly, in Coventry, this was an unsuccessful assembled light car with 1368cc Coventry-Climax or 1496cc Meadows engines.

WIKOV • Czechoslovakia 1927-1936

Made by an agricultural machine factory at Prostéjov, the Richter-designed Wikov had an ohc 1490cc four-cylinder engine, originally designed by Ansaldo in Italy. Most cars had four-seater bodies, but a few two-seater sports-racing cars were built, too. Driven by Szyzycki, Konecnik, Václavik, Kreml, and E. Wichterle (one of the factory owners,) Wikov cars gained many sporting successes. A streamlined prototype, built under Jaray Patents, appeared in 1931. Some of the last models had ohc 1740cc and 1960cc engines. A 3480cc eight-cylinder never saw production.

WILBROOK • England 1913

A 9 hp JAP-engined four-seat cyclecar with four-wheel brakes.

WILBURY • England 1900

The 5 hp "Vibrationless" Wilbury could attain a top speed of 20 mph claimed its maker, the Motor Fittings & Engineering Co of Redhill, Surrey. It was sold either as a complete vehicle or in component form for assembly by enterprising cycle traders.

WILCOX • USA 1910-1911

Designed by Claude E Cox, the 30/40 hp Wilcox had engine, clutch, and gearbox incorporated in the same casing.

WILFORD • Belgium 1897-c. 1901

Though it was powered by a single-cylinder heavy-oil engine, the lumpish Wilford was capable of rapid progress. One achieved 60 mph in 1899.

WILKINS • USA 1899

Mr Wilkins of San Francisco built a massive 12 hp car whose infinitely variable belt drive and steering were operated electrically by push-buttons. The prototype, fitted out as a primitive motor caravan, was scheduled by its optimistic inventor for a transcontinental tour "once it was proved roadworthy."

WILKINSON • England 1903-1907, 1912-1913

This famous London swordsmith sold the Belgian De Cosmo 24 hp under its own name in 1903-1904. The 1906 14 hp four had the "Tacchi" patent gear-change: in 1912 came a light car powered by the 7 hp watercooled four-cylinder engine of the Wilkinson-TMC motorcycle. A development of this became the first Deemster.

10/12 hp Windsor tourer, c. 1926

WILLYS (WILLYS-OVERLAND) • USA 1908-1956

See panel overleaf

WILLIS • England 1913

An 8 hp cyclecar "embodying many novel features."

WILLIS • USA 1928

Designed by D E Willis, this car had a nine-cylinder engine. The pilot model was based on a Gardner chassis, but the Willis never got into production. Willis also built a prototype three-cylinder car, and designed the DEW.

WILLS SAINTE CLAIRE • USA 1921-1927

Childe Harold Wills, an expert metallurgist, was the engineer behind the early Ford cars, including the Model T. He broke with Ford in 1919 and spent his $1,592,128 severance pay in developing 4400 acres at Marysville, Michigan, into a model industrial community, aiming to build a car ten years ahead of its time. Named for local beauty spot Lake Ste Claire, the Wills Sainte Claire, appearing in 1921, was a metallurgical masterpiece, the first car to use molybdenum steel. Its ohc 60 degree V-8 engine reflected the latest European thinking and bristled with refinements, such as a cooling fan which automatically cut out at speeds of more than 40 mph. But the Wills Sainte Claire Grey Goose was an ugly duckling as far as styling went; sales peaked at 1,500 in 1923 and then tailed off. An ohc 4.5-liter straight-six replaced the V-8 in 1925, succeeded by a pushrod unit in 1926, just before the marque's demise.

WILSON • England 1935-1936

This conventional looking electric car was built by Partridge Wilson & Co Ltd of Leicester. About 40 cars were made in the two years of production, making it the top-selling British electric car of the inter-war years!

1904 Wilson-Pilcher

WILSON-PILCHER • England 1901-1907

Fitted with an early form of preselector gear, the Wilson-Pilcher had an 8 hp four-cylinder horizontal engine. Latterly it was built by Sir W. G. Armstrong, Whitworth & Co.

WILTON • England 1913-1924

Wilton's first cars were an 8 hp JAP-engined twin which sold at £160 and a 1093cc own-make four, which continued into 1914. The post-1919 Wiltons had a 1490cc four-cylinder engine and worm final drive. The firm built its own bodywork in its Tooting factory.

WINDHAM • England 1906

King's Messenger Captain W G Windham's "Sliding Detachable Motor Bodies" were normally fitted to Renault and Mercedes chassis, but in 1906 he offered a 20/30 hp car under his own name.

WINDHOFF • Germany 1907-1914

A manufacturer of engines and components which entered car production at its Rheine/Westfalen works with 2012cc and 4960cc four-cylinder and 3018cc and 6125cc six-cylinder models. Fours of 1540cc, with ohc engine, and 2612cc, with ioe, appeared in 1912. The last Windhoff car was the C 15/40, with a 3920cc six-cylinder engine.

WINDSOR • England 1924-1927

The Windsor was a well-made light car, with a 10.4 hp 1353cc pushrod ohv engine of the company's own manufacture. A four-speed gearbox was another agreeable feature. Not surprisingly, the cars were not cheap, and at £400 each only a few were made, manufacturer J. Bartle & Co of London W11 ceasing production in 1927.

WINDSOR • USA 1929-1930

The Windsor "White Prince" was a Moon model, introduced as an eight in 1929. A Continental engine was employed and the price of the five-passenger sedan was $1,995. In 1930 the Windsor name superseded that of Moon; subsequent cars carried the Windsor insignia.

WINDSOR STEAM CAR • USA • Canada 1922-1923

The Windsor Steam Car was to have been the Canadian version of the Trask-Detroit Steam Car, later the Detroit Steam Car.

WINGFIELD • England 1909-1920

The 1913 15 hp WingRfield was a conventional four-cylinder shaft-driven car selling at £320 in chassis form.

1913 Windhoff tourer

1920 Winther six tourer

1915 Winter cyclecar

WING MIDGET • USA 1922

A one-passenger car, the Wing Midget resembled a racing car, was mounted on a 60-inch wheelbase and powered by a four-cylinder air-cooled Cameron engine. It featured double chain drive. Several Wing Midgets were built; some were featured in an early silent film.

WINNER • USA 1900

This 5 hp gasolene runabout was built by the Elgin Automobile Company, which also made the Elgin electric.

WINNIPEG • Canada 1921,1923

The Winnipeg was a bid by a Manitoba-based company to market an automobile to sell in the prairie provinces of Canada. The radiator emblem featured a sheaf of Manitoba's primary product, with the legend "Good as the Wheat." The one and only 1921 Winnipeg was a four, actually nothing more than a Hatfield car with changed badge. The company floundered for a while, but was back in business in 1923, this time with a six, of which between five and ten were shown for promotional purposes. The six, in truth, was the Davis car with the ubiquitous wheatsheaf emblem; again, the venture failed.

WINSON • England 1920

Precision or Blackburne 8 hp engines powered the Winson cyclecar from Rochdale, Lancashire. Friction drive was employed.

WINTER • England 1915

A sporting belt-drive cyclecar from Wandsworth with an own-make 988cc four-cylinder air-cooled engine.

WINTERS • USA 1909

Twin-cylinder air-cooled engines of 10 hp and 14 hp powered these high-wheelers from Coffey/ville, Kansas.

WINTHER • USA 1920-1923

A subsidiary of the Winther Truck Company, the Winther Motors Division built a creditable, if not exciting, assembled car in its four years of production. A Herschell-Spillman six-cylinder engine was used exclusively. Wheelbase was 120 inches and prices of the five-passenger touring model were $2,650 for 1920 and 1921 and $400 less in 1922 and 1923. An estimated 500 cars were produced. The basic Winther design was also used for the 1923 Harris Six.

WINTON • USA 1896-1924

See panel overleaf

WITHERS • England 1907-1915

The 1907 Withers was a 24/30 hp model built in Paddington, London. In 1913 20 hp, 25 hp, 30 hp, and 35/40 hp fours were offered, at chassis prices ranging from £430 to £600

WITTEKIND • Germany 1921-1925

Wittekind of Berlin concentrated on small cars with 780cc, 896cc, and 1280cc four-cylinder engines, but not many were made.

WIZARD • USA 1921-1923

Whether the Wizard was something of a hoax or not is a matter of guesswork today, as the company's only brochure hailed from "Wizard, North Carolina," a non-existent place on the map of America! The announcement called for a "Junior" and a "Senior" car featuring vee-twin and four-

WILLYS (WILLYS-OVERLAND) • USA 1908-1956

Salesman John North Willys took over the Overland company, which had been producing gas buggies since 1903, to save it from receivership, and re-formed it as the Willys-Overland Company in 1908. Initially a four-cylinder runabout with epicyclic gearing was produced, and the profits from the first year's sales of 465 cars enabled two new models, the Overland Six and the 45 hp Willys Six, to go into production. By 1910 Willys-Overland had outgrown its 300 ft-long tin shed works, and moved into the old Pope-Toledo factory in Toledo, Ohio. Sales in 1914 reached 80,000, due mainly to the 3949cc Overland Model 79 four-cylinder. Electric lighting and starting were adopted in 1914, in which year the first Willys-Knight was built. This 4529cc sleeve-valve four was based on the 1912-14 Edwards-Knight, and the Willys-Knight marque survived until 1932-1933. In 1920 a British venture, Willys-Overland-Crossley, was established, to assemble Overland Fours for the UK market, including a 1924 version of this model (distinguished by U-shaped transverse suspension) with a Morris-Oxford engine. The US company survived a major financial crisis in 1921-1923, and by April 1925 was building 250 Overland Sixes and 600 Overland Fours daily, plus 5,200 Willys-Knights a month. In 1926 came a new low-priced model, the Whippet, aimed at competing with the Ford and Chevrolet; it was eventually the cheapest car on the US market, priced at $495, but never secured the hoped-for market success. In 1929 John Willys

Julia Faye with her 1930 Willys-Knight coupé

1923 'British Built Overland (Willys)

unloaded his share in the company for $21 million and became US Ambassador to Poland. The company collapsed in the slump, and went into receivership again. Willys hurried back, but could not save the situation. He died in 1933, in which year the ugly aerodynamic Willys 77 was introduced. With more acceptable styling, it survived until 1942 as the "Willys-Americar." During the war Willys produced 361,349 Jeeps, and continued producing them for civilian use when hostilities ceased. An enclosed "Jeep Station Wagon" appeared in July 1946, and the 1948 range was extended to include several commercial models and the Brook Stevens-designed Jeepster Phaeton, current for four years, powered by sv Willys fours and sixes of 2196cc and 2425cc respectively. A brand-new range of passenger cars appeared in 1952, the Aero-Lark powered by the sv six, and the Aero-Wing, Aero-Ace, and Aero-Eagle with a 2638cc ohv six. A total of 31,363 Aero Willys was built in 1952, and 41,735 in 1953, when a gold "W" on the grille commemorated the 50th anniversary of Overland. That year the ailing Kaiser group bought Willys-Overland, but 1954 models were little changed except for the option of Kaiser's 3703cc sv six. A supercharger was fitted to some Aero Willys, boosting output to 140bhp. The 1955 models were mildly face-lifted, and the Aero name was dropped in favour of Custom (sedans) and Bermuda (hardtops.) After only 6,564 of the 1955 models had been sold the decision was taken to end US passenger-car production, though the Aero resurfaced in the Willys-Overland factory in Brazil, where it was built until 1962.

1962 "Aero'"Willys sedan

WINTON

The four- and eight-cylinder Winton Bullet racers for the 1903 Gordon Bennett race in Ireland

WINTON • USA 1896-1924

Scottish engineer Alexander Winton jumped ship in America and founded a cycle company in Cleveland, Ohio. In 1896 he built a two-cylinder car, and went into production with light phaetons in 1897. Twenty-five were built in the first year, the twelfth being bought by James Ward Packard. A 3.8-liter Winton single-cylinder took part in the 1900 Gordon Bennett race. In 1901 a twin-cylinder phaeton was introduced, and in 1903 Dr H Nelson made the first successful trans-America drive in one of these cars. Winton built two racers for the 1903 Gordon Bennett, low-profiled "Bullets," one with a 17,028cc straight-eight and only one speed. A flat-four, the Winton Quad, appeared in 1904; at the end of that year the twin was discontinued. Vertical fours of 16/20 hp, 24/30 hp, and 50/100 hp were standardized in 1905; they still featured the pneumatic speed governor that was characteristic of the marque. They introduced a new type of suspension; two superimposed semi-elliptic springs so shackled that on smooth roads only one spring was used, and on rough going both were called into play. In 1906 production was concentrated on the 5801cc Model K 30 hp: a 40 hp appeared in 1907. The Six-Teen-Six of 1908 boasted 7817cc, and in 1909 a 9505cc six incorporated a pneumatic starter; by 1911 it also had a built-in tyre pump. Conventional pair-cast sixes were built thereafter, acquiring electric lighting and starting in 1915. Car production ceased in 1924, when the company decided to concentrate instead on marine diesel engines.

1907 Winton 18/24 hp with detachable canopy

cylinder engines respectively; one "Junior" chassis is known to have been built, the two-passenger roadster being listed at $395. Wizard may have had some connection with Schuler, but this has not been proven.

WM • Poland 1927-1928

A flat-twin four-stroke engine powered this light car from Warsaw; the mass-production plans eventually came to nothing.

WOLF • England 1904-1905

A 5.5/6 hp three-wheeler with a two-speed constant-mesh gearbox from Wolverhampton.

WOLF • France 1913

An imported French 12/14 hp four-cylinder, sold by Seale & De Becker of London.

WOLFE • USA 1907-1909

Built in Minneapolis, the Wolfe was a conventional tourer with a choice of air-cooled 3294cc Carrico or 30 hp water-cooled Continental engines. From 1909-1912 the cars were known as "Wilcox."

WOLSELEY • England 1899-1976

See panel overleaf

WOLSIT • Italy 1907-c. 1908

License-built Wolseleys, 10/20 hp twin, 16/24, and 30/40 hp fours, and 45/60 hp six, from Legnano.

WOLVERINE • USA 1904-1906

Built by the Reid Manufacturing Company of Detroit, Michigan, the Wolverine was a 20 hp live-axle model.

WOLVERINE • USA 1927-1928

This was actually a small Reo, but as it carried its own advertising, specification listing and badge, it should be classified as a separate make. The Wolverine was iintroduced in April 1927. Engine was a six by Continental and wheelbase was 114 inches. Body styles included both a two-door and four-door sedan and a 2/4 seat cabriolet-roadster. It was readily distinguished by two groups of horizontal hood louvers.

WOLVERINE SPECIAL • USA 1917-1920

A sporty two-seater roadster, the Wolverine Special was powered by a Wisconsin four-cylinder engine, this being replaced in 1918 by a Rochester-Duesenberg four. The car featured a vee-type radiator, the motif being carried on into the wings. Door steps replaced running-boards and wire wheels were standard. Only three cars were completed.

WOODILL • USA 1958-1959

The Woodill Wildfire was created by Woody Woodill, a Willys/Dodge dealer. The glassfiber sports car body on an own-make frame used many Willys components, including the 90 hp F-head six-cylinder engine. Priced at $1,200 in kit form or from $2,900 as an assembled car, it was said to be the first glassfiber car to be produced in volume. Approximately 300 Woodills were made.

WOODROW • England 1913-1915

This cyclecar used initially an 8 hp air-cooled Jap vee-twin, subsequently a water-cooled 9 hp Precision. A sharp-nosed sports model was offered.

WOODS • USA 1899-1919

For the first 18 years of its existence Woods of Chicago built conventional, expensive electric cars. Then, in 1917, came the $2,650 Woods Dual Power, with a 12 hp Continental gasoline engine supplementing its electric motor, which was mounted where the gearbox would normally go. With both engines running the Dual Power could reach 35 mph.

WOODS MOBILETTE • USA 1913-1916

A soap-box cart reputedly inspired Francis A Woods to build "America's first cyclecar," a narrow tandem or staggered two-seater with a four-cylinder engine and underslung front suspension. Ease of storage was emphasized: "It will even climb the stairs to a second, a third, or any storey, if the turns of the stairs are not too sharp... it will go anywhere that you can put an upright piano."

WOOLER • England 1920-1921

The Wooler had a flat-twin engine with rotary valves. The whole device was rather crude, with belt drive to a worm-gear rear axle, but coil-sprung independent front suspension was featured.

WORLDMOBILE • USA 1928

Although seven prototypes were announced, only one may have been built. The Worldmobile used an eight-cylinder Lycoming engine and disc wheels, many other components being taken from other makes of car. The Lima Ohio-based Worldmobile announced that a sedan would be priced at $1,700, but production was not forthcoming.

WORTH • USA 1899-1901

A Chicago-built motor buggy which won five gold medals at the 1900 Chicago Auto Meet.

WSM • England 1961-1967

About 25 of the pretty WSM alloy-bodied Sprites were made, half of which were exported to the USA. The originator, Douglas Wilson-Spratt, also built one-off specials based on a Healey 3000, an MGB and even an MG 1100.

WYNER • Austria 1903-1905

A Vienna agent for Belgian Miesse steam cars, Wyner also built gasoline cars with one-, two-, and four-cylinder engines of 9 hp to 40 hp. Wyner also sold De Dion and Darracq cars; his own used De Dion engines.

WOLSELEY • England 1899-1976

In 1895 the Wolseley Sheep Shearing Company asked Herbert Austin, who had worked for them in Australia, to design a car with which they could enter the motor business. The result was a tricar fitted with a flat-twin engine, inspired by the French Léon Bollée. Four-wheeled prototypes appeared in 1899, and a 3.5 hp single-cylinder example competed in the 1,000-Mile Trial of 1900. A horizontal engine was a feature of all Wolseleys until 1905. But Colonel Siddeley, a Wolseley director and importer of French cars, insisted that vertical-engined Siddeleys or Wolseley-Siddeleys appear alongside the old horizontal engined models, a compromise that probably hastened Austin's departure, when he started building vertical-engined cars under his own name.

After he left in 1906, models were known variously as Siddeleys, Wolseley-Siddeleys, or Wolseley/Siddeley, the liaison lasting until 1910, with large four- and six-cylinder cars prevailing. During the First World War Wolseley built the ohc Hispano-Suiza V-8 aero engine under license, so it was no surprise to find this camshaft layout on its 1.3-liter 10 hp model after the war. Other variations on the same theme were the 12 hp and 15 hp models. In 1925 the 10 developed into the 11/22, while the ohc layout was replaced by a cheaper side-valve layout for the 16/35, which superseded the 15 in the same year. Although a new ohc six, the 16/45, appeared in 1927, the company had gone bankrupt in the meantime, being snapped up by William Morris in the face of opposition from Herbert Austin.

It was not long before the Wolseley-inspired ohc began appearing in the contemporary MG and Morris models, the 1928 Wolseleys being a 2.7-liter straight-eight and a four-cylinder 12/32. The 21/60, a six, followed, being a Wolseley edition of the Morris Isis. A significant event of 1930 was the appearance of the ohc 1.3-liter Hornet, while larger six- and eight-cylinder cars were also available. Although the Hornet was later increased to 1.4 liters, 1936 was the last year of the ohc Wolseleys. Pushrod-engined replacements included the Super Six and 1.8-liter 14/56. The post-war era saw the Morris-inspired ohv 8 and 10, while the four-cylinder ohc 4/50 and the six-cylinder 6/80 reverted to the old Wolseley tradition, the latter power unit being shared with Morris. However, the 4/44 of 1953 used a detuned MG TD engine, though rationalization was reflected in the 1500 of 1958, in effect an expanded Morris Minor. A variant of the Mini, the Hornet, appeared in 1962, while plusher versions of the fwd 1100 and 1800 models displayed the famous illuminated radiator badge, a feature of the marque since 1933.

1904 Wolseley 10 hp tourer

1912 Wolseley Roi des Belges 16 hp tourer

c. 1920 Wolseley

1957 Wolseley 15/50 sedan

1974 Wolseley Six

1917 Yale two-seater

XENIA • USA 1914

Designed by P E Hawkins, the Xenia cyclecar had an 1164cc vee-twin Deluxe engine and the odd combination of epicyclic gearbox and belt final drive.

YALE • USA 1903

"A car with the doubt and the jar left out," the 12 hp Yale from Toledo, Ohio, was claimed to have been "selected for export purposes by English experts... as the safest, simplest and most economical car made in America." One-, two-, and four-cylinder engines were used, in conjunction with epicyclic gearing.

YALE • USA 1916-1918

The Yale was built in Saginaw, Michigan, and used its own-make V-8 engine. Available both as a touring car and 2/4 passenger speedster, this car featured the "Neutralock," a theft-deterring device as standard equipment. Wire wheels and rakish lines made the Yale one of the sportier cars of the time, although production was small.

YAMABA • Japan 1904

Thought to be the first Japanese-built car, this was a heavy two-cylinder steam waggonette of crude appearance.

YAXA • Switzerland 1912-1914

"Y a que ça" ("It's the only one there is") was the phonetic rendering of this marque from Genéve, built by Charles Baehni, an early collaborator of Charles-Edouard Henriod. The Yaxa was a 1692cc light car with a four-cylinder Zedel engine. Central gear and brake levers were an advanced touch. Baehni drove a Yaxa to victory in the 1913 Coupe de la Gruyére.

YEOVIL • England 1895-1897

Petters of Yeovil, Somerset, was a gas engine manufacturer which collaborated with local coachbuilders Hill & Boll to build approximately 12 cars powered by Petter paraffin engines.

YLM • Taiwan 1953 to date

Founded as the Yue Loong Engineering Company, YLM formerly built jeeps and Nissan saloons, but then concentrated entirely on Nissans, from mini cars to mini buses. Latest is the Yue Loong 102, based on the old Nissan Stanza and launched in 1989.

Z (ZBROJOVKA) • Czechoslovakia 1927-1936

A big arms factory, Zbrojovka of Brno-Zidenice was part of the Skoda Group, but had, as far as car manufacture was concerned, no connection with Skoda cars. All Z cars were two-strokes, even the first model, the "Disk," a B. Novotny-designed 660cc twin-cylinder, which never went into quantity manufacture. The first production Z had a 1004cc twin-cylinder engine, followed by an improved version with a rotary inlet valve. In 1933 more two-strokes with rotary inlet-valves, a fwd 900cc twin-cylinder and a 1490cc four-cylinder model, also with fwd, appeared on the market. They sold well. Z works racing cars included 1100cc two-, four-, and six-cylinder and 1490cc eight-cylinder two-strokes, most of which had superchargers.

ZAGATO • Italy 1966-1968

Made by the famous coachbuilder who created many very sporting Alfa Romeo cars between the wars, the "new" Zagato was a modern version of the 1750cc Alfa Romeos of the late 1920s. It was a 100 mph "Gran Sport" open two-seater, with a 1600cc Giulia TI engine.

ZAPOROZHETS • Russia 1965 to date

Exported to Austria as the Eliette, and to other markets as the Yalta, this NSU Prinz-like rear-engined car from the Ukraine had its 881cc V-4 power unit replaced with a 1200cc unit in 1968.

ZASTAVA (Yugo) • Yugoslavia 1953 to date

Originally founded to make agricultural machinery, Zastava built old-style Fiats for years. The Yugo 45/55 of 1980 were reskinned Fiat 127s; a Yugo 55 Cabriolet was launched at the 1985 Belgrade motor show. In 1987 came the first "in-house" design – the Giugiaro-styled Florida (sold as the Miami or Sana in some markets.)

LE ZEBRE • France 1910-1931

The small Zébre was a popular car made at Suresnes, Seine, at first with a single-cylinder four-stroke 5 hp engine of 636cc. In 1913 Zébre presented two more models, a 6 hp of 785cc and a 10 hp of 1743cc, both four-cylinders. After the war Zébre resumed production with an 8 hp sv 997cc, the forerunner of the famous 5 hp Citroën (designed by Jules Salomon after he left Le Zébre.) The last production model was a 10 hp of 1974cc with a Ricardo head. The year Zébre closed it presented a prototype with a single-cylinder CLM diesel engine.

ZEDEL • France • Switzerland 1906-1921

Zurcher-Luthi was a well-known Swiss motorcycle maker whose first voiturette, an 1128cc four-cylinder, was built in 1906 in the factory at Pontarlier, France, which it opened to avoid customs duties. But production was really centered in a new factory at St Aubin, Switzerland. A 10 cv four of 1791cc appeared in 1908. In 1921 Zedel merged with the French marque Donnet to form Donnet-Zedel.

ZEILLER & FOURNIER • France 1920-1924

Made in Levallois, Seine, by MM Zeiller & Fournier, these were light 1130cc Ballot-engined cyclecars with friction drive.

1913 Coupé de l'Auto Zénia

1908 Targa Bologna Züst

1908 New York-Paris Züst

50/60 hp Züst Tipo America chassis, 1909

A Zeta coupé

ZENDIK • England 1913-1914

An 8 hp Chater-Lea-engined cyclecar with two-speed chain-and-dog transmission.

ZENIA • France 1913-1920

This Paris-based marque made a 2998cc car before the war. In 1919 it resumed production, offering three Altos-engined models of 1779cc, 2297cc, and 2950cc.

ZENITH, ZENITH-POPULAR • England 1905-1906

Zenith was better known for its motorcycles with infinitely variable Gradua belt drive than for its cars. The two-seater Zenith-Popular of 1906 was a light four-wheeler with a 6 hp twin-cylinder Stevens engine and underslung suspension.

ZENT • USA 1902-1907

Zent offered epicyclic-geared cars with two, three, and four cylinders. In 1908 its products were renamed "Bellefontaine" after the town in which they were built.

ZEPHYR • England 1914-1921

A 12 hp four-cylinder of 1944cc built by a firm in Lowestoft, Suffolk, more famous for its lightweight pistons.

ZETA • Australia 1963-1966

The highly original Zeta was another example of a locally designed car using a mixture of local and imported components. It came from Lightburn Industries, a major producer of car jacks, concrete mixers, industrial products, and power tools. The glassfiber body was an ungainly but ingenious design with huge doors. The seats could be laid flat or quickly removed to provide a large carrying area, and could also be placed on the roof to provide a grandstand view for sporting events. Total weight was 960 lb. Power came from a Villiers 324cc two-stroke engine driving the front wheels, with a Burman gearbox and Girling brakes. Despite plans to build 50 a week, only 363 were sold over a three-year period. The company also tried to build a Michelotti-styled rear-engined sports car, a diminutive design with a 500cc German FMR two-stroke engine developing 25 bhp. It, too, had a glassfiber body, built on a tubular chassis. Some 48 were made.

ZEVACO • France 1923-1925

M Zevaco of Eaubonne, Val d'Oise, made some light cars with 995cc Train vee-twin, and 950cc and 1350cc Chapuis-Dornier engines.

ZIL • Russia 1956 to date

Rivalling the Chaika as prestige transport for Soviet officials, the ZIL (Zavod Imieni Likhatchev) succeeded the ZIS (Zavod Imieni Stalina) of 1936-1956, originally inspired by the Buick straight-eight and since 1945 built with Packard body dies. Still Packard-inspired until 1963, the ZIL then acquired more modern US-type styling as the 111G. The 114 seven-seater appeared in 1967 and the Zil-117, a 7-liter V-8, dated from 1971.

ZIM • France 1922-1924

M Zimmermann of Epernay, Marne, made some cyclecars with a.sv 344cc single-cylinder engine and chain drive.

ZIMMERMAN • USA 1908-1914

Starting life as a wheel-steered high-wheeler with dummy hood, this marque from Auburn, Indiana, began building conventional four-cylinder cars in 1910, with a six appearing in 1912.

ZIP • USA 1914

A water-cooled four-cylinder 1287cc cyclecar from Davenport, Iowa.

ZITA • England 1971-1972

A very shapely two-seater based on VW mechanicals, the Zita ZS was intended to sell as a kit. However, the project was stillborn and only two cars were made.

ZUNDAPP • Germany 1957-1958

Still a leading manufacturer of mopeds and motorcycles, Zündapp of München built the unconventional Dornier-designed Janus mini-car, a four-seater in which the two rear passengers sat with their backs to those in front, looking through the rear window. Power was by a 248cc single-cylinder Zündapp two-stroke engine! Total production of the Janus was 6,900 cars.

ZUST • Italy 1905-1914

Excellent cars, designed and produced by Swissborn Ing Roberto Züst, whose first prototypes dated from the turn of the century. The range of models included a 10/15 hp three-cylinder of 1722cc, as well as 12 hp (2296cc,) 18 /24 hp (4082cc,) 20/35 hp (4982cc,) 28/40 hp (7429cc,) and 50/70 hp (9889cc) four-cylinder models. After the war OM cars were made at this Brescia works.

Silver Seraph

Cross-references

ABAM German license-built Kriéger.

ACCARY see Hédèa.

ADEX see Excelsior.

AERO MINOR see Minor.

AERO TYPE see Pagé.

AFG see Gorm.

AIGLE see AER.

AIGLON see Alliance 1905-1908.

AILSA CRAIG see Craig-Dörwald.

AIRETTE see Rex 1901-1914.

AIREX see Rex 1901-1914.

AIRPHIBIAN see US Continental.

AKD see Abingdon 1922-1923.

ALBANY (1902-1905) see Lamplough-Albany.

ALBRUNA see Brown 1899-1911.

ALLREIT see Allright 1908-1913.

ALVECHURCH see Dunkley.

AMEDEE BOLLEE see Bollée.

AMERICAINE see Cohendet.

AMERICAN MORS see Standard (USA) 1909-1910, Skelton.

AMERICAN MOTOR see Automobile Company of America.

AMERICAN TOURIST see American Underslung.

AMERICAN VOITURETTE Alternative name for Car-Nation (see Keeton.)

AMPLEX see American Simplex.

ANGLIAN British importer's name for Ariés.

AQUILA see Maillard.

ARIEL (USA) see Maryland.

AROP see Seidel-Arop.

AST-REX see Rex 1901-1914.

ATOM see Fairthorpe.

ATTICA Greek-built Fuldamobil.

AUGE see Troéïka.

AUTHI British Motor Corporation models license-built in Spain.

AUTOAR (ARGENTINA) see Cisitalia.

AUTO-FORE-CARRIAGE USA license-built Kuhlstein-Vollmer.

AUTO RED BUG see Smith Flyer.

AWE see EMW.

BABY FRISWELL British importer's name for 1906 6½hp Delage.

BAILEY & LAMBERT see Pelham.

BAMBI Chile-built Fuldamobil.

BANTAM see American Austin.

BARCAR see Phoenix 1903-1908.

BAUDOUIN see Déchamps.

BAYARD-CLEMENT see Clément.

BECKETT & FARLOW see Mathieu.

BEDFORD British importer's name for 1910-1914 Buick.

BELGA RISE Sizaire Fréres car built in Belgium from 1929.

BELLEFONTAINE see Zent.

BENOVA see Benjamin.

BERNARDI see Miari e Giusti.

BEVERLY see Upton.

BGS see Bouquet, Garcin & Schivre.

BIADA-ELIZALDE see Elizalde.

BINGHAMPTON Incorrect form of "Binghamton."

BLACK CROW see Crow-Elkhart.'

BRAMHAM see Stanhope.

BRENNA see Brennabor.

BRIGGS & STRATTON see Smith Flyer.

BRITISH IDEAL 6 & 8 hp Schaudels license-built in Birmingham.

BRITISH MERCEDES see Daimler-Mercedes.

BRITISH PEERLESS see Peerless 1902-1904.

BRIXIA-ZUST see Züst.

BROWN-WHITNEY see Brown.

BRUNAU see Weidmann.

BUAT see Léon Buat.

BUGGYAUT see Duryea.

BURLINGTON British importer's name for De Dietrich-Bugatti.

CAB see Automobilette.

CAESAR English importer's name for Schacchi.

CALEDONIAN see Argyl 1976 to date.

CANADIAN CROW see Crow-Elkhart.

CANELLO-DURKOPP see Durkopp.

CAR see Cosmos.

CAR-NATION see Keeton.

CATALONIA see Rebour.

CDS see Cognet de Seynes.

CELER An undocumented Nottingham make, possibly connected with **Binks** (Leader.)

CHAIKA see GAZ.

CHAMPROBERT see Electrogenia.

CHARETTE see International 1898-1904.

CHARRON see CGV.

CHAVANET see Automoto.

CHENU see Sixcyl.

LA CICOGNE see Bignan.

CID see Cottereau.

CLARKSON see Chelmsford.

CLEMENT-STIRLING see Stirling.

CLEMENT-TALBOT see Talbot (England.)

CLEVELAND SIX see Chandler.

COBRA see Shelby.

COCHOT see Lutéce.

COLOMBES see Villard.

COLONIAL (USA/Canada 1922) see Canadian.

COLT see Mitsubishi.

COLUMBIA (steam) see Crouch 1899-1900.

CONTAL see Mototri Contal.

CORONET see Powerdrive.

CROWN MAGNETIC see Owen Magnetic.

CSB see Cornilleau Ste Beuve.

CUMMIKAR see Ronteix.

DACIA Renault 12 license-built in Bucarest (Romania) since 1969.
DALGLEISH-GULLANE Scottish-modified 1907 De Dion Bouton.
DART (USA 1912) see Martin.
D'AUX see Causan.
DA VINCI see Scripps-Booth.
DAWFIELD, PHILIPS see DPL.
DE DIETRICH see Lorraine-Dietrich.
DE LUCA Coventry Daimlers license-built in Naples, Italy (1906-1911.)
DE LUXE see Car De Luxe.'
DEMEESTER see Jouffret.
DEW (1913-1914) Forerunner of Victor Cyclecar.
DICKINSON see Morette.
DLG see Dyke.
DONG-FENG see Hong-Ki.
DONINGTON see Johnard.
DOUGILL see Frick.
DOWNSHIRE see Chambers.
DREXEL see Farmack.
DUNAMIS see Miesse.
DUREY-SOHEY see Hanzer.
DUX see Damaizin & Pujos.
DyG see Diaz y Grillo.

EB DEBONAIR see LMB.
L'ECLAIR (1897) see Maison Parisienne.
EHV, **EISENHUTH** see Compound.
L'ELASTES c1907 name for Motobloc.
ELBURN see Ruby.
ELECTROBAT see Morris & Salom.
ELECTROCYCLETTE see AEM.
EL-FAY see Elcar.
ELIETTE see Zaphorozhets.
ELKHART see Elcar.
ELMO see Electromobile.
ENGLISH MECHANIC, EM see Hyler-White
EOLIA see Traction Aérienne.
ERCO see Eos.
ESPERANTO USA importer's name for Prunel.
ETOILE DE FRANCE see Darmont.
EUREKA see Victoria Combination.
EUSKALDUNA 1928 successor to CEYC (Spain.)

FAC see Victrix.
FACILE see Britannia.
FAIF see Isotta Fraschini.
FAS see Standard (Italy 1906-1908.)
FASA Spanish-built Renault models.
FAVORIT see Kroboth.
FEG see Erdmann.
FERNA see HH.
FIAT-HISPANIA see Seat.
FIDES Italian-built Brasier.
FJTA see Junior.
FRAM see Cantono.
LA FRANCAISE see Diamant.
FRISKY see Meadows.
FRONTENAC (Canada) 1931-1932 see De Vaux, Durant; 1933-1934 see Continental.
F-S see Petrel.

GAILLARDET see Doctoresse.
GARDNER-SERPOLLET see Serpollet.
GATSO see Gatford.
GEORGIA KNAP see Knap.
GLOBE (1906) see Kitchon-Weller.
GOGGOMOBIL (Germany) see Glas.
GORHAM see Lilla.'
GRAFFORD see Graf & Stift.
GREAT SMITH see Smith.
GTM see Cox.
GWYNNE-ALBERT see Albert.
GYROSCOPE see Blomstrom.

HAG see Hansa.
HAINSSELLIN see HL.
HANS VAHAAR Indian-built Fuldamobil.
HARDINGE see Pullman.
HARLE see Sautter-Harlé.
HARRIS-LEON LAISNE see Léon Laisne.
HERCULES see Ducroiset.
HEWBENZ 1901 English importer's name for Benz.
HISA see Hermes (Italy.)
HMC (1903) see Highgate.
HOFFMANN & CZERNY see Continental (Austria.)
HURMID see Hurst.
HYLANDER see Highlander.

IDEAL see TH (Spain.)
IMPERIAL (USA 1903-1904) see Columbus.
INDUCO see Marguerite.
ISETTA see ISO.
ITALIANA see Owen (England.)
IZZER see Model.

JACK ENDERS see Mourre.
JACK MULLER see BNC.
JACKSON-BUCKMOBILE see Buckmobile.
JACKSON-COVERT see Covert.
JANUS see Zéndapp.
JC see Corre.
JDS see Deasy.
LA JOYEUSE see Taine.
JUSTICIALISTA see Graciela.

KAISER CARABELA Original name for IKA-Renault.
KANE-PENNINGTON see Pennington.
KAUTZ see Ansbach.
KIBLINGER see McIntyre.

KNIGHT & KILBOURNE see Silent Knight.
KNIPPERDOLLING Small Dérkopp from 1908.

LACROIX ET DE LAVILLE see La Nef.
LAFAYETTE (USA 1934-1939) Nash model designation.
L & K see Laurin & Klement.
LEANDER see Cadogan.
LEONARD see Medici.
LEON BOLLEE see Bollée.
LEPRECHAUN Irish-assembled Stanhope.
LETHIMONNIER see Sultane.
LA LICORNE see Corre-LaLicorne.
LIEGEOIS Proposed Belgian license-built Duryea (1900.)
LITTLE GREG see Grégoire.
LITTLE KAR see Texmobile.
LLOYD & PLAISTER see L & P.
LM see Little Midland.'
LOCKE see Puritan (steam.)
LA LOCOMOTRICE 1905 24/30hp Rochet-Schneider license-built byNagant.
LORELEY see Ley.
LPC see Lewis (1913-1916.)
LUC (Germany) see Dinos.
LUCAS see Ralph Lucas.
LUXOR see Dagmar, Standish.
LYNX (1898) see Le Blon.

MA see Alvarez.
MAGIC Fischer sleeve-valve car sold by Withers.
MARCHAND-DUFAUX see Dufaux.
MARSHALL see Belsize.
MARTIN & LETHIMONNIER see Sultane.
MASS-PAIGE English importer's name for Paige.
MAYA GT see Camber.
McKAY see Whitney.
MENDELSSOHN see Passy-Thellier.
MERCEDES-ELECTRIQUE-MIXTE see Austro-Daimler.
METEOR (USA 1900-1904) see Automotor.
METEOR (USA 1902-1905) see Berg.
METROPOLITAINE see Cadix.
MGP 1912 name for Margaria.
MILDE-GAILLARDET see Mildé.
MINIATURE VELOX see Velox.
MLB see Landry & Beyroux.
MO-CAR see Arrol-Johnston.
MOHAWK-MANON see Manon.
MORANO-MARGUERITE see Marguerite.
MORRIS-LEON-BOLLEE see Bollée.
MOTOCAR see Micron.
MOTORMOBILE English importer's name for 1902-1904 Vilain.
MOYEA see Sampson.

NEW EAGLE see Eagle.
NEW KYMA see Kyma.
NEW LEADER see Leader.
NEW PARRY see Parry.
NEW PICK see Pick.
NEWTON-CEIRANO see Ceirano.
NEW TURRELL see Accles-Turrell.
NISSAN see Datsun.
NOBEL British-built Fuldamobil.
NO-NAME see Horley.
NUOVA INNOCENTI see Innocenti.

OAKMAN see Hertel.
OCTOAUTO see Reeves.
OLYMPIC see Gearless.
ONFRAY see Compagnie Franéaise.
OP see Phrixus.
OPELIT-MOPETTA see Brutsch.
OPPERMAN see Unicar.
ORIO & MARCHAND see Decauville.
ORLEANS see New Orleans.
OVERLAND see Willys.
PALM Modified 1918-1919 Model T Ford sold by E. W. Brown of Melbourne, Australia.
PALM (England) see Palmerston.
PAQUIS see SUP.
PARISIA see Owen (England.)
PASSE-PARTOUT see Reyrol.
PEGASUS British importer's name for Ader and Cottereau.
PENNANT see Barley.
PETELECTA see Owen (England.)
PETTER see Seaton-Petter, Yeovil.
PIERRON see Mass.
PLM Belgian-built Keller station wagon.
LA PLUS SIMPLE see Legros.
PMC see Premier (England.)
POBIEDA see GAZ.
LA POLAIRE see Leon Buat.
POLONEZ see Polski-Fiat.
PORTLAND (1903) see International.
POWERFUL British importer's name for Kriéger electric.
PREMIER-STRATTON see Stratton.
PRINCESS British Leyland marque succeeding Wolseley from 1976.
PROPULCYCLE see Madoz.
PTS see Vindelica.
PURITAN (1914) see Scripps-Booth.

QED see Marshall-Arter.

R & L see Rauch & Lang.
RAULANG see Rauch & Lang.
REGENT see Bock & Hollender.
REISSIG see RAW.
RELIABLE WAYNE see Wayne.

REMO see Rex (England 1901-1914.)
RENAUX see l'Energie.
RENNSTEIG see Schilling.
RENOWN 1920 successor to Palm.
REPLICAR see Glassic.
RGS-ATALANTA see Atalanta (1937-1939.)
RICHARD-BRASIER see Georges-Richard.
RIGS THAT RUN see St Louis.
RLC see Rubury Lindsay.
ROLLING see Dupressoir.
ROYAL CORONET see Cope-Bohemian.
ROYAL DETROITER see Detroiter.
ROYAL INTERNATIONAL see International (England.)
RUBAY see Leon Rubay.
RUGBY see Star (USA.)
RUTHERFORD see EJYR.

SABRA see Rom Carmel.
SAG see Pic-Pic.
SALVATOR see Underberg.
SARACEN see Reading.
SARATOGA TOURIST see Elite (1901.)
SASCHA see Austro-Daimler.
SAVENTHEM see Excelsior (Belgium.)
SCOOTACAR see Rytecraft.
SCOOTMOBILE see Martin 1920
SCORPION see Innes Lee.
SCOTT-NEWCOMB see Standard Steam Car.
SEIGFRIED see RAW.
SEM see Morisse.
SEVEN LITTLE BUFFALOES see De Schaum.
SEXTOAUTO see Reeves.
SEYMOUR see Turner.
SFA see Automotrice.
SHAVE-MORSE see SM.
SHERET see Carden.
SHOEMAKER see St Joe.
SIDDELEY-DEASY see Deasy.
SIENNA see Stevens.
LA SILENCIEUSE English importer's name for Vinot-Deguingand.
SINCLAIR see Clift.
SLIM-PILAIN see Pilain.
SMEDDLE-KENNEDY see SK Simplex.
SNOEK Bolide license-built in Belgium c1900.
SOCIETE CONTINENTAL D'AUTOMO BILES see Gautier Wehrlé.
SOCIETE PARISIENNE see Victoria Combination.
SPERRY 1900-1901 name for Cleveland Electric.
SRC see Matas.
SSS see Staines-Simplex.
STANLEY-WHITNEY see Whitney.
STAUGHTON English importer's name for Prosper-Lambert.
STORERO see Schacchi.
STRATTAN see Stratton.
SYMBOL see Status.
SYRACUSE see Van Wagoner.

TALBOT-DARRACQ see Darracq, Talbot (France.)
TAMA see Prince.
TEMPLE-WOODGATE see Temple-Westcott.
TESTE ET MORET see La Mouche.
TH (England 1906) see Farnell.
TOBOGGAN see Armadale.
TOULOUSE see Able.
TRASK-DETROIT see Detroit Steam Car.
TRIPLEX see Chicagoan.
TWEENIE see Ruby.
TWENTIETH CENTURY see Owen (England.)

UNION see Lambert.
URSUS see Menegault-Basset.
UTILITY see Pagé.

VCS see Schilling.
VELOCAR MOCHET see CM.
VELOMOBILE see Eastmead-Biggs.
VERNON-DERBY English importer's name for French Derby sports car.
VERTEX see James & Browne.
VESTA (1898) see Bamber & Lewis. Also English name for La Minerve (1899-1906.)
VICTOR English importer's name for Créanche.
VICTOR PAGE see Page.
VINDEC see Allright.
VOLGA see GAZ.
VOX see L & P.

WARD-LEONARD see Knickerbocker.
WATSONIA see Dürkopp.
WESTON see Grout.
WHIPPET see Willys.
WHITING-GRANT see Grant.
WILLYS-VIASA Jeeps built for Spanish market.
WINCO 1913-1914 twin-cylinder predecessor of Stringer-Winco.
WINDORA Ariés imported into England by S. A. Marples, whose aunts were named Winifred and Dora.
WOLSELEY-SIDDELEY see Wolseley.
WORTHINGTON see Berg.

YALTA see Zaphorozhets.
YORK see Pullman.
YUE LOONG see YLN.

ZEBRA English name for Le Zébre.
ZHIGULI see Lada.

GLOSSARY

Air cooled: An engine in which the heat generated by combustionin the cylinders is dispersed by convection, either by radiating fins or by forced draught.

ALAM horsepower rating: A formula used by the Association of Licenced Automobile Manufacturers in the early days of the US motor industry (and known as the SAE rating after its demise.)

ALAM hp equals cylinder bore (in inches) squared times number of cylinders plus 2.5, at a speed of 1000rpm.

Annular gear: A toothed wheel with the teeth formed on the inner circumference.

Armored chassis: A frame basically made of wood, but strengthened by steel flitch plates bolted on.

Artillery wheel: A road wheel with wooden or steel spokes, of greater strength than the conventional cart wheel.

Assembled car: A car whose engine, gearbox, axles, and other components were supplied by various proprietary makers, the factory merely assembling this kit of parts.

Axle, Dead: An axle on which the wheels revolve, but which itself does not revolve.

Axle, Floating: A live axle in which the half-shafts carry none of the car weight, but just carry the wheels. There are also"semi-floating" and "three-fourths-floating" axles.

Axle, Live: An axle containing the shafts which drive the wheels.

Axle, Swing: A form of independent rear suspension in which the outer axle casings pivot around a fixed differential unit.

Beau de Rochas cycle: An obsolete term for the four-stroke cycle.

Belt drive: A transmission system using leather or rubber belts and pulleys to transmit power to the driving wheels.

bhp: Short for "brake horsepower," though a visitor to the 1902 Crystal Palace Motor Show assured his girlfriend that it meant "British horse power." ("When an Englishman says "10hp" he means 10; when a Frenchman says "10hp" he means 8.")

Bi-block: An engine with its cylinders cast in two blocks (of two, three, or four cylinders each.)

Blower: A slang term for a supercharger (or a fan used to assist air cooling.)

Boiler, Fire-tube: A tubular steel boiler with end plates connected by open-ended thin tubes through which the hot gases pass, heating the water surrounding the tubes to boiling point.

Boiler, Flash: A steam boiler in which steam is generated almost instantaneously, the boiler carrying only a minimum of water.

Boiler, Water-tube: A steam boiler with the water carried in tubes around which the hot gases circulate.

Brake, Band: A brake contracting on the outside of a drum.

Brake, Disc: The most efficient form of car brake; callipers grip the faces of a revolving disc.

Brake, Drum: Commonly used, this type of brake has shoes expanding inside a drum.

Brakes, Mechanical: Little used since the 1950s except to operate parking brake mechanisms, this once-universal braking system uses metal rods or cables to actuate the brakes instead of hydraulic fluid operating in flexible pipes, as in all modern cars.

Cam: A shaped piece of metal revolving on a shaft and imparting a regular motion to a rod or lever. Most importantly used to operate the engine valves.

Cardan: A universally jointed shaft driving the rear axle.

Chain drive: Linking gearbox to rear axle by chains and sprockets instead of shaft, this transmission system was mostly obsolete by 1914.

Clincher tire: An obsolete design which has beads formed on the tyre which engage in channels on the wheel rims, air pressure in the tire locking it to the rim.

Clutch, Cone: Instead of flat discs of friction material, the driving and driven faces of this type of clutch are sections of a cone.

Clutch, Scroll: Used mostly by Mercedes in pre-1914 days, this type of clutch employs the gripping action of a powerful steel spring coiled round a shaft.

Coil, Trembler: In early ignition systems, trembler coils "buzzed" like a doorbell to make-and-break the primary ignition circuit.

Compound engine: A multiple-expansion engine in which the steam (or, in at least one case, the exhaust gases of a gasoline engine), after leaving the high-pressure cylinders, is exhausted into a low-pressure cylinder to make maximum use of its expansive energy.

Connecting rod: The rod which links piston to crankshaft.

Crypto gear: An epicyclic transmission using sun-and-planet gears.

cv: The French unit of horsepower (*cheval vapeur* = "steam horse.")

De Dion axle: Originally invented for De Dion Bouton steam carriages by Bouton's brother-in-law Trépardoux, this system uses a dead rear axle and independent universally jointed half-shafts to transmit power from a differential unit fixed to the frame.

Desaxé A cylinder offset relative to the center of the crankshaft, the theory being that the connecting rod gives a more direct thrust to the crankshaft on the working stroke, increasing mechanical efficiency and reducing wear.

Desmodromic: Valves which are both opened and closed mechanically. Normally only found in racing engines.

Diesel engine: An internal combustion engine in which the compression in the cylinders is so great that it ignites the fuel/air mixture.

dohc: Double overhead camshaft.

Dos-à-dos: A four-seater car with the passengers sitting back to back.

Drip feed: A primitive lubrication system in which oil was dripped through visible sight feeds on the dash before feeding the various engine bearings. Sometimes known as a "total loss" (or to disgruntled owners, "dead loss") system, as the theory was that, if you increased the drip rate to the point where the exhaust was just tinged with oil smoke, then the engine was being adequately lubricated.

Dry-sump lubrication: Generally used on racing engines, this system uses a remote oil tank with a feed pump supplying oil to the engine bearings and a scavenge pump taking it from the engine and returning it to the tank.

eoi: Exhaust over inlet valves; see F-head.

Epicyclic gear: An internally toothed drum containing "planetary" gears which revolve around the main shaft, which carries a "sun" gear wheel with which they mesh.

F-head: An engine with (normally) overhead inlet and side exhaust valves, though the alternative configuration of side inlet, overhead exhaust has been used.

Flat-twin (or-four): An engine with opposed horizontal cylinders.

Four-stroke engine: An engine operating on the four cycles (in two crankshaft revolutions) of induction, compression, ignition, exhaust (or, vulgarly, "suck, squeeze, bang, blow.")

4wd: Four-wheel drive.

Friction drive: Formerly used on light cars of feeble performance, this transmission system dispensed with gearing, using instead a friction wheel at right angles to the flywheel, and capable of being moved across its face so that varying drive ratios (and reverse) could be obtained.'

fwb: Front-wheel brakes.

fwd: Front-wheel drive.

Gasoline: Known as "petrol" in the UK, this colourless, inflammable and increasingly costly liquid distilled from crude gasolineeum is the most commonly used motor fuel. The word "Gasoline", however, is strictly speaking a trade name belonging to Carless, Capel & Leonard, of London, dating from the end of the nineteenth century.

Gasoline-electric: A transmission system in which an internal-combustion engine, running at more or less constant speed, drives a dynamo supplying current to electric motors, sometimes mounted in the wheel hubs, sometimes in the final drive. Because an internal-combustion engine running at a constant speed is most economical, this obsolete transmission system is being re-examined.

Gravity feed: A system for supplying fuel to the carburetor by mounting the tank above the level of the jet so that it flowed naturally without the need for a fuel pump. If the tank was mounted too low (as on the Model T Ford, where it was under the driver's seat), the car would have to be reversed up hills when the fuel level was low, to maintain sufficient head of fuel at the jet.

Horsepower: The rate of energy expended in a given time by a motor. One horsepower represents the energy expended in raising 33,000 lb by 1 foot in 60 seconds. Some early cars were advertised with two horsepower figures (e.g. 20/24 hp), representing power at 1000rpm, and a (usually optimistic) maximum power output.

Hot-tube ignition: An ignition system used on some primitive engines instead of electric ignition (or, where electric ignition was fitted and mistrusted, as an emergency ignition), in which a closed metal (usually platinum) tube projecting into the combustion chamber was heated outside the cylinder by a Bunsen burner fed by the gasoline supply. When the compressed gas/air mixture came into contact with this tube, ignition took place.

ifs: Independent front suspension.

ioe: Inlet over exhaust valves; see F-head.

irs: Independent rear suspension.

Jackshaft: In chain-drive transmission, a shaft running across the frame with a sprocket at either end from which the drive to the rear wheels by chain is taken.

Junk ring: The equivalent of a piston ring used to seal the sleeves in a sleeve-valve engine.

Knight engine: A sleeve-valve engine with two sleeves per cylinder.

Landaulette: A formal car whose rear portion may be opened.

L-head: A side-valve engine with inlet and exhaust valves on oneside of the block, actuated by a single camshaft.

Low-tension ignition: A magneto which initially generates a low-voltage current.

Magneto: Once the most common form of ignition, a magneto is an electric generator which produces the ignition current independently of any batteries. A low-tension magneto uses a coil to amplify the current, whereas a high-tension magneto produces sufficient current on its own.

Monobloc: An engine with all its cylinders cast in one piece.

ohc: Overhead camshaft.

ohv: Overhead valves.

Otto cycle: The four-stroke cycle of internal combustion, named after Dr Nikolas August Otto, who introduced it in his "silent gas engine" of 1876. (There was also a curious pedal-propelled two-wheeler called the Otto dicycle.)

Pair-cast: An engine with its cylinders cast in blocks of two cylinders.

Phaeton: An open touring car.

Planetary gear: Another name for Epicyclic gear.

Poppet valve: The conventional type of valve used in four-stroke engines.

Port: An aperture through which gases enter or leave the cylinder.

PS: The German unit of horsepower (*pferde stärke*)

Pushrods: Steel rods actuating overhead valves through the medium of rockers; pushrods are operated by cams low down in the crankcase.

RAC rating: Used mostly to determine taxation liability, this method of calculation of power output ignores the engine stroke. RAC rating is the bore in millimetres squared, multipled by the number of cylinders and divided by 1613.

Roi-des-Belges: An open car with elaborately contoured seat backs based, it is said, on the armchairs in the boudoir of Cléo de Merodé, dancer and *petite amie* of King Leopold II of Belgium, for whom the first body of this type was made (1902.)

Rotary engine: Early rotary engines had cylinders which rotated around a stationary crankshaft, the misapprehension under which their promotors labored being that the gyroscopic effect steadied the engine, while the revolving cylinders were better cooled than static cylinders. Modern rotary engines (the Wankel is the most successful, but has found only limited application) have rotating "pistons" running inside a specially shaped combustion chamber and geared to an output shaft.

Rotary valve: Driven by chain or gearing, rotary valves incorporated ports which communicated with inlet or exhaust ports. Supposedly more silent than poppet valves, they were very difficult to lubricate properly and therefore tended to seize.

rpm: Revolutions per minute.

Rumble seat: American equivalent of "dickey seat."

Runabout: A low-powered two-seater car.

Sleeve valve: The double sleeve-valve engine invented by C. Y. Knight has two concentric sliding sleeves surrounding the piston, operated by a shaft revolving at half engine speed. On the inlet stroke slots formed in the two sleeves coincide in register with the inlet port, on the exhaust stroke slots in both sleeves reveal the exhaust port, and on the compression and firing strokes the ports are out of line. Single sleeve-valve engines have one sleeve incorporating slots, which is twisted to and fro as it goes up and down to uncover the ports.

Slide valve: A relation of the sleeve valve, only the slide valves form just part of the cylinder wall, sliding up and down to reveal inlet and exhaust ports.

Splash lubrication: A system by which the big-end bearings are lubricated by the revolving crankshaft dipping into troughs, which are replenished by a pump or by scoops on the flywheel.

Supercharger: A device for forcing fuel/air into the cylinder for extra power.

Surface carburetor: The most primitive form of carburetor, consisting of a container in which gasoline, agitated by the motion of the car, gives off inflammable vapour, which is drawn into the cylinder and ignited.

sv: Side valve.

T-head: An early type of side-valve engine layout with the inlet valves on one side of the cylinder head and the exhaust valves on the other, necessitating the use of two camshafts.

Tonneau: An early form of four-seat car with back seats entered through a rear door.

Tourer: An open car, normally with four/five seats.

Town car: A formal car with an open driver's seat and the rear seats enclosed.

Conversion factors

TABLE OF CYLINDER BORES AND STROKES IN MILLIMETERS AND INCHES

The following figures are approximate, and intended only as a rough guide for comparison.

Millimeters	Inches
62 x 100	2 7/16> x 3 15/16
65 x 120	2 9/6 x 4 3/4
66 x 70	2 9/16 x 2 3/4
67 x 70	2 5/8 x 2 3/4
67 x 73	2 5/8 x 2 7/8
67 x 77	2 5/8 x 3
70 x 70	2 3/4 x 2 3/4
70 x 73	2 3/4 x 2 7/8
70 x 77	2 3/4 x 3
72 x 77	21 3/16x 3
73 x 73	2 7/8 x 2 7/8
73 x 80	2 7/8 x 3 1/8
77 x 77	3 x 3
77 x 80	3 x 3 1/8
77 x 83	3 x 3 1/4
78 x 78	3 1/16 x 3 1/16
80 x 80	3 1/8 x 3 1/8
80 x 86	3 1/8 x 3 3/8
83 x 83	3 1/4 x 3 1/4
83 x 86	3 1/4 x 3 3/8
86 x 86	3 3/8 x 3 3/8
84 x 90	3 5/16 x 3 9/16
90 x 90	3 9/16 x 3 9/16
90 x 110	3 9/16 x 4 5/16
95 x 115	3 3/4 x 4 9/16
100 x 115	3 15/16 x 4 9/16
105 x 118	4 1/8 x 4 5/8
108 x 120	4 1/4 x 4 3/4
110 x 125	4 5/16 x 4 15/16
112 x 128	4 7/16 x 5 1/16
114 x 130	4 1/2 x 5 1/8
116 x 134	4 9/16 x 5 5/16
118 x 138	4 5/8 x 5 7/16
120 x 140	4 3/4 x 5 1/2
122 x 143	4 13/16 x 5 5/8
124 x 146	4 7/8 x 5 3/4
126 x 148	41 5/16x 5 13/16
128 x 150	5 1/16 x 5 15/16
130 x 152	5 1/8 x 6
140 x 160	5 1/2 x 6 3/8

1 in	= 2.54cm
1 cu in	= 16.3871cc
1 meter	= 3.28ft
1 gallon (Imp)	= 4.546 liters
1 pint	= 0.568 liters
1 gallon (Imp)	= 1.2 gallon (US)
1 lb	= 0.454kg
1 ton	= 1016kg
1 liter	= 61.02cu in
1 mkg	= 7.233lb ft
10psi	= 0.703kg/sq cm
1bhp	= 745.7 watts

Liters/100km $= \frac{282.5}{\text{mpg}}$

Mph/1,000rpm $= \frac{60{,}000}{\text{gear ratio x rev/mile}}$

RAC hp $= \frac{D^2 \times N}{2.5}$ (D=bore dia.) (N=no. of cyl.)

B.m.e.p. $= \frac{2.47 \times \text{torque (lb ft)}}{\text{displacement (cc)}}$

Mean piston speed = 0.0656 x stroke (cm) x rpm

1 bhp = 1.014CV

To find the cubic capacity of an engine, square the bore diameter (in centimeters or inches), multiply by .7854, and multiply the result by the stroke. Then multiply by number of cylinders.

1 volume of gasoline yields 276 volumes of gasoline vapour.

1 lb of gasoline requires 200 volumes of air for complete combustion.

Gradients

A grade of	1 in 5	equals	20 per cent	or angle of	11° 19'
	1 in 6				9° 26'
	1 in 7		14		8° 09'
	1 in 8		12½		7° 08'
	1 in 9		11		6° 17'
	1 in 10		10		5° 43'
	1 in 11		9		5° 11'
	1 in 12		8		4° 46'
	1 in 13		7¾		4° 24'
	1 in 14		7		4° 05'

ACKNOWLEDGEMENTS

The publishers would like to thank the following for providing photographs used in this book.

Alfa Romeo Ltd
Associated Press Ltd
James O. Barron
David Burgess Wise
Peter Burns
Citroën Cars Ltd
Chrysler Jeep
Lance Cole
Daewoo Cars Ltd
Daimler-benz AG Bildarchiv
Pedr Davis
Mirco Decet
Andrew Dee
Mary Evans picture library
Michael Fear
Hyundai Car (UK) Ltd
Jaguar Car Ltd
Fiat Motor Company
Ford Motor Company
General Motors Ltd
Geoffrey Goddard
Nancy Hoffman Gallery, New York
Robert Lamplough
Mark Lawrence
Mansell Collection
Keith Marvin
Michelin Tyre Co.
Motor Magazine
Musée National des Techniques, Paris
National Motor Museum, Beaulieu
Orbis Publishing
Pininfarina
Jacques Potherat
Hervé Poulain
Renault Ltd
Rover Group
Rolls-Royce Motor Cars Ltd
Saab (GB) Ltd
Jasper Spence-Smith
Erwin Tragatsch
Toyota GB PLC
D. B. Tubbs
Volkswagen Group UK Ltd
Waddington and Tooth galleries ltd, London
Nicky Wright